Contents

Introduction vi

Dictionary A–Z 1

Textbooks and Reference Books by Subject Area 496
    Music Education 496
    Music Education Philosophy/Educational Philosophy 499
    Music Education History 499
    Sociology/Social Psychology 501
    Educational Psychology 502
    General Education 507
    Curriculum/Reports 510
    Music Psychology and Perception/Cognition 514
    Conducting Books 516
    Research 517

Tests and Measurement 518

Additional Resources 522
    Web sites 522
    Professional Music and Music Education Organizations/Associations . . .525

Professional Journals/Magazines 528

About the Authors 536

Introduction

Music education is a broad-based discipline, using terminology from several other areas of study including general psychology, sociology, physics, philosophy, research, technology, and general education. Language borrowed from these fields and applied in a musical context has become an important part of the profession's knowledge base. Music education students and professionals must possess an understanding of the terminology used in a wide variety of disciplines in order to read and comprehend the material effectively. Understanding literature relevant to music education is essential for individual growth, encourages openness and communication between the various emphases within the field, and advances the profession as a whole.

The music profession in general has many excellent, well-established reference books, including *New Groves Dictionary of Music and Musicians*, *New Groves Dictionary of American Music*, *The New Harvard Dictionary of Music*, *Norton's Concise Dictionary*, *Baker's Biographical Dictionary*, and the *Handbook of Research on Music Teaching and Learning*; however, no single source encompasses the breadth of terminology that music educators must know. Through the years, undergraduate and graduate students have frequently commented that their course readings contain too many unfamiliar words that make the readings difficult to understand. Students have also indicated that they cannot find definitions for many of these terms and that authors often do not define them in the readings. As a result, students do not fully understand the assigned readings or lectures and cannot contribute knowledgeably to discussions.

The purpose of this handbook is to provide students, teachers, professionals, and practitioners with a quick, easy-to-use reference for music education terminology. The design and writing style of the handbook are intended to provide the reader with a functional, working definition of each term presented. Each term chosen for this handbook meets at least one of the following criteria: 1) the term is commonly encountered during at least one standard university music education course; 2) the term is commonly encountered as part of the

Dictionary of Music Education:
A Handbook of Terminology

Dictionary
of **Music
Education:**

A **Handbook**
of **Terminology**

Mark C. Ely
and **Amy E. Rashkin**

GIA Publications, Inc.
Chicago

G-6233

Copyright © 2005, GIA Publications, Inc.
7404 S. Mason Avenue, Chicago, IL 60638

www.giamusic.com

ISBN: 1-57999-466-0

Cover design and book layout: Robert Sacha
Illustrations: Anastasia Ravestein

Printed in the United States of America

everyday experience of professional music educators; 3) understanding of the term is necessary in order to comprehend research and other professional literature relevant to music education; and 4) the term is not readily defined in other well-established music resources.

One important challenge music educators face is helping students understand the language of the profession. Many non-music majors take two years of general education preparatory courses prior to being admitted into specific degree programs. These students have time to learn terminology common to their fields of study. However, music education majors begin taking courses specific to their degree program during their freshman year. As a result, music education majors are exposed to unfamiliar terminology during their first term of study, placing them at a disadvantage.

Dictionary of Music Education: A Handbook of Terminology is a one-volume reference designed to facilitate understanding of terminology common to the music education profession. In addition, the reference listings at the back of the book are an invaluable resource. The listings are comprehensive, though not exhaustive. They provide teachers with bibliographic information on standard music education books, journals, and other resource materials designed to enhance teaching, learning, and musical skill development. These listings also provide students with a reference for identifying additional sources of information on a wide range of music education topics.

Content and Format

The terms appear in alphabetical order and are cross-referenced. Within each definition, terms that are defined elsewhere in the handbook appear in bold when appropriate. If definitions of other terms can assist the reader's understanding of a particular term, these terms have been indicated at the end of each entry. For example, for the term **Aesthetic Thinking**, the phrase "*See* Aesthetic/Aesthetics" appears at the end of the entry suggesting that the definition for **Aesthetics** may also be helpful to the reader's understanding of Aesthetic thinking.

The design and writing style of the handbook are intended to provide the reader with a functional, working definition of each term presented. The definitions are practical and succinct. When appropriate, analogies and examples are included to help clarify the definitions. These definitions are intended to provide the background information necessary to achieve higher levels of understanding. Efforts have been made to avoid defining terms that appear in other, well-established music reference books.

We have included a reference section at the back of the book. The reference section uses the following five categorical listings of music education resources: textbooks and reference books, tests and measurement, Web sites, professional music and music education associations, and professional journals and magazines.

These listings provide the reader with bibliographic information on standard music education textbooks and resource materials designed to enhance teaching, learning, and musical skill development.

A Priori Comparisons: In **Analysis of Variance (ANOVA)** research designs, a **simple effect** that enables researchers to determine what accounts for differences among the means. A priori comparisons belong to one category of simple effects, which are planned prior to data analysis, the other being post hoc comparisons. Orthogonal comparisons are commonly used for analyzing a priori comparisons. *See* **Post Hoc Comparisons; Analysis of Variance (ANOVA); Simple Effects**

"Aha!" Phenomenon: In psychology, the **perception** of relationships leading to the apparently sudden understanding and solution of a problem, or what is often called **insight**. The term "Aha" phenomenon is most often credited to **Max Wertheimer (1880–1943)**. *See* **Insight; Kohler, Wolfgang (1887–1967); Gestalt Psychology**

Ability: *See* **Musical Ability**

Abnormal Behaviors: Behaviors that are not normal or that are out of the ordinary in some way. Abnormal behaviors are often characterized as atypical, socially unacceptable, distressing, or maladaptive. *See* **Maladaptive Behaviors**

Abnormal Fixation: A stereotyped **habit** very resistant to change, or an abnormal attachment to a person or object. Abnormal fixations are often seemingly illogical and have no practical basis; that is, they are generally not necessary for efficient functioning nor do they contribute significantly to personal well being. For example, an individual who is virtually unable to function at work unless he or she sits in the same chair every day has an abnormal fixation. *See* **Fixation**

Absolute Expressionism: A form of **expressionism** characterized by the view that there is intrinsic value in the formal properties of artworks and that these formal properties should relate to the qualities or experiences of everyday life. Absolute expressionism involves relating a work of art to everyday life, which may make it more meaningful to some people because the value in any work of art is largely subjective. In music, significance or meaning is derived from the way a listener perceives a given piece of music and relates its qualities to his or her own life or experiences. *See* Referentialism; Formalism

Absolute Formalism: A philosophical view or belief that intrinsic value exists exclusively in the formal properties of artworks. In music, meaning is derived from the listener's **perception** and understanding of the formal properties or structure of the music and not from any external references, emotions, or feelings associated with the music. *See* **Referentialism; Expressionism**

Absolute Pitch: The ability to produce or label pitches on demand without the aid of a reference tone. Although it is not uncommon for individuals to have highly developed **relative pitch**, few individuals possess absolute pitch. Furthermore, individuals who possess absolute pitch vary in their abilities to produce and label pitches accurately. Whether or not absolute pitch is an innate ability or an ability that can be learned is unclear; however, studies show that absolute pitch can be learned in some instances. Individuals who have absolute pitch usually acquire the ability at a young age. Although this ability is somewhat prized among musicians, its practical value in musical performance is limited. *See* **Perfect Pitch**

Absolute Threshold: *See* Threshold

Absolutism: In music, the view that musical meaning exists within the content of the music itself, as opposed to the referential view that musical meaning is attached to external references. In **metaphysics**, absolutism refers to the theory that all of reality is an interconnected, single unity without conditions and without relationships. In **epistemology**, absolutism refers to the belief that objective truths exist and can be known. Ethically, absolutism refers to the view that ultimate values exist independently from the value human beings place on them. *See* **Referentialism; Expressionism; Formalism**

Absorption: In physics, the process whereby an object absorbs and retains a portion of the sound energy produced by a vibrating body. When sound **waves** strike an object, the object tends to vibrate in response. This vibration depletes energy from the sound source. That is, the object absorbs sound energy. Soft materials, like rubber and cork, vibrate easily and absorb sound effectively, while harder materials like concrete and hardwood do not. In education, the term absorption is sometimes used when referring to the process of taking in information. *See* **Reflection; Refraction**

Academic Achievement: In general, what has been learned or acquired through formal training but may also include academic knowledge that has been acquired in informal settings. The level of individual academic achievement is determined primarily through classroom **assessment** and performance on **standardized tests**. That is, a student's grade point average (GPA) along with scores on standardized tests are considered to be reflective of a student's level of academic achievement. Debates continue as to whether or not these types of assessments are true measures of academic achievement. Critics of traditional academic achievement assessment measures reject the testing process and the tests for being invalid, unreliable, and biased on the basis of such factors as **socio-economic status (SES)**, **race**, or **culture**. **Intelligence tests** have been shown to be somewhat reliable measures of academic achievement, but other factors, such as physical health, emotional well being, **motivation** level, and strength of ego, may also influence academic achievement. In music, researchers have studied the relationship between academic achievement and various aspects of music, including music achievement, **self-concept**, and **attitudes** toward music. *See* **Music Achievement**

Academic Freedom: In general, the opportunity for teachers to teach, research, or write in an environment free from coercion, censorship, or other restrictive interference. *See* **Tenure**

Academy, The: A school that opened in 1751 under the leadership of Benjamin Franklin (1706–1790). The Academy emphasized practical learning because it was more liberal and vocational in nature than were studies at the traditional **Latin schools** that dominated education at this time. These new academies offered study in English language, literature, oratory, and the sciences. The Academy led to a revolution in American education in the 1750s. As more academies opened, they gradually replaced Latin schools as the dominant secondary school. The academies influenced education for almost a century; however, because they were expensive, many people could not afford to attend. As the demand for affordable public school education for everyone grew in the 1820s and 1830s, the academies were gradually replaced by **common schools**.

Accelerated Schools: Schools designed to speed up the learning of economically disadvantaged or **at-risk students**. Accelerated schools became popular in the 1980s and 1990s as an alternative to more traditional schools and other methods of addressing student needs. The trend in education throughout the 1960s and 1970s had been to provide additional learning opportunities for students who were **gifted and talented**, while immersing less-capable and/or at-risk students into remedial programs. Such programs typically involved utilizing a simplified **curriculum**, moving at a slower pace, and emphasizing basic skills. In contrast, accelerated schools are designed to provide at-risk students with a wider range of learning opportunities by capitalizing on their strengths. In order to facilitate this process, **collaborative networks**, groups of people who meet on a volunteer basis to explore various educational issues, are formed. In addition, learning communities are sometimes formed to help students connect their school learning experiences with everyday life experiences based on their culture and their community. The effectiveness of accelerated schools has not been determined; however, some studies indicate that accelerated schools result in more positive student **attitudes** toward the learning process. *See* **Remediation**

Accelerated Schools Program: A school program designed by Henry Levin based on the fundamental premise that all children are **gifted and talented** rather than the premise that children have weaknesses and deficiencies. The Accelerated Schools Program was instituted in 1992 in about 150 schools. Accelerated schools focus on teaching to students' strengths rather than to their weaknesses as a way to bring about significant **curricular** change. The Accelerated Schools Program did not have a specified or planned system of curricular change because such change was supposed to be initiated from the communities themselves rather than from outsiders. Levin intended the program to create a culture for school reform as opposed to a set of techniques "for how to do school reform."

Acceleration: A teaching/learning process or **technique** that enables students to achieve at a rate that is appropriate for their ability levels. Acceleration is normally associated with allowing gifted and talented students to move through the school **curricula** at an accelerated rate, usually by skipping grade levels. *See* **Gifted and Talented/Giftedness**

Accidental Sampling: *See* **Haphazard Sampling**

Accommodation: In Jean Piaget's (1896–1980) **theory of cognitive development**, the process by which **cognitive** structures are modified. Piaget used accommodation in conjunction with **assimilation**, which is an individual's ability to internalize and conceptualize his or her environmental experiences. In other words, accommodation is the adjustment an individual makes to environmental **stimuli** that have been and are being assimilated. *See* **Assimilation**

Accountability: In general, the extent to which an individual or institution supports and takes responsibility for its output. In education, accountability involves efforts to systematically evaluate the effectiveness of instruction based on pre-determined **outcomes**. Several components of instruction for which teachers and schools may be held accountable include: 1) **curricular** programs, 2) **teaching methods**, 3) **lesson plans**, 4) **goals** and **objectives**, 5) **assessment** procedures, 6) instructional materials, 7) budgeting issues, and 8) classroom policies. Accountability has been a part of formal education since ancient times in various forms; however, the term itself and accountability "movements" have become more prevalent since the 1970s.

Accountability in education has lead to improved instruction and **curricular** design but has presented some difficulty for music educators. Potential problems with the testing and evaluation process, the role of music and the arts in curricula, and scheduling have been central to debates regarding its merits. Many methods of **assessment** and evaluation that work well in performance-based classes are not always considered appropriate for accountability purposes. Furthermore, traditional academic assessment measures are generally inappropriate for most **performance-based classes**. For example, many students, parents, teachers, and administrators consider a performance-based music class effective if, in their opinion, the ensemble performs well. This has led some to argue that accountability in a performance-based music class lies largely in the success of the performances. Unfortunately this method does not address critical issues regarding whether or not students actually learned what they were supposed to learn musically. Many music educators have made efforts to be more accountable by revising assessment processes to include testing more frequently, devising and administering a greater variety of written and performing tests, and more carefully monitoring student progress.

Historically, another problem with accountability is that the grading process in some **performance-based classes** is less than ideal. In many instances, if a student comes to class on time, prepares appropriately, pays attention in class, plays or sings the parts reasonably well, and attends all of the rehearsals and performances, that student receives an A. This manner of assessment does not address whether or not the student actually learned anything. Many music educators have revised testing procedures as mentioned above, but these assessments take away valuable rehearsal time because some aspects of student progress must be assessed individually. Ultimately, accountability is an issue that most music educators will have to face at some point. Each teacher should find a balance between musical and **nonmusical** assessment criteria based on the needs of their programs.

Accrediting Agencies: Agencies charged with accrediting teachers, administrators, service personnel, and/or educational degree programs. Accredited personnel and institutions are recognized nationwide as having met minimum **standards**. In addition, such agencies make sure high standards are maintained in educational institutions and ensure consistency of quality among programs. In music, the two most relevant accrediting agencies are the **National Council for the Accreditation of Teacher Education (NCATE)**, which accredits teachers, educational administrators, and school service personnel, and the **National Association of Schools of Music (NASM)**, which accredits music degree programs in colleges and universities.

Acculturation: In general, a strategy for cultural **assimilation** in which individuals are immersed in the dominant **culture**. The extent to which an individual becomes acculturated is largely determined by his or her ability to adjust to drastic changes effectively. In education, acculturation is the process of increasing students' awareness of their cultural traditions and **values** and instilling these values in students. Although part of the acculturation process is built into the educational design, acculturation is largely a by-product of the normal, daily functioning of any given society. *See* **Socialization**

Achievement: In general, knowledge and skills that have been learned or acquired through formal and informal training. *See* **Academic Achievement; Music Achievement**

Achievement Motivation: A term associated with the idea that individuals achieve solely for the sake of achieving without relying on other ulterior motives. Achievement motivation is linked with feelings of self-directed competence and a sense of personal satisfaction for a job well done. Achievement motivation is associated with the work of **David McClelland (1917–1998)**. *See* Achievement Motive

Achievement Motive: Any motive that enables individuals to accomplish something of value or importance. Achievement motives are typically intrinsic; however, they may occasionally be extrinsic. Achievement motives often facilitate academic achievement, and research has indicated that personal feelings of self-directed competence (an achievement motive) is the most important factor in determining **academic achievement**. Achievement motives are usually associated with self-directed feelings of social consciousness; people are often motivated to do what they feel is right. For example, a musician may perform in a nursing home or children's ward at a hospital simply because he or she believes it is the right thing to do. *See* Achievement Motivation

Achievement Tests in Music: A general term for tests that measure knowledge, skills, abilities, attitudes, and interests in music. Achievement tests typically measure aspects of music that have been learned or studied as opposed to **music aptitude tests**, which measure innate ability or potential to succeed in musical activities. The **Music Achievement Test (MAT)** by Richard Colwell and the **Kwalwasser-Ruch Test of Musical Accomplishment** for grades four through twelve are two well-known achievement tests in music.

Acoustic Center: The point in space where sound originates, also called acoustic origin.

Acoustic Environment: The complete set of all objects and their physical properties that influence the sound field surrounding the listener. The acoustic environment has a profound effect on perceived sound quality because the sound emitted by a source typically arrives to the listener through a variety of sound paths. **Reflection**, **diffraction**, **refraction**, and **diffusion** all occur as a result of the objects and their physical properties within the acoustic environment including corners, edges, openings, walls, chairs, stands, people, curtains, and other common objects. In addition, the size and shape of the objects and materials from which the objects are made all affect the acoustic environment.

Acoustic Origin: The point in time at which a signal or sound originates, also called acoustic center.

Acoustical Filter: In acoustics, any device or substance that blocks acoustical **waves** or prevents acoustical waves from passing through. Typically, acoustical filters are designed to block waves at a particular **frequency** or waves within a certain frequency **range**. For example, an A-weighting filter blocks out certain acoustical waves in certain high and low ranges to mimic the way the human ear works. *See* **A-weighting (dBA)**

Acquired Ability: An ability to do something as an **outcome** of formal education, training, and/or everyday experiences. Acquired abilities are achievement-related because they have been learned.

Acquired Motives: In psychology, motives that have been learned from birth, usually based on psychological needs, such as approval, affection, power, and prestige. Typically, acquired motives are dictated by the rules established by society and are not universal as was once believed. That is, acquired motives were once thought to be innate to all of humanity rather than culturally acquired.

Acquisition: In behavioral psychology, a stage of learning in which new responses are learned and gradually strengthened. Acquisition is also used synonymously with **encoding** to describe the first stage of **memory** in which information is initially acquired through the senses and coded into **short-term memory**.

Acronym: A memory recognition aid typically used with long titles or phrases formed by creating words using the first letters and/or syllables of each word in the title or phrase. Examples of acronyms include ERIC for **Educational Resources Information Center** or NATO for North Atlantic Treaty Organization. *See* **Mnemonics; Chunking**

Action Zone: In education, a physical area of a classroom where teachers are more likely to call on students to give responses. The location of action zones is influenced by a variety of factors, including 1) the location or arrangement of classroom furniture including desks, chairs, tables, or computer stations; 2) the relative location of furniture to the audio-visual equipment; and 3) the makeup of students seated in a particular area. A classic action zone in a traditional classroom runs across the front row and directly up the middle aisle.

Active Learning: In education, learning that involves active student participation or interaction; students learn by doing and experiencing. Active learning is in contrast to **passive learning**, in which students sit idly while information is presented to them. In performance-based music classes, students are almost always actively involved in the learning process because they are performing as part of an ensemble. In general music classes, students are often engaged in active learning through performance-based exercises. Most educators believe that active learning is generally more effective and more enjoyable than passive learning.

Active Recitation: In education, a memorization technique that involves repeating, reciting, or rehearsing the material to be memorized. Some experts suggest that active recitation should be used for at least half of the total time spent in memorization. Active recitation may be done aloud or silently. For example, a student trying to memorize a poem might recite each line several times. This step might be followed by reciting two lines at a time, then three lines, and so on until the entire poem is memorized.

Active School: Based on the work of **Jean Piaget (1896–1980)**, the conceptual idea that learning is enhanced through active, hands-on experiences in combination with thoughtful reflection. Active school is the idea that passive memorization does not necessarily mean that children have an understanding of the concepts they have memorized. According to Piaget, **intelligence** and physical activity are linked in that activity helps foster intellectual development. That is, he believed that engaging children in appropriate physical activities, especially during the sensorimotor stage (birth to age two), was vital to learning and understanding. The active school concept is consistent with other progressive educational ideas, most notably those of **John Dewey (1859–1952)**, who promoted the idea that learning should be active rather than passive and should involve more "doing" or "experiencing" and less talking. *See* **Active Learning; Passive Learning**

Activity: In education, something students do as a means of learning. Performing, reading, creating, describing, and listening to music are all musical activities.

Actuator: In vocal music, a general term referring to all parts of the vocal mechanism that start or actuate the flow of air. The actuator includes the lungs, the diaphragm, the muscles surrounding the ribs (intercostals), and the abdominal muscles.

Adaptation: According to **Jean Piaget (1896–1980)**, the ways individuals adapt to their environment. In Piaget's theory, adaptation involves two dynamic processes: 1) **assimilation**, which involves taking in new information and matching it to existing thought patterns, and 2) **accommodation**, which involves adjusting thought patterns according to the new information, which results in conceptual development. These two processes work together to facilitate learning. In **behavioral psychology**, adaptation is a process in which the sense receptors lose sensitivity to a particular **stimulus** because of the continued presentation of that stimulus. This type of adaptation occurs most rapidly with smell and taste, which is the reason most people have the greatest sensitivity to smells and tastes when they are first exposed to them. In education, adaptation is sometimes used to refer to the process of attaining a stable school climate that facilitates unbiased student learning about societal changes.

Adaptive Behavior: In behavioral psychology, any behavior that enables an organism to adjust to its ever-changing environment. Adaptive behavior is often used in association with behaviors that improve individual ability to function in everyday life. For example, individuals may adapt to a stressful work environment in a variety of ways, such as establishing a work routine to minimize stress, taking up a new hobby, or taking a walk on a lunch break. Adaptive behaviors also enable individuals to interact socially with others. For example, young children learn how to share toys and wait their turn on playground equipment, which enables them to socially interact in appropriate ways with other children. In education, students with mental and/or physical **handicaps** sometimes lack appropriate adaptive behaviors and have trouble interacting socially with others. The American Association on Mental Retardation has defined several adaptive behaviors, including: 1) communication, 2) self-care, 3) home living, 4) social skills, 5) community use, 6) self-direction, 7) health and safety, 8) functional academics, 9) leisure, and 10) work. *See* **Goal-directed Behavior; Maladaptive Behavior**

Adjective Circle: In music research, a technique or **experimental design** typically used to determine which musical elements are most likely to elicit certain emotional responses. A series of well-known studies conducted by Kate Hevner in the mid-1930s utilized adjective circles. In these experiments, Hevner grouped terms describing different emotions in clusters of similar meaning and put them in a circular pattern. Each adjacent cluster represented a slightly different emotion, while clusters opposite each other on the circle represented contrasting emotions. Subjects were given the adjective circles and asked to listen to music examples. After listening to each example, the subjects were asked to circle the cluster that best described their emotional reactions to the music. Variations in the examples and comparisons between responses given for each example allowed Hevner to conclude that tempo and musical mode (major or minor key) had the greatest impact on emotional response.

Adolescence: The period from puberty to maturity, usually occurring during the early to late teens. Adolescence is often characterized by dramatic physical, intellectual, and emotional changes. During adolescence, individuals may have difficulty coping with these changes and developing a sense of self-identity, **self-concept**, and **self-esteem**. Some psychologists and theorists believe that adolescence extends into the early twenties.

Adult Education: In general, the education and/or training of adults. Adult education has existed in America for many years and was an outgrowth of the immigration and industrialization in America around the turn of the twentieth century. Immigrants took classes to learn English and the skills needed to survive in a foreign **culture**. In addition, factories taught safety, and agricultural extension agents helped farmers improve their methods of growing crops and raising livestock. The **Chautauqua Movement** of the late nineteenth and early twentieth centuries is the most well-known **adult education** movement. It helped establish numerous civic music associations, correspondence courses, lecture-study groups, youth groups, and reading circles. In the 1930s, the federally funded community education project associated with the Tennessee Valley Authority (TVA) provided training in basic literacy and job skills. Today, education programs are readily available for adults of all ability levels. For example, corporations offer incentives for job-related education, colleges and universities offer adult education courses in a variety of subject areas, and volunteer adult education programs such as Literacy Volunteers of America, Reading Is Fundamental, and AmeriCorps exist to promote adult education.

Advance Organizers: An approach to learning developed by **David Ausubel (b. 1918)** in which students are informed in advance about the main points or **concepts** that will be presented during class. Advance organizers can be outlines, brief abstracts, or passages of the material to be learned, and they form a bridge between prior learning and new material that may help students focus their **attention** on subject matter more effectively. These organizers enable students to incorporate new material into existing cognitive structures by providing the groundwork needed to understand the relationship between what is known and what is being learned. According to Ausubel, advance organizers are at a higher level of abstraction than the new material. Thus, they form the conceptual framework, foundation, or readiness for learning. This enables students to learn in a "top-down" manner; that is, learners first develop a general conceptual framework and then learn the specifics involved. This approach is the opposite of most other cognitive approaches to learning, which typically suggest that learning takes place in a "bottom-up" manner. That is, through the learning of specifics, individuals develop greater conceptual understanding. Ausbel's advance organizers are an important component to his reception learning theory, which states that teachers should prepare and organize the new material in advance and then present it to the students. Reception learning is in direct contrast to Jerome Bruner's (b. 1915) discovery learning approach, in which students take a more active role in organizing the material to be learned. *See* **Discovery Learning, Bruner; Reception Learning/Method; Cognitive Learning**

Advance Placement (AP) Music Theory/AP Theory: A course offered in many high schools with course content similar to that found in many freshman-level college theory courses. Students seriously considering a college major in music often take AP Theory. Students learn the rudiments of music theory, ear training, and composition. The Advance Placement Examination in Music is usually offered at the completion of the AP theory course, and students who score sufficiently well may qualify for advance placement or college credit. Many colleges and universities do not accept the test scores for course substitutions, preferring their own testing procedures for making placement decisions.

Advocacy: The means by which a group or organization supports and promotes its views and raises awareness of issues that affect its welfare. Advocacy usually involves a combination of public awareness strategies and political activism at local, state, and national levels. Legislative involvement is crucial for successful advocacy.

Aesthetic/Aesthetics: Classically, a branch of philosophy usually dealing with the nature of the beautiful or with judgments concerning beauty, and less often with the nature of ugliness, tragedy, metaphor, or humor. Aesthetics is a distinct discipline about which much has been written; however, aesthetics are given great consideration in many disciplines. Aesthetics is frequently associated with the arts. In this context, aesthetics relates to ideas about the nature of beauty and the intrinsic value of artworks and has become somewhat synonymous with questions regarding the nature and value of the artworks. **Aesthetic experiences** provide human beings with **insight** and ways of knowing distinctly different from logical and analytic thought processes. Aesthetic sensitivity increases the awareness of human feelings and emotions. *See* Aesthetic Domain

Aesthetic Domain: In addition to the three traditional domains of learning (**cognitive**, **affective**, and **psychomotor**), many education specialists (especially in music and the arts) believe that a fourth domain should be added, the aesthetic domain. This domain offers insight into **humanistic** concepts and contributes to that area of human growth and development that involves human feeling and emotion. In music, authors including Abraham Schwadron, Charles Leonard, Benjamin Britton, Bennett Reimer, and Harry S. Broudy have written extensively about the aesthetic domain. *See* Aesthetic Experience; Aesthetics

Aesthetic Education/Philosophy: An approach to teaching that focuses on such **outcomes** as the development of values, character, and intellect, rather than on utilitarian outcomes such as job training skills. *See* Aesthetic Experience; Aesthetic Education Program; Aesthetic Questions in Music Education; Aesthetic Thinking; Aesthetic/Aesthetics; Aesthetic Domain

Aesthetic Education Program: A program designed to help schools develop a generalized course of study in aesthetics incorporating a wide variety of arts. **Curricular** plans were developed based on educational research, and included music, art, dance, film, literature, and theater. This program was successful in raising awareness of **aesthetic education**, an approach to teaching that focuses on such **outcomes** as the development of values, character, and intellect, rather than on utilitarian outcomes such as job training skills. This program was successful in raising awareness of aesthetic education, in clarifying aesthetic objectives, and in providing directions for future efforts in aesthetic education; however, its implementation was largely unsuccessful. On a practical level, teachers and administrators lacked sufficient interest in and understanding of aesthetics to successfully integrate aesthetic education into the general curriculum. The program was started by the Central Midwestern Regional Educational Laboratory (CEMREL). *See* **Aesthetic Education/Philosophy**

Aesthetic Experience: In the arts, a personally meaningful and sometimes life-changing experience resulting from the interaction between the art and the observer. Aesthetic experiences vary in quality and intensity in relationship to the quality of the art and the abilities and/or experiences of the observer. Although most people are capable of aesthetic experiences, those educated in the arts are often more aware of the **aesthetic** qualities of art works and are therefore more likely to have aesthetic experiences. Aesthetic experiences are first-hand; they cannot be transferred effectively to someone else through description. Such experiences require focused **attention** on the object. The value of an aesthetic experience is in the **insight**, satisfaction, and enjoyment derived from the interaction between the art and the observer.

In *Foundations of Music Education* by Abeles, Hoffer, and Klotman (1994), the authors identify six characteristics of an aesthetic experience:

1. An aesthetic experience has no practical or utilitarian purpose.
2. An aesthetic experience involves feelings. There is a reaction to what is seen and heard.
3. An aesthetic experience involves the intellect. Thought and awareness are necessary.
4. An aesthetic experience involves a focus of attention.
5. An aesthetic experience must be experienced. One cannot have secondhand aesthetic experiences.

6. The result of aesthetic experiences is a richer and more meaningful life.

Aesthetic Questions in Music Education: Questions that lend themselves to **aesthetic thinking** from a musical perspective. Such questions may be specific to music, for example: How is this piece of music meaningful? What characteristics make this piece of music valuable today, even though it was composed 300 years ago? Such questions may also be more general, for example: How are works of art aesthetically judged? What is the nature of art? What is the nature of beauty? Music education offers a unique opportunity to combine logical, objective, rule-based thinking with the goal of producing aesthetic works of art. Merely following the objective rules may result in a technically "correct" music performance but not necessarily an aesthetically moving one.

Aesthetic Thinking: A perspective used when contemplating and perceiving the qualities of art works that focuses on the meaningfulness and beauty in the work. Aesthetic thinking involves feelingful, subjective, and imaginative modes of thinking instead of logical, objective, or rule-based modes of thinking. Although an **aesthetic** component is present in many disciplines, the arts offer unique opportunities in education for students to learn to think aesthetically. It is important that students be exposed to aesthetic thinking through the study of the arts under the supervision of highly qualified teachers. Such teachers can help students learn and understand the various techniques involved in creating artworks. Qualified teachers can also help students interpret their impressions or reactions to artworks and can help students develop appropriate criteria for evaluating and understanding them. *See* Aesthetic/Aesthetics

Affective: A general term used to describe the wide variety of subjective feelings, responses, preferences, **values**, **attitudes**, and interests that individuals experience in everyday life. Items that fall into the affective realm usually do not have a right or wrong; they are matters of personal preference. Affective feelings and attitudes are influenced by genetic and environmental factors in conjunction with personal experiences and education. *See* Affective Assessment; Affective Domain; Affective Experience; Affective Response

Affective Assessment: In research, techniques used to determine whether **affective** behaviors have been learned. Affective behaviors are extremely difficult to assess because they can take a long time to develop and are not conducive to **quantitative assessment**. Verbal measures, behavioral measures, and the observation of several different behaviors have been used in affective assessment; however, the **observational method** is considered the most accurate, because the researcher can account for environmental factors. *See* Affective

Affective Domain: In education, the area or domain of learning that concerns subjective **attitudes**, feelings, personal preferences, and **values**, and part of **Taxonomy of Educational Objectives** by Krathwohl, Bloom, and Masia. The affective domain emphasizes **objectives** that involve a feeling tone, an emotion, or some degree of acceptance or rejection and focuses on subjective rather than objective aspects of **achievement** that impact success. These objectives vary from simple attention to selected phenomena to complex qualities of character and conscience. These qualities include interests, attitudes, appreciations, values, and emotional sets or biases. Traditionally, affective **outcomes** are considered less important in public schools than cognitive outcomes, perhaps because they are difficult to assess or because the development of the affective domain is not considered a primary responsibility of public school education. As a result, significantly more material exists to describe and assess the **cognitive domain** than exists to describe and assess the affective domain; however, such material is available. For example, Krathwohl's Taxonomy of the Affective Domain includes five categories arranged as a hierarchy from simple to complex: 1) receiving or giving attention to; 2) responding, or the willingness to interact with; 3) valuing, or demonstrating a commitment to something; 4) organizing of a constant and stable value system, and 5) displaying characteristic behavior consistent with one's value system. *See* Cognitive Domain; Taxonomy of Educational Objectives; Affective Assessment

Affective Experience: Any emotional experience, pleasant or unpleasant, that affects individuals in some way. *See* Affective Domain; Affective Response

Affective Measures: In research, any of a variety of testing methods or procedures for assessing **affective** behavior. *See* Affective Assessment

Affective Response: Any emotional reaction to a given **stimulus**. Affective responses include feelings, **values**, preferences, **attitudes**, interests, or desires and can range from being highly emotional to relatively indifferent. Affective responses are typically subjective; however, they may also be objective when the criteria for **evaluation** are established in advance. Generally, the focus of music research on affective responses has been on the relationship of music preferences to a wide variety of factors, including age, gender, **race**, **socioeconomic status (SES)**, **personality**, **aptitude**, **achievement**, and peer relationships.

Affiliative Motive: A natural social or psychological tendency for individuals to form friendships or associations with others.

Affirmative Action: A general term to describe any plan that is designed to prevent **discrimination** against racial minorities and women. Affirmative action was an outgrowth of the Civil Rights Movement and continues today. Its purpose is to ensure racial and gender balance, particularly in educational institutions and the workplace. In education, affirmative action typically involves giving preferential treatment to minorities and women to correct past discriminatory practices and to balance the faculty and student populations. This practice has been a source of controversy for decades, and some feel that it is a type of reverse discrimination. In 1978, the United States Supreme Court ruled against certain affirmative action practices in *Regents of the University of California v. Bakke*, a landmark case. Allan Bakke, a white male, was denied entrance into the University of California medical school in 1973 and 1974, even though the school had admitted minority candidates with lower grade point averages and lower test scores. The Court held that Bakke must be accepted into the medical school, citing that the admission procedures were unconstitutional. Since that time, various efforts have been made to legislate fair affirmative action policies, and while definite improvements have been made toward this end, segregation, inequality, and **discrimination** based on **race** and gender still exist today. *See* **Segregation; Desegregation**

After-only Experimental Design: An experimental **design** in which **measurement** occurs only after manipulation of the **independent variable**. It does not account for the background or abilities of the subjects. In addition, it may not be clear that the manipulation of the independent variable is the direct cause of the resulting measure. These weaknesses may be controlled somewhat by tracking possible alternative explanations for the results and by keeping the time of manipulation and measurement short to minimize interference. After-only experimental design may be done with one or two groups. In the case of two groups, one group acts as a control. *See* **Before and After Experimental Design**

After-school Programs: Programs typically designed to provide children with adult supervision, additional learning opportunities, and social interactions during after-school hours until parents arrive home from work. After-school programs may provide students with opportunities for academic assistance, to participate in sports, to be involved in music and arts activities, to join school clubs or student organizations, or to simply have more play or free time under supervision. The number of after-school programs has increased in recent years as the number of **latchkey children** has increased, and many school districts, community groups, and churches now offer after-school programs. After-school programs are also referred to as **enrichment programs** because of the additional opportunities they provide students. In addition, some schools provide after-school programs for **at-risk students**. Such programs often help raise awareness of problems like drug and alcohol use and are generally designed to help promote **academic achievement**, improve children's **self-esteem**, help students make good decisions, and improve students' knowledge of healthy and unhealthy lifestyles.

Aggression: Intentionally harmful behavior. While psychologists argue over whether aggression is inherited or essentially a by-product of the environment, the most likely reality is that both factors contribute. In education, aggression can be a serious problem in the classroom, particularly with younger children who do not possess a full range of social skills. Attempts to control aggression may involve behavioral techniques, psychiatric intervention, or medication. Children who display severe aggression may be labeled as having a **behavioral disorder** or as emotionally disturbed and may be moved out of the regular classroom until the aggression is under control.

Ainsworth Psalter: *See* **Book of Psalms**

Ainsworth, Reverend Henry Boston (c. 1570–1623): An influential religious leader and teacher who moved to Amsterdam in 1593 to avoid religious persecution. In music, Ainsworth is best known for his *Book of Psalms*, commonly referred to as the *Ainsworth Psalter*, which was published in 1612. The *Ainsworth Psalter* was brought to the American colonies by the Pilgrims and used extensively throughout the 1600s. *See* **Book of Psalms**

Alexander Technique: A relaxation technique developed by F. Matthias Alexander (1869–1955) in the late 1800s to reduce tension and pain caused by stress and poor body mechanics. The Alexander Technique involves identifying and correcting posture positions and body mechanics that cause tension and inhibit flexibility of movement. The general idea is to increase an individual's awareness of poor posture habits so that they can be relearned with the help of an instructor. Some musicians find the Alexander Technique beneficial.

Algorithm: Most generally, a term used to define any logical sequence of actions, or the process of following step-by-step instructions. Algorithm also refers to a precise rule or set of rules for solving a particular type of problem. The term is also used to describe a logical, methodical procedure for solving problems that guarantees some type of solution. Algorithms are commonly used in reference to **computer programs**, but the term appropriately describes applications in other contexts as well. For example, in order to solve a problem requiring long division, an individual applies an algorithm probably learned in elementary school. An individual wishing to bake a cake applies an algorithm called a recipe. *See* **Heuristics**

Aliferis Music Achievement Test: College Entrance Level: A test devised by James Aliferis at the University of Minnesota in 1954 for college freshmen or high school seniors designed to assess students' auditory-visual discrimination skills. The purpose of the Aliferis Music Achievement Test is 1) to determine the strengths and weaknesses of individual students in melody, harmony, and rhythm; 2) to make comparisons of individual students; and 3) to help with placement decisions in music theory classes. The material for the test was taken from freshman theory textbooks. The test can be administered using a piano or a prepared tape and takes approximately forty minutes to complete. It contains harmonic, melodic, and rhythmic sections, with sixty-four total test items. The test is in multiple-choice format, and test items are presented from simple to complex. The test has a total **reliability** coefficient of .88. The Aliferis-

Stecklein Music Achievement Test: College Midpoint Level is a similar test designed for students who have completed a two-year required course sequence in ear training and theory. The test has a total reliability coefficient of .92.

Alliance for Arts Education: A forty-six-state Alliance operating in partnership with the Kennedy Center dedicated to ensuring that the arts are included in American education. The Alliance for Arts Education was founded in 1973 as part of the authorizing legislature for the Kennedy Center.

Alpha Level: *See* Significance Level

Alternate-forms Reliability: A technique used to determine whether two alternative forms of a test are reliable or comparable in terms of difficulty and content. In testing, it is common to have two forms of the same test. In such cases, the secondary or alternative test should be as similar as possible to the original test. This is typically accomplished by having questions that are very similar, yet not identical. Alternate forms reliability is typically assessed by having individuals take two different forms of a test at two different times. Alternate forms reliability is appropriate when researchers want to assess stable variables such as **intelligence** and **achievement**. Alternate forms reliability assures that both forms of the test are as similar, or reliable, as possible. *See* Test-retest Reliability; Split-half Reliability; Reliability; Internal Consistency

Alternative Assessment: In general, any type of assessment that is unlike traditional **standardized tests**. Alternative assessments offer alternatives to the traditional multiple-choice format of standardized tests and may involve a variety of assessment techniques, including: 1) performance-based assessment, in which students are asked to demonstrate active skills, such as writing, drawing, speaking, acting, constructing, or repairing; 2) **problem solving**, in which students are asked to resolve problematic scenarios by applying major principles, theories, or formulae central to the discipline being studied; or 3) **interviews**, in which students are asked to explain or share information regarding what they know about a discipline. Alternative assessments are widely used in most subject areas, including music education, in which performance-based tests and teacher-made tests are common. *See* Alternative Education; Authentic Assessment

Alternative Education: A term used to describe any educational setting that does not follow a traditional curriculum and format. **Charter schools**, **independent schools**, **Montessori schools**, and **home schools** are all considered forms of alternative education. Although alternative education settings are more common at the elementary level, schools and programs are also available at the secondary and at the university levels. Alternative education programs are typically designed to be learner-oriented; that is, they allow learners more freedom to determine what, when, and how they learn than traditional schools do. *See* **Alternative Schools**

Alternative Licensure Programs: Programs that enable individuals who want to teach to bypass normal channels, usually requiring fewer courses for teacher **certification and licensure**. Alternative licensure programs were adopted in several states to alleviate recent teacher shortages. Individuals teaching under alternative licensure programs may not be compensated as well as a normally certified teacher for a time. While perhaps well intentioned, the practice of certifying individuals who are unprepared or experienced is disturbing to educators because alternative licensure programs provide cheaper teacher alternatives for school districts, lower the number of full-time teaching positions available for normally certified teachers, and lend credibility to the belief that anyone can teach.

Alternative Schools: A general term for **public schools** and **private schools** that are non-traditional in some way or that address specific needs or interests of particular student groups. Alternative schools may be self-contained or they may be organized as schools within schools. Alternative schools often have small school size, small class size, voluntary admission, minimum ability-grouping and labeling, **school-based management**, student involvement in governance, and expanded roles for teachers that may include counseling and guidance. Alternative schools are available for all types of students, although a common perception exists that they are particularly aimed at helping **at-risk students** or students with poor academic performance. Examples of alternative schools include **magnet schools**, **vocational-technical schools**, Montessori schools, Waldorf schools, **charter schools**, **parochial schools**, and **for-profit schools**. *See* **Montessori Schools; Waldorf Schools**

Ambience: In acoustics, the audible sense of a room or environment surrounding a sound source. **Reflections** and **reverberations** resulting from the basic physical construction of the room (general shape; hardness of the walls, floors, and ceiling; and ceiling height) and everything in the room (carpet, drapes, windows, chairs) contribute to ambience. *See* **Resonance**

America 2000 Schools: Experimental schools designed to achieve the **National Education Goals**. America 2000 Schools were an outgrowth of the **New American Schools Development Corporation (NASDC)**, a private, nonprofit, tax-exempt organization formed by American business leaders and the Bush administration in 1991. This group sponsored a national competition for innovative school design. The selected school designs were meant to serve as **models** that would lead the nation into the twenty-first century and restore American education to "world preeminence." By 1995, 9 plans had been chosen and tested in 155 schools in 18 states. For example, the "Roots and Wings" design was implemented in four elementary schools in Lexington Park, Maryland. The "Roots and Wings" design involved students in problem solving, hands-on activities, and teamwork. All of the group work was based on the students' abilities and interests rather than age. Students who had trouble received tutoring, family support services, and other outside help to master content. *See* Goals 2000: Educate America Act

American Association of Colleges for Teacher Education (AACTE): A national organization comprised of colleges and universities involved in teacher education. The AACTE is a politically active organization, representing the interests of collegiate-based teacher education in front of state and federal legislatures. In addition, the AACTE proposes and disseminates public policy initiatives for member institutions.

American Bandmasters Association (ABA): An organization established in 1929 to promote and improve bands and band music, originally conceived by Edwin Franko Goldman (1878–1956). Problems facing bands at the time included a shortage of repertoire other than marches, a lack of camaraderie among leading bandmasters, and a lack of universal instrumentation for band. The ABA has been continuously active since its inception, with the exception of cancelled conventions between 1942 and 1946 because of World War II.

American Choral Directors Association, The (ACDA): A national organization whose primary purpose is to promote choral music through performance, composition, publication, teaching, and research. Founded in 1959, the ACDA has more than 18,000 choral music teachers who teach at all levels in public and private schools, universities, and places of worship. The ACDA holds conventions and sponsors numerous national committees. Its official publication is the *Choral Journal*.

American College Testing Program (ACT): A testing program designed to assess the academic development of high school students and their readiness for college-level study. The ACT assesses English, mathematics, reading, and science abilities. The ACT is required for admission by many colleges and universities and is usually taken during the junior or senior year of high school and may be taken more than once. Scores are often used to determine scholarships and awards.

American Council for the Arts in Education: *See* Coming to Our Senses, The Rockefeller Report

American Educational Research Association (AERA): A prominent professional organization that promotes and advances educational research and its practical applications. The AERA has a diverse membership, including educators, administrators, testing agencies, behavioral scientists, and graduate students. The organization offers training fellowships, regular meetings, and a variety of scholarly publications, including *Educational Researcher, American Educational Research Journal, Educational Evaluation and Policy Analysis, and Journal of Educational and Behavioral Statistics*. The AERA consists of 12 divisions and more than 145 **special interest groups** covering a wide range of substantive and professional interests.

American Federation of Musicians (AFM): The first official national trade union for musicians, established in 1896 by the American Federation of Labor (AFL). Early activities included setting wage scales for musicians with traveling acts, discouraging the hire of foreign bands, and supporting copyright reforms. Throughout the years, the AFM has been an active advocate for professional musicians. Today, professional musicians face problems related to the availability of free music on the Internet. In music education, the AFM was one of three groups involved in a 1947 agreement called the Code of Ethics with Professional Musicians. This document defined which events and activities were appropriate for school music groups.

American Federation of Teachers (AFT): Founded in 1916 from the merger of 20 small teacher unions, the AFT is a political organization of 800,000 members devoted to the advancement of educational issues. The AFT has traditionally been closely allied with industrial labor unions and is affiliated with the American Federation of Labor-Congress of Industrial Organizations (AFL-CIO). As a result of its philosophical position, the AFT has periodically advocated various kinds of strikes or actions when its members feel they are not being treated fairly. The AFT has sponsored several projects and programs, such as Dial-A-Teacher and Learning Line. It has also supported teacher internship programs, adopt-a-school programs, and national conferences for paraprofessionals and other school personnel. The AFT was the primary labor union option for teachers until the **National Education Association (NEA)** became a labor union in the 1970s. The AFT and the National Education Association (NEA) compete for members and historically, these organizations have not always agreed on educational issues. Although efforts were made to merge the two organizations in the mid-1990s, disagreements regarding voting policies and organizational structure were not resolved.

American Orff-Schulwerk Association (AOSA): A professional organization of music educators dedicated to the teaching approaches developed by Carl Orff (1895–1982) and Gunild Keetman (1904-1991). The mission of AOSA is: 1) to demonstrate the value of the **Orff-Schulwerk** method and to promote its widespread use; 2) to support the professional development of its 10,000 members; and 3) to provide a forum for the continued growth and development of Orff Schulwerk that reflects the **diversity** in contemporary American society. *See* **Orff-Schulwerk; Orff, Carl (1895–1982)**

American String Teachers Association (ASTA): Formed in 1948 in Cleveland by a concerned group of string educators, a professional organization of string teachers, orchestra directors, and professional players that promotes excellence in string music. The ASTA is a non-profit organization founded in 1946 that is organized by state, with each state having its own organization, newsletters, and events. In addition, many universities, colleges, and high schools support student ASTA chapters. National School Orchestra Association (NSOA) merged with ASTA in the 1990s.

Americans with Disabilities Act of 1990 (ADA): Public Law 101-336, legislation enacted in 1990 to establish a comprehensive prohibition of **discrimination** based on **disability**. Title II of the Act prohibits discrimination on the basis of disability in all state and local government services, whether or not they are federally funded. Public schools fall under the ADA, and the statute mandates that school districts provide a **"free and appropriate public education" (FAPE)** to disabled students who fall under its protection. Title II of the ADA extends to all state and local governmental activities, whether or not they are federally funded. The ADA effectively expands the scope of section 504 of the **Rehabilitation Act of 1973**, which only covers programs that receive federal assistance. Individuals covered under the ADA may have one or more of a variety of both mental and physical disabilities. These disabilities can range from mild to severe and include impairments, learning disabilities, mental disorders, and physical disease.

Ameslan/American Sign Language: The most commonly used sign language for deaf and hearing-impaired individuals in the United States and Canada. Thomas Hopkins Gallaudet (1787–1851) is credited in part for the development of Ameslan, which is based on sign language used in France.

Amnesia: The partial or total loss of **memory** of past experiences, often the result of severe injury or trauma. The memories lost because of amnesia are usually not completely destroyed, and the forgotten experiences are often rapidly regained during the later part of the recovery process. Research with amnesiacs has lead to the development of a theory called implicit memory or priming. This theory proposes that memory can operate on the unconscious level and lets individuals know that they have experienced something before, even though they may not remember it. *See* Implicit Memory/Priming

Amplitude: The distance a vibrating body travels from its at-rest position during vibration. Amplitude decreases as the vibrating body loses energy. For example, a plucked violin string will have its greatest amplitude when first plucked; this amplitude will decrease steadily afterwards. In other words, the vibrations creating the sound will be moving

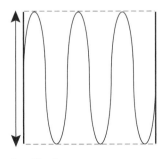

Amplitude

farthest away from the at-rest position when the sound is first produced. These vibrations will move toward the at-rest position as the energy decreases. *See* **Decay**

Amusia: A general term for the impairment of **musical ability**, usually because of physical abnormalities in one or both cerebral hemispheres. Research has suggested that impaired **pitch discrimination** ability is a primary cause for amusia. More specifically, it appears that the pitch-detecting mechanism located in the midbrain in some individuals is dysfunctional, which impairs musical discrimination abilities. *See* **Tone Deaf**

Anal Stage: *See* **Psychoanalytic Theory, Freud**

Analysis: In general, the process of breaking down something into smaller components, parts, or elements to facilitate understanding. In philosophy, analysis often involves breaking down theories and arguments into smaller units to refute them. That is, analysis enables philosophers to know and understand truth by showing what is not true. In philosophy, analysis is the opposite of **synopsis**, which is when philosophers use other theories and arguments to support their views. In psychology, analysis is commonly used to discover the source or sources of mental illness in various therapy programs such as **psychoanalysis**. In educational psychology, analysis is level five of **Bloom's taxonomy of educational objectives** in the **cognitive** domain. In music, analysis typically refers to the process of breaking down musical works according to the principles of music theory, including form, structure, tonality, harmony, melody, and rhythm. *See* **Taxonomy, Bloom's**

Analysis of Covariance (ANCOVA): A **research design** that controls for the effects of **extraneous variables** by parceling them out or separating them mathematically through statistical processes.

Music researchers often work with **intact groups**, such as full bands, choirs, and other classes, in which the researcher has little control over many variables. Because the population of the group is not altered, one **experimental group** may have an inherent advantage over another that could adversely affect the results of a study. This inherent advantage must be controlled for, and ANCOVA enables researchers to do this.

For example, a researcher may use two eighth-grade band classes. If 90 percent of the students in one group take private lessons and only 10 percent of the students in the other group take private lessons (i.e., an extraneous variable unaccounted for), the results of the study could be biased. In other words, assuming that the first group is able to perform better in some tasks than the second group, the researcher must be able to account for the private lessons in the statistical analysis so that differences found can be attributed to the variables under study rather than to private lessons (the extraneous variable). Such extraneous or nuisance variables are controlled statistically in the ANCOVA design and are called **covariates**. That is, the ANCOVA design helps ensure that any **statistically significant** differences found after data analysis are due to the **independent variables**.

In some research designs, researchers give each group a pretest to establish a **baseline** prior to variable manipulation. This is one of the most common procedures used in ANCOVA designs to control for extraneous variables. *See* Analysis of Variance (ANOVA); Factor Analysis

Analysis of Variance (ANOVA): Also called F ratio or F test, a parametric statistical test of **significance** developed by Sir Ronald Fisher (1890–1962) designed to establish whether a significant or nonchance difference exists among two or more **sample means**. ANOVA may be used in a variety of **experimental designs**, including those designs with only one independent variable, designs with two or more levels of **independent variables**, or designs with several independent variables. Thus, ANOVA is appropriate for both simple and complex experimental designs.

Technically, the F ratio is the ratio of two types of **variance**, **systematic variance** and **error variance**. Systematic variance is the difference between the group means and the means of all subjects in all groups and is also called between-group variance. Error variance is the deviation of individual scores in the group from the group's mean and is also called within-group variance. The larger the F ratio, the higher the likelihood that the results are significant; that is, they did not occur by chance alone.

Anechoic Chamber: A room without an **echo**, commonly referred to (although not entirely accurately) as a sound-proof room. In research, anechoic chambers are often used in acoustical testing. The lack of echo allows the sound source being tested to be measured without contamination or distortions from **reflections**.

Ann Arbor Symposia: Three meetings sponsored by the **Music Educators National Conference (MENC)** that took place between 1979 and 1981.

The purpose of these meetings was twofold: to discuss theoretical issues about teaching and **learning**, and to find ways these issues could be practically applied in the school music programs. The practical applications of both **cognitive** and **behaviorist** theories were discussed.

Anthem: Typically, a song about national pride, such as "The Star Spangled Banner." Historically, the term **anthem** has been used to refer to a religious song intended for liturgical performance.

Antinode: In acoustics, the point of maximum **amplitude** in a **standing wave**. *See* Node

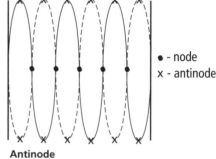

● - node
x - antinode

Antinode

Antisocial Behavior: A pattern of **behavior** that goes against social **norms** and is typically harmful to others. In children, two types of antisocial behavior are generally recognized. One occurs during **adolescence** and is usually limited to occasional, isolated episodes. This type of antisocial behavior is considered normal. The other type of antisocial behavior is typically exhibited in young children and persists beyond adolescence. It is often manifested as overly **aggressive** behavior toward others. This type of antisocial behavior is more serious. Research indicates that intervention is necessary to prevent increasingly more aggressive behavior in these children.

Anxiety: *See* Performance Anxiety

Anxiety Reaction: Also called generalized anxiety disorder, a debilitating type of irrational or unfounded fear that can last for months. Chronic, free-floating anxiety is the most defining characteristic of anxiety reaction, in which individuals have no idea why they are afraid. The physical symptoms of anxiety reactions include profuse sweating, pounding of the heart, and difficulty in breathing. Other symptoms include generalized fear, self-consciousness, constant worrying, shyness, tension, and difficulty in concentration.

AP Theory: *See* Advanced Placement (AP) Music Theory/AP Theory

Aperiodic Vibration: Any irregular and non-repeating vibration. Such vibrations produce sounds that are not integral multiples of the **fundamental**. Sounds produced by aperiodic vibrations generally do not sustain steadily for any length of time and include many percussive sounds such as those produced by bells and drums.

Aphasia: An acquired language disorder caused by brain damage or disease. Aphasia is characterized by complete or partial impairment of language skills, including speech and comprehension. *See* **Amusia; Asonia**

Apprenticeship: Generally, a period of time during which an individual gains practical work experience while learning a specialized skill or trade under the supervision of skilled workers or masters of that skill or trade. Historically, individuals were bound by contract or indenture to serve as apprentices. In exchange for learning a skill or trade, apprentices provided valuable, inexpensive labor for skilled tradesmen or journeymen. Today, apprenticeships are most common in trades such as carpentry, brick-laying, or construction work and typically involve a hands-on approach to learning.

Approval, Need For: An acquired social need for acceptance by others. Psychologists believe that the need for approval is acquired or learned in infancy and may be linked to the desire to be loved by one's mother or primary caregiver. The need for approval generally continues into adulthood and can be extremely powerful. In education, students are often highly motivated by the need for teacher approval and are willing to work hard to get it. As a result, approval can be a powerful motivator. On the other hand, approval may lose its effectiveness if overused or if students are asked to do too much to earn it.

Aptitude: In general, one's capacity to learn based on a combination of innate and acquired factors. *See* **Music Aptitude**

Aptitude Tests: *See* **Music Aptitude**

Archival Research: A type of research in which archived resources are the primary sources of information. Archival research sources include statistical records, survey archives, and written records.

Array: In research, the arrangement of numerical data according to magnitude from the smallest to the largest. For example, a group of scores including 3, 1, 10, 5, 8, 7 would be arranged as the following array: 1, 3, 5, 7, 8, 10.

Art Music: A general term for describing music written by composers who typically have a formal music education and who apply knowledge and theories of intellectual or formal techniques in the composing process. Art music is usually distinguished from popular music, whose primary purpose is entertainment or functional, while art music stands on its own merits. However, subjective value judgments often blur the distinction between art music and non-art music. In addition, attempts to objectify what is and is not art music are somewhat ambiguous and artificial. Even among professional musicians, debates concerning whether a particular piece of music is art are commonplace. Emotions, feelings, and intellectual understandings about the value of certain kinds of music contribute to this ambiguity. Ultimately, a work's musical complexity and the purpose for which it was intended are factors in determining its status as art.

Articulation: In education, the process of making what is learned in one class applicable and relevant in other classes, resulting in an interrelated educational program. That is, articulation involves transferring and supporting the material learned in one class to all other classes in a logical way and is sometimes referred to as **continuity**. Teachers sometimes tend to teach their own subject without regard for what other teachers are teaching in the other classes. For example, a music teacher may not feel that it is necessary to correct his or her students' grammar on written assignments or tests. This disregard is a hindrance to learning **transfer**. Articulation is also used to refer to the process of accepting credits or courses from one institution to another. In many cases, articulation guides established between educational institutions facilitate this process.

Articulators: Parts of the vocal mechanism that help form or shape particular vocal sounds. That is, articulators are those mechanisms that determine the distinguishable characteristics of each sound. Articulators include tongue, lips, teeth, lower jaw, the **hard palate**, and the **soft palate**.

Artificial Intelligence (AI): The simulation of human thinking by **computer programs** that attempt to parallel human thought processes. AI is usually based on theories of human thinking, and computer programs are created to simulate these theories. Computers have been successfully programmed to solve complicated logic problems, and can rival human abilities to think. For example, some computer chess programs have "beaten" world-famous chess masters; however, AI cannot begin to simulate the complexity of human thinking in many regards.

Artists-in-Schools Program, NEA: A program funded by the **National Endowment for the Arts (NEA)** that involved bringing artists into classrooms to share their talents and abilities with students. Funding for the Artists-in-Schools Program began in 1970, after the success of the visual artist-in-residence program in 1969. The program began by placing about 300 artists in elementary and secondary schools in 31 states. By 1974, more than 1,700 artists were placed in select schools in all 50 states. In 1980, the program became the Artists-in-Education Program and the scope was expanded to include grants for residencies in non-school settings, pilot learning projects, and technical services. Critics of the Artists-in-Schools Program questioned whether it was merely a work program for artists because the philosophies of working artists and educators were often at odds. Educational **goals** and **objectives** were often not defined in clear, concrete, and measurable terms, making evaluation of the program's success difficult. In addition, because the program was federally funded, many limiting policies were imposed on schools and artists. *See* **Arts-in-Education Program, NEA**

Arts Advocacy Project: A collaborative project between the Office of Education, the Alliance for Arts Education of the Kennedy Center, and the organizations of DAMT (dance, art, music, theater) in 1976. The Arts Advocacy Project was conducted over five weekends, featuring performances and discussions from a variety of organizations, including the Chief State School Officers and the National School Boards Association.

Arts and Humanities Program (AHP), USOE: A program funded by the United States Office of Education (USOE) in 1965, which sponsored research on **curricular** development and related programs for arts and humanities education. The AHP was well supported in the early years of its existence, and significant amounts of grant money were made available through the program. The AHP was considered to be the first cohesive national effort at art education research; however, the creation of the National Endowment of the Arts (NEA) redirected government efforts for funding the arts, and the program quickly declined. Although the NEA attempted to fill the gap left by the absence of the AHP, it was not until 1985 that Congress specifically recommended that the NEA support arts education. *See* **National Endowment for the Arts (NEA)**

Arts Education: A general term referring to the education students receive in the arts based on course offerings in school **curricula**. Arts courses typically include music, visual art, drama, and dance. Arts education may be mandated by state and/or local law or by local school boards if they consider the arts an important curricular component. Each area typically functions autonomously, although special projects combining different arts areas are common. In politics, arts education refers to all areas of the arts that have a presence in public schools and is usually used when broad-based policies are being considered or promoted that impact the arts.

Arts in Education: An approach to arts education in which the arts are incorporated directly into the educational program of the school. Most commonly used at the elementary level, Arts in Education integrates the arts into the general instruction received by every student rather than isolating them as a separate activity or including them as mere embellishment to the "real" **curriculum**. *See* **Disciplined Based Art Education (DBAE)**

Arts in General Education Approach (AGE): A phrase used in *Coming to Our Senses: The Significance of the Arts for American Education* meaning that arts should be implemented throughout the **curriculum** and used in an interdisciplinary manner. In this phrase, "general education" is used in a broad sense to mean unspecialized education. Critics of AGE claim that it defines the teaching and implementation of arts in education as a social service, merely an instrument through which other non-art goals may be reached or made more palatable to learners. *See* **Coming to Our Senses: The Rockefeller Report**

Arts-in-Education Program, NEA: A program intended to promote the arts in schools. Arts-in-Education funded grants to arts agencies to sponsor a number of arts-related activities, including residencies in schools and grants for promoting the arts as a basic and sequential component in school **curricula**. The Arts-in-Education program was formerly called the Artists-in-Education Program and the **Artists-in-Schools Program**.

Arts in Schools Basic Education Grant (AISBEG): A project designed to encourage state and local agencies to work in cooperation with schools to develop arts education programs that are a basic **curricular** component and are sequential from **kindergarten** through grade twelve. Supported by the **Arts-in-Education Program**, the primary purpose of the AISBEG project was to facilitate partnerships between local, state, and regional arts agencies and professional organizations, artists, and arts institutions as a way of providing leadership and support for improving arts education.

Asonia: The inability to discriminate between pitch differences in a normal manner. *See* **Amusia; Aphasia**

Aspiration/Aspirate h: A very soft, unvocalized noise heard in speech sounds created by a slight constriction of the vocal folds where the folds are brought closer together than at rest, but not close enough to be set into vibration. In English, the phonemes *h* and *p* are aspirated. When air is pushed through the vocal folds, a breathy *ha* or *pa* sound can be heard. These breathy sounds quickly dissipate following the release of an unvoiced consonant. For example, after an individual says the word "hi", listeners only hear the long *I* sound.

Assertive Discipline: In education, an approach to discipline developed by Lee Canter in 1976 and described in his book entitled, *Assertive Discipline: A Take-Charge Approach for Today's Educator*. Assertive discipline emphasizes the rights of teachers to enforce standards of behavior that allow them to be more effective. The focus is on clearly defined expectations linked to a system of **rewards** and **punishments**. Assertive discipline is an "if-this-then-that" approach to discipline in which actions and consequences are clearly established. For example, a typical assertive discipline punishment technique is to write the names of students who are misbehaving on the blackboard. This action may be followed by placing checkmarks next to these names for further misbehavior. Each checkmark leads to progressively harsher punishments, including time out from the classroom, notes to parents, or meetings with the principal. Assertive discipline has been very controversial. Proponents praise its effectiveness in creating a disciplined learning environment and promoting academic achievement. Opponents argue that assertive discipline places too much emphasis on threat and punishment as a means of maintaining classroom control.

Assertiveness Training: Also known as assertive training, a form of **counter-conditioning** that teaches and reinforces assertive responses to **stimuli** in an attempt to **extinguish** passivity or anxiety in individuals. Assertiveness training helps individuals learn to speak for themselves, exercise their right of choice, and negotiate appropriate solutions to conflicts. Assertiveness training develops healthy assertive techniques, not unhealthy **aggression**.

Assessment: In general, a term used to describe an evaluative process for determining what has been learned and/or levels of competency. Assessment encompasses a variety of **techniques** and **methods** and is often used interchangeably with **evaluation**, testing, or **measurement**. In education, a wide variety of assessment strategies are available. Some of the most common methods include: 1) a variety of teacher-constructed tests; 2) **standardized tests**; 3) subjective judgments of experts based on both specific or general criteria; 4) **portfolios**; 5) **authentic assessment** measures; and 6) **alternative assessments**.

Assimilation: In general, the process by which an individual or group is able to adapt and become part of a new culture. Assimilation is often associated with immigrant groups or other culturally distinct groups and may also apply to any individual or group confronting a new social or cultural situation or environment. In **Jean Piaget's (1896-1980) theory of cognitive development**, assimilation refers to the individual's ability to internalize and conceptualize environmental experiences. Piaget used assimilation in conjunction with **accommodation**, which refers to the adjustment an individual makes to environmental **stimuli**. *See* **Equilibration**

Associate Learning: In psychology, a therapeutic technique where individuals associate feelings of deep relaxation and calmness with ordinarily stressful or anxiety-producing situations. *See* **Desensitization**

Association for Supervision and Curriculum Development (ASCD): An international, non-profit organization that promotes and supports several aspects of effective teaching and learning, including professional development, educational leadership, and cultural diversity. ASCD membership includes a wide range of educational leaders from more than 135 countries. The ASCD was founded in 1943 as a division of the **National Education Association (NEA)**; however, in 1972 the ASCD became an independent organization. Throughout its history, ASCD has published several newsletters, journals, and yearbooks under titles such as Education Update and Curriculum Update.

Association for Technology in Music Instruction (ATMI): An organization devoted to issues regarding the use of technology in music teaching and learning. The ATMI provides technical information by and for specialists in the field of **computer-assisted instruction (CAI)** in music and for CAI users who are not technology specialists. This organization informs teachers of new technologies and of ways these technologies can be used. The ATMI publishes the Music Technology Directory yearly, which contains listings of freeware, shareware, and commercial software for both music and music instruction.

Associationism: Also known as connectionism, a school of psychological thought popular in the 1950s, or the belief that learning results from establishing meaningful connections between specific **stimuli** and **responses**. Edward L. Thorndike (1874–1949) was a leading proponent of associationism. **Behaviorism** was an outgrowth of associationism. *See* Thorndike, Edward L. (1874-1949)

Associative Play: A type of play classified by Mildred Parten in 1929, in which children interact with each other but do not appear to be actually playing together. In associative play, interaction can include sharing materials and asking questions. *See* Unoccupied Play; Solitary Play; Onlooker Play; Parallel Play; Cooperative Play

At-risk Students: A term commonly used to describe students who have a high risk for failure academically, economically, and/or socially. At-risk students often do not gain mastery of the fundamental skills necessary to succeed academically because of internal factors such as lack of **motivation**, low ability level, or psychological disorders. They can also be at-risk because of external factors such as home environment, **socioeconomic status (SES)**, and poor social skills. In addition, factors involving health, poverty, abuse, neglect, drug use, and pregnancy also contribute to being labeled at-risk. Criteria for identifying at-risk or potentially at-risk students include poor grades, high rates of absenteeism and tardiness, language difficulties, and the inability to function in traditional environments. Programs designed to help at-risk students are often restricted to remedial reading and rely heavily on teacher direction and instruction, a valuable and expensive resource. The financial burden involved in offering additional courses and hiring additional faculty and staff to work with at-risk students is substantial. In addition, some teaching techniques, such as ability grouping, can result in isolating at-risk students from others who are more highly motivated and academically successful. These factors often cause at-risk students to drop out of school altogether. Suggestions for helping at-risk students include intensive individualized instruction, early intervention, personal and social skills training, and interaction with other students. At-risk students do place a heavy burden on schools, but the inability of schools to meet the needs of at-risk students ultimately places a heavy, lifelong burden on society.

Atkinson-Shiffrin Model: A theory of memory developed by R.C. Atkinson and R. M. Shiffrin in 1968 suggesting that there are three distinct types of memory: 1) sensory memory, which is the awareness of sensations that disappear quickly unless given attention; 2) **short-term memory (STM)**, which is where information is first stored when given attention; and 3) **long-term memory (LTM)**, which is where information is stored once it has been rehearsed in short-term memory sufficiently. According to the Atkinson-Shiffrin model, information reaching the senses lasts for only a fraction of a second unless it is attended to. People are unaware of most sensory information; however, once selected information is attended to, it is processed in STM and held there for about 10–20 seconds. If rehearsed enough in STM, information is transferred to LTM, where it may be retained forever. The idea that forgetting occurs differently in STM and LTM is sometimes called the two-process theory of learning—a theory often associated with the cognitive **information processing model** of memory. *See* Information Processing Model

Attention: The focusing of perceptual abilities to heighten awareness of a particular object, event, task, person, or thought. Most individuals have the ability to give more attention to one thing than another, although precisely how this occurs is not known. Ideas regarding attention have focused on the following: 1) the degree to which the field is broad or narrow, 2) the degree to which an individual focuses on selected information within the field, 3) the role experience and learning have on attention, and 4) the conscious and unconscious preset for determining behavior. Lack of attention or the inability to focus attention is often cited as a reason for poor performance in most academic and performance-oriented areas. In musical performances, the potential for having a large number of distractions is great, and can be caused by the audience, extraneous noise, and mistakes. As a consequence, attention often plays a major role in determining performance proficiency. Efforts to improve attention have focused on: 1) **mental imagery**, 2) mental rehearsal techniques, 3) developing better mental presets, 4) increasing the awareness of individual actions and thoughts, 5) developing positive **attitudes**, and 6) ensuring that basic skills are learned properly. *See* **Mental Presets**

Attention-deficit/hyperactivity Disorder (ADHD)/Attention-deficit Disorder (ADD):

A neurobiologically based **disorder** resulting in abnormal impulsive and hyperactive behavior and the inability to maintain attention. Once called hyperkinesis, attention-deficit/hyperactivity disorder (ADHD) may also be called attention-deficit disorder (ADD). Behaviors indicating ADHD/ADD vary greatly from person to person and must persist for several months before a diagnosis may be made. These behaviors will usually interfere with social relationships and academic performance. Although the onset of ADHD/ADD is usually before age seven, it can persist well into adulthood.

Students with ADHD/ADD often display the following characteristics: 1) a consistent and often extreme difficulty staying on task; 2) the inability to focus **attention** on assigned tasks; 3) failure to complete assignments on a regular basis; 4) extraneous **off-task** behaviors that disrupt class; 5) failure to listen to the teacher's instructions; 6) prone to distraction; 7) turning in sloppy, incomplete assignments; and 8) failure to follow rules and directions. Identifying students with ADHD/ADD is difficult, and experienced professionals should be consulted when possible. ADHD/ADD may be treated with medication or with alternative therapies, such as **behavior modification**. One of the most common medications used for treating ADHD/ADD is Methylphenidate, a central nervous system stimulant that works by targeting the dopamine system in the brain. Methylphenidate is found in the following medications: Ritalin, Concerta, Metadate, Eqasym, and Medikinet.

Attenuation: In acoustics, the lessening of sound signal level because of environmental factors, including divergence, **absorption**, **reflection**, **refraction**, or **diffraction**. Attenuation is usually expressed in **decibels** (**dB**).

Attitude Measurement: In research, any process of assessing or measuring **attitudes** about something, usually experiences or **concepts**. Because attitudes are subjective **constructs**, one challenge researchers face is to clearly define the terms used to describe various attitudes to objectify responses. To this end, researchers often construct attitude **models**. **Variables** can be isolated from these models and questions can be derived for use in the **measurement** process. Although such models are generally accepted in research, critics point out that such research models artificially compartmentalize subject **responses** when used in attitude measurement. In reality several factors affect the **validity** and **reliability** of attitude measures, which may include the following: 1) the subjective nature of attitudes; 2) the fact that attitudes may change at any moment; 3) the inability of some people to articulate attitudes; 4) the ambiguity inherent within an individual concerning attitudes; and 5) the fact that people are often resistant about changing their attitudes. Numerous methods of attitude measurement are available, including Q-Methodology, Multidimensional Scaling, **Surveys**, **Content Analysis**, and Researcher Observation.

In music research, attitude measurement has generally taken three forms: 1) verbal or written responses, where attitudes are assessed based on what an individual says or writes about something; 2) **Likert scales**, where individuals are asked to respond to a scale (e.g., 1 = strongly disagree, 2 = disagree, 3 = undecided, 4 = agree, 5 = strongly agree); and the **semantic-differential** method, where pairs of bipolar adjectives (e.g., good/bad) are presented in conjunction with a numerical scale used to indicate the extent of "goodness" or "badness" perceived by the individual. Because music possesses an extremely strong **affective** component, attitude measurement studies in music education are particularly relevant. They provide valuable insights into current perceptions of music and music education, and they can assist music educators in determining future directions of the profession.

Attitudes: In general, how individuals feel about something or someone based on experiences and **perceptions**. As a **concept**, attitudes encompass a myriad of both psychological and perceptual components and are largely subjective. As such, they are difficult to describe in concrete terms. As a construct, educators and researchers have associated a variety of terms with attitude, including tastes, likes, dislikes, appreciations, preferences, interests, feelings, biases, prejudices, ideas, values, and opinions. *See* Attitude Measurement

Attitudinal Objectives: Educational **objectives** that focus on student **perceptions** and feelings toward new subject material or activities. Attitudinal objectives are usually not specifically oriented; however, achieving them can greatly facilitate learning. Examples of attitudinal objectives include sharing discoveries, developing openness and enthusiasm for the material, and engaging freely in class discussion and activities. Attitudinal objectives are particularly relevant when students are being asked to try new techniques or to use **discovery methods** when some students might feel intimidated, shy, or inadequate. *See* Affective Domain

Attribute-Treatment Interaction (ATI): In education, the interaction that takes place between a student and a teaching method. The attribute is the system of thinking that a student possesses, and the treatment is the **method** used to teach him or her. The **outcome** of the experience is the result of the combination of these two components. The general idea of ATI is that no generic teaching method can be applied to all students, because students will react differently to different teaching methods depending on their system of thinking.

Attribution Theory: A theory concerned with the psychological processes individuals use to attribute causes to behavior. According to attribution theory, individuals are motivated to explain their own behavior and the behavior of others by attributing the causes of the behavior to either a situation or a disposition. **Situational attribution** is when an individual attributes the cause of a behavior to something in the environment. For example, a runner who fails to run a qualifying time may blame the wind or the heat. **Dispositional attribution** is when an individual attributes the cause of a behavior to something inside the person. For example, a runner who fails to run a qualifying time may blame his natural lack of endurance or a lack of **motivation** to train properly. In reality, most people attribute the causes of behavior to a combination of both. *See* Fundamental Attribution Error; Self-serving Bias

Audiation: Edwin E. Gordon's (b. 1927) term for the process of hearing and comprehending music internally when there is no physical sound present. According to Gordon, audiation is fundamental to music aptitude and music achievement, and it is the basis of his **music learning theory**. Gordon makes a distinction between audiation and **aural perception**.

Audiation takes place when individuals hear and comprehend music, whereas aural perception takes place when individuals simply hear sound that is physically present. Sound is not comprehended as music until it is audiated.

Gordon also makes a distinction between audiation and imitation or inner hearing. Imitation is a product and audiation is a process. That is, individuals can inner hear without comprehending (aural perception), and one can imitate without audiating. There are eight types of audiation: 1) listening to music; 2) reading music; 3) writing music that is heard; 4) recalling music from memory; 5) writing music from memory; 6) creating or improvising music; 7) reading and creating or improvising music; and 8) writing and creating or improvising music. The types of audiation are not hierarchical; however, some serve as the readiness for others. Gordon's music learning theory is described in detail in his book entitled *Learning Sequences in Music*.

Audiometer: A handheld electronic device used to detect a person's response to sound stimuli. **Carl Seashore (1866–1949)** was instrumental in developing the audiometer in the early 1900s.

Auditory Association: The ability to associate verbally represented ideas or information with real things or **concepts**.

Auditory Blending: Connecting the necessary vocal sounds and syllables to create a single, integrated word when speaking.

Auditory Canal: The passageway leading from the **outer ear** to the **eardrum**. The auditory canal carries sound **waves** that are amplified by the eardrum and interpreted by the brain.

Auditory Localization: The perceptual ability to determine the direction and the distance of a sound source.

Auditory Memory: The ability to remember and recall information that is presented verbally. Auditory memory differs from aural memory. In auditory memory, it is the information represented by the words that is remembered. In aural memory, it is the aural characteristics of the words themselves that is remembered (e.g., the tone of voice and/or voice inflection. *See* **Aural Memory**

Aural Discrimination: The process of distinguishing between sounds (aural **stimuli**). In music research, aural discrimination tasks are often designed specifically for each study; however, common types of tasks have emerged over time. Tasks commonly used in music research involve listening to pairs of tones and making **pitch**, **timbre**, **loudness**, or **duration** judgments or listening to musical patterns and making melodic, harmonic, or rhythmic judgments. In addition, a variety of **tests** involve aural discrimination tasks, including: 1) **Musical Aptitude Profile** (1965) by **Edwin E. Gordon (b. 1927)**; 2) **Music Achievement Tests** (1969–70) by Richard Colwell; 3) **Wing Standardized Tests of Musical Intelligence** (1961) by H. D. Wing; 4) **Seashore Measures of Musical Talents** (1939) by **Carl E. Seashore (1866–1949)**; and 5) Measures of Musical Abilities (1966) by A. Bentley. *See* Aural-Visual Discrimination; Aural Recognition

Aural Imagery: **Mental images** evoked by sound. Aural images are subjective; that is, they vary from person to person. Aural images may be visual or conceptual. Visual images evoked by aural stimuli are usually associated with a particular event in an individual's past experiences or memories. Conceptual images evoked by aural stimuli contain an individual's subjective mental representations, thoughts, or ideas based on experience. *See* Imagery

Aural Memory: The ability to retain and recall sound information, including **timbres**, **pitches**, rhythms, melodies, and harmonies. For example, jazz players rely on aural memory to recall the harmonic and melodic outline of a tune when they use it to improvise melodies. *See* Audiation

Aural Models/Modeling: In education, the act of providing students with a sound representation to aid in the learning process. Aural modeling may be used to effectively demonstrate a variety of concepts, including tone quality, phrasing, vibrato, articulation, blend, and balance. Recorded sound or live sound with one or more instruments or voices may be used for aural modeling. For example, a band director may provide an aural model of phrasing and articulation by singing or playing a passage for students with the desired phrasing and articulation. Aural models are particularly useful in **performance-based classes** because they can provide a more efficient, accurate means of communication than verbal instruction alone. *See* Modeling

Aural Perception: *See* Music Perception

Aural Recognition: The act of making musical judgments regarding the various attributes or qualities of musical examples based on previously learned material. Aural recognition tasks are most commonly used in research and are also an integral part of the testing and **evaluation** process of many college-level music theory and history courses. Aural recognition tasks often involve: 1) identifying intervals, chord types, or **timbres**; 2) identifying melodic, harmonic, and rhythmic patterns; 3) identifying musical styles; and 4) identifying specific pieces. *See* Aural Discrimination; Aural-Visual Discrimination

Aural/Oral Level of Discrimination Learning, Gordon: *See* Skill Learning Sequence, Gordon

Aural-Visual Discrimination: The ability to recognize similarities and differences in aural and visual **stimuli**, such as music and notation. Aural-visual discrimination tasks are a typical component of **music achievement** and aptitude assessments at all levels of study. Some of the most common types of aural-visual discrimination tasks include: 1) listening to short musical examples and selecting the correctly notated example from several choices; 2) making judgments about whether a particular listening example is the same as or different from a given notated example; 3) identifying specific pitch, rhythm, melody, or harmony errors in notation based on a given musical example; and 4) associating pictures or icons that the listener believes reflect a given musical example. In addition, aural-visual discrimination tasks may also include a variety of melodic, harmonic, and rhythmic **dictation** tasks that are common in most theory and ear-training courses.

Ausubel, David (b. 1918): An educational **cognitive** theorist who has contributed, among other things, the concept of **advanced organizers** into an approach or strategy called **reception learning**. These advanced organizers allow students to incorporate new material into existing cognitive structures by providing the groundwork for developing and understanding relationships between what is known and what is being learned. According to Ausubel, these advanced organizers are at a higher level of abstraction than the new material. These organizers thus form the conceptual framework, foundation, or the readiness for later learning. This enables learning to take place in a "top-down" manner; that is, learners first develop a general conceptual framework and then learn the specifics involved. This approach is opposite most other cognitive approaches to learning, which suggest that learning takes place in a "bottom-up" manner. That is, through the learning of specifics, individuals develop greater conceptual understanding. The key to reception learning is that teachers should prepare and organize the material to be learned in advance and then present it to the students. Reception learning is in direct contrast to **Jerome Bruner's (b. 1915) discovery learning** approach, in which students take a more active role in organizing the material to be learned.

Ausubel devised two types of advanced organizers: 1) an expository organizer, which helps provide students with a subject overview and 2) a comparative organizer, which helps provide a link between information the students already know and the information they will be learning. That is, expository organizers are typically used to introduce new material in an overview manner, while comparative organizers are typically used to build on information that is already known in order to develop the unknown material. *See* Discovery Learning, Bruner; Reception Learning/ Method

Authentic Assessment: An **evaluation** process in which students are directly involved in assessing their work. Authentic assessment enables students to take control of their learning and to form meaningful connections to the material being learned. Students take responsibility for part of the learning process through student contracts. Authentic assessment places less emphasis on traditional written tests and instead focuses on assessments in which students can take an active role in assessing their work. Particular emphasis is placed on assessing skills, knowledge, and attitudes that extend beyond the classroom environment. For example, students may be asked to assess their communication skills, their ability to analyze issues, their ability to work with others, their problem-solving strategies, or their abilities to make choices and good decisions. Authentic assessment includes useful, practical, transferable items with focus placed on tasks that are realistic in nature. **Rubrics**, **graphic organizers**, **journals**, and **portfolios** are commonly used in authentic assessment.

Authoritarian Leadership: A style of leadership in which the individual holding the leadership position retains all the decision-making power and maintains control over as many aspects of the group as possible. Research has shown that this style of leadership is not as effective as those styles that allow group members to have some type of meaningful input.

Autism: A severe neurological disorder that can occur in early childhood. Such children may or may not possess normal **intelligence**, although some form of **mental retardation** is common with autism. Signs of autism include: 1) rigidity, or lack of ability to accept change; 2) hyperirritable attention, appearing as lack of **attention**; and 3) emotional instability, which may cause autistic children to react differently than other children. In music, studies with autistic children have shown a preference for music over other activities.

Autokinetic Effect: A visual effect produced when a small, stationary pinpoint of light in a dark room appears to move. The autokinetic effect is often cited as evidence that people "create" their own sense of movement within their minds and that the brain needs to experience a sense of motion. Because this movement is perceptual rather than physical, the autokinetic effect has been used in research to further the understanding of how group norms emerge.

Automation: *See* Task Automation

Autonomic Nervous System: A system of nerve cells and fibers regulating smooth muscle and glandular activities. The autonomic nervous system is closely integrated with the brain and spinal cord, although some cell bodies and synapses lie outside the brain and spinal cord.

Auxiliary Organizations, MENC: Organizations directly associated with the **Music Educators National Conference (MENC)**. Originally, two organizations were considered auxiliary organizations: the Music Industry Council (MIC) and the National Interscholastic Music Activities Commission (NIMAC). Today, several organizations are considered auxiliaries of MENC, including the **College Band Directors National Association (CBDNA)**, the **National Association of College Wind and Percussion Instructors (NACWAPI)**, the **American String Teachers Association (ASTA)**, the **American Choral Directors Association (ACDA)**, the **National Band Association (NBA)**, the **National Association for the Study and Performance of African-American Music (NASPAAM)**, and the **Organization of American Kodaly Educators (OAKE)**. In addition to its auxiliary groups, the MENC also maintains a close relationship with several other organizations, including the **National Association of Schools of Music (NASM)** and the Society for the Encouragement and Preservation of Barbershop Quartet Singing in America (SEPBQSA).

Availability Sampling: In research, a type of nonprobability sampling in which individuals who are readily available are included in the research sample. Like other nonprobability sampling techniques, availability sampling increases the chances of some types of research errors. *See* Nonprobability Sampling; Probability Sampling

Avant-garde: A term usually associated with the development of new or experimental ideas and **concepts** in the arts. Avant-garde artists are often pioneers of a movement in their fields, and their works often oppose established ideas, traditions, and/or styles. Avant-garde ideas and art are often considered experimental or innovative. In music, avant-garde is most commonly used to refer to some mid-to-late twentieth century compositions. Characteristics of avant-garde music include non-traditional compositional techniques including tone rows, unusual scales or pitch groups, and special effects. Performers often find themselves utilizing new or unusual performance techniques to meet the musical demands of a piece. Avant-garde is often associated with **electronic music**.

Average: *See* Mean

Aversive Behavior: *See* Avoidance Learning

Aversive Conditioning: The process by which an undesirable response is **extinguished** through the use of **punishment**. Aversive conditioning is sometimes used in **behavioral therapy**, although it is more often used in conjunction with other behavioral techniques.

Aversive Stimulus: Something painful or unpleasant, or a **stimulus** that decreases **behavior** when presented as a consequence (**punishing stimulus**). If an aversive stimulus is removed, the rate of behavior will increase. Thus, the aversive stimulus functions as a **negative reinforcer**.

Avocation: A secondary occupation or hobby. In general, avocations are not primarily money-making activities; they are usually pursued for the enjoyment and personal fulfillment they provide. Music is a popular avocation, and can be an enjoyable pursuit for a lifetime.

Avoidance Learning: Learning controlled by the threat of **punishment**. In education, avoidance learning occurs when students' actions become dictated by whether teachers are likely to punish them for certain behaviors. Thus, students learn to make choices and display actions that will not result in punishment. A primary problem with avoidance learning is that students learn to think in terms of which behaviors will not result in punishment, rather than in terms of which behaviors are most appropriate and why.

A-weighting (dBA): A system of filtering acoustical signals according to **frequency**. The purpose of A-weighting (dBA) is to compensate for the fact that the human ear does not respond equally to all frequencies; that is, human hearing is less sensitive at low and high frequencies than it is in the midrange, and the degree of variation depends on the **intensity** of the sound. A-weighting (dBA) filters roughly mimic the human ear's response to frequency and are typically used to modify sound meters. In addition, the dBA scale is easy to use and measure and is therefore used in variety of applications, including laboratory test systems, acoustic systems, and general-purpose signal modification.

Axiology: An area of philosophy concerned with the nature, types, and **criteria** of **values** and value judgments, particularly regarding **ethics**, or a branch of philosophy that seeks to explain how good something is or is not based on **analysis**. Questions emphasized in axiology are those questions regarding values or what "should be." Axiology is commonly divided into two main branches, the study of ethics, which encompasses moral values and conduct and the study of **aesthetics**, which encompasses questions regarding the nature of beauty and art. In axiology, philosophers often seek to assess value. That is, they seek to explain how good something is or is not based on analysis. The following are examples of axiological questions: Is Mozart better than Garth Brooks? Is country music better than classical music? Does any style of music contain more goodness than another?

Back-to-basics Movement: Originally, an economically driven movement resulting from the recession of 1974 that encouraged an emphasis on **basic subjects**. Many music programs suffered cutbacks or were eliminated during this time; however, many of these programs were restored once funding became available, affirming the value of music in public school education. Today, any move to reemphasize subjects like math, English, and the sciences is referred to as a back-to-basics movement.

Band Contests: Instrumental ensemble competitions that became popular in the late nineteenth and early twentieth centuries. In the late nineteenth century, small town brass bands were the most common entrants in band contests, with each community's band attempting to outperform the others. After World War I, the number of school bands and band contests increased. The first national school band contest was held in Chicago in 1923. Its success resulted in an increase in national, regional, and local band contests and festivals; however, national and regional contests declined rapidly at the end of World War II. Band contests today are typically held at the state and local levels.

Bandura, Albert (b. 1925): The originator of social learning theory, Bandura suggests that learning does not take place on the basis of reinforcement principles only but also takes place as a result of **modeling**. That is, Bandura believes that students can learn new responses simply by observing the behavior of others. He is also well known for his belief that individuals' expectations of their own effectiveness to master and achieve will play a significant role in determining the types of behavior these individuals will engage in. Bandura earned his bachelor's degree in psychology from the University of British Columbia in 1949 and his Ph.D. from the University of Iowa in 1952. In 1953 Bandura began teaching at Stanford University. *See* **Social Learning Theory, Bandura; Self-efficacy**

Bar Graph: A graph that uses horizontal and vertical bars to compare the values of the two different variables.

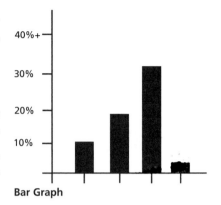

Bar Graph

Basal Mental Age: In individual intelligence tests (e.g., **Stanford-Binet**), the highest age level at which and below which tests designed to assess mental age are passed. *See* Mental Age (MA); Intelligence Tests

Baseline: In research, a measured performance taken in the course of many observations during a control period against which the effects of experimental **variables** can be assessed. Baseline is sometimes referred to as base rate or **operant level**.

Basic Concepts Commission: A commission organized by **Music Educators National Conference (MENC)** in 1954 to develop a unifying philosophy for music education. The yearbook *Basic Concepts in Music Education* was published in 1958 by the National Society for the Study of Education based on the work of the Commission on Basic Concepts. This yearbook included a variety of articles related to music education, articles on various philosophical systems used in American education, and guidelines for the development of a music education philosophy.

Basic Music Activities: The activities described in a widely used and distributed pamphlet entitled *Outline of a Program for Music Education* in the 1940s and 1950s. Basic music activities were divided into categories, including singing, rhythmics, listening, playing, and creating. In addition, an amount of time for each activity was recommended and activities for different grade levels were specified. This pamphlet and the basic music activities are historically important because they presented a **model** against which local school music programs could be measured. In addition, because basic music activities were widely available, they were used as the basis for music conference sessions.

Basic Subjects: A term that was popularized in the late 1950s after the Soviet launch of *Sputnik I* and the subsequent American concern with its educational system. Many people believed that American education did not properly emphasize subject matter that would develop the engineers and scientists necessary to maintain world supremacy both technologically and militarily. Subjects considered basic included mathematics, science, foreign languages, and reading. Although there was support for including the arts as a basic subject, such support was not universal. The result of this back-to-basics movement was to increase the amount of government money in education, especially for basic subjects. *See* **Back-to-Basics Movement; Sputnik I**

Basilar Membrane: The membrane of the inner ear within the coils of the **cochlea** supporting the **organ of corti** that vibrates in response to sound transmitted through the **outer** and **middle ear**. Movements of the basilar membrane stimulate the hair cells of the organ of corti, sending auditory signals to the brain. The basilar membrane has

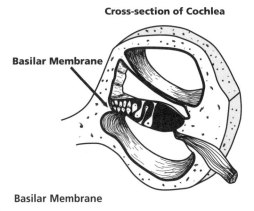

Cross-section of Cochlea

Basilar Membrane

Basilar Membrane

been used to explain the way pitch is identified in psychoacoustics. *See* **Place Theory**

Bawling Out: *See* **Lining Out**

Bay Psalm Book, The: Published around 1640, a revision of the **Ainsworth** edition of the psalms written by about thirty ministers who came to the colonies in 1636. *The Bay Psalm Book* is sometimes referred to as the first published songbook in America. The book relies on the **lining out** method, a type of call-and-response approach to singing commonly used in colonial times.

Beach Music Achievement Test: Published in 1920, the first standardized measure of **musical achievement**. The Beach Music Achievement Test is out of print but has historical significance because it provides insight into the musical skills and tasks being measured at the time and the way those skills and tasks were assessed. The test covered the following: 1) knowledge of music symbols; 2) recognition of measure; 3) tone direction and similarity; 4) **pitch discrimination**; 5) application of syllables; 6) time values; 7) terms and symbols; 8) correction of notation; 9) syllables and pitch names; 10) representation of pitches; and 11) composers and artists.

Beats: The pulsating **dissonance** that occurs when two tones produced simultaneously are slightly out of tune. The difference in wavelengths creates rapid changes in the **intensity** of the sound. This change occurs because the wavelengths alternate between reinforcing each other to create a greater **amplitude** and weakening each other by **masking** certain characteristics of the sound.

Before and After Experimental Design: An **experimental design** that measures the **dependent variable** before and after introduction of the **independent variable**. The purpose is to determine the effects of the independent variable on the dependent variable. A before and after experimental design may be used with one or two groups. When two groups are used, one serves as the **control group** and is not presented with the independent variable. By necessity, some time must pass between the first **measurement** and the second measurement. The use of a control group helps to ensure that any changes shown in the second measurement are likely caused by the independent variable and not by other extraneous factors. *See* **After-only Experimental Design**

Before-school Programs: Programs typically provided in conjunction with schools that offer a variety of student services before regular school hours. The number of before-school programs has increased in recent years because parents often need to take children to school early so that they can go to work. As a result, schools have assumed some of the traditional roles and responsibilities of parents. For example, many children do not eat breakfast, which has been shown to have a significantly negative impact on learning. Breakfast programs are among the most popular before-school programs. Federal, state, and local money has been allocated periodically to support these programs.

Behavior: Any observable and/or measurable act or **response** of an organism. Behavioral psychologists sometimes use the "dead man" test to determine whether something is or is not a behavior. Simply stated, if a dead man can do it, then it is not a behavior. For example, wearing glasses is not a behavior because a dead man can wear glasses. In his book entitled, *Teaching/Discipline: A Positive Approach for Educational Development*, Cliff Madsen defines behavior as "anything a person does, says, or thinks that can be observed directly and/or indirectly."

Behavior Disordered: A general term applied to individuals who may be afflicted with one or more of a variety of neuroses, psychoses, or other behavior-related conditions. Behavior disorders can range from mild to severe, and children suffering from behavior disorders often require special attention at school. Depression, anxieties, and phobias are examples of behavior disorders.

Behavior Genetics: The study of the inheritance of behavioral characteristics. Studies in behavior genetics attempt to discover relationships between observed behavior and genetic makeup. Studies with animals and humans support the theory that at least some characteristics of behavior are genetically determined. Animal studies generally involve selective breeding and inbreeding. For example, a typical study involves mating animals that are specifically strong in one area, such as aggressiveness. These studies show that behavioral characteristics can be isolated and reproduced with a significant degree of consistency. Human research in behavior genetics is severely limited by ethical considerations and, as a result, usually involves one of the following methods: 1) tracing lineage; 2) comparing adopted children and foster children to their biological parents; and 3) studying the similarities between identical twins who have been raised apart. *See* Genetics

Behavior Modification: A system for changing behavior based on the principles of **conditioning**. Behavior modification is usually applied in the classroom or to a patient undergoing **behavioral therapy**. When desirable **behavior** is exhibited, it is followed by a **reinforcing stimulus**; when undesirable behavior is exhibited, it is followed either by no **reinforcement** or, less commonly, by **punishment**. Defining **goals** precisely in behavioral terms and following a consistent coordinating schedule is important for successful behavior modification. *See* Behavioral Psychology/ Behaviorism

Behavioral Objective: *See* Objective

Behavioral Therapy: Also called **behavior modification**, a method of psychotherapy based on principles of learning. Behavior therapy includes the use of several techniques, including **conditioning, counter-conditioning, reinforcement**, and **shaping** to modify **behaviors** and/or to develop new ones. Behavior therapy does not involve seeking underlying reasons for behavior nor does it attempt to provide insight into the nature of the problem; its primary focus is on changing the undesired behavior.

For example, behavioral therapy is often used to help individuals learn to control aggressive behavior by rewarding appropriate behavior and/or by punishing or ignoring inappropriate behavior.

Behavioral Psychology/Behaviorism: A school of thought in psychology that promotes the **concept** that observable **behaviors** are the only **valid** measure of psychological **stimuli**. Although **B.F. Skinner (1904–1990)** is most often associated with behaviorism, **John B. Watson (1878–1958)** pioneered the school with his work and writings. In 1913, Watson outlined the behaviorist position in his paper *Psychology as the Behaviorist Views It*. Watson believed that concepts involving the mind or consciousness had no place in psychology.

Behavioral Sciences: A general term for those disciplines concerned in some way with behavior in man and lower organisms. For example, social anthropology, psychology, and **sociology** are behavioral sciences. Biology, economics, political science, history, and philosophy also include some aspects of behavioral science.

Behaviorists: Those who view learning as resulting from the forming of connections between **stimuli** and observable **responses**. The focus is on the observable action (response) and what caused it (stimulus). Some of the most well-known behaviorists include **Thorndike**, **Guthrie**, Hull, **Watson**, and **Skinner**. All of these psychologists viewed learning from a **stimulus-response** perspective, and although each had slightly different ideas regarding behavior, they all believed no need for **insight** or thinking existed. To behaviorists, learning is an **outcome** of **conditioning**. Behaviorists believe that the acquiring of knowledge is more of a muscular response, such as a reflex, than a thinking, or **cognitive** one. Examples of stimulus-response associations include: dogs salivating at the sight of food, babies waving bye-bye on cue, children memorizing that 8 x 8 = 64, and students reciting that a whole note gets four counts.

Berkeley Growth Study: A study initiated by Nancy Bayley in 1929 that tracked subjects throughout a lifetime in order to learn more about intellectual growth and development throughout the life cycle. The major findings of the study were: 1) **Intelligence quotients (IQs)** are not constant; 2) IQ variability is the greatest during the first few years of life; 3) intellectual growth may continue throughout life; and 4) the components of intellect change with age.

Between-class Ability Grouping: *See* Tracking

Bilabial Consonant: Four consonant sounds formed by the upper and lower lips. Bilabial consonants include *p*, *b*, *m*, and *w*.

Bilingual Education: In general, instruction in two languages, usually English and the students' native language. The primary **objective** of bilingual education is to teach non-native English speakers the rudiments of English to facilitate school **achievement**; however, bilingual education often implies language training in the native language as well. Bilingual education programs vary from school to school. For example, some programs offer instruction in both English and a student's native language throughout their entire school experience, while other programs help students make the transition from their native language to English by offering **English as a Second Language (ESL)** classes. Other programs involve removing students from regular classes and placing them in special classes in which they receive additional help with English or reading in their native language. Finally, bilingual education may involve immersing non-English speaking students in English-speaking classes in which non-English speaking students are typically provided with aides who speak both English and the student's native language.

Bilingual Education Act (1968): Also known as Title VII of the **Elementary and Secondary Education Act of 1965 (ESEA)**, legislation intended to address the needs of an increasing number of American children whose native language was not English. The act provides federal assistance to schools for children learning English. In 1974, as a result of the U.S. Supreme Court ruling in *Lau v. Nichols*, schools were required to provide remedial programs or **remediation** in English instruction and to provide subject matter instruction in a student's native language if the student's English proficiency was insufficient to understand the coursework in English.

Billings, William (1746-1800): A composer and Boston **singing school** master who was influential in the mid- to late-1700s. Billings was a tanner by trade and did not have a formal music education. Despite this fact, Billings composed several tune books using many folk idioms, including minor modes, irregular phrases, and pronounced rhythms. Billings' compositions are characterized by liberal use of parallel fifths and octaves with the melody line typically in the tenor. The tunes were often contrapuntal in nature, and many included imitative sections, or "fugues." Billings' works include: 1) *The New England Psalm Singer*, or *American Chorister* (which contains his most famous tune, "Chester"); 2) *The Singing Master's Assistant* (1778); 3) *Music in Miniature* (1779) (the only publication that was not entirely Billings' work); 4) *The Psalm Singer's Amusement*, (1781); 5) *The Suffolk Harmony* (1786); and 6) *The Continental Harmony* (1794). Although Billings was well known, his popularity declined toward the end of his life. He died in poverty in 1800. *See* **Yankee Tunesmiths**

Bimodal Distribution: A frequency distribution that contains two modes. A visual representation of all or part of the results from any data-gathering technique that shows the recurrence of two common results. That is, a high number of cases occur at two separate points along the frequency distribution. *See* **Frequency Distribution; Mode**

Binaural: In acoustics, hearing that utilizes two ears. Most hearing is binaural. *See* **Monaural; Diotic; Dichotic**

Binet, Alfred (1857-1911): A prominent French psychologist who developed the first modern **intelligence test** in 1905. Binet dropped out of medical school to study psychology and related topics. In 1894, he was appointed the director of the Laboratory of Physiological Psychology at the Sorbonne. Originally, these intelligence tests were designed to identify children who were mentally incapable of benefiting from a regular classroom environment. Instead of the sensorimotor tasks used by **Sir Francis Galton (1822–1911)**, Binet's tests used a series of intellectual tasks to determine intelligence. In addition, Binet introduced the concept of **mental age** as the basis for scoring his later tests beginning in 1908. Binet's tests were later used as the basis for the Stanford-Binet intelligence tests, published in 1916 in the United States. *See* **Stanford-Binet Test; Intelligence Quotient (IQ)**

Binomial Test: In research, a test used with data containing two categories such as good/bad, right/wrong, or yes/no (dichotomous data). Binomial tests indicate the probability of a particular response in a **data set**.

Biomechanics: The study of performance-related movement, particularly involving the fingers, hands, and wrists. Most research in biomechanics has focused on the physical measures of the hands, including size, width, and span as well as measurements of movements, including flexion, extension, and rotation of joints. Research in biomechanics has provided information useful in designing instruments more efficiently and in alleviating pain from stress-related performance movements. However, musicians' movements during performances have not been studied extensively because implementing appropriate scientific controls is not practical. A growing area of interest in biomechanics among music researchers involves the relationship between physiological movement and neurological control of this movement.

Birge, Edward Bailey (1868-1952): An important figure in music education who was recognized for several accomplishments. Birge received a bachelor of arts degree from Brown University in 1891 and a bachelor of music in 1904 from Yale University. That same year, he became music supervisor in Indianapolis, Indiana. Birge was one of the first teachers of music appreciation in the early twentieth century, when the mechanical (player) piano was the means for introducing children to classical music by great composers. He introduced mechanical pianos into nine elementary schools in Indianapolis, where twenty-minute recitals were given for the students twice per week and students were tested regularly. Birge was the chairman of the editorial board for the *Music Supervisors Journal*, which was renamed the *Music Educators Journal* (MEJ) in 1934, for fifteen years. Birge is perhaps best known for writing the first history book of American music education entitled *History of Public School Music in the United States*.

Black Music Caucus: *See* National Association for the Study and Performance of African-American Music (NASPAAM)

Block Grant: In education, a fixed lump sum of government money intended to fund several education programs in a designated locality, as opposed to a grant awarded for one specific project. The advantage of a **block grant** is that states and localities may distribute funds as they see fit, typically based on student enrollment or measures of student need. *See* Categorical Grant; Flat Grant

Block Schedules/Scheduling: School schedules characterized by fewer but longer class periods each day. Block schedules take many forms. In the 4 x 4 accelerated block, each day has four ninety-minute class periods, and courses change each semester, which enables students to take eight courses in one year. In the A/B eight block (expanded model) two four-period blocks rotate every other day for the entire school year, allowing students to take eight courses each year. In the modified block, block scheduling and traditional scheduling are mixed.

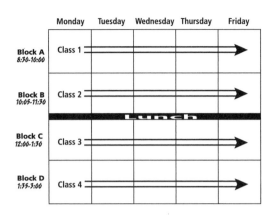

Debates continue as to whether or not the positive aspects of block scheduling outweigh the negative aspects. Proponents of block scheduling argue: 1) it allows students to take more classes than most trditional schedules; 2) students prefer it; 3) students achieve better grades using it; 4) students receive more individual attention; 5) students have more class time for homework; 6) teachers have more time to plan and prepare for classes; 7) teachers can

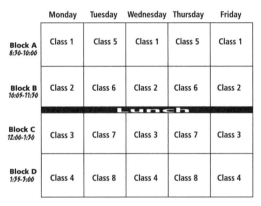

Block Scheduling

cover subject material in more depth; 8) teachers often use more interactive instruction because more time is available; 9) teachers spend less time with administrative processes, such as taking attendance, and more time with instruction; and 10) attendance is better. Opponents of block scheduling argue: 1) many teachers are not trained to devise lesson plans and/or implement a variety of instructional strategies appropriate for a ninety-minute class period; 2) less material can be covered; 3) students transferring from other schools have more trouble scheduling classes; 4) students do not retain material as well from one subject level to the next; 5) overuse of the lecture method; 6) lesson plans and teaching styles need to be modified or relearned to be effective in block scheduling; 7) students get bored with the material; 8) students have difficulty maintaining focus in one subject for ninety minutes; 9) in some block schedules, many students in performing arts groups can only participate for one semester instead of the entire year; and 10) the total amount of time spent in class is reduced, resulting in less time to cover course content.

While block scheduling has impacted all of education, the effect on performance-based music classes is particularly dramatic. Many teachers of performance-based ensembles are used to longer rehearsals because they have been involved in college ensembles that rehearsed for forty-five minutes or longer and prefer having longer blocks of time to work. On the other hand, many teachers find it more difficult to meet every other day, especially when vacation days and school-wide activities overlap rehearsal times. In addition, some block schedules allow students to take performance-based music classes for only half of each year or not at all. As a result, enrollment in these classes changes each semester, sometimes dramatically. Ultimately, students who want to stay enrolled in performance-based classes for the entire year need to plan carefully and work closely with counselors to ensure that their requirements are fulfilled.

Bloom, Benjamin S. (1913-1999): An eminent psychologist and scholar, well known for the development of *Bloom's Taxonomy of Educational Objectives*. Bloom completed his undergraduate and master's degrees at Penn State University before going to the University of Chicago, where he earned his Ph.D. and taught for more than thirty years. In addition to the taxonomy, Bloom also wrote a book entitled *Stability and Change in Human Characteristics*, in which he attempted to resolve the **nature/nurture controversy**. His later work involved studying the process of **gifted and talented** performance. Bloom has made significant contributions to psychology and education by showing the critical importance of early learning and experience in intellectual growth and development. *See* Taxonomy, Bloom's

Bloom's Taxonomy of Educational Objectives: *See* Taxonomy, Bloom's

Board of Education: The governing body of a school district whose powers are derived from state statutes. Boards of education usually consist of between four and nine elected members. Their primary responsibilities include approving the district's annual budget and employing a district superintendent. Other responsibilities may include levying taxes, approving salary schedules, hiring school district personnel, contracting for construction and maintenance, and setting school district policies. Boards of Education are policy-making groups that have the power to make and enforce reasonable rules and regulations. Typically, they do not actively administer the schools.

Bodily-kinesthetic Intelligence, Gardner: In Howard Gardner's (b. 1943) theory of multiple intelligences, the ability to perform or execute purposeful coordinated movements, actions, or tasks with part or all of the body. This **intelligence** enables difficult and complex movements, actions, or tasks to be developed at a very high level. For example, skilled athletes, musicians, surgeons, and dancers are said to possess bodily-kinesthetic intelligence. *See* **Multiple Intelligences**

Body Language: *See* **Nonverbal Communication**

Boethius (c. 480-524): A Roman statesman and scholar best known in music education for his *De Institutione Musica*, an early work that contained a discrete body of scientific knowledge about Greek music theory. *De Institutione Musica* preserved Greek music theory and is still studied today. In ancient times, music theory was a body of knowledge separate from actual music making. The work of Boethius contributed significantly to this separation. His writings emphasized reason, which appealed to scholars. Boethius thought that music could communicate on lower or higher levels of thinking. He believed that music communicated through the emotions on the lower levels, while on higher levels music communicated truth through reason according to abstract mathematical proportions from musical sounds.

Bond: In E. L. Thordike's (1874–1949) view, the association between sense impressions (**stimuli**) and an impulse to action (**response**). His concern was with what held the stimulus and the response together. In modern behavioral **psychology**, a bond is the association or link between a stimulus and a response. *See* **Associationism; Behaviorism**

Bonding: A process believed to produce a strong emotional attachment or bond between a mother and her newborn child through physical contact. Research suggests that bonding must occur within three days after birth. Failure to form this bond has been implicated as a possible cause or contributing cause for later episodes of neglect. Bonding is sometimes called maternal-infant bonding and is similar to the process of **imprinting** in animals.

Book of Psalms: Also known as the *Ainsworth Psalter*, a book written for the separatists in 1612 by the Reverend Henry Ainsworth to facilitate the singing of psalms for religious worship. The *Book of Psalms* was first printed in Amsterdam in 1612 and contained 342 pages and 39 psalm tunes. It was mainly circulated in Holland and England and was brought to the Colonies by Pilgrims. The *Book of Psalms* was the official Psalter of the Plymouth Colony until about 1692. The compositions contained in the book were taken from French, English, and Dutch sources, and a variety of meters were used to accommodate different psalms. The psalms themselves were translated into prose, allowing each one to be paired with several different melodies. The more complex tunes were too difficult for colonists to remember; as a result, the number of tunes in common use was reduced significantly. *See* Ainsworth, Reverend Henry Boston

Borduns: Drones of open fifths used by **Carl Orff (1895–1982)** in his first lessons on harmony. Borduns are considered effective accompaniments to pentatonic melodies and are conducive to improvisation. Harmonies evolve from the melodic movement of Borduns in the Orff system.

Boston Academy of Music: A music school run by **Lowell Mason (1792–1872)** and others from 1833 to 1847. Adults and children were taught in separate classes. Class sizes were large, and as many as 1,500 students were enrolled. Adults were charged a fee, but instruction was free to children over age seven who agreed to attend for at least one year. The Boston Academy of Music also supplied the community with adequately trained music teachers by offering annual teacher training classes at the Academy beginning in 1834. By the late 1830s, the school had an orchestra and was offering instruction in instrumental music. Mason's work at the Boston Academy of Music led the way for the inclusion of music classes in the curriculum of Boston public schools in 1838.

Boston Handel and Haydn Society: An amateur choral society founded in 1815 by Bartholomew Brown and others whose goal was to improve American tastes in art music. The Boston Handel and Haydn Society initiated many activities, including publications and concerts that furthered interest in amateur choral groups throughout New England. The Society helped familiarize Americans with European art music and was partially responsible for the wave of smaller societies that formed during this time throughout New England. The Society published Lowell Mason's (1792–1872) first compilation of sacred music in 1821, the *Boston Handel and Haydn Society Collection of Church Music*. *See* Mason, Lowell (1792–1872); Singing Societies

Boston Handel and Haydn Society Collection of Church Music: Lowell Mason's (1792–1872) first compilation of sacred music, published in 1821. Mason composed some of the music and compiled the rest, although he was not officially credited as editor of the book until the ninth edition. The *Boston Handel and Haydn Society Collection of Church Music* was the result of Mason's meeting with the Society's organist, Dr. George K. Jackson, who was very impressed with the collection and recommended it to the Society for publication. The book was a great success, and twenty-two editions were eventually published. It was also a financially profitable venture for both Lowell Mason and the Boston Handel and Haydn Society and was an important factor in Mason's decision to change his career from bank officer to professional musician.

Boston School Committee: The Boston Board of Education that approved the inclusion of music in the public school curriculum as a regular subject in 1838. The approval to include music as a curricular subject was accompanied by a report that included several reasons for making the decision to add music to the curriculum. The Boston School Committee stated in the report that music classes would benefit children intellectually, morally, and physically, and would also improve recreation, worship, and discipline.

Brainstorming: A technique for generating new and creative ideas in a group setting. Brainstorming encourages participants to present any ideas that come to mind in an open forum and to hold nothing back. Ideas are not criticized during the session. The idea behind brainstorming is that participants stimulate each other's creativity in such a way that each individual's creative problem solving ability is raised to a higher level than it would be in isolation. Research on brainstorming has shown that it may not be as effective as once believed. Some research suggests that people may produce more ideas considered unique and creative when they work alone than when they use brainstorming.

Brainwashing: A technique typically involving propaganda whereby someone is induced to accept regimented and sometimes extreme or antisocial ideas, often forsaking basic beliefs and attitudes to accept these new ideas. Brainwashing is most often used in political, social, or religious arenas, and implies a lack of control and choice on the part of the individual or group being brainwashed. Brainwashing is particularly dangerous because often the individual or group is not aware of its usage, particularly in the early stages of the process.

Branched Programs: *See* Programmed Instruction

Broudy, Harry S. (1905-1998): An eminent figure in educational philosophy who made significant contributions to music and the arts. Broudy was born in Poland in 1905 and came to the United States when he was seven years old. He received a bachelor of arts degree in Germanic literature and philosophy in 1929 from Boston University and a master's degree and Ph.D. in 1935 from Harvard. Broudy was named professor of philosophy and psychology by the Massachusetts Department of Education in 1937 and taught at North Adams and Framingham State Teachers colleges until 1957. He then joined the University of Illinois College of Education as a professor of philosophy of education, retiring in 1974 as professor emeritus. Broudy served as a general editor for the University of Illinois Press, the editor of *The Educational Forum*, and was also on the editorial board of the **Music Educators Journal (MEJ)**, *Educational Theory,* and *The Journal of Aesthetic Education* as well as being a senior faculty member at the Getty Institute for Educators on the Visual Arts.

Brown v. Board of Education of Topeka, Kansas: A landmark decision by the United States Supreme Court in 1954 that overturned the "separate but equal" doctrine established by the 1896 decision in *Plessy v. Ferguson*. This doctrine stated that public schools could be segregated based on race as long as the facilities provided for Negro children were the same as those provided for white children. The reality, however, was that facilities for Negro and white children were not "equal"; in fact, they were generally much poorer for Negro children. The plaintiffs in *Brown* successfully argued that "separate but equal" segregation was a violation of the equal protection clause of the Constitution. That is, the Court recognized that separate educational facilities were inherently unequal. In addition, the Court declared that implementing a new system in which public school admission was not based on race was the responsibility of the respective school boards. School boards across America, particularly in the South, were in a position of having to purposefully restructure the existing system of public school admission. The Supreme Court's ruling in *Brown v. Board of Education* had a monumental and lasting impact on American education and school desegregation. *See* Desegregation; Plessy v. Ferguson; Segregation

Bruner, Jerome S. (b. 1915): A researcher and psychologist well-known for his influence on cognitive psychology and for his **theory of instruction**. Bruner graduated from Duke University in 1937 and received his Ph.D. in psychology from Harvard University in 1941. During World War II, Bruner worked on psychological warfare under President Dwight D. Eisenhower. After the war, Bruner returned to Harvard and continued his work in psychological research. His studies on the effect of **need** on **perception**, the ways individuals obtain knowledge, and the ways individuals develop intellectually are now classic. Bruner's work was instrumental in the development of the American school of **cognitive psychology**. He also helped found Harvard's Center for Cognitive Studies. Bruner was awarded the Distinguished Scientific Award by the American Psychological Association in 1963 and was elected president of the American Psychological Association in 1965.

Bruner was the director of the **Woods Hole Conference**. Following the conference, Bruner wrote a book entitled *The Process of Education*, his account of what took place at the conference, along with his perceptions about how to improve education. In the book, Bruner emphasizes the importance of teaching the general nature, or "structure" of a subject. Second, Bruner states that any subject can be taught effectively to any child at any stage of development in some intellectually honest form. Third, Bruner stresses the importance of intuition in the learning process. He felt **insight** was an important problem-solving technique to provide children with understanding. *The Process of Education* remains one of the most influential books in education.

Bruner called his theory a theory of instruction, not a **learning theory**, because he wanted to emphasize that it was the teacher who was responsible for helping students learn. He also stressed the importance of **discovery learning**, believing that it was better to experience first and develop understanding later. Bruner placed very little importance on studying rats and other lab animals. Instead, he felt that the best way to find out how children learn is to study children in their natural learning environments. Bruner's theory of instruction has four major principles: 1) motivation; 2) structure; 3) sequence; and 4) reinforcement. *See* **Theory of Instruction, Bruner**

Buckley Amendment: Part of the Family Educational Rights and Privacy Act (FERPA) amended in 1993 that prohibits schools from releasing information about a student to third parties without parental or student permission.

Budget: In education, the amount of money allocated for all expenses necessary to fund a school, usually on a yearly basis. The term is also used to describe those portions of money that are allocated to certain areas and/or teachers to buy a variety of items, including teaching materials and supplies. In music education, budgets are often the means by which teachers purchase music, recordings, small instruments, and other supplies. More costly items, such as large instruments or uniforms, are usually not included in the regular music education budget. These items are often acquired through other means, including special requisitions or fundraisers. Budget management can have a significant lasting impact on the program. For example, the music library, teaching materials, recordings, instruments, computers, technological aids, and equipment maintenance are all impacted by budgetary decisions.

Bulletin of Historical Research in Music Education: A periodical founded in 1980 containing philosophical and historical research relevant in any way to music education. The *Bulletin of Historical Research in Music Education* contains articles of interest to music education historians, including research findings, general information, and forums.

Bulletin of the Council for Research in Music Education/CRME Bulletin: A periodical founded in 1963 by the University of Illinois and the Illinois Office of the Superintendent of Public Instruction to provide a source of information about research being conducted in music education. The *CRME Bulletin* is published quarterly and contains critiques of doctoral **dissertations**, book reviews, and original articles. In addition, the *CRME Bulletin* also publishes indices of music education doctoral dissertations in progress and of recently completed dissertations available for review.

Bureau of Education for the Handicapped, USOE: A federal bureau established in 1974 specifically for the benefit of Special Education. The Bureau of Education for the Handicapped eventually became the **Office of Special Education Programs**.

CAI: *See* Computer Assisted Instruction (CAI)

California Test of Mental Maturity: A test designed to measure the fundamental functional capacities necessary for learning, problem solving, and responding to new situations in comprehensive ways. The California Test of Mental Maturity was first published in 1959 and revised in 1963 and may be taken by individuals of virtually any age, from preschool to adult. The test is divided into twelve units that measure various aspects of mental ability. A complex summary of scores is computed, including the use of **mental ages, intelligence quotients (IQ), standard scores, stanines,** and **percentile ranks** that are interpreted using a framework of intra- and inter-individual differences. The California Test of Mental Maturity is intended as both a **survey** and as an analytical tool for educators, counselors, psychologists, and employers.

Call to Keokuk: An invitation by **Philip Hayden (1854–1925)** for music supervisors to attend a music conference in Keokuk, Iowa, in April 1907. Hayden extended this invitation personally to several music supervisors and also placed a notice in *School Music Monthly.* Hayden expressed the following three reasons for meeting in Keokuk. First, Hayden wanted to discuss his new rhythmic approach to music reading called "rhythm forms" and to have other music supervisors evaluate this approach. Second, the **National Education Association (NEA)** conference was meeting in California that year, which was a long way to travel. Hayden thought a conference in Keokuk would provide music educators with an alternative to the NEA conference. Third, Hayden hoped to exchange ideas about music education with other music supervisors. Approximately 100 people attended the Keokuk conference, many of whom were music supervisors. The success of this conference led to future meetings and ultimately, to the formation of the **Music Supervisors National Conference (MSNC)**, a name officially adopted in 1910. MSNC was renamed the **Music Educators National Conference (MENC)** in 1934.

Cannon's Theory/Cannon-Bard Theory: The theory that an emotion-producing stimulus also activates bodily **responses** at the same time, proposed by Walter Cannon and revised by his student, Philip Bard. The theory is based on the idea that emotion originates in the thalamus, a part of the brain believed to control emotions. That is, all emotions are physiologically similar, and physiological changes accompany emotional experiences. The Cannon-Bard Theory is opposed to the **James-Lange Theory**, which states that stimuli initiate physiological responses, and then the awareness of these responses constitutes emotional experience.

Canonical Correlation: In research, a method or technique for analyzing the relationship between two sets of continuous **variables**. Canonical correlations are generally used to determine the relationship or maximum degree of association between **predictor variables** and **criterion variables**. Predictor variables and criterion variables may be either linear sets or a weighted combination of two or more criterion variables. For example, in examining the relationships between a single variable (sight reading ability) and multiple variables (experience, gender, and instrument played), sight reading would be the criterion variable and experience, gender, and instrument played would be the predictor variables. Canonical correlations are an extension of **multiple regression analysis**. *See* **Discriminant Analysis; Factor Analysis**

Capacity: In education, the ability to learn or to perform a task. In music, capacity refers to the portion of an individual's **musical ability** either genetically endowed or due to **maturation**.

Carabo-Cone Method: A method developed by Madeleine Carabo-Cone (1915–1988) based on the belief that preschool children are capable of structured **cognitive** learning if properly integrated into their actions and environments at an early age. Carabo-Cone developed a series entitled *A Sensory-Motor Approach to Music Learning*, which contains instructions for implementing the sensory-motor approach. The Carabo-Cone method includes the use of audio, visual, and tactile learning tools that provide concrete representations of abstract musical concepts and encourages children to "become" various musical elements.

Cardinal Traits: In Gordon Allport's (1897–1967) **trait theory**, important individual traits that influence almost every aspect of a person's life. For example, someone who wants and needs to be working most of the time will likely structure their lives so that they are working most of the time and will be considered by others to be a "workaholic." *See* **Central Traits; Secondary Traits**

Career Ladder: In education, an **incentive program** that allows teachers to advance their career status within the teaching profession in a step-by-step manner. The idea is that experienced teachers should be given different, more complex roles and responsibilities within the profession than less experienced teachers. This approach differs considerably from the more traditional approach, where the "job" of being a teacher is essentially the same regardless of experience. Programs vary from district to district and from state to state and are typically structured to reflect a level of teaching experience and/or proficiency. As teachers gain experience, their **status** advances in several ways. First, teachers may advance from having a provisional teacher certificate/license to a regular teacher certificate/license. Second, teachers assume increased responsibility within their schools or districts, such as being asked to work on various in-service projects. Third, experienced teachers typically receive additional pay for their efforts. Career ladder programs are often successful in motivating teachers to advance, although the success of the programs is largely dependent upon the availability of funds to support them. *See* **Certification/Licensing**

Carnegie Report: A report released in 1983 that identified problems with American education. Fully titled *High School: A Report on Secondary Education in America*, the report was written by Ernest Boyer, former United States Commissioner of Education, based on a three-year study involving twenty-five educators at fifteen diverse senior high schools. Problems identified by Boyer included a sense of powerlessness among teachers, discipline problems, low teacher pay, and insufficient discretion in selecting textbooks and developing lesson plans. In addition, Boyer indicated that high schools lacked a mission statement or policy that indicated the school's educational priorities and common purposes. Several recommendations were made, including 1) the first two years of high school should be dominated by core **curriculum**, including the arts; 2) electives and specialized studies should be taken during the final two years; 3) teachers should not teach more than four regular classes and one small seminar; 4) teachers should have an hour per day for class preparation; and 5) teachers should not be responsible for monitoring halls, lunchrooms, or other recreation areas.

Carpal Tunnel Syndrome: A condition common among musicians that typically affects the wrists, fingers, and thumb. The nerve in the carpal tunnel, a narrow, rigid tunnel of ligament and bones that goes into the hand becomes pressed or squeezed at the wrist. Causes of carpal tunnel syndrome typically include irritated tendons or other swelling that narrows the tunnel and compresses the wrist. Symptoms of carpal tunnel syndrome include pain, weakness, or numbness in the hand and wrist that may radiate up the arm. Repetitive hand or wrist activity is a common cause of carpal tunnel syndrome, and individuals who suffer from it are often advised to decrease or stop the aggravating activity. In severe cases, surgery may be used to repair the damage caused by carpal tunnel syndrome.

Carry-over Effect: In research, a problem that can occur in **repeated block designs** (experiments in which multiple treatments or questions are posed to each subject) if the effects of one **treatment** are still present when the next treatment is given.

Case History: In research, a biography obtained for scientific study. Case histories may be obtained in several ways, including by interview or by collecting material over a period of years. *See* **Case Study**

Case Study: In research, a descriptive account of relevant factors usually concerning a specific individual or group of individuals who are related in some way. **Case studies** may include **behavior**, past history, **interviews**, and other relevant information. Case studies often involve individuals with unusual physical conditions or other circumstances that warrant in-depth personal study. Case studies may be used individually or collectively to reach general conclusions and principles.

Categorical Grants: Typically, a large grant program established through legislation. Categorical grants are often given to localities with large federal installations, such as military bases. Categorical grants are also given to help fund large-scale education programs designed for particular groups or for specific purposes. Some examples are **Education for All Handicapped Children Act of 1975**; **Individuals with Disabilities Education Act of 1990**; and **Project Head Start**. *See* **Block Grant; Flat Grant**

Cathedral Schools: Schools that began as centers for elementary-level learning around the time of Charlemagne in the ninth century. **Cathedral schools** were formed because Charlemagne and church officials were concerned about providing and preserving education for both religious men and royalty. Musical notation and chant were among the subjects taught in early Cathedral schools. Certain Cathedral schools attracted several teachers and scholars and eventually grew to become universities.

Cattell, James McKeen (1860-1944): An American pioneer in **intelligence testing**. Cattell studied in Germany under **Wilhelm Wundt (1832-1920)** and in England under **Sir Francis Galton (1822-1911)**. He brought his knowledge of European psychology back to America and was appointed to the first professorship in psychology at Columbia University in 1888, the first such appointment in the world. Patterning his work after Galton, Cattell devised a series of tests designed to measure human intellectual potential by testing sensorimotor capabilities. These tests included auditory range, visual range, and reaction time. Cattell is credited with first using the term "mental test" and in initiating the mental-testing movement in the United States.

Causal Comparative Research: A type of research involving a comparison of two or more groups to determine the "cause" of something. **Variables** are not manipulated in causal comparative research. Instead, **measurements** are made after the "treatment" has already occurred, also called *ex post facto* **research**. Medical researchers commonly use causal comparative research in attempts to discover the causes of illness. In music, causal comparison research is appropriate for many studies, such as determining why students drop out of music programs or determining which rehearsal method is the most preferable.

Causality: In research, a term used to describe a possible cause-effect relationship between groups of **variables**. Typically, causality is presented as questions written in a "What causes what?" format. Examples: Which teaching method yields the highest test scores in the least time? What study method results in the most memory retention?

Ceiling Effect: In research, the failure of a test or measure to detect differences between subjects and/or groups or to accurately measure achievement because the tasks or questions were too easy for all or most of the subjects. The ceiling effect prevents subjects from demonstrating their true capacity for achievement because of the limitations of the test or measure. *See* **Floor Effect**

Cell Assembly: In psychology, a concept of cognitive growth developed by Donald O. Hebb (1904–1985). Cell assembly occurs when groups of cells in the brain form cohesive units that increase the speed at which young children can learn. That is, children learn slowly and tediously at first because they are operating at the "single-cell level," but learning increases dramatically as cell assemblies are formed in the brain.

Census Studies: In research, a type of descriptive study in which researchers collect information from all members of a **population**. The **demographic** information collected every ten years by the United States Government regarding its population is a census study. In music, census studies are generally not practical and used on a very limited basis because of the expense and difficulty in reaching every member of a given population. For example, a music-related census study might involve collecting demographic information on all music students receiving bachelor's degrees at a particular university over the past ten years.

Cent/Cent Deviation: In acoustics, a measurement of pitch equal to 1/100 of an equal-tempered semitone. The usefulness of cents lies in the fact that they are consistent between tones; that is, each semitone is divided into 100 cents, even though the **frequency** differences between semitones vary according to range. Most tuning devices are based on cent deviation units, and musicians often use cents when describing how flat or sharp a pitch is relative to **equal temperament**. Research indicates that trained musicians can distinguish pitch differences as little as four or five cents between two consecutively presented tones. *See* **Just Noticeable Difference (jnd)**

Central Nervous System: Comprised of the brain and spinal cord, the core of the nervous system. Injuries or diseases of the central nervous system can severely restrict normal movement, activity, and functioning, both physical and mental.

Central Tendency: In research, a general term used to describe a single number, score, or value that describes the typical or central score among a set of scores. **Mean**, **median**, and **mode** are three common measures of central tendency. *See* **Normal Distribution**

Central Traits: In Gordon Allport's (1897–1967) **trait theory,** five to ten traits that define the characteristic way an individual behaves. For example, central traits might include being affectionate, fun-loving, humble, shy, competitive, or argumentative. *See* **Cardinal Traits; Secondary Traits**

Centrate/Centration: In Jean Piaget's (1896–1980) theory of **cognitive** development, a child's tendency to focus on only one aspect of a situation or to see only one point of view while neglecting all others. **Centration** is characteristic of Piaget's sensorimotor stage of development (birth to two years) and to a lesser extent the preoperational stage (ages two to seven) and is characterized by children's inabilities to understand the difference between their ideas and feelings and the ideas and feelings of others. Centration often makes a child's reasoning seem illogical. *See* **Decenter/Decentration; Piaget's Cognitive Growth Stages**

Certification and Licensing: In education, a process that qualifies individuals to become teachers in public schools. Certification and licensing are generally controlled by State Departments of Education. These agencies work with teacher training programs at higher education institutions to develop and establish certification and licensing requirements. These requirements include completion of courses and fieldwork that provide individuals with the education and experience necessary to become successful teachers in the public schools. Programs and requirements vary from state to state and are evaluated and changed periodically.

Chaining: In psychology, a form of **operant conditioning** in which a complex sequence of actions is learned by first rewarding the desired final response and then working backwards until a chain of behaviors is learned. Chaining is related to **shaping;** however, in chaining, only the final response is rewarded. Chained responses are formed by requiring more responses until the reward is given or by withholding the reward until other responses are demonstrated. Chaining also refers to the process of linking together previously learned stimulus-response associations into a sequence of behaviors, which enables individuals to perform complicated acts.

Challenge America Initiative, NEA: An initiative implemented in 2001 giving the **National Endowment for the Arts (NEA)** its first budget increase in almost ten years. The Challenge America Initiative is intended to make high-quality art available to all citizens in America. The initiative uses fast track grants to provide funding quickly by streamlining the review and administrative processes. This allows organizations to use the funds to leverage other public and private funds.

Changing Voice: In vocal technique, changes in the vocal mechanism of both boys and girls that occur during puberty as they mature physically. Girls' voices may drop a few tones; however, several changes brought about by testosterone can lower boys' voices by as much as an octave. The cartilage in the voice box grows thicker and larger, as do the vocal folds, which become approximately 60 percent larger than before puberty. The increased size and mass of the vocal folds dramatically slow the rate of vibration from approximately 200 vibrations per second to about 130 vibrations per second. In addition, testosterone affects the manner in which facial bones grow, creating larger cavities in the sinuses, nose, and back of the throat for resonance. During the maturation process, boys in particular may experience a stage in which they have difficulty controlling the voice, resulting in unexpected "breaks" or "squeaks" from the low to high register. This transitional process can be very uncomfortable or embarrassing for some, but it is typically short-lived.

Chaos Theory: A theory based on the belief that predicting the outcome of any sequence of events is impossible, regardless of how precise or scientific the information is regarding this sequence. The general idea is that so many **variables** and conditions are associated with any sequence of events that even small changes in one or more of these variables can lead to large changes in the outcome. This nonlinear attribute of variables or conditions is central to chaos theory. For example, despite having extremely sophisticated weather equipment and knowledgeable meteorologists, no one can predict the weather with an absolute degree of certainty.

Character Education: In education, a **curricular** approach that focuses on clarifying or teaching **values** or developing character. Character education has been emphasized in varying degrees since ancient times and has been associated with indoctrination and brainwashing. Today, because society is looking to schools to assume an increased role in the teaching of values, issues regarding character education are once again topics of discussion. However, research has shown that character education is largely ineffective and that character seems to develop as a result of the incorporation of democratic and humane values within the individual.

Charisma: A term used to describe a particular magnetic charge, energy, or hypnotic quality, usually associated with individuals who are considered leaders. An individual who possesses the ability to "charge" a room with energy upon entering and to draw others to them through sheer likeability and appeal is said to be charismatic.

Charity Schools: Schools operated by churches or other charitable organizations that were popular in America before the advent of common schools in the 1840s and 1850s. *See* **Common Schools**

Charter Schools: Schools operated by independent, usually private organizations. Charter schools are typically supported by state funds but are exempt from many district and state regulations governing traditional public schools. An alternative to traditional public schools, charter schools have grown in popularity since their inception in the early 1990s. There are now more than 1,400 charter schools in at least 27 states. The schools are based on a contract or charter between school organizers (typically a group of parents, teachers, or other concerned citizens) and a sponsor (typically a local or state board of education). The group organizers are responsible for devising an educational plan for their school that includes **curriculum**, staffing, and instructional **goals** and **objectives**. Organizers have almost total autonomy in running the school, including the power to hire and fire staff and to budget money as they see fit, which allows them to do what they think is necessary to meet student needs. In return, the organizers guarantee to their sponsors that certain academic **outcomes** will be met. Although the long-term effectiveness of charter schools has not yet been determined, in some cases, they have better attendance records and lower dropout rates than many traditional public schools. Critics question the use of public funds, particularly for start-up costs. In addition, they argue that charter schools take money away from regular public schools, do not have to follow state regulations, and have not been shown to be more effective than regular schools.

Chautauqua Movement: An education movement that began as a Methodist Sunday School Institute at Lake Chautauqua, New York, in 1874 and later became a secular institute for educating adults. The Chautauqua Movement developed in response to societal needs for adult education and led to the establishment of various types of civic associations, reading circles, correspondence courses, lecture-study groups, and youth groups. *See* **Adult Education**

Chi Square (x^2): In research, a statistical test of **significance** used to determine whether or not frequency differences have occurred on the basis of chance alone, often described as a "goodness-of-fit" test. That is, chi square (x^2) is used to assess whether or not observed frequency data fit into a theoretical distribution. When researchers are interested in the actual number of cases (i.e., frequency of occurrence) that fall into two or more discrete categories (e.g., good/bad; yes/no) chi square (x^2) is an appropriate statistical test. For example, if researchers want to know whether or not there is a significant difference in the proportions of students from either higher or lower (two discrete categories) socioeconomic backgrounds who complete three years of high school band, chi square (x^2) would be an appropriate statistical test. Chi square (x^2) is a nonparametric test since no **population** assumptions are required for its use. *See* **Nonparametric Statistics**

Chicago Band Tournament: An event held in Chicago in 1923 to promote school band programs and the sale of band instruments after World War I. Twenty-six high school bands and four elementary school bands participated in the tournament. The Chicago Band Tournament significantly contributed to the popularity of band tournaments and festivals popular during this time until around World War II.

Child Abuse: Intentionally inflicted physical, sexual, and/or psychological trauma and/or injury to a child. In most states, educators have a responsibility to report physical or psychological evidence of child abuse to school administrators or counselors. The Child Abuse Prevention and Treatment Act was passed by Congress in 1974 to provide financial support to any state that implemented programs leading to the identification, prevention, and treatment of child abuse or neglect.

Child Abuse Prevention and Treatment Act of 1974: See Child Abuse

Child Development: In psychology, the processes involved in individual growth from conception until adulthood. Typically, child development involves changes in three areas: 1) physical development, which includes changes in height, weight, and motor abilities; 2) intellectual or **cognitive** development, which includes changes in mental or cognitive abilities; and 3) personality/social/emotional development, which includes changes in feelings, emotions, relationships, and reactions. Some child psychologists believe that development occurs in small, incremental steps on a continual basis, while others believe that development occurs in a series of distinct, qualitatively different stages, often referred to as **stage theory**.

Child-centered: An instructional approach that focuses on the child's active participation in the learning process. That is, students are encouraged to actively experience, discuss, question, and discover instead of being instructed to passively sit and listen. Instruction at the elementary level tends to be more child-centered than instruction at the secondary level. The **Montessori Method** and **Carabo-Cone Method** are child-centered approaches.

Child-centered Education: Historically, a movement away from the standard of public education established by the mid-1800s that stressed systematic organization and efficiency. Child-centered education was developed to provide children with opportunities to learn through creation and discovery. One important outcome of child-centered education was **kindergarten**, which was designed to provide preschool children with creative outlets for self-involvement. Individuals associated with child-centered education include **Fredrich Wilhelm Froebel (1782–1852)**, **Johann Heinrich Pestalozzi (1746–1827)**, Amos Bronson Alcott (1799–1888), Colonel Francis W. Parker (1837–1902), and G. Stanley Hall (1844–1924).

Childhood: In psychology, a general term that refers to the developmental period that extends from about eighteen months to about thirteen years of age, when puberty marks the beginning of **adolescence**.

Chorus Effect/Choral Effect: The auditory sensation perceived when several nearly identical sounds almost become fused into one. The effect is commonly attributed to the **beats** that result from slightly out-of-tune **complex tones** and from other slight deviations always present in tones produced by traditional musical instruments or voices. These deviations result from slight differences in attacks, releases, and vibrato.

Chroma: *See* Tone Chroma

Chroma Helix: A graphic representation of **tone height** and **tone chroma** in the form of a helix. The tone height is the perceptual concept of pitch and represents the vertical dimension, while the tone chroma is the perception of similarity of two tones (such as octaves) and represents the circular dimension of the helix.

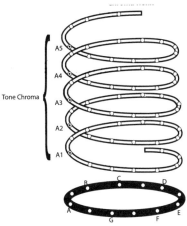

Chroma Helix

Chromesthesia/Chromasthesia: In music, a phenomenon or perceptual bridge between the senses that causes some individuals to see color images while listening to certain types of music, musical patterns, or specific pitches. Awareness of this relationship may facilitate the ability to discern musical patterns and/or pitches.

Chromosome: Threadlike pieces of protein contained in every cell of the human body. Each cell contains twenty-three pairs of chromosomes, with the exception of the reproductive cells (egg and sperm), which carry only twenty-three single chromosomes. At conception, the zygote has its full complement of twenty-three pairs of chromosomes, half from each parent. *See* **Zygote**

Chronological Age (CA): A time measurement of age that begins at birth. Chronological age is also referred to as calendar age. *See* **Mental Age**

Chunking: The process of grouping several separate items together in personally meaningful arrangements to facilitate memory **recall**. Because humans learn and perceive visual and auditory **stimuli** more easily in patterns than in isolated bits, chunking increases the amount of information remembered. Information should be chunked in logical ways. Creating patterns, ordering information in a more familiar manner, creating memorable links with familiar cues, devising word games or stories about the information, and substituting letters for words are all chunking techniques.

Examples of chunking can be found everywhere in society. For example, a ten-digit telephone number is broken down into three components: the area code, prefix, and number. Each component contains three to four numbers. Sometimes, one or more of these components form words which further aid **memory** (e.g., 1-800-Art Info). **Acronyms** (e.g., NOW for National Organization of Women) and **mnemonics** (Every Good Boy Does Fine for treble clef note names) are further examples of chunking. Another effective chunking technique is to organize and group related information on study guides into content areas, so that this material will be linked together. That is, grouping information about **Orff** and separating it from information about **Suzuki** or **Gordon** will aid the memory process. In short, chunking is grouping, and there are an infinite number of ways to group information to facilitate memory. *See* **Gestalt Learning**

Church Schools: Also known as parish schools, schools that provided elementary instruction during the Middle Ages. Church schools provided elementary reading, writing, and psalm singing, as well as some intermediate-level instruction to boys only. Church schools were originally established to prepare musicians for service in the church; however, by the end of the eighth century, the curricula included the seven liberal arts. Church schools also helped prepare young men for higher education at universities or at better monastery and **cathedral schools**.

CIJE: *See* **Current Index of Journals in Education**

Circadian Rhythm: A biological cycle lasting approximately twenty-four hours. Sleep, wakefulness, body temperature, and a number of behavioral and physiological aspects of human functioning follow a circadian rhythm.

Civil Rights Act of 1964: Legislation enacted by Congress making **discrimination** based on **race**, color, religion, or national origin unlawful. Because Congress used its power to regulate interstate commerce to reach the actions of individuals, the Civil Rights Act of 1964 originally prohibited discrimination in public establishments that had either a connection to interstate commerce or had financial support from the state. Such public establishments included hotels, motels, gas stations, restaurants, bars, taverns, and places of entertainment. In addition, the Act and subsequent legislation declared a strong legislative policy against discrimination in public schools and colleges. Title VI of the Act specifically prohibits discrimination in any federally funded programs.

Clark, Frances E. (1860-1958): An important figure in music education for her work in developing music curriculum, teaching and promoting music appreciation, and promoting music education. Clark was instrumental in organizing the **Call to Keokuk**, which would ultimately result in the creation of the **Music Supervisors National Conference (MSNC)**. While serving as music supervisor in Milwaukee, Wisconsin, she developed a graduated music curriculum from **kindergarten** through high school. This curriculum was designed to develop several aspects of musical literacy and ability, including a solid physical foundation for vocal tone production and pitch production, **music reading**, **sight reading**, part singing, music history, exposure to standard literature, and appreciation for art music. By the time students reached the high school level, they were able to sight read difficult literature and perform oratorios. Clark was a strong proponent of the phonograph, or Victor Talking Machine, a new invention at that time. She encouraged the placement of phonographs in her schools by demonstrating their usefulness. The phonograph enabled students to sing a piece and then listen to a master artist's interpretation of the same piece on the phonograph. In addition, programs and concerts for teachers were held in which student performances were alternated with phonograph performances. In 1910 Clark took a position with the Victor Company and focused on making children's recordings for educational purposes. A culmination of Clark's work in music appreciation was published in 1923, under the title *Music Appreciation with the Victrola for Children*, with the later 1930 edition simply titled *Music Appreciation for Children*.

Class Interval: In statistics, the small section of a scale in which scores of a frequency distribution are grouped. For example, the heights of a population may be grouped into class intervals of half an inch.

Classical Conditioning: In psychology, the conditioning techniques of **Ivan Pavlov (1849–1936)**. Classical conditioning involves the pairing of a **conditioned stimulus** with an **unconditioned stimulus** over many trials until the conditioned stimulus alone elicits the **conditioned response**. During conditioning trials, the conditioned stimulus acts as a signal that the unconditioned stimulus will follow. The organism eventually learns to respond to the conditioned stimulus alone. In Pavlov's classic experiment, a dog naturally salivated (**unconditioned response**) when presented with meat powder (unconditioned stimulus). Pavlov then paired the presentation of meat powder with the presentation of a tone (**neutral

stimulus). Over time, the dog learned to salivate (conditioned response) to the tone (conditioned stimulus), even when it was presented without the meat powder. That is, the tone had become a conditioned stimulus.

Classical Experimental Design: In research, the most common experimental research design in which researchers work with two groups, an **experimental group** and a **control group**. The following procedures are typically employed: 1) subjects are selected and assigned to groups randomly; 2) the experimental group is measured prior to and after the introduction of an **independent variable** or **variables (treatment)**; and 3) the control group is measured at the same time the experimental group is measured, except that the control group is not given the treatment.

Classroom Instruction: In education, a general term for teaching that takes place in the classroom. In music programs at the elementary, secondary, and university levels, classroom instruction generally takes two forms: 1) **performance-based** instruction and 2) non-performance-based instruction. Performance-based music instruction includes bands, orchestras, choirs, other ensembles, and private lessons. The majority of time in these classes is spent learning musical concepts and techniques through rehearsals and performances. Non-performance-based music instruction includes music theory and general music at the secondary level and music history and conducting at the university level.

Classroom Management: In general, the manner in which teachers and students interact within a classroom, or the manner in which a classroom is structured and maintained by the teacher. In most classrooms, teachers are almost entirely responsible for managing the classroom environment. Rules are devised and enforced according to the teacher's **goals** and expectations. Sometimes classroom management refers to the collective ability of teachers and students to agree upon, formulate, and implement a common **framework** for guiding social and academic interactions. Most aspects of teaching affect classroom management, including making **lesson plans**, choosing a **methodology**, completing administrative tasks, pacing and sequencing activities, and maintaining classroom discipline. Evidence of effective classroom management includes students who appear interested and on task, a teacher who is involved with the students, and lesson plans that are organized, clearly structured, and well planned. Evidence of ineffective classroom management includes students who are inattentive or unruly, a teacher who is unresponsive to student needs, and the inability or unwillingness to follow organized lesson plans.

Client-centered Therapy: *See* Person-centered Therapy; Rogers, Carl (1902-1987)

Closed Vowels: Vowels that are created by placing the tongue high in the mouth, resulting in a relatively small oral cavity. Closed vowels include *ee* and *oo*.

Closed-ended Questions: In research, questions used in the **interview** or **survey method** that limit subjects' responses by using a set of pre-selected, alternative answers. *See* Questionnaire

Closure, Principle/Law of: The perceptual ability of the brain to fill in gaps or missing information in order to perceive complete images or forms. The principle of closure enables individuals to recognize images or forms even though they may be incomplete or less than perfect. The principle of closure is a **gestalt concept** and is commonly employed in everyday life. *See* Continuity, Principle/Law of; Similarity, Principle/Law of; Proximity, Principle/Law of

Cluster Random Sampling: *See* Random Sampling

Cluster Sampling: In research, a **sampling** technique in which researchers draw a sample from groups or clusters selected from **large populations** based on predetermined **criteria** such as school size, race, or **socio-economic status (SES)**. In cluster sampling, researchers select clusters of potential subjects from the population being studied and then use simple **random sampling** techniques to select a final, smaller group of subjects to participate in the study. Cluster sampling is commonly used when a complete and accurate representation of an exceptionally large population is necessary. For example, cluster sampling would be appropriate in a study on the effectiveness of public school instruction throughout the United States.

CMP: *See* Contemporary Music Project

Coalition of Essential Schools: Types of **alternative schools** designed to serve the needs of targeted high school students through the implementation of school-based educational reform initiatives. Essential schools have grown in popularity since the mid-1980s and are based on the work of Theodore Sizer who believed it was important to build and maintain **collaborative networks** of parents, students, and educators who could work together to improve high school education. Essential schools are free to determine curricular specifics, although they are guided by common principles, including helping students master essential skills and knowledge, personalizing teaching and learning, helping students participate actively rather than passively in the learning process, and helping all students reach for the same ultimate goals in ways that match their individual learning styles. Teachers in essential schools make efforts to reduce their own disciplines to the essentials and to link instruction between the various disciplines and to daily life.

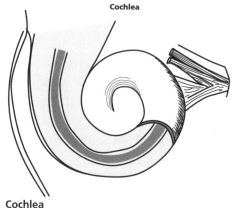

Cochlea

Cochlea

Cochlea: The portion of the **inner ear** that contains receptors for converting incoming sound into electrical signals that are transmitted to the brain. *See* Basilar Membrane; Organ of Corti

Coding: *See* Encoding; Recoding

Coefficient of Correlation: In statistics, a numerical index used to indicate the relationship between two paired sets of **measurements**. The most common coefficient of correlation is the **Pearson product-moment correlation coefficient, (Pearson r)**. While a correlation determines relationships between variables, it does not determine what causes what. A positive correlation indicates that variables vary together in the same direction. In other words, when one variable increases or decreases, the other variable increases or decreases accordingly. *See* **Correlation**

Cognition: In psychology, unobservable, internal mental processes that enable individuals to know. Cognition includes thought processes, **insight**, interpretations, understandings, knowledge, and ideas. *See* Cognitive Learning; Cognitivists

Cognitive Choral Music Achievement Test (CCMAT): An achievement test designed to assess performance-related objectives in high school choral settings. The CCMAT is based on R. W. Weymuth's 1986 doctoral dissertation and includes four parts: 1) interval identification; 2) rhythmic precision; 3) diction; and 4) vocabulary. The CCMAT has a **reliability** coefficient of .90.

Cognitive Dissonance: In psychology, a condition or state in which an individual feels uncomfortable because of inconsistencies in **attitudes**, beliefs, knowledge, or **behavior**. Cognitive dissonance theory was introduced by social psychologist Leon Festinger (1919–1989), and is based on the idea that individuals prefer to maintain a state of **equilibrium** or balance between attitudes, beliefs, and behaviors. Inconsistencies between thoughts and behaviors lead to an undesirable state of discomfort, or cognitive dissonance. This discomfort motivates the individual to change thoughts and/or behaviors in order to regain equilibrium. Cognitive dissonance theory is opposed to **self-perception theory**.

Cognitive Domain/Learning: The learning domain concerned with thought processes. *See* **Bloom's Taxonomy of Educational Objectives**

Cognitive Objectives: In education, desired **outcomes** that focus on whether the students have learned information and understand concepts. In many academic subjects, lesson plans consist largely of cognitive objectives. Students are required to learn information, theories, or **concepts**, and demonstrate understanding of this material through a variety of **assessment** processes. In music, particularly in **performance-based** classes, cognitive objectives are often learned through the development of **psychomotor** and listening skills. That is, with careful, purposeful instruction, students can learn about how music works, understand musical material, and develop knowledge about their instrument or voice through rehearsing and performing high-quality literature.

Cognitive Skills in Music: Those music skills that require information, knowledge, and understanding. Understanding the **framework** of Western music, including scales, intervals, chords, chord progressions, cadences, and song forms involves cognitive skills. In music performance, cognitive skills in music are combined with **psychomotor** skills and **aesthetic** sensitivity to create a sophisticated, artistic musical performance.

Cognitive Psychology/Cognitivism: In psychology, the view that **learning** is based on a restructuring of perceptions and thoughts occurring within the organism. This restructuring allows the learner to perceive new relationships, solve new problems, and gain understanding of a subject area. **Cognitivists** stress the reorganization of one's perceptions in order to achieve understanding. This view is opposed to **behaviorists** who stress the importance of associations formed between **stimuli** and **responses**. **Gestalt psychology** is normally associated with cognitive learning.

Cognitive Motivation Theory: In psychology, a theory of **motivation** based on the idea that individuals are motivated by both positive and negative **incentives**. These incentives are positive when the expectations are valued by the individual and negative when they are not. *See* **Positive Incentive; Negative Incentive**

Cognitive-Physiological Theory: A theory of emotion stating that emotion is the result of physical arousal interacting with cognitive processes. The state of bodily arousal or the physical sensation is then labeled by the individual and determines the type of emotion.

Cognitivists: Individuals who believe that the thinking process is central to learning and that learning results from reorganizing **perceptions** and forming new relationships. Cognitivists focus primarily on the way children think to explain human behavior. Some of the most well known **cognitivists** include **Jean Piaget (1896–1980), Max Wertheimer (1880–1943), Wolfgang Kohler (1887–1967),** Kurt Lewin (1890–1947), and **Jerome Bruner (b. 1915)**. **Insight** into a problem, **problem solving**, and thinking rather than going through a series of muscular or trial-and-error **responses** are all components of cognition. Cognitivists believe that learning is a matter of grasping the big picture in moments of insight. They essentially believe that the smaller, isolated bits of information are useless. This view is opposed to **behaviorists** who believe that small bits of information are taken together to form larger ideas and **concepts**. To cognitivists, training is one thing and learning is another. For example, a child can be trained to say that $8 \times 8 = 64$ without understanding the concepts; this training is not "real" learning. Knowing that $8 \times 8 = 64$ because $8 + 8 + 8 + 8 + 8 + 8 + 8 + 8 = 64$ demonstrates conceptual understanding beyond **stimulus-response (S-R)**; this understanding is cognitive.

Cohesiveness: In psychology, a group phenomenon that creates a sense of belonging in members of a group that tends to hold the group together. Cohesiveness is one of the few group **concepts** in **social psychology**. Groups can develop some degree of cohesiveness very quickly, even when the individuals involved do not know each other. For example, strangers waiting together at the airport after a flight cancellation will develop a degree of cohesiveness as they go through the rebooking and waiting process together. Group cohesiveness can be increased in several ways, including: 1) friendly interaction; 2) cooperation; 3) higher group status; 4) shared difficulty, challenge, or hardship; 5) an outside threat; and 6) democratic rather than authoritarian leadership. In education, cohesiveness is an observable phenomenon in most classrooms. That is, when a class first meets, they are strangers, but as the days and weeks go by, individuals develop a sense of togetherness and belonging that facilitates learning and well being. Cohesiveness is particularly strong in music classrooms, in which students often work together toward common goals over long periods of time.

Cohort: In general, a group of people born at about the same time and exposed to the same societal events. Cohort also refers to someone who is a member of a certain group of people. In education, groups of students who share common **goals** and interests are sometimes divided into groups or cohorts to facilitate the teaching/learning process.

Collaborative Network: In education, a group of parents, teachers, and concerned community members who come together voluntarily to help each other explore and advance specific educational issues. Collaborative networks are commonly used to improve the educational situations of targeted student groups, such as **at-risk students**, and are often associated with **accelerated schools**, **essential schools**, and other **alternative schools**. Collaborative networks for teachers are also common. Such networks help teachers focus on their content areas and their professional development through participation in collegial activities. In a sense, collaborative networks function as teacher support groups. Their purpose is to improve communication and understanding between teachers and to encourage professionalism by providing activities including symposia, internships, conferences, and workshops.

Collective Bargaining: In education, the process of negotiating the professional rights and responsibilities of teachers as a group. Collective bargaining is usually associated with matters related to contract issues and is typically handled by **teachers unions** and other organizations that support and promote the teaching profession.

Collective Unconscious: According to **Carl Jung (1875–1961)**, a psychic system within every individual that contains a collection of ancestral or inherited memories, including primitive ideas, images, and themes called **archetypes**. One common archetype is the shadow. According to Jung, the shadow represents the primordial fear of animals. The collective unconscious is the same for everyone and serves to unite all human beings.

College Band Directors National Association (CBDNA): An organization devoted to the study, teaching, and performance of music for wind bands. It functions largely as an organization that allows and encourages college band directors to communicate and share professional ideas and information.

College Board Study, The: A study conducted by the College Entrance Examination Board, sponsor of the **Scholastic Achievement Test (SAT)** college entrance exam, showing that test preparation courses for exams such as the SAT affect scores minimally. The study was conducted using scores obtained in 1995–96, and it created controversy with test preparation companies such as Kaplan and Princeton Review. These companies argued that the College Board benefits by finding that the test preparation courses are not very effective because effective test preparations would give an unfair advantage to those who could afford expensive tutoring or coaching. The College Board asserted that statistics compiled by test preparation companies did not include the score improvements of non-coached test takers, and that the testing companies benefit by showing a high effectiveness rating. The College Board Study brought into question the once little-questioned effectiveness of test preparation courses.

College Entrance Board Report: A report published in 1983 by the College Entrance Examination Board that strongly supported the arts in education. The full report was officially entitled *Academic Preparation for College: What Students Need to Know and Be Able to Do*. In addition to the arts, the College Entrance Board Report also included English, math, science, social science, and foreign language as six major areas of the curriculum. This report differed from another report issued in 1983 entitled *A Nation at Risk* in which the arts were not supported.

College Music Society, The (CMS): A consortium of college, conservatory, university, and independent musicians and scholars whose mission is to promote music teaching and learning, musical creativity and expression, research and dialogue, and diversity and interdisciplinary interaction. The first meeting of CMS took place in 1958. Currently, CMS publishes a newsletter and the journal *College Music Symposium*. In addition, CMS publishes *CMS Reports*, which addresses current issues in music and higher education. CMS also offers opportunities for professional development, including workshops, symposia, conferences, and summer institutes.

Combination Tone: In acoustics, a type of subjective tone that is not actually produced by the sounding device or instrument whose **frequency** is equal to the sum of the frequencies of the two primary tones that evoked its **perception**. *See* **Subjective Tone**

Comenius, John Amos (1592-1670): Author of the **Didacta Magna** (*The Great Didactic*) written in 1632, which is considered by many to be the first great educational treatise. Comenius was born in Moravia, Bohemia, and was one of the first to recognize the importance of **method** in teaching. The purpose of the *Didacta Magna* was "to seek and find a method of instruction, by which teachers may teach less, but learners may learn more." Comenius also wrote *The School of Infancy*, the first of a series of graded textbooks to illustrate how his method worked and was written to guide mothers in preschool training.

Comenius believed that education should begin at an early age and that careful supervision of the child's physical, moral, and emotional development was important. He also believed that everyone should have the right to a formal education and that all classes and sexes should be schooled together. Comenius thought that education should begin with vernacular instruction, which was uncommon at the time. Comenius advocated four stages of learning, each lasting six years: 1) infancy, 2) childhood, 3) boyhood, and 4) youth. He also advocated four types of schools to correspond with each stage of learning: 1) a mother school to train mothers, 2) a vernacular school in each town that included reading, writing, arithmetic, history, mechanics, religion, ethics, and music, 3) a classical school in every major city that included more intensive instruction in languages, arts, and sciences, and 4) a university for every regional area.

Coming to Our Senses, The Rockefeller Report: A report released in 1977 by the Arts, Education, and Americans Panel chaired by David J. Rockefeller, fully entitled *Coming to Our Senses: The Significance of the Arts for American Education*. The report summarized the Panel's position regarding the importance of art in education and the schools. In addition, the report suggested that the way to offset budget cuts and job losses was to utilize all resources available in the community to facilitate arts education, including employing local artists as teachers. Historically, *Coming to Our Senses* was an important report because it provided strong support for arts education, and it reflected America's cultural values and attitudes at that time. However, critics believed the report advocated that the arts should be used to make other learning activities more fun and exciting rather than for the inherent value within art itself. In addition, the report implied that the arts were a panacea for all that was wrong in education at the time. For example, the report indicated that the arts could increase energy levels, stimulate learning and creativity, lower the dropout rate, and help develop basic skills in other subjects, such as reading and math.

Commission on Basic Concepts: A commission organized in 1954 by the **Music Educators National Conference (MENC)** to develop a sound theoretical foundation for music education. The commission included both music educators and individuals outside of the music profession. The commission's work resulted in the 1958 publication of *Basic Concepts in Music Education*.

Commission on National Goals: A national commission established and appointed by President Eisenhower in 1960 consisting of eleven distinguished Americans. The commission addressed various topics in education and discussed ways to make sure that American children were adequately prepared for a modern, post-*Sputnik I* world.

Commission on Teacher Education, MENC: A commission appointed in 1972 by Wiley Housewright, then president of the **Music Educators National Conference (MENC)**, to make recommendations for improving music teacher education. The commission suggested that teacher certification be based on the demonstration of competencies rather than on the satisfactory completion of a course or set of courses. The competencies recommended by the commission included the following three categories: 1) personal qualities, 2) musical competencies, and 3) professional qualities. Each of these categories includes an extensive list of competencies at which music educators should be proficient.

Committee of Fifteen: An educational committee formed by the **National Education Association (NEA)** in 1895 to standardize elementary school curricula. The Committee of Fifteen focused on grammar, literature and art, mathematics, geography, and history, or what it called the five windows of the soul. The committee believed the school's role was to transmit Western cultural heritage through a graded and structured curriculum.

Committee of Ten: An educational committee established by the **National Education Association (NEA)** in 1892 to standardize high school curricula. The Committee of Ten suggested that all high schools offer four years of English, three years of history, three years of science, three years of mathematics, and three years of a foreign language. In addition, the committee suggested that modern and classical studies be given equal status.

Committee on Assessing the Progress of Education (CAPE): A committee initially formed in 1964 as the **Exploratory Committee on Assessing the Progress of Education (ECAPE)**, a name later changed to the **National Assessment of Educational Progress (NAEP)**. The goal of CAPE was to develop national assessments that could be used to provide the public with data on the educational achievements of American students, both children and adults. The Carnegie Corporation initially funded CAPE, and in 1969, the administration was transferred to the **Education Commission of the States (ECS)**.

Committee on Instruction (MENC): A committee formed in 1971 to identify issues and to develop position statements based on the **Goals and Objectives (GO) Project** sponsored by **Music Educators National Conference (MENC)** in 1969. The committee identified specific schools with outstanding programs in thirty-seven areas of American music education in a publication entitled *Selected Instructional Programs in Music*.

Common Schools: Free schools or tax-supported schools established in America during the early nineteenth century that allowed all boys and girls to have three free years of education. Common schools offered up to eight years of schooling and focused on reading, writing, arithmetic, and history. Common Schools were the predecessors of today's public schools.

Community Schools: Locally supported schools in which the educational program is an outgrowth of the life of a particular community. Interests and needs of the community are served in community schools, and all segments of the community are involved to some extent in determining **curricular** content. Community schools often operate as a type of service center in the community.

Community Sings: A popular activity in the early twentieth century, community sings were held in schools, factories, and for community events. The entire population would gather and sing songs, often of a patriotic nature. Community sings were especially popular during World War I, when feelings of patriotism were particularly high. Community sings also provided opportunities for music supervisors to get actively involved in the community and to promote music in the schools.

Comparative Music Education: In research, an area of study that examines relationships between music education programs and issues surrounding the functionality of music and its role in society, both nationally and internationally. Comparative music education researchers often study the practices and methodologies of school music programs to gain a greater understanding of the theoretical, philosophical, and historical bases of these programs.

Comparison Group: In research, a non-experimental group comprised of subjects who have *not* been randomly assigned and to which **experimental groups** will be compared. A comparison group is similar to a **control group**, except that subjects in a control group are randomly assigned.

Compensation: In psychology, a **defense mechanism** in which an individual attempts to hide or balance failure in, or lack of talent for, one activity by an exerted effort to excel in another activity. Effort may be spent in pursuing an activity either similar to or different from the failed activity.

Compensatory Education Programs (CEPs): Educational programs that offer supplementary instruction to **at-risk students** and/or students performing significantly below expected **achievement** levels, particularly in language, mathematics, and/or reading. CEPs are primarily intended to provide students who do not qualify for or need special education services with educational opportunities beyond those offered in traditional public school programs. CEPs are designed to compensate for factors that may be missing in children's lives such as individual attention and educational materials. CEPs are most common at the elementary level where such intervention and supplementary instruction have been shown to be most effective. CEPs often include: 1) Supplementary instruction only, not primary instruction, 2) an assessment component for identifying students eligible for the program and to determine student progress and program effectiveness, and 3) parental involvement. Examples: 1) **Title I**, 2) Upward Bound, and 3) Success for All.

Competence Motivation: A theory developed by personality theorist Robert White (b. 1904), which states all individuals have a basic, fundamental drive to become competent or to gain control or mastery over their environment. Increased competence results in increased enjoyment. Thus, competence is a driving force (**motivation**) for engaging and performing well in achievement-related activities. Several behaviors support this theory, including a preference for moderately challenging tasks and working alone, interest in the activity itself, persistence with the activity, and exploration. White believed that the competence motive was an intrinsic motive that may play a role in the survival of the human species. *See* Intrinsic Motivation

Competencies: The skills and techniques necessary to function in a particular activity or profession. Competencies are learned in formal and informal educational settings. In education, effective teachers often possess a variety of competencies related to knowledge of subject matter and teaching methods, professional attributes, personal characteristics, and teaching style.

Competency-based Teacher Education (CBTE): In education, the idea that prospective teachers must meet predetermined competencies, and the process of learning and developing these abilities. In many instances, prospective teachers are required to demonstrate predetermined competencies as part of teacher training programs. The push for CBTE began in the 1970s and continues today. The implementation of CBTE has brought positive changes in teacher education training programs, including the development of specific goals and objectives according to predetermined competencies.

Competition: In education, a teaching tool, technique, or event sometimes used to motivate students. Some research shows that competition may have negative effects on learning, while other research shows that competition can enhance learning. It appears that the intensity of the competition and the personalities of the participants influence the degree to which competition affects **motivation**. In music education, formal competition is common, especially as it relates to performance-based classes and activities. For example, full ensembles, small ensembles, and soloists often compete at a variety of festivals, contests, or competitions. Research indicates that the benefits gained from such events tend to be non-musical or extra-musical in nature.

Complex Tone: A tone consisting of a **fundamental** and upper **partials**. In music, the individual resonating properties of musical instruments enhance or suppress certain partials based largely on instrument construction, resulting in a wide variety of **tone colors** or **timbres**. Timbre enables individuals to distinguish one instrument from another. Almost all musical instruments naturally produce complex tones.

Composers in Public Schools: *See* Young Composer's Project

Composite Synthesis Level of Discrimination Learning, Gordon: The stage of learning where students comprehend the tonality and meter in written music. *See* Skill Learning Sequence

Comprehensive Arts Curriculum Model: A model proposed by Bennett Reimer (b. 1932) in 1989 designed to promote **aesthetic** literacy in children. In the comprehensive arts curriculum model, instruction is focused on developing students' perceptions and understandings of the creative process and interacting with artworks. These skills are intended to develop students' abilities to make informed judgments about the nature and value of art. The comprehensive arts curriculum model differs dramatically from traditional music instruction, where the focus is on skill development and musical performance.

Comprehensive Assessment: In education, a term used to describe **assessment** that measures a student's capacities for reasoning, thinking divergently, and solving problems creatively as opposed to assessment based on standardized **achievement** test scores. Comprehensive assessment places emphasis on measuring students' abilities to perform real-life tasks and to function effectively in real-world contexts. Although many questions remain about how this type of assessment can be implemented effectively and practically, there appears to be a trend in education toward comprehensive assessment. For example, having students demonstrate that they can apply what they have learned instead of having them complete a traditional pencil-and-paper test would be an appropriate comprehensive assessment technique.

Comprehensive Musicianship: An interdisciplinary approach to studying music in which students learn and understand the relationships between various music courses rather than treating each course independently. After the Soviet Union launched *Sputnik I* in 1957, the United States embarked on a mission to establish its supremacy among world superpowers. At the time, most Americans believed the United States had fallen behind the Soviet Union technologically and that it had become complacent in education. As a result, the attention and resources given to all areas of education were unprecedented over the next decade, and numerous conferences and seminars were held across the nation to address the problems in education.

Comprehensive musicianship was an outgrowth of these efforts. The original intent was to develop students' abilities to analyze, organize, and perform music, thus improving the quality of instruction in school music programs. The emphasis shifted to improving teacher education programs, and in 1965, the **Contemporary Music Project (CMP)** sponsored a four-day seminar entitled "Seminar on Comprehensive Musicianship—the Foundation for College Education in Music." After decades of use, the term comprehensive musicianship has become somewhat confounded. Some music educators use the term to describe an approach to teaching or a method of teaching, while others refer to it as a movement in music education. Overall, comprehensive musicianship has become almost synonymous with the teaching of music from a holistic, comprehensive perspective.

Compulsive Behavior/Compulsions: In general, repetitive actions that an individual is unable to resist. Compulsive behavior can be mild or severe. In mild cases, individuals engage in repetitive behaviors because they make them feel comfortable in some way. Most people exhibit mild compulsive behaviors, yet these behaviors do not interfere with their daily lives. For example, many baseball players develop a routine that they believe they must execute before batting in order to be properly prepared. Such a routine may involve adjusting the cap, pulling up the shirt sleeves, tightening the batting gloves, and taking a few preparatory swings before stepping into the batter's box. In severe cases, compulsions can interfere with daily life. That is, the repetitive and ritualistic behaviors inhibit normal functioning. People who are compulsive in this way spend an inordinate amount of time engaging in compulsive behaviors.

Computer Assisted Instruction (CAI): A type of instruction in which students interact with computers to learn materials. Music software programs are designed to help students develop musical skills in many areas including theory, history, **music reading**, aural training, and jazz **improvisation**. CAI is a non-competitive way to learn and allows students to take an active role in the learning process. Students interact with computer software programs in a variety of ways, but the most common use is for students to select appropriate responses from programmed choices. Although programs are typically not written for specific individuals, CAI is a form of **individualized instruction** in that it allows each student to progress at his or her own rate. In addition, programs provide students with immediate **feedback**, allowing students to track their own progress. *See* Programmed Instruction; Tachistoscope

Computer Programs, Music: Computer programs designed to facilitate music teaching and learning. Computer programs for music tend to fall into the following three categories: 1) interactive instructional programs designed to improve specific musical skills, such as rhythmic precision or interval recognition; 2) music writing and/or performing programs designed to aid student composition and performance; and 3) accompaniment programs that facilitate solo playing. Like most computer-related technology, these programs are continually updated and improved.

Computer-aided Music Instruction (CAMI): *See* Computer Assisted Instruction (CAI)

Computer-based Instruction (CBI): *See* Computer Assisted Instruction (CAI)

Computer-mediated Instruction (CMI): *See* Computer Assisted Instruction (CAI)

Concept: A set of attributes, properties, characteristics, relationships, or ideas that enable individuals to recognize, identify, and know something or someone. Concepts may be concrete or abstract. For example, a violin is a concrete concept referring to a given type of stringed instrument, and justice is an abstract concept regarding the nature of right and wrong or legal and illegal.

Concept Attainment: A teaching model developed by **Jerome Bruner (b. 1915)** in the early 1960s to help students learn concepts. Teachers using concept attainment typically prepare and present a finite series of positive and negative instances or examples of a given concept to students. Students are instructed to devise a list of similarities between the positive examples by engaging in **brainstorming** techniques and formulating their own definition of the concept and its essential attributes. Teachers then give the students another set of examples that can be used to test their definition. Concept attainment enables students to develop a deeper understanding of concepts by becoming actively engaged in the learning process.

Concept Formation: In psychology, the cognitive process whereby ideas are formed. These ideas are generalized from accumulated knowledge of qualities, aspects, and relations of actions and objects.

Concept Instances: Examples of a given concept. Concept instances are based on the idea that conceptual understanding is facilitated by providing many examples that illustrate the concept being investigated.

Concept Mapping: An organizational technique where concepts are arranged visually for easier understanding. Geometric shapes, icons, lines, and arrows are commonly used in concept mapping. Concept mapping is a learning aid that provides a visual picture of conceptual relationships.

Concept Not-instances: Examples of a concept other than the one being investigated. Concept not-instances are based on the idea that conceptual understanding is facilitated by providing many examples that illustrate a concept other than the concept being investigated. That is, not-instances facilitate the understanding of what the concept is not.

Concept Pair Analysis: A way of comparing and contrasting concepts by determining the similarities and differences in a pair of concepts. Concept pair analysis is used to facilitate **conceptual understanding**. For example, after determining the similarities and differences in a saxophone and clarinet and in a clarinet and a lamppost, most people would realize that a clarinet and a saxophone have more common characteristics and fewer differences than a clarinet and a lamppost.

Concept Structure Analysis: An analysis used to identify shared characteristics. For example, hot/cold and wet/dry are polar concepts that share the property of being two-member sets.

Conceptual Learning: Learning that places emphasis on concepts rather than on facts alone. In education, conceptual learning is generally considered higher level learning than factual learning. Conceptual learning is facilitated by encouraging students to think divergently and to openly express their thoughts and ideas. Conceptual learning also enhances the ability to **transfer** knowledge from one situation to another and aids in the memory process. *See* **Divergent Learning**

Conceptual Levels: According to David Hunt (b. 1926), the levels at which teachers operate or the ways in which teachers behave in the classroom based on their experiences. Hunt believes that teachers process experiences at different levels according to their own stage of conceptual development. Hunt identified three conceptual levels: 1) Level A, where teachers view knowledge as fixed truth and students are expected to memorize facts; 2) Level B, where teachers view their role as more interactive and begin promoting student development, and 3) Level C, where teachers are able to employ a variety of **teaching methods** to most effectively meet the needs of their students.

Conceptual Replication: The replication of research using different procedures for manipulating or measuring the **variables**. That is, the idea of the research study is replicated, but the data collection and/or statistical procedures are not identical.

Conceptual Understanding: A general understanding or idea about something or someone that is deeper and more sophisticated than basic factual knowledge. This understanding is based on a set of associated attributes, properties, characteristics, or relationships. For example, that George W. Bush (b. 1946) is the forty-third president of the United States is a fact; however, the **concept** of the president of the United States conjures up a variety of individuals, ideas, ideals, characteristics, and duties. As a concept, the president of the United States is understood somewhat differently by individuals based on circumstance, context, maturation, and experience.

Concrete Operational Stage: The third stage of Piaget's stages of cognitive development, approximately age seven to eleven, when children acquire the ability to think and reason logically and are able to understand **conservation**, classification, and other concrete ideas. *See* Piaget's Stages of Cognitive Growth

Concurrent Validity: *See* Validity

Conditioned Aversion: In psychology, something that an individual learns to dislike through a conditioning process.

Conditioned Reflex: *See* Conditioned Response

Conditioned Reinforcer: In psychology, a formerly neutral stimulus that has repeatedly preceded a **reinforcer** and acquires reinforcing power, also known as a **secondary stimulus**. In education, conditioned reinforcers often include things like good grades, social approval, and gold stars because their value to the learner has to be conditioned. *See* Classical Conditioning

Conditioned Response (CR): In psychology, a term used in **classical** and **operant conditioning** to indicate a learned or acquired **response** to a **stimulus**. *See* Conditioning

Conditioned Stimulus (CS): In psychology, a stimulus that does not elicit a response from the subject naturally; that is, it must be learned. *See* Conditioning

Conditioning: In psychology, the process in which new **stimuli** elicit **responses** that did not occur previously or naturally. Conditioning involves learning responses through training. Two general types of conditioning are classical and operant. In classical conditioning, a **conditioned stimulus** is presented, followed by or paired with an **unconditioned** (reinforcing) **stimulus**. Conditioning is exhibited when the organism responds to the conditioned stimulus alone. In operant conditioning, the response is allowed to occur and is immediately followed by a reinforcing stimulus. Operant conditioning is exhibited when the response rate increases over the original, preconditioned rate. *See* **Classical Conditioning; Operant Conditioning**

Conditioned Stimulus (CS): In psychology, a stimulus that does not elicit a response from the subject naturally; that is, it must be learned. A conditioned stimulus is created when a **neutral stimulus** is consistently paired with an **unconditioned stimulus**. Over time, the neutral stimulus alone will elicit the same response as the unconditioned stimulus. In **Ivan Pavlov's (1849–1936)** classic experiment, a dog naturally salivated (**unconditioned response**) when presented with meat powder (**unconditioned stimulus**). Pavlov then paired the presentation of meat powder with the presentation of a tone (**neutral stimulus**). Over time, the dog learned to salivate (**conditioned response**) to the tone (conditioned stimulus), even when it was presented without the meat powder. That is, the tone had become a conditioned stimulus. In operant conditioning, the response must precede the reinforcer. The conditioned response is defined in terms of either the rate of the response or its resistance to **extinction** rather than in terms of magnitude or latency. A strongly conditioned operant will occur far more rapidly and be far more difficult to extinguish than an operant that is weakly conditioned.

Conditioned Response (CR): In psychology, a term used in **classical** and **operant conditioning** to indicate a learned or acquired **response** to a **stimulus**. In **classical conditioning**, the conditioned response is the response being elicited by the **conditioned stimulus**. The stronger the conditioning, the greater the magnitude of the conditioned response and the shorter its **latency**. In operant conditioning, the response must precede the reinforcer. The reinforcer is meant to encourage the response. Therefore, the conditioned response is defined in terms of either the rate of the response or its resistance to **extinction** rather than in terms of magnitude or latency. A strongly conditioned operant will occur far more rapidly and be far more difficult to extinguish than an operant that has been weakly conditioned.

Conditions of Learning, Gagne: Eight conditions of learning described by Robert Gagne (1916–2002) in his book entitled *The Conditions of Learning* (1965). Gagne began with a description of various classifications of behavior; that is, he identified the various tasks and/or types of learning that seemed to be encountered in everyday life. His classification system or hierarchy progresses from the simple to the complex. Although Gagne referred to these classes as learning types, he was primarily interested in observable behavior, or the "products" of learning. Gagne fully acknowledged that there might be more than eight types of learning. Gagne's eight conditions of learning are as follows:

Signal Learning: This is basically **Ivan Pavlov's (1849–1936) classical conditioning**. At this stage, children develop conditioned responses to particular stimuli. Responses are diffuse, emotional, and reactionary. Learning is involuntary. Examples include calming down or going to sleep while listening to a lullaby or withdrawing the hand when seeing a hot object.

Stimulus-Response (S-R) Learning: This is basically **B. F. Skinner's (1904–1990) operant conditioning**. Responses are more precise rather than diffuse, emotional, or reactionary. S-R learning is used to acquire verbal and physical skills and involves "trained" responses. Examples include children waving without knowing why or saying "dada" or "mama" on request, or an adult learning the appropriate response to the stimulus of a word in a foreign language or seeing a second space A and automatically playing (fingering) the right note.

Chaining: The process of linking together previously learned stimulus-response associations. Chaining often occurs so naturally that the specific series of events goes unnoticed. Examples include a child saying the word doll, hugging the doll, laying the doll down, and saying "doll" again or the series of tricks performed by dolphins during a thirty-minute aquatic show.

Verbal Association: Verbal association is a type of chaining; however, the links are verbal units rather than other types of behavior. The simplest verbal association is the activity of naming an object, which requires two links: 1) an observing response enables the child to identify properly the object he/she sees and 2) an internal stimulus enables the child to say the proper name (translation response). Examples are when a child can name an object "ball" and also say "ball" or a music student can see an A and say it is an A.

Discrimination Learning: Discrimination learning is when individuals learn different responses for stimuli which might be confused, or when individuals learn to distinguish between motor and verbal chains previously acquired. An example is when an individual undertakes to identify all the new models of automobiles produced in the United States in a particular year. In this example, the individual must associate each individual model, with its distinctive appearance, with the correct model name, and with no other name.

Concept Learning: In concept learning, individuals respond to stimuli in terms of abstract characteristics like color, shape, position, and number. An individual's behavior is not under the control of particular physical stimuli, but rather of the abstract properties of each stimulus. Examples are learning what a cube is or understanding the concept of "cubeness," or developing ideas regarding tone quality characteristics of each instrument

Rule Learning: The process of relating two or more concepts. In effect, rules are chains of concepts and often follow an "if this, then that" format. For example, if a trumpet player uses more air or increases air speed, the tone will be louder, or if a clarinet player uses a soft reed, the tone quality will be thin, and the pitch will be flat in louder dynamic ranges.

Problem Solving: The process of using rules to achieve a desired goal or to solve problems. Basically, problem solving is thinking about how to do things. For example, a musician is engaging in problem solving when he or she makes decisions on how a piece in a particular style should be performed.

Conduct Disorders: A term for behavioral disorders involving **antisocial behavior**. Conduct disorders include the inappropriate use of language, fighting, throwing temper tantrums, and being overly aggressive.

Conflict Mediation/Management: In education, a strategy for teaching students how to resolve conflicts and disagreements in a responsible way. Conflict mediation is a voluntary, structured process in which students develop **problem solving** skills and strategies in negotiating and mediating differences among themselves. Typically, the students who have a conflict work together under the guidance of a mediator to resolve conflicts. In conflict mediation students: 1) state what they want and how they feel; 2) state the reasons for their wants and feelings; 3) discuss their understanding of each other's positions; 4) devise a few optional plans that may help resolve the conflict; and 5) agree on a plan to end the conflict peaceably. The number of conflicts between students in some schools has risen dramatically in recent years. Conflict mediation helps provide a peaceable means of dealing with these conflicts.

Confluence Model: A model of intellectual development showing that intellectual growth may be at least partially a function of other family members' intellectual growth. That is, the average of the intellectual levels of all other family members constitute the intellectual environment of any given child in that family. This model of intellectual development was proposed by Robert B. Zajonc (b. 1923), and the data reveal the following tendencies: 1) Eldest children tend to have higher **intelligence quotients (IQs)** than younger siblings; 2) The greater the number of children in a family, the lower the IQs of all children; 3) Twins have lower IQs than other siblings in the same family; 4) Children in homes with both parents present have higher IQs than children from one-parent homes; and 5) an only child tends to have a lower IQ than the eldest child in a two- or three-child family.

Conformity: In **social psychology**, a term used to describe the fact that individuals in groups tend to behave in a uniform way. Group pressure acts on individuals to force them into acting in accord with the rules or **norms** of the group. As a result, people tend to follow or accept what others do, say, or think. Several studies support the idea that people in a group will tend to modify their **behavior**, sometimes significantly, to conform to the group, even when they strongly disagree with what the group is thinking or doing. *See* Socialization; Group Polarization; Groupthink

Confounding: In research, the failure to control for the effects of a third variable or a nuisance variable in an **experimental design**. That is, confounding occurs when an **independent variable** outside the control of the researcher interacts or mixes with the independent variable being investigated, making it impossible to determine precisely the effects of the independent variable. Careful planning in the research design helps mitigate the possibility of confounding variables.

Congruence: According to **Carl Rogers (1902–1987)**, one of the three necessary and sufficient conditions for the promotion of learning, the other two being **empathy** and **unconditional positive regard**. Rogers uses the term congruence to mean total and complete honesty, and he believed that teachers must be "real" and honest with students to promote learning. According to Rogers, teachers should not merely go through the motions of teaching, pretending to be interested in students' progress and pretending to be interested in the material being taught. Rogers believed that individuals who do not possess congruence should not teach.

Connectionism: *See* Associationism

Connotative Meaning: The suggestions, undertones, and emotional meanings of a word, phrase, or symbol that are deeper than the literal, or **denotative, meaning**. For example, the words collision and crash can be used to describe a car accident, but they have somewhat different connotations; that is, each word conjures up a slightly different mental picture and emotional response.

Conscience: An internal valuing and recognition of standards, typically involving right and wrong. Each individual uses these standards to judge his or her own behavior. In **Freud's psychoanalytic theory**, the conscience tries to prevent morally objectionable behavior, including thoughts, and comprises one part of the superego. *See* Id; Ego; Superego

Conservation: A term used by **Jean Piaget (1896–1980)** in his theory of cognitive growth for the ability of a child to recognize that certain properties of objects, such as mass, volume, and number do not change despite transformations in the appearance of the objects. A classic illustration of conservation typically involves pouring water from a tall, thin glass into a short, wide glass without changing the amount of water involved and asking children to indicate which glass has more water in it.

Children who correctly indicate that both glasses have the same amount of water can conserve. According to Piaget, children typically acquire the ability to conserve at about age seven when they reach the **concrete operational stage**. An example of conservation in music occurs when students demonstrate an understanding that a quarter note gets one count, yet the length of that count varies according to the tempo. *See* **Piaget's Stages of Cognitive Growth**

Consistency Paradox: The discrepancy between what appears intuitively true regarding the consistency of **personality** behaviors and what has been shown by research. That is, even though personality appears to be consistent across time, it appears to be inconsistent across situations. Researchers have attempted to explain the **consistency paradox** by pointing out that while individuals may be honest at work or when they are with other people, they may not be honest in their personal lives or when they are alone. In other words, individuals sometimes act one way when they believe others are watching and evaluating and another when they feel that no one is watching.

Consolidation Hypothesis: In memory, the **hypothesis** that memories must be consolidated or set in the brain before they can be stored in **long term memory (LTM)**. The general idea is that if information is interfered with before it has been consolidated, it will be lost.

Consolidation Theory: The theory that learning produces changes in the nervous system that need time to become permanent. During the consolidation process, these changes in the nervous system are particularly vulnerable to obliteration.

Consonance: In music, combinations of tones considered to be "pleasant" and stable. Major thirds, perfect fourths, and perfect fifths are considered consonant intervals. In psychology, consonance is a desired state of consistency and **equilibrium** within individuals and within groups. In individuals, consonance occurs when thinking and behavior are in agreement. For example, if someone who is trying to lose weight passes up the opportunity for a fast food meal, he or she will maintain a state of consonance because the actions and the thoughts are congruent. In groups, consonance occurs as a function of the successful interaction of different personalities. In education, teaching style and discipline are significant factors that determine the amount of consonance in the classroom.

Consonants: Vocal sounds resulting from the restriction of air created by articulate movements of the lips, tongue, and jaw. Consonants provide clarity and intelligibility to vocalization.

Construct: In psychology, an unobservable hypothesized characteristic whose presence is inferred by linking observed responses to stimulus events, activities, or situations. Constructs include a wide variety of characteristics including **aptitude**, verbal aptitude, **anxiety**, leadership, and ego strength. For example, one could infer a musician's high level of performance anxiety (the construct) if he or she started to shake, perspire, and turn pale (the response) when walking on stage to perform a violin solo for an audience (the stimulus). Similarly, one could infer a high level of **music aptitude** (the construct) by receiving a high score (the response) on a standardized music aptitude test (the stimulus).

Construct Validity: *See* Validity

Constructivism: In education, a term sometimes used to describe a movement to modify the **curriculum** and instruction to reflect a **cognitive** or student-centered point of view. Constructivists favor **student-centered instruction** over **teacher-centered instruction**. That is, a teacher's role is to provide students with conceptual bases upon which students can construct meaning or make sense of information for themselves. Teaching students to think for themselves, helping students develop effective study skills, and helping students develop effective **problem solving** strategies are common components of constructivism. Constructivism is structured around a process called **scaffolding**, in which knowledge is constructed or built up in layers by individuals acting within a social context.

In philosophy, constructivism is the epistemological concept that the world as each individual knows it is a product, or construction, of that individual's mind. The outside world is transformed within the mind of each individual. In constructivism, knowing is a subjective rather than an objective reality. In music education, constructivism provides a natural basis to explore and research epistemological foundations by focusing on aspects of music that are inherently constructive. These include listening, performing, composing, and improvising. Music education and constructivism work well together because much of the knowledge imparted in music courses relates to feeling, understanding, or representation.

Contemporary Music Project (CMP): Funded by the **Ford Foundation**, CMP ran from 1963–73 and was the result of the success of the **Young Composers Project**. In the proposal to the Ford Foundation, the **Music Educators National Conference (MENC)** states the following five goals for the CMP: 1) to increase the emphasis on the creative aspect of music in the public schools, 2) to create a solid foundation or environment in the music education profession for the acceptance (through understanding) of the contemporary music idiom, 3) to reduce the compartmentalization that now exists between the profession of music composition and music education for the benefit of composers and music educators alike, 4) to cultivate taste and **discrimination** on the part of music educators and students regarding the quality of contemporary music used in the schools, and 5) to discover, when possible, creative talent among students. CMP consisted of several pilot programs designed to introduce contemporary music into the public schools and to educate teachers and students on the value of contemporary music. CMP included workshops, seminars, and the sponsorship of composers in selected public schools.

Content Analysis: A type of descriptive research in which the content of documents or journals is systematically analyzed using specific coding systems. In general research, content analysis typically involves analyzing data that is in written form; however, in music research, content analysis often involves analyzing musical notation. Inferences or conclusions can be made once the data has been organized, categorized, and analyzed in a logical manner. For example, a researcher may choose a variety of band method books from a particular time frame and analyze the content to determine the emphasis placed on certain **skills** or **concepts**.

Content Based Instruction (CBI): In education, an approach commonly used for learning a second language in which the subject matter is used to practice and learn a second language but is not the teacher's primary learning objective. In language study, CBI focuses on integrating language teaching and subject matter in such a way to facilitate the learning of language. Typically, students focus on learning about a topic of general interest in the language being studied. For example, students may use a second language to learn about their favorite entertainers or other topics of interest. The topic of interest facilitates the use of the new language.

Content Learning Sequence: *See* Tonal Content Learning Sequence, Gordon; Rhythm Content Learning Sequence, Gordon; Music Learning Theory, Gordon

Content Validity: *See* Validity

Contests: *See* Band Contests

Context, Input, Process, Product (CIPP): A systems-oriented evaluation **model** developed by Daniel Stufflebeam in the mid-1980s. CIPP is commonly used in business and in education, and the model's primary components are identified in the name. Context involves identifying the target audience and determining what needs are going to be met. Input involves determining how the needs are going to be met. This process includes evaluating available resources and assessing possible alternative strategies. Process involves examining how successfully the plan was implemented. Product involves examining the results obtained by the actions including whether needs were met and what planning might be required for the future.

Contingency: In psychology, a term that refers to the delivery of consequent **stimuli** under specific conditions. Contingency implies an "if-then" relationship; if response A occurs, then reinforcer or punisher B will be given. *See* Operant Conditioning

Contingency Contracting: In education, an agreement between students and teachers in which students receive various **reinforcements** contingent upon meeting specified requirements. Contingency contracting is based on the behavioral principles of reinforcement, and the type of reinforcement varies according to pre-determined levels of performance. Reinforcement menus or systems typically vary among students and may include rewards such as bonus points, free time, or tokens that can be exchanged for larger rewards. *See* Token System; Schedules of Reinforcement

Contingent Reinforcement: *See* Contingency

Continuing Education: Formal education that extends beyond the undergraduate level. Continuing Education can be used in reference to graduate level study in one's area of expertise, typically pursued to obtain a masters or doctoral degree. Continuing education is also commonly used to refer to classes or courses offered for the purpose of learning a new skill or developing skills already acquired. Typically, these courses do not have stringent prerequisites for attendance. Many colleges, universities, and community colleges offer a variety of continuing education courses across disciplines.

Continuity: *See* Articulation

Continuity, Principle/Law of: The ability to perceive lines and patterns as following a predictable pattern in time and space, usually based on experience. Continuity is a **gestalt concept**. *See* Closure, Principle/Law of; Similarity, Principle/Law of; Proximity, Principle/Law of

Continuous Reinforcement: *See* Schedules of Reinforcement

Control Group: In **experimental research**, a group that does not receive experimental **treatment** (**independent variable**). Results obtained from a control group are compared to the results obtained from the group or groups that received the experimental treatment (experimental group) to determine whether the treatment had an effect. **Treatments** usually involve the manipulation of one or more **variables** whose effect(s) (**dependent variable**) are under study. A control group should resemble the experimental group in all respects. The use of a control group is critical in evaluating the effects of the independent variable on the subjects' measured responses. *See* Experimental Group

Control Processes: In psychology, the processes or operations that facilitate the selection and use of **cognitive** processes or that organize cognitive processes in ways that enable individuals to choose the ones that are most suited to accomplishing a given task or goal. During multicomponent tasks, there are many cognitive processes or mental representations active at the same time; however, only some of these processes will be used to guide an individual's actions or thoughts. Control processes control and organize the myriad of cognitive processes that are active during multicomponent tasks and determine which ones will be used. Thus, control processes are independent of or separate from cognitive processes. That is, they do not lead to action; rather, they facilitate the cognitive processes that lead to action.

Controlled Association: In psychology, an activity used in **word-association experiments** in which the subject is instructed to provide a specific type of associated word. For example, a subject may be asked to give a word opposite to that of the **stimulus** word.

Conventional Moral Reasoning: *See* Moral Development, Kohlberg

Conventional Morality: *See* Moral Development, Kohlberg

Convergent Thinking: A mode of thinking where the **goal** is to produce a specified response in accordance with truth and fact. Most **convergent thinking** involves finding only one correct response. In testing, true/false questions, multiple-choice questions, and fill-in-the-blank questions all require convergent thinking because they require only one correct answer. Convergent thinking is opposed to divergent thinking in which multiple, creative responses are sought and encouraged. *See* **Divergent Thinking**

Cooperating Teacher: Public school teachers who supervise and mentor student teachers during the **student teaching** experience. Cooperating teachers serve as **role models** for student teachers and are usually experienced teachers who are well respected in the teaching community. Typically, a cooperating teacher will work together with **university/college supervisors** and the student teacher to structure appropriate student teaching experiences.

Cooperative Learning: Learning that occurs in groups in which students are encouraged to work together toward achieving common **goals**. **Cooperative learning** is versatile because it can be adapted to almost any group setting, including like-ability groups, different-ability groups, and groups formed for a larger purpose, such as band, orchestra, or choir. The ways groups are formed can help teachers accomplish social, personal, and academic objectives. Cooperative learning is becoming increasingly popular because it promotes **self-esteem**, improves student relations, and improves student attitudes about learning. In addition, many teachers find that cooperative learning teaches students to work together and be more accepting of individual differences. In music, almost all **performance-based** classes involve cooperative learning.

For years, music teachers have been aware of the positive benefits of cooperative learning, and music classes often serve as exemplary models. However, critics point out several problems with the use of cooperative learning. They are concerned that the work is not shared equally among students, which can cause tension in the group. Learning efficiency can be inhibited because some students focus better alone than they do in a group environment. In addition, cooperative learning is more conducive to lower level, fact-based activities. Several programs using cooperative learning have been developed including: 1) Learning Together; 2) Group Investigation; 3) Teams-Games-Tournament; 4) **Student Teams-Achievement Divisions (STAD)**; and 5) Team-Assisted Individualization (TAI).

Cooperative Play: A type of play classified by Mildred Parton in 1929 in which children actively play together. Cooperative play may involve something as simple as taking turns with other children or may involve creating a new game. Cooperative play is emphasized at the preschool and elementary levels. *See* **Unoccupied Play; Associative Play; Solitary Play; Onlooker Play; Parallel Play**

Coping: In psychology, a method of direct **problem solving** in which an individual learns to co-exist with a problem in some tolerable way, often by developing strategies to minimize undesirable effects caused by the problem. Coping is often used when problems cannot be eliminated. The general idea is that if the problem cannot be eliminated, the individual must learn how to coexist with it so that it causes as little interference as possible. *See* **Defense Mechanisms**

Core Curriculum: In education, a term used in a variety of ways to refer to courses, credits, knowledge, and **skills** that all students should complete, know, or be able to perform by the end of an academic program. Core curriculum is commonly used in the context of public school education and refers to those academic courses that all students must complete prior to graduation. Some educators consider the core curriculum to be the foundational components of education from **kindergarten** through high school. Mastery of the core curriculum is considered the minimum adequate preparation for success in higher education and throughout life. Individual states determine which courses are included in the core curriculum. These decisions are often based on budgetary and political factors. Music and art educators have fought for inclusion of the arts as an integral component of core curricula, and they have succeeded in many instances; however, each time new concerns arise about the poor quality and high cost of American education, discussions ensue about whether or not to reduce or eliminate music and arts courses from the core curriculum.

Correlation: In statistics, the amount or extent to which two variables are related. Correlations are usually expressed on a scale between +1.0 and –1.0. The closer correlations are to +1.0 or –1.0, the greater the relationship among **variables**. Correlations around zero indicate no consistent relationship among the variables; a correlation is said to be positive when high scores on one variable are associated with high scores on another, or when low scores on one variable are associated with low scores on another. A correlation is said to be negative when high scores on one variable are associated with low scores on another and vice versa. For example, rising ambient temperature and ice cream consumption may show a strong positive correlation (closer to +1.0), while rising ambient temperature and parka sales may show a strong negative correlation (closer to –1.0). Correlations do not show causation; that is, it cannot be accurately stated that because there is a strong correlation between two variables that one causes the other. Consider the ambient temperature and ice cream example. As the temperature rises, so proportionally does ice cream consumption; however, one cannot assume that the rising temperature causes ice cream consumption. Even though it may be true, a statistical correlation does not permit such an inference.

Correlation Coefficient: In research, an index showing how strongly two **variables** are related to each other in a group of subjects. *See* **Correlation; Pearson Product Moment Correlation (Pearson *r*)**

Correlational Method: In research, a **method** of determining whether two **variables** are related by measuring or observing the variables. There are a variety of correlational techniques that can be used depending on the type of variables (e.g., continuous or ranks) involved and what relationships the researcher wants to assess. The **Pearson Product Moment Correlation (Pearson *r*)** is the most common correlational method. Other methods include: Rank-difference Correlation (Spearman *rho*), Point-biserial Correlation Coefficient, and the Spearman-Brown Formula. In addition, a variety of correlational methods or techniques are available that are extensions of correlation. These include path analysis, multiple regression, discriminant analysis, canonical correlation, and factor analysis.

Correlational Research: A type of research that enables researchers to study the relationships or interrelationships between or among **variables**. Correlational research is nonmanipulative; that is, researchers observe or measure variables of interest as they occur naturally. Data may be gathered by directly observing specific behavior, by asking people to describe their behaviors regarding variables under investigation, or by examining already existing data. *See* **Pearson Product Moment Correlation (Pearson *r*)**

Council for Research in Music Education (CRME): An organization dedicated to the promotion of professional research in music education. CRME was founded at the University of Illinois in 1963 by professors Richard Colwell and Charles Leonard. CRME also publishes a quarterly journal, the *Bulletin of the Council for Research in Music Education*. The *Bulletin* publishes four types of articles: 1) reports on original research; 2) research summaries and issue discussions; 3) doctoral **dissertation** critiques; and 4) book reviews. Summaries or reports based on one's own doctoral dissertations are not appropriate for this publication. Instead, the CRME publishes indices of recently completed doctoral dissertations in music education, and of music education dissertations in progress.

Council on Basic Education (CBE): A national non-profit organization that promotes high academic standards and academic achievement in America's public schools founded in 1956 by a group of concerned citizens. In 1975 CBE added the arts to its list of subjects that it considers basic. CBE focuses on strengthening the liberal arts as a way of fostering the love of learning in students and of preparing students to be responsible citizens in their adult lives. CBE also works to improve the quality of teacher education, and in 1996 CBE collaborated with the **American Association of Colleges for Teacher Education (AACTE)** on the Standards-based Teacher Education Project (STEP), a project designed to improve teacher education programs and to strengthen **curricula** and **assessment** measures. In addition, CBE is also involved in strengthening and improving instruction in other nations through its Schools Around the World (SAW) program. *See* **Standards-based Education**

Counseling Psychologist: In education, trained psychologists who treat students with personal problems not classified as illness, such as academic, social, or vocational problems. Counseling psychologists usually have a university degree and are often part public school staffs.

Counterbalancing: In research, a method used to control the order of effects in a **repeated measures design**. Counterbalancing may be achieved by either randomly determining the order for each subject or by including all possible order combinations of **treatment** presentation.

Counter-conditioning: In **behavioral psychology**, the process of replacing a particular response to a **stimulus** with another, usually incompatible, **response**. Counter-conditioning may be used to replace unacceptable or inappropriate responses with acceptable and appropriate ones. For example, an individual may respond to stress by reaching for chocolate. If the individual is trying to lose weight, he or she may use counter-conditioning to learn to respond to stress by reaching for an apple or by going on a walk instead.

Counting/Rhythm Syllable Systems: Systems designed to help musicians learn rhythm. Typically, counting systems use numbers, letters, syllables, and words alone or in combination to represent notated rhythms. Below is a summary of counting systems with brief examples of how the rhythmic pattern of four sixteenth-notes followed by two eighth-notes would be counted.

1.	Traditional method	1-e-and-a	2-and
2.	Middleton	1-ti-te-ta	2-te
3.	Tucker 1	1-a-an-du	2-an
4.	Tucker 2	1-ta-ti-ta	2-an
5.	Breath Impulse	ta-a-a-a	ta-a
6.	Gordon (1971)	1-ta-ne-ta	2-ne
7.	Gordon/Froseth (1980)	du-ta-de-ta	du-de
8.	Benham	1-e-and-a	2-and
9.	Kodaly	ti-ri-ti-ri	ta-ta
10.	Word	Miss-iss-ip-pi	U-tah
11.	Sueta	T-T-T-T	Ta-Ta
12.	Winslow-Dallin	1-e-&-a	2-&

Triplet rhythms and rhythms commonly found in compound meters generally pose more difficult problems for counting systems. The methods each of the above systems use for three eighth-note groupings and six sixteenth-note groupings are:

1. Traditional method	1-2-3	4-and-5-and-6-and
2. Middleton	1-la-li	[not accounted for]
3. Tucker 1	1-an-du	2-ta-an-ta-tu-ta
4. Tucker 2	1-la-le	2-ta-la-ta-le-ta
5. Breath Impulse	a	ta-a-a-a-a
6. Gordon (1971)	1-na-ni	2-ta-na-ta-ni-ta
7. Gordon/Froseth (1980)	Du-da-di	Du-ta-da-ta-di-ta
8. Benham	1-ta-te	[not accounted for]
9. Kodaly	tri-o-la	[not accounted for]
10. Word	mer-ri-ly	knickerbockermaker
11. Winslow-Dallin	1-la-lie	1-e-la-e-li-e
12. Sueta	Da-Da-Da	[not accounted for]

No rhythm syllable system has been definitively "proven" to be superior to the others, but several of these systems have very strong advocates. The effectiveness of any system partly may be a matter of how consistently a teacher uses that particular system. Several considerations for choosing a counting system include: 1) consistency of the system, which involves the duplication of counting syllables on different parts of the beat or using different notational representations for the same rhythm; 2) ease of utilizing the system, which relates to whether or not the syllables are easy to speak, learn, and understand; 3) completeness of the system, which involves the ability of the system to account for a wide range of duple, triple, and unusual meters; 4) relationship between the system to the rhythmic function rather than simply to note length; and 5) how comfortable teachers feel about utilizing the system. Because counting systems are sometimes taught concurrently with musical notation and with the mechanics involved to play a musical instrument, students can become overwhelmed and confused. This confusion often hinders students' ability to understand how to use any counting system effectively. In addition, students are sometimes unable to make connections between the visual and the aural aspects of reading rhythms. If these connections are not made, no counting system can effectively improve rhythm reading skills. This points to the critical importance of proper sequencing of instruction.

Covariate: In research, an **extraneous variable** that changes along with the other experimental variables in a study to help ensure that any statistically significant differences found after **data analysis** are due to the **independent variables**. Covariates are common in Analysis of Covariance (ANCOVA) research designs. *See* **Analysis of Covariance (ANCOVA)**

Covered Tone: A sound produced by firming the vocal mechanism to modify the vowel sound being produced toward the *uh* vowel. Male singers typically use covered tone in the upper register. This technique produces a full, resonant sound with no **falsetto** characteristics.

Creativity: A general term used to describe innovation and/or talent. Some psychologists have identified three distinct **cognitive** operations that appear to be linked to creativity: 1) fluency, 2) flexibility, and 3) originality. The process of creativity has also been linked to divergent thinking. In music, creativity takes many forms and includes composing, improvising, arranging, and performing. Some well-known tests of creativity include: 1) **Torrance Tests of Creativity** (1966, 1988, 1990), 2) The Miniscat Measure of Creativity (1974), 3) **Rimm's GIFT** (Group Inventory for Finding Creative Talent, 1980, 1981), and 4) the PRIDE Tests of Creativity (1985).

Creative Thinking: A type of thinking usually associated with being particularly innovative or productive. Individuals who have a high ability for creative thinking may be good at **problem solving**, often in unusual ways; inventive or innovative; devise new plans, ideas, or theories; be adept in an art-related activity such as painting, drawing, or music; be able to "see" what others do not; and be aware of relationships others are not. Creative thinking involves a combination of **cognitive** and **affective** processes. The ability to think creatively is influenced by both **genetics** and the environment.

Creativity/Improvisation Level of Inference Learning, Gordon: *See* Skill Learning Sequence, Gordon

Criterion Validity: *See* Validity

Criterion Variable: In research, a behavior that the researcher wishes to predict using a **predictor variable**. *See* Dependent Variable

Criterion/Criteria: In general, a rule or standard for making judgments about something or someone. In research, a criterion is an accepted or **valid** standard upon which the measure of a **variable** or variables is based.

Criterion-referenced Test: In education, a test scored or based on an arbitrary, fixed standard of performance rather than on the scores of other test-takers. That is, criterion-referenced tests compare a student's score with predetermined, desired **outcomes** rather than other students' scores. In music, playing tests are generally criterion-referenced, because the objective is for each student to play the test material with 100 percent accuracy and musical fluency, not to compare one student's score to another's. Criterion-referenced tests are frequently used in public schools because teachers can use individual test scores to modify instruction to help meet each student's needs. *See* **Norm-referenced Test**

Criterion-related Validity: *See* **Validity**

Critical Band: In physiology, an area along the **basilar membrane** that vibrates in response to sound stimulation. When a sound source reaches the ear, the basilar membrane vibrates over a range or band of frequencies.

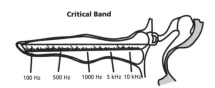

Basilar Membrane & Critical Band

The critical band is dependent upon the frequency of the sound source causing the vibration. In acoustics, critical band refers to the part of the frequency range that is necessary for two identical tones to become two different tones. That is, as two identical frequencies separate, beats and roughness are heard before two distinct, smooth-sounding tones are heard. The critical band is the frequency range that occurs between roughness and smoothness.

Critical Listening: A **technique** used by educators and professional musicians to teach and analyze music at a sophisticated level. In education, students are asked to listen to and for specific things in music, such as melody, harmony, intonation, or a particular instrument or section. Students are usually asked questions or asked to perform to determine whether they heard correctly. Critical listening can be used while students are performing or as a separate exercise. Professional musicians use critical listening for a variety of tasks, including score analysis, a critique of a particular performance, and interpretation development.

Critical Period: A concept used by Konrad Lorenz (1903–1989) and other ethologists to define certain ages or periods in an organism's life in which it is more receptive to and capable of learning than at any other time. For example, Lorenz found that goslings were capable of **imprinting** on moving **stimuli** for about thirty hours after hatching.

Critical Score: The minimum test score necessary to be deemed qualified for a task or position. Critical scores are based on experience with tests used for a given purpose. That is, experience with certain tests shows that most individuals falling below the critical score are unlikely to succeed at the task or position for which they are being tested. For example, if an individual does not make the critical score on a test used to determine college entrance, then the individual will not be given any further consideration for admission.

Critical Thinking: A general term for a conceptual mode of thinking that can involve a variety of processes, including reflection, logic, **analysis**, synthesis, **problem solving**, directed thought (concentration), focus, **evaluation**, investigation, and thoughtful consideration. In education, a great deal of **attention** is given to developing critical thinking skills. While this seems a worthy **goal**, there is not enough specificity in the term "critical thinking" to clearly define what those skills are. Tests designed to measure critical thinking, such as the Cornell Tests of Critical Thinking and the Ennis-Weir Critical Thinking Essay Test, provide some guidance. For example, the Ennis-Weir Critical Thinking Essay Test (1985) requires students to do the following: 1) think logically; 2) find fallacies; 3) solve problems; 4) hypothesize; 5) identify underlying assumptions; 6) evaluate material; and 7) generalize. In music, studies involving critical thinking tend to focus on problem solving skills and identifying relationships between musical and non-musical **variables** on measures of critical thinking tasks.

Criticism: In general, the process of evaluating something, including work, progress, process, or product. In education criticism is a necessary part of the learning process, and without it improvement is difficult. Research has shown that the manner in which criticism is presented can have a dramatic effect on students' **achievement** and **self-esteem**. In music education, particularly in **performance-based** classes, unfair or poor criticism can have negative consequences, including disinterest and **performance anxiety**. Conversely, lack of criticism can also have significant negative impacts, including disinterest, lack of student progress, and poor to mediocre performances. A great deal has been written about ways to be both positive and critical that allow for constructive criticism in the music **curriculum**.

In research, criticism is the process of evaluating scholarly writings. Criticism typically involves systematically analyzing each part of a work and making judgments about its consistency, accuracy, relativity, and its meaning as a whole. Such criticisms typically include a statement of the information, its accuracy and completeness, and the value of the information in the field of study. The focus of any criticism should be on the work itself and the information contained within the work. Personal views or subjective biases can lead to unfair and inaccurate criticism. Although criticism can be a healthy part of any profession, its value is dependent upon the **objectivity** of the review process and the integrity of the critic.

Cross Loading: In **factor analysis**, when one item or factor in a research design is strongly related to several items or factors. Cross loading is when items in a factor structure matrix have relatively strong loadings on more than one factor.

Cross-age Tutoring: A teaching technique in which older students help younger students in the classroom; for example, a fifth-grade student may help a second-grade student with math. Typically, the teachers in the respective classes work together to arrange specific times for cross-tutoring. Research has shown that cross-age tutoring can have positive effects on student **attitude** and **achievement**. Cross-age tutoring is most common at the elementary level, although it is employed somewhat at the secondary and even university level. *See* Peer Tutoring

Cross-cultural Research: Research that focuses on the relationships between **variables** across different cultures.

Cross-domain Transfer of Learning: In psychology, the **hypothesis** that learning can be transferred across domains. For example, a musician who engages in **mental practice** or rehearsal can **transfer** what is learned to improved physical performance. The amount of transfer depends upon several factors, including the individual's skill level, how well the material is learned, and the difficulty of the material. *See* Learning Domains

Cross-impact Matrix Method: In research, a refinement of the **Delphi Method** in which possible future events are predicted by synthesizing the predictions of a number of experts to account for their interdependencies. *See* Trend Analysis

Cross-sectional Method: A developmental research method in which persons of different ages are studied at only one point in time. Cross-sectional method is conceptually similar to an **independent groups design**. *See* Cross-sectional Research

Cross-sectional Research: A type of post-facto research often used in place of **longitudinal research** or to determine possible growth trends in a **population**. Cross-sections of two or more populations are selected for purposes of comparison. Typically, the populations are different age groups. Although cross-sectional research can compare two sample populations, it cannot accurately answer questions about the effects of a single population over time. In addition, cross-sectional research can be misleading because individuals of different age groups are likely to have had different upbringings, backgrounds, and educational experiences that would skew the outcomes.

Cue-dependent Forgetting: The **hypothesis** that **forgetting** is due to the lack of cues needed to locate and retrieve information, rather than the loss of the actual information in the **memory**. An individual may be unable to **recall** information in memory at one time but may be able to do so later, when appropriate **retrieval cues** become available. For example, a person talking to a friend might not be able to recall lyrics to a favorite song, but those lyrics are immediately available when the introduction to the song plays on the radio. *See* Retrieval Strategies

Cultural Awareness: In education, being aware and sensitive to students' cultural backgrounds. Cultural awareness enables teachers to address the diverse needs of all students and to structure **curricula** accordingly.

Cultural Identity: In general, an individual's association with a given **culture**. An individual's cultural identity is determined in large part by several factors including **race**, **ethnicity**, **socioeconomic status (SES)**, gender, religious affiliations, language, **disability**, and sexual orientation.

Cultural Literacy: Typically, the ability to share and understand the common information and knowledge of a given **culture** in order to function within that culture. In a broader sense, cultural literacy refers to the ability to understand and share knowledge about many cultures with others in an **intelligent**, informed manner.

Cultural Pluralism: A term used to describe a society in which people of diverse ethnic, racial, religious, and social backgrounds maintain autonomous participation within a common civilization, or the idea that culturally different groups can each maintain their cultural heritage while also functioning as part of a larger society.

Cultural Relativity: In psychology, an approach to labeling that defines normalcy relative to **standards** established by a particular social structure.

Culture: In general, a civilization or group of people and their characteristics including their customs, language, religion, social mores, artistic expression, and sexual behavior. Culture is often used when describing people of various **ethnic groups**, especially when describing **minority** students. Teachers should possess a thorough and varied understanding of culture for several reasons. First, culture exerts a great influence on virtually every aspect of a student's life. Second, culture shapes students' identities, beliefs, and behaviors about learning. Third, understanding culture helps teachers learn to value and appreciate **diversity** and to use diversity as an aid to the instructional process. Finally, culture is often used in narrow ways. For example, society talks about the drug culture, the feminist culture, or the sports culture. In these cases, inclusion in these "cultures" is based on whether individuals exhibit behaviors typically associated with them. Knowledge of these cultures and the behaviors associated with them can give teachers valuable **insights** into the lives of their students.

Cumulative Curve: In psychology, a graphic representation of **responses** given in a session of **operant conditioning**. The slope of the cumulative curve indicates the rate of response during the session.

Curiosity Motivation: In psychology, an inborn **motive** or **drive** usually satisfied by simply discovering the answer or seeing or finding something for curiosity's sake. The general idea is that human beings are naturally curious and that this natural curiosity drives or motivates people to behave in certain ways.

Current Index of Journals in Education (CIJE): One of two monthly indices published by **Educational Resources Information Center (ERIC)** that provides full bibliographic citations and abstracts for all entries, including subject and author indices. Of particular interest to music educators, CIJE contains the indices of the *Music Educators Journal (MEJ)* and the *Journal of Research in Music Education (JRME).*

Curriculum: In education, a term used in several different ways. Curriculum can refer to all course offerings at an institution, or it can refer only to those courses that lead to a particular degree or certificate. Curriculum can also refer to those courses or offerings in a particular area of study. For example, music teachers may refer to the music curriculum and math teachers may refer to the math curriculum. Finally, curriculum may be used when discussing the content of a particular course. In higher education settings or vocation/technical institutions, curriculum typically refers to a sequence of required and elective course offerings, classes, or studies in formal educational settings leading to completion, graduation, or certification. Most curricula consist of courses that meet during the school day and count for credit toward program completion.

Curricular: Anything having to do with **curriculum**. Generally, curricular courses are courses taken for credit. Such courses usually meet during the school day; however, curricular courses may be taken for credit even though they meet outside of regular school hours. *See* **Extracurricular**

Curriculum Development: In education, changes in the content and design of curricula. Curriculum development also refers to designing curricula for new courses to meet the needs of a changing nation. As a formal movement, curriculum development began in the 1950s and was geared toward updating the educational system in the United States without disturbing the organizational **framework** of the schools. Curriculum development encouraged change within the subject matter itself rather than through the organizational structure of American education. In addition, curriculum developers favored conceptual approaches to various disciplines. Using this approach, students learn **concepts**, principles, and modes of inquiry instead of a body of factual knowledge that soon becomes obsolete. The ability to resolve unfamiliar problems through **inductive reasoning** was a primary **goal** for curriculum developers.

Curriculum Evaluation: In education, the process of gathering and analyzing information pertinent to curricular programs for evaluation purposes. Curriculum evaluation can include a wide range of topics, including course offerings, course content, balance of subject areas, effectiveness of curricula, effectiveness of instruction, teaching style, testing and grading practices, national **standardized tests**, **goals** and **objectives**, social relevance, and materials and resources for instruction. Such topics range in scope from broad to narrow and from general to specific. Curriculum evaluation typically focuses on the following issues: 1) what material should be taught; 2) why this material should be taught; 3) how this material should be taught; 4) when this material should be taught; and 5) in what ways students can be assessed to determine whether the material has been learned.

Curwen Hand Signs: A set of hand signs designed to facilitate the teaching of melodic reading skills. Developed by John Curwen (1816–1880), each sign corresponds to a specific solmization syllable and is thought to provide an additional physical and mental connection between the notes and their corresponding sounds, thus improving reading abilities. Curwen hand signs are commonly used in and associated with the **Kodaly Method**.

Cycle: *See* Period

Cyclical Learning: *See* Spiral Learning

Cyclical Sequence: A theory regarding the presentation of subject matter developed by **James Mursell (1893–1963)** in 1948. Mursell believed that material should be presented in a variety of settings and at a variety of complexity levels based on the age, experience, and **readiness** of the learner. *See* **Spiral Curriculum**

Dalcroze: *See* Jaques-Dalcroze (1865-1950)

Dalcroze Method: An approach to teaching music developed by **Emile Jaques-Dalcroze (1865–1950)** that focuses on the development of **musicality** rather than technique. To Dalcroze, technique was merely the means to an artistic, musical end. The Dalcroze method focuses on three main areas: 1) **eurhythmics**, 2) **solfege**, and 3) **improvisation**. Study usually begins with two to three years of eurhythmics, which consists of movement to music that is specific to meter, rhythm, character, tempo, dynamics, flow of the music, and accompaniment. Although improvised, right and wrong movement styles are recognized, and improvised movements must be appropriate. Improvised accompaniment may follow movement later; this accompaniment may include the use of speech, percussion instruments, and keyboards. After eurhythmics, music reading and writing are introduced using solfege and solfege-rhythmique. Solfege is used to help develop tonal memory, or what Dalcroze called inner hearing. Students are presented with various singing and listening exercises in a certain key until they learn to "hear" in that key. Exercises involve singing songs and intervals using solfege syllables and improvising vocally. Once one key is mastered, students perform a similar set of exercises in a new key. A fixed-do system of solfege is used. That is, students are expected to learn **absolute pitch** relationships rather than **relative pitch** relationships. Students are also expected to improvise on the piano or another instrument. The instrumental improvisation should be reflective of the child's naturally improvised body movement to the music.

Dalcroze Society of America, The: An organization founded on Jaques-Dalcroze's approach to teaching music education.

Data: In research, information collected on a particular subject or area of study for the purpose of reasoning, discussion, or statistical analysis.

Data Analysis: In research, a general term for the processes used to manipulate and analyze data. Data analysis enables researchers to test **hypotheses**, answer research questions, and interpret results. The **research design**, the type of data being collected, and the nature of the research questions or hypotheses determine which data analyses are most appropriate. In most **quantitative research**, data analysis requires the use of appropriate statistical tests or procedures for determining **significance**. In most **qualitative research**, statistical procedures are often not appropriate, and data analysis typically involves presenting the data in logical ways and drawing conclusions using more subjective, common sense measures.

Data Sets: In research, sets of data collected in an **experimental study**.

DATRIX: A computerized search service from University Microfilms (UMI) for individuals who lack library access to the Dissertation Abstracts database online or on CD-ROM. DATRIX retrieves up to 500 titles per search based on keywords and provides a printout of the relevant citations including ordering information.

dBA: *See* A-weighting (dBA)

DBAE: *See* Discipline Based Art Education (DBAE)

De Institutione Musica: An early work containing a discrete body of theoretical, scientific knowledge about Greek music theory. Written in the early sixth century by **Boethius (c. 480–524)**, a Roman statesman and scholar, *De Institutione Musica* was commonly studied by musicians and theorists for more than a millennium and through the Middle Ages. *De Institutione Musica* focuses on the scientific aspects of music rather than on aspects of musical performance. Boethius believed that music communicates truth through reason according to abstract mathematical proportions from musical sounds. *De Institutione Musica* was such a significant contribution to the study of musical theory that it is still studied today at some institutions.

Debriefing: In research, the process of explaining the purpose of a research study to the subjects following their participation in the study.

Decay: In psychology, the passive loss of **memory** due to inactivity or lack of **rehearsal**. In this sense, the phrase "use it or lose it" is appropriate. In **acoustics**, decay is the decrease in sound over time resulting from a decrease in sound energy. For example, the sound of a tuning fork will be the strongest when initially struck; afterwards, the sound level will decrease steadily as the energy that produced the sound is spent. Decay is also used to specifically describe the dissipation of sound from the time the sound source stops until silence.

Decenter/Decentration: In Jean Piaget's (1896–1980) **stages of cognitive growth**, the ability to think about several different aspects of a given situation simultaneously or to see more than one point of view. Decentration occurs at the end of the **sensorimotor stage** (birth to two) or at the beginning of the **preoperational stage** (age two to seven) and is characterized by children's abilities to understand the difference between their ideas and feelings and the ideas and feelings of others. The ability to decenter is the opposite of the ability to **centrate**, or to focus on only one aspect of a given situation or see only one point of view. *See* Centrate/Centration

Decibel (dB): A unit used to measure sound **intensity**, a decibel is one-tenth of a Bel. Decibels are logarithmic; that is, they are multiples or powers of ten. A 10 dB increase in a sound's intensity level results in a sound 10 times more powerful (10^1), while a 20 dB increase results in an intensity level 100 times more powerful (10^2). The lower **threshold** of hearing is zero decibels and the upper threshold (i.e., threshold of pain) is about 120 decibels; these limits are not absolute. A normal conversation is between 50 and 60 decibels. A 60 dB sound (normal conversation level) is a million times (10^6) more powerful than the lower threshold of hearing. In other words, a small variation in decibels (dB) can result in a relatively large difference in sound level.

Deduction/Deductive Reasoning: A type of reasoning in which one starts with a general principle that is accepted as true, applies the principle to a particular case, and arrives at a conclusion that must be true if the **premise** is true. That is, the conclusion follows necessarily from the premise. Deductive statements must result in fact. Example: In 4/4 time, a quarter note gets one count. Half notes are twice as long as quarter notes. Therefore, half notes get two counts. *See* Induction/Inductive Reasoning

Defense Mechanisms: In general psychology, an adjustment made by an individual either through action or the avoidance of action that prevents one's own awareness of personal qualities or **motives** that might lower **self-esteem**, cause unpleasantness, or heighten **anxiety**. Most defense mechanisms are initiated unconsciously. For example, denial, which is the act of **self-deception**, is a common defense mechanism. In psychoanalytic theory, **Freud** thought that defense mechanisms were unconscious distortions of reality that protected the **ego** against anxiety. His defense mechanisms included: 1) **regression**, which is returning to behavior of an earlier age; 2) **repression**, which is blocking feelings and experiences that arouse anxiety from consciousness; 3) **sublimation**, which is channeling disturbing sexual or aggressive impulses into acceptable activities; 4) **projection**, which is attributing unacceptable thoughts and motives to another person; and 5) **reaction formation**, which is saying the opposite of what one really thinks or feels.

Deferred Imitation: When a child imitates something they have seen or heard after some time has passed, even though the **model** is no longer present. Deferred imitation is evidence that children are able to hold events or actions in **memory** and imitate them later. Deferred imitation is characteristic of **Jean Piaget's (1896–1980) preoperational stage** (age two to seven) and is one type of **symbolic function**. Example: A child sees a parent playing a guitar and at the time does nothing. One hour later, the child pretends to be playing the guitar.

Definition: In acoustics, the degree to which individual strands can be differentiated from one another in a musical presentation. Definition can be horizontal or vertical. Horizontal definition is the degree to which consecutive sounds stand apart. Musical factors in composition and performance contribute to horizontal definition. Such factors include tempo, repetitions of tones, relative loudness of successive tones, and melodic contour. Acoustical factors affecting horizontal definition include the length of **reverberation** and the ratio of the **loudness** of the early sound and the loudness of the reverberant sound. Vertical definition is the degree to which simultaneous sounds are heard separately. Composers specify vertical definition by choosing the **pitches** of simultaneous tones (i.e., voicing), their relation to the tones around them (i.e., intervals), and the instruments on which they are played (i.e., **timbre**). Performers can alter vertical definition by varying the dynamics of simultaneous sounds (i.e., balance) and by performing with good or poor precision and intonation. Acoustical factors such as the energy ratio of early sound to reverberant sound also affect vertical definition.

Degrees of Freedom (df): In research, the number of observations or scores that are free to vary in a study. The degrees of freedom (df) is equal to the total number of subjects in all groups minus the total number of groups in a study. For example, if there are 8 subjects in one group, then there are 7 degrees of freedom, because 8 (subjects) minus 1 (group) is 7.

Deindividuation: A process in which a person loses individual **identity**. Deindividuation usually occurs when an individual is part of a large group and receives very little or no individual recognition over a long period of time. Deindividuation can also occur in an environment where an individual's identity is concealed or hidden in some way, such as a username on the Internet. As identity is reduced, social restraints are weakened and impulsive, aggressive, and regressive tendencies are often released. For example, people who take part in masked parties, such as those that occur during Mardi Gras, often behave in ways that are out of character.

Delayed Conditioning: In psychology, a process used in **classical conditioning** in which the **unconditioned stimulus** begins several seconds before the **conditioned stimulus**. Both **stimuli** continue until the **response** occurs.

Delphi Method: In research, a technique used to obtain a group consensus on issues. The Delphi Method involves the use of repeated questioning, often written in the form of questionnaires. Individuals are selected as **subjects** based on whether or not their opinions or judgments would be considered of interest. The subjects are all initially questioned and the information is compiled and provided to each subject on subsequent **questionnaires**. Each individual is encouraged to reconsider and, if appropriate, to alter the reply based on the information from the rest of the group. Typically, after two or three rounds, an averaging technique is used to arrive at a consensus.

Delusion: A term used to describe false beliefs that often accompany psychotic disorders. Delusion is often manifested in fantasies regarding self-grandeur and/or persecution from others.

Demand Characteristics: In research, cues that inform the subject about how he or she is expected to behave. Demand characteristics are usually unintentional and may be manifested in several ways: 1) **subjects** may try to confirm the **hypothesis**; 2) subjects may try to disprove a hypothesis (reactance); or 3) participants wish to be judged favorably and may hide true **attitudes**, beliefs, and responses (evaluation apprehension). Several techniques are commonly used to reduce demand characteristics when conducting **experimental research**. For example, experimenters may: 1) provide subjects with a false hypothesis, 2) observe behaviors to determine implicit and explicit attitudes, 3) make subjects believe they are assisting the experimenters when they are actually being used as subjects, and 4) measure the **dependent variable** in a context separate from the experiment so the subject is less likely to associate the two.

Demographics: In research, the relevant characteristics of a given **population**. **Demographics** often include such characteristics as gender, age, **race**, education, religious affiliation, marital/family status, and **socio-economic status (SES)**. Such information provides a background or context for the participants and is important in designing research studies and interpreting their results.

Denial: In psychology, the act of self-deception. Denial is frequently used to avoid facing serious personal problems, such as alcohol abuse, drug abuse, the death of a loved one, or the diagnosis of serious illness. *See* **Defense Mechanisms**

Deoxyribonucleic Acid (DNA): Large molecules found in the **chromosomes** of cell nuclei primarily responsible for genetic inheritance. DNA molecules are responsible for the body's growth and development; they are arranged to reproduce themselves precisely and exactly. Along with ribonucleic acid (RNA), DNA constitutes the chemical composition of the **gene**.

Dependent Variable: In research, the variable or variables in an experiment that are measured in some way. Dependent variables are **responses** of some kind. These responses can be actions or changes in **behavior**. Often, the dependent variable is a subject's response to, and is dependent upon, the level of the manipulated independent variable. Dependent variables are also referred to as dependent measures. Other terms such as output, outcome, and response are used to refer to dependent variables.

Depression: A mood disorder that alters emotion, behavior, **cognition**, and body function. Symptoms of depression include excessive sadness for long periods of time, crying frequently without reason, loss of interest in normal activities, general apathy, persistent and distorted thoughts of hopelessness and despair, feelings of worthlessness, low self-esteem, loss of appetite, general fatigue, and thoughts of death or suicide. Depression differs from normal sadness and grief in that it affects self-worth and **self-esteem**. Individuals suffering from depression typically see themselves as worthless and unlovable. Depression is often triggered by traumatic emotional experiences, such as the loss of a loved one, the loss of a job, or a divorce. Depression is usually treated with medication, therapy, or a combination of both.

Descriptive Statistics: In research, a term used to refer to measures or summarizing statements describing the results of a study or the measurements made on a population, or statistical measures that describe the results of a study. Descriptive statistics include **measures of central tendency** (e.g., **mean**, **median**, **mode**), **variability** (e.g., **standard deviation, variance**), and **correlation** (e.g., **Pearson r**). Strictly speaking, descriptive statistics apply solely to **populations**, rather than to **samples**, but the term is used loosely for summarizing statements about samples when they are treated as populations. Analyzing standardized test results, determining students' **grade point averages (GPA)**, or computing basic demographic information all involve descriptive statistics. *See* **Inferential Statistics**

Desegregation: In general, the elimination of separation or **segregation** on the basis of race. In education, desegregation usually refers to eliminating the practice of placing students into public schools based on racial factors. Prior to the ***Brown v. Board of Education*** Supreme Court decision in 1954, many school districts had all-white and all-black schools, particularly in the southern United States. During the two decades following the Brown decision, schools were forced to become more racially integrated by implementing several techniques for desegregation, including mandated busing and reorganizing school boundaries. Today, efforts to ensure that schools remain desegregated are ongoing; however, geography and **socio-economic status (SES)** are powerful influences on the racial composition of any school. As a result, many schools are still racially unbalanced and will continue to be racially unbalanced in the future.

Desensitization: The process of becoming less sensitive to a particular **stimulus** or stimuli, typically after repeated presentations. *See* **Adaptation**

Developmental Theory: A general term for any theory that attempts to explain how people change physically, mentally, and socially as they age. In education, developmental theories related to learning and **child development** are most relevant. Identifying developmental milestones enables parents, educators, and other adults to structure learning more appropriately and effectively. **Jean Piaget's (1896–1980)** theory of cognitive development and **Erik Erikson's (1902–1994)** stages of psychosocial development are developmental theories.

Dewey, John (1859-1952): One of the most well-known American philosophers, Dewey wrote extensively on education. Dewey was born in Burlington, Vermont, and received his undergraduate degree from the University of Vermont in 1879 and his Ph.D. from Johns Hopkins in 1884. Dewey held positions at the University of Michigan, the University of Chicago, and Columbia University. John Dewey is often associated with **pragmatism**. His works include: *Human Nature and Conduct* (1922); *How We Think* (1933); *A Common Faith* (1934); *Art as Experience* (1934); and *The Child and the Curriculum* (1956).

df: *See* **Degrees of Freedom (df)**

Dialectical Thinking/Reasoning: The process of solving problems, determining truth, or resolving differences by thinking critically about all opposing points of view and weighing and comparing all of the available facts and information. Dialectical thinking enables individuals to arrive at the "most correct" answer when considering **open-ended** issues. For example, addressing the issue of whether a **voucher** system should be utilized in education can involve dialectical thinking. The ability to utilize dialectical thinking is dependent upon being open-minded and impartial. *See* **Dialogical Thinking**

Dialogical Thinking: A term used by Richard Paul to describe a strong sense of **critical thinking** involving the awareness of one's thinking skills and the ability to be critical of one's thought processes. That is, dialogical thinkers are able to reason rationally and logically while analyzing the **validity** of their own thoughts. They can listen to opposing views and make decisions based on the information presented, and they can also process other alternatives when making judgments. Dialogical thinking is a dynamic process that involves considering and integrating new information into thought processes. *See* **Dialectical Thinking/Reasoning**

Diaphragm: A broad muscle located between the chest cavity and the abdomen vital to the breathing process. At rest, the diaphragm is dome-shaped. As the diaphragm contracts, it moves downward, flattens, and expands, pushing against the abdominal organs. The rib muscles expand outward as the diaphragm contracts. This process reduces air pressure in the lungs, causing air to enter (inhalation). When the diaphragm relaxes, it resumes its original position. This process pushes on the filled air sacs in the lungs, causing exhalation.

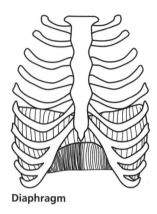

Diaphragm

Dichotic: In acoustics, the presentation of tones or sounds separately to each ear. Dichotic listening does not usually occur naturally. In everyday life, both ears receive all available incoming sounds. *See* **Diotic**

Dictation: In music, the act of writing notation for music that is heard. Dictation is commonly used to help develop listening and notational skills in the context of music theory courses, particularly at the college or university level. Exercises involving dictation may include notating rhythm, pitches, melodic lines, intervals, harmonic progressions, or part-writing examples. Musicians also use their dictation skills to transcribe music from recordings, particularly in jazz.

Diction: A general term for language pronunciation. In vocal performance, diction focuses on shaping vowels and articulating **consonants**. At least three common types of diction are taught: legato, staccato, and marcato. In legato diction, the consonants and vowels are smoothly connected, minimizing any explosive qualities of the consonants. In addition, the final consonant sound is usually carried over to the beginning of the next word. In staccato diction, all notes and words are distinctly detached. In marcato diction, the explosiveness of the consonants is exaggerated, and most of the notes are accented.

Didacta Magna/The Great Didactic: Written by John Amos Comenius (1592–1670) in the 17th century, the first treatise to address the need for **method** and **curriculum** in music teaching; it is considered by many to be the first great educational treatise. *Didacta Magna* emphasized the singing of well-known melodies and the elements of advanced music. *See* Comenius, John Amos (1592–1670)

Difference Threshold: In general, the minimum difference that can be perceived between two stimuli under experimental conditions. In music, difference threshold is sometimes used to indicate the minimum difference that can be perceived between two pitches presented consecutively under experimental conditions. Difference thresholds are not absolute; they vary according to the **frequency range**, **timbre**, **duration**, and **intensity** of the tones. As a general rule, the smallest difference that can be perceived by trained musicians between two pitches presented consecutively is approximately four cents. *See* Cent; Just Noticeable Difference (jnd); Threshold

Differential Reinforcement: In **behavioral psychology**, a process of **reinforcement** in which selected **responses** are reinforced in the presence of **stimuli** while others are not.

Differentiated Education: The implementation of instruction and learning activities designed specifically for gifted or advanced students. *See* Giftedness/Gifted and Talented

Diffraction: The bending of sound **waves** around solid objects. To a large degree, diffraction enables sound to be heard even when the sound source is on the other side of a building or other solid structure. The **frequency** of sounds greatly affects diffraction. Low-frequency sounds with longer **wavelengths** have a greater capacity to bend around objects than high-frequency sounds with shorter wavelengths. In music, the most obvious example of diffraction occurs during parades. Before the marching band can be seen around the corner, the low sounds coming from the bass drum and low brass are dominant. However, as the band turns the corner and marches toward the listener, the higher instruments can be easily heard because diffraction is greatly reduced. When more solid objects are between the listeners and the band, more diffraction occurs.

Diffusion: In acoustics, when sound energy spreads out in all directions after striking hard surfaces. Diffusion occurs as a result of the objects and their physical properties within the **acoustic environment,** including corners, edges, openings, walls, chairs, stands, people, curtains, and other common objects. The size and shape of the objects and materials from which the objects are made all affect diffusion. Generally speaking, harder, larger, and more angular objects increase the amount of diffusion.

Diffusion of Responsibility: The psychological tendency for feelings of responsibility to be diffused across a group, resulting in no action being taken by anyone. Diffusion of responsibility is common in emergency situations and is also called bystander apathy.

Diotic: In acoustics, the presentation of identical tones or sounds to both ears simultaneously. *See* **Dichotic**

Diphthong: A compound or double vowel that transitions smoothly from one sound to the other. For example, the word "sound" contains the diphthong *ou*.

Diplacusis: An abnormal hearing condition in which the pitch of a single tone is perceived differently by each ear, or when the **frequency** of a sound source reaching one ear is different from the frequency of a sound source reaching the other. In everyday life, **diplacusis** is usually not problematic and its effects in musical environments are usually negligible.

Direct Instruction: A highly structured teaching strategy or **model** formally introduced in the 1960s that involves utilizing behavioral techniques to promote and enhance learning such as modeling, **feedback,** and **reinforcement**. Direct instruction is primarily **teacher-directed**. That is, the teacher is responsible for the following: 1) providing and maintaining a classroom environment conducive to learning; 2) presenting and explaining new material to the class in a logical manner; 3) guiding students through each step of the learning process; 4) providing appropriate experiences, exercises, and activities; and 5) reviewing the material to ensure that students have learned. Direct instruction is often considered to be the traditional teaching method. *See* **Mastery Learning**

Disability: Something that limits normal human functioning in some way. Disabilities can involve the loss of physical functioning, or they can refer to other types of difficulties in learning and social adjustment that interfere with normal growth and development. A disability is generally more specific than a **disorder**. *See* Specific Learning Disability

Disciplined Based Art Education (DBAE): A program intended to establish the arts as a more meaningful part of school **curricula** by broadening content, emphasizing the relationships between the arts, helping students understand the place of arts in the history of civilization, and making course requirements more rigorous. DBAE was founded in the 1980s by the *Getty Center for Education in the Arts*, an entity of the J. Paul Getty Trust. It was believed that most art education programs focused too much on creating products of questionable **value** and too little on understanding the cultural and historical contributions of art, valuing art, and analyzing and interpreting art. DBAE focuses on the concepts and methods of four interrelated disciplines: 1) **aesthetics**, which involves developing informed opinions and/or judgments about art works; 2) **criticism**, which involves in depth study and analysis of art works; 3) history, which involves using relevant past and present art works to help students understand the role of the arts in civilization; and 4) production, which involves learning the techniques and skills that enable students to create meaningful art works. DBAE has been shown to be an effective program, although its adoption in classrooms across the country has been limited.

Disciplined Based Music Education (DBME): A music education program intended to strengthen the position of music education in school **curricula** modeled after the **Disciplined-Based Art Education (DBAE)** program. DBME aims to foster musical understanding and appreciation within students so they become knowledgeable about music and to help students become discriminating music listeners so that they will be knowledgeable consumers as adults. DBME is based on four areas or disciplines similar to those developed for DBAE: 1) **aesthetics**, which involves understanding the nature of music; 2) **criticism**, which involves establishing a basis for judging or valuing music; 3) history, which involves the contexts in which music is composed; and 4) production, which involves the processes and techniques necessary for composing and performing music. Western and non-Western music of various cultures is used in this program.

Discovery Approach: In general, an educational approach to learning in which students are encouraged to explore educational topics, arrange or organize subject material, and discover information largely on their own, with minimal purposeful guidance from a teacher. The discovery approach provides students with the freedom to manipulate material and to participate directly in the learning process, which enables them to learn in personally meaningful ways.

Discovery Learning: A teaching technique where teachers question students about a topic. Often, teachers ask students to think through something without prior instruction. Students are led to discover (learn) things for themselves through the thinking process. Discovery learning is typically used to supplement traditional **methods** of instruction.

Discovery Learning, Bruner: An educational approach to learning in which students are encouraged to discover answers to questions and solutions to problems through their own explorations. Bruner's discovery learning goes beyond simple memorization of factual material and contributes to conceptual understanding. According to Bruner, information that students learn or discover on their own is often more meaningful, more easily retained, and generally more useful. Bruner believed that teachers need to engage students in discovery learning on a regular basis, even though discovery learning is more time-consuming than **teacher-directed** learning approaches. *See* Bruner, Jerome (b. 1915); Theory of Instruction, Bruner

Discovery Method: A teaching **method** where students are led to discover answers for themselves and to learn on their own with appropriate teacher guidance. The discovery method is typically used in less-structured learning environments, and its use is largely dependent upon the teacher or facilitator. Generally, students are given a certain amount of information and then given suggestions about where or how to find additional information through various activities, including reading, experiencing, critiquing, and performing.

Discriminant Analysis: In research, an extension of **correlation** that enables researchers to predict a single discrete grouping **dependent variable** based on several other **independent variables**. The independent variables selected by researchers have a relationship with the dependent variable being studied. Discriminant analysis involves determining discriminant functions, or sets of weighted **predictor variables**. Discriminant functions allow persons or objects to be classified into a dependent variable group that allows for discriminant analysis. For example, discriminant analysis would be appropriate if researchers wanted to predict in which sport (single discrete grouping dependent variable) students would be the most successful based on a set of independent variables such as speed, strength, hand-eye coordination, parental support, and desire.

Discrimination: In general, the ability to distinguish between one thing and another. In behavioral conditioning, discrimination refers to the differential responses an organism makes to stimuli as a result of positive and **negative reinforcement** and is the opposite of **generalization**. For example, a child who has been bitten by a dog may be afraid of all dogs for a period of time afterwards. However, as time passes, the child learns to discriminate between dogs that are likely to bite and those that are not. In education, discrimination enables students to distinguish or discriminate between appropriate and inappropriate **behavior**. For example, talking loudly and running around the room may be perfectly acceptable during gym class, yet extremely inappropriate during math class. In some developmental **stage theories**, the ability to discriminate is often linked to a particular stage of development. For example, in **Piaget's stages of cognitive growth**, the ability to discriminate is acquired during the preoperational stage (ages two to seven). In social psychology, discrimination refers to an individual's prejudicial attitudes or treatment of others, often based on race or gender. In **perception**, discrimination refers to the ability to detect differences between **stimuli**. *See* Discriminative Stimulus

Discrimination Learning, Gordon: In Edwin E. Gordon's (b. 1927) **Skill Learning Sequence**, the lower level of two types of skill learning including discrimination learning and inference learning. Discrimination learning includes the following five levels: 1) aural/oral, 2) verbal association, 3) partial synthesis, 4) symbolic association, and 5) composite synthesis. *See* Inference Learning, Gordon

Discriminative Stimulus: A type of **stimulus** presented to which a particular **response** is most likely to lead to **reinforcement**. Responses reinforced in the presence of a discriminative stimulus will more likely occur when the stimulus is presented at a later time. The response is not reinforced in the absence of the stimulus. For example, a knock leads an individual to open the door. The door opening is reinforced by the presence of the person who knocked. Opening the door when no one has knocked will not result in the same reinforcement; no one will be waiting there. The consistent presence of someone at the door whenever there is a knock will increase the likelihood that the individual will open the door when the knock is heard. *See* Discrimination

Disorder: A broad term referring to a disturbance or abnormality in normal functioning. Disorders may involve mental, physical, and/or psychological processes. *See* Disabilities; Learning Disorders; Learning Disabilities

Displaced Aggression: The act or process of behaving aggressively toward a person or thing that is not the source of **frustration**. In everyday life, displaced aggression occurs when individuals take their frustrations out on someone or something else. Example: A teacher yelling at students in the classroom when he or she is really angry at administrators. Displaced aggression is related to displacement; however, displacement does necessarily involve **aggression**. *See* Displacement; Projection; Sublimation

Displacement: In psychology, a defense mechanism in which feelings and needs are transferred from one situation, object, activity, or person to another. **Sigmund Freud (1856–1939)** believed that displacement is the result of energy that cannot be expressed because it is blocked and must be expressed onto a substitute. Children and adolescents commonly use displacement to release pent-up frustration or anger over matters they cannot control. For example, a child whose parents are divorcing may become aggressive or angry toward peers and teachers, even though those feelings of anger are the result of the parents' divorce. Displacement can be expressed positively or negatively. When displaced energy is used for a beneficial cultural or social purpose, it is called **sublimation**. For example, it is a common perception that artists produce better quality art when they are personally in states of turmoil and need an outlet for expression. *See* Defense Mechanisms; Displaced Aggression; Projection; Sublimation

Display Rules: In psychology, social and cultural rules or mores that determine when, how, and where individuals may or may not express their emotional feelings. Display rules differ from culture to culture, and are typically learned and used by most individuals without much conscious awareness. For example, while some societies mourn the death of an individual with sadness, others rejoice and celebrate the life of the deceased. Most people in a given culture do not realize they are following a set of display rules established by that culture; they simply respond according to learned expectations. For example, in American society it is common to be sad at funerals, happy at weddings, proud at graduations, and loving toward family members. People who do not behave in these ways are often considered to be weird, antisocial, or unfeeling. Other types of display rules frequently accompany one's job. For example, waiters and waitresses are expected and often required to act friendly, cheerful, and helpful regardless of how they really feel. *See* **Antisocial Behavior**

Dispositional Attribution: In psychology, attributing peoples' actions or the causes of their behavior to personal, internal characteristics, such as **attitudes** and **traits**. Dispositional attribution is the opposite of **situational attribution**, which is attributing an individual's actions to external or environmental causes. Attributing the act of donating to charity to the individual's generous nature is an example of dispositional attribution.

Dissertation: In general, a formal discussion of a particular issue or topic. At the college or university level, a dissertation is the culminating written project of a doctoral student.

Dissertation/Thesis Guide:

Preliminary Headings

1. Title page – One page
2. Table of Contents (main heading) – Typically one or two pages
   a. Acknowledgments (subheading)
   b. List of tables (subheading)
   c. List of figures (subheading)

The Five Chapters

1. CHAPTER 1 – Introduction to Study
   a. Begin with a general abstract of your topic
   b. Need for the study (heading example)
   c. The problem (heading example)
   d. Purpose of the study (heading example)
   e. Questions or hypotheses (heading example)
   f. Definition or clarification of terms (heading example)
   g. Limitations of the study (heading example)

2. CHAPTER 2 – Review of Related Literature
   a. Introduction (heading example)
   b. Related studies (heading example)
   c. Summary of the general state of things with pertinent opinion

3. CHAPTER 3 – Methodology and Procedures
   a. Subjects (heading example)
   b. Description of measures employed
   c. Stimuli (heading example)
   d. Apparatus or equipment (heading example)
   e. Procedures
   f. Research design

4. CHAPTER 4 – Presentation and Analysis of Data or Results
   a. Analytic Techniques or statistical analysis of data (heading example)
      • What constitutes the data
      • How was the data treated statistically
   b. Results (heading example; a description of results/findings pertinent to each hypothesis)
   c. Other findings (probably not a heading, but placed at the end of this chapter)

5. CHAPTER 5 – Summary and Conclusions
   a. A review of the study (heading example), may include a review of the study's purposes, questions and/or hypotheses, results, and findings
   b. Conclusions
   c. Discussion (heading example)
   d. Implications for now (heading example)
   e. Implications for future research (heading example)
   f. Recommendations for further research (heading example)

Appendices

   1. Subject consent form (example)
   2. Pearson correlation – raw data (example)
   3. Group responses – raw data (example)

Reference Materials

   1. Bibliography
   2. Index

Dissonance: In psychology, a term for a perceived inconsistency between one's **attitudes** and one's behavior. In music, dissonance refers to any inharmonious combination of sounds. *See* **Consonance**

Distance Cues: In acoustics, cues that enable individuals to perceive the distance and direction of a sound source. Distance cues are primarily provided by the **intensity** of a sound and the difference between the amount of time it takes for the sound to reach each ear. *See* **Auditory Localization**

Distance Learning: In general, any **method** of learning in which teachers communicate interactively with students over long distances. Distance learning opportunities are especially important when students live in remote areas or where traveling back and forth to traditional classes would be difficult. Distance learning is best suited for instruction in math, science, and other academic disciplines. In music, distance learning is not appropriate for **performance-based** music courses; however, some academic music courses such as theory, history, and music appreciation are now offered in some distance learning programs.

Distributed Practice/Learning: Also referred to as spaced practice, the idea that small amounts of practice time at regular intervals help students learn more effectively than large amounts of practice time at less regular intervals. In other words, more will be learned and retained if a student practices an hour each day for a week than if he or she practices three or four hours once a week. *See* **Massed Practice/Learning**

Distribution: An ordered and systematic arrangement of data based on magnitude. A distribution enables researchers to observe general trends in the data more efficiently than with unordered raw data. *See* **Frequency Distribution; Normal Distribution**

District Power Equalization: An educational funding plan in which localities establish the tax rate for educational spending, generating a fixed amount of revenue. The state then guarantees a set amount of money proportional to this locally generated revenue.

Divergent Thinking: A mode of thinking in which the **goal** is to produce a variety of diverse **responses** in accordance with truth and fact. Divergent thinking often requires individuals to think in unconventional ways and has been linked to **creativity**; however, the precise nature of this relationship has been the subject of debate. In education, students in the classroom may be asked to solve a problem by arriving at several possible solutions instead of only one. A common technique for encouraging divergent thinking is to ask open-ended questions. For example: What are the advantages of studying? In music education, the subject material naturally lends itself to fostering creativity and divergent thinking through the processes of listening to and performing music. *See* **Convergent Thinking**

Diversity: In education, an all-inclusive term used to describe the wide range of differences among students. Diversity is often used to describe differences based on ethnicity, **race**, and/or cultural background; however, diversity is also used to describe differences based on characteristics such as gender, sexual orientation, **intelligence**, **disabilities**, and social class. **Concepts** surrounding diversity are complex because they typically involve **variable** attributes, such as personal preferences and **traits**, as well as critical attributes such as one's physical characteristics. In addition, people often use terminology associated with diversity imprecisely and inconsistently when describing racial, ethnic, and cultural identities. *See* **Ethnic Group/Ethnicity**

DNA: *See* **Deoxyribonucleic Acid (DNA)**

Domains of Learning: *See* **Learning Domains**

Dominant Genes: In a pair of **genes**, the one that is most likely to be expressed in the organism's **phenotype**. That is, the gene that will most likely determine a particular physical characteristic. For example, the gene for brown eyes is dominant over the gene for blue eyes. If one parent contributes a brown eye gene and the other parent contributes a blue eye gene, the organism will have brown eyes. *See* **Genotype; Recessive Gene**

Doppler Effect: In acoustics, the relative **perception** of changing **frequency** or **pitch** that occurs when a source producing a sound and an observer listening to or measuring the frequency of the sound are moving relative to one another. Sounds approaching at a rapid rate tend to sound higher as they get closer and lower as they get farther away. The speed of this **displacement** affects the degree of perceived pitch change. The Doppler effect is commonly experienced when listening to sirens on a police car passing on the street. The perceived pitch of the siren will continue to rise as it approaches and fall as it passes.

Double-blind Method/Study: In research, an **experimental design** in which neither the investigators nor the participants know who is in the **experimental** (treatment) **group** and who is in the **control** (non-treatment) **group** until the experiment has been completed. Double-blind experiments are often used in drug research to prevent the drug manufacturer or developer from biasing the study. *See* **Single-blind Method/Study**

Down's Syndrome/Trisomy 21: A form of **mental retardation** or mental deficiency resulting from an extra **chromosome** on the twenty-first chromosome pair. Physical characteristics of individuals with Down's syndrome include a thick tongue, extra eyelid folds, and short, stubby fingers. Also called mongolism, the risk of having a baby with Down's syndrome increases significantly when the mother is over thirty-five years of age.

Drake Musical Aptitude Test: Published in 1954, a battery of standardized tests designed to measure musical memory and rhythm. While these tests are no longer published, they are historically significant because of their approach to musical **aptitude** measurement. Most tests at this time were designed to test musical achievement or musical skill learning. The Drake Musical Aptitude Test required little or no musical training and measured the ability to perform certain tasks that were considered important for successful **musical achievement**. That is, the test was intended to measure fundamental attributes of innate **musical talent** instead of measuring several musical abilities, many of which may be unrelated to musical success.

Dramatic Play: Any type of play that involves taking on a social role and acting it out in some manner. Children can engage in dramatic play alone and with others. Dramatic play can be based on reality or fantasy. For example, children may act out the **roles** of parent and child, or they may act out the roles of superhero and villain. Flexibility is an important component of dramatic play, and children contribute to the direction and outcome of the play. In education, dramatic play facilitates social development by allowing students to try out or experience various social roles in a controlled environment. It also promotes interaction and cooperation between students.

Drive-reduction Theory: A psychological theory of **motivation** developed by Clark Hull (1884–1952) based on the idea that physiological needs create or lead to an aroused psychological state that drives an organism to behave in a manner that will help meet or reduce this **need**. When the **goal** state is attained, the drive is reduced, and the goal state functions as a reinforcer for learning. Drive-reduction theory typically implies drives that are survival-oriented such as hunger, thirst, sexual interest, and feeling cold. That is, the primary aim of drive reduction is **homeostasis**, or a steady internal state. Hull believed that these drives and the behaviors developed to fulfill them were a significant part of the evolutionary process. Drive-reduction theory has been criticized because it fails to explain some aspects of human behavior, including the fact that some human action is designed to produce tension rather than to reduce it. For example, many people enjoy activities that may cause fear and tension, such as riding roller coasters or hang gliding.

Drives: Observable changes in **behavior**, usually triggered by physiological and/or psychological **needs** or internal deficits. Drives are directed toward or away from a **goal** or **motive**/motives. *See* **Drive-reduction Theory**

Dual Code Theory/Encoding: A theory developed by Allan Paivio in his 1971 book entitled *Imagery and Verbal Processes* stating that encoding concrete words in memory as both verbal symbols and visual images will facilitate retention and recall. Dual code theory is believed to increase the likelihood of **recall** because two **memory** retrieval routes are established instead of one. Words are stored in memory as **verbal codes**, and visual images are stored in memory as analogue codes. In education, dual code theory supports the use of video and other multimedia in the classroom as an effective way to increase retention. Dual code theory appears to work best with concrete words that are readily converted into images. Abstract words are likely to activate only a verbal representation and do not work as well for applications of dual code theory. *See* **Verbal/Linguistic Code; Visual Imagery**

Dualism: In general, any theory that reduces subject matter to two fundamental **principles** such as good and evil, or natural and supernatural. In philosophy, dualism refers to the theory that both physical and psychic (mental) phenomena are real but that they are fundamentally different in nature. Specifically, physical phenomena (objects) can be measured and explained physically or mechanically, whereas psychic phenomena (thoughts) cannot. In other words, understanding the physical makeup of the brain does not lead to understanding the mind. Dualism is a time-honored philosophical theory and has been discussed in some form by Plato, Hume, Kant, Heidegger, Russell, and Descartes.

Dunn's Multiple Comparison Procedure: In research, a statistical procedure often used following a significant Kruskal-Wallis one-way analysis of variance (ANOVA) test to determine the exact location of the mean rank differences. In other words, if the Kruskal-Wallis test indicates that there is a difference overall, then the Dunn's Multiple Comparison Procedure allows the researcher to determine where the differences occur among the **populations**. *See* Analysis of Variance (ANOVA); Kruskal-Wallis Analysis of Variance

Duration: In acoustics, the length of time a physical sound lasts. Psychologically, there is a difference between the perceived duration and the actual duration of a sound. For example, studies have shown that individuals tend to perceive sounds with a duration of less than one second as being longer than they actually are and to perceive sounds with a duration of more than one second as being shorter than they are.

Dyslexia: A learning **impairment** that affects the ability to read and write that is most common among males. Dyslexia typically involves confusing the order of letters or numbers in a word or number sequence. For example, an individual with dyslexia might look at the number 354 and perceive the number 543, or they might look at the word "from" and perceive the word "form." Forms of dyslexia can range from mild to severe, and studies have shown that dyslexia does not correlate with a lower IQ level, as was once believed. Although there is no cure for dyslexia, people can learn to compensate for and function effectively despite its limitations. Both Thomas Edison and Woodrow Wilson had dyslexia.

Ear Canal: *See* Auditory Canal

Ear Training: The process of learning to recognize, write, and sing unwritten musical material. In most undergraduate music programs, ear training courses are typically coordinated with or a component of music theory. Practical aspects of ear training are almost always learned and/or applied in other **performance-based** music courses. *See* **Music Theory Courses**

Eardrum: The thin membrane at the inner end of the **auditory canal** leading to the **middle ear** that vibrates when sound **waves** strike it. Sound waves enter the **outer ear** and travel down the auditory canal. These waves then strike the eardrum, which separates the outer ear and the middle ear. The eardrum is also called the tympanic membrane.

Early Intervention Programs: Educational programs designed to provide care and support for children from the prenatal period through the first years of life. Early intervention programs help prepare these children to enter school ready to learn, increasing the likelihood of academic success. The most well-known early intervention program is the Perry Preschool Program, which began in 1962 in Ypsilanti, Michigan. The program provided preschool experiences and home visits to three- and four-year-old children from economically disadvantaged families. Data collected on the children enrolled in the program over a three-decade period indicated that these children were more successful socially and economically than children from similar backgrounds who did not receive preschool experiences. Other early intervention programs include Project Head Start and Early Head Start. *See* **Project Head Start**

Ebbinghaus, Hermann (1850-1909): One of the earlier pioneers in **memory,** sometimes referred to as the "father of the experimental study of learning." Ebbinghaus received a Ph.D. from the University of Bonn in 1873, and in 1885 he was appointed professor of philosophy at the University of Berlin. After several years in Berlin, he eventually took a position at Breslau. Ebbinghaus is best known for developing a curve of forgetting. He discovered that forgetting follows a predictable pattern. First, individuals remember best right after they have learned new information. Second, after a brief period of time, there is a relatively rapid decrease in memory abilities. Third, after this rapid decrease, an individual's ability to remember information declines steadily as time passes. *See* **Forgetting**

Echo: The sound produced when sound waves reflect off of a surface and return in a very similar form. Shouting into a rocky canyon often yields several echoes, each with decreasing energy. These echoes occur because canyons usually contain an enormous amount of two or more very hard surfaces that are arranged at a variety of angles, allowing the sound to reflect off of several surfaces and maintain much of their original integrity. *See* **Reflection; Refraction**

Echoic Memory: The part of **memory** associated with remembering sound. Research has shown that an unattended sound lasts only about an eighth of a second before fading from memory. *See* **Semantic Memory**

Echolalia: A meaningless repetition or **imitation** of words. Echolalia is common in very young children and is often associated with a variety of mental **disorders**.

Eclectic: In education, a person who combines what they perceive to be the best elements from different systems of thought is said to be eclectic. Most people tend to be eclectic in nature, although some adhere strictly to the principles of one system of thought, such as **behaviorism**.

Educability Expectation: A parameter of classification that represents a prediction of expected educational **achievement**. Educability expectation is often used with special needs students to predict what they may be capable of learning. *See* **Mentally Retarded/ Mental Retardation**

Educable Mentally Retarded (EMR): A classification of individuals based on educability expectation who are considered to be mildly retarded and who have an **intelligence quotient (IQ)** of approximately 55–70, which is lower than what is considered normal, yet higher than other classifications of mental retardation. EMR is a higher IQ classification than trainable mentally retarded (TMR) or **profoundly mentally retarded (PMR)**. EMR individuals often appear normal in the first few years of life, although they are generally slower than normal in learning to walk, talk, and feed themselves. EMR individuals can acquire social skills and practical skills, and by the end of high school, they may be able to read and calculate at between a third- and sixth-grade level. As adults, many EMR individuals are able to care for themselves with only a modest amount of guidance and support. *See* Mentally Retarded/ Mental Retardation

Education Amendments of 1974: Public Law 93-280, legislation which had a significant impact on education with two laws in particular: 1) the Education of the Handicapped Amendments of 1974, which addressed education for all disabled children, and 2) the Family Education Rights and Privacy Act, which gave parents and students over the age of eighteen the right to examine those records kept in a student's personal file.

Education Commission of the States: A commission responsible for overseeing the administration of assessments developed by the **National Assessment of Educational Progress (NAEP)**.

Education Consolidation and Improvement Act (ECIA): An act of Congress in 1981 that consolidated many education programs into one **block grant** instead of having separate **categorical grants** for funding many smaller programs. ECIA contained two major programs, Chapter I and Chapter II, and was a move toward giving state and local education agencies more discretion for dispersing federal funds. *See* Title I

Education for All Handicapped Children Act of 1975/Public Law 94-142: A law requiring due process and a "**free appropriate public education**" (FAPE) for all disabled children. The Act, which went into effect in 1977, mandated that children be taught in the **least restrictive environment (LRE)** and that each child be provided with an **individualized education plan (IEP)**. Public law 94-142 provides the core of Federal funding for special education. The law has been amended twice, once in 1983 and again in 1986. These amendments were added primarily to provide more benefits for infants and preschoolers. In 1990, the legislation was renamed the **Individuals with Disabilities Education Act (IDEA)**.

Education International (EI): An organization devoted to improving the teaching profession and educational programs worldwide. EI replaced the World Confederation of Organizations of the Teaching Profession (WCOTP) in 1993 and has united more than 240 national educator unions and professional associations from around the world, including the **National Education Association (NEA)** and the **American Federation of Teachers (AFT)**. EI membership includes more than 20 million educators and staff personnel at all levels of education. EI is committed to the following: 1) improving the quality of education throughout the world; 2) upgrading the working conditions of education employees; 3) fighting for adequate educational funding; 4) sharing curricular programs and information; 5) assuring human rights in education; 6) promoting gender and racial equality in education; and 7) building stronger educational organizations.

Education Professions Development Act of 1967 (EPDA): Legislation that provided funding for several teacher education and related programs. EPDA supported teacher-training projects to alleviate teacher shortages in certain subject areas. EPDA also encouraged organizations involved in the teacher training and certification process, such as state and local educational agencies and university departments, to combine resources and work together. EPDA also supported programs that promoted teacher training for **paraeducators**, preparing them for licensure, particularly through the Career Opportunities Program (COP). COP was developed to help minority and disadvantaged individuals become effective teachers to better meet the needs of low-income or otherwise disadvantaged students.

Education Through Music (ETM): A non-profit corporation that promotes the integration of music into elementary and middle school **curricula** to enhance student development and academic performance. ETM was founded in 1991 by Edmund Schroeder and Eldon Mayer and is currently incorporated in several elementary and middle schools in the New York area, Connecticut, and Pennsylvania. Music instruction is comprised of a sequential skills-based curriculum that includes learning frameworks, sample lesson plans, integration strategies, and assessment tools.

Educational Psychologist: A psychologist whose research focus is on the application of psychological principles to school education. Educational psychologists work with both children and adults.

Educational Resources Information Center (ERIC): The world's largest educational database. ERIC contains more than 500,000 educational documents, journal articles, **curriculum** guides, conference papers, and information on career opportunities. ERIC is an invaluable source of information for researches, educators, administrators, students, and other teacher-related professionals. ERIC is accessible either by computer or through two printed monthly indexes, *Resources in Education (RIE)* and *Current Index to Journals in Education (CIJE)*.

Educational Testing Service (ETS): An organization that publishes, administers, and scores a variety of tests. ETS has four different **music achievement** tests available. These are **The Graduate Record Examinations (GRE) Advanced Music Test** (1951), **The National Teacher Examinations – Music Education** portion (1957), The Undergraduate Program Field Tests (originally published in 1969 under the title The Graduate Record Examination), and **Advanced Placement Examination in Music** (1971). Administration of these tests is restricted to maintain the confidentiality of test materials. ETS tests are **norm-referenced**. As a result, test-takers receive information regarding how well they performed on the test compared to others who have taken the test (**standard scores**). In addition, test-takers' scores are converted into **percentile ranks**. ETS also provides this statistical information to designated institutions or agencies.

EEG: *See* Electroencephalogram (EEG)

Efferent Nerve: Those nerves responsible for transmitting impulses toward peripheral organs from the central nervous system. Efferent nerves, or motor nerves, usually end in muscles or glands.

Efficacy Expectations: Individuals' **perceptions** about their own abilities to perform tasks or behaviors. *See* Self-efficacy Expectations

Efficacy Perceptions: *See* Self-efficacy Perceptions

Ego: In Sigmund Freud's (1856–1939) **psychoanalytic theory**, one of the three components of **personality** that corresponds most nearly to the perceived self. Ego is the part of an individual's personality that holds back or controls the instinctual impulses of the **id** until gratification can be found (delayed gratification) in socially acceptable ways. *See* Id

Ego Identity: *See* Erikson's Stages of Psychosocial Development

Egocentric: A term used to describe individuals who are self-centered or who believe that they are the center of all things. Most theories of child development acknowledge that egocentric **behaviors** and **attitudes** are a normal and necessary part of the growth process.

Eidetic Imagery: The ability to retain visual images of pictures almost photographic in clarity. Those who possess this ability can describe images in far greater detail than those who do not.

Electra Complex: In psychology, the sexual feelings girls have for their fathers along with feelings of hostility toward their mothers. The Electra complex occurs in the phallic stage (ages three to seven) of psychoanalytic development, and is commonly referred to as "penis envy." According to Freud, the Electra complex arises from the normal culmination of the infantile period of development, although the Electra complex is considered more ambiguous than the Oedipus complex. *See* **Freud, Sigmund (1856-1939); Psychoanalytic Theory; Oedipus Complex**

Electroencephalogram (EEG): A record obtained by attaching electrodes to the scalp or brain and amplifying the spontaneous electrical activity of the brain. An EEG is useful in studying some forms of mental disturbance and in research on brain function.

Electroencephalograph: An apparatus used in medicine and research to measure electrical activity in the brain. *See* **Electroencephalogram (EEG)**

Electronic Music: In general, music composed and/or performed on electronic equipment, usually an electronic keyboard or synthesizer. In music education, equipment and funding for electronic studios began on a limited basis in the late 1960s and became more popular as equipment was designed and priced for educational use. Electronic music has served a variety of functions in music education. Electronic instruments have been used in performance, particularly as accompaniments and in stage bands. They have also been used as teaching tools for theory, acoustics, form and analysis, and keyboard techniques.

Elementary and Secondary Education Act of 1965 (ESEA): Public law 89-10, federal legislation designed to improve the quality of education and to equalize educational opportunities for all children. ESEA provided funds to improve education in several ways, including: 1) establishing and improving arts education programs; 2) purchasing learning materials and equipment; 3) establishing regional laboratories for the development of **curriculum** and instructional materials; 4) supporting research activities in universities and development centers; and 5) strengthening state departments of education. It signified the government's desire to take a more active role in education and resulted in a shift of policy-making power from state and local agencies to the federal government. Several amendments were made to this legislation in 1965, 1966, 1968, and 1970. These amendments were specifically targeted to special needs students and special education. In 1994, ESEA was revised and renamed the **Improving American Schools Act (IASA)**.

Elementary Music Achievement Tests: *See* Music Achievement Test (MAT)

Emotionally Disturbed Children (ED): One of nine types of **handicaps** specified by the **Individuals with Disabilities Education Act (IDEA)** that can involve one or more emotional problems exhibited to the extent that a student's educational performance is adversely affected. ED classification requires that a student exhibit problematic characteristics over a period of time and to a degree that warrants intervention. ED children may display one or more of the following: 1) an inability to learn that cannot be attributed to other factors; 2) an inability to engage in or sustain appropriate interpersonal relationships; 3) inappropriate behaviors or emotions; 4) an overall mood of depression or unhappiness; and 5) a tendency to develop physical symptoms over emotional situations. Children with some clinical mental illnesses, such as schizophrenia, and most socially maladjusted children are not considered emotionally disturbed under IDEA. The emotionally disturbed classification is categorized as "high incidence." That is, approximately 8 percent of all children with handicapping conditions as defined by IDEA are emotionally disturbed. *See* Behavior Disordered

Empathy: In general, the ability to realize, understand, and appreciate another person's feelings, or the ability to experience and "see" the world through another person's eyes. According to **Carl Rogers (1902–1987)**, empathy is one of the three necessary and sufficient conditions for learning, the other two being **unconditional positive regard** and **congruence**. Empathy allows teachers to connect with students by showing an understanding of feelings and emotions that students are experiencing.

Empiricism: In philosophy, the belief or acceptance that things are what they appear to be and that ultimate, ideal truths that defy reality do not exist. Empiricism is based on the idea that reality is that which is clear to everyone and is contrary to **rationalism** or idealism. Empiricism, also called **realism**, has been a part of Western philosophy since ancient times, beginning with Aristotle (384–322 BC). John Locke (1632–1704) and **William James (1842–1910)** are well-known advocates of empiricism. In education, empiricism greatly influences much of the **curriculum**, especially in **teacher-centered** classes in which teachers dispense knowledge and there is little opportunity for thinking about or considering seemingly unlikely ideas. *See* **Idealism**

Enactive Representation: In psychology, the first stage of **cognitive** development and a method of communication introduced by **Jerome Bruner (b. 1915).** Enactive representation involves thinking and communicating without the use of words. Children at this stage understand best through action. Adults may also find it helpful to use enactive representation when learning a new skill, especially a motor skill. For example, an adept ski or golf instructor will often model physical actions and ask students to imitate them. This instruction is often far more helpful than using verbal instruction alone. *See* **Theory of Instruction, Bruner**

Encoding: The creation of **memory traces** or mental abstractions based on the most prominent features of the incoming information in the **information processing model**. The encoded information, which represents the external object or event, can thus be used for **storage**. For example, a piano is recognized as a piano because of specific visual and aural characteristics that have been encoded in **memory** through experience.

Encoding Specificity Hypothesis: In memory, a hypothesis based on the idea that the effectiveness of a **retrieval** cue depends on its relationship to the way information is encoded or stored in memory, or the idea that a retrieval cue will be effective to the extent that it helps tap into the encoding process. The encoding specificity hypothesis helps explain why appropriate retrieval cues can often bring back "forgotten" memories, and it helps explain why some memories are recalled easier when the contexts in which the memories were created are similar. That is, an individual's ability to recall an event will be better facilitated if the information from the retrieval cue matches what is in the **memory trace**. As a result, environmental context serves as a retrieval cue in specific situations. The encoding specificity hypothesis is related to another concept called state-dependent learning, which proposes that the ability to recall information will be enhanced if people are in the same physiological state when they try to recall the information as they were in when they learned the information.

Encounter Group: A general term for any group that meets in order for individuals to learn more about themselves in relationship to other people. Encounter groups are also referred to as sensitivity groups.

Enculturation: *See* Socialization

English as a Second Language (ESL): An instructional program designed to teach English to non-English speaking students. The need for ESL classes increased dramatically during the 1980s and 1990s in response to the increasing numbers of immigrants and other non-English speaking people. *See* Bilingual Education; Limited English Proficient (LEP)

Engram Hypothesis: In psychology, a term referring to the hypothesized physical location of memory. The Engram Hypothesis states that when learning has been demonstrated by new behaviors, accompanying changes within the nervous system also occur. Accordingly, these changes within the organism's nervous system should be measurable; however, no one has been able to do so. *See* Memory Trace

Enrichment: In education, experiences for gifted students that enhance thinking skills and extend their depth and breadth of knowledge. Enrichment is based on four principles: 1) every learner is unique; 2) learning is more effective when it is enjoyable; 3) learning is more effective when it is individualized or personalized; and 4) activities should be designed to enhance or enrich the knowledge and **skills** gained from formal instruction. Enrichment experiences typically involve providing special projects, taking field trips, and supplementing regular classroom instruction in creative ways. Sometimes enrichment is facilitated by creating full-time **gifted and talented** classes; however, generally students are taken out of their regular classrooms periodically for enrichment opportunities. *See* Acceleration

Enrichment Programs: *See* After-school Programs

Enunciation: In vocal performance and speech, a general term used to refer to the clarity and distinction with which vowels and **consonant** sounds are produced. Enunciation is considered satisfactory when the words pronounced can be clearly and distinctly heard by the listener.

Envelope: In physics, the attack, **decay**, sustain, and release of a tone.

Epigenetic Principle: Erik Erikson's (1902–1994) theory of personal growth based on built-in mechanisms for growth and development. Erikson's epigenetic principle represents the ground plan for **personality** development through six psychosexual stages that span from birth through the early twenties. Each stage involves the resolution of opposite tendencies, and the successful resolution of those tendencies depends on the **acquisition** of a sequence of virtues. These virtues are hope, will, purpose, competence, and fidelity. *See* Psychosocial Theory/Stages, Erikson

Episodic Memory: A type of memory that enables individuals to recall an act or event in its entirety, rather than only remembering specific facts or details. Episodic memories may include special events or instances of outstanding personal achievements or failures.

Epistemology: In philosophy, the theory or study of what knowledge is, how knowledge is acquired, and what the limits of knowledge are. The following are examples of epistemological questions: How do we know music? How do we learn? What is knowing and understanding? What is the nature of musical knowledge as it relates to knowing?

Equal Access Act (EAA): A 1984 law that addresses the issue regarding the separation of church and state. Specifically, the EAA recognizes that secondary-school students are mature enough to understand that a school does not condone religion simply because it allows prayer clubs on public property. The EAA stipulates that if secondary public schools accept federal aid, then they must treat student religious groups and other **extracurricular** clubs in the same way. As a result, if a school allows non-curricular student groups (e.g., chess club) to meet on school property outside of regular school hours, then it must also allow other groups to meet on school property, regardless of their religious, philosophical, or political views. In other words, if schools sanction any noncurricular student organization, then they cannot discriminate against other student organizations.

Equal Educational Opportunity: The idea that students deserve to have equal access to educational resources, choices, and encouragement. In addition, students have a right to achieve full potential in educational settings, regardless of **race**, color, national origin, gender, **disability**, or **socioeconomic status (SES)**. Equal educational opportunity is linked with the **Education for all Handicapped Children Act of 1975/Public Law 94-142** and, more recently, with the **Individuals with Disabilities Education Act (IDEA)** of 1990.

Equal Temperament: The most commonly used tuning system today for fixed-pitched instruments, such as the piano. Equal temperament is a compromise system that divides the octave into twelve equal semitones and facilitates modulation to all keys. The ability to modulate freely is a great advantage; however, a disadvantage of equal temperament is that no beatless intervals occur within the octave other than the octave itself. *See* Temperament; Beats

Equal-loudness Curves/Contours: Graphs developed by Fletcher and Munson in 1933 showing that higher **frequencies** are perceived as being louder than lower frequencies at the same volume. Equal-loudness curves illustrate the results of research on the effects of frequency on subjects' **perceptions** of **loudness**. Equal-loudness curves were adopted by the Committee of Acoustical Measurements and Terminology of the American Standards Association and established the standards for such a phenomenon.

Equilibration: In psychology, the innate tendency for individuals to organize experiences to assure maximum **adaptation**, and the driving force behind intellectual growth according to **Jean Piaget (1896–1980)**. Equilibration is an adjustment between the twin **concepts** of **assimilation** and **accommodation** that allows children to grow intellectually.

Equilibratory Senses: Psychological mechanisms that enable individuals to be aware of body position in space and of body movement in general. For example, mechanisms within the ears contribute significantly to the ability to balance properly when standing or walking.

Equilibrium: In psychology, a comfortable and desirable state within an individual that occurs when **attitudes**, beliefs, and actions are in balance. Generally, equilibrium is reached when individuals behave in accordance with their thoughts. Equilibrium is a desirable state for most individuals, and those who do not experience it are motivated to modify either thoughts or behaviors to regain equilibrium. *See* **Cognitive Dissonance**

Equivalent Groups: *See* Matched Groups

ERIC: *See* Educational Resources Information Center (ERIC)

Erikson, Erik H. (1902-1994): A German-born **personality** theorist who studied under **Sigmund Freud (1856–1939)** at the Psychoanalytic Institute in Vienna. Erikson met Freud when he was traveling in Europe earning money as an artist and was commissioned to paint a portrait of Freud's child. Following many informal discussions, Freud invited Erikson to attend the Psychoanalytic Institute and study child analysis. Erikson moved to the United States in 1936 and was a professor at the University of California from 1939–51 before moving to the Austen Riggs Clinic in Pittsburgh. In 1950, the White House Conference on Children adopted a national charter for child and adolescent development that was modeled after Erikson's theories. Erikson's theory of personality development has its roots in psychoanalytic theory. His theory describes eight stages of personality development throughout the life cycle, and each stage is characterized by attempting to resolve a particular crisis. Through the attempts to resolve these crises, the healthy personality emerges. Erikson's stages are sequential, and if an individual fails to resolve a particular crisis, the ability to resolve a similar crisis at a later stage becomes even more difficult to develop. According to Erikson, mature individuals should have a sense of identity and a healthy personality.

Erikson's Stages of Psychosocial Development: *See* Psychosocial Theory/Stages, Erikson

Error Variance: In research, random variability in a set of scores that is not the result of the **independent variable**. Error variance is the variability of each score from its group mean.

Escape Learning: A form of **learning** controlled by painful stimulation (**punishment**). Escape from the punishment brings an end to the unpleasant or painful situation and is therefore rewarding.

ESL: *See* English as a Second Language (ESL)

Essential Schools: *See* Coalition of Essential Schools

Essentialism: The philosophical belief that a body of knowledge exists that all people must learn in order to function effectively in society. Essentialism is often associated with the work of William Bagley (1874–1946), founder of the Essentialistic Education Society in the 1940s as a reaction against progressive and pragmatic trends in education. Bagley believed that the moral and intellectual standards of young people were declining. He advocated that schools teach a common, essential core of knowledge to all students. This essential core should focus on helping students become better prepared to solve contemporary problems in society, rather than learning for learning's sake. According to this view, teachers should instill values such as discipline, self-control, and hard work into their students by structuring and controlling learning in ways that enable students to master the material.

Ethics: The study of human conduct and moral judgment. The term ethics is often used when describing a system or code of moral behavior adopted by a person or group of people. For example, questions regarding corporal **punishment** or discussions of sexuality in the public schools are ethical in nature.

Ethnic Group/Ethnicity: In general, a term used to describe a group of people who share a common language, religion, traditions, and sense of identity. Various ethnic groups often function as subgroups within a larger societal structure. For example, people refer to the Hispanic community, the African-American community, and the Asian community within American society. The determination of ethnicity is based on **race**, cultural heritage, national origin, and whether an individual chooses to be identified with a particular ethnic group.

Ethnocentrism/Ethnocentric: The belief that one's own group, **culture**, or country is superior.

Etiology: The cause or causes of a condition. Etiology is generally used in the context of physical or mental illness. Examples: What are the causes (etiology) of **anxiety** disorder? What are the causes (etiology) of cancer?

ETM: *See* Education Through Music (ETM)

Eurhythmics: A system of teaching rhythm developed by Swiss musician-educator **Emile Jaques-Dalcroze (1865–1950)**. Eurhythmics is one part of a three-part approach to teaching music that also includes **solfege** (the study of **pitch**, melody, and harmony through various singing, ear training, and theory exercises) and **improvisation** (applying or synthesizing what has been learned through eurhythmics and solfege on an instrument). Although eurhythmics was developed in Europe around 1900, it did not become popular in the United States until the 1950s and 1960s. Eurhythmics is based on the idea that rhythmic sensitivity is developed by allowing students to respond to rhythmic exercises physically with their entire bodies. Jaques-Dalcroze believed that musical **concepts** are internalized through rhythmic movement. Movement activities include walking, running, skipping, conducting, nodding, and creating or improvising individual movements to music. Students are often encouraged to move freely to the music and to create movements that express the music. The term eurhythmics is often used to describe the entire Dalcroze method in which rhythmic movement, ear training, and improvisation are integrated. This usage is understandable because many of the exercises and concepts involve all three parts of the system. Eurhythmics has had a major influence on music education, especially at the elementary level. In practice, the manner in which eurhythmics is implemented in **curricula** varies considerably; however, the basic concepts of integrating rhythmic movement to music remains constant.

Eurocentric: Any view that depicts Europe as the cradle of Western culture.

Evaluation: *See* Assessment; Formative Evaluation

Ex Post Facto Research: Research focused on determining relationships, usually causal relationships, between the **variables** being studied. Ex post facto research is conducted after the "**treatment**" has already occurred naturally, without researcher manipulation. That is, ex post facto research does not involve manipulating variables or treatments like experimental and quasi-experimental **research** studies do. Two common types of ex post facto research are causal comparative research and correlational research. *See* **Causal Comparative Research; Correlational Research**

Exceptional/Exceptional Learner: In psychology, a general term for individuals whose physical, mental, or behavioral performance deviates substantially from the **norm**. In education, an exceptional learner is any student who has a special ability or **disability** that sets him or her apart from the other students. Approximately 10 percent of all students are exceptional in some way. Additional services are necessary to meet the needs of exceptional learners. *See* **Gifted and Talented/Giftedness; Disability**

Exclusion: In education, the formal process of excluding individuals from various social groups typically because of the determination that the groups are inappropriate for the student. Students may be excluded for a variety of reasons, including learning **disorders**, **behavior disorders**, speech and language disorders, physical characteristics, **personality** traits, giftedness, and other distinguishing factors. Exclusion is often associated with **stereotyping**, labeling, and **discrimination**. The trend today in education, largely due to legislation such as the **Individuals with Disabilities Education Act (IDEA)**, is to include rather than exclude students when at all possible by modifying **curricula** and employing aids and **paraeducators**.

Existentialism: In philosophy, a viewpoint emphasizing that every individual has the freedom to make vital choices and to assume responsibility for his or her own existence. Existentialism is based on the idea that humans are not "ready-made machines" and emphasizes **subjective** experiences as sufficient criteria for truth.

Expectancy: *See* **Researcher Bias**

Expectation of Failure: A psychological source of **motivation** that may cause individuals to behave in certain ways because they expect to fail. The expectation of failure is related to **self-fulfilling prophecy**, in that individuals who are motivated by the expectation of failure often fail as a result of these expectations. Expectation of failure plays a powerful role in determining behavior and is based primarily on experience. *See* **Expectation of Success; Fear of Failure; Fear of Success**

Expectation of Success: A psychological source of **motivation** that may cause individuals to behave in certain ways because they expect to succeed. The expectation of success is related to **self-fulfilling prophecy**, in that individuals who are motivated by the expectation of success often succeed as a result of these expectations. Expectation of success plays a powerful role in determining behavior and is based primarily on experience. *See* Expectation of Failure; Fear of Failure; Fear of Success

Expectation-value Theory: A theory centered around **motivation** and decision-making. Expectation-value theory accounts for making choices on the basis of values.

Experimental Design: In general, the way a particular study is designed by the researcher to answer one or more research questions or to test one or more **hypotheses** or **null-hypotheses**. More specifically, experimental design refers to the techniques used in **experimental research** for creating equivalent groups of subjects. Three basic experimental designs are: 1) after-only, in which subjects are randomly assigned to control and experimental conditions and the **dependent variable** is measured only after the introduction of the **independent variable**; 2) before-after, in which a group of subjects is used as its own control, and the dependent variable is measured both before and after the introduction of the independent variable; and 3) matched-subjects, in which subjects are matched or equated based on some relevant **variable** or variables. Experimental design varies within and across disciplines. In addition, the terms experimental design and quasi-experimental design are often used interchangeably. However, in an experimental design, the groups are formed from a single subject population and all subjects are "equal" prior to administering the treatment. In a quasi-experimental design, the groups are not always formed from a single subject population and all subjects may not be "equal" prior to administering the treatment.

Experimental Group: In research, the group of subjects given the **treatment** whose effect is under investigation in an experimental study involving two similar groups. For example, in a study designed to measure the effects of a guided method of instruction on sight reading skills, the experimental group is the group that actually received the guided method of instruction. The results of this guided method would usually be compared to the results obtained from a control group that did not receive the treatment. *See* Control Group

Experimental Method: In research, a method for determining whether variables are related in experimental studies. The experimental method typically involves researcher manipulation of an **independent variable** and control of as many other variables as possible by using **randomization** methods or by direct experimental control.

Experimental Realism: In research, the extent to which the manipulation of an **independent variable** impacts the subjects in an experiment.

Experimental Research: Research conducted using the **experimental method** in which an **independent variable** is manipulated to bring about a change in the **dependent variable**. Experimental research requires the researcher to control as many variables as possible to establish the pure effects of the independent variable. Typically, **matched groups** of subjects are formed or selected in some way, exposed to different **treatment** conditions, and then observed to see if **response** differences exist. Experimental research enables researchers to make cause-and-effect inferences about the data.

Experimenter Bias/Expectancy: *See* Researcher Bias

Explicit Curriculum: Any **curriculum** or part of a curriculum based on clearly written policies and procedures, instructional materials, books, and other printed materials that state directly what and how students are to learn. Official program descriptions, course descriptions, and goals and objectives for both teachers and students are all part of the explicit curriculum. Schools are almost always accountable for explicit curriculum, although they may not be accountable for implicit curriculum. *See* Implicit Curriculum

Exploratory Committee on Assessing the Progress of Education (ECAPE): A committee established and funded by the Carnegie Corporation in 1964 to examine the feasibility of conducting a nationwide **assessment** of educational **achievement** among students of all ages. The committee was formed because of concerns about the lack of information available regarding **academic achievement** in America. In 1969, when the feasibility of such an assessment was established, the Education Commission of the States took over administration of the committee, and the name was changed twice, first to the **Committee on Assessing the Progress of Education (CAPE)**, then to the **National Assessment of Educational Progress (NAEP)**.

Exploratory Studies: In research, studies designed to examine aspects of a particular topic. Exploratory studies are often conducted to determine characteristics of potential subjects or subject groups or to determine the feasibility of a study on a larger scale. The results of exploratory studies generally provide a direction for further research or more in-depth study.

Expository Method: A teacher-dominated approach to teaching in which teachers present information to students. The **lecture method** is the most common example of the expository method. Information generally includes facts, terms, descriptions, definitions, and **principles**. When the expository method is used in this manner, very little interaction between teacher and students occurs. **Modeling** is another example of the expository method that is widely practiced among music teachers, usually in performance-related activities such as ensemble rehearsals and private lessons.

Expressionism/Expressionist: In music, the philosophical viewpoint that meaning lies beyond the music itself, or that music expresses feelings associated with non-musical aspects of human life. These feelings and meanings that each listener takes from the music are unique and based on individual experiences. More than one interpretation and meaning may be derived from listening to the same piece of music. Expressionist thought may be encouraged by having students listen for the expressive qualities in music, encouraging students to describe how music makes them feel emotionally and asking students to describe the things they are associating with the music. *See* Absolute Expressionism; Formalism

Extended Learning Programs (ELP): In education, programs designed to provide additional learning opportunities for intellectually gifted students in grades K–8. ELP programs seek to vary pace, depth, method, and breadth of the material to be learned, and are generally designed to accommodate individual student's needs.

External Validity: *See* Validity

Extinction: In behavioral psychology, a term used by **conditioning** theorists to describe a forgetting process in which the **stimulus-response** associations are eroded. In **classical conditioning**, extinction occurs when the **conditioned stimulus** is presented without being followed by the **unconditioned stimulus**, and the magnitude of the **conditioned response** returns to zero. In **operant conditioning**, extinction occurs when the conditioned operant is allowed to occur without being followed by a reinforcing stimulus.

Extinguish: In behavioral psychology, the process used to stop a response or behavior. The process of extinguishing a response or behavior often requires repeated efforts because of a phenomenon called spontaneous recovery. That is, the undesired response or behavior has a tendency to spontaneously reappear after it has been initially extinguished. By repeating the extinguishing process, spontaneous recovery will occur less frequently and with less intensity over time, until the response or behavior is fully extinguished. *See* Extinction

Extraneous Variables: In research, variables that may affect the results of a study not controlled or accounted for by the experimenter. Extraneous variables are also referred to as nuisance variables and are generally detrimental to research design. In music education research, extraneous variables such as eye color, height, or weight typically do not influence the results of a study; however, other uncontrolled variables, such as practice time or a subject's home environment can negatively affect the outcome of a study. *See* Analysis of Covariance (ANCOVA)

Extra-musical: A term used by some music educators to describe educational outcomes of music classes that are not directly musical. For example, extra-musical outcomes in a high school band class might involve learning teamwork, how to march, and how to properly care for an instrument. These outcomes occur in addition to musical outcomes. Extra-musical is sometimes used to describe activities that involve music as a secondary component or when music is used to enhance activities. For example, dancing, studying while listening to music, and driving while listening to music are extra-musical activities. Extra-musical is also used to describe activities that do not directly involve music but are related in some way. Sorting music into folders, keeping instrument and music inventory, and repairing instruments may be considered extra-musical. Some music educators would consider these activities to bo non-musical; however, the distinction between extra-musical and non-musical is often blurred. *See* Non-musical

Extracurricular Activities: Activities not included in the school curriculum. Usually, these activities take place before or after school and are not offered for credit. Sports and other various school clubs and organizations generally fall into this category. *See* Curricular

Extravert/Extraversion: One of two basic **personality** types or orientations as laid out by **Carl Jung (1875–1961)** to describe an individual who is outgoing, energetic, assertive, sociable, warm, and highly active. That is, extraverts are preoccupied with social life and the external world and less concerned about their inward experiences. Extraverts tend to display these characteristics consistently over time. The terms extravert and extrovert are often used synonymously. *See* **Introvert/Introversion**

Extrinsic Motivation: The linking of **task** performance to positive and negative external consequences valued by the performer. Extrinsic motivation is external to whatever satisfactions or annoyances are inherent in the task itself. In other words, extrinsic motivation is linked to the possibility of receiving positive or negative external consequences to behavior that are either valued or disliked in some way rather than to "feeling good" about the task itself. In education, common forms of extrinsic motivation include: 1) tangible rewards, such as prizes; 2) intangible rewards, such as teacher praise or approval; 3) punishment; and 4) making the task relevant to the student by placing emphasis on its value. Extrinsic motivation can help create the desire to perform tasks and often helps initiate and drive the learning process. As students mature and learn, they derive greater personal satisfaction (intrinsic motivation) for completing the **task** and the need for extrinsic motivators diminishes. Thus, extrinsic motivation is most effective and used most extensively at the elementary level, although it is used to some extent throughout the education process. *See* **Intrinsic Motivation**

Extrinsic Motives/Motivators: External **reinforcers** that encourage and drive **motivation**. Extrinsic motives often initiate and drive the learning process, and can include a variety of desirable **rewards** or undesirable **punishments**. Earning good grades or extra credit, winning a prize, earning special recognition, avoiding a parent-teacher conference, or avoiding other punitive measures are all **extrinsic motives**. *See* **Extrinsic Motivation**

F Test/F Ratio: *See* Analysis of Variance (ANOVA)

Face Validity: *See* Validity

Factors: In research, a term often used interchangeably with **variables**. In **factor analysis**, factors are generally those variables or dimensions that account for the **variance** in intercorrelated measures.

Factor Analysis: In statistics, a procedure that allows researchers to determine the underlying relationships between a large number of **variables**. Factor analysis is commonly used to help identify underlying traits or attributes in data sets and to determine or define smaller sets of derived variables or factors that have been extracted statistically from the data set. Factor analysis explains how the **variance** can be accounted for in a set of inter-correlated measures. Common factor analysis is often used in music research, although several types of factor analysis exist.

Factor Approach, in Intelligence: A model of intelligence that uses correlational statistical methods for mathematically determining various components or factors of **intelligence. Charles Spearman (1863–1945)** identified two factors, *s* (specific) and *g* (general). **Louis Thurstone (1887–1955)** identified seven factors. These included: 1) verbal comprehension; 2) word fluency; 3) numerical ability; 4) spatial visualizations; 5) associative memory; 6) perceptual speed; and 7) reasoning. **Jay P. Guilford (1897–1988)** identified a potential 120 factors of intelligence in his structure of intellect model.

Factorial Design: In statistics, a design in which all levels of each **independent variable** or factor are combined with all levels of other independent variables. A factorial design allows investigation of the separate **main effects** and interaction effects between two or more independent variables.

Fading: The gradual removal of a **prompt** or the gradual removal of reinforcers. In a special **reinforcement** system, such as a **token system**, fading facilitates a smooth transition from using the reinforcers to not using the reinforcers while maintaining the desired behaviors. Fading is often used to facilitate the **transfer** of **motivation** from **extrinsic** to **intrinsic.**

Falsetto: A light head voice that lies above the natural or normal **range** of the male voice. Only the inner edges of the vocal folds vibrate when using a falsetto tone.

Fear of Failure: A condition that results from an individual's fear that he or she will fail in task performance. Fear of failure can either drive an individual to put forth a monumental effort to achieve, or it can inhibit an individual from putting forth their best effort. *See* **Self-fulfilling Prophecy; Fear of Success; Expectation of Failure; Expectation of Success**

Fear of Success: A condition that results from an individual's fear that he or she will succeed and that this will be accompanied by negative consequences. Typically, the fear of success inhibits individuals from achieving or from putting forth their best effort to achieve. People who experience the fear of success tend to focus on the possible negative consequences that success may bring, such as social rejection, unpopularity, and loneliness. Studies have shown that the fear of success affects more women than men, a finding most often attributed to cultural **stereotypes.** *See* **Self-fulfilling Prophecy; Fear of Failure; Expectation of Success; Expectation of Failure**

Feedback: In general, verbal and non-verbal responses to answers, comments, or actions that indicate whether the answer, comment, or action was considered correct or appropriate. In education, both teachers and students give and receive feedback. For example, students receive teacher feedback on a regular basis through daily verbal comments, written feedback on assignments, and a variety of assessment measures. Teachers receive student feedback through daily verbal comments, classroom participation, and test scores. Feedback can be direct or indirect. For example, teachers can simply tell students that their answer is right or wrong (direct), or teachers can guide students to the appropriate response (indirect). Ultimately, feedback from teachers, supervisors, researchers, peers, students, or colleagues have positive or negative effects on learning.

Field Experiences: In higher education, in-school visitations associated with teacher training programs in which the main purpose is to provide prospective teachers with hands-on training in the schools. Field experiences vary in format across programs and range from passive observations to active teaching. Although many educators believe that field experiences are an extremely valuable part of teacher training, much research in this area does not support this view. In addition, some educators believe that negative experiences early in the teacher-training program may actually do more harm than good.

Field-based Instruction: In education, a type of instruction in which knowledge is acquired primarily through **field experiences**. Some field-based instruction is commonly used in teacher-training programs.

Field Experiment: An experiment conducted outside of a laboratory setting. Field experiments involve going to where the subjects are, rather than bringing the subjects to an artificial environment. Field experiments are common in music education, especially when **intact groups** (e.g. music classes) are used as subjects.

Field Observation/Fieldwork: Written or oral descriptions of observations made in subjects' natural environments or other complex social settings.

Field Theory: A theory developed by Kurt Lewin (1890–1947) based on the psychological context of learning, which Lewin referred to as "**life space**." Life space involves the choices that an individual is faced with on a daily basis. Individuals must make decisions based on the attractiveness or unattractiveness of the possible options. For this reason, arranging positive/attractive alternatives or experiences would be most beneficial in an educational environment. Factors that can influence an individual's life space include: 1) school setting or environment; 2) organization of the classroom; 3) classroom atmosphere; 4) teacher characteristics; 5) student behavior; 6) teacher behavior; and 7) teaching style.

Figure-Ground Perception/Discrimination: The perceptual ability to perceive a pattern or object as the foreground against a background, even when the background is visually ambiguous or confusing, or the process of distinguishing an object from its background even though the background can be perceived as the object and the object can be perceived as the background. In some cases, the foreground-background relationships are reversible. That is, one can perceive the pattern or object as being in the foreground or the background depending on one's **perception** at a given moment. Figure-ground perception is often associated with **gestalt psychology**.

Filler Items: In research, items included in a **questionnaire** unrelated to the measure's purpose. Filler items are often used to help hide the true purpose of a measure.

Fine Arts: In general, a term used to describe primarily artistic endeavors, including dance, drama, music, painting, and sculpture. The term fine arts is commonly used to describe departments in high schools and departments or colleges at higher education institutions that encompass all of the arts. The term is also used in reference to courses that offer an overview of one or more fine arts.

Fine Motor Skills: In general, relatively small, intricate muscle movements of the fingers, hands, and arms. Writing, drawing, cutting with scissors, and typing all involve fine motor skills. Fine motor skills are carried out when the brain, nervous system, and muscles work together; however, unlike gross motor skills, fine motor skills involve deliberate and controlled movements requiring highly refined muscle development and maturation of the central nervous system. In addition to developing fine motor skills in the fingers, hands, and arms, musicians often develop fine motor skills involving the wrists, lips, jaw, and tongue. Such development is essential to high levels of musical performance. Proper technique, tone production, vibrato, rhythmic control, and intonation all require fine motor skills. Fine motor skills develop systematically over time and can be developed and enhanced through practice. *See* **Gross Motor Skills**

Fixation: In psychoanalytic theory, the inability of an individual to move beyond an earlier stage of development or to change objects of attachment. **Sigmund Freud (1856–1939)** believed that individuals who are fixated at an earlier stage of development have problems in later life. *See* **Psychoanalytic Theory, Freud; Abnormal Fixation**

Fixed Interval: *See* **Schedules of Reinforcement**

Fixed Ratio: *See* **Schedules of Reinforcement**

Flat Grant: A uniform or variable grant provided by states to the local school districts. Uniform flat grants are structured to provide equal amounts of money on a per-student basis to districts, regardless of district needs or financial status. By contrast, variable flat grants are structured or weighted to provide more money to schools and/or programs based on differing classroom needs. For example, high schools with vocational, **bilingual**, or **special education programs** often receive more grant money than schools that do not offer such programs. *See* **Block Grant**

Floor Effect: In research, the failure of a test or measure to detect differences between subjects and/or groups or to accurately measure **achievement** because the tasks or questions were too difficult for all or most of the subjects. The floor effect prevents subjects from demonstrating their true **capacity** for achievement because of the limitations of the test or measure. *See* **Ceiling Effect**

Ford Foundation: A philanthropic foundation that has provided a significant amount of support to various aspects of music and music education. For example, the Ford Foundation helped found the **Young Composers Project** in 1959 after receiving ideas and suggestions from leaders in the arts. The Foundation also gave **Music Educators National Conference (MENC)** a grant to extend the **Contemporary Music Project (CMP)** an additional five years in the late 1960s. The Ford Foundation continues to support many worthwhile causes and programs, including the arts.

Forgetting: The inability to **recall** or remember previously learned information. Although no one is certain how or why people forget, there are several theories of forgetting and several factors that affect our abilities to recall information. These theories and factors usually involve the three main components of the **information-processing model** of memory. These include: 1) **encoding** or **acquisition**, which is how information is initially acquired through the senses and coded; 2) **storage**, which is the way information is stored in the sensory register, short-term memory, and long-term memory; and 3) **retrieval**, which is the way information is recalled when needed. Specific factors or considerations related to forgetting include: 1) the nature of the material being learned; 2) the importance of the material to the individual; 3) amount of time spent rehearsing or practicing the material; 4) how well the material is organized in the learning process; 5) how information is transferred from **short-term** to long-term memory; 6) how well the material is understood; 7) memory aids and retrieval cues; and 8) physical and mental condition.

Formal Discipline Theory: In education, an early theory stressing a **curriculum** focused on mental discipline. Formal discipline theory was predicated on the idea that the mind was like a muscle and, as such, needed systematic exercise to become strong. The curriculum included logic, Latin, and Greek for their ability to facilitate mental strength, not because they had an immediate or practical use. Formal discipline theory originated in ancient Greece and remained popular until the early twentieth century. **William James (1842–1910), E. L. Thorndike (1874–1949),** and Charles Judd (1873–1946) refuted the position with independent studies in positive transfer. *See* **Transfer**

Formal Operation: A one-step rule, often used in mathematics and science. Example: Density equals weight divided by volume. *See* **Formal Operational Stage**

Formal Operational Stage: The fourth and final stage of **Jean Piaget's (1896–1980)** theory of **cognitive** development in which the child can use abstract rules. The formal operational stage usually occurs between eleven and sixteen years of age and is characterized by the ability to develop complete, formal patterns of thinking based on abstract symbolism. Individuals can reason logically at the abstract level, develop symbolic meanings, and generalize to other situations. Formal operations is the most advanced level of thinking, and Piaget indicates that it requires the maturation of certain structures in the brain to be fully developed. *See* **Piaget's Stages of Cognitive Growth**

Formalism: In music, the philosophical view that the meaning of music exists within the music itself. That is, the **value** of music as an art is found only in the formal properties of the music, such as musical structure, rhythm, and harmony. Considerations related to feelings or expression are not considered relevant to formalists. Basically, formalism is "music for music's sake." In music education, focusing students' attention on qualities such as harmony, melody, rhythm, form, and timbre helps students listen formally. Formalism is in contrast to expressionism. *See* **Expressionism; Absolute Expressionism; Referentialism**

Formant: In acoustics, a region of specific fixed frequencies unique and prominent for each type of musical instrument regardless of the **fundamental**. The theory that incorporates formants suggests that they give each instrument (including voice) its unique sound quality. The number, size, and position of the formants determine the tone quality of any particular instrument. It is unclear whether or not formants exist for all instruments, and the theory is usually associated with sound research, not with music instrumental performance.

Formative Assessment: A form of teacher **evaluation** designed to enhance teaching performance. Evaluators help teachers assess their own strengths, weaknesses, and overall effectiveness to make them more aware of what is actually happening in their classrooms. Formative assessment focuses on improving teacher knowledge and performance and is in contrast to summative assessment that focuses on evaluating teacher competence and outcomes.

Formative Evaluation: A term coined by M. S. Scriven in 1967 to describe the evaluation of educational programs in progress instead of evaluating educational programs after completion. *See* **Formative Assessment**

For-profit Schools: Alternative **schools** run by businesses to make money. For-profit schools became popular in the 1980s and 1990s. Because these schools are for profit, they do not have tax-exempt status. The creation of for-profit schools was part of a larger movement to privatize education. Advocates believe that for-profit schools can provide a better education for less money than public schools. The Edison Project is one of the most well known efforts to support and sustain for-profit schools.

Forward Stepping Multiple Regression: *See* Multiple Regression Analysis

Foundation Program: A funding program in which the funding for educational expenditures is split between the state and its localities. In foundation programs, the state guarantees a certain amount of money to local school districts per pupil or per classroom and determines what proportion of educational costs should be shouldered by localities. The amount of money provided by localities is usually based on property tax rates and expressed as a **millage rate**. Foundation funding varies inversely with the wealth of a given locality; in localities where the revenue from property taxes is low, the state contributes more money than in localities where the revenue from property taxes is high.

Four-Way Agenda of Teaching: In education, the idea that four major components interact at all times during the educational process. These are: 1) student characteristics, 2) teacher characteristics, 3) subject matter, and 4) teaching strategies.

Frames: A strategy for organizing or **chunking** information into a visual display to facilitate **memory** and the learning process. Frames are particularly helpful to students who learn visually because they are spatial in nature. By breaking down material and reorganizing the parts in a meaningful way, the learner is given or creates a visual picture of the material. A frame is normally constructed as a two-dimensional grid matrix representing the information to be learned.

Framework, Hunt: In general, the basic underlying structure or fundamental concepts upon or around which other concepts or ideas can be built or developed. In education, a term used by David Hunt suggesting that effective teaching should match the developmental stage of the learner and the content and process of the teaching program. According to Hunt, students at various conceptual levels have different needs regarding the amount of structure teachers should provide and the way concrete or abstract **concepts** should be presented. An effective framework requires starting at an appropriate level for each student, gradually removing the structure, and gradually increasing the abstractness of the concepts taught.

Free and Appropriate Public Education (FAPE): Part of the Education For All Handicapped Children Act (PL 94-142) of 1975 and the Individuals with Disabilities Education Act (IDEA) of 1990, the mandate that all students with disabilities are entitled to a "free and appropriate public education" based on an individual's abilities and needs. The Supreme Court in *Hendrick Hudson District Board of Education v. Rowley* (1982) ruled that disabled students are entitled to a FAPE consisting of special instruction and related services that are individually designed to provide educational benefit. Commonly referred to as the "some educational benefit" standard, this ruling mandates that states must provide disabled students with an education that offers tangible benefits, although it need not be ideal. **Individualized Education Plans (IEPs)** are the vehicles for ensuring that every student with a **disability** receives a FAPE. *See* **Individualized Education Plan (IEP); Least Restrictive Environment (LRE)**

Free Associations: In psychoanalysis, a method of recovering unconscious conflicts by having individuals say whatever comes to mind. The general idea is that the therapist helps individuals arrive at the source of the conflict. Free associations usually involve discussing dreams, fantasies, and early memories to discover the root of a problem. *See* **Psychoanalytic Theory, Freud**

Free Schools: During the 1700s and into the 1800s, schools that could be attended by both wealthy and poor children. Those children whose parents could afford to pay the tuition did so, and those whose parents could not attended for free. These schools are historically significant because they were among the first efforts to provide free public education. More recently, the term free school was used in the 1960s and 1970s to describe a type of **alternative school** where students and administrators participated equally in the governance of the school and the **curricular** design. Free schools were an outgrowth of social unrest and a larger, nationwide movement to reform education at all levels. Ultimately, free schools failed as a result of disagreements over how much freedom students should have, the inability to agree on curricular content, and the inability to improve the quality of educational instruction.

Frequency: In general, the rate at which something occurs over a specified period of time. In acoustics, the rate or speed of a **periodic vibration**. Although an absolute relationship between frequency, a physical measurement, and **pitch**, a perceived phenomenon, does not exist, higher tonal frequencies will usually produce higher pitches. Frequency is commonly measured in **hertz (Hz)** or cycles per second (cps).

Frequency Distribution: In statistics, a set of scores arranged from lowest to highest that visually indicates the number of times each score was obtained.

Frequency Polygon: In statistics, a graphic display of a **frequency distribution** in which the frequency of each score is plotted on the vertical axis and the plotted points are connected by straight lines.

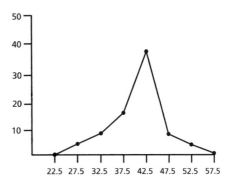

Frequency Polygon

Frequency Theory: In psychoacoustics, a theory about hearing which assumes that neural impulses arising in the **organ of corti** are activated by the ear's **basilar membrane** according to the **frequency** of the vibration, not according to the place along the basilar membrane where movement occurs. Frequency theory is in contrast to H. L. F. von Helmholtz's (1821–1894) place theory, which suggested that the **perception** of **pitch** relates directly to the area of stimulation on the basilar membrane. *See* **Place Theory**

Freud, Sigmund (1856-1939): One of the most influential figures in psychology, best known for developing **psychoanalytic theory** and **psychoanalysis**. Freud graduated from the University of Vienna medical school and planned to do scientific research; however, he went into private practice instead. Freud specialized in the treatment of nervous disorders, which was a relatively new field of medicine in the late 1800s. Freud's treatments initially involved hypnosis; however, he began experimenting with methods that involved talking with patients about their problems. His success encouraged him to expand and develop his therapeutic technique, which became known as psychoanalysis. Freud's ideas were shocking at the time, yet he was able to articulate his views clearly and provide support for these views, which bolstered his support in the psychological community. Many of Freud's ideas have become ingrained in American society. The importance of infantile sexuality, the significance of dreams, the influences of the unconscious mind, and the introduction of several **defense mechanisms** have become fundamental concepts in psychology. *See* **Psychoanalytic Theory; Psychoanalysis**

Freudian "Slips": A colloquial term for slight errors in speech, memory, and/or action believed to be the result of some unconscious motive. **Sigmund Freud (1856–1939)** called these slips *Fehleistung*, which means faulty action. He believed that they resulted from an individual's unconscious wishes or conflicts. *See* **Psychoanalytic Theory, Freud**

Fricative: A speech sound produced by forcing air through a constriction in the vocal tract. Examples of fricative sounds are *s* and *f*.

Friedman Test: In research, a common statistical test appropriate for use in studies in which subjects are asked to rank two or more items on a continuum (ordinal level measurement). The Friedman test is a multiple-sample test generally used to determine whether three or more matched sets differ significantly among themselves on the basis of mean ranks for each set. *See* **Ordinal Level Measurement**

Froebel, Friedrich Wilhelm (1782-1852): An eminent German educator best known as the founder of **kindergarten**. Froebel attended the University of Jena and later taught in **Johann Pestalozzi's (1746–1827)** school at Yverdon. Froebel was influenced by the educational ideas of Pestalozzi, and he felt that "self-activity" and play were crucial to child development in education. Froebel believed that the teacher's role was to encourage self-expression rather than to force students to learn, and he formulated three pedagogical postulates: 1) educational growth proceeds in its own way; 2) the unfolding process of education follows a genetic order of development; and 3) education must be structured around the child's interests and spontaneous behaviors. Froebel is also credited with two complimentary laws of learning: 1) the law of opposition or polarity, which states that all things have contrasting opposites and that the inner nature of a child and the environment must align, and 2) the law of connection, which states that the child must comprehend the relationships among things in a contrasting or opposite manner.

Frustration: In general, a state of being usually the result of being thwarted, disappointed, or defeated. In psychology, frustration typically results from events or circumstances that interfere with goal-directed action. Frustration is often triggered by circumstances over which there is no control or after an individual has given a best effort and still has not achieved the desired results.

Frustration-aggression Hypothesis: Also known as frustration-aggression theory, a hypothesis developed by Dollard, Doob, Miller, Mowrer, and Sears in 1939 that frustration induces a drive that causes aggressive behavior. Some controversy exists as to whether the theory works as an explanatory **model**. For example, while some individuals may react aggressively when they are late for work and the car does not start, others in the same situation may respond by sitting quietly and seething inwardly. In addition, frustration-aggression hypothesis is not an inclusive explanation for **aggression**, because many aggressive behaviors are triggered by other causes. For example, being annoyed or attacked by another person may lead to an aggressive response. The frustration-aggression hypothesis was revised by Leonard Berkowitz (b. 1926) in 1989. Berkowitz proposed that frustration leads to anger rather than aggression.

Fuging Tunes: A style of Psalm tunes that was popular in the mid- to late-eighteenth century in New England and Britain. Church choirs of this period used fuging tunes extensively. Fuging tunes were not really fugues but simplistic imitations performed by singers with little musical training that allowed some freedom of interpretation and performance on the part of the singers.

Full Inclusion: In education, the practice of teaching students with **disabilities** in regular education classrooms for as much of the school day as is reasonably possible. Full inclusion is a controversial topic in education. Proponents believe that full inclusion is more cost effective, because **special education programs** are ineffective and costly. In addition, students are provided social benefits they would not receive in special education classrooms. Opponents believe that because special education programs are designed to meet the needs of students with disabilities, they provide benefits that regular classrooms cannot. In many instances, districts and schools strike a balance between integrating students with disabilities into regular classrooms when appropriate to do so while also providing additional classes specifically designed to meet their needs. Generally, teachers, parents, and other professionals work together to determine what is best for each child. Full inclusion typically involves developing an **Individualized Education Program (IEP)** for each child based on a child's strengths and weaknesses, setting long- and short-term **goals**, and determining the amount of time that will be spent in general education classrooms. Full inclusion is often used interchangeably with **mainstreaming**; however, full inclusion is meant to move beyond the principles of mainstreaming. That is, mainstreaming implies placing **exceptional** children into regular classrooms as often as possible and full inclusion implies placing exceptional children into regular classrooms unless good reason exists not to do so.

Full State Funding: Funding provided by the state that pays for the educational expenses of all school districts within the state through revenue generated by a statewide tax.

Full-service Schools: Schools designed to meet the basic needs of students by providing such necessities as food, clothing, shower facilities, health care, and counseling services. Full-service schools often collaborate with local health and social service agencies to provide students with services they would not otherwise receive. These schools offer a range of services for children, including weight and drug counseling, treatment of illness and minor injuries, and testing for pregnancy and sexually transmitted diseases. When appropriate, the educational **curriculum** is linked to these services. For example, teachers can address health concerns by linking them to issues regarding teen pregnancy and drug use. Full-service schools have been around since the 1970s and are located throughout the United States.

Functional Age: An individual's level of ability to perform various tasks relative to the average age of others who can perform those tasks. Functional age is often used with **mentally retarded** individuals to provide a general idea of the skills and abilities of which an individual is capable. For example, an adult whose functional age is ten years can be expected to perform those tasks and thought processes that the average ten year old can perform.

Functional Autonomy: A theory of **motivation** proposed by Gordon Allport (1897–1967) that attempts to account for those human motives that appear to have no basis in biological need. The theory states that many human motives arise when the means to an end becomes the end itself. That is, the initial motive becomes detached from its origin and begins to develop a life of its own. For example, an individual may want to accumulate money because he or she is able to exchange it for food, clothing, shelter, and other things necessary and desirable (**primary reinforcement**). As the accumulation of money continues, the individual comes to value money for itself, not for what it can provide.

Functional Design: In research, an experiment that contains many levels of the **independent variables** to determine the exact functional relationship between the independent and **dependent variables**. For example, if experience is used as an independent variable to determine its effects on rhythmic accuracy, the researcher may want to determine subjects' various levels of experience. The researcher may ask subjects to place themselves in one of the following categories: one year of experience, two years of experience, three years of experience, or more than three years of experience. The results from this functional design would reflect four levels of experience, thus four levels of the independent variable.

Functional Fixedness: In psychology, the general tendency for individuals to consider only the most common function of an object and to overlook other possibilities. Functional fixedness is one type of **learning set** and often leads to rigidity in **problem solving**. An example of functional fixedness is the inability to realize that a pocket knife can be used to remove a screw in the absence of a screw driver.

Functionalism: In psychology, a general set of ideas that relate to the usefulness, practicality, or adaptive significance of mental processes. Functionalism focuses on the functions of conscious experience and **behavior** unlike **structuralism**, which focuses on the content of the mind. Functionalism is often associated with the ideas of **John Dewey (1859–1952)** and **William James (1842–1910)**.

Fundamental: In acoustics, the **partial** with the lowest **frequency** in a tone. The fundamental is often responsible for the perceived **pitch** of a tone; however, the perceived pitch may also result from a combination of upper partials in certain frequency ranges. In such combinations, the fundamental tone is perceived by the listener, even though it is not physically present. This **perception** is the reason listeners hear bass sounds from even the smallest radios.

Fundamental Attribution Error: In **attribution theory**, the tendency for people to prefer **dispositional attributions** over **situational attributions** when explaining other peoples' behaviors. Fundamental attribution error typically occurs when individuals attribute the causes of behavior almost exclusively to **personality** factors rather than to environmental or situational factors. For example, when an actor "acts" mean or cruel, people tend to believe that he or she is indeed mean or cruel, even though they know the actor is simply acting out a role. *See* Attribution Theory; Self-serving Bias

Fundraising: In general, an activity designed to generate additional revenue, usually used by organizations, clubs, or school groups. Many school music programs, particularly at the secondary level, engage in some type of fundraising activity. Fundraising takes many different forms and can include such activities as raffles, car washes, sales, and performances. Fundraisers may be used to provide items for the entire program, such as new uniforms for the marching band. They may also be used to help individuals pay for something music related, such as the cost of a band or choir tour. Fundraising usually requires a significant amount of teacher time to select, prepare, and implement. The amount of fundraising done by a program is often determined by such factors as the amount of fundraising used in the past, the purpose of the fundraising, the needs of the program, and the needs of the students. Fundraising should not be expected to pay for items that are traditionally covered by the school budget, such as instruments and sheet music.

Gagne, Robert Mills (1916-2002): An eminent experimental psychologist who was a pioneer in instructional design. Gagne's work significantly impacted contemporary educational technology. Gagne received his bachelor of arts from Yale University in 1937 and his doctorate in experimental psychology from Brown University in 1940. His professional career spanned fifty years and included appointments at Princeton University, University of California at Berkeley, and Florida State University. Gagne also developed tests and instructional design models for the military during World War II and later in the early 1950s and the early 1990s. Although Gagne has published several books, the most well known is *Conditions of Learning*, which was published four times between 1965 and 1985. In this and other publications, Gagne describes a **Taxonomy of Learning Objectives** and eight **conditions of learning** that include nine instructional events and provide specific strategies based on a hierarchy of intellectual skills.

Galton, Sir Francis (1822-1911): Considered by many to be the "father of intelligence testing," Galton went to medical school in Cambridge and London, England, between 1840 and 1844. He later devised the first series of tests designed to measure intellectual ability. He believed that **intelligence** was dependent on the quality of the human sensory apparatus, which he believed was largely inherited. His tests measured such abilities as reaction time, visual and auditory range, and sensory acuity. Galton's emphasis on the relationship between sensory ability and intellect foreshadows much of today's research on the importance of sensory stimulation in determining **cognitive** growth. Galton was one of the first researchers to quantify **data** and is credited with shaping the direction of psychological testing.

Galvanic Skin Response (GSR): The way that sweat affects the ability of the skin to conduct electricity. Traditional lie detector testing machines use GSR measurements to determine the likelihood that someone is answering questions truthfully.

Gaston Test of Musicality: *See* Test of Musicality

Gehrkens, Karl W. (1882-1975): An influential figure in public school music education, particularly in the area of teacher training. Gehrkens' formal education included the study of educational psychology with **John Dewey (1859–1952)** and William Heard Kilpatrick (1871–1965) at Columbia University Teachers College. He spent his early career as a high school teacher, choir director, and piano teacher before taking charge of all music teaching in the public schools in Oberlin, Ohio. Gehrkens spent the majority of his professional career at the Oberlin College Conservatory of Music, where he was recruited as Teacher of Public School Music in 1907. At Oberlin, Gehrkens developed a teacher-training **curriculum** for public school music teachers, and in 1923 Oberlin became the first institution in America to offer a bachelor of school music degree. In addition to his work at Oberlin, Gehrkens was also active in the promotion of music education at the national level. He was a member of the **Music Teachers National Association (MTNA)** for thirty-six years, serving as its president from 1934–1935 and as the editor of the *MTNA Proceedings* from 1917 to 1939. Gehrkens was president of the **Music Supervisors National Conference (MSNC)** in 1923, and was part of its first Education Council. He also served on MSNC's Executive Committee from 1930–1934 and is credited with coining the catch phrase "Music for Every Child—Every Child for Music," which became MSNC's official slogan. Gehrkens also wrote several books for school music, including *The Essentials of Conducting Music Notation and Terminology, An Introduction to School Music Teaching,* and *Fundamentals of Music.*

Gender Bias: Any type of discriminatory behavior that unfairly favors or disfavors individuals solely on the basis of gender. Gender bias is often related to gender **stereotypes** that have been cultivated in society and can be overt, subtle, or unconscious. Research on gender bias in schools indicates that girls receive less teacher attention than boys and that teachers tend to choose classroom activities that interest boys rather than girls. Research also indicates that teachers expect boys to be more active, less attentive, and more likely to have behavioral and academic problems than girls. In music, gender bias may at least partially explain why boys gravitate toward trombone, tuba, or trumpet, while girls gravitate toward flute or clarinet.

Gender Identity: In general, the awareness an individual has of his or her own gender and the gender of others. In education, many strongly believe that gender identity is largely a matter of the **socialization** process. The way males and females are treated affects the manner in which they behave. Stereotypical views about the ways males and females should behave have contributed to distinctive behaviors within each gender group. Traditionally, research has revealed differences in mathematical, verbal, and spatial skills that can be attributed to gender; however, more recent research indicates that these differences are decreasing as efforts to avoid stereotyping have increased. It has been suggested that children may be more flexible regarding gender, attitudes, and behaviors once they are secure with their own gender identities. **Disorders** related to gender identity typically involve problems an individual has reconciling his or her biological sex with his or her gender identity.

Gender Roles: Behaviors and attitudes considered appropriate by a **culture** that are specific to each gender. Gender roles are often created by **stereotypes**. For example in many cultures, women are expected to be compliant, dependent, and nurturing while men are expected to be dominant, aggressive, and independent. Children assume these gender-role stereotypes early, and the brightest children tend to display these characteristics the earliest. *See* Gender Identity; Gender Bias

Gender Sensitivity Training: **Curricula** designed to help eliminate gender-role stereotyping. Although gender sensitivity training may be structured for both men and women, it is often designed for men who treat female colleagues and subordinates in the workplace inappropriately. Such inappropriate behavior can include remarks and actions of an unwelcome sexual nature, passing over qualified females for job promotions or assignments, or compensating females less than males for equal work.

Gender-typing: The idea that individuals may have preconceived ideas about how males or females should behave. Gender-typing is a type of **stereotyping**. A central issue surrounding gender-typing is the degree to which socialization affects **perceptions** about appropriate behavior for each gender. Socialization and gender are important to gender-typing because individuals tend to realize expectations, or to realize self-fulfilling prophecies. In music education, gender-typing has been shown to occur in class choice and instrument choice. For example, more girls want to play the flute and clarinet, while more boys want to play the trumpet and trombone.

Gene: A tiny particle that contains hereditary information responsible for hereditary transmission. Genes are located in the **chromosomes** of each of the body's cells, and current estimates of the total number of genes in a human being range between 25,000 and 150,000. *See* **Chromosome**

General (g) Factor: A type of general **intelligence** or general ability that underlies intelligence test scores and one of two types of intelligence (general and specific) identified by **Charles Spearman (1863–1945)**. He used *g* to describe the general ability to perform well on many mental tasks and *s* to describe other specific abilities to perform well on particular mental tasks. In other words, general intelligence (*g*) accounted for similar levels of performance across many test items or tasks, whereas specific intelligence (*s*) accounted for performance on a particular task only. Spearman believed that the *g* factor was the most important aspect of intelligence and that it was the overriding element in all human tasks. To Spearman, the *g* factor was a kind of dynamic brain energy that acted as a driving force for the *s* factors.

General Music Today (GMT): A publication of the **Music Educators National Conference (MENC)** that contains articles of interest for those teaching general music.

Generalization: The detection by the learner of a characteristic or principle common to a class of objects, events, or problems. Generalization is common in **concept** formation, **problem solving**, and **transfer** of learning. In **conditioning**, generalization refers to the principle that once a **conditioned response** has been linked to a given **stimulus**, similar stimuli will also evoke that same response. *See* **Discrimination**

Generalization Level of Inference Learning, Gordon: *See* Skill Learning Sequence, Gordon

Genetic Determiners: Genetic makeup that predisposes an organism to display certain physical or psychological characteristics. Certain genetic determiners have a propensity for developing certain physical or psychological **traits**. Although genetic determiners are inherited, parents and their offspring may or may not display the characteristics of genetic determiners because the traits may be expressed or latent. *See* Latent Trait

Genetic Epistemology: Jean Piaget's (1896–1980) theory that attempts to trace intellectual development. In Piaget's use of the term, genetic refers to developmental growth rather than biological inheritances, and epistemology refers to the study of knowing or learning.

Genetics: The branch of biology concerned with heredity and the means by which inherited characteristics are transmitted. Geneticists study both the continuity and the variation of traits across generations. Gregor Mendel (1822–1884) conducted the first studies in genetics in the 1860s. Mendel discovered that the color of flowers could be predicted from one generation to the next. In the 1910s, Thomas Hunt Morgan (1866–1945) suggested that genes are arranged in the **chromosomes** in an ordered sequence after studying fruit flies. James Watson (b. 1928) and Francis Crick (1916–2004) won the Nobel Prize in 1962 for their pioneering work on genetic composition. *See* **Behavior Genetics**

Genital Stage: *See* Psychoanalytic Theory, Freud; Freud, Sigmund (1856–1939)

Genotype: In **genetics**, all characteristics that an organism has inherited and will transmit to descendants, or one's genetic composition. The genotype includes genetic properties that are both expressed and latent. For example, someone may possess a gene for blue eyes (genotype), but will have brown eyes (**phenotype**) because the brown eye gene is dominant. This individual may have children with blue eyes depending on the genotype of the other parent. *See* Latent Trait

Gestalt Psychology: A school of thought maintaining that the organized whole, configuration, or totality of psychological experience should be the proper object of study. Gestalt psychology was founded in the early 1900s by **Max Wertheimer (1880–1943)** whose interest in **perception** shaped the early ideas. Gestalt psychology was later expanded by **Wolfgang Kohler (1887–1967)** and Kurt Lewin (1890–1947) with their studies on learning and **motivation**. Gestalt psychologists tend to emphasize **cognitive** processes in the study of learning. Gestaltists stress that true understanding occurs only through the reorganization of ideas and perceptions, not through memorization or **conditioning**.

Gestaltist: Someone who adheres to the principles of gestalt psychology. **Max Wertheimer (1881–1943)**, **Wolfgang Kohler (1887–1967)** and Kurt Lewin (1890–1947) are the names most commonly associated with gestalt psychology. They believed that children could memorize a great deal of information but that this information is virtually useless without understanding and is not real learning. Gestaltists believe that the idea that learning can be explained by **stimulus-response (S-R)** associations **(behaviorism)** is nonsense and that real learning involves developing meaningful relationships **(cognitivism)**. The **goal** of teaching is to lead students to understand the structure of a subject so that they can see how each part relates to the whole.

Getty Center for Education in the Arts: An entity that strongly supports the arts and music and a well-known advocate for **Discipline Based Arts Education (DBAE)**. The Getty Center has focused much attention on the visual arts but has also supported efforts in music education. The Getty Center is a strong advocate for incorporating the arts into school **curricula** as a substantive subject rather than promoting it as a social service to aid in the teaching of other subjects. *See* **Discipline Based Music Education (DBME)**

Gifted and Talented/Giftedness: Individuals with extraordinary abilities or the potential for high levels of performance in one or more areas. Gifted and talented students generally progress rapidly in these areas and are capable of superior performance. In addition, giftedness is often accompanied by high levels of **motivation** and task completion. Traditionally, **academic achievement** levels and **intelligence quotients (IQ)** have been determiners of giftedness. Giftedness has been recognized in the past several decades as an attribute that merits special attention, in much the same way that disabled children are afforded special attention. In 1972, the U.S. Department of Education published the Marland Report (Public law 91-230, Section 806), which contains a definition of giftedness that has been adopted in many states. According to this definition, students are gifted and talented if they excel in one or more of the following areas: general intellectual ability, specific academic **aptitude**, creative or productive thinking, leadership ability, ability in the visual or performing arts, and psychomotor ability. Giftedness is related to a combination of several different capacities and **cognitive** abilities, some of which can be tested and some of which cannot. *See* **Acceleration; Enrichment**

Gifted and Talented Programs: Programs designed to provide advanced educational opportunities for students with extraordinary abilities in one or more areas. Programs for gifted and talented students fall into two general categories: 1) enrichment programs, which involve supplementing regular instruction in some way, and 2) acceleration programs, which allow students to progress more quickly through traditional **curricula**, often skipping grade levels.

Gilmore, Patrick S. (1829-1892): An influential figure in the history of early concert bands, Gilmore came to America from Ireland ca. 1848 and is remembered for several contributions to the development of bands in America. First, he incorporated the best European band traditions into his own bands, establishing a "prototype concert band" consisting of both woodwind and brass instruments. Second, his band traveled throughout the country playing in small towns, often providing townspeople with their first exposure to the music of European composers. Third, Gilmore was famous for organizing fantastically large events. For example, in 1864, Gilmore organized a concert for the newly elected Governor of Louisiana involving a 500-piece band and a chorus of 5,000 children. In 1869, he organized the National Peace Jubilee to commemorate the end of the Civil War, which included a 1,000-piece band and a 10,000-member chorus. An International Peace Jubilee three years later included a 2,000-piece band and a 20,000-member chorus.

Ginn Co. Institutes: Music schools designed to train music supervisors and music classroom teachers for public school service, sponsored by Ginn and Company. The institutes were a means to train individuals in the use of the *National Music Course*, a series of books published by Ginn and Company. Other publishers, such as Holt and Silver Burdett & Company, also sponsored institutes. These institutes became part of the established **normal school** movement in the late 1800s. Normal schools provided vocational teacher training beyond the high school level but did not require attendance at a university. By 1920, the Ginn Company had closed their institutes because public school music instruction was being offered at numerous colleges, universities, and normal schools.

Global Village Concept: In music, a term introduced by Marshall McLuhan recognizing that a more global view and acceptance of world music is replacing feelings of Western cultural superiority. The acceptance of world music and the advances in communications, media, and technology have all contributed to the global village concept.

Glottis: Anatomically, a fissure or opening between the vocal folds. Research has shown that the glottis opens and closes once for each vibrating cycle. This action causes the air to travel through the glottis in short puffs, although this puffing is not audible in the sounds produced. When singing or speaking, the vibrations of the glottis result

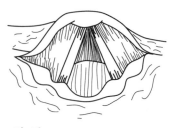

Glottis

in a tone filled with partials, which is the reason why some voices often sound rich and full. Tone qualities vary considerably from one individual to the next because no two vocal mechanisms, including the glottis, are identical.

Goal: An end state or condition toward which students work. Goals are typically long-ranged and broad-based and are achieved when several specified **objectives** are met. For example, a goal might be to have all students play all of the major and minor scales from memory by the end of the school year. An objective leading to accomplishing that goal might be to have students play a C major scale, ascending and descending with the quarter note at mm=60, without errors by the end of the first week. *See* Objective, Behavioral

Goal-directed/Goal-oriented Behavior: Any behavior that is conscious and deliberate rather than accidental. Goal-directed behavior is one of two forms of behavior that researchers focus on when studying **intelligence**, the other being adaptive behavior. *See* Adaptive Behavior

Goals 2000: Educate America Act: Legislation passed by the federal government in the early 1990s to elevate the standards in several areas of education to "world class." Enacted as Public Law 103-227, Goals 2000 is based on the idea that students will achieve more if more is expected of them. To that end, the legislation provides resources to states and communities to raise expectations and achievement. In addition to providing funding, Goals 2000 codified eight educational goals, which appear as stated in the Act:

1. All children in America will start school ready to learn.
2. The high school graduation rate will increase to 90 percent.
3. All students will leave grades 4, 8, and 12 having demonstrated competency over challenging subject matter…[and] be prepared for responsible citizenship, further learning, and productive employment in our nation's modern economy.
4. The United States will be first in the world in mathematics and science achievement.
5. Every adult American will be literate and will possess knowledge and skills necessary to compete in a global economy and exercise the rights and responsibilities of citizenship.
6. Every school in the United States will be free of drugs, violence, and the unauthorized presence of firearms and alcohol.
7. The nation's teaching force will have access to programs for the continued improvement of their professional skills and the opportunity to acquire the knowledge and skills needed to instruct and prepare all American students for the next century.
8. Every school will promote partnerships that will increase parental involvement and participation in promoting the social, emotional, and academic growth in children.

The **Music Educators National Conference (MENC)** was among the professional organizations to receive grants to reassess curriculum standards.

Goals and Objectives (GO) Project, MENC: A project implemented in 1969 in response to recommendations made at the **Tanglewood Symposium**. Issues addressed by the GO Project centered around cultural **diversity**, **ethnic** and world music, changing **demographics** in American society, and music education in urban settings. The **Music Educators National Conference (MENC)** National Executive Board officially adopted the goals and objectives of the GO Project in 1970. MENC appointed two commissions to help implement the recommendations made by the GO Project. The Project had a marked influence on music education and, ultimately, played a role in the development of the **National Standards for Music Education** adopted by MENC in 1994.

Gordon, Edwin E. (b. 1927): One of the most well-known contemporary researchers in the field of the psychology of music education, Gordon has made significant contributions to music education with the study of **music aptitudes**, **audiation**, **music learning theory**, and musical development in infants and very young children. Gordon earned his bachelor's and master's degrees from the Eastman School of Music in string bass performance and earned his Ph.D. from the University of Iowa in 1958. Gordon taught at the State University of New York at Buffalo, the University of Iowa, Temple University in Philadelphia, and at Michigan State University. Gordon has authored six **musical aptitude tests** and several publications, including *Learning Sequences in Music: Skill, Content, and Patterns* (1989), *A Music Learning Theory for Newborn and Young Children* (1990), and *Guiding Your Child's Musical Development* (1991). The complete collection of Gordon's professional materials are housed at the University of South Carolina/Columbia (USC) Music Library in the Edwin E. Gordon Archive. *See* Audiation; Music Aptitude; Music Learning Theory; Rhythm Content Learning Sequence, Gordon; Tonal Content Learning Sequence, Gordon; Skill Learning Sequence, Gordon

Gordon Institute for Music Learning, The (GIML): An organization dedicated to promoting the concepts pioneered by **Edwin E. Gordon (b. 1927)**. GIML offers workshops, certifications, and mastership programs for individuals who want to become familiar with and proficient at using the concepts presented in Gordon's Music Learning Theory and other materials.

Gordon's Music Learning Theory: *See* Music Learning Theory, Gordon

Gordon Musical Aptitude Profile: *See* Music Aptitude Profile (MAP)

Grading: *See* Assessment; Evaluation

Graduate (Music) Teacher Education Report (1982): A report based on an examination of graduate music teaching programs at colleges and universities during a four-year period from 1976–1980. The commission was appointed by Robert Klotman, then president of **Music Educators National Conference (MENC)**. The commission made several recommendations regarding the general competencies that students in masters and doctoral programs should possess or develop. The report stated that all graduate students in music education should have or develop: 1) knowledge and competence in teaching and performance; 2) insight into the nature and acquisition of musical knowledge; 3) a rational basis for professional commitment and continued growth; 4) research competence;

and 5) added breadth and depth in musical knowledge. In addition, the committee recommended that masters students should be able to analyze, synthesize, and generalize at a higher level than undergraduates and that doctoral students should develop in-depth, comprehensive knowledge in one major area of music education such as research, history, or philosophy.

Graduate Record Examination (GRE): A test published, administered, and graded by the **Educational Testing Service (ETS)** consisting of a general test and various subject tests, often required for admission to graduate programs. The GRE is a restricted test; that is, it may only be taken at specific times and at specific locations. Entrance requirements for each graduate program determine which tests must be completed. The GRE General Test measures analytical writing skills, verbal skills, and the quantitative skills a college graduate should possess. These skills are not specific to any particular field of study. The GRE Subject Tests are designed to assess the qualifications of graduate school applicants in specific areas of study, including biochemistry, biology, chemistry, computer science, literature in English, mathematics, physics, and psychology. Additional specialized tests are available.

Graduate Record Examination (GRE) Advanced Music Test: A test published by the **Educational Testing Service (ETS)** to assess **music achievement**, often taken in conjunction with other GRE subject tests. The GRE is a restricted test; that is, it may only be taken at specific times and at specific locations. The test was originally published in 1951 but is revised periodically because of its widespread use. The GRE Advanced Music Test contains items that are designed to measure achievement in music theory, music history, and form and analysis. It includes a limited number of questions on instrumentation and orchestration.

Graphic Organizer: A general term for organizing and presenting information in a visual form. Webs, concept maps, matrices, and flow charts are all types of graphic organizers. Graphic organizers can be used to describe, compare and contrast, classify, and sequence information and can be used to illustrate causal inferences or facilitate decision-making.

GRE: *See* Graduate Record Examination (GRE)

Great-leader Theory: The theory that certain individuals possess inherited leadership qualities that are not a result of environmental or social factors. Great-leader theory states that certain individuals possess the "right" blend of certain **traits**, involving looks, **personality**, and **intelligence**, that predispose them to assume leadership positions. *See* **Charisma**

Gretsch-Tilson Musical Aptitude Test: A battery of tests intended to replace or offer an alternative to the original **Seashore Measures of Musical Talents**. The Gretsch-Tilson Musical Aptitude Test was published at approximately the same time as the Seashore revised measures (1939) and was designed to quickly provide an accurate assessment of musical potential in students from grades four through twelve. Farnsworth found that the reliability of the Gretsch-Tilson Musical Aptitude Test was comparable to the Seashore test battery for grades five through eight. The test is not appropriate for university students.

Gross Motor Skills: Movements that incorporate the large muscles in the arms, legs, feet, and torso. Crawling, walking, running, and jumping are all gross motor skills. Gross motor skills are carried out when the brain, nervous system, and muscles work together. *See* **Fine Motor Skills**

Group Dynamics: A branch of **social psychology** that studies the processes that create and maintain group life. The focus of group dynamics is a systematic understanding of group functioning, the discovery of general laws concerning group properties, and the application of those laws to enhance group life. In the classroom, students develop a mode of behavior based on the roles that have been established through interaction with each other. Expectations about the way individuals are supposed to behave within the group become a powerful force in determining the way those individuals actually do behave. In this sense, the group's expectations become a self-fulfilling prophecy. Group dynamics are powerful and can influence behavior positively and negatively. **Master teachers** use group dynamics to foster an environment conducive to learning. *See* **Self-fulfilling Prophecy**

Group Polarization: A phenomenon that occurs when members of a group move toward a position that is a more pronounced version of pre-existing tendencies. When people in a group are in decision-making positions, they typically have a preexisting attitude toward the situation. During a discussion, the group's preexisting attitude may be strengthened, resulting in group polarization. Take the case of a group of educators discussing whether their school should move from a traditional schedule to a block schedule. Initially, the group as a whole is somewhat in favor of moving to a block schedule, but after a discussion the group indicates that they are now strongly in favor of the move to a block schedule. In this example, the group's general attitude toward block scheduling was strengthened, and the group became polarized against the traditional schedule.

Group Test: A test administered to several individuals at one time by a single tester. The **Scholastic Assessment Test (SAT)**, the **American College Test (ACT)**, and **Advance Placement (AP) Examinations** are examples of group tests.

Group Tests of Intelligence: Tests designed to measure **intelligence**, usually administered to large groups at a single sitting. Also called "paper-and-pencil tests," group tests of intelligence were developed during World War I to test large groups of men quickly. The Army Alpha test was used with men who could read, and the Army Beta test was used with men who could not. The Alpha test proved successful and resulted in the development of other group tests, which have been utilized in the public schools. Tests used in schools today include the **California Test of Mental Maturity** and Tests of General Ability (TOGA). Because such intelligence testing can significantly impact a child's future, heated debate continues regarding the prerequisites for administering such tests, which tests should be administered, and whether group intelligence tests should be given at all.

Groupthink: The tendency of a group to make faulty judgments or poor decisions instead of careful or high-quality decisions as a result of feeling pressured to attain unanimity. Groups experiencing groupthink are typically highly cohesive and do not consider alternatives, expert opinions, or contingency plans. In addition, these groups are often selective about the information they consider, do not criticize each other's ideas, and may apply pressure to those inclined to disagree. Groupthink was identified by Irving Janis and has often been found to affect groups that are highly task-oriented and goal driven. Groupthink often results in poor decision-making and a lack of creativity.

Guided Participation: A type of learning in which a child actively solicits or engages the help of others within his or her social environment to help solve a problem. The ultimate goal of guided participation is to develop independence. Guided participation requires the child to take an active role in solving the problem while learning from people who are more skilled or experienced in a particular area. In this regard, the child's learning is directly dependent upon the effort they put into the **problem solving** process. Guided participation contains three phases: 1) choosing tasks or activities and structuring them appropriately; 2) offering support and monitoring student participation and progress; and 3) altering the level of support as students become more competent and independent with the activity or task.

Guilford, Jay P. (1897-1988): A prominent psychologist most known for his work in the field of **intelligence**. Guilford studied at Cornell University and the University of Nebraska, where he also served as an associate professor. In 1940, he taught at the University of Southern California and became Director of Psychological Research for the U.S. Army in 1941. An expert in statistics, Guilford developed a three-dimensional model of the structure of intellect constructed through the use of **factor analysis**. Each dimension was divided into categories: 1) contents (figural, symbolic, semantic, and behavioral); 2) products (units, classes, relations, systems, transformations, and implications); and 3) operations (evaluation, convergent thinking, divergent thinking, memory, and cognition). The categories of Guilford's operations dimension are most relevant to learning and have become fundamental concepts in education. Guilford's model theorized that there are 120 traits of intelligence. He believed that intelligence is comprised of a series of distinctly different modes of thinking rather than being a single trait. In this regard, Guilford was an early proponent of multiple intelligences, a concept made popular in recent years by Howard Gardner. *See* Multiple Intelligences; Structure of Intellect Model, Guilford

Gunther Schule: A school founded in Munich in 1924 by Carl Orff (1895–1982) and Dorothee Gunther for gymnastics, music, and dance. The primary purpose of the school was to train teachers in movement and rhythm and to develop their **creativity**. Orff was the musical director of Gunther Schule and was responsible for the students' musical training. He believed that music education should be related to the natural tendencies of young children to move and learn and that rhythm was the central element in music, dance, and speech. Orff also believed that rhythm was the basis for musical learning and that rhythm should evolve from dance movement; his approach to teaching is based on these beliefs. As a result, he emphasized the use of body sounds and gestures to help teach rhythm and incorporated a wide variety of drums into his teaching at Gunther Schule. Orff also emphasized the use of the voice as the first and most natural musical instrument. Improvisation and creation were also central to his teaching method, and the ostinato helped provide the musical form in all improvisations. Gunther Schule was quite successful. It grew rapidly and flourished for well over a decade until it was destroyed during World War II. Following the war, Orff began focusing on early childhood music education, and his method, **Orff-Schulwerk**, grew in popularity. Today, it is one of the most popular music education methods for young children. *See* Orff, Carl (1895-1982)

Guthrie, Edwin R. (1886-1959): A well-known behaviorist and learning theorist best known for his Law of Contiguity, which states that a combination of **stimuli** that accompany a movement (**response**) will upon recurrence tend to be followed by that movement. In other words, if an individual behaves a certain way in a particular situation, the next time that situation occurs, the individual is likely to behave in the same manner. Guthrie believed that all learning could be explained on the basis of the Law of Contiguity, or the contiguous association of stimuli and responses. Guthrie also believed that learning is complete after only one pairing between the stimuli and the response and that learning appears incremental because there are so many stimuli and movements. Guthrie's Principle of Recency states that that which was done last in the presence of a set of stimuli will be that which tends to be done when that stimulus combination next occurs. Guthrie believed that forgetting occurs in one trial, when an alternative response has been caused in the presence of a stimulus pattern. Guthrie believed that all forgetting was the result of **retroactive inhibition**, a type of interference that results when newly learned material interferes with previously learned material. Guthrie also proposed that movements are simple muscle contractions, acts are a large number of movements, and a skill is made up of many acts. Guthrie joined the faculty at the University of Washington in 1914.

Haas Effect: In psychoacoustics, when two sounds with the same **intensity** level reach the listener at slightly different times. The perceived location of both sound sources is based on which of the two sounds reaches the listener first. The Haas Effect is also known as the precedence effect and was named after Helmut Haas, who described the phenomenon in his doctoral dissertation.

Habituation: In **behavioral psychology**, the weakening of an organism's **response** to stimuli due to repeated exposures to that **stimuli**. Habituation is related to extinction in that both involve a weakening of a response to stimuli. Extinction refers to the weakening of a conditioned response that has not been rewarded sufficiently. Habituation refers to a weakening or waning of a response due to an innate orienting reaction, such as boredom or disinterest. Habituation can be avoided or interrupted by presenting a new stimulus. *See* **Conditioning; Extinction**

Habit/Habit Chain: A learned **stimulus-response** sequence. Habits are generally automated; they occur without conscious thought. Individuals may or may not be aware that they are exhibiting habitual behaviors, and they are often unaware of the causes of these behaviors. A habit chain is formed when the stimulus produced by making one response provides or becomes the cue for another response. This process may be repeated indefinitely. In habit chains, the sequence of responses remains unchanged. *See* **Mental Presets**

Hallucination: An experience in which an individual hears, sees, smells, tastes, or feels something that is not physically present; the sensory experience only exists within an individual's mind. Hallucinations can include hearing voices and/or seeing things that are not physically present. Hallucinations are most often the result of mental illness or drug-induced states.

Halo Effect: A phenomenon that occurs when someone is viewed positively because of one **trait** and as a result is also thought to possess many other positive traits. Advertisers rely heavily on the halo effect because people are susceptible to it. That is, consumers believe that an expert in one area must also be an expert in another. This impression of expertise is why well-known personalities are paid to endorse various products. In education, the halo effect can be a pitfall for teachers in two ways: 1) teachers may assume that students who perform well in one area will also perform well in others and 2) teachers may assume that students who perform poorly in one area will also perform poorly in others. The halo effect also includes the idea that a student's **personality** significantly affects teacher **perceptions** of that student. For example, a student with a pleasant, agreeable, **extroverted**, and energetic personality will be thought of as more capable than a student with a difficult, disagreeable, **introverted**, or lethargic personality. Such unfounded expectations can have positive or negative consequences on the teaching and learning process. It is important for teachers to be aware of the halo effect to maintain objectivity when assessing students' abilities. In research, the halo effect is a common error. In experimental studies that require observations about subjects' behavior, researchers must be careful not to form early impressions that could influence later judgments. Forming early favorable or unfavorable impressions may subconsciously affect the researcher's ability to remain objective.

Handicap: In general, a term used to describe a physical, mental, emotional, or other condition that limits normal human functioning. *See* Education for All Handicapped Children Act of 1975/Public Law 94-142

Handicapping Conditions: A physical, mental, emotional, or other condition recognized by Public Law 94-142. The law specifies nine categories and mandates that education must be provided for all individuals in these categories until graduation from high school or until the age of twenty-one. *See* Education for All Handicapped Children Act of 1975/Public Law 94-142

Haphazard Sampling: In research, a type of **nonprobability sampling** in which subjects are selected in a casual manner, usually on the basis of availability and without regard as to whether the sample is representative of the **population**. Selecting subjects by standing on a street corner and asking people who happened to walk by to participate in a study is haphazard sampling. *See* Sampling; Nonprobability Sampling

Haptic: A term referring to touch sensation and usually associated with information being transmitted through feel, body movement, and/or body position.

Hard Palate: A bony structure covered with a layer of tissue located at the roof of the mouth between the alveoli and the soft palate. The positioning of the hard palate is a factor in vocal production. *See* **Soft Palate**

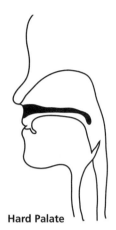

Hard Palate

Hawthorne Effect: A common research error. The error results from **response** differences that occur because the researcher was paying too much attention to or being too nice to the subjects rather than from the action of the **independent variable**. That is, individual behaviors may be altered because they know they are being studied. Any research in which subjects are measured, then subjected to a **treatment**, then measured again, has the potential for the Hawthorne Effect. Normally, this potential is minimized by using an equivalent group as a **control group** in the study. This process allows the researcher to be reasonably confident that any response differences are due to the pure effects of the independent variable and not the researcher. The Hawthorne Effect is named after experiments conducted from 1927 to 1932 at the Western Electric Hawthorne Works in Cicero, Illinois, where Elton Mayo, a professor from Harvard Business School, studied productivity and work conditions.

Hayden, Philip Cady (1854-1925): The music educator credited with founding the **Music Supervisors National Conference (MSNC)**, which became known as the **Music Educators National Conference (MENC)** in 1934. In 1900, Hayden became the music supervisor in Keokuk, Iowa, and founded the *School Music Monthly*, a journal dedicated to public school music education issues. Hayden was the editor of this publication for many years and wrote several articles for the journal, which was later renamed *School Music*. In 1907, Hayden decided to call a meeting of music supervisors to promote his *Music Forms* and to discuss issues in music education. Hayden called this meeting as an alternative to the **National Educators Association (NEA)** meeting. This call is now known as the "**Call to Keokuk.**" The success of this historic meeting of music supervisors ultimately led to the formation of the MSNC, of which Hayden was the first president.

Head Start: *See* Project Head Start

Head Start/Perry Preschool Program: A famous **longitudinal study** on the effects of head start, which showed that the program produced positive effects on participants, including increased academic achievement and decreased criminal activity. Head Start is a government-funded program designed to help disadvantaged children reach their intellectual potential. Measures were taken on a group of nineteen year olds who were enrolled in the Head Start program and on a control group of similar individuals who were not enrolled in Head Start.

Hearing Disorder: A general term pertaining to physical conditions that affect normal hearing, which result in partial hearing impairment or total deafness.

Hedonism: In psychology, the idea that the pursuit of pleasure and the avoidance of pain motivate behavior. In philosophy, hedonism is an ethical principle, which states that the achievement of pleasure or happiness is the highest form of "good" and is the ultimate goal of moral behavior.

Heredity: *See* Genetics

Heritability: In research, the proportion of the total **variability** of a given **trait** in a **population** that is due to genetic factors rather than to environmental factors. Heritability is expressed numerically as a value between 1.00 and 0.00. For example, if 100 percent of the variation in a population's **intelligence quotient (IQ)** scores was attributed to genetic factors, the heritability would be 1.00. If 100 percent of the variation in a population's IQ scores was attributed to environmental factors, the heritability would be 0.00. Studies in heritability indicate that children raised in healthy socioeconomic conditions generally have higher heritability values (i.e., closer to 1.00) than children raised in unhealthy socioeconomic conditions. In addition, studies indicate that heritability tends to be magnified over time. That is, a child who has a low heritability will have an even lower heritability value as time passes, unless steps are taken to intervene.

Hertz (Hz): A unit used to measure the wave **frequency** of sound. Hertz is measured in terms of the number of cycles vibrating molecules complete in one second. One hertz equals one cycle per second.

Heterogeneous Classes: In education, classes comprised of students who vary widely in their abilities and/or skill levels. In music education, heterogeneous or heterogeneity is often used to refer to music classes in which several different instruments are taught simultaneously. For example, beginning instrument classes in which flute, clarinet, and saxophone are taught simultaneously are heterogeneous classes. Most performing ensembles are also heterogeneous classes because they typically include students at several grade levels, at various levels of **musical achievement** and **aptitude**, and with a wide range of musical skill development.

In general education, while all classes contain some heterogeneous characteristics, the term implies that the level of heterogeneity has negatively impacted the learning process. Strategies for making classes less heterogeneous and more similar (homogenous) include grouping students according to ability and achievement levels, typically determined by a variety of test scores. *See* **Homogeneous Classes; Tracking**

Heuristics/Heuristic Strategies: The process of learning or discovering possible solutions to problems quickly through informal methods or strategies including guesswork, trial-and-error, and **insight**. Heuristic strategies do not follow more formal step-by-step plans, established formulas, or other organized methods. Phrases sometimes used to describe heuristics include "seat-of-the-pants," "educated guessing," "winging it," or "cookbook solutions." Heuristics is also used to describe the use of general knowledge gained through experience or common sense. That is, heuristics involves following one's own set of rules, or what some refer to as basic "rules-of-thumb." Other common heuristic strategies include: 1) simplification, which involves reducing the number of steps in solving a problem while emphasizing its key elements, 2) analogous plans, which involve solving complex problems by solving similar, less complicated problems first, and 3) computer programs, which are designed to employ heuristic strategies. *See* **Algorithm**

Hidden Agenda: The discrepancy between goals that are stated and those which underlie the **attitudes** and expectations of teachers. Hidden agendas exist in every classroom because every teacher has certain expectations that are not stated explicitly and generally not considered to be formal curricular goals and are also known as **implicit curriculum**. Hidden agendas have been shown to be a powerful influence on student learning in both positive and negative ways. Example: Most teachers expect students to respect authority, yet respect for authority is not typically a written **curricular goal**. *See* Explicit Curriculum

High-forward Resonance: In vocal technique, a tone produced in the frontal cavities of the head, commonly referred to as the "mask." The physical conditions necessary to produce high-forward resonance are an open throat and an arched **soft palate** (velum).

High-interference Variables: *See* Observational Research

High School: A Report on Secondary Education in America: *See* Carnegie Report

High Stakes Tests: In general, any test that has significant consequences to test-takers, including those required to obtain a drivers license, mandatory state **competency tests** required for teacher **certification**, and tests required for admission to state bar associations. In education, high stakes tests are used to evaluate students' performances to determine whether they should be promoted to the next grade level, be allowed to graduate, or be permitted access to special programs or specific fields of study. The use of high stakes tests was a reaction to the minimum competency movement that began in the 1970s in which tests were designed and used to assess whether or not students met the "lowest acceptable levels" of academic performance. Supporters of high stakes tests believe they help ensure that students have met minimum **standards**. Critics believe that too much emphasis has been placed on these tests and that reliance on high stakes tests limits curricular content and forces teachers to employ a "teach-to-the-test" mentality. *See* Minimum Competency Movement

Higher Education Facilities Act of 1963/Public Law 88-204: Legislation authorizing financial assistance for funding the construction, rehabilitation, and improvement of facilities for both public and nonprofit undergraduate and graduate institutions. The act was passed to construct new facilities and update existing ones at universities, colleges, and community colleges nationwide because of a rapid increase in the number of people wanting a college education.

Higher-level/order Questions: Complex questions that require conceptual and abstract thinking beyond simple recall of factual information or basic comprehension. Higher-level questions also involve analytical, critical, or divergent thinking skills. Higher level questions often begin with "how" or "why" and are often open-ended. These questions are most effective when students have an adequate knowledge base of factual information, and experienced teachers typically build this base by asking **lower-level questions** before asking higher level questions. Examples of higher-level questions include: Why is freedom a good thing? How did the Colonists survive their first winter in America? What were the issues that led to the Civil War? *See* Lower-level/order Questions

Histogram: *See* Bar Graph

Historical Research: Research in which factual information is obtained and evaluated as objectively as possible to determine what actually occurred or is occurring at a given time and place in history. Historical researchers place the highest value on primary sources, including eyewitness accounts, written accounts, original documents, letters, and video recordings. Secondary sources are also valuable. These sources include stories passed down through generations, second-hand accounts, and written or verbal accounts that recall documents or letters that no longer exist. The accuracy and **objectivity** of any source is of the utmost concern to historical researchers. One task of the historical researcher is to make informed, yet subjective judgments regarding the accuracy of their sources so that sound conclusions can be drawn. Logic and reason are often used instead of statistics to draw conclusions in historical research. A primary concern with historical research is that the conclusions drawn rely almost completely on the quality of the research materials and the ability of the researcher to interpret them, arguably resulting in a higher degree of subjectivity than other research methods.

Holistic Development: In general, the growth and development of the whole person, rather than the growth and development that occurs in one area, skill, or context. In education, holistic development is usually associated with the idea that schools should be equipped to help students in all areas of development, rather than limiting their focus to helping students achieve academically. That is, schools should be concerned with the students' behavior, health, emotional development, and social development as well as their academic performance. As schools assume some of the traditional roles and responsibilities of parents, it becomes increasingly important for schools to consider the holistic development of every student.

Holmes Group, The: A consortium comprised of education deans and chief academic officers from major universities in all fifty states. Beginning in 1983, the consortium studied teacher education programs over a two-year period and developed ideas for improving teacher education. The Group made several recommendations, including: 1) making teacher education intellectually solid, 2) recognizing differences in knowledge and skill among teachers, 3) creating relevant and defensible standards to the teaching profession, 4) connecting teacher training programs with schools, and 5) making schools better places for teachers to work and learn.

Some recommendations were highly controversial. The consortium recommended that professional certificates should involve requirements in addition to an undergraduate degree. Teachers without the requirements would be called instructors and receive only a temporary certificate until they completed a professional development course and passed a general abilities test. The first full professional certificate would be given only after instructors completed work leading to the completion of a master's degree. This degree would involve advanced study in one's major or minor field, working with at-risk children, a year of supervised teaching, and additional competency testing. To receive a career professional certificate, the culminating license in one's field, teachers would need to complete all previous requirements, have demonstrated outstanding teaching performance over time, and complete additional study in one's teaching field. The consortium believed that the way to improve the quality of education was to improve the quality of teachers and to improve teacher salaries. *See* **National Board for Professional Teaching Standards (NBPTS)**

Home Schools/Homeschooling: An **alternative** form of education in which students are educated at home rather than in a traditional school. Homeschooling was a common practice in colonial America, where opportunities to attend formal schools were limited. Today, the number of students being homeschooled is increasing because many people believe it provides more freedom to practice their particular religious beliefs and that schools do not adequately meet the needs of their children. Most states allow children to be homeschooled; however, the laws, rules, and policies governing homeschooling vary from state to state. Some considerations with home schooling include choosing a curriculum, keeping records, providing appropriate activities, and meeting state laws.

Becoming a member of a support group is often recommended. Methods and/or approaches commonly used in homeschooling include the

Charlotte Mason Method, the Classical Education Method, the Eclectic Homeschooling Method, the **Montessori** Method, the Unit Studies Approach, Unschooling (or the Natural Learning Method), and the **Waldorf** Education Method. Proponents of homeschooling argue that children receive more individual attention and more appropriate attention than they would in a public school. They also believe that their children are not exposed to the social problems and inappropriate behaviors often found in public schools. Finally, proponents believe that homeschooled children are able to complete lessons more efficiently and productively. Opponents of home schooling argue that many parents are not qualified or capable of providing an appropriate, professional educational experience for their children. They also believe that homeschooling does not provide children with an appropriate or sufficient variety of activities and that the social experiences of homeschooled children are narrow and inadequate. Finally, opponents are concerned that some parents may actually abuse the right to homeschool their children by promoting or exposing them to various types of abusive or anti-social behavior.

Homeostasis: An optimal level of organic function maintained by regulatory mechanisms known as homeostatic mechanisms. In other words, homeostasis is the tendency of the body to maintain a steady state or to maintain balance between the body's physiological components (i.e., internal organs, blood, and hormones). The body tends to maintain homeostasis automatically. For example, the body sweats in **response** to being too hot; this physiological response helps cool the body; however, one can make conscious efforts to assure balance such as removing clothing, turning on the air conditioner, taking a break, and doing other things that will help cool the body. *See* **Drive-reduction Theory**

Homogenous Classes: In education, classes comprised of students who are similar in their abilities and/or skill levels. In music education, the term homogeneous is often used to refer to music classes in which the same instruments are taught simultaneously. For example, beginning instrument classes in which one instrument type is taught together (e.g., all violins) are homogeneous classes. Most performing ensembles are heterogeneous classes because they typically include students at several grade levels, at various levels of **musical achievement** and **aptitude**, and with a wide range of musical skill development.

In general education, while all classes contain some heterogenous characteristics, the term implies that the level of heterogeneity has negatively impacted the learning process. Strategies for making classes less heterogenous and more homogenous include grouping students according to ability and achievement levels, typically determined by a variety of test scores. *See* **Heterogenous Classes; Tracking**

Horace's Compromise: The Dilemma of the American High School: A book written by Theodore Sizer in 1984 describing a choice that a teacher named Horace must make regarding school curricula. Specifically, Horace must choose between brief coverage of many low-level skills in the curriculum or in-depth coverage of fewer important concepts. Ultimately, Sizer recommends that the curriculum be divided into four major areas: 1) inquiry and expression, 2) mathematics and science, 3) literature and the arts, and 4) philosophy and history. One unique aspect of Sizer's view is that he does not advocate adding courses to the curriculum. Instead, he believes students should learn course material in-depth and that student expectations should be raised. "Horace's compromise" has become a common phrase in education for the dilemma described in his book.

Hostile Aggression: Aggression that is manifested by actions intended to inflict injury.

Housewright Symposium, Vision 2020: Fully titled Vision 2020: The Housewright Symposium on the Future of Music Education, a symposium held in Tallahassee, Florida, in 1999 that focused on the future of music education in America and the necessity of music in American society. The Housewright commission, representing various interests related to music education, presented responses to six questions concerning Vision 2020. The questions were:

1. Why do humans value music?
2. Why study music?
3. How can the skills called for in the National Standards best be taught?
4. How can all people continue to be involved in meaningful music participation?
5. How will societal and technological changes affect the teaching of music?
6. What should be the relationship between schools and other sources of music learning?

One important result of the Housewright Symposium was the Housewright Declaration, which includes a list of twelve agreements made at the symposium. The agreements are:

1. All persons, regardless of age, cultural heritage, ability, venue, or financial circumstances, deserve to participate fully in the best music experiences possible.

2. The integrity of music study must be preserved. Music educators must lead the development of meaningful music instruction and experience.

3. Time must be allotted for formal music study at all levels of instruction such that a comprehensive, sequential and standards-based program of music instruction is made available.

4. All music has a place in the curriculum. Not only does the Western art tradition need to be preserved and disseminated, music educators also need to be aware of other music that people experience and be able to integrate it into classroom music instruction.

5. Music educators need to be proficient and knowledgeable concerning technological changes and advancements and be prepared to use all appropriate tools in advancing music study while recognizing the importance of people coming together to make and share music.

6. Music educators should involve the music industry, other agencies, individuals, and music institutions in improving the quality and quantity of music instruction. This should start within each local community by defining the appropriate role of these resources in teaching and learning.

7. The currently defined role of the music educator will expand as settings for music instruction proliferate. Professional music educators must provide a leadership role in coordinating music activities beyond the school setting to ensure formal and informal curricular integration.

8. Recruiting prospective music teachers is a responsibility of many, including music educators. Potential teachers need to be drawn from diverse backgrounds, identified early, led to develop both teaching and musical abilities, and sustained through ongoing professional development. Also, alternative licensing should be explored to expand the number and variety of teachers available to those seeking music instruction.

9. Continuing research addressing all aspects of music activity needs to be supported, including intellectual, emotional, and physical responses to music. Ancillary social results of music study also need exploration as well as specific studies to increase meaningful music listening.

10. Music making is an essential way in which learners come to know and understand music and music traditions. Music making should be broadly interpreted to be performing, composing, improvising, listening, and interpreting music notation.

11. Music educators must join with others in providing opportunities for meaningful music instruction for all people beginning at the earliest possible age and continuing throughout life.

12. Music educators must identify the barriers that impede the full actualization of any of the above and work to overcome them.

Humanistic Psychology/Humanism: A philosophy, a branch of psychology, and an educational approach that emphasizes the natural goodness of each human being and seeks to promote or enhance individual development based on their personal needs and desires. In philosophy, humanism is often linked to existentialism and the writings of Jean Jacques Rousseau (1712–1778) because of its emphasis on the individual as the source of great ideas.

In psychology, humanism focuses on a learner's **personality** rather than on the interaction between learners and problems. Humanism became popular in the 1960s and is often associated with the work of A. S. Neill, **Abraham Maslow (1908–1970)**, and **Carl Rogers (1902–1987)**. All three believed that learners should be given choices and that they should have an active role in decision-making processes regarding their own learning.

In education, demonstrating respect and kindness toward students and using developmentally appropriate instruction in liberal arts, social conduct, and moral principles are central to the humanistic concept. A humanistic approach is one that focuses on the individual and helps them become self-actualized and autonomous thinkers. Characteristics of a humanistic approach include: 1) giving students freedom to explore their world; 2) focusing on the feelings of each student; 3) allowing students to make choices in the educational process; 4) basing instruction on the student's interests, abilities, and needs; 5) encouraging students to think independently and divergently; and 6) providing an environment that is open and not restricted in traditional ways (e.g., utilizing open spaces without walls in the classroom).

Historically, humanism is rooted in ancient Greek and Roman thought, and it flourished as an historical movement in Europe during the twelfth and thirteenth centuries. Humanism was the basis for the Renaissance period. Today, the idea that people behave intentionally according to their value systems is a central theme in humanism. It is a holistic approach. Humanists focus on the development of the whole person over the lifespan, with an emphasis on studying the self, motivation, and setting personal goals. *See* **Summerhill**

Humanities: In general, **curricular** study that emphasizes historical and philosophical concepts, including fine arts courses. At many universities, the term humanities is often used to designate a college within the university.

Hyperactivity: Refers to an excess of any behavior in inappropriate circumstances. *See* **Attention-deficit/hyperactivity Disorder (ADHD)/ Attention-deficit Disorder (ADD)**

Hyperkinetic: *See* **Hyperactivity**

Hypothesis: In research, a statement that makes an assertion about what is true in a particular situation or about the relationship between two or more **variables**. Most hypotheses are two-tailed hypotheses. Two-tailed hypotheses predict only a general difference; that is, they do not specify the direction of difference. Example: There will be a significant difference between groups' scores on **sight reading** tasks that can be attributed to **intelligence**. One-tailed hypotheses are less common because they specify the direction of difference. Example: Group A will score higher than Group B on sight reading tasks as a result of intelligence. One-tailed hypotheses are limiting and should only be used when no logical possibility of the result coming out in the opposite direction exists. For example, if stated that Group A will score higher than Group B and the data reveals that Group B scored higher than Group A, then the study is complete. Further statements or inferences about the study, **population**, or **sample** cannot be made. *See* **Null Hypothesis**

Hypothesis of Association: A research hypothesis that states that two or more measured variables will be found to correlate with each other in the measured sample and in the population being represented by that sample.

Hypothesis of Difference: A research hypothesis which states that two or more groups of **subjects** will differ on some measure of the **dependent variable** in the measured sample and in the population being represented.

Iconic Memory: A type of sensory memory that enables individuals to remember visual stimuli for a brief moment after seeing it, or a photographic-type image of what is seen that lasts only a fraction of a second. Although iconic memory is short-lived, it allows visual information to be processed in the sensory register. Iconic memory is also referred to as after-image. *See* **Echoic Memory; Memory**

Iconic Models: A general term for **models** that represent something visually. For example, a fingering chart for bassoon is an iconic model.

Iconic Representation: In **Jerome Bruner's (b. 1915) theory of instruction**, both a mode of communication and the second stage of **cognitive** growth. At the iconic representation level, objects become conceivable as images within the brain, and a child's ability to visualize an object or **concept** as an image is no longer dependent upon muscular action. The use of pictures and diagrams illustrates iconic communication. *See* **Enactive Level**

Id: According to **Sigmund Freud (1856–1939)**, the part of **personality** that reflects unorganized, instinctual impulses. The id seeks immediate gratification of primitive needs if left unchecked. *See* **Psychoanalytic Theory, Freud**

Idealism: In general, the idea that behavior or thought is guided by the pursuit of individual concepts of perfection, or the ideal. In philosophy, idealism refers to a theory based on the belief that perceived objects are actually manifestations of the mind and that it is possible to know mental life. Ethically, idealism refers to the idea that individuals should seek to realize universal values. *See* **Realism**

Identification: The process of acquiring social **roles** in childhood by consciously and unconsciously copying adult behavior. Typically, children copy the behavior of adults who play significant roles in their lives, such as parents, by adopting their values, beliefs, and sense of morality. **Identification** also occurs as children interact in social situations with friends who share common interests. In Freud's psychoanalytic theory, identification refers to a child's tendency to identify with the same-sexed parent at the resolution of the **Oedipus complex**. *See* Psychoanalytic Theory, Freud

Identification Figures: Parents and other adult models copied by a child during the **identification** process.

Identity: *See* Gender Identity; Cultural Identity

Identity Crisis: In Erik Erikson's (1902–1994) **psychosocial theory**, a psychosocial crisis that occurs during **adolescence** when an individual's ego identity is being formed. During the identity crisis, children try to find out who they are and who they want to be. *See* Psychosocial Theory/Stages, Erikson; Ego

Identity Formation: In psychology, the process of acquiring adult personality integration. Identity formation is an outgrowth of earlier identifications and other influences. *See* Identification

Ideology: In general, a manner of thinking characteristic of an individual, group, or culture. In philosophy, ideology is a systematic body of concepts about human life or culture.

IEP: *See* Individualized Education Program (IEP)

Illusion: In general, a misinterpretation of the relationships among presented stimuli, resulting in a **perception** that does not accurately reflect physical reality. Illusions are most often optical or visual, although other types can occur as well.

Imagery: Anything related to mental sense impressions produced by imagination. The most common types of imagery include: **visual imagery**, **verbal imagery**, and **aural imagery**. In memory, imagery is believed to facilitate **encoding** in the memory process. In music, researchers have investigated the mental images music elicits under a variety of conditions. Typically, these images are expressed as colors (**chromesthesia**), pictures, or words. *See* Echoic Memory

Imagery Memory: Memory processes that enable individuals to form mental images of the material they want to memorize. Images may be formed from auditory stimuli, although most images are either visual or verbal. Imagery memory is also used to describe the ability to memorize large quantities of material with limited exposure.

Imitation: The act of directly copying or otherwise modeling the behaviors and actions of others. In **Edwin E. Gordon's (b. 1927) music learning theory**, imitation refers to the repetition of music just heard without musical meaning or understanding.

Immediate Memory Span: In memory, the number of items an individual can repeat after a single presentation. Items can include such things as digits, letters, and words. In 1956, George Miller wrote a famous article entitled "The Magical Number Seven, Plus or Minus Two: Some Limits on Our Capacity for Processing Information." In the article, he proposes that individuals can hold approximately seven items (plus or minus two) in short-term memory at any one time. This proposition has been proven repeatedly and is accepted almost universally.

Immunization Against Persuasion: Also known as inoculation against persuasion, a technique used to develop resistance to persuasion by exposing individuals to weak counter-arguments against their own beliefs along with appropriate refutations of these opposing views. Immunization against persuasion is designed to provide individuals with material to combat unwanted persuasion in a specific area.

IMPACT: *See* Project IMPACT

Impairment: A general term referring to a physical deviation or defect. Impairments may be either congenital or acquired. The term is commonly used when referring to disabilities involving speech, hearing, and vision. *See* Disability; Handicapped

Implicit Curriculum: The unwritten, unspoken, and sometimes unintended lessons or instructional expectations contained within classroom and school **curricula**. In the classroom, **implicit curriculum** is influenced by several factors, including the teacher's values and teaching style, the choice of subject material and the way it is presented, and the general atmosphere. Common components of an implicit curriculum include expecting students to stay on task most of the time, to raise their hands before talking, and to treat each other and the teacher with respect. *See* Hidden Agenda; Explicit Curriculum

Implicit Memory/Priming: A type of memory that lets individuals "know" that they have experienced something before, even though they may not remember the experience. Implicit memory operates on the unconscious level and is based on research with amnesiacs. Researchers discovered that individuals with **amnesia** learn certain things faster as a result of previous learning, even though they cannot remember the previous learning. Implicit memory appears to be related to **long-term memory (LTM)**. *See* Forgetting

Implicit Personality Theory: A theory in which **traits** and **behaviors** are correlated with other traits and behaviors based on a set of assumptions or preconceptions. Implicit personality theories usually involve making over-generalizations about people based on previous knowledge and experiences. These theories often involve forming a detailed impression of someone based on a few observations and limited information. For example, if an individual is well-groomed, well-dressed, and well-mannered, people are more likely to conclude that this individual is also trustworthy, intelligent, and well-educated. **Stereotypes** are special kinds of implicit personality theories because they involve particular sets of expectations that have been learned. *See* Halo Effect; Stereotype

Imprinting: A special form of learning that is acquired or activated early in life when the organism is most susceptible to surrounding **stimuli**. Imprinting usually occurs during a very specific time period, often immediately after birth, and remains relatively unchanged over time and is not reversible. Konrad Lorenz (1903–1989) demonstrated this phenomenon by presenting himself as a moving stimulus to a group of newly hatched goslings. The goslings imprinted on Lorenz and followed him around as though he was their mother. *See* Critical Periods

Improving American Schools Act (IASA): A 1994 revision of the **Elementary and Secondary Education Act (ESEA) of 1965**. The IASA was intended to improve education in several ways, including funding professional development and technical assistance programs, promoting safe and drug-free schools and communities, and promoting school equity.

In addition, IASA amended Chapter 1, which was updated and renamed **Title I**.

Improvisation: In music, the act of creating music spontaneously within a framework of selected notes or scales and/or specific chord progressions. Improvisation is most often associated with jazz performance, elementary music, and general music. In jazz performance, improvisation requires mastery of scales and general technique, gaining a working knowledge of chord structures, and developing critical melodic and harmonic listening skills. More advanced improvisation requires the ability to manipulate more complex patterns and chord changes. Students learning to improvise may begin with written patterns or phrases and begin to create their own phrases and patterns as their skills develop.

In elementary music and general music, improvisation is commonly used in several ways, including having students explore the sound possibilities of an instrument, creating parts within a specific, pre-determined framework, making up an accompaniment, adding rhythmic patterns to a given melody, and imitating musical styles. Improvisation is also one part of a three-part approach to music teaching and learning developed by Swiss musician and educator **Emile Jaques-Dalcroze (1865–1950)**. In this approach, improvisation refers to applying or synthesizing what has been learned through **eurhythmics** and **solfege** on an instrument, usually the piano. This means creating music spontaneously by incorporating learned concepts regarding phrasing, rhythm, melody, harmony, and dynamics of time and energy.

In loco parentis: When an individual assumes care and supervision of a minor in the absence of supervision by the minor's guardian. The Latin phrase literally means "in place of a parent." In loco parentis is temporary and occurs with no formal legal approval. Legal issues regarding whether teachers are acting in place of the parents or as agents of the state are sometimes raised in education.

Incentive: In psychology, a tangible **goal** or object that provides the **motivation** that leads to action. Incentives are typically associated with **extrinsic motivation**. For example, the desire to receive a music scholarship may provide the incentive for an individual to practice his or her instrument.

Incentive Programs: In education, programs designed to encourage academic success by offering students outside incentives for good attendance and good grades. For example, the Hope Scholarship Program in Georgia offers a free college education to all Georgia high school students with a B average who choose to attend a public college, university, or technical institute in that state. If students choose to attend a private school, they receive an annual scholarship. Several states have passed similar legislation.

Incentive Theory: In psychology, the general belief that individuals are motivated by **positive** and **negative stimuli** or incentives. Incentive theory is based on the idea that individuals will be attracted to things they find pleasant and repelled by things they find unpleasant. Incentive theory is related to but not identical to Maslow's need theory. **Needs** must be met, and they push or drive people to behave in certain ways, almost without choice. Incentives are desirable but not absolutely necessary, and they pull people to behave in certain ways primarily by choice. *See* **Needs Hierarchy, Maslow**

Incidence: In education, the number of times something occurs within a specified time period. Usually, incidence refers to the number of times a particular student engages in inappropriate activity over a certain period of time.

Independent Groups Design: In research, a general term for any experiment in which each group consists of different subjects. An independent groups design is also referred to as a between-subjects design. For example, in a study involving an **experimental group** and a **control group**, each group is comprised of different subjects and would therefore be considered an independent groups design. *See* **Repeated Block Design**

Independent Schools: *See* **Private Schools**

Independent Variable: In research, usually a variable manipulated in some way so that its effect(s) on the **dependent variable** can be measured. Independent variables may also be assigned. An assigned independent variable is a categorization of subjects on the basis of some pre-existing **trait** measured by the researcher. Whether the independent variable is manipulated or assigned determines whether the research is experimental (manipulated) or post-facto (assigned). In experimental research, the independent variable is the potential causal half of the cause-and-effect relationship, while the dependent variable is the effect half. In **correlational research**, the independent variable is the measure from which the prediction will be made, and is called a **predictor variable**.

Individual Attention: In education, one-on-one time between a teacher and a student. Individual attention is often necessary to address student concerns that cannot or should not be addressed in front of the entire class. Such concerns may be of a more personal nature, or they may require a considerable amount of time, detracting from regular class activities. Because of the time involved, individual attention usually takes place outside of scheduled class time. In music education, particularly in **performance-based** classes, providing individual attention in a rehearsal setting can be difficult if a problem requires more than a simple pedagogical comment or a brief moment of attention. Individual attention is extremely important for developing musicians. Some states and school districts include private lessons in the school day as part of performance-based music classes. In other states and districts, teachers often schedule such lessons outside of the normal school day, or make arrangements for them with an outside teacher. Giving each student an appropriate amount of individual attention is an ongoing concern of many performance-based music educators.

Individual Differences: Originally noted by **Sir Francis Galton (1822–1911)**, differences among members of the same species on a wide variety of measurable traits. Researchers use individual differences to measure relative standing. For example, a person's height or weight is more meaningful if expressed in terms of its relative position to others of like gender or age than if expressed as an absolute number. The **concept** of individual differences is also used to find a common ground between different types of **measurements**. For example, height and weight cannot be compared directly because they are expressed in different units of measurement; however, they can be compared in the amount that each may vary from its own **norm**, or average.

Individual Relativity: *See* Internal Relativity

Individualization: In education, a **student-centered** approach to instructional design, or the process of making instruction directly relevant to each student's needs based on strengths and weaknesses. Individualization is a central goal of most **special education programs**.

Individualized Instruction: A type of instruction that provides a unique learning program for each child. Individualized instruction involves assessing current abilities, determining the need for growth, and providing appropriate experiences to help the child learn. Individualized instruction became popular in the 1970s and is commonly used today in **special education programs**. Aspects of individualized instruction are incorporated into most classrooms and are considered by many teachers to be essential components of effective teaching.

Individualized Education Plan (IEP): A plan of instruction mandated by the **Education for All Handicapped Children Act of 1975** and the **Individuals with Disabilities Education Act (IDEA)** of 1990 for all children classified in any category of **special education**. A team that may include teachers, psychologists, social workers, counselors, administrators, parents, and the child establishes a series of educational **goals** and timetables. IEPs are reviewed on a regular basis. Each child must be placed in the **least restrictive environment (LRE)** consistent with achievable educational attainments.

Individuals with Disabilities Education Act (IDEA): The name given to the new and expanded version of the **Education for All Handicapped Children Act of 1975/Public Law 94-142** in 1990. IDEA continued mandates for a **"free and appropriate public education" (FAPE)** and **Individualized Education Plans (IEPs)** carried out in the **least restrictive environment (LRE)**. The term "handicapped" was replaced with "**disability**" to more accurately reflect current trends in educational thought. IDEA mandated transitional services, reauthorized and expanded several discretionary programs, and defined several devices and services related to new technology. In addition, IDEA added **autism** and traumatic brain injury to the existing category list of children eligible for special education and related services. IDEA was amended in 1992 and 1997, and this legislation is now implemented through the Office of Special Education and Rehabilitative Services (OSERS) and the units it oversees: the Office of Special Education Programs (OSEP), the National Institute in Disability and Rehabilitation Research (NIDRR), and the Rehabilitative Services Administration (RSA). *See* **Zero-exclusion Principle**

Induction Program: In education, programs that provide special assistance to beginning teachers, usually in the form of mentor teachers. Induction programs allow teachers who have taught from one to three years to receive **feedback** from more experienced teachers to improve their teaching skills. *See* Mentoring

Induction/Inductive Reasoning: A judgment about what is probably true given the facts and circumstances, although such reasoning does not necessarily result in truth. Example: An individual may listen to a flute sonata, note that all of the stylistic elements are consistent with those found in the Baroque period, and conclude it was composed by J. S. Bach (1685–1750) when it was actually composed by another Baroque composer. *See* Deduction

Inductive Fallacy: The act of making inaccurate generalizations based on too few observations. Inductive fallacy occurs when a person observes a particular characteristic in one individual of a particular class and then assumes that all members of that class must also possess the characteristic. For example, it would be an inductive fallacy for an individual to assume that all musicians have good memories based on the fact that the one musician they know is able to memorize music quickly and accurately.

Infancy: In developmental psychology, the period immediately following birth during which time infants (or other organisms) are dependent and helpless. In humans, infancy lasts from birth to about eighteen months. The end of infancy is marked by the ability to represent things and people through the use of language. At this point, infancy ends and **childhood** begins.

Inference Learning, Gordon: According to Edwin E. Gordon (b. 1927), the higher of two types of skill learning, the other being discrimination learning. Inference learning includes the following three levels: 1) generalization, 2) creativity/improvisation, and 3) theoretical understanding. *See* Skill Learning Sequence, Gordon; Discrimination Learning, Gordon

Inferential Statistics: Statistics designed to determine whether or not results obtained from **sample data** may be generalized to a **population**. That is, inferential statistics enable researchers to arrive at conclusions that extend beyond the sample statistics to the population from which the sample was drawn. Inferential statistics include numerous statistical tests or procedures, such as **factor analysis** and **analysis of variance (ANOVA)**.

Information Processing: A theory of learning and remembering based on the way a computer functions. The sense organs respond to incoming information. This information is then passed along and encoded in the memory and nervous system. This encoded information is then processed, stored, and ultimately retrieved for use. Terms often associated with information processing include sensory input, processing, **encoding,** **storage, retrieval,** and **output.**

Information Processing Model: In memory, this term most commonly refers to a three-stage model for processing and remembering information. The three stages are: 1) information comes in through the **sensory registry;** 2) information that has been sufficiently attended to and/or rehearsed is temporarily stored and processed in **short-term memory (STM);** and 3) information that has been sufficiently rehearsed or otherwise has personal meaning is stored in **long-term memory (LTM).** The **Atkinson-Shiffrin Model of Memory** is a variation of the classic information processing model.

Informed Consent: In research, the ethical principle that potential experimental subjects should be informed in advance of all aspects of the research that might influence their decisions about whether to participate. Informed consent is a standard component of most research involving human subjects, particularly when conducted as part of a graduate degree program.

Infrasonic: A term used to describe any sound with a **frequency** below the range of human hearing. Typically, infrasonic sounds are below approximately 15 Hz. *See* **Ultrasonic**

Ingroup Bias: In research, when characteristics of the **subjects** in a group affect the outcome or results of a study. Ingroup bias is normally controlled by using **random sampling** techniques.

Inhibition: In psychology, the process of holding something back. Inhibition occurs when ideas, emotions, **attitudes,** or another inner force inhibits an individual's impulses or desires. In memory, inhibition is used to describe two types of **interference: proactive inhibition** and **retroactive inhibition.**

Innate Releasing Mechanism (IRM): Similar to instinct, an innate **stimulus-response** pattern that is built into the central nervous system. The IRM is a response or set of neurological responses triggered by specific external stimuli. For example, a male stickleback fish is induced into a set of attacking responses when presented with red color.

Inner Ear: The part of the ear inside the oval window. The inner ear contains the **cochlea**, which is filled with fluid and divided by the **basilar membrane**. The inner ear is separated by the oval window and round window. *See* **Outer Ear; Middle Ear**

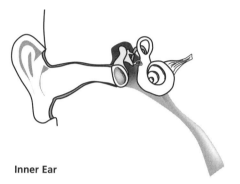

Inner Ear

Inquiry Learning/Method: A type of learning strategy or instructional approach in which students try to answer questions and solve problems based on facts and observations. Inquiry learning involves helping students discover answers or solutions to problems on their own by analyzing **data**, creating and testing theories and **hypotheses**, and expanding their conceptual abilities. The central idea behind inquiry learning is that as new information is discovered and new theories are formed, old ideas are modified or no longer relevant. The Suchman Inquiry Model is one of the most popular examples of inquiry learning. In this model, teachers present students with a problem and then guide them through five steps: 1) defining the problem, 2) formulating hypotheses, 3) gathering data, 4) organizing data and modifying hypotheses accordingly, and 5) generalizing about findings. In this sense, inquiry learning is a scientific approach to learning. Inquiry method is more suitable for longer class periods such as those found in block schedules.

Inservice Teachers: Teachers who are actively employed. Inservice teachers are distinguished from preservice teachers, including college students in teacher training programs and student teachers.

Insight: In psychology, a gestalt concept introduced by **Wolfgang Kohler (1887–1967)** to explain the spontaneous, sudden appearance of a solution to a problem or the sudden perception of relationships leading to the understanding and solution of a problem. This process is sometimes called the "Aha!" phenomenon. Many believe that insight results from the reorganization of ideas and **perceptions**, rather than from simple trial-and-error behavior. *See* **"Aha!" Phenomenon; Wertheimer, Max (1880-1943)**

Instinct: In psychology, unlearned, patterned, goal-directed behavior and responses that are usually innate. In **Sigmund Freud's (1856–1939) psychoanalytic theory**, instincts are what drive individuals to behave in certain ways. According to Freud, there are two types of instincts: 1) eros, which are the instincts for pleasure-producing activities such as sex, and 2) thanatos, which are the instincts for **aggression** or destruction.

Instinct Theory: A discredited theory that attempted to explain behavior by simply describing it in other terms, then calling it instinct. The popularity of instinct theory was one reason why the study of heredity did not begin in earnest until the middle of the twentieth century. Instinct theory uses circular reasoning and confuses description with explanation. For example, humans are seen as going to war because of an "aggressive instinct" or have a habit of biting fingernails because of a "nail-biting instinct." *See* **Nominal Fallacy**

Institutional Review Board (IRB): In research, an **ethics** review committee established to review research proposals. The IRB is usually composed of scientists, nonscientists, and legal experts. *See* **Informed Consent**

Instruction: In education, a general term for a set of procedures or techniques used to promote learning. *See* **Instructional Models; Method; Techniques**

Instructional Evaluation: A general term for evaluating or assessing teaching, which involves testing and **measurement**. The three phases are 1) pre-assessment, evaluation that takes place prior to instruction and is used to determine what students know before instruction; 2) **formative assessment**, evaluation that takes place during the instructional process; and 3) **summative evaluation**, a culminating evaluation that occurs at the end of the instructional process. *See* **Assessment**

Instructional Models: In education, complete plans, systems, or strategies for teaching based on certain principles or beliefs about the teaching/learning process. Many types of instructional models are available that use a variety of instructional strategies or techniques, including inquiry learning, **mastery learning, direct instruction, computer-assisted instruction (CAI), synectics, cooperative learning, peer tutoring, reciprocal teaching, outcomes-based education,** and **individualized instruction.** Although teachers may favor one model over another, effective teachers use a variety of these strategies to meet student needs.

Instrument Decay: In research, when the characteristics of a **measurement instrument** change over time and influence the results of a study and negatively affect internal **validity.** Instrument decay often occurs when observers used to measure or record behaviors become fatigued and/or distracted.

Intact Groups: In research, groups used for study that are already formed for some other purpose and are not further divided or separated in any way. In educational settings, intact groups usually involve studying particular classrooms, involving all or most of the students in those classrooms. For example, researchers who use two or more fifth-grade classes in their study without making changes are using intact groups.

Integrated Curriculum: In education, any **curriculum** that combines **concepts, skills,** and information from various subject areas to enhance learning and understanding or the blending of content areas around a central theme or focus of study. The general idea behind an integrated curriculum is that the subjects become mutually reinforcing because the teachers often collaborate with each other in planning and implementing curricular content.

Integration/Integrated: Placing students with disabilities into regular classroom settings. Integration is also used when referring to social policies designed to make certain that minority students are educated with non-minority students. *See* **Desegregation**

Intellectualization: In psychology, a **defense mechanism** used by individuals to emotionally detach themselves from a situation by excusing or dismissing it through logic and reasoning. *See* **Defense Mechanisms**

Intelligence: In general, the degree to which an organism can function on many levels. Higher functioning usually equates to higher intelligence. Intelligence is viewed from a variety of perspectives and is a difficult concept to pinpoint because it cannot be directly observed; it must be inferred from **behavior**.

Intelligence is believed by many to be a combination of hereditary and environmental factors. **Charles Spearman (1863–1945)** identified two factors early in the twentieth century: 1) an underlying **general factor (g)**, and 2) a series of specific factors (s). **Louis L. Thurstone (1887–1955)** hypothesized in the early 1920s that intelligence was a composite of special factors, each peculiar to a specific task. **J. P. Guilford's (1897–1988)** factor approach included up to 120 separately identifiable traits for intelligence.

Howard Gardner (b. 1943) described seven intelligences in his book *Frames of Mind*. Gardner's approach is based on eight criteria: 1) the potential isolation by brain damage; 2) the existence of idiot **savants** and prodigies; 3) identifiable core operations such as sensitivity to pitch and rhythm relations; 4) a developmental history that leads to expert performance; 5) an evolutionary history; 6) support from experimental psychological tasks; 7) support from psychometric findings; and 8) the ability to encode the information with a symbol system.

Several other views of intelligence exist. For example, Robert Sternberg (b. 1949) views intelligence from an information-processing perspective. P. E. Vernon (b. 1933) suggests three basic meanings of the concept of intelligence: genetic capacity, observed behavior, and as a test score.

Intelligence Quotient (IQ): A numerical measure of intelligence. IQs were originally calculated using the ratio method in which the subject's mental age is divided by his or her chronological age and the result is multiplied by 100. The deviation method is a newer method for determining IQ and is computed based on how far an individual's score deviates from the **mean** score obtained for an entire group of the same **chronological age**. This technique is based on a **standard score** concept and assumes a **normal distribution** for each age group. IQs are controversial measurements. Proponents believe that calculating and knowing a child's IQ allows parents and educators to better tailor that child's education and to make maximum use of available resources. Critics argue that IQs do not provide a full picture of intelligence; some theories of intelligence hypothesize that several types of intelligence exist, many of which cannot be determined in a traditional IQ test. In addition, when children and adults know an IQ number, they are more likely to develop expectations of each student's abilities based on that number. These expectations may not be accurate and may eventually prevent the children from reaching his or her full potential.

Intelligence Tests: Usually refers to **standardized tests** designed to measure intelligence. The most well-known intelligence test is the **Stanford-Binet Test**, developed by Alfred Binet (1857–1911) in 1905 in France and last revised in 2003. Originally, Binet's tests were designed to identify children who were mentally incapable of benefiting from a regular classroom environment. Instead of the sensorimotor tasks that were used by Sir Francis Galton (1822–1911), Binet's tests used a series of intellectual tasks to determine intelligence. In addition, Binet introduced the concept of **mental age** as the basis for scoring his tests. David Wechsler (1896–1981) is also well known for devising intelligence tests including the **Wechsler Adult Intelligence Scale (WAIS)**, which has been revised (WAIS-R), the **Wechsler Intelligence Scale for Children (WISC)**, which has been revised (WISC-R), and the **Wechsler Preschool and Primary Scale of Intelligence (WPPSI)**. Wechsler defined intelligence as "the global capacity of an individual to think rationally, to act purposefully, and deal effectively with his environment." All of the Wechsler tests report three separate scores, including a verbal IQ, a performance IQ, and a full-scale IQ. *See* **Binet, Alfred (1857-1911); Galton, Sir Francis (1822-1911); Wechsler, David (1896-1981)**

Intensity, Sound: In physics, the energy content of a sound wave and the physical measure of a sound's strength or power. Intensity can be measured in **watts** or **decibels (dB)**. Physically, intensity is proportional to the square of the **amplitude**. Musically, intensity is related to the **loudness** of a sound; greater intensity produces louder sound.

Interaction Effects: Simply stated, interaction effects take place when independent variables affect each other as well as the dependent variable. In research involving factorial designs, interaction effects occur when the effect of one independent variable is dependent upon a particular level of another independent variable. In factorial designs there are two types of effects: 1) main effects, a term which refers to the effect of each independent variable by itself, and 2) interaction effects, a term which refers to how various levels of one independent variable affect another independent variable's effect on the dependent variable. *See* **Main Effect; Dependent Variable; Independent Variable**

Interactive Method: In education, a **method** of teaching in which students learn by doing. This method involves interaction between teacher and students and includes discussion, discovery, and **problem solving** activities. Exchanges of viewpoints and opinions are encouraged, and the teacher often structures the discourse so that students are encouraged to discover new ways of behaving, believing, or thinking.

Interactive Multimedia: *See* Computer Programs; Electronic Music

Interaural Amplitude Difference (IAD): In acoustics, the difference between the amplitude of a sound measured at both ears. IAD is one of the perceptual cues that enables an individual to determine the location of a sound source. *See* Auditory Localization; Interaural Time Delay (ITD)

Interaural Time Delay (ITD): In acoustics, the difference between the arrival time of a sound at both ears. ITD is one of the perceptual cues that enables an individual to determine the location of a sound source. *See* Auditory Localization; Interaural Amplitude Difference (IAD)

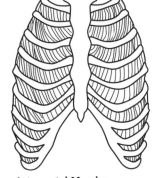

Intercostal Muscles: The muscles that lie between the ribs. Intercostal muscles play a significant role in the breathing process, and are important in proper breathing technique necessary for wind instrumentalists and vocalists.

Intercostal Muscles

Intercultural Education: In education, the evaluation and acknowledgment of the importance cultural **diversity** plays in the education process. Intercultural education involves promoting and encouraging cultural views in an **objective** manner. *See* Multicultural Education

Interdisciplinary Model Programs in the Arts for Children and Teachers (IMPACT): *See* Project IMPACT

Interference: In psychology, when the learning of or knowledge of some information hinders memory processes. There are two types of interference: 1) **proactive inhibition**, when previously learned information inhibits one's ability to learn new information, and 2) **retroactive inhibition**, when the learning of new information inhibits one's ability to **recall** previously learned information. Organizing material properly can help offset the effects of interference.

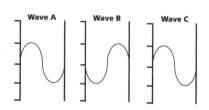

In acoustics, interference occurs when two tones that are slightly out of tune are sounded together. There are two types of acoustical interference: 1) constructive interference, when the two **waves** are completely in phase and reinforce each other, resulting in an increase in **amplitude** and **intensity**; and 2) destructive interference, when

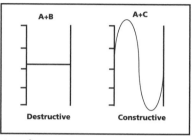

Interference

the two waves are completely out of phase, (i.e., the high pressure point of one wave aligns with the low pressure point of the other) and the waves partially cancel each other out, resulting in a decrease in amplitude and intensity. The fluctuation in intensity and amplitude results in beats, which occur when two tones slightly out of tune are sounded together. *See* **Beats**

Interindividual: Literally, between individuals. Interindividual generally refers to the comparisons of one individual's performance with the performance of others.

Interlochen Center for the Arts: Originally, a National High School Orchestra Camp founded by Joseph Maddy and T. P. Giddings in 1928. Located in Michigan, Interlochen has grown to become one of America's premier sites for developing young musicians, dancers, actors, visual artists, and writers. The Interlochen Arts Center is a year-round fine arts school in addition to its extensive summer program and annual Interlochen Arts Festival.

Intermediate Educational Unit (IEU): In education, a collaborative organization or joint facility maintained by separate districts to provide educational services. IEUs enable participating school districts to benefit from expensive educational services that they would not be able to afford otherwise. **Vocational schools** are one of the most common types of IEUs, which are sometimes called educational service agencies or boards of cooperative educational services.

Intermittent Reinforcement: In psychology, a method of **reinforcement** in which only some correct responses are reinforced. *See* **Schedules of Reinforcement**

Internal Consistency: In research, methods of assessing **reliability** in which subjects are measured at only one point in time or the extent to which a measure or test is consistent or reliable across items. Internal consistency is usually determined by examining item subsets within the measure. The methods of reliability include: 1) split-half reliability, the correlation between an individual's score on the first half of the test and his or her score on the second half of the test; 2) odd-even reliability, the **correlation** between an individual's total score on the odd-numbered items and his or her score on the even-numbered items; and 3) item-total reliability, the correlation between an individual's total score and each item of a measure. *See* **Test-retest Reliability; Alternate-forms Reliability; Split-half Reliability; Reliability**

Internal Validity: *See* **Validity**

International Association of Jazz Educators (IAJE): An organization that promotes jazz **curricula** in the public schools in America and internationally as a legitimate and serious art form. *Jazz Education Journal,* its official publication, includes philosophical and practical articles about jazz education. The IAJE was originally formed in 1968 as the National Association of Jazz Educators (NAJE) and changed its name in 1989 to more accurately reflect the organization's global perspective and outreach.

International Comparative Education: In research and education, the study of education or educational systems of different societies for comparison purposes. Researchers and educators believe that international comparative education helps individuals develop new insights into other societies as well as a deeper understanding of their own society. In addition, such education encourages multicultural understanding, broadens perspectives, and promotes better relations between cultures.

International Institute for Comparative Music Studies: A society devoted to the promotion and understanding of the music of non-Western and Western cultures.

International Journal of Music Education (IJME): A publication started in 1983 that features articles covering different aspects of international music education. Articles include detailed descriptions and discussions of the music education systems of many countries in general education schools and in specialized schools.

International Phonetic Alphabet (IPA): An alphabet commonly used by singers that illustrates proper pronunciation (diction) of a word in any given language. The alphabet is universal and facilitates the understanding of pronunciation. The idea behind IPA is that the reader need not rely on knowledge of the sounds of different letters and letter combinations in a language.

International Society for Music Education (ISME): An organization that promotes and coordinates international perspectives in music education. ISME was an outgrowth of The Role and Place of Music in the Education of Youth and Adults conference held in Brussels in 1953 and organized by the United Nations Educational, Scientific, and Cultural Organization (UNESCO) and the International Music Council (IMC). ISME publishes journals, including the *International Journal of Music Education (IJME)* founded in 1983 to help promote international music education. ISME has also formed area-specific commissions to facilitate the international exchange of ideas. These commissions focus on several aspects of music education, inluding community music, early childhood, mass media policy, music therapy and special education, research, schools and teacher training, and the education of the professional musician.

Interpersonal Intelligence, Gardner: In Howard Gardner's (b. 1943) theory of **multiple intelligences**, the ability to understand other people's verbal and **nonverbal behaviors** (i.e., actions, emotions, thoughts, and intentions) and to respond verbally and nonverbally to these behaviors appropriately and effectively. Effective teachers, counselors, politicians, and therapists are said to possess interpersonal intelligence.

Interpretation: In Sigmund Freud's (1856–1939) **psychoanalysis**, a technique used by psychoanalysts to help individuals become aware of their resistances to facilitate the flow of associations. Freud used **interpretation** to explain the symbolic meaning of dreams as a way of understanding the unconscious mind. In music, interpretation is commonly used to refer to the way or ways a musician consciously decides to perform music. Although related to style, interpretation is often used when referring to subtle nuances in a musical performance unique to an individual performer.

Interrupted Time Series Design: A research design in which the effectiveness of a **treatment** is determined by examining a series of **measurements** made over an extended period of time. These measurements are made both before and after the treatment, which is introduced at a specified point in time. For example, an interrupted time series design could be used to examine student drop-out rates in the school orchestra over a four-year period after the initiation of a new retention program.

Interval Scale: In research, a **measurement scale** without an absolute zero point in which the intervals between scale numbers are all equal in size. Because the intervals between scale numbers are all equal, interval scales allow for meaningful comparisons. For example, a thermometer measures temperature on an interval scale, allowing people to understand the difference between 50 degrees and 100 degrees Fahrenheit. The absence of a zero point means that ratio comparisons cannot be made accurately. That is, 100 degrees Fahrenheit is not twice as warm as 50 degrees Fahrenheit. *See* Ratio Scale; Measurement/Measurement Scales

Intervening Variable: In research, anything that occurs between the presentation of a **stimulus** and the **response** that can be used to account for differences in the response. Intervening variables may be inferred from the data without further specification, or they may be given concrete properties and investigated further. *See* Independent Variables; Dependent Variables

Interview Method: In research, a method of gathering **data** in which researchers ask a subject or subjects questions either in person or by telephone. In-person interviews allow for more in-depth information and allow the researcher to make visual observations about the subject during the interview process. In-person interviews typically involve a greater investment of researcher and subject time. Depending on the nature of the study and the information desired by the researcher, interviews by telephone are often adequate.

Interview Structure: The way in which interviews are organized and conducted by researchers. There are three standard approaches to interviews: 1) the structured interview, 2) the semistructured interview, and 3) the unstructured interview. Each is used in different contexts and yields different types of data. The structured interview has a well-defined format allowing only limited clarification and elaboration. Structured interviews, such as objective **questionnaires**, tend to be factually oriented and are designed to obtain specific, relatively brief information. Structured interviews may be used when the type of information needed fits readily into a structured format and when accurate and complete information from all respondents is necessary. Semistructured interviews are used when researchers want information that is too complex or elusive to obtain in a more structured interview. Semistructured interviews allow researchers to probe for further information after asking the core of structured questions in order to discover underlying **factors** or relationships. Conducting semistructured interviews is more complex than conducting structured interviews because the tendency to bias subjects is greater. In unstructured interviews, the subjects have much more freedom to express themselves. Unstructured interviews are commonly used in counseling sessions, and such interviews were the basis of the client-centered therapy of **Carl Rogers (1902–1987)**. Information obtained in unstructured interviews tends to be highly personal and potentially threatening to the subject. The tendency for researcher bias or other errors is greatest with unstructured interviews.

Interviewer Bias: In research, when interviewers intentionally or unintentionally influence respondents so that **responses** are consistent with the interviewer's expectations. *See* **Researcher Bias**

Intraindividual: Literally, within an individual. Intraindividual generally refers to comparisons made between an individual's performance in one area with his or her performance in other areas. Individuals are compared to themselves to describe their own strengths and weaknesses rather than being compared to others. *See* **Interindividual**

Intrapersonal Intelligence, Gardner: In Howard Gardner's (b. 1943) theory of **multiple intelligences**, the ability to understand one's own verbal and **nonverbal behaviors** (i.e., actions, emotions, thoughts, and desires) well. Social workers, therapists, and counselors are said to possess intrapersonal intelligence.

Intrinsic Motives/Motivation: Motivation that occurs when the action and the results of the action are inherently motivating. In other words, intrinsic motivation comes from within the individual. Intrinsic motives include **curiosity**, internal drives, and the desire to learn and achieve because these things are rewarding in and of themselves. In education, students have different levels of intrinsic motivation for different learning tasks at different stages of the learning process. Research has shown that learning prompted and sustained by intrinsic motivation lasts longer than learning prompted and sustained by extrinsic motivation, including external reinforcers. *See* **Extrinsic Motivation; External Reinforcers**

Introspection: In psychology, a process used in the late 1800s and early 1900s by **Wilhelm Wundt (1832–1920)** and Edward Bradford Titchener (1867–1927) of the Structuralist school for gathering psychological data or information. The process involved having **subjects** look within themselves and then report all feelings, sensations, and images. **John B. Watson (1878–1958)** and other **behaviorists** rejected the use of introspection because they believed it was too subjective. In its original form, introspection is no longer used to gather data; however, forms of introspection in which individuals are asked to describe their feelings and experiences are still practiced today. *See* **Structuralist Psychology/Structuralism**

Introvert/Introversion: One of two basic personality types or orientations identified by **Carl Jung (1875–1961)** referring to an individual who is shy, withdrawn, quiet, calm, timid, cautious, and reflective. Introverts tend to withdraw into themselves and to avoid other people, especially in time of emotional stress. Introverts are normally passive, tend to think rather than act, and are viewed by others as being shy or unsociable. These characteristics are typically displayed consistently over time. *See* **Extravert/Extraversion**

Intuition: In psychology, a term used to describe a way of knowing in which individuals perceive and understand information apparently without reflection, logic, or reason. In other words, individuals know something because they know they know it. Intuition often involves knowing and understanding without awareness of how it is known. *See* **Insight**

Invariant Sequence: In general, any unchanging sequence of events. In psychology, an invariant sequence usually refers to the idea that human development occurs in stages arranged in an unchanging sequence that only move in an upward or forward direction. In an invariant sequence, stages or steps cannot be skipped; they occur in order, one step at a time. **Cognitive** development and moral growth theories are often expressed in an invariant sequence, progressing from the simple to the complex. Examples: 1) **Piaget's Stages of Cognitive Growth**; and 2) **Moral Development, Kohlberg**

Iowa Test of Basic Skills (ITBS): A national standardized test used to assess elementary students' understanding of core subjects. The ITBS has been used to identify low-performing students and low-performing schools. In recent years, using the ITBS for determining low-performing schools (i.e., **accountability**) has been controversial, because the ITBS has not been validated for that purpose. As a result, some researchers believe that the ITBS should be replaced with a test that is more appropriate.

Iowa Tests of Music Literacy (ITML): A comprehensive music achievement test battery developed over an eight-year period by Edwin E. Gordon (b. 1927) ending in 1970. The ITML is designed to sequentially measure and evaluate basic **music achievement**. The test is offered at a variety of difficulty levels to accommodate students of different ages. The ITML is comprised of two major divisions: Tonal Concepts and Rhythmic Concepts. Each division contains three subtests. Composite score reliabilities range from .87 to .94. See **Gordon, Edwin E. (b. 1927)**

IQ: *See* Intelligence Quotient

ISME: *See* International Society for Music Education (ISME)

Item-total Reliability: *See* Internal Consistency

Ives, Elam (1802–1864): In music education history, a Connecticut singing school master and church choir director who made a significant impact on music education with his work applying the principles of **Johann Heinrich Pestaozzi (1746–1827)** to music teaching in the United States. Ives' *American Elementary Singing Book* is believed by many to have been the first music book in America to advocate the principles of Pestalozzi.

James, William (1842-1910): America's first and probably most revered psychologist, James spent his entire academic lifetime at Harvard University, first as a student and later as a professor. Although James received an M.D. degree, he is best known for his work as a professor of both psychology and philosophy. James created and taught the first psychology course ever offered in the United States in 1876 and had a great interest in and respect for classroom teachers. He felt that students' success in education was determined in large part by the performance of classroom teachers. James is also credited with originating the school of **functionalism** in psychology, which is interested not so much in what the elements of consciousness are but in the ways they are used.

James-Lange Theory: In psychology, the theory that stimuli initiate bodily responses and that the awareness of these responses constitutes emotional experience. James-Lange Theory is a classical theory of emotion named after the two men who independently arrived at essentially the same conclusion, **William James (1842–1910)** and Carl Lange (1834–1900). The James-Lange Theory is in contrast to the Cannon-Bard Theory. *See* **Cannon's Theory**

Jaques-Dalcroze, Emile (1865-1950): An eminent Swiss music educator best known in music education for developing a method of learning music that is still widely used today, particularly with young children. Jaques-Dalcroze studied composition with Bruckner, Fauré, and Delibes and became professor of harmony at the Geneva Conservatory in 1892. While at the Geneva Conservatory, Jaques-Dalcroze believed that too much emphasis was placed on developing technical skills rather than musical skills. In the early twentieth century, Jaques-Dalcroze experimented with new methods of teaching music education involving eurhythmics. In 1914 Jaques-Dalcroze left the Geneva Conservatory and founded the Institute Jaques-Dalcroze in Geneva to teach and promote his new method.

To Dalcroze, the development of **musicality** and self-expression through the art of music should be the central focus of training, not the development of performance skills. He believed developing tonal and rhythmic skills was vital to musicality. Dalcroze also advocated the use of **solfege** and **improvisation** to help develop critical listening skills. These beliefs resulted in the Dalcroze method, which consists of rhythmic movement, ear training, and improvisation. Heavy emphases are placed on singing vocal exercises and on the coordination of body movement to music. Dalcroze's views on learning were progressive at that time and were not directly incorporated into music education programs, although his method is still studied in some detail by most music educators during their teacher-training programs. Dalcroze's ideas are still influential and are clearly reflected in the **National Standards for Music Education**. *See* Dalcroze Method; Eurhythmics

Jitter: In acoustics, the rapid and subtle **frequency** and/or **amplitude** modulation of a tone and/or its partials.

jnd: *See* Just Noticeable Difference (jnd)

Jones Music Recognition Test: A test designed to measure the recognition of representative musical repertoire, originally published in 1949. The Jones Music Recognition Test includes a level for elementary and junior high students and one for high school and college students. It is not standardized.

Journal of Music Teacher Education (JMTE): A music education journal that focuses on topics related to music teacher training, issued twice per year and published by **Music Educators National Conference (MENC)**. The *JMTE* disseminates information regarding teacher education reform, **curricular** issues, and other topics related to teacher training. It is only available to members online.

Journal of Research in Music Education (JRME): The premiere research journal in music education, founded in 1953 by Allen P. Britton. The *JRME* is published quarterly by the **Music Educators National Conference (MENC)** and contains information about the latest music education research and related topics. One primary goal of the JRME is to disseminate research results to and enhance the knowledge of MENC members.

Journaling/Journals: In education, having students maintain a written record of their thoughts or ideas about what they are doing in school or in a particular class. Journaling is often used for reading courses and often involves having students relate the content of readings to their own experiences. Journals are sometimes included in a student's **portfolio** as a sample of their work and can be an integral component of the **assessment** process.

JRME: *See* Journal of Research in Music Education (JRME)

Juilliard Repertory Project: A project intended to improve the quality of elementary school music instruction by researching and compiling a library of the highest quality music literature in the field for use in **kindergarten** through sixth grade. The Juilliard Repertory Project was made possible through a grant received by the Juilliard School of Music in 1964 from the United States Office of Education and was a direct result of the **Yale Seminar**, which took place in 1963. The project resulted in the **Juilliard Repertory Library**, a collection of quality music in a variety of periods and styles appropriate for younger students.

Juilliard Repertory Library: The collection of "appropriate and authentic" musical pieces that resulted from the **Juilliard Repertory Project** intended for use in the public schools, particularly from **kindergarten** through the sixth grade. The Juilliard Repertory Library contains 230 vocal and instrumental works divided into seven period/style categories: pre-Renaissance, Renaissance, Baroque, Classical, Romantic, Contemporary, and Folk. Pieces of music for the library were selected and compiled by music educators, researchers, and educators after being reviewed and tested for their suitability in classroom situations.

Jung, Carl (1875-1961): An eminent Swiss psychiatrist whose writings have influenced many fields, including psychology, education, and, to an extent, religion. Jung received a medical degree in 1902. Afterward, he researched and studied mental illness with Eugen Bleuler (1857–1939) in Zurich. During this time, Jung began developing his ideas regarding the effects of the unconscious mind on behavior. In 1907 Jung became close friends with **Sigmund Freud (1856–1939)**, and for several years they exchanged ideas and collaborated on several projects. Jung was primed to continue Freud's work in **psychoanalysis**; however, Jung did not agree with Freud's view that an individual's neuroses had a sexual basis and as a result their relationship was permanently damaged. Jung later founded the field of analytic psychology in response to Freud's psychoanalysis. His ideas and concepts about **introvert** and **extravert** personalities, **archetypes**, and the **collective unconscious** are now classic. Jung also formulated new psychotherapeutic techniques designed to reacquaint an individual with his or her unique place or "myth" in the collective unconscious. Jung believed that an individual's place in the collective unconscious was expressed in dreams and in one's imagination. His works include *The Psychology of the Unconscious* (1912), which was revised as *Symbols of Transformation*, *Psychology and Religion* (1938), and *Memories, Dreams, Reflections* (1962).

Just Intonation: A tuning system in which pure intervals are mathematically related in a way that **beats** are not present when the tones are sounded together. In just intonation, the intervallic ratios are selected and related based on the harmonic series. While just intonation works well on a limited basis, it does not provide flexibility for modulation as does **equal temperament** tuning. *See* **Temperament/Tuning Systems**

Just Noticeable Difference (jnd): A measure of human ability to perceive small changes in **pitch** between two tones presented sequentially. In this sense, the jnd is a measure of pitch difference threshold. The jnd varies according to the pitch register. That is, for tones with frequencies up to about 1000 Hz, the jnd is 3 Hz or about 5 cents. The jnd increases in the low and high ranges. That is, as sounds go lower or higher, the difference in the frequency between the two tones must be greater for listeners to perceive pitch differences.

Just-world Phenomenon: In psychology, the tendency to believe that the world is a fair place and that people get what they deserve and deserve what they get. Some psychologists believe that the just-world phenomenon is related to the idea that good is rewarded and that evil is punished, which most people are taught during childhood. If someone is punished, people tend to believe that he or she must be evil; if someone is rewarded, people tend to believe that he or she must be good. In either case, the **punishment** or **reward** is perceived as being deserved. This phenomenon is reflected in the fact that people will often stand by and watch someone being harmed unjustly and actually begin to believe that the person deserves it.

Justification for Music Programs: In education, the reasons for keeping or including music as a core subject in school **curricula**. In many schools, music programs are threatened by budget cuts, especially when budgets are tight, because music is often not considered a core subject. Music educators must often provide justifications for continuing or adding a music program that will be supported by administrators, parents, and the community. Some justifications for music programs include the following: 1) music is important in American life; 2) children need a well-rounded education; 3) music provides opportunities for **aesthetic experience** that other courses do not; 4) the skills learned in music **transfer** to other areas of study; 5) music contributes to overall mental health and well-being of students; and 6) music provides many individuals with a lifelong avocation.

Kindergarten: An educational program designed to prepare young children for first grade. The first kindergarten was established in 1837 by **Friedrich Wilhelm Froebel (1782–1852)**.

Kindermusik: A music education program designed to provide musical experiences that are both fun and educational for children from birth through age seven. Kindermusik integrates music and movement activities into age-appropriate **curricula** that typically include singing, chanting, listening, and playing instruments. Kindermusik programs are based on the following beliefs: 1) parents are a child's most important teacher; 2) a child's home is an ideal environment for musical learning; and 3) music nurtures **cognitive**, emotional, social, language, and physical development.

Kinesthesis/Kinesthesia/Kinesthetic: In physiology, an internal sense that facilitates awareness of body movements, including where, when, and how body parts move. Kinesthesis utilizes sense receptors located in the muscles, joints, and tendons to collect sensory information. This sensory information is combined with additional information from the other senses, such as sight and hearing, and is interpreted by the brain, enabling individuals to determine body location. Kinesthesis is often associated with the ability to perform motor skills. For example, touching your nose with your finger with your eyes closed, dancing without stepping on your partner's feet, driving a car, playing baseball, and performing on a musical instrument all involve kinesthesis. Kinesthesis is sometimes called proprioception because it involves cues that provide information about activity within the body and body movement. Kinesthesis is also related to vestibular sense because it is part of the process that enables individuals to maintain a sense of balance or **equilibrium** despite changes in body position. *See* **Proprioceptive Cues; Vestibular Sense**

Knuth Achievement Tests in Music: A test designed to measure the ability to recognize mistakes in rhythm and melody, originally published in 1936 and reissued in 1967. The Knuth Achievement Test is available in three divisions to accommodate a variety of age groups. The test is relatively easy to administer, and Knuth reports a split-half reliability of .92 for all three Divisions. *See* Snyder Knuth Music Achievement Test

Kodály Method: A system of music education based on the general idea that every child should have a music education and should be musically literate, developed under the guidance of **Zoltan Kodály (1882–1967)** in the mid-twentieth century. Central to the Kodály Method is the idea that children should learn music through singing, playing instruments, and moving to folk songs of their own culture. The musical **objectives** of the Kodály Method include: 1) children should be able to sing, to play instruments, and to otherwise create music from memory using a large repertoire of native folk song material and later incorporating music from other cultures; 2) children should listen to, analyze, and perform great art music of the world; 3) children should master several musical skills, including music reading, writing, singing, and part-singing; and 4) children should improvise and compose using the musical vocabulary they have learned at each level of development. The Kodály Method incorporates a variety of musical practices from other existing methods, including solfege syllables with accompanying hand signals and movable "do." The Kodály Method remains influential and is widely used today.

Kodály, Zoltan (1882-1967): An eminent Hungarian composer, ethnomusicologist, and music educator, Kodály studied at the Budapest Academy of Music and at the university in Budapest where he earned diplomas in composition and teaching and a doctorate in Hungarian folk song. Kodály spent a great deal of time developing a national school music **curriculum** in Hungary and, with Béla Bartók (1881–1945), compiled the well-known *Hungarian Folk Songs* (1906). Kodály's other works include *Psalmus Hungaricus* (1923) and the opera *Hary Janos* (1926). In the United States, Kodály is best known in music education for developing the Kodály Method, one of the most influential elementary teaching methods. *See* Kodály Method

Kohlberg, Lawrence (1927-1987): *See* Moral Development, Kohlberg

Kohler, Wolfgang (1857-1967): One of the founders of **gestalt psychology**, Kohler was a student of **Max Wertheimer (1880–1943)** at the University of Frankfurt. Kohler performed gestalt psychology's most famous animal learning study. While studying an ape, Kohler noticed that sometimes learning occurred on the basis of insight rather than the slow accumulation of specific associations. Insight, or the **"Aha!" phenomenon**, is learning that occurs suddenly as new relationships among perceptions are discovered. *See* Insight

Krathwahl's Taxonomy of the Affective Domain: *See* Affective Domain

Kruskal-Wallis Analysis of Variance: In research, a common **nonparametric statistical** test of **analysis of variance (ANOVA)** appropriate in studies involving more than two independent samples and ranked **data**. The Kruskal-Wallis Analysis of Variance (ANOVA) assumes that the independent samples have been selected randomly and that the variable being assessed is at least ordinal. *See* Analysis of Variance (ANOVA); Ordinal Level Measurement

Kwalwasser-Ruch Test of Musical Accomplishment: Published in 1924 and revised in 1927, a battery of tests designed to measure **musical achievement** in grades four through twelve. The Kwalwasser-Ruch Test contains ten subtests: 1) Knowledge of Music Symbols and Terms; 2) Recognition of Syllable Names; 3) Detection of Pitch Errors in a Familiar Melody; 4) Recognition of Time and Errors in a Familiar Melody; 5) Recognition of Pitch Names; 6) Knowledge of Time Signatures; 7) Knowledge of Key Signatures; 8) Knowledge of Note Values; 9) Knowledge of Rest Values; and 10) Recognition of Familiar Melodies from Notation.

Laban Movement Education: An approach to music education developed by Rudolf von Laban (1879–1958) in the early twentieth century that centered on movement activities. Laban movement education emphasized developing awareness of the body and its movement in space. The direct benefits of this approach have not been researched.

Labeling: In education, the classification of students in categories other than normal based on pre-determined criteria. Labeling includes a wide variety of classifications, including **learning disabled**, speech handicapped, **mentally retarded, emotionally disturbed**, and **gifted and talented**. Labeling can help teachers use methods that match the intellectual and cognitive levels of students. However, labeling can also be problematic. First, the criteria for labeling often include assessment procedures and measures such as **intelligence quotient (IQ) tests** that may be misleading or biased. For example, many believe that some **standardized tests** are culturally biased, yet standardized test scores are commonly used for categorizing students. Second, unfair and often inaccurate assumptions about a student's potential are frequently associated with student labels. These assumptions can be detrimental and create serious problems with student achievement and **self-esteem**.

Labiodental: Consonants formed by the lower lip making contact with the upper front teeth. Labiodental consonants include *f* and *v*.

Land Grant College: Institutions of higher learning founded through land grants provided for by the Morrill Acts of 1862 and 1890. Each state was allowed to grant 30,000 acres for each congressman to establish and maintain a college for the state. These colleges were intended to provide more practical education than existing schools funded privately or by religious organizations. Agriculture, military tactics, and "mechanical arts" were the educational focus of these land grant colleges. Several states chose to construct schools away from existing cities, creating such towns as State

College, Pennsylvania; College Park, Maryland; and College Station, Texas. The Second Morrill Act of 1890 was passed to fund colleges for African Americans who could not otherwise attend college in their home state because of **segregation** laws.

Laryngeal Muscles: Muscles that regulate the size of the glottis, control the tension of the vocal folds, and close off the larynx during swallowing.

Laryngeal Muscles

Larynx: Commonly called the voice box, the sound-producing structure at the top of the windpipe (trachea) that contains the vocal folds. Air travels from the lungs, through the trachea, to the **larynx**, where the vocal folds are set into vibration. The larynx is made of cartilage.

Latchkey Child: In education, a term used to describe any child who is home without adult supervision for several hours each day, particularly the time in the afternoon before parents arrive home from work. Increasing numbers of school districts, community groups, and churches offer after-school programs to provide latchkey children with supervision and social interaction. Leaving children home unsupervised for extended periods of time has been linked to low **self-esteem** and failure to reach full potential.

Latency: In behavioral psychology, the time delay between the occurrence of the **stimulus** and the onset of the **response**. In **Freud's (1858–1939) psychoanalysis**, a period in middle childhood during which a child's sexual and aggressive impulses are somewhat subdued. *See* Latency Period

Latency Period: In **Freud's (1858–1939) psychosexual stages**, the period between the phallic stage and the mature, genital stage. According to Freud, during this period (ages six to twelve), children repress memories of infantile sexuality, and their sexual and aggressive impulses are somewhat subdued. As a result, children's attention is directed toward the outside world and their curiosity about their environment is heightened, which makes them receptive to learning.

Latent Content: In Freud's (1856–1939) **psychoanalytic theory**, the true meaning of a dream, as determined through **psychoanalysis**. Latent content includes repressed wishes or desires that are disguised symbolically within the dream. Latent content is opposed to manifest content, which refers to what a person actually remembers about the dream.

Latent Learning: In psychology, a type of learning that does not always manifest itself immediately. Rather, latent learning may become apparent or be demonstrated by a child only after the presentation of an appropriate incentive. Latent learning is sometimes used as proof of cognition, because it demonstrates that learning can occur without reinforcement.

Latent Trait: In general, a trait that is present but hidden in some way or a trait that is not manifested overtly. For example, an individual may possess feelings of anger or hostility inwardly, yet appear quite calm most of the time. In this instance, anger and hostility are latent traits, because they are present within the individual but not readily observable by others. Psychologists believe that latent traits are important components of one's **personality**. In genetics, latent traits are inherited traits that are not immediately or readily observable in the organism. These traits may be passed down from one generation to the next. In research, a latent trait refers to an underlying trait or **variable** that can be identified through **factor analysis**.

Latent Trait Modeling: In research, a statistical process for measuring variables which are otherwise difficult to measure, such as concepts. The process usually involves developing a conceptual model, devising a graph of the model, and testing the model. Latent trait modeling also provides information about the interrelationship of these **variables** and the model being tested and can be viewed as a blend of **multiple regression** and **factor analysis**.

Latin Grammar School: The first formal type of secondary school in the American Colonies. The first Latin grammar school was established in Boston, Massachusetts, in 1635. The students were nine- and ten-year-old boys who could already read and write English. Latin grammar schools focused on teaching Latin and Greek; however, they also offered arithmetics, geography, algebra, trigonometry, and rhetoric. Latin Grammar Schools were used to prepare students for college entrance tests.

Latin Schools: Secondary schools that primarily taught Latin in preparation for college; however, Greek was also taught. Latin schools existed in America, but were unpopular because students who finished the program were qualified only for the ministry, the magistracy, or for teaching in a Latin school. Latin schools were eventually replaced by academies, which emphasized subjects of immediate practical use.

Laws of Learning, Thorndike: From the results of his research, **E. L. Thorndike (1874–1949)** created three major laws of learning, the Law of Effect, the Law of Exercise, and the Law of Readiness.

Law of Effect: One of the three main laws of learning, this states that when an association between a **stimulus** and **response** is followed by a satisfying state of affairs, the association is strengthened. When the association is followed by an annoying state of affairs, it is weakened. In other words, Thorndike believed that the consequences of an activity determine whether or not it will be learned. Reward strengthens and punishment weakens the connection between stimuli and responses. Thorndike's Law of Effect is considered by many psychologists to be the cornerstone on which **B.F. Skinner (1904–1990)** built his system of operant conditioning.

Law of Exercise: This law is comprised of the Law of Use and the Law of Disuse and states that connections are strengthened as they are used (Law of Use) and weakened when they are not used or if the neural bond is not used (Law of Disuse). The Law of Exercise states that the more frequently a **stimulus-response** connection occurs, the stronger the resulting association and the stronger the learning will be. Later, the Law of Exercise was amended to incorporate the importance of the consequences to learning. Thorndike found that practice without knowledge of the intended outcomes is not nearly as effective as practice when the intended outcomes are known to the learner. Generally speaking, the Law of Exercise is similar to the common phrase "use it or lose it."

Law of Readiness: It states that learning occurs when neurological conduction units are primed or ready to conduct. The Law of Readiness refers to momentary readiness rather than maturational readiness. Generally speaking, the Law of Readiness indicates that when one is ready to learn, one will learn.

Learned Helplessness: In psychology, when individuals learn to believe that they cannot do anything to improve their abilities to perform or their situation in a particular environment or a particular type of personality response in which individuals learn to appear helpless. Martin Seligman found that some individuals acquire external behaviors that give the impression they are not competent in some way. People who are more likely to develop learned helplessness include those who are economically disadvantaged, ethnic minorities, those excluded from the mainstream of society, handicapped children, and children who are overprotected or rejected by their parents. Seligman suggests that teachers need to pay careful attention to such children to prevent them from being caught in the syndrome. Setting reasonable objectives in a firm yet supportive atmosphere will avoid reinforcing learned helplessness.

Learning: A relatively permanent change in behavior that occurs as the result of practice and experience. Learning may be conscious or unconscious, adaptive or maladaptive, and overt or covert. Although learning is often associated with observable and measurable performance or **achievement**, such as test scores, learning also involves unobservable changes within the nervous system. Acquiring physical skills, memorizing poems or music, developing attitudes and prejudices, and even tics and mannerisms are all examples of learning. Behavioral changes that are not considered learning include those produced by **maturation**, fatigue, or the influence of drugs are not considered learning.

Learning Curve: A graphic presentation of learning performance that represents the course of learning over a period of time, the shape of which is a direct reflection of the learning process. The amount learned or a measure of proficiency is plotted on the vertical axis (ordinate) and the amount of practice or a measure of practice is plotted on the horizontal axis (abscissa). Proficiency is an indication of the amount learned or errors made in a specified unit of time, while the amount of practice is represented by specified periods of time or the number of trials. Typically, the acquisition of new information follows a predictable sequence. When new material is first introduced, students learn slowly. Soon afterwards, the speed of learning increases dramatically. As students gain mastery of the material, learning speed slows dramatically and improvements are made in smaller increments. When there is no further increase in performance, the learning curve levels off or plateaus. As a result, the classical learning curve is negatively accelerated, although learning curves can take many shapes.

Learning Disability: In general, problems in learning that cannot be attributed to **mental retardation**, sensory impairments, or emotional disturbances. Generally speaking, the term learning disability has become an all-encompassing term for any of the myriad of problems children may experience in the learning process. Learning disabilities may be mild or severe, specific or general, and can result from physiological, psychological, and/or emotional conditions. In 1988, the National Joint Committee on Learning Disabilities defined learning disability as "a general term that refers to a heterogeneous group of disorders manifested by significant difficulties in the acquisition and use of listening, speaking, writing, reasoning, or mathematical abilities." According to the committee, learning disabilities are intrinsic. They occur across the life span and are often due to central nervous system dysfunction. Individuals with learning disabilities often have problems with self-regulatory behaviors, social perception, and social interaction; however, these problems do not necessarily constitute learning disabilities. *See* Disability

Learning Disordered/Disorders: In general, a term applied to individuals who are significantly below average in learning performance in one or more areas when compared to others of similar **chronological age**. The term learning disordered is commonly used interchangeably with **learning disabilities**. However, there seems to be a general move toward using the term learning disabilities as a general, more global term that includes learning disordered. For example, a student who is significantly below average in one subject area, such as math, may be classified as learning disordered, whereas a student who is significantly below average in several areas may be classified as learning disabled. These designations or categorizations are somewhat subjective. *See* Disability; Learning Disability

Learning Domains: *See* Cognitive Domain; Psychomotor Domain; Affective Domain; Aesthetic Domain

Learning Programs: Pre-planned programs designed to help students learn on their own and at their own pace. Learning programs are presented in a systematic sequence and typically increase in difficulty in a progressive manner. Students are rewarded for correct responses.

Learning Sequence Activities: In Edwin E. Gordon's (b. 1927) music learning theory, activities designed to facilitate musical learning by focusing on three sequences: 1) **skill learning sequence,** 2) **tonal content learning sequence,** and 3) **rhythm content learning sequence.** These activities are to be incorporated into the first ten minutes of a class or rehearsal. *See* Music Learning Theory, Gordon

Learning Set: The tendency for individuals to solve problems or learn tasks in a certain way based on prior experiences with solving similar problems or learning similar tasks. Learning sets may be helpful in that they can make learning and problem solving more efficient; however, they can also be problematic. For example, people can become so rigid in their thinking that they are unable to consider different solutions to some problems because they have become "set" in their ways.

Learning Sets, Harlow: A concept developed by Harry Harlow (1905–1981) to describe the phenomenon of learning how to learn. Learning sets are based on the idea that individuals learn or develop rules, relationships, or strategies for learning that are used for processing new information. According to Harlow, the development of learning sets frees the learner from the slow process of trial and error learning. In his studies with monkeys, Harlow found that they became increasingly skilled at solving **discrimination** problems with practice and that they also improved on novel problems as well as those previously learned. He attributed this improvement to the acquisition of learning sets and used learning sets to explain the **gestalt** term **insight.** To Harlow, insight does not occur as the result of a sudden reorganization of **perceptions;** rather, they are a result of learned rules or relationships. Learning sets do not occur suddenly; they are learned or developed through experience over time and can be transferred from one learning situation to the next. In Harlow's view, insight is merely an extension of this type of **transfer.**

Learning Theory: In general, any theory that attempts to explain how learning occurs. In **behavioral psychology,** learning theories are based on the idea that most behavior is learned from environmental experiences (nature) as opposed to inborn **capacity** (nurture). Individuals learn as behaviors are reinforced within their environment. For example, children learn to talk by first imitating their parents and by being praised or positively reinforced for this behavior. In **cognitive psychology,** learning theories are based on the idea that learning results from thinking processes within the brain. In **humanistic psychology**, learning theories are based on the idea that every human being possesses a natural goodness that helps promote or enhance individual development according to personal needs and desires. The most well-known theory about how music is learned is **Edwin E. Gordon's (b. 1927) music learning theory**. Although his music learning theory is quite involved, the key component is **audiation**, or the ability to hear music that is no longer or may never have been physically present.

Least Restrictive Environment (LRE): Language in the **Education For All Handicapped Children Act of 1975/Public Law 94-142** and the Individuals with Disabilities Education Act (IDEA) of 1990 requiring that **disabled** children be educated in the regular classroom with as much interaction as possible with his or her non-handicapped classmates. Disabled children should only be removed from the regular classroom when the environment no longer promotes satisfactory educational progress, even with the help of supplementary aids, **paraeducators**, and other services. Two circuit court decisions, *Daniel R. v. State Board of Education* (1988) and *Roncker v. Walters* (1983), established the most widely used tests for determining whether a student is being accommodated in the least restrictive environment. The *Daniel* test has two parts. First, it must be determined if a disabled child can receive a satisfactory education in a regular classroom with the help of additional services. Second, the school must determine whether the child is being **mainstreamed** "to the maximum extent appropriate." The court acknowledged that mainstreaming offers models for behavior and opportunities for social growth in addition to academic benefits. The Roncker test requires school districts to consider whether services provided in special education schools or programs could be provided in a regular classroom setting. A "**segregated** placement is indicated" if the student's behavior disrupts other students, or if the student is receiving "little or no educational benefit from the educational setting." The *Daniel* test is more commonly used and has essentially been written into the Individuals with Disabilities Education Act (IDEA). *See* Individuals with Disabilities Education Act (IDEA)

Lecture Method: A method of teaching in which the teacher imparts information by talking to or lecturing students. When the lecture method is used, students generally sit passively, and typically take notes or answer occasional questions. The lecture method has been utilized for centuries and is still one of the most popular teaching methods at the high school and college levels. However, some research indicates that methods in which students are more actively involved are more effective in some circumstances.

Lesson Plan: Usually a detailed outline for structuring class time. Lesson plans may include the following: 1) educational objectives for the class, 2) procedures for accomplishing the objectives, 3) materials needed to teach the objectives, 4) the amount of time and in what order information should be presented (pacing and sequencing), 5) assessment of students' progress, and 6) evaluation of the lesson's effectiveness. In **performance-based classes**, lesson plans often include information regarding the warm-up period, secondary and primary pieces to be rehearsed, and the amount of time planned for each piece.

Libido: *See* Psychoanalytic Theory, Freud

Licensing: *See* Certification and Licensing

Life Space: A concept developed by Kurt Lewin (1890–1947) that refers to the psychological context of learning. Life space involves the everyday choices that individuals must make and is the basis of his **field theory**. Specifically, individuals must make decisions based on the attractiveness or unattractiveness of the possible options. For this reason, arranging attractive alternatives or experiences is most beneficial to learning. In education, factors that can influence a student's life space include: 1) school setting or environment, 2) organization of the classroom, 3) classroom atmosphere, 4) teacher characteristics, 5) student behavior, 6) teacher behavior, and 7) teaching style. *See* **Field Theory**

Life-span Psychology: In psychology, the sequence of biological changes that take place over a lifetime. Life-span psychology encompasses all of the mental and physical changes that help mark or define an individual's growth from birth (or conception) to death. *See* **Child Development; Psychosocial Theory/Stages, Erikson's**

Likert Method of Attitude Measurement: In research, one of the most common methods of **attitude measurement** in which data is collected using Likert scales or Likert-type scales. The Likert method was proposed by

Renis Likert in 1932 as an alternative to the Thurstone method. *See* Thurstone, Louis L. (1887-1955); Likert Scale

Likert Scale: The most common scale of **attitude measurement** in music research. Likert scales commonly include five categories, for example: 1) strongly agree, 2) agree, 3) undecided, 4) disagree, and 5) strongly disagree. In most studies involving the use of Likert scales, respondents are asked to choose the scale category which best describes their attitude toward a statement. The following statement is an example: Music Methods was the most valuable course in your teacher-training program at the university level. **Reliability** issues surround the use of Likert scales or Likert-type scales. These issues generally relate to two factors: 1) the number of categories in the scale and 2) the perception of equality between any two consecutive categories. Regarding the first, research has shown that reliability does not necessarily improve by having more than five categories. Regarding the second, because categorical responses are assigned numbers to facilitate quantitative, statistical analyses, researchers must make certain that the perceptual distinction between any two consecutive points on the scale is as equal as possible. *See* Quantitative Analysis

Limited English Proficient (LEP): A designation for students who qualify for instruction in English as a Second Language (ESL) because of limited proficiency in English. Students who are designated LEP are typically not native English speakers and otherwise possess normal learning capacities. *See* Bilingual Education; English as a Second Language (ESL)

Linear Programs: *See* Programmed Instruction

Lingua-alveolar: Refers to the consonants formed by the tip of the tongue touching or near the alveoli, or the area near the teeth ridge. These consonants include: *t, d, n, l, s,* and *z*.

Lingua-dental: Refers to the consonants formed by the tip of the tongue touching the upper front teeth. Example: the *th* consonants in words like thousand, three, or there.

Lingua-palatal: Refers to the consonants formed by contacting the tongue with the hard palate. These include: *sh, zh, ch, dzh, j,* and *r*.

Linguistic Intelligence, Gardner: In Howard Gardner's (b. 1943) theory of multiple intelligences, the ability to use language, either written or spoken, at a very high level. Linguistic intelligence can be used in many ways, including writing, speaking, or storytelling. *See* Multiple Intelligences

Linguistic-relativity Hypothesis/Theory of Linguistic Relativity: The theory that thought processes and perceptions of the world are related to language and the different ways languages are constructed and used. This theory is most often associated with Benjamin Lee Whorf (1897–1941), who, after studying a variety of peoples and their languages, suggested that language affects both **cognition** and **perception** and that the language individuals speak affects their views of reality. While no definitive proof of Whorf's linguistic-relativity hypothesis exists, language's relationship to cognition has been well documented.

Lining Out Method: Also known as deaconing or bawling out, a method for singing psalms to memorized melodies popular in Colonial America. In the lining out method, a deacon called out each line of the psalm and the pitch for the tune was provided by a precantor. The precantor then led the congregation in singing one of the tunes that they had memorized. In Calvinist doctrine, the psalm words were of the utmost importance. Thus, having a deacon read each line first enabled the congregation to understand the words and repeat them correctly. The lining out method also accommodated congregations whose members could not read music and relied on a handful of memorized tunes to which any of the psalms could be sung.

LISREL: In research, a statistical program commonly used in latent trait modeling. *See* Latent Trait Modeling

Literature Review: In research, an in-depth review of studies and other relevant material pertaining to a particular topic being studied or investigated. A literature review typically comprises the second chapter of a thesis or dissertation.

LM Learning: *See* Logico-mathematical (LM) Learning

Localization: *See* Auditory Localization

Location Constancy: The tendency to perceive the place where a resting object is located as remaining the same despite the changing position of the observer. *See* **Perceptual Constancies**

Locus of Control: In psychology, the type of personal control an individual uses. When the locus of control is internal, individuals view themselves as being personally in charge of their own destinies. When the locus of control is external, individuals view themselves as being at the mercy of external circumstances. *See* **Learned Helplessness**

Logical-mathematical Intelligence: In Howard Gardner's (b. 1943) theory of multiple intelligences, the ability to complete complex mathematical computations and to reason inductively and deductively. Individuals who are exceptional with numbers, who are able to calculate figures quickly and accurately, and/or who are adept at reading and using symbols are said to possess logical-mathematical **intelligence**. *See* **Multiple Intelligences**

Logico-Mathematical (LM) Learning: A concept developed by **Jean Piaget (1896–1980)** to describe learning that results from the actions of the learner on the physical environment rather than from the physical environment acting on the learner. LM learning occurs when individuals organize and reorganize actions in a continuous manner based on previous experiences, which leads to understanding. According to Piaget, LM learning is internally motivated. *See* **P (Physical) Learning**

Longitudinal Research: A developmental research method in which the same persons are observed repeatedly as they grow older (usually at pre-determined periodic intervals). Researchers interested in growth and development sometimes conduct studies over a lifetime. **Lewis Terman's (1877-1956)** study of growth trends among intellectually gifted children is an example of longitudinal research. Longitudinal research requires a great deal of researcher patience, but data obtained over long periods of time are often considered to be more valid than those obtained in other research methods. Example: Panel Study Survey.

Longitudinal Study/Method: A research method that involves studying individuals or groups of individuals over a long period of time and taking measurements at periodic intervals. Subjects can be involved in a longitudinal study for several years, or even decades. Longitudinal studies can provide insight into developmental processes, and they are often used to detect possible growth trends or changes in populations over time. The primary problem with longitudinal studies is the extended amount of time they take to complete. As a result, cross-sectional research studies, which involve less time, are often conducted as an alternative. *See* **Cross-Sectional Research**

Longitudinal Waves: *See* Waves

Long-term Memory (LTM): In the **information-processing** model, the second of the two main storage systems. The first, **short-term memory (STM)**, contains information that may be passed along for processing and storage into long-term memory (LTM) after a period of time if sufficient attention (**rehearsal**) has been given to it. Interestingly, traumatic, important, or exciting events may be placed in long-term memory forever without rehearsal. Long-term memory may have the potential for holding encoded information for a lifetime. Verbal representations play a major role in long-term memory and are perhaps why little, if anything, is remembered prior to language acquisition.

Loudness: A subjective, perceptual dimension of hearing closely related to the **amplitude** and **intensity** of a sound source. As a rule, greater amplitude and intensity increase the loudness of a sound; however, sometimes intensity, which is an objective, physical measure, can change without any perceived change in loudness. To a lesser degree, loudness perception is also affected by **pitch** and **timbre**. Research has shown that the human ear is less sensitive to **sine tones** in the very low and very high ranges than to sine tones in the 3,000-5,000 Hz range, and the perceived loudness of **complex tones** differs from that of sine tones. The terms **phon** and **sone** have been used by some researchers to describe subjective loudness levels.

Low-interference Variables: *See* Observational Research

Lower-level/order Questions: Questions requiring responses that emphasize simple **recall** or basic comprehension of factual information rather than conceptual, abstract, analytical, critical, or **divergent thinking** skills. Lower-level/order questions often begin with the words "what," "when," "where," or "who." Some examples of lower-level questions are: When was the Declaration of Independence signed? What year was Johann Sebastian Bach born? Who wrote *The Rite of Spring*? Lower-level questions tend to focus on the memorization of facts rather than on the development of conceptual understanding and are often used to provide a foundation for higher-level/order questions or thinking. *See* **Higher-level/order Questions**

Lyceum: A term commonly used in the eighteenth century referring to out-of-school programs designed to improve the education of adults. Reading circles and debate clubs were common examples of lyceums, and some lyceums offered special musical training. Lyceums were largely replaced by **normal schools** by the mid-1800s, although some exist today.

Macrobeats: In Edwin E. Gordon's (b. 1927) music learning theory, the fundamental beats or the longest beats of equal duration in a rhythmic pattern. A macrobeat is what musicians commonly refer to as the beat. That is, in 2/4 and 6/8 time (usual meters) the quarter note and the dotted quarter note, respectively, are macrobeats. In 5/8 and 7/8 time (unusual meters), the macrobeats are combinations of quarter notes and dotted quarter notes, depending on the structure of the rhythm within the measure. *See* **Microbeats**

Maddy, Joseph (1891-1966): The first supervisor of instrumental music in America, in Rochester, New York (1918). Maddy formed the first National High School Orchestra in 1926 to perform for the **Music Supervisors National Conference (MSNC)** in Detroit, Michigan. The orchestra consisted of more than 200 high school musicians from across the country. After organizing subsequent orchestras, Joseph Maddy and Thaddeus P. Giddings (1868–1954) decided to find a summer home for the orchestra. Maddy and Giddings founded the National High School Orchestra and Band Camp at Interlochen, Michigan, in 1928. *See* **Interlochen Center for the Arts**

Magna Charta of Music Education (1838): A vote passed in August 1838 by the Boston School Board that permitted the committee on music to contract with a vocal music teacher to teach in several Boston public schools. It was the first time that a teacher was contracted by a school board to teach music in the public schools. **Lowell Mason (1792–1872)** was hired to fill the position. Most music educators consider this contract to mark the beginning of public school music education in America. The introduction of music in the Boston public schools was extremely successful, and it ultimately led to the hiring of more music teachers in Boston and other cities. *See* **Boston School Committee**

Magnet School: A type of alternative school that offers a **curriculum** based on a special theme or instructional **method** such as mathematics, the arts, the sciences, foreign languages, or college preparation and honors courses. Magnet schools operate within a public school system and draw students from the entire district. Students who meet predetermined **criteria** attend by choice. Some magnet schools exist as independent structures, while others exist within traditional schools. For example, while a school may offer a traditional educational curriculum, it may also offer a special-ized curriculum for the **gifted and talented**. *See* **Alternative Schools**

Maidstone Movement: A movement toward instrumental class instruction in music education that resulted from the formation of the first violin class in Maidstone, England, around 1905. The Maidstone movement is generally considered to be the key factor in the rapid growth in instrumental class instruction in America, particularly after Albert F. Mitchell, a music supervisor in the Boston public schools, visited in 1910. Murdock and Company, a London music dealer, sponsored class instruction. The Murdock Company supplied the instruments, music, and other equipment, and students were charged only a small amount per week to participate. This arrangement allowed many children, including poor children, to participate in the successful program.

Main Effect: In experimental research, a term used to describe the direct effect of an independent variable on a dependent variable. The main effects are typically related to "answering" the primary questions. For example, if the primary purpose in a research study is to investigate the effects of practice time on sight reading ability, then the main effect would be finding that, in fact, there was a significant effect of practice time (**independent variable**) on **sight reading** ability (**dependent variable**) as determined by a statistical test.

Mainstreaming: In general, placement of persons who might be classified as **handicapped** or disabled within the mainstream of society, particularly in the workplace. In education, mainstreaming usually refers to placing stu-dents who are handicapped, disabled, or **learning disabled** in regular school classrooms for all or part of the school day. Mainstreaming has been the pol-icy since passage of the **Education For All Handicapped Children Act of 1975/Public Law 94-142**. *See* **Inclusion**

Maladaptive Behaviors: Behaviors that are self-defeating, harmful, and/or nonproductive to the individuals who exhibit them. Some examples are drug and alcohol abuse, overeating, and sleep deprivation. *See* Abnormal Behaviors

Malleus: *See* Ossicles/Ossicular Chain

MANCOVA: *See* Multivariate Analysis of Covariance (MANCOVA)

Manhattanville Music Curriculum Program, The (MMCP): A program funded by the U.S. Department of Education in 1965 whose purpose was to develop a sequential music learning program for primary and secondary school students. The project originated at Manhattanville College in Sacred Heart, New York. Grant money was given to achieve the following four objectives: 1) a curriculum guide and materials for a sequential music program; 2) meaningful sequencing of basic musical concepts; 3) a spiral curriculum to help unify music curricula at all levels; and 4) a teacher reeducation curriculum to help them work with the MMCP. The fundamental premise of the program was that real education is not a study about things but an experience inside things. As such, a music curriculum should be designed to promote the teaching and learning of music as a creative art form. The program contained three phases. The first phase (1966) was to gather information on curricula, classroom procedures, and the ways students learn. The second phase (1967) was to refine and synthesize this information into a course of study. The third phase (1968) was to field test the program and make refinements as needed as well as to plan for teacher training and program assessment. The result of the program was the development of a comprehensive curriculum for grades three through twelve (synthesis) and an early childhood curriculum (interaction). In addition, three feasibility studies and twenty-three workshops were conducted to offer music educators alternatives to traditional practices and techniques. Because the requirements for successful implementation were extensive, and because the program was so different from traditional music programs, MMCP was not widely used in its original form; however, the concepts and strategies introduced in the program have been widely adapted for use in traditional school music programs.

Manipulation Check: In research, the process of determining whether the manipulation of an independent variable has the intended effect(s) on subjects. Manipulation checks can take several forms including self-reports, behavioral measures, or physiological measures. For example, if researchers were manipulating anxiety, a self-report manipulation check could tell researchers whether subjects in the high-anxiety group really were more anxious than subjects in the low-anxiety group. There are two main advantages to manipulation checks. First, if a manipulation check is done prior to conducting the actual experiment and it indicates that the **independent variable** does not affect the **dependent variable**, then researchers are saved the time and expense of actually conducting the experiment. Second, if researchers find that there is no relationship between the independent variable and dependent variable or if they obtain nonsignificant results after conducting an experiment, a manipulation check can help identify whether these nonsignificant results are due to problems in the way the independent variable was manipulated. If the manipulation check reveals no relationship between variables, then the nonsignificant results seem logical.

Mann, Horace (1796-1859): One of the most well known advocates for American public education. Mann studied law at Brown University and was later elected to the Massachusetts State Legislature. From 1837 to 1848 Mann was secretary of the Massachusetts State Board of Education, during which time he fought vigorously for educational reform. Mann believed that education in a democratic society should be free and universal and that the key to improving education was to implement a tax-supported system. In addition, Mann believed that well-trained teachers were essential for a proper education, and he helped establish normal schools to prepare future teachers. Mann is often referred to as the "Father of the American Common School."

Mann-Whitney U Test: In research, a test commonly employed in music education when researchers want to determine differences between two independent, randomly drawn **samples**. This **nonparametric** test is appropriate when using small samples and ordinal data. The test measures whether the two groups came from the same **population**. *See* Ordinal Level Measurement

Masking: The perceptual erasure of one sound by another. Generally, higher-pitched, weaker tones tend to be masked by lower-pitched, louder ones. In music, masking occurs in virtually every ensemble experience; however, common playing characteristics of acoustic instruments such as attacks, releases, vibrato, and other factors all reduce the effects of masking by creating non-periodic **transients**. *See* **Timbre**

Maslow, Abraham (1908-1970): An eminent American humanistic psychologist best known for the development of a need hierarchy and for his theory of "**self-actualization.**" Maslow earned his degrees at the University of Wisconsin, culminating with a Ph.D. in psychology in 1934. Maslow taught at Brooklyn College from 1937 to 1951 and at Brandeis University from 1951 to 1969. In *Motivation and Personality* (1954) and *Toward a Psychology of Being* (1962), Maslow suggested that individual needs can be arranged in a hierarchy and that these needs must be met to become self-actualized. According to Maslow, as each need is satisfied, the next higher level need in his hierarchy dominates conscious functioning. *See* **Need Hierarchy, Maslow; Humanism/Humanistic**

Mason, Lowell (1792-1872): Known as the "Father of Music in American Schools," Mason was a bank clerk for fifteen years before pursuing musical activities full-time as an outstanding organist, conductor, music educator, composer, and compiler of music collections. Mason is known for the **singing schools** he organized, particularly the **Boston Academy of Music**, which was established in 1833. In 1834, Mason organized an annual teacher-training class at the Boston Academy. In 1838, he obtained approval from the Boston School Committee to add music as a regular part of the **curriculum**; thus, Mason is credited with bringing music into the public schools. Mason also traveled extensively to promote music education and published more than 100 different music collections for a variety of organizations. These collections include *The Boston Handel and Haydn Society Collection of Church Music* (1822), *The Child's Introduction to Sacred Music* (1829), *The Juvenile Lyre* (1831), *The Boston Academy's Collection of Church Music* (1835), *The Modern Psalmist* (1839), and *The Psaltery, A New Collection of Church Music* (1846).

Mason, Luther Whiting (1828-1896): An innovative and influential music educator best known for developing the *National Music Course*, a graded series published by Edwin Ginn and Company. Mason was a music teacher in Louisville, Kentucky, and in Cincinnati, Ohio, in the 1850s before moving to Boston, where he organized public school music instruction. The *National Music Course* was the first completely planned method book series, and it was modeled after *Hohmann's Practical Course* by Christian Heinrich Hohmann (1811–1861). Mason is often referred to as the father of the American graded series, and his method books influenced American education for more than half a century. The *National Music Course* was used nationwide and translated into other languages. *See* National Music Course, The

Massachusetts School Law of 1642: The first public education law passed in the colonies. The Massachusetts School Law of 1642 required that children be provided a compulsory elementary education, although the law did not require the establishment of schools or indicate the manner in which towns should comply. The law did specify the minimum essential requirements for education and was followed by additional legislation requiring the establishment of schools and specified the subjects to be taught.

Massed Practice/Learning: Learning accomplished in large blocks of time with no break, as opposed to distributed learning accomplished in significantly smaller blocks of time with breaks in between. Cramming for a test the night before is an example of massed practice. Studies indicate that massed practice is less efficient than distributed practice or spaced learning for many activities, especially motor activities. However, massed practice may be more efficient for some intellectual tasks, such as memorizing a passage of poetry or working through a single problem. *See* Distributed Practice/Learning

Master Teacher: A teacher who has demonstrated a high level of competency over an extended period of time. The term master teacher may be used unofficially or may be an official designation in a given district.

Mastery Learning, Bloom: In education, a learning concept developed by **Benjamin S. Bloom (1913–1999)** in the 1960s based on the idea that all students can learn the material or achieve mastery if given sufficient time and that educational institutions should be structured to provide this time. Mastery learning is in contrast to the more traditional idea that some students can master the material and some cannot. Traditional systems typically involve teaching subject matter for a specified length of time and then moving on to new material. In mastery learning, students do not move on to new material until they have mastered old material. This approach necessarily results in the need to adjust curricula based on individual needs. Task selection, time allocation, and efficient instruction are the key elements in mastery learning. In addition, clearly specified learning **objectives**, predetermined performance **standards**, sequenced learning units, **feedback**, testing, and retesting are all integral components of mastery learning. While the **concept** of individualizing **curricula** to ensure mastery is a worthwhile ideal, the implementation of mastery learning was not practical. In reality, students who learn faster were being held back in the education process, and slow learners were falling farther and farther behind. In short, no amount of time guarantees mastery learning in all situations, and determining how to maximize teaching efficiency in classrooms where learning abilities vary widely is always difficult. Ultimately, finding an appropriate balance between these issues is an important consideration for successful mastery learning.

Mastery Play: Any form of play that leads to gaining mastery of new skills. During childhood, certain types of mastery play, such as skipping or jumping rope can help develop physical skills. As children mature, mastery play may include more intellectual games such as chess or other intellectual activities such as playing with words and ideas. *See* **Play**

Matched Groups: *See* Matched Random Assignment

Matched Random Assignment: In research, a **method** of assigning subjects to groups in which pairs are first matched based on some characteristic and then assigned randomly to a group. For example, matching pairs of students on the basis of grade point average or years of private music instruction and assigning one to an **experimental group** and one to a **control group** randomly is matched random assignment.

Matching and Mismatching: In education, a teaching method that involves discovering a student's **cognitive** stage of development, matching learning content and structure to that stage, and gradually introducing mismatches to help stimulate development to the next stage. In other words, a teacher first matches instruction to the student's ability level and then provides modest challenges that will facilitate progress to the next stage of development. Critics point to several problems inherent in this method. First, it is not always possible to accurately determine a student's cognitive stage of development. Second, because students learn differently, matching content and structure for the various learning styles may not be practical in a traditional classroom setting. Third, some students may experience **anxiety** when new material is introduced or when going through developmental transitions. Fourth, some students may be advanced thinkers in certain subjects, but not in others. For matching and mismatching to be effective, all of these **variables** must be controlled for in some way.

Maturation: In general, the normal growth processes resulting in orderly and systematic changes in behavior as human beings and other organisms age. The timing and patterning of these changes are relatively independent of exercise or experience but can be influenced by the surrounding environment. In research, maturation may threaten the internal **validity** of a study. If researchers do not account for maturation changes within individual subjects, the results of a study may be flawed because any differences found may be a result of maturation rather than the **independent variables**.

McClelland, David (1917-1998): A well-known psychologist associated with achievement motivation. McClelland received his undergraduate degree in 1938 from Wesleyan University and his master's degree in 1939 from the University of Missouri. He earned a Ph.D. in experimental psychology from Yale University in 1941. McClelland taught at Connecticut College for Women, Wesleyan University, and Harvard University. McClelland studied the problems of **underachievement** from the viewpoint of both the individual and the entire society. His studies indicate that the achievement motive is composed of the ability to compete with some standard of excellence, to take moderate risks, and to make use of concrete **feedback**. *See* **Achievement Motivation**

Mean: In research, the mathematical average of a group of numbers. The mean is a statistical measure of central tendency, found by adding all of the scores in a **distribution** and dividing by the total number of scores. For example, the mean of 5, 6, 11, and 14 is 9. *See* **Descriptive Statistics; Measure of Central Tendency**

Means-end: A type of heuristic, or problem solving strategy, in which the difference between the desired **goal** and current progress toward reaching the desired goal is assessed and then a way of reducing the difference is found. *See* Heuristic

Meantone Scale/Temperament: A tempered scale or **tuning system** in which the major thirds are pure and all of the tones are made equal to the average, or **mean**, of a major tone and a minor tone. In other words, the thirds are "split in half" to produce the seconds. It is this averaging process that gives the meantone scale or temperament system its name. *See* Temperament

Measures of Central Tendency: In statistics, the average, central, or most frequent scores in a **distribution**. Measures of central tendency describe a group as a whole on the basis of its most common **measurement**. These measures are also used when researchers want to know which score best represents a group of differing scores. The three measures of central tendency are the **mean**, **median**, and **mode**. *See* Frequency Distribution

Measure of Variation: In research, a measure of the dispersion or spread of scores in a **frequency distribution**, which visually shows the range of scores. *See* Dispersion

Measurement/Measurement Scales: In research, the way **data** is measured or recorded. Generally, measurement involves assigning numbers to **observations** according to certain rules (quantification) so that statistical tests can be applied. In experimental research, there are four basic measurement scales: nominal, ordinal, interval, and ratio. Measurements are generally taken using a **measuring instrument** of some kind; however, the precise nature of how data is measured varies considerably. Measurement also helps to objectify the data being collected. *See* Nominal Level Measurement; Ordinal Level Measurement; Interval Level Measurement; Ratio Level Measurement

Measurement Error: In research, the degree to which a **measurement** deviates from the **true score** value, or any variation in measurement that is unrelated to the **variable** or variables being measured.

Measurement Instruments: In research, generally something used to measure or record data. Often simply referred to as "instruments," measurement instruments take many forms including a wide variety of tests, **surveys** and **questionnaires**, forms designed by researchers to collect or record data specific to a given study, and a wide range of mechanical testing equipment designed for specific types of **measurements**.

Medial Consonant: A **consonant** situated within a vowel.

Median: A statistical measure of central tendency and the middle-most score in a **distribution** of scores. The median divides the distribution in half and can be determined by ordering the scores from lowest to highest and determining which score is in the middle. For example, in a distribution of scores including 1, 2, 4, 6, 7, 9, and 10, the median is 6. *See* **Measures of Central Tendency**

Mediation Theory: The theory that learning is facilitated by the use of internal mediators that help form associations between a **stimulus** and a **response**. Internal mediators may be words, concepts, sets, and images that help make stimuli more distinctive, thus making **discrimination** easier. For example, children will learn to distinguish between a flute, clarinet, and oboe more quickly if they attach verbal labels to these instruments. Mediation theory has also been used to explain certain types of learning, such as **paired-association learning**. That is, studies indicate that subjects learn paired words more quickly when there is a meaningful association between the words.

Medium: In acoustics, any solid, liquid, or gas that transmits vibrations from one place to another. Mediums can be one-dimensional, such as the vibration of a string, two-dimensional, such as the vibration of a drum-head, or three-dimensional, such as vibration in the air. In education, medium is also used to describe a discipline, when, through involvement in that discipline, students learn something "outside" of the discipline itself. For example, music teachers may use music as a medium to teach self-discipline and responsibility. Through participation in music, students learn about **nonmusical** or **extra-musical** things. In this case, music is a medium. *See* **Propagation**

Melting Pot: A popular concept used to describe American society throughout most of the twentieth century, related to the idea that people of all **ethnic** backgrounds would be assimilated into American society once they had experienced American life and education. The belief was that immigrants would adopt American **values**, **ideals**, and **standards** and give up those of their cultural heritages. Although this has happened to some degree, many ethnic groups are not fully assimilated into American society. For example, many ethnic groups have formed their own societies, which allow them to maintain, and in many cases showcase, their cultural heritages. In addition, members of a particular ethnic group often live in the same areas or regions of the country; this allows people with similar cultural backgrounds to live in a familiar environment and to support others with similar value systems. Today, many Americans value the social, ethnic, and **cultural diversity** in America. As a result, the term melting pot is not an accurate reflection of American society. *See* Pluralism; Multiculturalism

Memory: Everything a person remembers and the processes involved in remembering. Memory is also used to indicate specific remembrances. The nature of memory is important in education, and there are many theories regarding memory. Efforts have been made to understand the way people perceive, encode, store, and recall information in the learning process.

Memory Trace: According to proponents of the trace decay theory of forgetting, an inferred or hypothesized neurological change (trace) in the brain as a result of learning. Many believe that learning information actually results in new physiological traces that become more permanent or resistant to forgetting with practice, **rehearsal**, and experience. *See* Trace Decay; Trace-dependent Forgetting

MENC Goals and Objectives (GO) Project (1969): *See* Goals and Objectives (GO) Project

MENC Professional Certification: A special certification offered through **Music Educators National Conference (MENC)** to music teachers with eight or more years of experience. To qualify for MENC professional **certification**, candidates must complete the application process. The certificate is renewable every five years. Although not required by states as a prerequisite to teach music in the public schools, it is the "seal of approval" from the leading nationally recognized organization of music educators.

MENC—The National Association of Music Education (NAME): *See* Music Educators National Conference (MENC)

Mental Age (MA): A relative measure of mental growth determined by how well a child performs on certain tasks compared to the average child of the same age. **Alfred Binet (1857–1911)** arranged a series of tasks in order of difficulty and presented them to a group of French children. He discovered the average number of tasks that any age group could pass and defined mental age in terms of the age at which a given number of test items are passed by an average child. Specifically, an average child's mental age is exactly the same as his or her natural age. *See* Intelligence Quotient (IQ); Chronological Age; Basal Mental Age (IQ); Norm-referenced Test

Mental Combinations: In psychology, mentally playing-out a course of action before actually engaging in the action. According to **Jean Piaget (1896–1980)**, the ability to use mental combinations is expressed between eighteen and twenty-four months of age during the **sensorimotor stage** of development. *See* Mental Representation

Mental Imagery: In memory, mental pictures often used to facilitate the memory process. *See* Imagery; Eidetic Imagery

Mental Practice: The process of practicing or rehearsing something in the mind rather than executing the act. In music, mental practice may enhance performance skills, and some musicians use it on a regular basis. Research indicates that mental practice coupled with traditional practice may be the most beneficial way to enhance performance skills. In addition, it appears that individuals must possess the necessary physical skills and understanding of what is involved in performing the act prior to engaging in mental practice for mental practice to be effective. That is, mental practice without the physical ability to perform the act may not be an effective way to improve performance.

Mental Presets: In music, mental models of musical knowledge, skills, and values deeply set or imbedded in memory and based on an individual's prior experiences and learning. When needed, mental presets can be called upon or involved as models of exemplary musical behaviors, helping individuals focus **attention** and guide musical learning. Research on presets has focused on the way mental presets affect the ability to focus attention, the way individuals practice, and the way presets affect musical performance.

Mental Rehearsal: *See* Mental Practice

Mental Representation: In psychology, creating mental images of objects, events, or people that have been seen or experienced previously but that are not actually in view. According to **Jean Piaget (1896–1980)**, the ability to use mental representation is expressed between eighteen and twenty-four months of age, during the **sensorimotor stage** of development. *See* Mental Combinations

Mentally Retarded/Mental Retardation: A general term for individuals with below-average general intellectual abilities accompanied by deficits in the ability to perform normal daily routines. Some consider any child with an **intelligent quotient (IQ)** below 80 to be mentally retarded or mentally subnormal. Most mentally retarded individuals have problems in two or more of the following areas: 1) communication, 2) social skills, 3) health and safety, 4) self-direction, 5) functional academics, 6) emotional control, 7) self-care, 8) work, and 9) leisure activities. Mental retardation has been classified on the basis of IQ scores using both **Stanford-Binet** and **Wechsler** scores, respectively, as follows: 1) mild retardation (52–68 and 55–69), which encompasses approximately 90 percent of those individuals classified as mentally retarded and includes individuals who can function independently in some areas but need help and guidance in others; 2) moderate retardation (36–51 and 40–54), which encompasses approximately 6 percent of those individuals classified as mentally retarded and includes individuals whose abilities are very limited and function on a five-year-old level; 3) severe retardation (20–35 and 25–39), which encompasses approximately 3 percent of those individuals classified as mentally retarded and includes individuals whose abilities are extremely limited and who typically are almost totally dependent on others for basic needs; and 4) profound retardation (below 20 and below 25), which encompasses approximately 1 percent of those individuals classified as mentally retarded who cannot master the simplest tasks and require constant care and supervision.

Most individuals who are mentally retarded are typically impaired from birth; however, some children develop retardation later in infancy or childhood through disease, injury, or physical and emotional neglect over prolonged periods of time. In addition, three general categories of retardation are recognized for educational and training purposes: 1) **educable mentally retarded (EMR)**, 2) trainable mentally retarded (TMR), and 3) dependent mentally retarded. Educable mentally retarded (EMR) children can generally function in regular classrooms. Trainable mentally retarded (TMR) children are generally not capable of traditional academic class work but can learn self-care, safety rules, and social adjustment. Dependent mentally retarded individuals must be under supervision at all times, and many are bedridden.

Mentally Subnormal: *See* Mentally Retarded

Mentoring Program: In education, support systems or programs designed to enhance students' academic success and to help boost the **self-esteem** of **at-risk students**. Mentoring programs often involve pairing younger students with older students who can assist them in the learning process and serve as **role models** for them. These so-called "buddy" programs are common in most states. Mentoring programs are also used to describe programs designed to help new teachers be more effective and productive. *See* Mentors; Peer Tutoring; Cross-age Tutoring

Mentors: Individuals who serve as **role models** or guides for others who are younger or less experienced. Mentors can be anyone in the community, school, or workplace with whom an individual has developed an association or bond. In educational settings, mentors are sometimes individuals who have been selected through a formal process. Mentoring programs are becoming more common and are designed to facilitate the transition into the teaching profession and to provide guidance during the first year or so of teaching. Ideally, a mentor is someone who exemplifies positive attributes and serves as a role model for the person being mentored. People often use the terms mentor and role model interchangeably; however, role models may be anyone a person admires and tries to emulate, such as a famous athlete or performer. Mentors typically play a more active, "hands-on" role in the mentoring process and are usually selected for their experience and expertise.

Merit Pay: In education, a type of **incentive program** that rewards teachers for outstanding performance. Merit pay is typically given in the form of base-salary increases or one-time cash awards. Merit pay programs are intended to supplement and augment the step-by-step progression of traditional salary schedules; however, they are often problematic. Issues regarding the fairness and **objectivity** of decisions regarding merit pay are difficult to resolve, and the money to support merit pay programs is inconsistent from year to year. *See* **Career Ladders**

Meta-analysis: In research, a specific set of statistical procedures for combining the results of a number of studies to provide a general **assessment** of the relationship between **variables**.

Metacognition: In education, the process of "knowing how we know" or of "thinking about thinking." Metacognition involves knowing how to use what an individual knows to full advantage. In practice, metacognition is a kind of self-reflection that enables an individual to strategize, to develop ideas, to solve problems, to correct oneself, and to clarify thinking processes. Metacognition also involves thinking about what one does not know and being aware of a variety of learning strategies.

Metaphysics: A branch of philosophy that deals with the nature of reality. Metaphysics encompasses two main areas: 1) ontology, which is concerned with the nature of being, and 2) cosmology, which is concerned with the nature of the cosmos or universe. *See* **Ontology**

Method/Methodology: In education, an orderly and systematic process of imparting information to students based on philosophical beliefs. Methods or methodologies are often associated with the people who devise them (e.g., Orff; Jaques-Dalcroze) and are purposeful and specific in nature. Teaching **techniques**, **curricular** content and design, teaching styles, types of activities involved, and types of **pedagogical** approaches used are important factors or considerations in establishing any methodology. The manner in which these factors are incorporated, emphasized, or used characterizes each methodology.

Some disagreements exist among educators as to exactly what constitutes a method, and the term itself is often used interchangeably with other terms such as technique or style. Method can also refer to a way of teaching unique to a specific teacher, or it can refer to a recognized system of instruction adopted by many teachers. In music education, the most commonly recognized methods are: **Kodály, Dalcroze, Gordon, Orff, Suzuki, Disciplined-Based Music Education (DBME),** and **Education Through Music (ETM).** Other methods include: **Related Arts, Eclectic, Outcomes-based Education, Integrated,** and **Content Based.**

In general education, some of the commonly recognized methods are: **Expository Method (Lecture Method), Interactive Method, Individualized Instruction, Non-graded School Instruction, Programmed Learning, Performance Contracting, Montessori Method, Outdoor Education, Community Schools, Team Teaching, Microteaching,** and **Open Education.** Keywords or phrases often associated with method include: **child-centered, teacher-centered,** group or individual, and structured or flexible.

Method of Loci: In memory, the process of transforming verbal material into mental images and locating these images at successive positions along a visualized path or route. That is, the **method of loci** involves visually placing items to be remembered in familiar locations. For example, if individuals want to remember a list of items needed from the grocery store, they could visualize these items at various locations throughout their home. If a person needs to buy milk, bananas, laundry detergent, and flour, they could imagine milk being on the doorstep, bananas hanging on the door, laundry detergent on the washing machine, and flour on the countertop. The method of loci is based on the same principles used in the **pegwords method**; however, pegwords involve using a set of words for reference, while the method of loci involves using a set of locations. *See* **Pegwords/Peg Method**

Microbeats: In Edwin E. Gordon's (b. 1927) music learning theory, equal divisions of macrobeats or what musicians commonly refer to as subdivisions. Gordon states that macrobeats may be divided into microbeats in three ways: 1) macrobeats in usual duple meter may be divided into two microbeats of equal duration; 2) macrobeats in usual triple meter may be divided into three microbeats of equal duration; and 3) macrobeats in unusual meter may be divided into various combinations of two and three microbeats, depending on the meter and rhythm. For example, in usual meters, a quarter note may be divided into microbeats of two eighth notes in 2/4 time. In 6/8 time, the dotted-quarter note may be divided into microbeats of three eighth notes. In unusual meters, such as

5/8 time, the quarter note may be divided into macrobeats of two eighth notes and the dotted-quarter note may be divided into microbeats of three eighth notes, or vice-versa. *See* **Macrobeats**

Microteaching: A type of teaching/learning experience often employed in teacher-training courses in which college students are videotaped teaching a short lesson, usually five to ten minutes in length. The tape is played back and critiqued almost immediately. The lesson may be repeated as part of the **learning** process. Microteaching was popularized in the 1960s at Stanford University.

Middle Ear: An air-filled cavity in the ear containing the ossicles (malleus, incus, and stapes) that transmits vibrations to the **inner ear**. The middle ear connects the **eardrum** to the **oval window**. *See* **Ossicles/Ossicular Chain**

Middle-school Movement, The: An educational movement in which the traditional school organization for grouping grade levels is varied. Traditional elementary schools contain grades one through six, junior high schools contain grades seven through eight, and senior high schools contain grades nine through twelve resulting in a six-two-four organizational design. Other organizational designs have been implemented during the last half of the twentieth century. The most common middle school groupings include grades six through eight and grades seven through nine; however, some middle schools include grades five through eight. The general idea behind the middle-school movement is to ease students' transition between late childhood and early adolescence.

Millage Rate: The rate of taxation expressed in mills per dollar, where a mill is equal to $.001, or one-tenth of a cent. In education, millage rate is used to refer to the amount of property tax dollars to be paid within a geographical region to finance educational costs.

Minimal Brain Damage/Dysfunction: A categorization of individuals with average or above-average **intelligence** who display problems or difficulties in language, memory, motor, and impulse-control. Because individuals with minimal brain dysfunction are average or above average in intelligence, they are not considered to be mentally retarded. *See* **Mentally Retarded/Mental Retardation**

Minimum Competency Movement, The: In education, a movement to ensure that students are learning a common body of knowledge and that they can demonstrate at least a minimal level of learning by meeting minimum competency standards. Minimum standards are often defined in terms of what educators, parents, and administrators believe that children will need to know and/or be able to do to become productive members of society. Supporters believe that having students meet minimum competencies will ultimately raise the overall level of **academic achievement**. Critics believe the minimum competency movement has led to an emphasis on and overuse of **minimum competency tests** or **high stakes tests**. They point out that important subject matter is being dropped from **curricula** in favor of training for basic skills tests or **standardized tests**.

Minimum Competency Tests: Tests designed to assess the lowest acceptable level of student performance. Minimum competency tests help ensure that students learn a basic body of knowledge and skills, and are often used to determine if students should move on to the next level. *See* High Stakes Tests

Minority: In general, any group or subgroup within a society that has fewer members than another group within the same society. Members of a minority group often share similar identifiable characteristics, backgrounds, or beliefs that may result in differential treatment. Legally, minority is often used to refer to an individual who is not of legal adult age, or who has not attained the age of majority (eighteen).

Missing Fundamental: In psychoacoustics, the perceived **fundamental pitch** of a **complex tone** as a result of the tone's **partial** structure. Studies show that listeners can perceive the fundamental of a complex tone on the basis of its partials alone, even when the fundamental is missing. That is, the fundamental can be perceived even though there is no physical energy present at that **frequency** level. This **perception** is the reason that the bass can be heard on an inexpensive transistor radio, even though the speakers are too small to produce the fundamental frequencies. *See* Place Theory

MMCP: *See* Manhattanville Music Curriculum Program (MMCP)

Mnemonics: A system for improving or triggering **memory** often involving a set of symbols, words, phrases, or letters. Some examples are Every Good Boy Does Fine for treble clef note names (EGBDF) and My V-Eight Motor

Jumps Sideways Under Normal Pressure for the arrangement of planets from the sun.

Modality: The general idea that individuals have separate senses or sensory departments such as vision, hearing, and smell with which they experience phenomena. Experiences within one modality can be arranged along continuous dimensions with intermediate values. For example, vision may be 20/20, 20/40, or 20/60 where these numbers represent levels of visual acuity. Because these numerical representations fall along a single dimension, it is possible to imagine an experience of 20/30 or 20/50 vision. However, there is no similar way or simple way of moving from one modality to another. For example, it is difficult, if not impossible, to imagine an experience lying halfway between a color and an odor.

Mode: In research, the most frequently occurring score in a distribution of scores. Mode is a measure of central tendency. For example, in the series 2, 3, 4, 2, 2, 5, 6, 4, the number 2 would be the mode. *See* **Central Tendency; Normal Distribution**

Model: In music, an individual who performs or demonstrates exemplary or representative behaviors to be imitated. A model can also refer to the exemplary behavior itself (e.g., producing the desirable articulation), or to the act of demonstrating an exemplary behavior. That is, a model (teacher) models (demonstrates or performs) a model (exemplary behavior). Models also include exemplary recordings that provide an aural illustration of the musical qualities students are learning. All of these models help students understand concepts and are typically used to facilitate musical performances.

In education, a model is generally some form of graph, diagram, flowchart, or other symbolic, visual representation of a concept, process, or other complex phenomenon. The purpose is to organize data based on certain principles to facilitate understanding. Models are constructed in a logical manner in accordance with the information, knowledge, and experience of the person devising the model. Models are often hierarchical and almost always indicate a direction of flow. That is, models indicate what leads to what. The term model has become all-inclusive and somewhat confounded. That is, educators use the term model to describe any program, form, or graphic representation that suits their needs in some way. Furthermore, terms like conceptual **framework**, **paradigm**, network, and

theory are often used interchangeably with model, adding to the confusion. *See* Modeling

Modeling: In music, the process of performing behaviors as examples to facilitate learning either vocally or instrumentally. Modeling is common in **performance-based** classes such as choir and band. Modeling is also common in private lessons and typically involves having students imitate the teacher. Most teachers believe that modeling is an effective "non-verbal" technique for developing **conceptual understanding** and enhancing performing abilities. In research, modeling refers to the construction of research models to facilitate statistical analyses of the **variable**(s) in question (e.g., latent trait modeling). *See* Model; Latent Trait Modeling

Moderator Variable: In research, a **variable** such as age, gender, or **intelligence** that influences or moderates the **correlations** found in **personality** trait research.

Modes of Knowing: In general, a phrase commonly used to describe the ways individuals can know. Philosophers and educators have attempted to explain knowing by identifying schools of thought regarding the nature of what it means to know and how individuals gain knowledge and understanding. In addition, questions regarding the process of knowing and learning are central to all areas of academia, and theories about how individuals know are abundant. In reality, there are many modes or ways of knowing, and an individual's depth of understanding is influenced by several factors including personal experiences, professional education/ training, knowledge of research, environmental influences, and natural abilities.

Modes of knowing are often associated with the four domains of learning: **cognitive, psychomotor, affective,** and **aesthetic**. It is widely accepted that each of these domains contributes to learning in different but important ways. In music, discussions about how music helps individuals to know have focused on all learning domains because music is one of the few disciplines that actively involves all domains at a substantive level. Justifications for music as a curricular subject have also focused on all four learning domains; however, music educators and researchers have focused extensively on how affective components relate to knowing. Specifically, it is believed that affective components such as expression and emotion as well as musical processes such as listening, performing, and composing all contribute significantly to the ability to know. The general idea is that the processes involved in music learning facilitate increased self-awareness, provide insights into relationships and interrelationships that exist within and between individuals and cultures, and open pathways to **creativity**.

Modulation: In physics, a term used to describe any variation in the attributes of a sound. Musically, the lip/jaw vibrato commonly used on the saxophone produces what may be thought of as a kind of frequency modulation because the manner in which the vibrato is produced results in slight, regular variations in **pitch** or **frequency**. The diaphragmatic vibrato produced on flute may be thought of as amplitude modulation, because the manner in which the vibrato is produced results in slight, regular variations in loudness or amplitude. Typically, modulation is used to refer to more regular fluctuations produced at much higher frequencies, such as those used in broadcasting, including frequency modulation (FM) and amplitude modulation (AM).

Monaural: In general, relating to or having to do with only one ear. *See* Binaural; Monotic; Dichotic; Diotic

Mongolism: *See* Down's Syndrome

Monitorial Method: In education, a **teaching method** in which master teachers instruct monitors, and the monitors, in turn, instruct students. This method was designed to facilitate the teaching of large numbers of students and is most common at the university/college level.

Monotic: In acoustical research, when sound is presented to only one ear. *See* Diotic; Dichotic

Montessori Schools/Method: Schools based on the ideas of **Maria Montessori (1870–1952)** or what is commonly referred to as the Montessori Method. Although most Montessori schools are designed for preschool education, some schools provide education through the sixth grade. Montessori's method is based on the premise that children and adults are distinctly and fundamentally different. She believed that it was important to develop a child's creative potential, their natural drive or will to learn, and their right to be treated as individuals. The Montessori method also stresses the importance of the learning environment to the teaching/learning process. As a result, Montessori proposed that educational activities should be correlated with the basic principles of child development and that children learn more effectively in a natural environment conducive to learning.

Montessori, Maria (1870-1952): A well known Italian educator, Montessori earned a medical degree in 1894 and worked in a clinic for mentally retarded children before teaching at the University of Rome. Montessori opened her first children's school in 1907, and for more than four decades she traveled throughout Europe, the United States, and India lecturing and writing about education and setting up Montessori schools. Although most Montessori schools are designed for preschool education, some schools provide education through the sixth grade. Montessori's method or system of education is based on developing children's creative potential, their natural drive or will to learn, and their right to be treated as individuals. Montessori also stressed the importance of the learning environment to the teaching/learning process. These principles are **humanistic** in nature, even though they predate that movement by several decades. Like **John Dewey (1859–1952)**, Montessori believed that children learn and develop new knowledge more effectively by experiencing and doing, by making their own observations, and by learning on their own. In this regard, Montessori's work contributed to the development of **progressive education**. Today, there are hundreds of Montessori schools in the United States and Canada. *See* **Montessori Schools/Method**

Moral Anxiety: In Sigmund Freud's (1856–1939) psychoanalytic theory, the guilt individuals feel about their own unacceptable feelings, thoughts, or deeds. *See* **Psychoanalytic Theory, Freud**

Moral Development, Kohlberg: The developmental processes that enable individuals to learn and adopt guiding principles for determining right and wrong. Moral development is usually based on such factors as age, intelligence, and experience. Individuals use these principles throughout their lives to do what is right and to resist temptations to engage in unacceptable conduct. Although **Jean Piaget (1896–1980)** pioneered the idea that morality develops in a series of growth stages similar to those espoused in his theories of cognitive development, **Lawrence Kohlberg (1927–1987)** is credited with shaping modern thinking about moral development and education. Like Piaget, Kohlberg believed that moral development occurs in a sequence of invariant growth stages and that moral character gets more complex and comprehensive over time. Kohlberg identified three levels, each with two stages, of morality.

Kohlberg identified three levels of morality, with each level containing two stages. At the preconventional level of morality (stages 1 and 2), people make decisions based on their own needs. At the conventional level of morality (stages 3 and 4), people weigh social mores and laws as they make judgments. At the postconventional level of morality (stages 5 and 6), people consider moral issues in keeping with abstract personal or universal principles.

Preconventional Morality (Level 1)
Stage 1: Punishment-Obedience Outlook—where decisions are made on the basis of power. People behave in ways that indicate a desire to avoid severe punishment.

Stage 2: Personal Reward Outlook—where actions are taken to satisfy one's own needs. People make trades and exchange favors but try to come out a bit ahead in the bargain.

Conventional Morality (Level 2)
Stage 3: Social Conformity Outlook—where people make moral judgments to do what is "nice" and what pleases others.

Stage 4: Law and Order Outlook—where people believe that laws are right and they are to be obeyed. They believe that people should respect authority and maintain order.

Postconventional Morality (Level 3)
Stage 5: Social Contract Outlook—where morality is governed by a system of laws based on socially accepted standards. Judgments are not based exclusively on the situation or on a particular rule but viewed in relation to the system.

Stage 6: Universal Ethics Outlook—where behavior is judged on principles, not necessarily written, of justice, of concern for human rights, and of respect for human dignity.

Moratorium: Erik Erikson's (1902–1994) term for a stage of **identity formation** that normally occurs during late **adolescence**. According to Erikson, moratorium is a time for experimentation in which adolescents explore alternatives and possibilities without making final choices. Moratorium typically precedes a commitment to an adult career.

Mortality: In research, the loss of subjects who drop out of an experiment. Mortality is a threat to **internal validity** when the mortality rate is related to the nature of the experimental manipulation or affects the outcomes of the study.

Mother-tongue Method: *See* Suzuki Method

Motivated Forgetting: A type of **forgetting** caused by conscious or unconscious desires to eliminate painful or unpleasant experiences or information. During times of emotional stress, individuals have been known to forget specific events, information, and even friends and relatives; however, they tend to remember historical events and can form new memories normally.

Motivation/Motives: A psychological term used to explain behavior initiated by **needs** and directed toward a **goal**. In general, motivation is what causes individuals to behave in certain ways. Motives may be biologically-based (biogenic) or acquired. Biologically based motives stem from physiological needs within the organism such as the need for food and water. Acquired needs are learned through interaction with the environment, especially the social environment, and include the desire for respect and **self-esteem**. Almost all **personality** theorists have developed their own lists of important human motives, and debates have occurred over which are of greatest importance. **Abraham Maslow's (1908–1970)** hierarchy of needs is arguably the most well-known classical theory of motivation. Among learning theorists, **Jerome Bruner (b. 1915)** placed a great deal of emphasis on the role motivation plays in the learning process. Bruner believed that most children have a built-in "will to learn," which motivates them to achieve. *See* Need Hierarchy, Maslow

Motor Learning/Abilities: The process of learning and developing skills involving movement. Children begin developing **motor skills** during infancy as they move instinctively to environmental stimuli. As children mature, their movements become more coordinated and purposeful. In music education, motor learning is facilitated through a variety of movement activities usually associated with musical performance. The development of motor skills in music generally begins with large muscle groups and involves incorporating body awareness activities into daily lesson plans. These activities typically include clapping, stepping, marching, swaying, running, and jumping. Motor learning activities gradually become more refined as children mature and replace instinctive movement with thoughtful, deliberate movement. Sophisticated movements are required to perform at a high level and require careful control of muscle movement by the mind. Musical performance activities designed to facilitate the development of motor skills include a wide variety of scales, etudes, and solos. *See* **Psychomotor Domain; Psychomotor Skills**

Mozart Effect: In general, the idea that studying music makes an individual smarter. The Mozart Effect became well known after a study entitled "Listening to Mozart enhances spatial-temporal reasoning" by Rauscher, Shaw, and Ky (1995) appeared in *Neuroscience Letters*. The researchers found a relationship between increased **intelligence** and listening to Mozart's music. Controversy surrounding the Mozart Effect centers on the inability of other researchers to replicate the original study. The Mozart Effect has become a more inclusive term for describing the positive benefits of music instruction.

MTNA Professional Certification Program: A certification program of the **Music Teachers National Association (MTNA)** intended to improve the level of professionalism among music teachers. The MTNA Professional Certification program contains five **standards** based on teacher competencies. These include professional preparation, teaching practices, business management, partnerships, and personal renewal. Teachers who meet all five standards are granted certification and designated a National Certified Teacher of Music (NCTM). Teachers must continue to fulfill the five standards through renewal processes to maintain certification.

Multicultural Curriculum: A general term for a curriculum that includes multicultural or multiethnic concepts. Multicultural curricula provide students with opportunities to study various world cultures and **ethnic** heritages and to gain insight into their contributions to the world. Various laws have promoted multicultural curricula, but the most well known are the Education Amendments of 1972, most notably **Title IX.**

Multicultural Education: A movement in education to include information about world cultures into school **curricula**.

Multicultural Music Education: The integration of music from many cultures into music curricula. The purpose of multicultural music education is to increase awareness and understanding of other cultures through music. America is a **pluralistic** society comprised of many cultural heritages and **ethnic groups**. Studying music from these cultures allows students to develop respect and tolerance for **diversity** and to realize that there are many other valid forms of musical expression apart from Western traditions. *See* Ethnic Groups/Ethnicity; Pluralism; Melting Pot

Multifactorial Characteristics: Abilities, qualities, characteristics, or **traits** that are determined by the interaction among both genetic and environmental influences. **Intelligence, personality, talent, ability**, and **achievement** are multifactorial characteristics.

Multimodal Distribution: In research, a distribution curve with more than one mode, or score that recurs most frequently. *See* Mode; Frequency Distribution

Multiple Baseline Design: A research design in which the researcher observes **behavior** before and after a **variable** or variables are manipulated in some way. This manipulation can occur under multiple circumstances, including across different individuals, behaviors, or settings. *See* Baseline

Multiple Correlation: In research, a **correlation** between one **variable** and a combined set of **predictor variables**. *See* Correlation

Multiple Intelligences: The idea that individuals possess many different types of **intelligences** or **cognitive** abilities that, when viewed collectively, constitute intellectual ability. The concept of multiple intelligences is often associated with **Howard Gardner (b. 1943)**, who described seven intelligences in his book *Frames of Mind:* 1) **linguistic,** 2) **logical-mathematical,** 3) **musical,** 4) **spatial,** 5) **bodily-kinesthetic,** 6) **intrapersonal** (knowledge of self), and 7) **interpersonal** (understanding of others). Before Gardner's theory was developed, theories of multiple intelligences, or at least multiple components of intelligence, were proposed by other psychologists. **Louis L. Thurstone (1887–1955)** hypothesized in the early 1920s that intelligence was a composite of special factors, each peculiar to a specific task. **J. P. Guilford's (1897–1988)** factor approach included up to 120 separately identifiable traits for intelligence. Guilford suggested that the ways individuals think, what they think about, and the results of this thinking all help define how intelligent individuals behave.

Multiple Regression Analysis: In research, a statistical procedure in which many variables are related to a single **variable**. Multiple regression is an extension of simple correlation. In a simple correlation, a relationship is found between two variables such as **intelligence** and **creativity**. In a multiple regression analysis, relationships are found between a single variable (e.g., sight reading ability) and multiple variables (e.g., experience, gender, and instrument played). The variables being related to a single variable are called **predictor variables**. In the example above, experience, gender, and instrument played are predictor variables. The single variable to which the **independent variables** are being related is the **criterion variable**. In the example above, sight reading is the criterion variable. The degree of relationship between the predictor variables and the criterion variable is called the **multiple correlation coefficient** (R). This coefficient ranges from -1.00 to $+1.00$ as it does in a simple correlation. *See* Correlation

Multivariate Analysis of Covariance (MANCOVA): In research, MANCOVA is appropriate when the research design has more than one **dependent variable** and when researchers need to statistically control for extraneous variables that might affect the results of the study. As is the case with other analysis of variance designs (ANOVA, ANCOVA, MANOVA) subanalyses or subtests are used to provide information about the data. In other words, once a significant overall test has been identified, it is common to then look at the **univariate** subanalyses of variance in which each dependent variable is analyzed separately. MANCOVA allows researchers to identify which of the dependent variables is producing significant differences for the particular effect while controlling for extraneous variables. *See* Analysis of Covariance (ANCOVA)

Multivariate Analysis of Variance (MANOVA): In research, a statistical procedure appropriate when researchers want to investigate more than one dependent variable in an experimental design. As is the case with other analysis of variance (ANOVA) designs, subanalyses or subtests are used to provide information about the data. In other words, once a significant overall test has been identified, it is common to then look at the univariate subanalyses of variance in which each dependent variable is analyzed separately. MANOVA enables researchers to identify which of the dependent variables is producing **significant** differences for the particular effect. **Wilks' lambda** is one of the most common subtests used in ANOVA designs.

Multivariate Statistics: In research, any number of statistical procedures appropriate in research designs in which researchers analyze the simultaneous effects of phenomena on a number of **variables** instead of just one variable. That is, multivariate statistics allow researchers to determine first whether the **independent variable**(s) produce a significant effect on the **dependent variables**. If significant differences are found, subanalyses are then performed to determine if the significant effect occurred for each of the dependent variables individually. Some examples are **Analysis of Variance (ANOVA)**, **Multivariate Analysis of Variance (MANOVA)**, **Analysis of Covariance (ANCOVA)**, **and Multivariate Analysis of Covariance (MANCOVA)**.

Mundane Realism: The extent to which the **independent variable** manipulation is similar to events that occur in the real world.

Mursell, James (1893-1963): An eminent psychologist best known for introducing **gestalt** concepts to music education. Born in England, Mursell earned an undergraduate degree from the University of Queensland in Australia and a Ph.D. in philosophy from Harvard University. Mursell's first teaching position involved psychology and education courses at Lake Erie College. In music education, Mursell is best known for the **Omnibus Theory**, which proposed that musical talent or musicality is an all-pervasive ability that can only be described as a "whole" and not as a series of fragmented or separate abilities as **Carl Seashore (1866–1949)** suggested in his **Theory of Specifics**.

Music/Musical Ability: A general term for being able to do things musically. Musical ability encompasses a wide variety of skills and other factors including **musical capacity**, **musical aptitude**, **musical talent**, **musical achievement**, and **musicality**.

Music/Musical Achievement: In general, everything that has been learned or acquired through formal musical training, which also includes what has been learned in informal settings. Music achievement is determined in everyday life by performance prowess. In non-performance settings, music achievement is often measured by written and/or listening tests. Music achievement tests measure what has been learned in both general and specific areas including **music reading**, general music knowledge, and aural, visual, performance, and composition skills. The most well-known tests of music achievement include: 1) **Aliferis Music Achievement Test,** 2) Elementary Music Achievement Tests, and 3) **Music Achievement Tests.**

Music Achievement Test (MAT): A music achievement test developed by Richard Colwell in 1969. Originally published as the Elementary Music Achievement Tests, the MAT is comprised of four main tests. Each test is subdivided into three or four subtests: 1) Test 1, which includes pitch **discrimination**, interval discrimination, and meter discrimination; 2) Test 2, which includes major-minor mode discrimination, feeling for tonal center, and auditory-visual discrimination; 3) Test 3, which includes pitch recognition, tonal melody, and melody recognition; and 4) Test 4, which includes musical style, auditory-visual discrimination, chord recognition, and cadence recognition. The tests are in multiple-choice format, and the musical examples are performed on cello, piano, viola, or violin. The MAT may be the most widely known, comprehensive music achievement test in music education.

Music Appreciation: In general, a term sometimes used to describe music courses taught at the high school or college level in which students learn basic facts and knowledge about music. These courses include information about instrumentation, composers, musical styles, and compositional forms. The primary **objective** of music appreciation courses is to develop students' musical **discrimination** skills and to increase their general understanding of the role music plays in their lives.

Music/Musical Aptitude: The potential for learning music or for developing musical skills. Musical aptitude includes **music capacity** plus the results of environmental influences. **Edwin E. Gordon (b. 1927)** has written extensively on music aptitude from a developmental perspective. He believes that one's music aptitude level is highest at birth and becomes stabilized at age nine. Gordon also believes that the musical environment in the early years is critical to the development of music aptitude. Tests have been devised to measure aptitude for music. Such tests often include a series of **discrimination** tasks involving such elements as **loudness, pitch, timbre**, duration, tempo, phrasing, balance, style, form, melody, harmony, and rhythm. Skepticism regarding the accuracy, validity, or usefulness of aptitude tests in predicting music potential exists within the profession. Two main factors contribute to this skepticism: 1) research shows that **nonmusical** factors like **academic achievement, intelligence**, and socioeconomic background are significant predictors of musical ability and 2) the discrimination task format of traditional **aptitude tests** may be nonmusical and thus inappropriate. The most well known music aptitude tests include **Seashore Measures of Musical Talents**, Gordon Musical Aptitude Profile, and Measures of Musical Ability.

Music Aptitude Profile (MAP): *See* Musical Aptitude Profile (MAP)

Music Aptitude Tests: Tests designed to measure an individual's **aptitude** in music. *See* Music/Musical Aptitude

Music Babble/Music Babble Stage: In Edwin E. Gordon's (b. 1927) **music learning theory**, the stage during which very young children produce musical sounds that are not recognizable as melodic patterns. The music babble stage is similar to the speech babble stage of language development, during which very young children make speech sounds that are not recognized as words. According to Gordon, there are basically two types of music babble: tonal babble, which includes developmental aspects of pitch and tonality, and rhythm babble, which includes developmental aspects of rhythm. In the early stages of music babble (birth to eighteen months), children audiate subjectively, and the syntax of this audiation is not influenced by culture. Children emerge from music babble at around eighteen months, when they audiate objectively and the syntax is influenced by culture.

According to Gordon, the following statements can be made about music babble. First, children should be expected to emerge from music babble at an early age; however, some children will do so before others. Second, children can emerge from tonal babble before they emerge from rhythm babble, and vice versa, based on their level of **music aptitude**. Third, with appropriate music guidance and instruction, most children should emerge from music babble between the ages of five and nine, both tonally and rhythmically. Fourth, children who receive music guidance during this stage will emerge from music babble sooner than those who do not. Finally, some individuals never emerge from music babble; that is, they cannot distinguish among tonalities, sing with good intonation, distinguish among meters, perform with continuous flowing movement, or perform with coordinated body movements at a consistent tempo. *See* Audiation; Musical Syntax; Music Learning Theory, Gordon

Music Content: In Edwin E. Gordon's (b. 1927) music learning theory, the actual music materials or elements used when making music. Tonality, meter, and melody are examples of music content, which cannot be realized without music skills. Music skills and music content are combined to accomplish the act of making music, including reading, writing, performing, and listening. *See* Music Skills; Music Learning Theory; Gordon, Edwin E. (b. 1927)

Music Educators Journal (MEJ): An official publication of the **Music Educators National Conference (MENC)** and one of the most widely read journals in music education. The *MEJ* focuses on articles related to teaching methodologies, philosophies, current trends and issues in music education, and current products and services. The *MEJ* is published five times per year. Originally the *Music Educators Journal (MEJ)* was called the *Music Supervisors Bulletin* and was published four times per year. In 1915 the name was changed to *Music Supervisors Journal*, and in 1934 the name was changed to *Music Educators Journal (MEJ)*.

Music Educators National Conference (MENC): The leading national organization for music education. MENC is an advocate for all of music education at all levels of instruction. Founded in the early 1900s as the **Music Supervisors National Conference (MSNC)**, the organization became the Music Educators National Conference in 1934. In the late 1990s, the name was modified to: MENC—The National Association for Music Education (NAME). In addition to extremely high rates of membership among professional music educators, many colleges and universities have active college chapters. MENC offers a wide range of materials of interest to music educators and publishes several journals for a wide audience, including *General Music Today (GMT)*, *Journal of Music Teacher Education (JMTE)*, *Journal of Research in Music Education (JRME)*, *Music Educators Journal (MEJ)*, *Teaching Music (TM)*, and *UPDATE: The Applications of Research in Music Education (UPDATE)*.

Music Educators Research Council (MERC): The branch of the **Music Educators National Conference (MENC)** responsible for research activities. Historically, MERC began as the Educational Council in 1918 and was responsible for publishing bulletins on **curricular** matters, music supervisor training, and other topics related to music education. The name of the Educational Council was changed to the National Research Council on Music Education in 1923 and finally to the Music Education Research Council (MERC) in 1932. Today, MERC is the governing body of the **Society for Research in Music Education (SRME)**.

Music Intelligence: A type of **intelligence** that enables individuals to excel in music. Music intelligence has been examined by several psychologists, including **James Mursell (1893–1963)**, **Carl Seashore (1866–1949)**, and **Howard Gardner (b. 1943)**. Theories about music intelligence vary considerably among these psychologists. Gardner suggests in his book *Frames of Mind* that intelligence is a multifaceted concept and that there is indeed a musical intelligence. One of the greatest controversies regarding music intelligence is whether such intelligence is a general, all-pervasive measure as Mursell suggested or whether it is task-specific, as Seashore suggested. This debate has become a classic in music education. While the concept of music intelligence is accepted by many psychologists and music educators, the precise relationship between intelligence and musicality is not known. *See* **Multiple Intelligences, Gardner**

Music Learning Theory, Gordon: A comprehensive theory of the music learning process that attempts to explain how individuals learn **music skills** and **music content** developed by **Edwin E. Gordon (b. 1927)**. Music Learning Theory is based on evidence from research in the psychology of music and related disciplines and on concepts borrowed from the work of **Robert Gagne (1916–2002)** and **Jean Piaget (1896–1980)**. Music Learning Theory is not a method or a set of techniques; rather, it is a theory explaining how individuals learn music and a skill-learning hierarchy of musical development. Gordon's learning theory consists of three music learning sequences: skill learning sequence, tonal content learning sequence, and rhythm content learning sequence. Each of these sequences consists of two general types of learning, **discrimination learning** and **inference learning**. Gordon's music learning theory is based on audiation, or the ability to hear and comprehend music in the brain without the physical presence of sound. That is, audiation is fundamental to music aptitude and music achievement and is the basis of Gordon's music learning theory. *See* Audiation; Tonal Content Learning Sequence; Rhythm Content Learning Sequence; Skill Learning Sequence

Music Literacy: A general term used to describe the processes of understanding music from both an aural and a visual perspective. Research on music literacy has focused on several areas, including: 1) reading music notation, 2) aural and visual **discrimination** skills, 3) performing skills, 4) compositional skills, 5) the effects of instructional methods on music literacy, 6) music **perception**, and 7) critical thinking skills. In recent years, much has been made of the importance of learning literacy in general education, and attempts to link music literacy with non-music literacy have been somewhat problematic at the university level. Problems stem from the fact that the processes involved in music literacy are fundamentally different in many regards from those involved in learning literacy.

Music Memory Contests: In music education, contests that tested students' memory of musical selections. Music memory contests were popular in America from World War I to about 1930. People associated with music memory contests include **Edward Bailey Birge (1868–1952)**, who used music memory contests informally in Indianapolis schools as early as 1909, and C. M. Tremaine, who used music memory contests in Westfield, New Jersey. Typically, music memory contests involved playing excerpts of pieces and having students identify the title and composer of the composition, although some contests asked students to answer questions about style, form, and history. Training and studying for the contests often became a community effort involving music clubs, music dealers, and the local press. Music memory contests were generally not strongly supported by music supervisors, who preferred to emphasize music performance over academic exercises like music memory contests.

Music Perception: The way individuals perceive music through the senses, encompassing both the psychoacoustical and the cognitive aspects of musical sound. More specifically, music perception involves the sensory and cognitive attributes of **pitch, timbre, loudness,** and **duration** (time and space) and the perceptual awareness of how music incorporates these attributes. *See* Aural Discrimination

Music Psychology: The study of the ways music influences human behavior and of the ways music is used by human beings.

Music Reading: The process of seeing music notation, interpreting this notation, and performing accordingly. Music reading is the process of identifying visual cues (notes, expression markings, tempo indications, etc.) and performing a series of physical and mental actions necessary to produce the desired sound or sounds. Music reading has been a fertile area of research. Researchers have focused on the psychological and musical connections between the musical symbols, physical actions, and sound. Specific areas of research include rhythm, melody, the relationship between music and language reading, notation, context, and eye movement.

The results of such studies indicate the following:

1. When good musicians sight read, they add an expressive component to the notes played; that is, they not only "read" the symbols, but they add their own sense of musicality to the performance based on previous experience.
2. Musical training and experience improve music reading skills.
3. The precise relationship between music reading and language reading is not known; however, although some studies have not found close relationships between music reading and language reading, most studies have shown a strong relationship between the two.
4. There seems to be an accepted belief among educators that music reading leads to improvement in language reading as well as in other subject areas.
5. Music readers tend to fill in missing information and to correct "wrong" information based on previous experience and expectation, a phenomenon similar to what language readers refer to as "proof-readers' error."
6. The eyes move in rapid jerks during which time there is no clear vision; they scan material very quickly, then pause briefly, and it is during these pauses that individuals actually comprehend the material.
7. Music reading is affected by the type of notation and by the complexity of the notation.
8. The average visual grasp is three to five notes.
9. The rate of music reading is dependent upon improvement in the ability to grasp rhythmic figures.

10. Skilled music readers observe more dynamic and expression markings than non-skilled readers.

The major challenge for educators is how to teach students to translate what they see on paper into musical sounds in the most efficient manner. *See* Sight Reading

Music Skills: In Edwin E. Gordon's (b. 1927) music learning theory, the physical act of engaging in music activity, including reading, writing, listening, performing, and improvising. Music skills are used to realize music content. Music learning theory categorizes the ways individuals learn, perform, create, and listen to music.

That is, music skills and music content are combined to accomplish the act of making music, including all of the musical activities mentioned above.

Music Societies: In the United States and other countries, usually amateur organizations that provide outlets for musical creation and expression. Music societies gained considerable popularity in the United States in the early 1800s. They were sometimes established to maintain music in communities after singing school masters moved on to other locations. One of the most famous music societies in America is the **Boston Handel and Haydn Society.**

Music Supervisors Bulletin: The first official publication of the **Music Supervisors National Conference (MSNC).** The purpose of the bulletin was to increase the awareness of MSNC. The *Music Supervisors Bulletin* began in 1914 and was renamed *Music Supervisors Journal* in 1915.

Music Supervisors Journal: Originally named the *Music Supervisors Bulletin,* this journal was the official publication of the **Music Supervisors National Conference (MSNC)** from 1915 to 1934, when it was renamed *Music Educators Journal (MEJ).*

Music Supervisors National Conference (MSNC) (1907): An organization whose purpose was to promote music education in the public schools. Before MSNC was established, the music section of the **National Education Association (NEA)** represented the interests of music education. MSNC was established in 1907 as a result of a national meeting of music supervisors in Keokuk, Iowa, in 1907. The meeting is usually credited to **Philip Cady Hayden (1854–1925)**, the music supervisor of Keokuk. He was interested in promoting his new method of practice called "rhythm forms" as well as offering an alternative to the meeting of the music section of the NEA held in California. The group officially adopted a constitution and a board of directors in 1910 and officially became known as the Music Supervisors National Conference (MSNC). The organization flourished, and in 1934 became the **Music Educators National Conference (MENC)**. *See* Music Supervisors Journal; Call to Keokuk

Music Teachers National Association (MTNA): An organization founded in 1876 to promote the welfare of music education, music study, and music making in American society. MTNA was founded by Theodore Presser and his colleagues in Delaware and Ohio and is the oldest non-profit music teachers' association in the America. Membership includes a wide variety of professional music teachers and college students.

Music Technology: *See* Computer Programs, Music

Music Tests: A general term used to describe any evaluation or **assessment** of **musical ability**, **achievement**, **attitude**, or **aptitude**. Music tests may be published, or they may be teacher-constructed. Music tests often ask test-takers to perform aural recognition tasks, aural/visual **discrimination** tasks, preference/sensitivity tasks, and performance tasks. Music tests may appear in several formats, including: 1) paper-and-pencil tests, 2) performance tests, and 3) **computer-based** tests. Examples of well known music tests include the **Watkins-Farnum Performance Scale (WFPS)**, the **Music Aptitude Profile (MAP)**, and the **Music Achievement Test (MAT)**.

Music Theory Courses: Courses that emphasize the basic fundamentals of music notation, scales, intervals, chord structures, chord progressions, harmonies, and four-part writing. Music theory courses are sometimes offered at the high school level as Advanced Placement (AP) theory for advanced music students and are almost universally part of core curricula for music degree programs at the university level. A very solid background in music theory is recommended for teaching theory courses and at least some piano skills can be very helpful. Music theory, particularly at the college freshman level, is sometimes called Basic Musicianship or Fundamental Musicianship.

Musical Anxiety: *See* Performance Anxiety

Musical Aptitude Profile (MAP): A music aptitude test devised by **Edwin E. Gordon (b. 1927)** in 1965. Designed to be used in grades four through twelve, the MAP consists of three main sections: 1) tonal imagery, which includes melody and harmony; 2) rhythm imagery, which involves tempo and meter; and 3) musical sensitivity, which includes phrasing, balance, and style. The test uses "real" musical examples played on violin and cello as opposed to electronically-produced examples. In the first two sections of the test, students are asked to indicate whether two phrases are the same or different. The differences are the result of manipulating a single **variable** such as tempo. The third section of the test asks students to indicate their preference for pairs of phrases. The test takes about three hours to administer or approximately one hour per section. Administration requires a test manual, a tape of musical examples, and answer sheets. MAP is probably the most widely known music **aptitude** test in music education.

Musical Attitudes: A general term describing what people like and do not like about music or how people feel about music. Music educators help shape student attitudes about music by increasing students' understanding, knowledge, and appreciation of musical attributes. Through involvement in music education programs, students learn to develop more sophisticated attitudes toward music by learning to make more informed, knowledgeable choices about music.

Music/Musical Capacity: The portion of a person's **musical ability** either genetically endowed or due to **maturation**. Capacity refers to innate abilties or biological potential to be musical or execute musical behaviors.

Musical Concepts: The properties, characteristics, or relationships common to musical attributes that facilitate understanding or recognition. Concepts may be concrete, such as the length of a quarter note in 4/4 time at various tempi, or abstract, such as what constitutes a "good" tone quality on a given instrument. Musical concepts are used to classify or organize ideas or thoughts about music, and they are often difficult to define or explain verbally. Musical concepts can be broad, such as understanding the difference between Baroque style and Rock, or narrow, such as understanding the subtle stylistic differences between two similar Baroque pieces. In both instances, the development of musical concepts leads to musical thinking and understanding within individuals. *See* Conceptual Understanding

Musical Intelligence: In Howard Gardner's (b. 1943) theory of multiple intelligences, the capacity to discriminate between musical pitches, to identify musical themes and formal properties of music, to sense and understand rhythm, to detect timbral differences, and to recognize and understand musical texture at a very high level. Outstanding performers, composers, conductors, and listeners are said to possess musical intelligence. *See* Multiple Intelligences, Gardner

Musical Modeling: *See* Modeling

Musical Syntax: The organization and patterns of sound in a piece of music and the way these sounds relate to each other in a musical context. Listeners derive meaning from musical syntax based on such things as experience, background, training, and education, but this meaning may vary among individuals. Musical syntax is related to language syntax; however, in language, words and sentences generally have concrete meanings. By contrast, a musical phrase can have different meanings to different individuals.

Musical Talent: In general, a special or natural ability or **aptitude** in some area or areas of music. **Musical talent** is generally associated with musicians who perform at a high level, although the term is used inconsistently in music education literature to describe a variety of abilities, **aptitudes**, and acquired skills.

Musicality: The state of being musical or being sensitive to changes in musical stimuli. Musicality is usually, but not always associated with someone who has outstanding performance and/or listening skills. Some individuals possess excellent listening skills and a deep appreciation of music with limited or no performing skills.

Musicing: A term used by David Elliott when discussing the fact that even though there is no biological reason for the existence of music, music is an integral part of most, if not all, societies. In his view, life without musicing and music-listening would not be human as we know it.

Nn

Nägeli-Pfeiffer: A music method emphasizing the study of music in the context of rhythm, melody, and dynamics developed by Hans Georg Nägeli (1773–1836) and Michael Traugott Pfeiffer (1771–1849) in the early 1800s. The Nägeli-Pfeiffer method is based on the teaching principles of **Johann Heinrich Pestalozzi (1746–1827)** and was the first to apply these principles specifically to music learning. The original manuscript contained no songs and no harmony; however, songs and/or harmony were added in later editions. The works of Nägeli and Pfeiffer were used by **Lowell Mason (1792–1872)** and others in early American music instruction.

Nation at Risk, A: A 1983 report from the National Commission on Excellence in Education on the state of America's educational system, fully entitled A *Nation at Risk: The Imperative for Educational Reform*. The report indicated that American students were academically behind students from other industrialized nations in certain areas and made several criticisms regarding teaching and learning in America. They include: 1) educational **curricula**, educational leadership, and teacher preparation programs lack vision and promote poor educational standards; 2) students do not spend enough time doing homework; 3) curricula have been diluted and diffused to the point that a central purpose no longer exists; 4) there is a shortage of qualified teachers, particularly in math, science, and foreign languages; and 5) teachers are underpaid. The report indicated that wholesale changes in education were needed, and several recommendations were made, including: 1) that a basic curriculum for high school graduation include a minimum of four years of English, three years of mathematics, three years of science, three years of social studies, and one-half year of computer science; 2) that, in addition, college-bound students take two years of a foreign language; 3) that the standards and expectations of students should be raised; 4) that teacher-training programs need to be improved; and 5) that teachers' salaries need to be raised to improve teacher quality.

A *Nation at Risk* caused great controversy throughout the country. Some educators agreed with the report, while others felt that it was unfairly critical and an inaccurate reflection of the educational system. Arts educators were generally upset because the report placed virtually no emphasis on improving arts education, including music education. Instead, the committee placed emphasis on what it considered to be the new "basics" including English, math, science, social studies, and computer science. *A Nation at Risk* caused national alarm in much the same way as when the Soviet Union launched *Sputnik I* in 1957. The report and subsequent discussions about it led many people to believe that American students were not achieving academically as well as many foreign students. Although this perception was not entirely accurate, public concern was real, and the demand for educational **accountability** and reform grew. *A Nation at Risk* helped change American education. It resulted in an increased emphasis on math, science, social studies, computer science, and English courses, changes in curricular design and content, and changes in school schedules. For example, **alternative school** schedules such as **block scheduling** are outcomes of *A Nation at Risk*.

National Alliance for Arts Education: An organization devoted to strengthening arts in education at the national, state, and local levels. The National Alliance for Arts Education was founded in 1973 by the John F. Kennedy Center for the Performing Arts and the United States Office of Education (USOE), in cooperation with national arts education organizations, including the **Music Educators National Conference (MENC)**. The National Alliance for Arts Education supports a variety of arts activities, including music, that are designed to promote and facilitate art education.

National Assessment of Educational Progress (NAEP): A congressionally mandated battery of **achievement tests** developed and overseen by the **Educational Testing Service (ETS)** to assess the effects of schooling across the nation. Since 1969, the NAEP has been actively involved in helping maintain high **standards** of achievement through its testing programs.

National Association for the Education of Young Children (NAEYC): The largest professional association for early childhood educators. NAEYC was founded in 1926, and its focus is early childhood education through the third grade.

National Association for the Study and Performance of African-American Music (NASPAAM): A nonprofit organization dedicated to promoting, performing, and preserving African-American music. NASPAAM was founded in 1972 in Atlanta, Georgia, as a protest to being excluded from the **Music Educators National Conference (MENC)** divisional and national planning sessions and programs. Originally called the National Black Music Caucus (NBMC), the name was changed in 1997. NASPAAM publishes the quarterly national newsletter *Con Brio* for its members.

National Association of College Wind and Percussion Instructors, The (NACWPI): An organization formed to facilitate communication between applied music instructors on college campuses. NACWPI is open to university, college, and conservatory teachers and is dedicated to promoting several aspects of wind and percussion performance and teaching at the college level.

National Association of Jazz Educators, The (NAJE): *See* International Association of Jazz Educators (IAJE)

National Association of Schools of Music (NASM): The accrediting agency for music and music education programs at the university/college level. NASM publishes curricular recommendations and requirements for member institutions. These institutions are reviewed and required to report to NASM to ensure minimum requirements are met. The NASM standards significantly influence college music and music education programs. *See* Accrediting Agencies

National Association of Teachers of Singing (NATS): The largest association of vocal instructors and teachers of singing in the world. NATS is a nonprofit organization dedicated to excellence in vocal teaching, performance, and research. NATS is comprised of members from more than twenty-five countries, including the United States and Canada. NATS promotes professional development for its members through conventions, workshops, and a professional publication, *Journal of Singing*.

National Band Association, The (NBA): The largest band directors' professional association dedicated to the promotion of excellence in all aspects of wind bands, including band performance, education, and literature. Any individual associated with bands in any way may become a member. The NBA provides members with publications, mentor opportunities, and literature lists. The NBA was founded in 1960 by Traugott Rohner, then publisher and founder of *The Instrumentalist* magazine.

National Black Music Caucus, The: *See* National Association for the Study and Performance of African-American Music (NASPAAM)

National Board for Professional Teaching Standards (NBPTS): A nonprofit organization charged with the task of creating a national system to regulate advanced certification for outstanding teachers. The NBPTS was formed in 1987 in response to a recommendation made by the Carnegie Task Force on Teaching as a Profession and is comprised of teachers, administrators, curriculum specialists, state and local officials, union and business leaders, and higher educators.

National Center for Education Statistics (NCES): An arm of the United States government's executive branch responsible for collecting and analyzing statistics on education.

National Certification: In education, a system of certification in which individual teachers are recognized for outstanding service to the profession. *See* National Board for Professional Teaching Standards (NBPTS)

National Congress of Parents and Teachers (PTA): The largest non-profit volunteer organization for child advocacy in the United States. The PTA's membership includes parents, educators, students, and citizens active in their schools and communities. The primary goals of the PTA include: 1) promoting legislation designed to benefit children at the state and national levels, 2) bringing parents and teachers together in cooperative ways to improve education, and 3) bringing teachers and the general public together in cooperative ways to provide maximum advantages for all children.

National Council for the Accreditation of Teacher Education (NCATE): A coalition of thirty-five professional organizations that acts as a professional accrediting body for teacher education. NCATE is recognized by the United States Department of Education (USOE) and the Council for Higher Education Accreditation (CHEA). More than 500 institutions are currently accredited by NCATE. The primary goal of NCATE is for accrediting and state licensing authorities to coordinate their activities to bring a level of consistency to teacher education standards. Partnerships between NCATE, states, and higher education institutions have facilitated the matching of licensing requirements and preparation standards between these entities. NCATE promotes a performance-based accreditation system or a licensing system that evaluates teaching candidates' knowledge and skills, rather than "seat time" in courses. The council also works with the **Educational Testing Service (ETS)** to align licensing assessments with the profession's standards in various subject areas. Most states have integrated NCATE's professional review of colleges of education with their own review processes as a way of strengthening teacher preparation programs.

National Defense Education Act (NDEA): Federal legislation passed in 1958 providing funds for education at all levels in both public and private institutions. NDEA was primarily designed for the advancement of subjects considered basic, including science, mathematics, and modern foreign languages. NDEA also provided some funds for other areas as well, including technical education, vocational training, geography, **English as a second language (ESL)**, school libraries, and educational media centers. NDEA authorizes funds to institutions of higher education for 90 percent of the capital used for low-interest loans to students and provides a number of fellowships. The act also provides federal support for improvement and change in elementary and secondary education. It specifically prohibits federal direction, supervision, or control over the **curriculum**, program of instruction, administration, or personnel of any educational institution.

National Education Association (NEA): An organization dedicated to the advancement of education. Founded in 1857, the NEA has more than two million members, including teachers, administrators, higher education faculty, college students, guidance counselors, librarians, secretaries, bus drivers, and custodians. The NEA is actively involved in virtually all aspects of education including negotiating teacher salaries, reporting educational research, and supporting teachers' professional development. In addition, the NEA is one of the most effective lobbying organizations in the nation and was instrumental in creating the **National Council for Accreditation of Teacher Education (NCATE)**, an organization that monitors the quality of collegiate teacher education programs at the national level. *See* **American Federation of Teachers (AFT)**

National Education Goals, The: Goals established in the 1990s under the leadership of Presidents George H. W. Bush and Bill Clinton. In 1989 President George Bush and the nation's governors met in Charlottesville, Virginia, to begin crafting the National Education Goals; they set the year 2000 as the target date for achieving these goals. To ensure the success of this endeavor, the National Education Goals Panel was established. The panel included eight governors, four members of Congress, four state legislators, the U.S. secretary of education, and the president's domestic policy advisor. By 1994, six goals had been established. Under President Clinton, two more goals were added. In 1994, eight National Education Goals were formalized into law with the passage of the **Goals 2000: Educate America Act**.

National Education Goals Panel: A panel established under President George H. W. Bush in 1989 preceding the passage of **Goals 2000: Educate America Act**. The National Education Goals Panel was formed to develop and draft the National Education Goals, which were to provide a national framework for education reform. The panel published a report entitled *National Education Goals Report: Building a Nation of Learners* in 1997 and was dissolved in 2002 after helping establish eight National Education Goals.

National Endowment for the Arts (NEA): Established by Congress in 1965, an independent agency dedicated to promoting excellence in the arts, bringing art to all Americans, and providing leadership in arts education. The NEA funds more arts programs than any other endowment, bringing art to cities, rural areas, and military bases nationwide. The goals of the NEA 2003–2008 strategic plan are artistic creativity and preservation, learning in the arts, access to the arts, and partnership for the arts. A primary function of the NEA is to award grants to further its goals. Grant awards are made in several areas of the arts, including music, dance, literature and theater and are designed to promote access to the arts, arts learning, creativity, folk arts, leadership initiatives, technology, and organization.

National Goals and Standards: *See* Goals 2000: Educate America Act; National Education Goals

National Interscholastic Music Activities Commission, The (NIMAC): An auxiliary commission of the **Music Educators National Conference (MENC)** that represented the contest and festival movements. Several organizations merged after World War II to eventually become NIMAC, including the National High School Band Association, the National High School Orchestra Association, and the National School Vocal Association. An important activity of NIMAC, beginning in 1952, was the publication of lists of selected pieces of music for use in contests and festivals, and the publication of prepared adjudication forms. In 1963, NIMAC published the *NIMAC Manual,* a guide for those engaged in interschool music activity. NIMAC was dissolved in 1968 because too many contests and festivals were being controlled by other state and regional organizations.

National Music Course, The: A graded music series written by Luther Whiting Mason (1828–1896) and published by Edwin Ginn and Company in 1870. The *National Music Course* was a series of seven graded books and included a set of charts to assist instruction. The song material in the *National Music Course* was taken largely from German sources and included numerous German folksongs. The *National Music Course* was a significant departure from the traditional **singing school** books in use at the time. The *National Music Course* was successful in both the United States and Japan, and other graded music courses were published, eventually making **tunebooks** obsolete. *See* **Mason, Luther Whiting (1828-1896)**

National Network for Educational Renewal: A network established by John Goodlad and his colleagues at the University of Washington to enhance collegiality among educators from universities and partner schools. The network's goals are to promote exemplary performance by universities in instructing educators, exemplary performance by schools in educating young people, and constructive collaboration between schools and universities when they have overlapping mutual self-interests. The general idea behind the network is that it allows educators and institutions to pool their resources to provide more educational opportunities.

National School Orchestra Association, The (NSOA): *See* American String Teachers Association (ASTA)

National Standards, Music Education: Explicit standards for music education intended to reflect what every child should know and be able to do in music at specified grade levels. The national standards were developed voluntarily in response to growing concerns over the state of public school education. Many believed that all educational subject areas needed to have "world-class" standards that reflect America's aspirations and not the status quo. The general hope was that developing standards in music and other arts would help secure a place for music and the other arts among the basic disciplines of the K-12 **curriculum**. Similar standards are being or have been developed in history, science, language arts, foreign languages, geography, civics, and mathematics.

The movement toward developing national standards began in 1992 with the formation of the America 2000 arts partnership and continued with the **Goals 2000: Educate America Act** in 1993. The **Music Educators National Conference (MENC)** appointed a task force to develop the national standards for music education. These standards were revised several times in response to comments and suggestions made by various reviewers, including MENC members. MENC joined with the American Alliance for Theatre and Education, the National Art Education Association, and the National Dance Association to form a Consortium of National Arts Education Associations. This association worked to coordinate the national standards among the various disciplines for K-12 instruction. In addition, input was received from the National Committee for Standards in the Arts, comprised of educators, artists, business people, and government representatives.

The national standards in music education are arranged according to three grade levels: K-4, 5-8, and 9-12. They describe the skills and knowledge students are to have learned by the end of grades four, eight, and twelve. Within each grade level, the standards are organized into three broad categories, which are divided into general areas, such as singing and playing instruments. These general areas are divided into content standards which identify broad subject matter, and these content standards are further divided into several achievement standards specifying desired levels of attainment or stating how students will demonstrate attainment of the desired level. In addition, the standards for grades 9-12 are divided into "proficient" and "advanced" levels of achievement. The proficient level is for students who choose to take music courses for one to two years beyond grade eight, and the advanced level is designed for students who choose to take courses for three to four years beyond grade eight.

The National Standards for Music Education as published by MENC include:

1. Singing, alone and with others, a varied repertoire of music.
2. Performing on instruments, alone and with others, a varied repertoire of music.
3. Improvising melodies, variations, and accompaniments.
4. Composing and arranging music within specified guidelines.
5. Reading and notating music.
6. Listening to, analyzing, and describing music.
7. Evaluating music and music performances.
8. Understanding relationships between music, the other arts, and disciplines outside the arts.
9. Understanding music in relation to history and culture.

National Teacher Examinations: In education, tests designed to assess the skill and knowledge levels of prospective teachers. Most states require a national teacher examination before granting initial certification. Furthermore, some states require prospective teachers to reach a minimum level of performance on such tests for certification. The Praxis Series is the most well-known national teacher examination test series. *See* **Praxis Series, The**

National Teacher Examination, Music Education: A restricted test published by the **Educational Testing Service (ETS)** first published in 1957, which is frequently revised. The National Teacher Examination in Music Education is designed to assess an active or prospective teacher's knowledge about music education. Several areas of music are covered in the test, including music theory, music history, music teaching concepts, teaching techniques, and music education philosophy. In addition, the music education portions of the exam require working knowledge about all areas of music education, including general music, instrumental music, and vocal music. Some states use or have used the National Teacher Examination in Music Education for state certification.

Natural Frequency: In acoustics, the **frequency** at which a vibrating body oscillates in its natural state.

Naturalism: In education, an approach involving a minimal amount of teacher intervention in the learning process. Naturalism enables students to follow their natural tendencies in development. Students often work with a teacher to determine learning content and structure, and the teacher serves as a facilitator of knowledge.

Naturalistic Observation: In research, a method in which scientists test **hypotheses** by observing people in their natural environments, such as at home, at school, or in the work place. The idea behind naturalistic observation is to observe behavior without influencing it. Naturalistic observation typically involves special training using specific methods of data collection to make the data-gathering process as objective as possible.

Naturalistic Research: A type of **qualitative research** conducted in subjects' natural environments. Naturalistic research is based on gathering data in natural settings under normal conditions rather than in contrived or artificial environments. For example, recording observations about musical or **nonmusical** behaviors exhibited during a typical rehearsal in a choir class would constitute naturalistic research.

Nature/Nurture Controversy: In education, one of the oldest debates regarding the influences of behavior. The central question of the controversy is whether nature (heredity) or nurture (environment) is more influential in determining behavior. While both sides have strong arguments, most educators agree that both play vital roles in determining behavior.

NEA: *See* National Education Association (NEA); National Endowment for the Arts (NEA)

Need for Positive Regard, Rogers: In psychology, a universal need that may cause an individual to distort experiences that is inconsistent with positive self-regard or self-esteem. The need for positive regard is a component of **Carl Rogers' (1902–1987) humanistic** approach to psychology. *See* **Self-esteem**

Need Hierarchy, Maslow: In psychology, a theory proposed by **Abraham Maslow (1908–1970),** which suggests that human needs can be arranged in a hierarchy. In his book **Conditions of Learning,** Maslow describes five different kinds of needs. Starting with the most basic, his hierarchy includes: 1) physiological needs, 2) safety needs, 3) love needs, 4) esteem needs, and 5) self-actualizing needs. *See* **Self-actualization**

Needs: The part of the motivational cycle that involves deficits (needs) within the individual. These needs may be physiological, such as the need for food, or psychological, such as the need for approval. Needs must be satisfied to correct deficits. *See* **Drives; Motives**

Negative Identity: According to **Erik Erikson (1902–1994)**, when individuals choose identities that directly oppose the expectations of parents or societies. *See* **Psychosocial Theory/Stages, Erikson**

Negative Incentive: In cognitive motivation theory, anything that causes an individual to behave in certain ways to avoid expected negative consequences. For example, if a student expects to be punished for poor grades, the **punishment** acts as a negative incentive to induce the student to study harder. In music, fear of embarrassment from a poor performance may be negative incentive for an individual to practice and to be properly prepared for a public performance. *See* **Cognitive Motivation Theory; Reinforcer; Reinforcement**

Negative Reinforcer/Reinforcement: In psychology, when the removal of a **stimulus** increases the probability of a **response**. Negative reinforcers are usually unpleasant or aversive. For example, during the first six weeks of the term, every student is given verbal praise if they practice three hours that week. After six weeks, the teacher stops praising students for practicing, yet the practice time actually increases. In this case, practice time (the behavior) increases (reinforces) after the praise (the **stimulus**) is removed (negative). Unlike **punishment**, which reduces **response** rates, negative reinforcement increases response rates. *See* **Positive Reinforcement**

Negatively Accelerated (Intellectual) Growth Curve: A graph depicting the relationship between intellectual growth and chronological age. Some researchers have suggested that the relationship between intellectual growth and chronological age is negative. In other words, a child's potential for intellectual growth decreases as chronological age increases. It appears that children derive the most benefit from an enriching environment when they are younger and less benefit as they get older.

Negativism: In psychology, a type of behavior characterized by resistance to suggestion. Negativism may be manifested either passively or actively. When an individual fails to do what is expected, it is called passive negativism. When an individual does the opposite of what is expected, it is called active negativism.

Neurosis: A mental or emotional **disorder** characterized by **depression**, **anxiety**, abnormal fears, and/or compulsive behavior. People often confuse neurosis with psychosis; however, a neurosis is less severe than a psychosis.

Neutral Stimulus: In behavioral psychology, any **stimulus** that does not evoke a **reflex response**. When paired repeatedly with an **unconditioned stimulus**, a neutral stimulus begins to elicit the same response as the unconditioned stimulus and is called a **conditioned stimulus**. This process is known as classical conditioning. *See* **Classical Conditioning**

New American Schools Development Corporation (NASDC): A private, nonprofit, tax-exempt organization formed by American business leaders and the George H.W. Bush administration in 1991. The corporation is best known for sponsoring a national competition for "break the mold" schools. The competition encouraged individuals and groups to design innovative schools that could serve as models for the twenty-first century. *See* **America 2000 Schools**

New England Psalm Singer, The/American Chorister: A collection of 120 vocal works published in 1770 by **William Billings (1746–1800)** and the first published edition of American music. *The New England Psalm Singer* changed choral singing in America and included many of Billings' pieces, including the well-known song "Chester."

No Child Left Behind (NCLB): Legislation passed in 2001 that reauthorizes the **Elementary and Secondary Education Act of 1965 (ESEA)**. NCLB incorporates the principles and strategies proposed by President George W. Bush. These include the following: 1) increased **accountability** for states, school districts, and schools; 2) increased opportunities for school choice; 3) increased flexibility in the way states and local educational agencies use federal education funds; and 4) increased emphasis on reading, especially in the younger grades.

Node: In acoustics, the point of least **amplitude** in a **standing wave**. *See* Antinode

Nominal Fallacy: An error in logic resulting from the attempt to explain an event by describing the same event in a different way. For example, saying that the way to prevent school music programs from being cut is to make sure school programs stay in the schools is a nominal fallacy. *See* Circularity

Nominal Level Measurement: In research, a level of **measurement** or a **measurement scale** used solely for classification. A nominal level measurement is sometimes referred to as the naming scale because the scale categories are used to merely indicate what something is or is not or whether something is the same or different. The nominal scale does not indicate less-than or greater-than properties. Some examples are male or female; flat or sharp; green or purple.

Nondirective Model: In education, a teaching strategy that emphasizes helping students develop effective learning styles, problem solving strategies, and positive self-concepts. Teachers who employ a nondirective model generally assume the role of facilitator or educational guide. Their role is to encourage students to define their problems, to help students understand their feelings, to encourage students to assume responsibility for solving their own problems, and to help students determine how their personal goals might be reached. The nondirective model is based on the work of **Carl Rogers (1902–1987)**.

Nonequivalent Control Group Design: In research, an experimental design in which the groups of subjects participating are nonequivalent in some way or ways that does not use a pretest (a **measurement** of an experimental **variable** before the experimental **treatment** is administered). A nonequivalent control group design is sometimes necessary, especially when working with intact groups; however, the risk of error is also greater. Using random sampling techniques and/or giving a pretest may reduce the risk of error. *See* Random Sampling; Nonequivalent Control Group Pretest-posttest Design

Nonequivalent Control Group Pretest-posttest Design: In research, an experimental design in which the groups of subjects participating are nonequivalent in some way or ways that use a pretest (a **measurement** of an experimental **variable** before the experimental **treatment** is administered) and a posttest (a measurement of an experimental variable after the experimental treatment is administered). A pretest allows assessment of equivalency based on pretest-posttest changes. A nonequivalent control group pretest-posttest design is sometimes necessary, especially when working with intact groups; however, the risk of error is also greater. Using random sampling techniques and/or giving a pretest may reduce the risk of error. *See* Random Sampling; Nonequivalent Control Group Design

Nongraded Classrooms: In education, classrooms in which children are grouped heterogeneously based on their abilities or **achievement** levels rather than by **chronological age**. Nongraded classrooms are sometimes referred to as multiage, multi-grade, or family grouping programs and are most common at the elementary level. Research has shown that nongraded classrooms are most effective when students are grouped for one academic subject only.

Non-graded School Instruction: In education, a type of instruction in which students are allowed to progress at their own rate without receiving traditional grades. Some educators believe that assigning grades may cause students who do not achieve to be "labeled" in some way, negatively influencing learning. Non-graded school instruction greatly reduces or eliminates such **labeling**.

Nonmusical: A term used by some music educators to describe educational outcomes of music classes that are not musical. For example, sorting music into folders, keeping instrument and music inventories, and repairing instruments are often considered nonmusical. Some music educators would consider these activities as being **extra-musical**, because they do not involve making or listening to music in any way, yet they are related to music classes. Sometimes the term is used to describe positive **nonmusical outcomes** in music classes. For example, developing leadership skills, teamwork skills, and confidence in front of an audience are nonmusical benefits of music classes. In this regard, the distinction between extra-musical and nonmusical is often blurred.

Nonmusical Outcomes: Those outcomes considered by many music educators to be positive by-products of music education. In addition to the music-related benefits of music classes, students may also receive several positive nonmusical benefits, including emotional release, improved

self-esteem, social interaction, improved achievement in other academic areas, positive work ethic, and good practice/study habits.

Nonparametric Statistics: In research, statistics appropriate when the **samples** involved are not representative of the **population**. Nonparametric statistics are appropriate under the following conditions: 1) a sample has not been drawn according to accepted randomization procedures; 2) a sample is very small; 3) it is believed that a sample's distribution could be skewed or biased in some way; and 4) the **data** represent **nominal** or **ordinal levels of measurement**. Disagreement exists among statisticians regarding the point at which the shape of a **frequency distribution** does not allow researchers to use parametric statistics for data analysis. Examples of nonparametric statistics include **Chi-square (x^2)** and **Friedman Two-Way Analysis of Variance (ANOVA)**. *See* **Parametric Statistics**

Nonperforming Classes: In music education, music classes in which musical performance is not the primary focus of the class. General music, **Advance Placement (AP) Music Theory**, and **music appreciation** classes are often nonperforming classes. Generally, teachers of nonperforming classes do incorporate some performance **activities** into their **lesson plans**. Such activities often include singing and playing simple instruments. *See* Performance-based Classes

Nonprobability Sampling: In research, a type of sampling that does not guarantee that each member of any given **population** has an equal chance of being selected for inclusion in the sample. Nonprobability sampling techniques include: 1) **purposive sampling**, when **subjects** are selected according to specific criteria; 2) **quota sampling**, when researchers deliberately seek a sufficient number of participants who are representative of the groups being investigated or compared in a study; 3) **systematic sampling**, when a system is used for selecting subjects; and 4) **haphazard sampling**, when researchers use people who just happen to be available as subjects. *See* Probability Sampling; Sampling

Nonsense Syllable: In research, an item used in **rote memorization** experiments, usually consisting of two **consonants** with a vowel between. The combination of letters must not form a word in familiar languages. "Geb" or "bup" are nonsense syllables. In music, nonsense syllables are sometimes used in elementary songs. In addition, young children are often encouraged to improvise using nonsense syllables to familiar tunes.

Nonsignificant Results: In research, results based on statistical analyses that lead to a decision not to reject the **null hypothesis**. In other words, nonsignificant results indicate that any differences found in a study could have occurred by chance alone. *See* **Significant Result; Statistical Significance**

Nonverbal Behavior: Also referred to as body language, any non-speech behavior that can be observed. In education, nonverbal behaviors are generally associated with nonverbal means of communication, and they provide important cues that help both teachers and students understand and interact with each other. Nonverbal behaviors indicate mood, likes and dislikes, approval or disapproval, emotions, and **attitudes**. Sensitivity to nonverbal behaviors and the ability to understand what these behaviors mean are crucial elements in developing healthy student/teacher relationships. In addition, teachers can use a variety of nonverbal behaviors to facilitate instruction and to create a disciplined and productive learning environment. *See* **Nonverbal Strategies in Music Instruction**

Nonverbal Responses: Responses that do not involve words. Nonverbal responses typically include facial expressions, gestures, and posture; however, they may also involve physiological reactions such as increased heart rate, shallow or heavy breathing, and increased brain wave activity. *See* **Nonverbal Behavior; Nonverbal Strategies in Music Instruction**

Nonverbal Strategies in Music Instruction: In music education, the use of **nonverbal behaviors** to facilitate music teaching and learning. Nonverbal strategies in music instruction include: 1) **aural modeling**, when teachers sing or play the passage being learned, providing a model of the desired performance, and 2) using physical gestures, such as conducting gestures, body positioning, and facial expressions to illustrate a point or to facilitate performance of desired behaviors. Nonverbal strategies vary widely among individual teachers and are often employed in reaction to student behaviors in a "live" performance situation. A teacher's nonverbal gestures are often intuitive in nature and not preplanned. Most teachers agree that nonverbal strategies are effective in facilitating music instruction, and the limited research in this area supports this view; however, it has also been shown that students do not always understand nonverbal gestures. Ensuring that students understand nonverbal strategies leads to more effective instruction.

Norm-referenced Test: Any test that uses a specific comparison technique for scoring. A norm-referenced test is any test that scores an individual based on their performance in relation to others taking the same test. Most **standardized tests** are norm-referenced. For example, the **Scholastic Achievement Test (SAT)** compares each individual test taker's score to the scores of all other test takers. Norm-referenced tests are commonly used for teacher-made tests, because it is easier to account for a test that is too easy or too difficult. Such tests are commonly referred to as being graded on a "curve," because the grading is determined by scores of everyone taking the test. Heated debates about the **validity**, **reliability**, usefulness, and appropriateness of norm-referenced tests have been and continue to be common in educational and political arenas. Yet, the results of these tests are central to issues regarding **accountability**, admission processes, and scholarship considerations. *See* **Criterion-referenced Test**

Normal Curve: In statistics, a linear graph (curved line) representing a **normal distribution**. The normal curve is a theoretical curve where the **frequency distribution** is plotted on the horizontal axis (x) and the **frequency** of occurrence is plotted on the vertical axis (y). Shaped like a bell, the normal curve is sometimes referred to as a

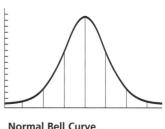

Normal Bell Curve

bell curve. Although the normal curve is a statistical construction, it has many applications in everyday life, because it represents roughly the proportions in which most human phenomena occur. *See* **Normal Distribution**

Normal Distribution: The standard symmetrical, bell-shaped **frequency distribution** whose properties are commonly used in making statistical inferences from measures derived from **samples**; it is theoretical. In a normal distribution, most of the scores cluster around the center; as scores move away from the center in either direction, they decrease in **frequency**. As a result, 68 percent of all scores fall within one **standard deviation** of the **mean**, 28 percent fall within two standard deviations of the mean, and the remaining 4 percent are at the extreme ends of the **distribution**. When plotted on a graph, the scores fall in a symmetrical bell shape, each half of the curve being a mirror image of the other. The **mean**, **median**, and **mode** all fall at precisely the same point (the center) in a normal distribution, and the areas of standard deviation remain constant.

Normal Music Course: A series of music instruction books by Hosea Holt and John Tufts originally published in 1883 by D. Appleton and Company. The *Normal Music Course* was a five-book series and one of the most significant series in the history of music education. During the late nineteenth and early twentieth centuries, its scientific approach to music instruction based on note-reading skills was standard in music instruction. **Sight singing** exercises were a fundamental component of the *Normal Music Course*, and the songs were based on what was learned in the exercises.

Normal School: An educational program established in the 1800s dedicated solely to teacher training. The first normal schools were established in Lexington, Massachusetts, in 1839, during **Horace Mann's (1855–1937)** term as secretary to the Massachusetts State Board of Education; however, normal schools did not become widespread until after the Civil War. The normal school **curriculum** included courses in the history and philosophy of education, instructional principles and teaching methodologies, and practice teaching.

Norms: In general, an average, common, or standard performance under specified conditions. For example, wind bands typically perform a concert B-flat scale to warm-up and orchestras tune to the pitches of the open strings; these behaviors are norms. In research, norms refer to statistical averages on selected attributes of a large, representative **sample** from a given **population**. For example, the norm for an infant's first step is about twelve months. In testing, norms typically refer to scores and **percentile ranks** of a large, representative sample from a given population for which the test was constructed. These scores are distributed into a **normal curve**, which serves as a reference for making comparisons between individual scores. In social settings, norms refer to the expectations people have for one another or to the understood rules for acceptable or unacceptable behavior. *See* Conformity

Null Hypothesis: In research, a statistical **hypothesis** indicating that any difference observed among treatment conditions or **variables** occurs by chance alone and does not reflect a true difference. Rejection of a null hypothesis means that the **treatment** conditions or variables actually had an effect on the results. For example, there will be no significant difference between groups' scores on **sight reading** tasks that can be attributed to teaching **method**. *See* Hypothesis

Object Constancy: The tendency to see objects as relatively unchanged under changing conditions. For example, individuals can recognize a car as a car regardless of changes in distance, position, or illumination. *See* Perceptual Constancies; Shape Constancy; Size Constancy; Location Constancy

Object Permanence: A psychological term used by **Jean Piaget (1896–1980)** referring to a child's realization or understanding that an object continues to exist even though it is hidden from view. Object permanence becomes obvious when a child learns that mom is not really gone but simply in the other room. According to Piaget, object permanence occurs at about ten months.

Objective Scoring: Scoring a test or other **measurement** according to a finite code of right and wrong so that any scorer would arrive at precisely the same score. That is, objective scoring involves clearly defined right and wrong answers. Objective scoring is in contrast to subjective scoring, in which more than one answer on a given test item may be considered correct. Most questions in a true/false test or a multiple-choice test are graded using objective scoring. *See* Subjective Scoring

Objectives, Behavioral: In education, statements typically regarding what students should learn, how well they should learn it, and how long it should take them to learn it. Behavioral objectives are often used interchangeably with **goals**; however, goals are usually broader and more long-range. Objectives can be viewed as being short-range steps to accomplishing long-range goals. The following is an example of a goal: students will be able to recognize all wind and string instruments heard in solo listening examples with 100 percent accuracy by the end of their first year of study. The following is an example of a behavioral objective: students will identify the appropriate brass instruments heard in solo listening examples with 100 percent accuracy after one hearing by the end of the first two weeks of study.

Objectivity: In research, the process of observing, verifying, or measuring through scientific and/or common sense **methods**. The use of standard procedures for gathering, scoring, and interpreting data often assures objectivity in **research designs**. *See* **Subjectivity**

Observational Learning: Learning that occurs when individuals learn new responses by observing the behavior of others, rather than learning through direct experience or direct instruction. Observational learning usually does not require direct **reinforcement**, and occurs in both formal and informal settings. *See* **Modeling; Vicarious Learning**

Observational Method: In research, the process of studying events as they occur in nature without controlling **variables**. Examples include studying the numbers of negative and positive comments in the classroom over a specific period of time or studying the mating habits of mule deer. *See* **Naturalistic Observation**

Observational Research: Any type of research in which predetermined observational procedures are used to obtain **data**. Observations are normally recorded using some type of **measurement instrument** according to a designed system. This system can be open or closed. In an open system, information is written or recorded in its original form, without categorical considerations. In a closed system, categorical considerations for information have been predetermined and may include the use of rating scales or checklists. Low-interference and high-interference **variables** are typically associated with observational research. Typically, low-interference variables are clearly defined and easily observed. Classroom examples of low-interference variables include the teacher smiling or giving verbal praise. High-interference variables are not as clearly defined or easily observed. Classroom examples of high-interference variables include the teacher being supportive of students, using humor effectively, and having good rapport with students. In education, observational research is normally used in studies where researchers want to know more about what occurs in classrooms. Teacher effectiveness, student behaviors, and **attitudes** about learning may be considerations for observational research.

One problem with observational research is that it can be limiting. For example, the process of teaching and learning is complex and conceptual, yet, observational research commonly uses only one measurement instrument to collect data. As a result, the data may not be as representative or comprehensive as researchers would like. Researchers employing the observational method often expand their collection techniques to include more than one of the following: 1) using both closed and open systems; 2) using separate systems for recording objective versus more subjective data; and 3) double-checking all information through the use of audio and video recordings. These techniques help researchers establish the **validity** and **reliability** of the measuring instruments used in observational research.

Obsessions: In psychology, persistent thoughts, ideas, or feelings that interfere with normal daily functioning. Obsessions are often irrational, and individuals have little conscious control over them. When obsessions lead to action, these actions are called compulsions. *See* Compulsions; Obsessive-compulsive Behavior/Reaction

Obsessive-compulsive Behavior/Reaction: In psychology, neurotic, usually uncontrollable behavior involving thinking about and/or doing something excessively. Obsessive-compulsive behaviors fall into three basic categories: 1) recurrent thoughts, often disturbing and unwelcome (**obsessions**); 2) repeated **stereotyped** or ritualistic acts (**compulsions**); and (3) a combination of obsessions and compulsions. *See* Neurosis

Occam's Razor/Ockham's Razor: A principle that states that entities should not be multiplied unnecessarily; that is, the simplest, most obvious answer or solution is probably correct. In logic, Occam's Razor dictates that any argument should be stated in its simplest form. In the evaluation of scientific theories, Occam's Razor dictates that one should choose the simplest theory that fits all of the available facts. Occam's Razor was devised by the English philosopher William of Occam (c. 1280–1347).

Oedipal Stage: In **psychoanalytic theory,** another name for **Sigmund Freud's** (1856–1939) **phallic stage** of **psychosexual development**. The phallic stage is sometimes called the Oedipal stage because it is at this stage that the Oedipus complex arises. *See* Electra Complex

Oedipus Complex: In psychology, the sexual feelings boys have for their mothers along with feelings of hostility toward their fathers. According to **Sigmund Freud (1856–1939)**, the Oedipus complex occurs in the **phallic stage** of **psychoanalytic development**. The Oedipus complex derived its name from a character (Oedipus) in Greek mythology who unknowingly killed his father and married his mother. The **Electra complex** is a similar concept for the sexual feelings girls have toward their fathers; however, the term Oedipus complex is sometimes used to refer to the same psychological phenomenon occurring in either gender. *See* **Psychoanalytic Theory, Freud**

Off Task: In education, when students are not following the instruction or direction of the teacher. That is, students are not doing what they are supposed to be doing. *See* **On Task**

Office of Special Education Programs (OSEP): An office of the United States Government dedicated to helping infants, toddlers, children, and youth with disabilities from birth through age twenty-one by providing financial support, leadership, and assistance to state and local district programs. The OSEP operates within the Office of Special Education and Rehabilitation Services (OSERS) to implement legislation authorized by the **Individuals with Disabilities in Education Act (IDEA)**.

Omnibus Theory, Mursell: In music, a **gestalt theory** that **musical talent** or **musicality** is an all-pervasive ability that could only be described as a "whole" and not as a series of fragmented or separate abilities as **Carl Seashore (1866–1949)** had suggested in his **Theory of Specifics**. The Omnibus Theory was first proposed by **James Mursell (1893–1963)**.

On Task: In education, when students are following the instruction or direction of the teacher. That is, students are doing what they are supposed to be doing. *See* **Off Task**

Onlooker Play: A type of play classified by Mildred Parten (b. 1929), where children merely watch or observe other children at play. That is, onlooker play is when children are more interested in watching others play than they are in playing themselves. *See* **Unoccupied Play; Solitary Play; Parallel Play; Associative Play; Cooperative Play**

Ontology/Ontological Questions: Philosophical questions regarding the nature of being and reality. Many ontological questions begin with the phrase, "What is the nature of...", which reflects the importance of thinking through issues. Most ontological questions are often sources of debate and contention among educators and philosophers. In music, as in all fields, exploration of these types of questions is essential for developing an in-depth understanding of conceptual issues. Ontological questions are typically open-ended. Examples: 1) What is the nature of any musical experience? 2) When does learning occur? *See* **Open-ended Questions**

Open Education: In education, a program or environment in which students take an active role in determining **curriculum**; the teacher serves as a guide to or facilitator of learning experiences. Open education environments often use non-traditional classroom settings. The goal is to build the student's **self-esteem** by promoting positive learning experiences and developing positive attitudes about **learning**. As a movement, open education was popularized in the 1970s. *See* **Summerhill School**

Open-ended Questions: In research, questions used in the **interview** or **survey method** that do not limit the subject's responses by allowing only pre-selected, alternative responses, such as yes or no. *See* **Closed-ended Questions**

Operant/Operant Response: In behavioral psychology, a term coined by **B.F. Skinner (1904–1990)** to describe a freely emitted (voluntary) response/response pattern or a response for which no **stimulus** can be identified. Operant responses occur within or operate on the environment. The likelihood of an operant response continuing is directly dependent upon the consequences of that response (**reinforcement**). If the consequences are positive, the operant responses will most likely be strengthened. *See* **Operant Behavior; Operant Conditioning**

Operant Behavior: In behavioral psychology, a term used by **B. F. Skinner (1904–1990)** to describe behavior involving **operant responses** operating on the environment in some way. The consequences of operant behavior can be observed, even though the **stimulus** is not known. For example, if a rat presses the lever in a Skinner Box, and this action results in **reinforcement**, an increase in operant rate will be observed even though no stimulus initiated the original press of the bar. In **operant conditioning**, reinforcement is contingent on the operant first being emitted. The organism must "operate" on the environment for reinforcement to follow. Operant behavior leads to a reward of some kind.

Operant Conditioning: In behavioral psychology, a form of **conditioning** described by **B. F. Skinner (1904–1990)** in which an **operant response** (not contrived or controlled) is followed by a **reinforcing stimulus** that increases the likelihood of the operant occurring again. It is important that the reinforcing stimulus be presented if, and only if, the desired **response** occurs. For optimum conditioning, the reinforcing stimulus should follow the operant immediately. Teachers use operant conditioning regularly in their classrooms when they praise desired behaviors so that these behaviors are reinforced. *See* **Operant Level**

Operant Level: In behavioral psychology, the original, preconditioned rate of operant responding before reinforcing **stimuli** have been introduced. In **B. F. Skinner's (1904–1990)** experiments, rats were reinforced with food each time they pressed a lever; as a result of the **reinforcement**, the rats pressed the lever more often. Prior to the beginning of such an experiment, if a rat happens to press the lever three times an hour without being reinforced, pressing the lever voluntarily is the free operant, and the operant level for that response would be three per hour. In other words, the operant level is the rate at which the free operant is typically emitted prior to **conditioning**. In education, the operant level is the rate at which a behavior occurs naturally in the classroom. For example, if a student raises his or her hand to answer questions two times in a one-hour period, the operant level would be two per hour. The general idea for establishing an operant level is to help devise a reinforcement schedule that will lead to an increase in the desired behavior(s). *See* **Operant Conditioning**

Operation: In behavioral psychology, the common effect of a set of behaviors under **stimulus** control usually involving what is done, how it is done, and why it is done. In **cognitive** psychology, operations refer to mental abilities that enable children to understand abstract principles such as cause-and-effect relationships. According to **Jean Piaget (1896–1980)**, operations are cognitively reversible. For example, multiplying 2 x 6 = 12 and understanding that 6 x 2 = 12 is an operation. These kinds of operations occur during Piaget's concrete operational stage (approximately age seven to eleven) but not at the preoperational stage (age two to seven). *See* **Piaget's Stages of Cognitive Growth**

Operational Definition: In research, the definition of a **construct** or **concept** written to clarify and specify the precise operation that will be used in a study to measure said construct or concept. Because constructs and concepts are difficult to define, researchers attempt to define them in objective ways or in some form of objective procedure or measure. This process allows researchers to apply **quantitative** analysis to otherwise **subjective** terms. Operational definitions help readers understand the study. They also enable researchers to more accurately replicate the study by using the same terminology.

Opportunity-to-learn (OTL) Standards: Linked to **Goals 2000: Educate America Act**, standards designed to make certain that students have a fair chance to succeed in their classes by holding schools accountable for providing students with appropriate support, including books, technological equipment, effective teachers, and other educational support tools. Schools meet OTL standards only if they provide the resources necessary to ensure student success. The basic idea behind the OTL standards is that if students are going to be held accountable for meeting national **minimum competency standards**, then schools must be held accountable for providing the opportunity for ensuring student success.

    In music, the OTL standards for K-12 describe the conditions necessary for students to meet the national content and achievement standards in music and focus primarily on curriculum and scheduling, staffing, materials and equipment, and facilities. The OTL standards in music are based on the **national standards** and are comprehensive. These standards are strictly voluntary; however, they are recommended by **Music Educators National Conference (MENC)**, either for adoption or as a basis for adaptation. A full listing of the OTL standards can be accessed from the MENC Web site. *See* **National Standards, Music Education**

Oral Cavity: The space inside the mouth. The oral cavity is the primary resonance chamber in vocal production. It can be modified by changing the position of the tongue, throat, and the mouth opening. Along with the nasal cavity, the oral cavity facilitates vocal resonance. As the oral and nasal cavities resonate, they create formants and emphasize various partials within the sound. This **resonance** adds to the richness of the vocal **timbre**. *See* **Formants**

Oral Stage: In psychoanalysis, the first of **Sigmund Freud's (1856–1939) psychosexual stages** of development. During this stage, babies derive pleasure from sucking and eating. In a sense, babies live, love, and know the world through their lips and mouth during this stage. According to Freud, the oral stage occurs between birth and about age eighteen months and permanently affects the child's later feelings of independence and trust. *See* Psychoanalytic Theory, Freud

Order Effect: In a **repeated measures research design**, the effect that the order of introducing a **treatment** has on the **dependent variable**.

Ordinal Level Measurement: In research, a level of **measurement** or a **measurement scale** that indicates the position of items in a set arranged from the smallest to the largest. Ordinal level measurement does not indicate the degree to which items in the set are different, only that they are different. Examples: 1) first place, second place, and third place in a pie-baking contest; 2) in instrumental ensembles, first chair, second chair, and third chair in the tuba section. *See* Measurement/Measurement Scales

Ordinal Scale: A scale of measurement in which the categories form a rank order along a continuum. *See* Measurement/Measurement Scales

Orff, Carl (1895-1982): A German composer and music educator best known for his approach to teaching elementary music. Orff studied at the Munich Academy. As a music educator, Orff was influenced by the theories of **Emile Jaques-Dalcroze (1865–1950)** and his emphasis on dance-movement or **eurhythmics**. As a result of this influence, Orff and Dorothee Gunther founded a school for gymnastics, music, and dance called **Gunther Schule** in 1924. The purpose of the school was to train teachers in movement and rhythm and to develop their **creativity**.

Orff also believed that music education should be related to the natural tendencies of young children to move and learn. He also believed that rhythm was the basis for musical learning and that rhythm should evolve from dance movement. Orff published a five-volume series of books entitled *Music for Children* in the 1950s, describing his approach to teaching music. The books were translated into many languages and adapted for music instruction in many countries around the world. Orff's approach to teaching music education, which is often called Schulwerk or **Orff-**

Schulwerk, has been one of the most significant influences on teaching music at the elementary level. As a composer, Orff's compositions were based on Greek tragedies or Bavarian comedies and were written for the stage. His most well known piece is *Carmina Burana*, which was written in 1937. *See* **Jaques-Dalcroze (1865-1950)**

Orff-Schulwerk: An approach to teaching music developed by **Carl Orff (1895–1952)** in the 1950s. The approach is based primarily on rhythmic development. Emphasis is placed on enabling students to develop creative improvisational skills with a limited formal knowledge base. Orff believed that children should be exposed to rhythm first and that other musical elements would follow as a natural outgrowth of rhythmic training. In his approach, playing progresses from imitation to experimentation and creation. Orff devised rhythmic patterns based on chants, games, and other vocal sounds already familiar to young children. Through free and uninhibited movement activities such as clapping, dancing, chanting, and singing, children develop vocabularies of rhythmic, melodic, and harmonic patterns. These vocabularies help foster creativity and are the foundations of his approach. They are used for improvising, composing, and performing music. When these foundational skills have been mastered, specially designed Orff instruments (the "Orff Instrumentarium") are introduced, usually by the third grade. Because of the emphasis on rhythm, percussion instruments are predominantly used, including xylophones, bells, drums, cymbals, woodblocks, and rattles. Playing progresses from imitation to experimentation and creation.

Orff-Schulwerk has become almost synonymous with the playing of simple percussion instruments in elementary classrooms. Later, at about the fifth grade, recorders are introduced. Orff-Schulwerk has dramatically influenced the way elementary music is taught in the public schools. The method allows children to actively participate in the learning process, fosters creativity and self-expression appropriate to a child's experience level, encourages children to explore the nature of sound and music production, and allows children to enjoy the music learning process.

Organ of Corti: The actual receptor for hearing located in the **inner ear**. The organ of corti is about an inch long and lies on the **basilar membrane** in the **cochlea**. It contains approximately 24,000 hair cells that function as receptors for hearing. The organ of corti is where the fibers of the auditory nerve originate. *See* **Basilar Membrane; Cochlea**

Organism: In psychology, a term referring to a human being or non-human animal. In biology, organism refers to any form of plant or animal life.

Organization of American Kodaly Educators (OAKE): An organization founded on Zoltan Kodály's (1882-1967) ideas about music education. *See* Kodály Method; Kodály, Zoltan (1882-1967)

Orienting Reflexes: Typically, head or body movements that help orient the organism's receptors to those parts of the environment in which changes in the **stimulus** are occurring. Orienting reflexes help individuals focus attention and/or prepare for changes in the environment. They are often nonspecific **responses** to changes in stimulation that may involve changes in **galvanic skin response**, pupillary dilation, and depression in alpha waves. *See* Proprioception/Proprioceptive Cues

Oscilloscope: An electronic device for displaying **waveforms** onto an illuminated screen. At one time, the oscilloscope was the primary research tool for sound analysis. Although still used to some extent, technological advances have made its use limited.

Ossicles/Ossicular Chain: The three small bones that transmit vibrations through the middle ear cavity to the **inner ear**. These include the malleus, incus, and stapes, commonly referred to as the hammer, anvil, and stirrup, respectively.

Outcome Expectation: An individual's belief or perception about the consequences of his or her behavior or performance.

Outcomes: In psychology, the results or consequences of behavior. In education, outcomes usually refer to the results or consequences of teaching. In music education, outcomes can be general or specific. General outcomes include making, understanding, and valuing music. Specific outcomes include improved tone quality, improved rhythmic accuracy, and increased historical knowledge.

Outcomes-based Education (OBE): An educational approach that emphasizes what students are to learn or be able to do (**outcomes**) as a result of the activities they engage in. Characteristics of outcomes-based education include: 1) clearly focusing desired outcomes; 2) devising a **curriculum** based on achieving these outcomes; 3) providing students with realistic challenges and opportunities that will lead to achieving desired outcomes; 4) rewarding students for demonstrating improvement toward desired outcomes; and 5) providing students with the assistance needed to achieve the desired outcomes. Criticisms of OBE are usually centered on the nature of the outcomes. Some educators and parents believe that outcomes tend to extend beyond the scope of appropriate school curricula by focusing on **attitudes** and values. Outcomes-based education is also known as Outcomes-driven developmental model (ODDM) and goal-based education (GBE).

Outdoor Education: In education, interaction with natural resources that assist students in the learning process. Outdoor education involves active participation and direct learning experiences in a natural setting. Taking a field trip to study various rock formations in a particular location is an example of outdoor education.

Outer Ear: The visible portion of the ear consisting of the external fleshy portion (the pinna) and the ear canal (auditory meatus). The outer ear functions as a sort of radar station to detect and funnel sound through the rest of the hearing mechanism. *See* **Hearing**

Oval Window: An oval opening in the bone between the air-filled middle ear cavity and the fluid-filled inner ear. The oval window is approximately twenty times smaller than the tympanic membrane and is also covered by a thin membrane. The **stapes** is connected to the oval window, which is part of the mechanism that transmits vibrations through the liquid of the **inner ear**.

Overachievers: Individuals who have the potential and capability to perform specific tasks at a certain level, yet who consistently perform above this level. Research shows that **achievement** and **motivation** are closely linked and that overachievers tend to possess qualities or traits that enhance or facilitate motivation for success. Such traits include the willingness and/or ability to work hard or to focus on the task at hand. *See* **Underachiever**

Overlearning: The idea that if one learns and relearns material it will become more permanent in **memory**. Studies show that retention is longer and retrieval easier when material is overlearned. This is most valuable when studying material that is difficult to learn initially and is important for learning permanence. In musical performance, overlearning is beneficial because it often results in better performances. When musicians experience anxiety-inducing stress, the performance is less likely to suffer if the material is overlearned. *See* Cyclical Learning; Spiraling

Overtones: A common, but somewhat outdated term for the tones that sound above the **fundamental** in a **complex tone**. The terms **overtones**, **harmonics**, and **partials** are all used to describe components of a complex tone and are often incorrectly used interchangeably. Overtones only include the upper partials of a complex tone, not the fundamental. Partials, on the other hand, refer to any part of a complex tone including the fundamental. Harmonic refers to any partial of a complex tone whose frequency is an integral multiple of the fundamental **frequency**.

P (Physical) Learning: A form of learning described by **Jean Piaget (1896–1980)** that results from the action of the physical environment on the child rather than the actions of the child on the environment. According to Piaget, the physical properties of certain objects acting on an individual are potentially reinforcing to that individual. Piaget's physical learning is virtually identical to **B. F. Skinner's (1904–1990)** concept of operant conditioning. *See* **Operant Conditioning**

Pacing: In education, the rate at which information is transmitted from the teacher to the students. When pacing is too fast, it is difficult for students to absorb or learn the information. When pacing is too slow, students have difficulty absorbing, focusing, and learning. Both can result in decreased attention, discipline problems, and a poor learning environment. *See* **Sequencing**

Paired-associate Learning: In psychology, a method used to study verbal learning and memory, in which a subject is presented with a list of word pairs such as "black-ball," "hot-dog," "play-toy," or "quarter-note" and then tested by being asked to repeat the second word of the pair (the **response**) each time the first word (the **stimulus**) is introduced. Typically, subjects are given about a dozen word pairs for memorization. Research has shown that subjects respond more quickly to word pairs when they are able to make meaningful associations between the two words. For example, subjects will usually learn "hot-dog" faster than "orange-dog." Many psychologists believe that the learning of word pairs is a fundamental process in thinking and memory. Paired-associate learning is the most common technique employed in the study of verbal learning.

Palate: The area commonly called the "roof" of the mouth. The palate is made up of both the hard palate and the soft palate, or velum. *See* **Hard Palate; Soft Palate**

Panic Attack: Typically, a brief feeling of intense fear characterized by rapid breathing, rapid pulse, sweating, dizziness, shakiness, feelings of helplessness or being out of control, and feelings of impending doom or death. Panic attacks can last from a few moments to a few hours. They are often stress-related, may occur suddenly, and are usually triggered by a particular situation. *See* **Performance Anxiety**

Paradigm: In research, a conceptual framework designed to describe the manner in which "reality" is viewed. A paradigm may be thought of as a set of assumptions or ideas about the way things are or about the way an individual sees things. Paradigms influence the types of questions asked by researchers and the types of research modes employed. Paradigms both positive and negative characteristics. While they help define and clarify what is being studied and its context, paradigms may limit the focus of research and may not be an accurate reflection of reality. In education, the term paradigm is often used synonymously with example or model. For example, in a grammatical context, a word in all its inflections is considered a paradigm. *See* **Model**

Paraeducators: In education, individuals who are not certified teachers who help teachers, students, and parents in educational settings. Typically, paraeducators are used in **special education** contexts, serving as additional supports for students with **disabilities** in the regular classroom as part of a policy of **full inclusion**. *See* **Individuals with Disabilities Education Act (IDEA)**

Parallel Play: A type of play classified by Mildred Parten in 1929, where children play without interacting with other children. In parallel play, children may play with similar toys and in similar ways as children around them. *See* **Unoccupied Play; Solitary Play; Onlooker Play; Associative Play; Cooperative Play**

Parameters: In research, numerical characteristics of a population, in contrast to **statistics**, which are numerical characteristics of a sample. In reality, researchers often use the term statistics even though they are really describing parameters. *See* **Population; Sample**

Parametric Statistics: In research, statistics appropriate when the **samples** involved are not representative of the **population**.

Parish Schools: *See* Church Schools

Parochial Schools: A general term for schools established, maintained, and operated by religious groups that include religious instruction in one or more components of the curriculum. Public policy and constitutional considerations regarding separation of church and state prevent most government funding of parochial schools; however, in some instances, governmental funds have been allocated to parochial schools. For example, in 2000 the United States Supreme Court in *Mitchell v. Helms* ruled that the use of federal funds for computers, instructional equipment, and library books to both parochial and private schools was constitutional. All schools with a religious affiliation are generically referred to as parochial, including Catholic schools, Jewish schools, and other Christian schools.

Partial: In acoustics, any of the **simple tones** that are contained within or comprise a **complex tone**. Individuals sometimes use the terms partials, **overtones**, and **harmonics** interchangeably. However, the term partial refers to every simple tone within a complex tone including the **fundamental**, while the terms overtone and harmonic refer only to the tones in a complex tone above the fundamental. That is, the fundamental is the first partial, and the first overtone or harmonic is the second partial and so on. *See* **Harmonic Series**

Partial Correlation: In statistics, the correlation between two **variables** for which the influence of a third variable is statistically controlled. *See* **Correlation**

Partial Inclusion: In education, a system of instruction in which students, typically those with **disabilities** or those who are gifted in some way, receive the majority of instruction in regular classrooms. These students are usually removed from the regular classroom for part of the day and placed in other instructional settings to help meet their individual needs. *See* **Disabled; Gifted and Talented/Giftedness; Full Inclusion**

Partial Reinforcement: In **behavioral psychology**, reinforcing a given response only some of the times it occurs, rather than each time it occurs. Partial reinforcement is also known as **intermittent reinforcement**. *See* **Reinforcement**

Partial Synthesis Level of Discrimination Learning, Gordon: *See* Skill Learning Sequence, Gordon

Pass-fail Grading: In education, a system of grading in which students receive a passing or failing grade, with no other indications of **achievement** reflected in the grade. Typically, pass-fail grades are not computed in grade point averages (GPA). Proponents of pass-fail grading point out that it enables students to try new areas of study without the fear of receiving low grades. Critics of pass-fail grading claim that students may not make as much effort in a class where they only need to make a passing grade, resulting in lower levels of achievement. They also argue that pass-fail grading provides significantly less information regarding student achievement than the traditional grading system using A-to-F indicators.

Passive Decay: *See* Decay

Passive Learning: In education, learning that involves little or no active student participation or interaction. During passive learning, students often sit idly or take notes while information is presented to them. The traditional **lecture method** is an example of passive learning. *See* Active Learning

Path Analysis: In research, a statistical technique for determining the possibility of cause-and-effect relationships among a series of time-ordered, correlated **variables**. Path analysis is an extension of **correlation**. It allows researchers to determine whether a variable is being influenced by the variables that precede it and/or those that follow it. Path analysis is often used to test the validity of a theory about causal relationships between three or more variables that have been studied using a **correlational research** design. When used in this manner, path analysis is similar to other **multivariate** procedures such as **multiple regression, discriminant analysis, canonical correlation,** and **factor analysis.** However, whereas these procedures are used primarily to maximize the correlation between various combinations of variables, path analysis is used solely to test theories about causal links between variables. A path diagram is usually drawn to indicate the direction of the relationships between variables in path analysis.

Pavlov, Ivan (1849-1936): An eminent Russian psychologist associated with classical conditioning, Pavlov bypassed seminary study to pursue physiology. In 1875 he received a degree in natural sciences and continued studies at the Academy of Medical Sciences until 1879. In 1890, Pavlov organized and directed the department of physiology at the Institute of Experimental Medicine and was the director for a period of forty-five years. Pavlov's contributions to psychology are largely the result of his observations of animal behavior during conditioning experiments. Pavlov found that dogs would salivate (**unconditioned response**) naturally when food was presented (**unconditioned stimulus**). This behavior was reflexive in nature; nothing was learned. However, Pavlov noted that if he paired a tone (**neutral stimulus**) with the food that the tone would eventually elicit the same **response** as the food. The response to the tone (**conditioned stimulus**) was a **conditioned response** because it had been learned. That is, the dog associated food with the tone and salivated. This experiment is the cornerstone of classical conditioning. In addition, Pavlov found that other tones would elicit the same response as the original test tone. This phenomenon is known as **generalization**. Pavlov won the Nobel Prize in medicine for his work on the digestive activity of dogs. *See* **Classical Conditioning**

Peace Jubilee: A musical celebration organized by **Patrick S. Gilmore (1829–1892)** in Boston, Massachusetts, in 1869 to celebrate the end of the Civil War. An orchestra of 1,000 musicians and a chorus of 10,000 singers performed at this peace jubilee. The event was a huge success, and in 1872 Gilmore organized an eighteen-day International Peace Jubilee to celebrate the end of the Franco-Prussian War.

Peak Experience: In psychology, a term associated with **Abraham Maslow (1908–1970)** referring to an intensely pleasurable insight or experience during which an individual is extremely happy and fulfilled. According to Maslow, peak experiences are more likely to happen to a self-actualized person. *See* **Need Hierarchy, Maslow; Self-actualization**

Pearson Product-moment Correlation (Pearson *r*): The most common type of **correlation**, a statistical test for determining the degree of relationship between two **variables** or whether there is a relationship between two sets of **measurements**. Correlations range from +1.00 (a perfect positive correlation) through zero to −1.00 (a perfect negative correlation). The further the Pearson *r* is from zero in either a positive or a negative direction, the stronger the relationship. The Pearson *r* can be used for making better-than-chance predictions about phenomena, but it cannot be used for directly determining causal factors. That is, while a correlation determines relationships between variables, it does not determine what causes what. A positive correlation indicates that variables vary together in the same direction. In other words, when one variable increases or decreases, the other variable increases or decreases accordingly. For example, as study time increases, test scores increase; or in wind playing, as the amount of air decreases, the loudness decreases. A negative correlation indicates that variables vary in opposite directions. In other words, when one variable increases, the other variable decreases and vice versa. For example, as practice time increases, the number of mistakes in performance decreases; or as the number of teachers in a school increases, the teacher/pupil ratio decreases.

Pedagogy/Pedagogical Content Knowledge: Teaching knowledge associated with a particular discipline necessary to teach or impart the content knowledge of that discipline. Knowledge of the subject matter and of the processes involved in "doing" is an important component of pedagogy. In teacher preparation programs in music, pedagogy courses focus on teaching the "nuts-and-bolts" aspects of music. Typically, college and universities require some type of pedagogy courses for music education majors, including courses that cover the fundamentals of playing and teaching woodwind, brass, string, and percussion instruments as well as courses in vocal technique.

Peer Tutoring: In education, when one student tutors another student of the same age, usually in the same class. Teachers who employ peer tutoring in their classrooms typically set aside specific times for this activity. Peer tutoring can be a positive experience. First, students who are having trouble in an area may feel more comfortable working with another student than they do working with an adult. Second, students are sometimes able to explain material in terms that other students can relate to more readily because of their peer status. Peer tutoring can also be a negative experience. First, care must be taken to avoid making students who are being tutored feel inferior to the tutors. Second, peer tutoring can lead to resentment between students, which negatively impacts group dynamics within the classroom. In general, social issues often make peer tutoring less effective than cross-age tutoring. *See* **Cross-age Tutoring**

Pegwords/Peg Method: In memory, a **mnemonic** device that involves memorizing a list of words or things onto which new material to be memorized can be "hung." Pegwords are based on the same principles used in the method of loci; however, the method of loci involves using a set of locations, while pegwords involves using a set of words for reference. *See* Method of Loci

Per-pupil Expenditure: In education, the amount of money allocated by educational services divided by the number of pupils to be served, or the amount of money spent for each student.

Percentile Rank: In statistics, the percentage of cases falling at or below a given score, typically a test score. That is, if an individual scored at the 95th percentile, that individual would exceed 95 percent of all persons taking that particular test. *See* Percentile

Percentiles: In statistics, actual numbers that divide a **distribution** into 100 equal parts. Individual scores along this distribution are percentile ranks. In education, percentiles are used to place students in comparison to other students on **standardized tests**. *See* Percentile Rank; Normal Curve

Perception: The process of becoming aware of objects, qualities, or relations through the senses. While sensory content is always present in perception, perceived information is influenced by training, education, and experience. As a result, perception is more than a passive registration of **stimuli** impinging on sense organs.

Perceptual Constancies: The ability to identify an object correctly even though the object may change its location, distance, or position from the observer. That is, changes in retinal images do not affect the ability to recognize and correctly identify most objects. For example, one can easily recognize a trumpet as a trumpet or a car as a car regardless of its position in the visual field. Due to perceptual constancies, people do not have to treat every perceptual change as if it were a new experience. This ability allows an individual's ever-changing environment to remain relatively stable in a general sense. The main types of perceptual constancies include: 1) **shape constancy,** 2) **size constancy,** 3) **location constancy,** and 4) **object constancy.**

Perceptual Patterning: In psychology, the tendency to perceive stimuli according to **gestalt** principles including **proximity**, **similarity**, **continuity**, and **closure**. Gestalt psychologists place a great deal of emphasis on perceptual patterns. *See* **Figure-ground Perception; Gestalt Psychology**

Perceptual Set: In general, a habitual or ingrained way of perceiving stimuli based on preconceived expectations. Perceptual sets are formed through individual experiences and are based on how things normally look or sound. Perceptual sets can be helpful in daily life, because they enable individuals to understand language or visual signs, symbols, or messages even when part of the information is missing. For example, if part of a road sign is covered up, most drivers can understand the sign because they are able to "fill in" missing information based on perceptual sets. In fact, people are often unaware of the missing information; the brain simply "sees" or "hears" the information intact. Perceptual sets can be problematic, because they can keep individuals from perceiving certain things. That is, individuals can get "locked" into a certain way of thinking that inhibits their abilities to think creatively.

Perennialism: In educational philosophy, shaping the thinking about education by looking both backward through history and forward in time. Perennialism was introduced by Robert Hutchins (1899–1977) and Mortimer Adler (1902–2001) in the 1930s in reaction to **progressive** educational approaches. These progressive approaches involved **curricula** being viewed as relative to a time and a culture and placing emphasis on child-centered teaching strategies and problem solving skills instead of knowledge acquisition. Perennialists believe that all individuals need the same basic education in history, language, mathematics, science, literature, and the humanities. Perennialists also believe that fundamental, enduring principles of education are central to all cultures and should be studied everywhere. These principles include the universality of truth, the importance of rationality, and the power of aesthetics. Perennialists believe that students should study the classics of Western culture as a means of developing intellectual capabilities and a solid knowledge base. In this regard, perennialists prefer a teacher-centered approach in which the teacher is the authority. They believe it is the teacher's responsibility to teach the essential **core curriculum** to the students.

Perfect Pitch: In music, the ability to produce or label **pitches** on demand without the aid of reference tones. Although it is not uncommon for individuals to have highly developed relative pitch, few individuals truly possess perfect pitch. Debates about whether perfect pitch is an innate ability are ongoing. *See* **Absolute Pitch; Relative Pitch**

Performance: In psychology, overt behavior or behavior that can be observed in some way. Performance is distinct from other types of knowledge or information that is not translated into action. The distinction is often addressed in learning theories. In music, the term performance is used in several ways. First, it refers to the act or process of playing or singing in a formal or informal setting (a rehearsal or performance). Second, performance can refer to a particular concert, festival, or other event in which someone is performing for others (last week's performance). Third, performance can be used when referring to how well an individual played in a particular venue. ("His performance was brilliant.")

Performance Anxiety: Often called stage fright, the stress sometimes experienced by performing artists before and/or during concerts, recitals, or competitions. Symptoms of performance anxiety can include: 1) trembling, 2) weak knees, 3) rapid heart rate, 4) dry mouth, 5) shortness of breath, 6) memory lapses, and 7) impaired motor function. As a result of stress, physiological changes can occur in a matter of seconds. These changes include: 1) the slowing or stopping of the glandular activities of digestion, which causes the salivary glands to stop functioning, resulting in dry mouth; 2) circulation changes resulting in an increased heart rate and rise in blood pressure; 3) increased activity of the body's sweat glands; 4) contraction of the muscles around the hair follicles, resulting in bristling; 5) a sudden release of stored sugar from the liver; and 6) an increased secretion of adrenalin.

While some nervousness before and during performance is normal and may actually be beneficial, extreme nervousness reaching the level of performance anxiety generally results in poor performances or the inability to perform at all. Several measures may be taken to reduce and control performance anxiety. These include: 1) being organized and well-prepared; 2) developing and following a pre-performance routine; 3) forming realistic expectations about the performance beforehand; 4) rehearsing the program mentally (**mental practice**); 5) visualizing as many aspects of the performance as possible, including the audience, the performing venue, the lighting, and the attire; and 6) performing more often. Although the symptoms of performance anxiety are physiological, their causes are typically psychological in nature; thus, developing a sense of emotional stability and self-confidence is important for overcoming and preventing performance anxiety. Research suggests that stage fright may result from physiological changes instead of psychological ones, implying that no amount of preparation or mental practice can overcome it. Therapy and medication are often used when such physiological changes are determined to cause stage fright.

Performance anxiety is also often associated with competition; however, the nature of the relationship is unclear. Some researchers have found that competition may have negative effects on performance, while others have found that competition can actually enhance performance. The intensity of the competition and **personality** factors contribute to the level of performance anxiety individuals experience in competitive situations.

Performance Assessment: In education, the measure of actual performance for assessment purposes. The idea behind performance assessment is that students should be assessed while they are actively engaged in what it is they are learning. For example, if a student is learning to read and speak French, then they should be assessed while they are actually reading and speaking French. In music education, particularly in **performance-based** classes, performance assessment has long been part of many programs. Having students play or sing scales, **sight read**, and perform excerpts from performance literature are all frequently used methods of performance assessment.

Performance-based Classes: In education, classes in which **objectives** and **goals** are met or accomplished primarily by emphasizing the development of performance skills. **Fine arts** classes that involve performing outside the classroom in concerts, festivals, and other venues are considered performance-based. These include band, orchestra, choir, theater, and dance. Often the majority of class time is spent rehearsing for upcoming performances in performance-based classes.

Performance-based Music Classes: *See* Performance-based Classes

Performance-based Teacher Education: *See* Competency-based Teacher Education (CBTE)

Performance Contracting: In education, a contract between a school system and a business to carry out a specific instructional task.

Performance IQ: In psychology, a term used by **David Wechsler (1896–1981)** to describe the **nonverbal** component of **intelligence**. Wechsler believed that the **Stanford-Binet** test placed too much emphasis on verbal items and for this reason made a pointed effort to include a section designed to tap visual-motor abilities. These abilities are reflected in terms of a performance IQ on Wechsler's tests. That is, the Wechsler IQ tests are scored on the basis of a verbal IQ and a performance IQ. The performance IQ portion of the test consists of five subtests, including picture arrangement, picture completion, block design, digit symbol, and object assembly. In Wechsler's tests, verbal and performance IQ scores are combined to arrive at a full-scale IQ score. Wechsler believed that this approach to testing IQs more accurately reflected the intelligence of individuals who did not possess strong verbal skills. *See* **Wechsler, David (1896-1981)**

Performing Groups: The traditional band, orchestra, and choir classes found in most public school music programs. Class time is largely spent rehearsing music for performance outside the classroom. Such performances include concerts, festivals, athletic events, and assemblies. Less common performing groups include percussion ensemble, madrigals, pit orchestras, guitar ensembles, and swing choirs.

Period: In physics, the time required for a vibrating system to complete one **cycle**. For example, in string playing, a string is in an **at-rest** position when it is not vibrating. When a player bows or plucks the string, it is set in vibration. The string vibrates in a back-and-forth or up-and-down motion. As a result, the string passes through the at-rest position on both the up side and the down side repeatedly during vibration. The range of motion the string travels from the at-rest position to the up side, back through the at-rest position to the down side, and then back to the original at-rest position, is one cycle. The period is the time it takes to complete one cycle and is measured in seconds. The period is a useful term in physics; however, in music, frequency is a much more useful measure of vibration. *See* **Frequency**

Periodic Vibration: In acoustics, any vibration produced by a sound source that repeats itself at regular intervals. For example, a bowed violin produces periodic vibrations when playing long tones because the vibration patterns repeat regularly. This phenomenon is true of other string and wind instruments as well. The amount of time it takes for the vibration to complete one **cycle** is one **period**. In reality, because neither traditional musical instruments nor musical performers are capable of producing perfectly consistent tones, most musical sounds fluctuate slightly and are more accurately characterized as quasi-periodic sounds.

Periodicity Theory: In psychoacoustics, the theory that the **pitch perception** of a **complex tone** is determined by the **periods** of the **upper tone partials** rather than by the **fundamental frequency** of the tone. The periodicity theory was an **alternative theory** proposed by J. F. Schouten to H. L. F. von Helmholtz's (1821–1894) **place theory**. *See* **Missing Fundamental**

Person Variables: In Walter Mischel's (b. 1930) **cognitive social learning theory** (1979), a set of cognitive and behavioral attributes that help determine the way individual experiences affect **cognition**. The general idea is that the same experiences can affect individuals in different ways. Mischel identified five person variables: 1) **competencies**, which includes **problem solving** abilities; 2) **encoding** strategies, which includes how an individual processes or interprets information; 3) **expectancies**, which are things an individual thinks are likely to happen; 4) **subjective values**, which is how an individual feels about expected outcomes; and 5) **self-regulatory** functions, which is how an individual regulates his or her own behavior by means of self-reinforcement, **criticism**, and plans.

Person-centered Therapy: Originally known as **client-centered therapy,** or the Rogerian approach, a therapy devised by **Carl Rogers (1902–1987)** in the 1950s to treat individuals with mild emotional or mental disturbances. Person-centered therapy was based on the idea that being warm, empathetic, and genuine would have therapeutic benefits to individuals and was developed as an alternative to **Sigmund Freud's (1856–1939) psychoanalysis**. Person-centered therapy is considered to be a **humanistic** approach even though it was developed a decade before the humanistic movement of the 1960s and 1970s because of its emphasis on the individual.

Person-centered therapy is a nondirective approach to treatment because the individual has the primary responsibility for solving his or her own problems with help from the therapist. The major themes of the approach include: 1) focusing on the here and now, rather than on an individual's childhood experiences or past events; 2) being empathetic to the individual; 3) the use of unconditional positive regard, or the acceptance of the individual despite what he or she may say or do; 4) being warm and sensitive to the individual's situation; 5) working to improve an individual's self-concept; and 6) helping individuals learn to accept themselves for who they are. Person-centered therapy has significantly influenced psychological counseling and therapy, and research has repeatedly confirmed its effectiveness.

Personality: In general, the patterned ways individuals behave based on their reactions to people and experiences. Personality factors tend to be stable across time and include emotions, moods, actions, and responses.

Personality Assessment: In general, the appraisal or **evaluation** of the ways individuals behave in a variety of situations. Personality assessment is usually based in part on the ways individuals behave in contrived social situations. Personality is typically assessed through observations and judgments.

Personality Disorders: Ingrained, habitual, and rigid patterns of behavior that limit an individual's adaptive potential. Typical symptoms of personality disorders include being anxious, extremely shy, or unusually sad much of the time. Society acknowledges that these behaviors are maladaptive, although individuals with personality disorders often will not acknowledge the maladaptive nature of their **behavior**. *See* Maladaptive Behaviors

Personality Inventory: An inventory or form that can be used for self-appraisal, personality inventories generally consist of statements or questions about personal characteristics and behavior. Typically, individuals determine whether they can apply certain statements or questions to themselves. The individual's choices help determine **personality** type. *See* Projective Test

Pestalozzi, Johann Heinrich (1746-1827): A Swiss educator best known for his ideas and work regarding educational reform. Pestalozzi was director of the Yverdon Institute between 1805 and 1825, an institute which accepted students from across Europe. One of his most famous students was **Frederic Wilhelm Froebel (1782–1852)**, founder of the **Kindergarten.** Pestalozzi's **teaching method** was based on a number of principles considered innovative at the time and included the following concepts: 1) emphasis on group rather than individual recitation; 2) focus on participatory activities such as drawing, writing, singing, physical exercise, model making, collecting, mapmaking, and field trips; 3) making allowances for individual differences; 4) grouping students by ability rather than by age; and 5) encouraging formal teacher training. Pestalozzi's principles of teaching and his teaching methods were widely studied throughout Europe and America, and his ideas influenced teaching in European and American singing schools, including those of **Lowell Mason (1792–1872)**.

Phallic Stage: In Sigmund Freud's **(1856–1939) psychoanalytic theory,** the third stage of **psychosexual** development. During the phallic stage (ages three to seven) a child's gratification is associated with sex organ stimulation, and the sexual attachment is to the parent of the opposite sex. According to Freud, conflict results from the child's attachment to the parent of the opposite sex and a fear of retaliation from the parent of the same sex. During this period, the child is searching for sexual identification. The conflict resolves itself at about age seven, when the child begins to identify with the parent of the same sex. The phallic stage is sometimes called the Oedipal stage because it is at this stage that the Oedipus complex arises. *See* **Oedipus Complex**

Phenomenalism: In philosophy, the view that human beings can only know physical reality through their **perceptions**, or that all knowledge of the physical world is limited to what is learned through human perceptions.

Phenomenology: In philosophy, looking at and describing phenomena without preconceived ideas about their underlying structure. That is, phenomenology involves viewing things from a "new" perspective. In **philosophical research**, phenomenology centers on the analysis of phenomena that individuals experience and the ways individual **perceptions** affect knowing and understanding. In behavioral psychology, phenomenology refers to the idea that individuals may behave in destructive ways due to faulty perceptions or feelings related to **self-esteem** or image.

Phenotype: In genetics, the inherited traits, genetic properties, characteristics, or observable properties that are expressed or displayed by an individual organism. Phenotypes can include such characteristics as eye color, intelligence, and temperament and are opposed to genotypes, which are traits that may be carried genetically but are not necessarily displayed. *See* Genotype

Philosophical Research: A method of research that addresses philosophical questions. Philosophical researchers often seek to enlighten or to answer questions by clarifying terminology, evaluating underlying assumptions, analyzing available information, and developing a structurally sound, organized body of thought. Statistical analysis is not a common component of philosophical research as it is in experimental research. Instead, one role of philosophical research is to generate the types of questions that experimental researchers may wish to investigate or test. The evaluation of assumptions helps to refine philosophical ideas leads to and critiques of philosophical thought. Philosophical assumptions are often evaluated using the following techniques: 1) appeals to precedent, 2) weight of authority, 3) logic, 4) moral claims, 5) realism of expectations, 6) ease of application, and 7) aesthetic appeal. Philosophical researchers analyze ideas in an attempt to clarify and to help justify their points of view. Careful, methodical, and thoughtful analysis helps philosophers develop a "theory" or a conceptual framework that can be coherent, consistent, and insightful.

Philosophy: Etymologically, philosophy is the love of wisdom. Generally speaking, philosophy is the branch of science that investigates general facts, values, and principles of reality and human nature. Philosophy deals with the study of truths or principles and the underlying knowledge surrounding them. Philosophers attempt to answer questions critically by investigating what makes such questions puzzling or confusing and by trying to eliminate vagueness and confusion that surround them. Aesthetics, ethics, metaphysics, epistemology, ontology, axiology, realism, idealism, existentialism, progressivism, and logic are all philosophical areas of investigation or thought.

In *Foundations and Principles of Music Education* (1972), Leonard and House suggest that music philosophy embraces reasoned underlying beliefs about music, its power, and the qualities that make music a worthwhile pursuit. They see music philosophy as a way of answering questions such as: What is there about music that impels us to spend our lives and our substance preparing to teach it? What is there about music that can sustain us through a lifetime of contact with it? What is the nature of the aesthetic musical experience? What qualities do music and the musical experience have that justify their inclusion in the school curriculum? Why teach music? They further indicate that the answers to these questions constitute the framework for a philosophy of music education. Classic philosophers include Plato, Aristotle, Descartes, Kant, Hume, Locke, Hobbes, James, Dewey, Huxley, and Russell. Music educators who have written extensively about philosophy include Schwadron, Langer, Broudy, Reimer, Bowman, and Elliott.

Phobia: In psychology, an irrational fear that interferes with normal, daily functioning. Phobias are usually exaggerated fears or responses to mildly or potentially fearful situations that are not logical or reasonable. Some of the most common phobias include: 1) claustrophobia, a fear of enclosed places; 2) aquaphobia, a fear of water; 3) agoraphobia, a fear of open spaces; 4) acrophobia, a fear of high places; 5) hematophobia, a fear of the sight of blood; 6) mysophobia, a fear of dirt or germs; 7) xenophobia, a fear of strangers; 8) lalophobia, a fear of public speaking; and 9) zoophobia, a fear of animals.

Phobic Reaction: In psychology, an excessive fear of something in the absence of any real danger. *See* **Phobia**

Phon: In acoustics, a unit used to indicate degrees of **loudness**. Phons are similar to decibels (dB), which are used to indicate **intensity** levels. *See* **Decibel (dB); Sone**

Phonation: *See* **Phonetics**

Phoneme: The smallest sounding unit in a language system. Phonemes are the distinctive sounds that certain letters have when spoken. They help characterize the sound of a particular language. Example: The *b* in bat and the *c* in cat are phonemes that enable the listener to distinguish between the two words.

Phonetics: The science of speech sounds, the pronunciation of language, and a branch of linguistics. Phonetics is the study of speech production, including the way speech is produced (i.e., **articulators**), the sound waves associated with speech, and the auditory effect of speech on listeners.

Phonetics also refers to the body of speech sounds contained in any particular language, including the way these speech sounds are articulated and their relation to one another. Singers commonly use the International Phonetic Alphabet (IPA) to understand precise pronunciation, particularly of words in foreign languages. *See* International Phonetic Alphabet (IPA)

Phonology: A system of speech sounds, or the study of a language's sound system. Phonology within a particular language system helps determine which sound sequences will occur and which sequences will not. These sequences help give a language its characteristic "sound." *See* Phonetics; Phonemes

Physical (P) Learning: *See* P (Physical) Learning

Physical Disorders: A general term for physical abnormalities that interfere with an individual's mobility, coordination, communication, learning, and/or personal adjustment. *See* Handicapped; Impairment

Physical Prompting: In education, when a teacher physically moves the student in some way through the desired responses. Physical prompting is common in music education because of music's emphasis on **motor skill** development. Some examples include: 1) physically placing a student's hands or fingers in the proper position on the instrument; 2) manipulating a singer's body in order to achieve proper positioning for vocal production; and 3) pulling a trumpet player's elbows out from the body to a proper position.

Physiological Measures: Measures of bodily responses involving the brain and nervous system such as brain waves, heart rate, pupillary response, and sweating.

Physiological Motives: Motives based on physiological needs or physical deficits within the body. Physiological motives cause individuals to find ways of eliminating these deficits to return the body to its normal state. Physiological motives are based on needs such as food, water, sleep, sex, and body temperature regulation.

Physiological Psychology: A branch of psychology that deals with the physiological basis of behavior. That is, physiological psychology emphasizes the relationships between bodily functions and changes in bodily functions and associated feelings, actions, and thoughts.

Physiological psychologists are particularly interested in the interaction between the two.

Piaget, Jean (1896-1980): A Swiss psychologist who spent most of his adult life studying **cognitive** development. Piaget received a zoology degree from the University of Neuchâtel in 1918. He studied with **Carl Jung (1875–1961)** and **Eugen Bleuler (1857–1939)** before working with **Alfred Binet (1857–1911)** administering intelligence tests to children. In 1929, Piaget became professor of child psychology at the University of Geneva. Through detailed observations of developing children, Piaget formulated a theory of the way children learn. He believed that children learn **concepts** as they progress through a sequential series of biologically based developmental stages. Piaget's **stages** are: 1) sensorimotor (birth to two years); 2) preoperational or intuitive (two to seven years); 3) concrete operational (approximately seven to eleven years); and 4) formal operational (approximately eleven to sixteen years). *See* **Piaget's Stages of Cognitive Growth**

Piaget's Stages of Cognitive Growth: In psychology, an invariant sequence of four age-related stages describing the way children think and/or behave during certain growth periods. **Jean Piaget's (1896-1980)** theory of **cognitive** development is probably the most well known **stage theory** of cognitive development. According to Piaget, the stages of cognitive growth begin at birth and are completed by approximately age sixteen. Children cannot skip stages, and the progression from one stage to the next constitutes a major breakthrough or transformation in thought processes. The four stages are: 1) sensorimotor (birth to two years); 2) preoperational or intuitive (two to seven years); 3) concrete operational (approximately seven to eleven); and 4) formal operational (approximately eleven to sixteen years). A summary of characteristics of each stage is presented below.

Sensorimotor (birth to two years): Children learn primarily through their senses and are strongly affected by the immediate environment. They begin to follow objects with their eyes (visual pursuit). They also begin to realize that objects still exist, even though they may be out of sight. Their movement progresses from simple reflex actions or responses, such as grasping and sucking, to more goal-directed behaviors or purposeful responses, such as reaching for and deliberately holding onto things.

Preoperational (two to seven years): Vocabulary development and the ability to understand and use words increase dramatically during this stage. Children tend to talk *at* rather than *with* others. Symbolic thinking begins during this stage, and ideas begin to replace the need for concrete experience. At this stage, children have imaginary friends and make up creative stories. They also have difficulty realizing the reversible nature of relationships; that is, they have not mastered conservation concepts.

Concrete Operational (approximately seven to eleven years): During this period, children develop the ability to solve problems logically through the use of hands-on materials. That is, they develop the ability to understand and use logic and apply this logic to abstract, hypothetical situations. They also develop conservation concepts and can classify objects according to dimensions such as color, height, weight, and volume. Children take things quite literally at this stage and are very fact-oriented.

Formal Operational (approximately eleven to sixteen years): During this stage, children are able to solve abstract problems in logical ways by applying abstract rules and thinking hypothetically. Children are able to hypothesize, are more reflective in their thinking processes, are able to generalize from one situation to the next, and are aware of the differences regarding the way others think.

Piaget's Theory of Cognitive Development: In psychology, one of the most well-known theories of cognitive development. **Jean Piaget (1896–1980)** believed that the fundamental development of all intellectual abilities occurs during the first two years of life and that the ability to think at higher levels is a direct result of both maturation and experience. According to Piaget, mental functioning is dependent upon the ability to adapt to new experiences, a process he called **adaptation**. Piaget also believed that adaptation takes place through the twin processes of **assimilation**, which relates to the way information is absorbed into existing cognitive structures, and **accommodation**, which relates to the way existing cognitive structures are modified in response to new information. He noticed that children of different ages used different cognitive strategies to solve problems. Piaget's theory of cognitive development centers around his stages of cognitive growth, which includes: 1) **sensorimotor** (birth to two); 2) **preoperational** (two to seven); 3) **concrete operational** (approximately seven to eleven); and 4) **formal operational** (approximately eleven to sixteen). *See* **Piaget's Stages of Cognitive Growth**

Pilot Study: A small-scale research study involving fewer subjects than a full-scale study. Pilot studies are usually designed to test and refine procedures for a larger study or to see if an area of research interest warrants further investigation.

Pitch: In acoustics, a qualitative dimension of hearing, or the perceptual attribute of tone height correlated with the **frequency** of sound. In music, pitch generally refers to a specific tone in a specific register, such as middle C. Pitch is also used in reference to being in or out of tune. That is, musicians often refer to someone's pitch as being flat or sharp. The ability to hear pitch is affected by several factors, including **intensity**, **duration**, frequency, **timbre**, and the context of the tone.

Pitch Discrimination: In acoustics, the ability to distinguish between two pitches of nearly the same **frequency**. Pitch discrimination abilities are dependent upon physical factors such as frequency **range**, **loudness**, **timbre**, **duration**, and other factors, such as aural acuity, training, experience, and the manner in which tones are presented to the listener. Research on pitch discrimination has focused on the way these factors affect pitch discrimination alone and in combination. *See* **Just Noticeable Difference (jnd)**

Pitch Structure: In acoustics, the relationships between the components of a complex tone. Pitch structure is often used synonymously with pitch class, tone chroma, or pitch set.

Pitch-reading Systems: Any system utilizing syllables and/or other symbols to facilitate pitch-reading abilities. Pitch-reading is almost always used synonymously with sight singing. In the United States, a **number system** and the solfege system are both commonly used pitch-reading systems. *See* **Sight Singing Systems; Solfege**

Place Called School, A: A book written by J. I. Goodlad in 1984 that many consider the impetus behind **block scheduling**. Goodlad believed that traditional high school schedules did not allow sufficient time to promote high levels of learning and that these schedules were inefficient. Specifically, he felt that the time spent moving from class to class was wasted. Goodlad proposed that schedules be modified to include fewer but longer class periods. He strongly supported the need for arts education in the schools and felt that longer class periods would help develop student interests and talents.

Place Theory: H. L. F. von Helmholtz's (1821–1894) theory (1863) of **pitch perception** suggesting that the perception of pitch relates directly to the area of stimulation on the **basilar membrane**. The theory was criticized after it was shown that **partials** of a **complex tone** can stimulate several areas on the basilar membrane, yet only one pitch is perceived. In fact, studies show that listeners can perceive the fundamental of a complex tone, even when it is physically missing from the tone, on the basis of its partials alone. As a result, **place theory** was determined to be only a partial explanation of the way individuals perceive pitch. *See* **Missing Fundamental**

Placebo: In general, a substance or other aid purported to have beneficial qualities that it really does not possess. The idea behind using a placebo is that something that normally would have no beneficial effect actually does have a beneficial effect because the beneficiary believes it does. In medical research, a placebo is an inert substance used in place of an active drug and given to placebo groups in drug research.

Placebo Groups: In drug research, groups that receive an inert substance rather than an active drug to assess the psychological effect of receiving a **treatment**. Typically, placebo groups are unaware that they are being given a placebo. Studies have shown that groups receiving a placebo rather than the drug being tested sometimes exhibit the positive effects of the drug. It appears that the mere thought of taking a drug designed to better health is often enough to improve health in some way.

Plateau: In a learning curve, a **period** of no improvement usually preceded and followed by periods of improvement. *See* **Learning Curve**

Play: In educational psychology, a general term used to describe spontaneous activity undertaken for the sake of itself or for the pleasure that results. In education, play usually implies freedom on the part of the child to choose an activity for the sake of exploration alone, although that does not preclude teacher or parent direction and supervision.

Play is an important component of the learning process. The value of play in education was introduced by **Friedrich Wilhelm Froebel (1782–1852)** in the early part of the nineteenth century and continues to be an important component of preschool and elementary school education today. Play has been shown to benefit children in many ways, including enhancing social interaction and developing social skills; promoting physical development of both large- and small-motor skills; and assisting in **personality** and emotional development. **Jean Piaget (1896–1980)** identified several types of play, including **sensorimotor** or **functional play, symbolic play,** playing games with rules, and constructive play. Finally, Mildred Parten (1929) identified several types of play, including **unoccupied play, associative play, solitary play, onlooker play, parallel play,** and **cooperative play**.

Pleasure Principle: In Sigmund Freud's (1856–1939) psychoanalytic theory, the principle by which the **id** operates. The pleasure principle involves the immediate gratification of instinctual or primal impulses, avoiding pain, and seeking pleasure. *See* **Hedonism**

Plessy v. Ferguson: An 1896 United States Supreme Court decision stating that "separate but equal accommodations" were required for "white" and "colored" passengers on the railroad. In the majority opinion, Justice Brown discusses the fact that state laws had upheld the "separate but equal" doctrine for public schools, even in states that aggressively pursued political rights for African Americans. This opinion effectively placed the constitutional stamp of approval on the "separate but equal" doctrine, which remained in effect for over fifty years following the *Plessy* decision. This "separate but equal" standard was upheld until the 1954 United States Supreme Court decision in *Brown v. Board of Education of Topeka, Kansas*.

Pluralism: A term used to describe any society comprised of many types of people with differing **ethnic** and cultural backgrounds, ideologies, religions, value systems, and other diverse elements. A distinction is often made between pluralism and the **melting pot** concept of American society. Pluralism refers to a society comprised of ethnic groups who have maintained their cultural heritages to a large extent. The melting pot concept implies forsaking cultural heritages and assimilating into a new culture. Sensitivity to issues regarding pluralism is a major focus in education today. As a result, integrating music of various cultures into curricula is an important, enriching component of music education. Pluralism is often used synonymously with multiculturalism. *See* Multicultural Education

Pluralistic Ignorance: In a group situation, the tendency to view an emergency as a non-emergency because others are remaining calm and are not taking action.

Plus One: In education, the **concept** that students can understand reasoning consistent with their current level or stage of reasoning, and that they can gradually be attracted to reasoning that is slightly more complex than their current level. That is, students are attracted to reasoning one stage higher than their current level, or plus one. The **concept** of plus one is based on the idea that students cannot understand reasoning two or more stages higher than their current level. This concept is consistent with the idea that presenting students with modest challenges motivates them to achieve at higher levels.

Polygenic Traits/Inheritance: Inherited **traits** or characteristics that result from the combination of large numbers of **genes**. Polygenic traits include characteristics such as **intelligence**, height, and emotional stability and are different from those physical traits determined by a single pair of genes, such as eye and hair color.

Population: In research, the total number of individuals, things, or events falling into a particular group based on defined **parameters** or **traits** from which a sample is drawn. For example, all individuals with an **intelligence quotient (IQ)** over 180 would be a **population**.

Portfolio: In education, a collection of a student's works over a specified period of time typically used for assessment purposes. Portfolios are one of the most popular forms of **alternative assessment** today. Depending on the nature of the course, a portfolio may include samples of a student's writings, artwork, musical compositions, tests, assignments, or other items representative of a student's work in that course. Portfolios often contain samples of a student's best works as well as other "average" works so that the collection is truly representative. Portfolios are **performance-based** and can be used in most courses. In addition, because they contain a collection of works over a period of time, student progress can be easily tracked, and many portfolios contain written student critiques of their own work. These self-critiques enable students to be actively involved in the assessment process.

Considerations for building portfolios include the following: 1) determining its purpose, 2) determining its desired outcomes, 3) choosing its contents, 4) determining scoring criteria for its contents, 5) determining specific timelines for adding contents to the portfolio, 6) determining specific timelines for evaluating the contents of the portfolio, and 7) arranging conferences with all parties involved to discuss the portfolio. In music, portfolios may not be practical for evaluating performance-based classes for two main reasons. First, when done properly the amount of time involved in portfolio assessment is extensive and would detract from rehearsal time, negatively impacting the performance level of the ensemble. Second, performance-based classes do not typically involve many written materials or projects.

Positive Discipline Techniques: In education, techniques for disciplining students that are positive, fair, and encouraging. Positive discipline techniques include the use of positive reinforcers, allowing the class to participate in the rule-making process, facilitating group projects that promote **cohesiveness**, and making the consequences of misbehaving reasonable and fair. These techniques are "hands-off" techniques designed to encourage self-discipline.

Positive Incentive: In cognitive motivation theory, anything that causes an individual to behave in certain ways because of positive expectations. In education, anything that constitutes a reason for students to work toward a goal or goals. Positive incentives can be objects or they can be intangibles, such as praise or feelings of accomplishment. *See* **Cognitive Motivation Theory; Negative Incentive; Reinforcer; Reinforcement**

Positive Reinforcement: Any added **stimulus** that increases the likelihood of the **response** recurring. Food and money are common examples of positive reinforcers, because the addition of either typically leads to an increase in the desired behavior. In the classroom, positive reinforcement may be provided by primary reinforcers, such as food, or by conditioned reinforcers, such as gold stars, grades, or approval.

Positivism: In philosophy, the general belief that an ultimate reality exists beyond a human being's **subjective** and often inconsistent abilities to know it. Common in the seventeenth and eighteenth centuries, positivism was based on the idea that knowing was the product of gathering knowledge via the scientific method. It was believed that individuals could discover this ultimate reality through scientific investigation and/or rational thought. In research, positivism is the idea that knowing is based on the scientific method of gathering data. That is, emphasis is placed on information gleaned from scientific, empirical studies.

Post Hoc Comparisons: In research, **data** comparisons that have been unplanned by the researcher prior to data analysis in **analysis of variance (ANOVA)** statistical designs. That is, post hoc comparisons are determined after an ANOVA research design has shown **significant** differences for the main and **interaction effects**. Their purpose is to determine which of the differences of the **means** are significant. Common post hoc tests include Duncan's multiple range test, Scheffe's contrast vectors test, and Tukey's post hoc comparisons test. *See* Simple Effects; Main Effects; A Priori Comparisons

Postconventional Morality/Moral Reasoning: In Lawrence Kohlberg's (1927–1987) moral **development** stages, the highest stage of moral reasoning. At this stage, individuals formulate and follow the universal ethical principles or rules of society. However, individuals also realize that these principles or rules may need to be overridden in certain circumstances, such as when or if they become destructive. *See* Moral Development, Kohlberg

Post-Facto (P/F) Research: A type of research that allows researchers to compare an individual's responses on two or more measured **traits** or dimensions. P/F research does not involve manipulating **variables** and does not allow researchers to make direct cause-and-effect conclusions; however, it does allow researchers to make better-than-chance predictions about the traits or dimensions being investigated. For example, if researchers wanted to know if student participation is related to teacher enthusiasm, they could find a reliable and valid scale for measuring both student participation and teacher enthusiasm. If they find that indeed a relationship does exist (i.e., the student participates more when the teacher is more enthusiastic), then researchers could predict with greater accuracy than a guess that the more enthusiastic the teacher is, the more students will participate. What the researchers cannot say is that the teacher's enthusiasm is the cause of the student participation.

Posttest: In research, a **measurement** of an experimental **variable** after the experimental **treatment** is administered. A posttest is often compared with the results of a pretest to determine whether the experimental treatment had a significant effect on the experimental groups' performance. *See* **Pretest**

Power: *See* **Statistical Power**

Pragmatism: A philosophy or philosophical method in which the truth and meaning of ideas are based on the physical consequences and practical value of these ideas, or the idea that the validity of something is directly related to its practical application in daily life. In philosophy, pragmatism has its roots in ancient Greece, but it flourished as a philosophy in the nineteenth and twentieth centuries.

In education, pragmatism is virtually synonymous with practicality. That is, something is pragmatic if it is viewed as being practical. Educators who say they have pragmatic concerns are normally talking about logistical, functional aspects. In this regard, pragmatism is often viewed as a "common sense" philosophy. Like many philosophers, pragmatists concern themselves with the dualistic concept of mind and matter, or the subjective versus the objective worlds. Pragmatists believe that objective reality is meaningful only if individuals can associate meaning with this reality based on its practical consequences. As a philosophical method, the goal of pragmatists is to determine what is true by examining the consequences of particular beliefs. That is, if an individual's beliefs "work," then these beliefs must be true.

Although Charles Sanders Pierce (1839–1914) is the originator of modern pragmatism, most people associate the philosophy with **William James (1842–1910)** and **John Dewey (1859–1952)**. Dewey wrote extensively on the importance of educational preparation for life in a democracy and on pragmatic views of education. For example, Dewey believed that education should prepare students to solve problems encountered in everyday life, to govern themselves, to assume responsibility for their own actions, and to enhance their human potential. He also stressed the importance of teaching thinking and problem-solving skills that would enable students to function effectively in society.

Praxis Series, The: In education, a battery of tests devised by the **Educational Testing Service (ETS)** to assess the skills and knowledge of beginning teachers. These tests are often taken prior to receiving certification and licensure. The Praxis Series tests measure teachers' basic skills in reading, writing, and mathematics, as well as professional education and subject matter knowledge. They also assess abilities related to planning instruction, teaching, **classroom management**, and student assessment.

Precedence Effect: *See* Haas Effect

Precise Teaching: A method of individualized instruction commonly used for newly mainstreamed children. Precise teaching involves utilizing a very structured classroom environment along with **behavior modification** techniques to help students master educational tasks. Students are allowed to proceed at their own pace and receive **positive reinforcement** for accomplishments in order to accumulate successes in the classroom. Components of precise teaching often include the following: 1) selecting a highly specific task, 2) setting up a contract with the student that includes a way to visually track student progress, and 3) negotiating a significant reward or choice of rewards to serve as **reinforcements** for desired behaviors. Precise teaching is most effective when used in single subjects areas for brief periods of time.

Preconventional Morality/Moral Reasoning: In Lawrence Kohlberg's (1927–1987) theory of **moral development**, the first stage of **moral reasoning**. At this stage, an individual's own welfare is the primary concern, while society's customs and mores are relatively unimportant. *See* Moral Stages, Kohlberg

Prediction: In research, a statement that makes an assertion concerning what will occur in a particular study.

Predictive Validity: *See* Validity

Predictor Variable: In research, a measure used to predict behavior on another measure. Predictor variables are typically subsets of a larger pool of **variables** that allow researchers to make accurate predictions. The use of predictor variables is made possible when many of the variables in the larger pool are intercorrelated. The general idea is that a minimal number of predictor variables can account for the majority of the **variance** within a larger set, facilitating the practicality of the research design. Predictor variables are common in **multiple regression analysis.**

Preferred Style of Learning: In education, the style or system of **problem solving** preferred by a student according to his or her stage of **conceptual development.** David Hunt believes this system is neither fixed nor permanent and students can be encouraged to grow conceptually and increase the complexity of their thinking. This growth is accomplished by matching and mismatching appropriate materials and/or methods according to the student's stage of development. *See* **Plus One; Matching and Mismatching**

Prejudices: **Attitudes** firmly fixed in an individual's mind, often based on false perceptions or lack of knowledge. Prejudices are frequently difficult to change or overcome, and people who are prejudiced in some way are not always open to discussing related issues in a free and rational manner. Prejudices against people based on **race** and gender are often discussed in today's society; however, prejudices regarding religion, **ideology**, education, and politics are also very common.

Premack Principle: Introduced by David Premack, a principle of **behavior modification** based on the idea that **behavior** that occurs at a naturally high rate of frequency may be used to reinforce behavior that occurs at a naturally low rate of frequency. In the classroom, teachers can determine which **activities** the students like the best by how often they engage in these activities during their free time. These activities can then be used as **positive reinforcers** for those that the students do not like as much. For example, in music classes, teachers may find that their students enjoy listening to popular music more than they enjoy listening to classical music during their free time. As a result, teachers could allow students to listen to popular music as a reward for listening to more classical music. The Premack principle is sometimes referred to as "Grandma's rule."

Premise: In general, an assumption, foundational idea, or postulate upon which something is based. For example, American democracy is built on the premise that certain types of freedom are highly valued, such as freedom of speech and freedom of association. In logic or argument, premises are statements assumed to be true from which logical conclusions can be drawn.

Preoperational Stage: *See* Piaget's Stages of Cognitive Growth

Preschool Measures of Musical Audiation (PSMMA): A test developed by **Edwin E. Gordon (b. 1927)** to measure preschoolers' **audiation** abilities. Gordon found that age and **intelligence** are related to preschoolers' abilities to audiate. *See* Primary Measures of Musical Audiation (PMMA)

Pretest: In research, a **measurement** of an experimental **variable** before the experimental **treatment** is administered. Pretests are often given when researchers want to know how something (**independent variable**) affects something else (**dependent variable**). Pretests provide baseline scores that can be compared to posttest scores following the administration of the treatment(s). Differences in pretest and posttest scores can then be attributed to the treatment(s). *See* Posttest

Primacy Effect: In memory experiments, the tendency for individuals to remember the initial information they received longer than subsequent information. For example, when presented with a list of words to memorize, individuals are more likely to remember the first few words than they are the others. The **primacy effect** is generally associated with long-term memory (LTM). *See* Recency Effect; Long-term Memory (LTM)

Primary Control: In psychology, a **coping mechanism** in which individuals attempt to modify or influence external reality by changing other people, the situation or circumstances, or relevant events. Primary control is in contrast to **secondary control** in which individuals change their own attitudes and **perceptions** to accommodate external reality. *See* Secondary Control

Primary Emotions: In psychology, emotions considered to be universal and biologically based. Primary emotions include fear, anger, grief, happiness, surprise, and disgust. *See* Secondary Emotions

Primary Measures of Music Audiation (PMMA): A music aptitude test developed by **Edwin E. Gordon (b. 1927)** in 1979 for students from kindergarten through third grade. The test has two sections: tonal stimuli (forty sets) and rhythm stimuli (forty pairs). Students are asked to make same/different judgments regarding the musical examples, which are produced electronically on a synthesizer. In the tonal section, students listen to the first example, then to a second example, and are asked to indicate if the second is the same or different than the first. In the rhythm section, students listen to rhythmic pairs produced on one tone, and are asked to indicate whether the pairs are the same or different. The test has an **internal consistency** reliability of .90 and a **test-retest reliability** of .75.

Primary Mental Abilities: According to **Louis L. Thurstone (1887–1955)**, hypothesized mental abilities that cannot be further reduced. Primary mental abilities include memory, reasoning skills, verbal abilities, and spatial abilities. Primary mental abilities are believed to underlie performance on **intelligence tests.**

Primary Punisher: In **behavioral psychology,** any **stimulus** that is inherently or naturally **punishing,** or any stimulus that weakens or reduces the probability that the response will follow the presentation of a stimulus. *See* Punishment; Primary Reinforcer

Primary Reinforcer: In **behavioral psychology,** any **stimulus** that is inherently or naturally reinforcing, or any stimulus that strengthens or increases the probability that the response will follow the presentation of a stimulus. Primary reinforcers typically satisfy a physiological **need** such as the need for food. *See* Reinforcement; Primary Punisher

Priming/Implicit Memory: *See* Implicit Memory/Priming

Primitivation: *See* Regression

Principle of Recency: *See* Guthrie, Edwin (1886-1959)

Private Schools/Independent Schools: Nonprofit, **tax-exempt schools** usually governed by a board of trustees and financed through private funds including tuition, endowments, and/or grants. Private schools are accredited by state departments of education; however, like public schools, they must meet the rules and laws governing health, safety, and mandatory attendance. Private schools differ from public schools in several ways. First, private schools can set their own admission requirements as they see fit. Second, private schools can recruit students or admit students without concern for district boundaries. Third, private schools have the freedom to adopt philosophies that appeal to specific groups of people, while public schools are driven by inclusiveness. The once-clear distinction between private schools and public schools has become blurred in recent years. The acceptance of new ideas about how schools should be structured, the increased involvement of businesses and the private sector in educational policies, and the increased use of public revenues, such as vouchers, to help fund private education have done much to blur the distinction between private and public schools.

Proactive Inhibition: In psychology, when previously learned information inhibits the ability to learn new information, or when old learning interferes with new learning. For example, if a new phone number has several digits in common with a previously learned phone number, knowledge of the old phone number can interfere with learning the new phone number. *See* Interference; Retroactive Inhibition

Probability: In research, the likelihood that a given event will occur among a specific set of events. *See* Statistical Significance; Probability Value

Probability Sampling: In research, a general term for sampling procedures in which each member of a **population** has a specifiable probability of being chosen for inclusion. Probability sampling decreases the likelihood of error in a study and includes **simple random sampling**, **stratified random sampling**, and **cluster sampling**. *See* Nonprobability Sampling; Random Sampling; Sampling

Probability Value: In research, a number used to indicate whether or not the results obtained via statistical procedures are **significant**. The most common probability value is .05. This value means that the results are considered significant when there is a .05 probability or less of getting the results, or that there is only a 5 percent chance that the results occurred by chance alone. *See* Statistical Significance

Problem Solving: In education, a term used to describe an exercise whereby students use new **skills** and **concepts** to work through hypothetical scenarios or problems. Problem solving is often used to gauge a student's understanding of information, skills, or concepts and offers opportunities for students to practice and manipulate new information, skills, and concepts.

Procedural Memory: A type of memory that enables individuals to perform specific **motor skills** or physical actions. Riding a bicycle, driving, or swimming all involve procedural memory.

Processing Capacity: In memory, an individual's ability to hold information in **short-term memory (STM)** or working memory, where information is processed and where reasoning and thinking occur. Evidence suggests that older children have a greater processing capacity than do younger children, which helps explain why older children are better at solving problems.

Product-moment Correlation: *See* Pearson Product-moment Correlation (Pearson *r*)

Professional Development: The process of continuing to develop and enhance teaching, musical and/or professional skills in some manner after the college degree is earned. Several states legally require teachers to engage in professional development activities to maintain certification. Professional development activities include special classes or clinics, seminars, conferences, research, and graduate study. Professional development may lead to merit pay and/or salary increases. In addition, some districts allow some time off for participation in professional development activities and will sometimes help defray the costs of participation.

Professional Development Schools (PDS): Schools devoted to the development of both novice and experienced professionals, in which individuals at public schools and universities work together to explore problems of teaching and learning. The establishment of professional development schools was a primary initiative of the **Holmes Group**. The focus of professional development schools is on sharing ideas and information about teaching, questioning assumptions and routines, taking part in research and development projects, and seeking ways to improve the teaching and learning process. In professional development schools, professors, public school teachers, and prospective teachers address teaching issues and establish **goals** in an effort to promote higher levels of professionalism and advance the teaching profession. Although a few schools were established in various locations across the country, they are not common. Other avenues for encouraging collaboration between universities and public schools are more common. *See* **Collaborative Networks; Holmes Group, The**

Profoundly Mentally Retarded (PMR): A classification of individuals who score from 0 to 20 on the **Stanford-Binet intelligence test** or 0 to 25 on the **Wechsler intelligence test**. Profoundly mentally retarded (PMR) individuals typically have some form of brain damage coupled with mental and physical limitations, and they cannot care for themselves. Profoundly mentally retarded (PMR) individuals usually attend special schools and are not mainstreamed. *See* **Mentally Retarded/Mental Retardation**

Program: In education, a course of study related to the teaching and learning processes within a particular discipline, such as a music program. Also in education, the term program is used to describe a step-by-step plan or approach to **problem solving** and is commonly associated with computer instruction. The term is often used interchangeably with "routine" and specifies the precise sequence of instructions to be followed. In this context, a program generally refers to a set of materials arranged in a particular order and designed to facilitate learning efficiency. *See* **Programmed Instruction; Computer Programs, Music**

Program Evaluation: In general, the process of determining the effectiveness of educational programs. Program evaluation is generally associated with the large-scale testing programs that began under **Title I** of the **Elementary and Secondary Education Act of 1965 (ESEA)** to assess the progress of at-risk elementary and secondary students. Program evaluation was specifically geared toward meeting the educational needs of low-income, low-achieving students and resulted in the formulation of **pull-out programs** in the public schools. In the 1970s, a move toward **minimum competency testing** began, in which all students were given large-scale, **standardized achievement tests** as a visible measure of program evaluation, student progress, and general accountability. The use of standardized tests as a method of program evaluation and effectiveness continues today, and the ESEA has been amended with the No Child Left Behind (NCLB) Act of 2001. *See* **No Child Left Behind (NCLB)**

Programmed Instruction: The arrangement of instructional material in a stepwise sequence designed to help students attain specified **goals**. The material being presented is broken down into small units called **frames,** which organize information into a visual display. The two general approaches to programming are linear and branched. In **linear programs,** students progress through each step, and the frames gradually increase in difficulty. In branched programs, students do not necessarily complete the steps sequentially. That is, students may skip forward or backward in the program as a result of the success or failure experienced in responding. Traditionally, programs were designed for teaching machines or **tachistoscopes.** Today, computer-assisted instruction (CAI) is the most common example of programmed instruction. Programmed texts, slides, films, pictures, diagrams, and tape recordings are also commonly associated with programmed instruction. The concept of programmed instruction is credited to **B. F. Skinner (1904–1990).**

Programmed Learning: *See* Programmed Instruction

Progressivism/Progressive Education: A system of education that emphasizes matching course content with each student's individual abilities and interests rather than expecting students to adapt to a given curriculum. Progressive education is based predominantly on the ideas and principles of **John Dewey (1859–1952)** and is a student-centered rather than a teacher-centered approach to education. Progressive teachers rely on class discussions, debates, and demonstrations to facilitate learning rather than on direct instruction or rote learning from textbooks. Progressive teachers also involve their students in practical learning experiences with relevance outside the classroom whenever possible. Students are usually actively involved in the learning process, and teachers function as facilitators, helpers, or guides. In addition, progressive teachers work to integrate subjects when possible, drawing connections from one subject to the next. Critics of progressive education believe that it lacks structure and that it does not focus on a specific body of knowledge. They also feel that it places too much emphasis on making students happy and too little emphasis on academic rigor.

Project Head Start: The first major early prevention program subsidized by the federal government. Project Head Start began in the 1960s during President Lyndon B. Johnson's administration and was designed to provide various kinds of nutritional, health, and social services to three- and four-year-old children from low-income families. Parental involvement is an important component of Head Start. Parents participate in its governance, take parenting classes, and often assist in Head Start classrooms. The success of Project Head Start, commonly called Head Start, has been well documented, and federal money continues to be used to support the program.

Project IMPACT: In education, an acronym for Interdisciplinary Model Program in the Arts for Children and Teachers, a program funded by the United States Office of Education (USOE) in the early 1970s to evaluate the arts in schools. The main purpose of the program was to assess the effectiveness of arts programs and to find ways to improve arts instruction and **curricula**.

Project-based Learning: A type of learning involving relatively long-term, problem-based units of instruction in which students are encouraged to pursue solutions to real-life, often complex problems posed by students, teachers, or **curriculum** developers. Students attempt to solve these problems in several ways, which include asking and refining questions, collecting and analyzing information, formulating **hypotheses** and testing them experimentally, engaging in debates, discussing the problem with others. Project-based learning encourages students to draw information from several different curricular areas, to utilize current technology, and to make cross-curricular connections.

Projection: In psychology, the tendency for individuals to attribute or project their own feelings, ideas, or **personality traits** onto another individual or group. Projection is a common **defense mechanism**, especially when the trait being projected is undesirable. Examples include acting like someone else is in a bad mood because you are in a bad mood or acting like someone is jealous of your success when you are jealous of theirs. *See* **Defense Mechanisms**

Projective Tests: In psychology, **personality** tests in which test-takers reveal or project themselves through products of their imaginations. Projective tests are used to measure or assess both conscious and unconscious thoughts, feelings, **perceptions**, or conflicts within an individual. Projective tests allow for much freer responses than the fixed-alternative personality inventory, which limits an individual's potential responses. The general idea is that test-takers will project their feelings onto or through the test. In **psychoanalysis**, projective techniques are used as a means of examining and understanding unconscious conflicts. Examples: **Rorschach Test**, where ink blots are interpreted, and **Thematic Apperception Test (TAT)**, where pictures elicit stories.

Prompt: In memory, any cue that helps jog an individual's memory. More specifically, **prompts** are previously learned discriminative stimuli that can be used to facilitate **recall**. Prompts are sometimes called retrieval cues and can be also be used to elicit a response to a new stimulus. *See* **Cue-dependent Forgetting**

Propagation: In acoustics, the spread of the vibration from one part of a vibrating body to another. Once something is set in vibration, the vibrating parts exert forces on adjacent parts, which cause them to vibrate. This process continues, moving or propagating the vibration. Propagation can be viewed as the path or paths that the vibration travels or moves along as it spreads from the original point of vibration.

Proportionate Stratified Random Sampling: In research, a method of random sampling in which the same proportion of each **stratum** in the **research design** is included in the **sample**. *See* **Random Sampling**

Proprioceptive Cues: Internal sensory cues that provide an individual with information regarding bodily movements and other internal sensations. **Kinesthesis** is a type of proprioceptive cue that increases an individual's awareness of body movements, including where, when, and how body parts move. Other types of proprioceptive cues include stomach upset or a sense of balance. *See* **Vestibular Sense**

Protocol Analysis: A type of **descriptive research** technique in which researchers attempt to assess an individual's thought processes. Protocol analysis is accomplished by having subjects verbally explain how or what they are thinking as they are actively engaged in an activity. In essence, protocol analysis involves having subjects think aloud while they are performing.

Proximity: In general, how close or far one person or thing is from another. Teachers use proximity to maintain discipline and to help students stay focused. Generally, the closer teachers are to students, the more attentive students tend to be, although sometimes moving farther away may help students feel more relaxed and independent. Proximity can be used effectively in performance-based music classes to direct attention and give individual instruction without disrupting the rehearsal.

Proximity, Principle/Law of: In perception, the tendency for individuals to perceive elements that are close together as belonging together, or the tendency to group elements that are near each other as a whole figure. *See* Closure, Principle/Law of; Similarity, Principle/Law of; Continuity, Principle/Law of

Psalmody: In general, the art or practice of singing psalms or hymns, especially as part of religious service. Psalmody also refers to the composing and arranging of psalm tunes. Psalmody was popular in the American colonies in the 1700s.

Psychiatry: A branch of medicine concerned with mental health and mental illness. *See* Psychoanalyst; Psychoanalysis/Psychoanalytic Method

Psychoanalysis/Psychoanalytic Method: In psychology, a method for treating various kinds of **neuroses** developed by **Sigmund Freud (1856–1939)**. Psychoanalysis is based on Freud's **psychoanalytic theory**. The general idea is that psychoanalysts attempt to help their patients by revealing to the patients the unconscious source of their anxieties. This **insight** into the nature of their problems provides patients with a sort of emotional release.

Psychoanalyst: An individual trained to use **psychoanalysis**. Psychoanalysts are usually trained psychiatrists. Psychoanalysts attempt to help their patients by revealing to the patients the unconscious source of their anxieties. *See* Psychoanalytic Theory, Freud; Freud, Sigmund (1856-1939)

Psychoanalytic Theory, Freud: Sigmund Freud's (1856–1939) **psychological theory** of human behavior concerned with the way unconscious forces motivate human behavior. Freud developed psychoanalytic theory to help his patients understand their thoughts and actions, and it was through his work with patients that he refined his therapeutic technique known as **psychoanalysis**. Freud believed that the human mental state consisted of three levels: 1) the conscious level, which is when an individual is aware of their thoughts and actions, 2) the preconscious level, which consists of the content an individual is able to bring to the conscious state, and 3) the unconscious level, which is a level about which an individual is unaware. Freud believed that the unconscious level constituted the largest part of the mind and that it exerted the greatest influence on behavior. In other words, Freud believed that all behavior is determined by specific motives that lie at the unconscious level, which is why people are unaware of the reasons for most of their own behavior.

To Freud, neurotic tendencies or behaviors result from an individual's inner conflicts, and these inner conflicts are a product of childhood trauma and/or anxiety. Psychoanalytic theory is based in large part on the idea that individuals want to avoid pain and pursue pleasure (hedonism). Although Freud's theory was designed to be therapeutic, his ideas regarding the meaning of dreams, the unconscious mind, repressed sexual feelings, and slips of the tongue (**Freudian slips**) have impacted society on a fundamental level, and they have had a major influence on the understanding of learning in general.

Freud's views are consistent with **E. L. Thorndike's (1874-1949) Law of Effect** and with basic behavioral stimulus/response principles of punishment and reward. However, in psychoanalytic theory individuals are driven by an internal force or psychic energy based on sexual urges or what Freud called **libido**. The libido drives behavior and helps define one's personality. Freud believed that the human personality was made up of three elements or mental structures: the **id**, the **ego**, and the **superego**. The id is the unconscious source of motives and desires and is present at birth. The id is motivated by the **pleasure principle**; it seeks immediate gratification of needs. The ego emerges during the first year of life and represents reason, rational thinking, and common sense. It seeks acceptable ways of obtaining gratification and helps strike a balance between the id and the superego. The superego develops around age four or five. It represents the values of society that have been learned by a child through interaction with parents and other adults. That is, the superego incorporates socially approved behaviors into the child's value systems or conscience.

Freud believed that development takes place in a series of **psychosexual stages**. Each developmental stage is characterized by the focusing of sexual interest or gratification on a particular part of the body. Children who are gratified too little or too much at a particular stage may become fixated at that stage. These **fixations** manifest themselves in certain behaviors later in life and become sources of conflict within the individual. Freud also believed that the way parents help their children resolve the conflicts that emerge during these stages determines their personalities for life. According to Freud, the adult personality is determined by age five or six.

Freud's stages of psychosexual development are described briefly as follows:

Oral (birth to twelve to eighteen months): During this stage, the child's focus is on the mouth. Mouth-oriented activities such as sucking and eating are the primary sources of pleasure.

Anal (twelve to eighteen months to three years): During this stage, the child's focus is on the anal area. Sensual gratification is gained from withholding and expelling feces.

Phallic (three to six years): During this stage, the child's focus is on the genital area. It is also during this stage that the **Oedipus complex** in boys and the **Electra complex** in girls emerge.

Latency (six years to puberty): During this stage, students are rather calm and conducive to learning. Children identify with the parent of the same sex.

Genital (puberty through adulthood): At this stage, mature adult sexuality emerges.

Psychodrama: A form of spontaneous play-acting used in **psychotherapy**.

Psychodynamics: In Sigmund Freud's (1856–1939) psychoanalytic theory, the perpetual conflict among the **id**, **ego**, and **superego**. *See* Psychoanalytic Theory, Freud

Psychological Defenses: A variety of **defense mechanisms** used during **adolescence** to counter threats to an individual's developing sense of self or **self-esteem**. Defenses such as **displacement**, reversal of affect, and withdrawal are considered normal, while **regression**, asceticism (extreme self-denial), and being uncompromising may be signs of psychological problems. The concept of psychological defenses is often attributed to Anna Freud (1895–1982). *See* **Defense Mechanisms**

Psychological Motive: A motive that is primarily learned rather than based on biological needs. The desire to be wealthy or popular is a psychological motive.

Psychology: In general, the science that studies human behavior and mental processes. As such, psychology is an extremely broad discipline that transcends and benefits many other disciplines to varying degrees. When used in the context of the "psychology" of an individual or group, psychology refers to the emotional and behavioral characteristics of that individual or group. In education, psychological theories and research provide a wealth of information that contributes significantly to the understanding of teaching and learning processes.

Psychometric Approach/Perspective: In education, the belief that **intelligence** or intellectual **aptitude** can be measured with tests. Typically, test measurement is conducted by assigning a number of tasks, observing responses to these tasks, and inferring intellectual capabilities from students' performances. Test items assess intellectual abilities such as attention, verbal comprehension, and reasoning. Psychometric testing has been common since the late 1800s. Early pioneers of psychometric testing include **Sir Francis Galton (1822–1911), Alfred Binet (1857–1911),** and Theophile Simon (1873–1961).

Psychometrics: An area of psychology that focuses on measuring and assessing abilities, **aptitudes,** and **personality** characteristics. *See* Psychometric Approach/Perspective

Psychomotor Domain: A learning domain that focuses on motor skill development. The psychomotor domain, the **cognitive domain,** and the **affective domain** are the three most-frequently mentioned domains of learning. The psychomotor domain emphasizes muscular or motor skill, manipulation of material and objects, and acts that require neuromuscular coordination. The psychomotor domain is involved in any educational objectives that require "doing," including writing, drawing, acting, and music-making. In public school **curricula,** learning objectives in the cognitive domain typically far outweigh learning objectives in the psychomotor domain; however, psychomotor skills are extremely important in **performance-based classes**. For example, in a typical band class, instrument position, hand or holding position, embouchure formation, posture, technical fluidity, air support, and proper articulation are all dependent upon psychomotor skill development. As a result, knowledge of this domain is crucial for successful music teaching.

Elizabeth Simpson's psychomotor domain is divided into the following seven large categories:

Perception: Perception is becoming aware of objects, qualities, or relations through the senses. This definition of perception includes three components: 1) sensory stimulation, which is information being picked up by the senses, 2) cue selection, which is deciding what cues to respond to and what cues are important for task completion, and 3) translation, which is determining the meaning of the cues needed for action.

Set: Set is the readiness for learning. Simpson identifies three types of readiness: 1) mental set, which includes being ready to perform mentally, 2) physical set, which is being ready to perform physically, and 3) emotional set, which is having a favorable attitude about what is being learned.

Guided Response: Guided responses are overt behavioral actions performed under the guidance of an instructor. Guided responses can include imitation, which is the act of imitating another person and/or trial and error, which is trying a variety of responses until the right one is found.

Mechanism: Mechanism involves making guided responses learned habits.

Complex Overt Response: Complex overt responses involve the smooth and efficient performance of a complex motor act. They have two components: resolution of uncertainty, which is knowledge of the sequence and confidence in executing the sequence, and automatic performance, which is the ability to perform finely coordinated motor skills with ease and muscle control.

Adaptation: Adaptation is the ability to change a performance to make it more suitable for the situation at hand.

Origination: Origination is the ability to develop new skills. *See* **Psychomotor Research; Psychomotor Skills**

Psychomotor Learning: Aspects of learning that have a physiological component requiring precise and unique brain-muscle connections. Psychomotor learning is important for developing many musical skills, including playing an instrument, singing, reading music, and writing music notation. *See* Psychomotor Domain

Psychomotor Research: In research, studies involving **psychomotor skills.** Psychomotor research studies in music tend to fall into several broad categories, including: 1) development, musical growth, and readiness; 2) **biomechanics** and efficiency of movement; 3) physical problems in performance; 4) influences of training, practice, and/or education on psychomotor skills; and 5) the relationships between muscle and brain activities. *See* Psychomotor Skills

Psychomotor Skills: Skills that involve brain-body coordination, or skills involving psychological processes and motor skill development, must work together with great precision. In musical performance, psychomotor skills are extremely important. Instrument position, hand or holding position, embouchure formation, posture, breath support, and articulation are all dependent upon psychomotor skill development. *See* Psychomotor Research; Psychomotor Domain

Psychosexual Stages/Development, Freud: In psychoanalytic theory, the idea that development takes place through a series of stages. Each developmental stage is characterized by the focusing of sexual interest or gratification on a particular part of the body. These stages include: oral, anal, phallic, latent, and genital. *See* Psychoanalytic Theory, Freud; Freud, Sigmund (1856-1939)

Psychosocial: A general term used to describe the interrelationships of psychological and social processes and disciplines. The term psychosocial is used in **Erik Erikson's (1902–1994)** theory of human development. *See* Psychosocial Theory/Stages, Erikson

Psychosocial Development: In psychology, changes in the way an individual's social and emotional needs are met through relationships with others. Psychosocial development is affected by factors such as age, **intelligence**, and experience. **Erik Erikson (1902–1994)** is most often associated with psychosocial development. His stages of psychosocial development include: 1) trust versus mistrust (birth to age six), 2) autonomy versus shame and doubt (ages two to three), 3) initiative versus guilt (ages three to six), 4) industry versus inferiority (ages six to twelve), 5) adolescence (ages twelve to eighteen), 6) intimacy versus isolation (ages thirteen to twenty-five or young adulthood), 7) generativity versus stagnation (middle adulthood), and 8) ego integrity versus despair and disgust (old age). *See* Psychosocial Theory/Stages, Erikson

Psychosocial Domain: The domain of human development that involves emotions, feelings, **personality**, and relationships with other people. *See* Psychosocial Theory/Stages, Erikson

Psychosocial Theory/Stages, Erikson: A psychosocial theory of human development that emphasizes social growth and change over the life span. **Erik Erikson's (1902–1994)** psychosocial theory was influenced by the ideas of **Sigmund Freud (1856–1939)** and was based in part on Freud's **psychoanalytic theory**. Erikson extended Freud's concept of **ego** and its role in establishing **behavior**; however, Erikson also emphasized society's influence on the developing **personality**. That is, Erikson believed that people are motivated by psychological, social, and cultural forces, not only by sexual motives as Freud believed. In addition, Erikson's theory also extends into adulthood, whereas Freud's did not.

In Erikson's theory, every individual passes through eight developmental stages that ultimately lead to wisdom and maturity. Each stage involves a combination of biological drives and societal demands, and at each stage there is a "crisis" that must be resolved before an individual can proceed to the next stage. Each crisis emerges based on an individual's maturation level. As an individual resolves each crisis, development continues toward the next crisis, and so on. Failure to resolve a crisis satisfactorily will interfere with healthy ego development. For example, according to Erikson, an individual who puts off making choices about his or her future goals indefinitely may develop an identity crisis.

In order for each crisis to be resolved successfully, individuals must find a balance between a positive trait and a corresponding negative trait. Although the positive quality should predominate, a lesser degree of the negative trait is needed as well. For example, trust versus mistrust is the first crisis of infancy. Most would agree that a large degree of trust is necessary for people to live and work together; however, a lesser degree of mistrust allows people to protect themselves from potential dangers In Erikson's theory, successful resolution of a crisis leads to the development of a particular virtue. For example, resolution of the trust versus mistrust crisis leads to hope.

Erikson's eight psychosocial stages are summarized below according to the crisis that occurs at each stage:

Basic trust versus mistrust (birth to twelve to eighteen months): At this stage, a baby develops a sense of whether or not the world can be trusted. This trust is based on whether others provide things such as food, comfort, love, warmth, and security. A child may never develop the basic trust necessary to function comfortably in the world if these needs are not met. At this stage, the virtue is hope.

Autonomy versus shame and doubt (twelve to eighteen months to three years): At this stage, a child develops a balance of independence over shame and doubt. For example, the child must learn to stand on his or her own two feet without feeling ashamed of the newly learned behavior or without doubting their newly discovered abilities. At this stage, the virtue is will.

Initiative versus guilt (three to six years): At this stage, a child develops the initiative to try new things without being overwhelmed by failure. The child is acquiring new physical and mental skills, setting goals and enjoying newfound talents and abilities. At the same time, the child must learn to control impulses and energies. The danger lies in developing too strong a sense of guilt over his or her fantasies, newfound power, and childish instincts. At this stage, the virtue is purpose.

Industry (competence) versus inferiority (six years to puberty): At this stage, a child must learn the skills of the culture or experience feelings of inferiority. The child begins developing the skills necessary to function in the adult world both at home and at school. Failure to attain mastery and competence results in feelings of inadequacy and inferiority. At this stage, the virtue is skill.

Identity versus identity confusion (puberty to young adulthood): At this stage, an individual must determine his or her sense of self. The onset of puberty triggers the crisis at this stage. Individuals must make choices regarding who and what they are going to be in the future. Successful resolution of the crisis results in a strong identity and a plan for the future. Failure results in confusion and the inability to make decisions, or what Erikson called an **identity crisis**. At this stage, the virtue is fidelity.

Intimacy versus isolation (young adulthood): At this stage, individuals attempt to make commitments to others. People know who they are and want to share themselves with others. The inability to make commitments may lead to a sense of isolation and self-absorption. Erikson believed that individuals are not developmentally complete until they are capable of intimacy. At this stage, the virtue is love.

Generativity versus stagnation (middle adulthood): At this stage, mature adults are concerned with establishing and guiding the next generation, otherwise they will become complacent and self-serving. Although parenthood is the most common way to resolve the crisis at this stage, many people resolve the crisis through coaching, teaching, or working with children in other ways. Erikson felt that adults need children as much as children need adults. In addition, this stage often reflects an individual's need to create his or her own legacy. At this stage, the virtue is care.

Integrity versus despair (old age): At this stage, elderly individuals either develop a sense of acceptance of their lives, including the acceptance of death, or they fall into despair. As this stage, people strive for wisdom and spiritual tranquility. Erikson believed that healthy adults will not fear death. At this stage, the virtue is wisdom.

Psychotherapy: A psychological method or technique for treating mental or emotional disorders. Psychotherapists attempt to change an individual's thoughts, moods, and/or behaviors through the use of verbal and symbolic techniques.

Public Law 94-142: *See* Education for All Handicapped Children Act of 1975/Public Law 945-142

Public Relations: In music education, the relationships school music programs have with businesses and people within the community and surrounding areas. Music programs are commonly active within schools and communities, particularly at the secondary level. School music ensembles often perform at assemblies, pep rallies, athletic events, and a wide variety of community functions. Music teachers also play a key role in fostering and maintaining healthy relationships between the music programs, schools, and communities by being reasonably accommodating regarding the number and length of performances given by their ensembles.

Public Schools: Schools operated and governed by state education systems and funded through federal, state, and local tax dollars. **Public schools** must abide by laws and regulations mandated by federal and state governments to receive funds. Public schools comprise the majority of educational institutions in the United States and cover the full range of educational levels, from **kindergarten** through institutions of higher education.

Pull-out Programs: In education, programs in which individual students are removed from regular classes for a period of time each day for special instruction. **Pull-out programs** were an outcome of **Title I of the Elementary and Secondary Education Act of 1965 (ESEA)**, one of the largest federally funded education programs for **at-risk** elementary and secondary students. The purpose of pull-out programs was to increase the achievement of at-risk students; however, the effectiveness of pull-out programs has been questioned. A 1993 study by the U.S. Department of Education revealed that pull-out programs have had little or no effect in closing the achievement gap between low-income children and other disadvantaged students not in the program. On the other hand, many teachers and administrators feel that pull-out programs do, in fact, help at least some at-risk students achieve at higher levels academically despite the reported statistics.

Punisher/Punishing Stimulus: In behavioral psychology, any **behavior** or **stimulus** that weakens or decreases the probability of an undesirable behavior or **response**. Examples: time out, detention. *See* **Aversive Stimulus; Primary Punisher**

Punishment: In general, a **method** for controlling behavior through the use of aversive stimulation that produces pain or annoyance. Typically, as long as the **aversive stimulus** is present, the rate of responding will be reduced. Punishment is often confused with negative reinforcement. However, punishment involves the addition of an aversive stimulus, or the removal of a stimulus to reduce the **response** of the behavior, while negative reinforcement involves the removal of a stimulus, which leads to an increase in the behavior.

Punishment, like reinforcement, can be positive or negative; that is, it can involve the process of adding something to or taking something away from a situation. Punishment is positive when the addition of an aversive stimulus leads to a decrease in a particular behavior. For example, making a child write "I will not talk without raising my hand" fifty times, resulting in a reduction of the number of times the child talks without raising his or her hand, is positive punishment. Punishment is negative when the removal of a stimulus leads to a decrease in a particular behavior. A common musical example of negative punishment is when less practice time results in decreased quality of performance on a musical instrument. Both of these stimuli (talking without raising the hand and decreased quality of performance) are punishing because they result in a decrease in behavior. *See* **Negative Reinforcement**

Pure Tone: *See* **Sine Tone**

Purposive Sampling: In research, a nonprobability sampling technique in which researchers select **subjects** based on specific, predetermined characteristics. Purposive sampling is employed when researchers believe that finding a sufficient number of subjects at random would be difficult, or when the **population** having the desired characteristic(s) is small. Examples: 1) individuals with **perfect pitch** and 2) musical **savants**. *See* **Nonprobability Sampling**

Pythagorean Tuning/Temperament: Developed by Pythagoras, an approach to tuning based on the circle of fifths in which each consecutive fifth is tuned mathematically to a beatless 702 cents. However, when this process is taken to its entirety (i.e., eleven fifths), there is a "leftover" fifth that contains only 679 cents, which is 23 cents short of a beatless 702 cents. This shortage is referred to as the Pythagorean comma. In practicality, this out-of-tune fifth creates such significant problems with intonation as to render this tuning system unusable. *See* **Temperament/Tuning Systems**

Quadrivium: *See* Seven Liberal Arts

Qualitative Development: In psychological **stage theories**, the idea that **cognitive** growth and **maturation** occur in a sequence of qualitative transformations or changes. Qualitative development is analogous to the change from an egg to a caterpillar and then to a butterfly. That is, each change or transformation leads to a major shift to a more complex system of thinking or to the next stage. Some of the most common stage theories include **Jean Piaget's (1896–1980) stages of cognitive growth**, **Erik Erikson's (1902–1994)** stages of personal development, **Lawrence Kohlberg's (1927–1987) stages of moral development**, and **Sigmund Freud's (1856–1939) psychosexual stages**.

Qualitative Research: A type of research that emphasizes **subjective** judgments in the data-gathering process; the opposite of **quantitative research**. Qualitative research is concerned with the different meanings that actions and events have for different individuals. Researchers place an emphasis on observing people in their natural settings and making judgments about these observations. Thus, qualitative research is interpretive and often field-oriented.

The researcher is the key instrument in qualitative research because he or she interprets what is being observed. Researchers must often rely on **intuition**, since many important research criteria are not specified in qualitative studies. **Data** often take the form of words rather than numbers and include contextual descriptions of people and events. Data collection techniques include observations in natural settings with minimal researcher intervention and taped **interviews**, photographs, videotapes, audiotapes, films, and musical artifacts. Analyses of data typically involve only a limited amount of quantitative analyses. These analyses are usually descriptive in nature and often involve coding and classifying information. In addition, quantitative data are usually organized around and based on the notes and stories the researcher keeps. As a study progresses, researchers tend to narrow their focus to a relatively small number of issues or themes. **Triangulation**, or the checking of data against multiple sources and methods, is common in qualitative research, and researchers try to disconfirm their own interpretations.

Common types of qualitative studies include **case studies, field studies, naturalistic studies**, and **ethnographic studies**, which are often comparative in nature. Qualitative reports are designed to assist readers in making their own interpretations and to recognize subjectivity. In music, many qualitative studies are ethnomusicological in nature. **Comparative studies** of musical systems and cultures of the world are examples of ethnomusicological studies.

The strengths of qualitative research include: 1) it is a holistic, systemic approach designed to reveal the inner workings and contexts of a particular situation; 2) it provides researchers with the flexibility to interpret data from a "human" perspective rather than a statistical one; 3) it gives researchers the opportunity to analyze all of information from the data; and 4) because researchers can relate in an empathetic way to what they are observing, the interpretation of the data is often directly relevant to educational practice. Weaknesses of qualitative research include: 1) subjectivity may be excessive in observations; 2) the language used in qualitative reports is sometimes vague; 3) the reports are sometimes long and unwieldy; 4) it is difficult to generalize qualitative research findings to other situations; 5) the amount of time and costs involved can be excessive; and 6) qualitative methods can be intrusive.

Quantitative Analysis: *See* Quantitative Research; Statistics

Quantitative Development: In psychology, a theory of intellectual development based on the idea that growth occurs in a linear fashion rather than in stages. According to this theory, **cognitive** growth takes place as steady, accumulative additions to the intellect and not as sudden changes in thinking processes. One example is **Jerome Bruner's (b. 1915) theory of instruction**.

Quantitative Research: A type of research that emphasizes the quantification of data and the application of statistical procedures to this data to draw conclusions. **Experimental** and **quasi-experimental studies** are quantitative in nature. Quantitative researchers follow a rigid experimental process or scientific method that generally includes the following basic components:

1) a statement of the problem, 2) a **hypothesis** or hypotheses, 3) a review of literature, 4) established and controlled **methodologies** and procedures, and 5) statistical procedures for analyzing the data.

Evaluating the experimental design is a primary concern. Quantitative researchers are concerned with questions such as: 1) Are the experimental variables singular and not confounded with other factors or each other? 2) Are all nonmanipulative variables randomized? 3) Has consideration been given to the possibility of the experimenter or experimental procedures biasing the results? 4) Are all precautions taken to obtain equivalence of subjects, groups, or other necessary aspects of the experiment? 5) Are the samples adequate in kind and number? 6) Are the techniques of the pairing or matching of subjects valid? 7) Are there test items, factors, measures, or instruments that might bias the results in some way? 8) Are the materials, instruments, facilities, and other necessary equipment adequate for the study? 9) Are the statistical procedures appropriate for data analyses? 10) Does the design ensure that experimental findings are the result of intended manipulations?

Quasi-experimental Design: *See* Experimental Design

Questionnaire: In research, written or printed sets of questions used to gather information (data) from individuals. Questionnaires may contain closed- or open-ended questions. *See* Survey Method

Quota Sampling: In research, a **nonprobability sampling** technique in which researchers choose a **sample** that is representative of the groups being compared. Often a quota sample is based on the numerical composition of various **ethnic** subgroups in a given **population**. For example, choosing a sample that contains 60 percent Caucasian Americans, 20 percent African Americans, 10 percent Hispanic Americans, 5 percent Asian Americans, and 5 percent Native Americans is a quota sample because it closely reflects the makeup of the general population. *See* **Sampling**

Race: Traditionally, any of the major divisions of humankind based predominantly on physical characteristics, especially skin color, ancestry, and national origin. Race is often used in conjunction with the terms ethnicity or **ethnic group**. However, whereas ethnicity or ethnic group refers to people who share a common language, religion, traditions, or sense of identity, racial traits are more specifically heritable.

Random Sampling: In research, a technique in which every member of a given **population** has an equal chance of being selected for inclusion in a sample. Random sampling is the most commonly used sampling technique in research. Today, computer programs are commonly used to generate random samples. *See* **Sampling**

Randomization/Random Assignment: In research, assigning **subjects** to groups in a random manner such that assignment is determined entirely by chance. *See* **Random Sampling**

Randomized Response Technique: In research, a technique used when researchers want to obtain honest responses to questions that are highly sensitive. This technique is based on the notion that subjects will respond honestly to questions such as "Do you use drugs?" or "Do you cheat on your taxes?" if they know that they have complete anonymity. Typically, subjects are shown two questions, one sensitive and the other not. Subjects are given only two response choices—yes or no. They will respond to only one of the questions presented based on the outcome of a random event. For example, a subject may be asked to flip a coin and answer the first question if the upside of the coin is heads and the second question if the upside of the coin is tails. In this way, not even the researcher knows which question the subject answered, assuring anonymity.

Range: In music, the distance from the lowest note to the highest note in a given section or piece of music, or the distance from the lowest note to the highest note that can be played or sung on a given instrument or voice.

Range is also used to describe where a note or group of notes is located in relation to high and low frequencies. For example, teachers often refer to the high range, middle range, or low range when describing where notes lie.

In research, range is a statistical measure of **variability** and the variation of scores in a **frequency distribution** from the lowest to the highest score. The range represents the entire width of a distribution and is found by subtracting the lowest score from the highest score. Generally, the range increases as the number of cases under investigation increases and vice versa. For example, in a group of scores where the low score is a 60 and the high score is a 100, the range would be 40. *See* **Tessitura**

Rank Correlation: In research, a **correlation** computed from ranked data. Rank correlation is an approximation of the Pearson product-moment correlation (Pearson r). The rank correlation coefficient is designated by the small Greek letter rho (p) to distinguish it from the Pearson product-moment correlation (Pearson r). *See* **Correlation; Pearson product-moment Correlation (Pearson *r*)**

Ranked Data: In research, data ranked or arranged in order on the basis of a specified criterion or dimension. For example, arranging test scores from the highest to the lowest constitutes ranked data.

Rate of Response: In general, the frequency with which a particular response is made within a specific period of time. For example, in a research context, the rate of response might involve recording the number of times a rat pushes a button to obtain a food reward in a thirty-minute period. In an educational context, the rate of response might involve the number of positive comments given in a fifty-minute class period.

Ratio Scale: In research, a measurement scale used when the **variables** involve physical measures such as weight, height, length, or width. Ratio scales have an absolute zero point, which indicates the absence of the variable being measured. The numbers on a ratio scale are relative, in that statements can be made about the relationships between scale points. For example, if weight is a variable, it is possible to say that someone who weighs 200 pounds weighs twice as much as someone who weighs 100 pounds, which is expressed as a two-to-one ratio. *See* **Measurement/ Measurement Scales**

Rationalism: The philosophical belief that the mind contains a base of fundamental truths that can be discovered through rational thought processes. These fundamental truths are believed to represent the ultimate or ideal forms of all phenomena. The general **premise** is that physical objects are imperfect representations of the ideas they represent and that ideals exist within the mind, not as physical manifestations of the mind. Sometimes called **idealism**, rationalism was a common philosophy of the Western world from ancient times to the eighteenth century. Rationalism has its roots in ancient Greece. Well-known philosophers who have expressed rationalistic thoughts include Socrates, Plato, Descartes, and Kant. In music education, teachers may incorporate rationalistic concepts by encouraging students to search for meaning and understanding in music, presenting several models to help students develop a concept of the ideal, and placing emphasis on performing only high-quality literature.

Rationalization: In psychology, a defense mechanism that enables individuals to maintain **self-esteem** by providing acceptable reasons for or otherwise justifying unacceptable behavior. Rationalization often involves distorting the truth. In other words, individuals use rationalization to "save face." For example, a student may use rationalization to explain failing a playing test in band for which he or she was not prepared by saying the following: "I would not have failed the playing test if the teacher had not made me nervous. I could play it perfectly at home yesterday." *See* **Defense Mechanisms**

Reaction Formation: In psychology, a defense mechanism in which individuals speak or act in a manner that is the opposite of the way they actually think and feel. Individuals employing reaction formation often tend to overreact in the opposite direction of their true feelings. For example, a person who lies frequently may give the impression that he or she absolutely hates lying in general and cannot tolerate other people's lies. For example, a student may use reaction formation to cope with a disappointing audition by saying: "I'm glad I didn't audition well because I was getting tired of playing first chair anyway; now I can sit next to my friend." *See* **Defense Mechanisms**

Reaction Time: In behavioral psychology, the time between the presentation of a **stimulus** and the occurrence of a **response**. In other words, reaction time is how long it takes a person to react or respond to something. *See* **Latency**

Reactive Effects/Reactivity: In research, a problem of **measurement** in which the measure changes the behavior being observed. Reactive effects occur when subjects' responses are affected or influenced by their awareness of being observed and are relatively common threats to both internal and external **validity**.

Readiness: Also referred to as **maturation**, the term is used in education to gauge students' **capacity** for **learning** a particular thing at a particular time. Both physical and mental components must grow and develop sufficiently so students have the capacity to achieve learning **goals** at a level appropriate to their abilities. Although each child grows and develops at his or her own pace, general consistency in human growth and development exists. This consistency allows educators to set achievable, yet challenging learning goals for most students. While age is a significant factor in determining **readiness**, it is not the only factor. **Intelligence, motivation,** and experience also play significant roles in determining one's readiness to learn.

Reading Patterns: In music, a term typically used to refer to melodic or rhythmic note groupings that are read more easily together than they are separately. For example, a melodic pattern might involve recognizing a broken major triad in a melodic line that allows the performer to comprehend three notes at once instead of one. Rhythmic patterns are often beamed together according to the meter to facilitate pattern recognition. For example, reading a beamed pattern consisting of an eighth note followed by two sixteenth notes is easier than trying to decipher the same notes written individually. The ability to recognize common patterns in music is particularly important for **sight reading.** *See* **Music Reading**

Realism: In general, the tendency of individuals to think and behave according to what they believe is real, practical, and functional. In art and literature, realism describes a way of looking at and representing the world as it actually is rather than as an ideal. In philosophy, realism refers to the belief that physical objects and reality exist independently from the conscious mind.

Recall: In memory, the ability to bring information to consciousness on demand or to demonstrate retention by repeating previously learned information. Remembering the name of the first president, reciting a poem from memory, and performing a scale from memory are all examples of recall. *See* Memory

Recency Effect: In memory experiments, the tendency for recent information to be recalled more easily than information acquired earlier. *See* **Primacy Effect**

Reception Learning/Method: A **teacher-directed** method or strategy in which teachers arrange or organize subject material in advance in a way that they believe the students will most easily understand. Reception learning is associated with **David Ausubel (b. 1918)** and is contrary to **Jerome Bruner's (b. 1915)** discovery learning approach. Some research indicates that reception learning is most appropriate with younger students, while discovery learning is most appropriate with older students. In practice, both approaches can be used effectively at all levels. *See* **Discovery Approach; Discovery Learning, Bruner**

Recessive Gene: In a pair of **genes**, the one least likely to be expressed in the organism's phenotype. That is, the recessive gene will not determine the characteristic trait unless both genes in the gene pair are recessive. For example, brown eye color is dominant over blue eye color. In order for an individual to have blue eyes, the eye color gene from both parents must be blue. If one of the parents contributes a brown eye color gene, and one contributes a blue eye color gene, the organism will have brown eyes because brown eye color is dominant. *See* **Dominant Gene**

Reciprocal Teaching: In education, a teaching/learning process or method in which teachers and students work together in a partnership. Teachers focus on teaching students effective learning strategies, and students focus on using these strategies to facilitate learning. In practice, teachers give instruction on how to summarize, outline, or organize material, how to ask pertinent questions about the material, and how to anticipate test questions. In addition, teachers guide students through the learning process, convincing them that these learning strategies really do work. The idea of reciprocal teaching is that becoming familiar with learning strategies helps students learn content and vice-versa. Reciprocal teaching is often used to help poor readers develop reading comprehension strategies, and research has shown that reciprocal teaching positively impacts the teaching/learning process.

Reciprocity: In general psychology, the idea that people tend to like other people who like them or who show them respect, kindness, or approval. In this context, reciprocity is also referred to as reciprocal liking. In **Jean Piaget's (1896–1980)** stages of cognitive growth, reciprocity is a conservation principle that states that a change in one dimension of an object affects a change in another dimension. For example, a ball of modeling clay the size of a golf ball can be reshaped to look much longer and thinner, yet the same amount of modeling clay will be present. According to Piaget, children begin to understand reciprocity during the **concrete operational stage** (approximately age seven to eleven). *See* Conservation; Piaget's Stages of Cognitive Growth

Reciprocity Agreement: In education, an agreement between states in which professional licensure for teaching in one state is recognized as valid for licensure in another state. Reciprocity agreements are made on a state-by-state basis; not all states have them. In addition, states often have specific rules governing reciprocity agreements. The certification office in the receiving state typically has the necessary information for transfer of teacher certification to that state.

Recoding: In memory, the reorganization of information in logical ways to decrease the likelihood of **forgetting**. Recoding can involve any of three types of **memory** codes: 1) verbal codes, the association of concrete objects with words; 2) imaginal codes, the process individuals use to form mental images of what they are trying to remember; and 3) motor codes, the way individuals remember how to perform physical skills. The **dual code theory** of memory is based on the idea that forgetting is less likely to occur if the information to be learned is represented in both imaginal and verbal codes. *See* Encoding

Recognition: In memory, the ability to identify a previously learned item when presented with a series of choices that includes the correct item. In education, one of the most common ways to test for recognition is to provide students with a series of multiple-choice test questions. That is, absent a lucky guess, students must recognize the correct item in order to select it.

Redintegrative Memory: The process of remembering all of an earlier experience after being provided with partial cues. Redintegrative memories typically involve the recollection of events in an individual's personal history along with the circumstances surrounding these events. *See* **Memory; Cue-dependent Forgetting**

Reference Group: Any group individuals refer to or use for making comparisons, judgments, and/or decisions regarding one's own opinions and behaviors. In education, the student's class, smaller sub-groups of the class, clubs, and sports teams are common **reference groups**. In research, a reference group is any group to which an individual's performance can be compared to in some way. *See* **Norm-referenced; Criterion-referenced**

Referentialism: In music, a philosophical view or theoretical position of music listening asserting that the **value** and meaning of music is directly related to its references to ideas, events, or objects outside of the music itself. In other words, music's value and meaning lie not in the music itself, but in the **nonmusical** meanings to which the music may refer. Referentialism is contrary to absolutism, a view characterized by the belief that the meaning in music lies within the music itself, rather than to outside referents. One problem with referentialism in music education is that referentialism is by definition nonmusical. That is, if one is listening to music and deriving meaning from references made to things outside of the music, those meaningful references are necessarily not musical. On the other hand, non-musical references applied to a theme or musical section can often help students identify or recognize form in certain styles of music. These references help in the teaching/learning process. Programmatic music, such as *Peter and the Wolf*, is largely referential. Music used as a background for movies where nonmusical associations are attached to the music is referential. Listening to music and reminiscing about old times is referential. In short, when the value and meaning in music lies outside of the music itself, it is referential. In music education, the term referential is used when discussing any nonmusical benefit gained from music. Examples of referentialism include statements such as "Music makes students better in other subject areas," "Music develops self-discipline in students," and "Music keeps students out of trouble." *See* **Absolutism; Expressionism; Formalism; Absolute Expressionism; Absolute Formalism**

Reflection: In acoustics, when sound energy bounces off of a hard surface, prolonging the vibration of sound. Reflection occurs because all of the energy is not absorbed when sound strikes a hard surface. The material from which the surface is made determines the amount of reflection or absorption that occurs. A single bounce off of a surface is referred to as a first-order reflection, while two bounces off of a surface is a second-order reflection, and so on. Each time a sound reflects off of a surface, the material properties of the surface affect the sound. *See* **Absorption**

Reflex: Relatively simple, unlearned, involuntary responses to specific stimuli. Sneezing, perspiring, blinking, breathing, sucking, and grasping are all reflexes.

Refraction: The bending of sound due to differences in air temperature. Sound **waves** bend away from warmer air toward cooler air because the sound is traveling more quickly through the warmer air. This phenomenon is the reason that a sound that cannot be heard clearly during the day can often be heard more clearly at night. During the day, the air near the ground is generally warmer than the air above. As a result, sound waves are drawn in an upward direction, making it more difficult to hear at a distance. At night, the air near the ground is frequently cooler than the air above. As a result, sound waves are drawn downward, making sound easier to hear at a distance.

Registers: In vocal and instrumental music, groups of notes that share certain characteristics, usually related to **pitch range** or **timbre**. In vocal music, registers have been established based on singers' abilities to sing in a particular range without significant adjustment to the vocal folds. The most common vocal registers are the chest and head registers; however, some vocalists consider the middle range of the voice as a third register. Some vocalists deny the existence of vocal registers altogether. In instrumental music, the names of registers vary according to the instrument; however, almost all instrumental teachers refer to the low, middle, and high registers. Other register names are instrument specific. For example, clarinetists sometimes use the terms chalumeau when referring to the low range, the term throat tones when referring to open G to B-flat, and the term clarion when referring to the high register. In addition, almost all wind instrumentalists use the term altissimo when referring to the extremely high register on their respective instruments. Register and range are often used interchangeably. *See* **Range; Tessitura**

Regression: In psychology, when an individual returns to more primitive or infantile behavior. Two primary types of regression are commonly recognized: 1) **retrogression**, when individuals revert to behavior they engaged in when they were younger, and 2) **primitivation**, when individuals revert to more infantile or childlike behavior, but not necessarily behavior they engaged in when they were younger. At the onset of puberty, adolescents commonly display regression as a result of a desire to remain a child. For example, individuals may dress and play as though they were in elementary school.

Regression is also caused by unusual stress. For example, a twelve-year-old may begin wetting the bed for a period of time following a traumatic event, such as a divorce. Typically, when the crisis fades and the individual is able to deal with the problem, the inappropriate behavior disappears. In research, regression is a type of statistical procedure in which many **variables** are related to a single variable and commonly refers to multiple regression. *See* **Multiple Regression**

Rehabilitation Act of 1973: Legislation authorizing grants primarily for vocational rehabilitation services. The Rehabilitation Act (the Act) authorized specific programs and provided a statutory basis for the establishment of several governmental agencies, including the Rehabilitation Service Administration, the Department of Health, Education, and Welfare, and the Office for the Handicapped. **Section 504** of the Act has had a significant impact on education. It specifically "prohibits recipients of federal funds from discriminating on the basis of disability" and requires that "school systems receiving federal funds provide a free and appropriate public education to children with disabilities." In addition to requiring a **"free and appropriate education" (FAPE)**, Section 504 also requires that education for disabled children occur in the "least restrictive setting," including evaluation, placement, and additional safeguards. Often, the **Americans with Disabilities Act (ADA)**, the **Individuals with Disabilities Education Act (IDEA)**, and the **Rehabilitation Act of 1973** are discussed together for their impact on education.

Rehearsal: In memory, a technique that can be used to facilitate learning and remembering. Rehearsal involves practice and/or repetition of behavior and can lead to learning permanence. Some psychologists believe that rehearsal is the primary factor in encoding and storing information in **short-term memory (STM)** and **long-term memory (LTM)**. In music, rehearsal refers to the process of practicing one's musical skills instrumentally or vocally alone or in an ensemble setting. The majority of time in **performance-based** classes is spent rehearsing. Musical rehearsals are typically structured around preparing pieces for performance. Educational **objectives** are generally met through the rehearsal process. *See* Encoding; Storage

Rehearsal Buffer: In memory, the array of information being rehearsed and continuously regenerated in short-term memory (STM). The rehearsal buffer facilitates the short-term recall of information and its transfer to long-term memory (LTM). *See* Memory; Short Term Memory (STM); Long Term Memory (LTM)

Reimer Curriculum Model: In music education, a performance-based curriculum model articulated by Bennett Reimer in his book *A Philosophy of Music Education*. The Reimer curriculum model involves seven interacting phases. The first phase is the Values Phase, which is the development of "philosophically justifiable reasons" for performance-based music classes. This philosophy should be "centered around the act of musical creation." The second phase is the Conceptualization Phase, which is the application of an overall teaching and learning approach in the classroom designed to promote and realize the philosophy. Teachers should consider several factors when developing the approach or concept, including psychology, **child development**, current educational trends, the nature of the subject matter, and the developmental level of the students. The third phase is the Systematized Phase, which involves structuring learning appropriately within and across each year of schooling. The fourth phase is the Interpreted Phase, which is the manner in which individual teachers choose to implement the previous phases. The fifth phase is the Operational Phase, which is the actual daily operations of the music program, including all activities that occur as a part thereof. The sixth phase is the Experienced Phase, which is what students receive from and give to the process. In other words, what should and what do students experience as a result of the previous phases? The final phase is the Expectational Phase, which is what others outside the classroom expect from performance groups. Teachers should educate both students and the community regarding educational foundations, philosophies, and goals of performance-based music classes to set appropriate expectations.

Reinforcement: The process whereby a **stimulus** increases the likelihood of a **response** recurring. Reinforcement may be used in either **classical** or **operant conditioning**. In **classical conditioning**, the **unconditioned stimulus**

serves as the reinforcement. In operant conditioning, the presentation of any stimulus following the emitted response can be considered reinforcement if it results in a higher response rate. In education, reinforcement occurs as the result of a teacher's actions when those actions increase a behavior or behaviors. Most commonly, reinforcement occurs as the result of feedback provided to students after a task is completed. For example, when students behave appropriately, teachers often praise them (positive reinforcer), which increases the desired behavior (reinforcement). Reinforcement occurs both positively and negatively. Comments and actions, or the lack of them, can reinforce desirable as well as undesirable behaviors. Purposeful, constructive reinforcement helps students achieve educational **objectives** and helps foster an effective learning environment.

Reinforcement Schedules: *See* Schedules of Reinforcement

Reinforcer/Reinforcing Stimulus: In behavioral psychology, a **stimulus** that follows a **response** and strengthens or increases the future occurrence of that response. In classical conditioning, a reinforcing stimulus is an unconditioned stimulus. In operant conditioning, a reinforcing stimulus is any stimulus that reinforces the **operant behavior.** *See* **Reinforcement; Classical Conditioning; Operant Conditioning**

Relative Pitch: The ability to produce or label **pitches** with minimal aid from a reference tone. This ability can become highly developed, and musicians are often trained to identify pitches in a wide variety of musical contexts. Experienced musicians will often memorize the tone qualities of the various pitches on their instruments. Such musicians often appear to have perfect or absolute pitch when, in fact, they have developed their relative pitch skills to a high level. *See* **Perfect Pitch; Absolute Pitch**

Relativism: In philosophy, the ethical view that the appropriateness of an individual's moral behavior is based on the principles deemed acceptable in that individual's culture or society. Moral behavior deemed appropriate in one society may not be appropriate in another.

Relearning: In memory, the ability to relearn material when it is presented on subsequent occasions. That is, when individuals "forget" what they learn, they typically need less time and/or fewer trials to relearn the material at a later date.

Reliability: In research, the consistency of a **measurement instrument** (e.g., a test) over time. A reliable test tends to produce roughly the same results when used repeatedly under the same conditions. In addition, reliability is also a concern when more than one experimenter is manipulating **variables** in an experiment. Specifically, the concern is whether experimenters are behaving in the same manner when evaluating or recording **data**. *See* Internal Consistency; Test-retest Reliability; Alternate-forms Reliability

Remediation: In education, a general term for courses or a **curriculum** designed to strengthen students' weaknesses. Remediation typically involves less advanced subject material and course work. It allows students to repeat the learning process more slowly to learn and absorb what they missed and to get more practice in the area or areas in which they are having difficulty.

REMs: *See* Rapid Eye Movements (REMs)

Repeated Block Designs: In research, an **experimental design** in which **subjects** are measured more than once during the experiment. That is, subjects are assigned to more than one group and tested repeatedly. A repeated block design is also commonly referred to as a repeated measures design or a within-subjects design. It may be used when the researcher wants to determine the effects of a treatment a number of times, at several points throughout the experiment, or when subjects are given a variety of treatments. For example, a repeated block design may be used to determine the effects of timbre on students' abilities to detect intonation problems in a series of listening tasks.

Repeated Measures Design: *See* Repeated Block Design

Repetition: In research, when one researcher conducts a study that is similar to but not identical to another researcher's study in order to validate the findings of the original study. *See* Replicate/Replication

Replicate/Replication: In research, when a study or experiment is repeated or duplicated as identically as possible. Replication is commonly used to strengthen research in an area or to validate findings of earlier studies. *See* Repetition

Representative Sample: In research, a **sample** that matches the **population** being studied on important characteristics such as age, gender, and experience. In other words, a representative sample is representative of the population from which the sample is drawn. *See* **Sampling**

Repression: A **defense mechanism** that enables traumatic or anxiety-producing feelings and/or memories to be removed from conscious memory. Repression may be serious or mild. Anxiety-producing events, such as a serious car accident or the loss of a loved one may produce serious repression including the inability to remember or consciously acknowledge that the event ever occurred. Daily stresses may also produce milder forms of repression. For example, a severe dislike for geometry homework may result in regularly **forgetting** about homework assignments. Repression can be confused with ordinary forgetting; however, there are two important distinctions between repression and forgetting. First, repression results in a total loss of memory. Second, repression is always triggered by **anxiety**.

Reproduction: In memory, the process of performing or reproducing previously learned material. Example: Playing or singing a solo from memory for a concert or competition. *See* **Retrieval; Recall; Memory**

Research Design: In research, the way a study is or will be conducted. The following steps are typically used to develop a research design: 1) formulating the problem, 2) reviewing related literature, 3) establishing the methodology and procedures, 4) determining the results and drawing conclusions from them, and 5) a discussion of the results. Theses and dissertations commonly follow a research design format. *See* **Experimental Design**

Researcher Bias: In research studies, an error resulting from unintended preferential treatment being shown or given to certain subjects in a study. Researcher bias is a threat to a study's **external validity** and can be a problem when the researcher knows which subjects are in the **experimental group** and which subjects are in the **control group**. **Double-blind studies** are often used to control for researcher bias. Researcher bias is sometimes referred to as **experimenter bias, expectancy**, or Rosenthal Effect. *See* **Rosenthal Effect**

Resistance: In psychology, when responses to stimuli are not easily changed, altered, or extinguished. For example, research has shown that providing **intermittent reinforcement** or **reinforcement** according to a variable schedule results in a greater resistance to extinction than does **continuous reinforcement**. *See* **Schedules of Reinforcement**

Resonance: A phenomenon that occurs when a vibrating object causes a non-vibrating object to vibrate due to the frequency of the vibration. Physical contact with the vibrating object is not necessary for resonance to occur because vibrations travel through air and other media, including solids and liquids. Resonance occurs most easily when the natural vibrating **frequencies** of the involved objects are harmonically related; that is, they share **partials**. For example, household objects commonly rattle or ring when music is playing. In instrumental music, resonance can be beneficial or detrimental. Resonance can increase the number and balance of partials in a sound, and professional performers are careful to select instruments that resonate in ways that dramatically enhance their overall tone quality. Unwanted resonance can ruin a performance; for example, if a percussionist forgets to turn off the snares during an exposed lyrical section of music, the resulting resonance is extremely distracting. In vocal performance, resonance typically refers to the amplification and enrichment of vocal tone through manipulation of the body's resonance cavities.

Resonator: In vocal and instrumental music, any part of the sound-producing mechanism that amplifies or enriches the tone, contributing to its characteristic **timbre**. In vocal performance, resonators include the **larynx**, mouth, nasal cavity, and sinuses. Some vocalists believe that the **trachea**, the bronchi, and the chest cavity are also resonators. *See* **Resonance**

Resource Room: Any room equipped with special learning materials designed to help children learn. Resources rooms are common in most regular schools and are often designed to help children with **learning disabilities** without disrupting their sense of being part of a regular class in a regular school.

Resources in Education (RIE): One of two monthly indexes published by the **Educational Resources Information Center (ERIC)** that provides an abstract and full bibliographic citations for each entry, including subject and author indexes. RIE documents are available on microfiche in many library collections, and virtually all libraries now have computer access to the database.

Respondent: In research, a term usually associated with someone who responds to a **survey**, is interviewed as part of a study, or answers questions as an experimental subject. In **behavioral psychology**, respondents are what **Ivan Pavlov (1849–1936)** called **reflexes**. They are **unconditioned responses** that may be elicited or triggered automatically by a specific unlearned or **unconditioned stimulus**.

Respondent Behavior: In behavioral psychology, a type of behavior corresponding to reflex action. *See* Respondent; Reflex

Respondent Conditioning: B. F. Skinner's (1904–1990) term for classical conditioning, in which a **conditioned stimulus** that has been paired with an **unconditioned stimulus** over a period of time also evokes the **conditioned response**, even in the absence of the conditioned stimulus. *See* Classical Conditioning

Response (R): In psychology, any **activity** that occurs as the result of **stimuli**. Although responses are typically observable, mental images or thoughts are not.

Response Sets: In research, a "standard" response or the tendency to respond in a socially acceptable way to questions on a self-report measure that are not related to the content of the questions or do not reflect how the individual really feels or believes. Response sets typically involve answers that are inaccurate and misleading and are most common when the questions being asked are sensitive in nature. For example, an individual is likely to provide a response set on such questions as "Have you ever used cocaine?" or "Have you ever had an affair?" *See* Randomized Response Technique

Responsive Approach: A qualitative assessment model or a method of evaluating arts and music classes that relies primarily on subjective information for evaluation rather than objective measures. The responsive approach includes examples of the student's music or artwork and commentary from both the teacher and the student. The responsive approach involves evaluating each student's work independently rather than comparing each student's work to the work of other students or to intended outcomes.

Retention: In memory, the ability to store information for **retrieval** after it has been presented. Teachers use a variety of techniques to aid in retention, including drill, repetition, exercises, activities, and review. In education, retention refers to the act of not promoting students from one grade level to the next at the expected time because of unacceptable grades. The term retention also refers to those students who remain in a particular school or school district over time. As a professional term, retention refers to the act of retaining teachers at a particular educational institution.

Retrieval: In memory, the ability to **recall** and utilize stored information, or the output end of the memory process in the **information-processing model**. When information is available but not accessible to the individual, this information is said to be irretrievable for reasons not fully understood. However, **prompts** and other cues are useful tools for helping individuals access available information from memory. For example, reminding an individual of a fact or two about an event can often "jog" his or her memory, enabling the individual to remember more details about the event. *See* Cue-dependent Forgetting; Forgetting

Retrieval Strategies: *See* Forgetting

Retroactive Inhibition (RI): In memory, interference in which an individual's ability to **recall** or retrieve previously learned material is disrupted by learning new material. Retroactive inhibition (RI) occurs when new learning interferes with old learning. Retroactive inhibition is the opposite of proactive inhibition (PI) in which an individual's ability to recall or retrieve new information is disrupted by previously learned material. *See* Proactive Inhibition; Forgetting; Interference

Retrogression: *See* Regression

Reverberation/Reverberance: In general, when a sound continues to be heard well after the source has stopped vibrating. More specifically, reverberation refers to the extended length of time it takes for a sound to decay due to the number of reflective surfaces. In a room filled with reflective surfaces, the sound can be heard for longer periods of time because the sound waves keep bouncing or reflecting off of surfaces rather than being absorbed by them. *See* **Resonance; Reflection**

Reversibility: The **conceptual understanding** that something altered in a certain way can be returned to its original state by reversing the process. For example, a ball of modeling clay that has been rolled out into a long, thin rope can be reshaped into a ball. According to **Jean Piaget (1896–1980)**, reversibility is central to a child's ability to reason and is characteristic of the **concrete operational stage** (approximately age seven to eleven). *See* **Conservation; Operation; Piaget's Stages of Cognitive Growth; Reciprocity**

Reward: A positive **incentive** that acts as a **reinforcing stimulus**. In education, rewards are used to encourage desired behaviors or to acknowledge students for exhibiting desired behaviors.

Rhetorical Questions: Questions asked by individuals to which they already know the answer. Rhetorical questions are common in education. For example, teachers ask rhetorical questions to help get students involved in class discussion and to assess student progress and preparation for class. Rhetorical questions may be used constructively to contribute to the learning experience. They may also be used in a negative and antagonistic manner.

Rhythm Content Learning Sequence, Gordon: In Edwin E. Gordon's (b. 1927) **music learning theory**, one of three learning sequences (rhythm content learning sequence, **tonal content learning sequence**, and **skill learning sequence**). Rhythm in the context of music learning theory has three fundamental elements: **macrobeats**, **microbeats**, and melodic rhythm. According to Gordon, syntactical meaning is given to rhythm through a sense of meter, and all of these rhythmic elements must be audiated simultaneously to establish rhythmic syntax. Macrobeats are the longest beats of equal duration, such as the quarter note in common time. Macrobeats are fundamental because microbeats and melodic rhythm are superimposed in audiation on macrobeats. Microbeats are subdivisions of macrobeats, and there are numerous ways to subdivide macrobeats. For example, a quarter note in common time may be divided by several combinations of microbeats, such as two eighth notes, four sixteenth notes, an eighth note followed by two sixteenth notes, or other combinations.

Melodic rhythm refers to the ongoing series of rhythm patterns in a piece of music and can incorporate a variety of macrobeats and microbeats depending on the complexity of the music. Rhythm content learning sequence is hierarchical; mastery of one skill is a necessary prerequisite for moving on to the next skill. This hierarchy involves several classifications of meters and tempi from simple to complex. In addition, there are several classifications of rhythmic patterns (a variety of combinations of macrobeats and microbeats), which also range from simple to complex. Gordon's book *Learning Sequences in Music* devotes an entire chapter to fully describing and explaining the rhythm content learning sequence. *See* **Music Learning Theory, Gordon**

Rhythm Syllable Systems: *See* Counting/Rhythm Syllable Systems

Rimm's GIFT, GIFFI, and PRIDE Tests of Creativity: A series of tests designed by S. B. Rimm in the 1980s for determining characteristics of **creative** children. These tests include: the Group Inventory for Finding Creative Talent (GIFT), the Group Inventory for Finding Interest (GIFFI) tests I and II for secondary school students, and the Preschool Interest Descriptor (PRIDE) test for preschoolers or kindergartners, which is completed by parents for their children. Rimm's tests focus on preferences, **personality** characteristics, interests, independence, imagination, and, with older students, characteristics such as confidence and inventiveness. Rimm's tests are very easy to administer and take and require only yes or no responses.

Risky Shift: In social psychology, the tendency for individuals in a group situation to be less cautious and more prone to taking risks than they are when they are alone. Risky shift affects both attitudes and behavior.

RNA Synthesis Theory: A theory of memory based on the idea that memory is controlled, at least in part, by chemical changes within the brain. Specifically, it is believed that ribonucleic acid (RNA) is either the physical site of the memory itself or involved in the process that leads to the physiological formation of memory. Proponents of the theory suggest that chemical compounds help consolidate short-term memories, allowing them to become long-term memories. This consolidating process is facilitated by rehearsing and organizing the material to be learned and is also affected by the meaning or importance learners attach to the material.

It has also been suggested that the physiological processes involved in committing something to memory are set as follows: 1) neuronal activation leads to RNA synthesis; 2) RNA synthesis leads to protein synthesis; and 3) protein synthesis leads to synaptic growth, the physiological basis of long-term memory. The RNA synthesis theory is supported by the fact that the production and decline of RNA levels in the brain closely parallel the efficiency of the human memory cycle. In addition, researchers have observed changes in the RNA content of trained animals. Finally, drugs that affect memory work directly on the RNA.

Rogers, Carl (1902-1987): An eminent American psychologist, Rogers trained at Columbia University's Teachers College where he received his Ph.D. in 1931. Rogers directed a children's agency in New York before teaching at the university level with stints at the Ohio State University in 1940 and the University of Wisconsin in 1957. In 1945, Rogers set up a counseling center at the University of Chicago. In 1963, Rogers helped found an institute devoted to the study of the person in La Jolla, California. Rogers is best known for the development of **client-centered therapy**, a nondirective approach to treating individuals. Client-centered therapy, known today as **person-centered therapy**, was originally developed as an alternative to Freud's **psychoanalysis**. Rogers is often associated with humanistic psychology even though his client-centered therapy was developed in the 1950s, a decade before the humanistic movement. Rogers emphasized the potential for good in all of his clients, which became a central theme of humanism. Rogers has had a significant influence on the methods of psychological counseling, and many of his techniques are standard practice today. His writings include *Counseling and Psychotherapy* (1942), *Client-Centered Therapy* (1951), *Psychotherapy and Personality Change* (1954), and *On Becoming a Person* (1961).

Role: In **social psychology**, the actions and behavior expected by individuals due to their position or status within a group or society. An individual's role is the behavioral repertoire or collection of responses associated with his or her **status** in society's prestige hierarchy. Society expects individuals of a given status to behave in certain ways. As a result, individuals feel obliged to behave according to society's expectations. **Role** is tied to status, which carries with it perceived expectations of behavior. Examples: 1) Lawyers and university professors are expected to conduct themselves with more decorum than a truck driver. 2) There is constant pressure on teachers to act "teacherly" and professional even when they are not at school. Failure to do so may result in loss of respect in the community and the inability to function effectively at school as a result. *See* **Status**

Role Diffusion: *See* **Psychosocial Stages, Erikson's**

Role-playing: An instructional method in which students play a position or role and interact in a simulated, realistic environment. Role-playing often involves having students pretend to be someone else to help students understand all sides of issues. Because role-playing involves acting out scenes or situations in dramatic fashion, both personal and social dimensions can be addressed. Using props and staging equipment is common and helps make the situation more realistic. Role-playing has been used in some form for centuries; however, it has been used regularly as an instructional method since the 1960s. In the classroom, role-playing is commonly employed when teachers want students to "experience" a particular social issue. It is also commonly used to help students understand a variety of principles that affect interpersonal relationships and to help students develop better communication skills.

Rorschach Inkblot Test: A projective test that consists of ten symmetrical inkblots presented on separate cards. Individuals are asked to look at and then describe what each inkblot looks like or might be. Like other projective tests, the Rorschach Inkblot Test is used to assess **personality** by assessing the ways individuals reveal or project themselves through their imaginations. Such tests enable individuals to respond as they wish; there is no correct interpretation of the inkblots. The general idea is that individuals will project their thoughts and feelings onto the test, which allows the researcher or therapist to understand them better. *See* **Projective Tests; Thematic Apperception Test**

Rosenthal Effect: In research, a phenomenon described by Robert Rosenthal in the 1960s based on the idea that researchers can inadvertently bias the results of their studies through a variety of verbal and non-verbal cues, such as facial expressions, posture, or tone of voice. The Rosenthal Effect, also referred to as **researcher bias** or experimenter bias, has implications for teaching. For example, teachers often form expectations about student performance and behave in a suggestive manner according to these expectations. Students may believe in and respond to teacher expectations, which results in a **self-fulfilling prophecy**. That is, if a teacher has high expectations of a particular student, this student may do well because of these high expectations. On the other hand, if a teacher has low expectations of a particular student, this student may not do well because of these low expectations. Furthermore, teachers may actually treat students differently, which further enhances this effect. In short, students often act in accordance with teacher expectations, which manifest themselves in overt ways. *See* Self-fulfilling Prophecy

Rote Learning: A method of learning that usually involves listening to someone else perform, read, or model the material to be learned. Individuals rely on memory alone to reproduce the information presented to them. In elementary music, rote learning provides a foundation for higher levels of musical learning. The **Suzuki Method** is an elementary method that uses rote learning extensively. As students advance, rote learning is used to develop performance and listening **skills**.

Rote Memorization: Verbatim learning that is often done without regard for understanding the content or context of the material. For example, it is not necessary to read notation or understand musical concepts to learn a song using rote memorization. Rote memorization can be beneficial when it is used as a basis for gaining further understanding. For example, a performer may memorize a piece of music so that he or she can focus on the artistic and musical aspects of the performance, rather than focusing on notes and rhythms on the printed page.

Rubric: Currently, one of the more popular methods of **alternative assessment** in today's schools in which certain **criteria** are selected to evaluate student performance. A wide variety of rubrics are in use, but the following three are the most common: 1) Particular Trait Rubrics, which are designed to single out one or two criteria for **evaluation** of a complex performance while ignoring other elements; 2) Analytic Rubrics, which are designed to track all of the criteria for evaluation individually, providing a separate score for each criteria; and 3) Holistic Rubrics, which are designed to combine all of the criteria for evaluation into one comprehensive description of the performance. *See* Alternative Assessment

Ss

Sample: In research, a group of **subjects** chosen from a given **population** for use in experimental studies. As a general rule, if proper sampling procedures are followed, then the larger the sample, the more reliable and **valid** the resulting **data** will be. *See* **Sampling**

Sampling: In research, the process of choosing sample subjects from a given **population**. **Random sampling** is the most commonly used sampling technique. This technique helps ensure that every member of a given population has an equal chance of being selected, which contributes greatly to the **reliability** and the **validity** of the results. Computers are commonly used to generate random samples. Other types of sampling include **cluster sampling, stratified random sampling, quota sampling,** and **haphazard sampling.** *See* **Probability Sampling; Nonprobability Sampling**

Sampling Errors: In a research study, the chance variations in a **sample** that can be attributed to chance **variables** rather than to non-chance variables. That is, because a sample is comprised of a relatively small number of individuals within a larger **population**, it is always possible, if not likely, that the sample will not precisely represent the population. Sampling error affects researchers' abilities to generalize from a sample to a particular population and their abilities to determine whether two or more samples were drawn from the same population. Researchers control sampling error by using proper sampling techniques. *See* **Probability Sampling; Nonprobability Sampling; Random Sampling**

Savants/Savant Syndrome: Individuals, typically mentally retarded or autistic, who display remarkable abilities in at least one particular area such as math, music, art, or memory. These abilities are often very specific, narrow in range, and outstanding in nature. For example, someone may be classified as a savant who has unusual and exceptional abilities in one area, such as drawing, memorizing large amounts of information, or performing specific mathematical calculations. Savants are often severely handicapped physically and/or intellectually and typically score low on **intelligence tests**. In addition, savants often have severe language deficits and behave in socially inappropriate ways. About 75 percent of those diagnosed with savant syndrome are males. At one time, the term "idiot savant" was commonly used to describe individuals with savant syndrome; however, the word "idiot" is an outdated term for mental retardation, and it has been dropped in recent years.

Musical savants can often play instruments they have never been trained to play and can perform thousands of songs from memory. In addition, savants can often listen to long musical compositions and, after only one hearing, perform the composition from memory. The existence of musical savants may be an indication that intelligence, as traditionally measured, may not be necessary for at least some abilities generally considered to be musical. *See* **Autism; Mentally Retarded/Mental Retardation**

Saving Score: In memory, a measure of retention that indicates the amount of time saved in the process of **relearning** material. A saving score is shown as a percentage of time saved as related to the amount of time it took to learn the material the first time. *See* **Relearning**

Sawtooth Wave: In acoustics, a type of **wave** produced by a **complex tone** in which the second **partial** is twice the **frequency** of the **fundamental** and has half the **amplitude** of the fundamental; the third partial is three times the frequency and has one-third the amplitude of the fundamental; the fourth partial is four times the frequency and has one-fourth the amplitude of the fundamental, and so on. *See* **Waveform**

Scaffolding: In education, a process in which teachers provide support for student learning and then remove the support so that students become self-reliant. The idea behind scaffolding is to provide the necessary structure, guidance, and teaching that students need to learn as well as fostering student independence by removing the support. Ideally, the students will continue to develop skills and acquire knowledge on their own. Scaffolding can involve providing all needed support beforehand, or it can involve ongoing guidance and discussion, depending on the nature of the subject material. Scaffolding is an especially useful technique for technology-based learning because it is an area in which students need to be more self-reliant.

Scale: A set of ascending or descending values usually arranged in ascending order. Most scales are numerical, in which numbers are typically assigned to the various scale degrees. Scale degrees generally have a logical or quantitative relationship to each other and are often designed to allow estimations of value or substance. For example, on a scale from one to ten, ten is twice as much as five. Certain types of scales, such as Likert Scales, are more qualitative in nature and use descriptive terms instead of numbers for scale degrees. *See* Likert Scale; Measurement/Measurement Scales

Scapegoating/Scapegoat Theory: A form of **displaced aggression** in which an innocent, but helpless victim is blamed for the mistakes of others. In a classroom setting, scapegoating is common. For example, blaming one person for the low quality of work on a group project when, in fact, everyone was responsible, is scapegoating. Scapegoats are often unpopular students who are shy or different in some way, or they may be students who are not part of a particular group of friends. Students who disrupt class on a regular basis are also used as scapegoats because students know that displacing blame onto students who are disruptive will most likely be accepted as fact by their teachers. *See* Defense Mechanisms

Scattergrams/Scatterplot Diagrams: In research, the plotting of individual data points on a graph according to magnitude of two **variables** such as years of experience and percentage scores. One variable is represented on the *x* axis (horizontal axis) while the other variable is represented on the *y* axis (vertical axis). When lines are drawn from point to point, relationships or lack of relationships can be seen. For example, if the line starts in the lower left portion of the graph and ascends diagonally toward the upper right portion of the graph, the relationship is positive. If the line starts in the upper left portion of the graph and descends diagonally towards the lower right portion, the relationship is negative. No relationship is indicated when the points are dispersed in no discernible pattern.

Schedules of Reinforcement: In **behavioral psychology**, a series of well-defined procedures for reinforcing a given **response**. Schedules of reinforcement can be based on either the time elapsed or the number of responses emitted. The five major schedules of reinforcement are: 1) **continuous**, where reinforcement is given continually; 2) **fixed ratio**, where reinforcement is given after a specified number of responses; 3) **fixed interval**, where reinforcement is given after a set amount of time has elapsed; 4) **variable ratio**, where reinforcement is given after a certain number of responses, when this number keeps changing; and 5) **variable interval**, where reinforcement is given after a certain amount of time has elapsed, when the amount of elapsed time keeps changing. Responses reinforced periodically, rather than each time they are emitted, tend to be conditioned more strongly and are thus more resistant to extinction. *See* Conditioning; Reinforcement

Scheme/Schema/Schemata: In **cognitive** theory, patterns or structures within the brain that enable individuals to know. That is, schema are the mental structures, the rules for processing information, or the internal **framework** that represents what individuals know about objects, situations, events, actions, and processes. Schema enable an individual to **assimilate** new knowledge and experiences. Cognitivists such as **Jean Piaget (1896–1980)** believed that schema undergo fundamental transformations during development.

Scholastic Achievement Test (SAT): One of the most popular **standardized tests** of **academic achievement** used in high schools. The SAT test battery includes the SAT I and the SAT II. The SAT I measures verbal and mathematical reasoning skills and takes approximately three hours to complete. The SAT II consists of subject tests designed to measure how much students know about a particular academic subject and how well they can apply that knowledge. Subject tests are largely multiple-choice tests, and each test takes approximately one hour to complete. Twenty-two subject areas have specialized tests, including literature, U.S. history, math, biology, chemistry, French reading, German reading, and Spanish reading. Many colleges and universities use SAT scores as one indicator of a student's readiness to complete college-level work. In addition, test scores are often used as criteria for awarding various types of scholarships. Most colleges and universities require students to take the SAT test prior to admission. In addition, colleges and universities often set minimum score requirements for admission.

School Administrators: Superintendents, principals, vice principals, counselors, and other specialists within a school or district whose primary responsibilities are associated with running the school rather than with teaching students. School administrators are generally responsible for activities that occur within their own schools. Music teachers must generally seek administrator approval for several types of activities. These activities often include fundraising, trips and tours, concert dates, additional rehearsals, music program expenditures, and certain disciplinary actions. Music teachers typically work closely with administrators because most music programs involve large amounts of extracurricular activity, and most are very visible to the rest of the student body and the community.

School Choice: In general, the idea that parents and guardians should be free to choose schools for their children. Specifically, children should not be forced to attend a school on the basis of geographical location. Parents and guardians should have freedom to choose a school based on what they believe is best for their children.

School Music Monthly: The first successful music education publication, which focused on a wide range of topics pertinent to music teaching. *School Music Monthly* was founded in 1900 by **Philip C. Hayden (1854–1925)**, the music supervisor in Keokuk, Iowa. In 1907, the name *School Music Monthly* was changed to *School Music*, which remained in print until 1936.

School Music Program: The Description and Standards (1986): A list of **goals** for school music programs established by **Music Educators National Conference (MENC)** in 1986, which was a revision of the goals established in 1974. The 1986 standards include: 1) the ability to make music, alone and with others; 2) the ability to improvise and create music; 3) the ability to use the vocabulary and notation of music; 4) the ability to respond to music aesthetically, intellectually, and emotionally; 5) the acquaintance with a wide variety of music, including diverse musical styles and genres; 6) the understanding of the role music has played and continues to play in the lives of human beings; 7) the ability to make aesthetic judgments based on critical listening and analysis; 8) the development of a commitment to music; 9) the support of the musical life of the community and desire to encourage others to do so; and 10) the ability to continue musical learning independently. These standards and descriptions served as the basis for the National Standards in Music developed in the early 1990s. *See* **National Standards, Music Education**

School Psychologist: A professional psychologist employed by a school or school district whose primary responsibilities include student testing and guidance. School psychologists help students work through problems associated with school-related activities as well as personal problems that affect a student's abilities to function at school.

School-based Budgeting: The process of allocating resources at the school level rather than at the central administration level. In school-based budgeting, teachers, parents, principals, and other concerned taxpayers are involved in the decisions regarding how money will be allocated for school-related expenditures. The central idea behind school-based budgets is that the entities that control the money represent a balance of community values.

School-based Management: *See* Site-based Management

Schoolwide Enrichment Model (SEM): A **model** for fostering **creativity** and gifted behaviors in children developed by J. S. Renzulli and S. M. Reis (1985, 1997). SEM emphasizes identifying children's areas of strength and interests and developing them by providing students with an enriched learning environment. SEM is based on the belief that adult creative productivity is associated with an interaction of three areas, which Renzulli and Reis referred to as the Three-Ring Conception of Giftedness. The three components of **giftedness** include: 1) above-average general and specific abilities, 2) high degrees of task commitment to specific projects and problem-solving initiatives, and 3) the ability to develop creative solutions and products to address these problems. This Three-Ring Conception of Giftedness is the basis for the SEM model. In the classroom, the teacher's role is to help students discover and articulate their particular interests and to provide them with appropriate activities that will encourage them to pursue these interests in addition to regular classroom work. In this regard, teachers in the SEM model are facilitators of student interests. *See* Enrichment; Gifted and Talented/Giftedness

Scientific Method: A sequential method used in research to test **hypotheses** or to answer research questions. The **scientific method** consists of the following steps: 1) identify the problem, 2) gather all pertinent data, 3) formulate hypotheses or questions, 4) conduct an experiment, 5) interpret results, and 6) draw conclusions.

Seashore, Carl (1866-1949): One of the most influential leaders in the psychology of hearing, best known in music for the **Seashore Measures of Musical Talents** test battery and for his **Theory of Specifics**. Seashore attended Gustavus Adolphus College in St. Peter, Minnesota, before getting a Ph.D. from Yale in 1895. Seashore taught for many years at the University of Iowa. While there he founded one of the first psychological laboratories in the country and was instrumental in the development of the **audiometer** in the early 1900s. Seashore was interested in individuals' abilities to hear mentally, a concept he called inner music. Seashore studied this ability in musicians and believed that it was the defining characteristic or mark of the best musicians. Seashore believed that the way to measure **musicality** was to measure several different musical capacities separately with as much experimental control as possible in order to eliminate the effects of previous training. He believed that being musical was a reflection of how an individual performed on each test, rather than on the battery as a whole. Seashore called this idea the Theory of Specifics. **James Mursell (1893–1963)** and other critics of Seashore's theory indicated that assessing music **aptitude** in this manner was unmusical and that music should be assessed in a holistic manner. Mursell developed his own theory in opposition to Seashore's, which is called the **Omnibus Theory**. The debate between Seashore and Mursell is well documented in the literature.

Seashore Measures of Musical Talents: The first and probably the most well-known standardized test battery of musical **aptitude** ever written, originally published in 1919 by **Carl E. Seashore (1866–1949)**. The Seashore Measures of Musical Talents were designed to measure what Seashore considered to be the basic attributes of musical individuals. In his view, it was important to measure several different **musical capacities** separately with as much experimental control as possible to eliminate the effects of previous training; however, the resultant test is anything but musical. Seashore utilized laboratory instruments instead of real musical instruments, measured only a single capacity at a time, and devised examples that are almost completely unmusical in nature. In addition, the presentation is boring, and some students find it humorous. To Seashore, being musical was a reflection of how an individual performed on each test, not on the test battery as a whole. Critics pointed out that assessing **music aptitude** in this manner was not a true reflection of **musicality** or musical aptitude.

Seashore's original test battery contained five tests: Sense of Pitch, Intensity Discrimination, Sense of Time, Sense of Consonance, and Tonal Memory. Seashore added a sixth test for Sense of Rhythm in 1925, and in 1939, the test was revised. The revision was significantly different from the original. Changes included the following: 1) the consonance test was eliminated and replaced by the timbre test; 2) the term "intensity" was replaced with "loudness"; 3) the task on the time test was altered; and 4) the length of each test was reduced. Although the test manual has undergone minor revisions, the current edition of the test itself is basically the same as the 1939 test version.

Secondary Control: In psychology, an individual's effort to accept external reality by changing his or her attitudes, goals, or emotions. Secondary control enables an individual to accept the way things are and is a "learn to live with it" **coping** mechanism. *See* **Primary Control**

Secondary Reinforcer: In **behavioral psychology**, any **stimulus** that has become reinforcing through prior association. Secondary reinforcers differ from primary reinforcers, such as candy, which have inherently reinforcing properties. Most secondary reinforcers do not have reinforcing properties naturally; they have reinforcing value because such value has been learned. For example, teachers can make gold stars or praise a secondary reinforcer. *See* **Primary Reinforcer; Reinforcement**

Secondary Traits: In Gordon Allport's (1897–1967) **trait theory**, specific, narrow traits that exert less influence on behavior than central traits. Secondary traits are generally less important aspects of **personality** than central traits and change more often than central traits according to the situation or mood. Secondary traits include preferences for food, colors, movies, and clothes. *See* **Cardinal Traits; Central Traits**

Section 504 of the Vocational Rehabilitation Act: A section of the Vocational Rehabilitation Act of 1973 that is broader in scope than the **Individuals with Disabilities Education Act (IDEA)** regarding eligibility to receive accommodations in education. The Section 504 definition of **disability**, which has been incorporated in the **Americans with Disabilities Act of 1990 (ADA)**, may include individuals with a variety of conditions, including drug addiction, alcoholism, or a variety of diseases, such as HIV infection and heart disease. The idea behind Section 504 is to "create a fair and level playing field" in educational programs, which is typically accomplished through incorporating a number of accommodations and modifications into education programs, including: 1) allowing extra time to complete assignments, 2) arranging seating to accommodate reduced vision or hearing, 3) allowing students to take untimed tests, 4) using taped textbooks, 5) using supplementary materials, and 6) providing access to peer tutors or paraeducators. *See* **Individuals with Disabilities Education Act (IDEA); Americans with Disabilities Act (ADA)**

Segregation: In general, the act of separating individuals based on some characteristic, such as race or religion. In education, the term segregation has historically been used to refer to the separation of African American and Caucasian students, usually into different schools. Such segregation was common in American schools, particularly in the South, until the 1954 United States Supreme Court decision in **Brown v. Board of Education of Topeka, Kansas**. The term segregation is also used in education to refer to the act of placing disabled or **handicapped** children into separate classrooms or other facilities to accommodate special needs. Laws and public policy in education currently favor inclusion over segregation to accommodate the needs of disabled students, employing **paraeducators** and modifying **curriculum** to keep students in regular classrooms whenever possible.

Selection Bias: In research, a threat to a study's internal validity that sometimes occurs when the subjects selected for the groups are different from each other in ways that affect the results of a study. Selection bias occurs when groups are not initially equivalent. **Random sampling** techniques help control for selection bias. *See* **Researcher Bias**

Selectivity: The process of responding to some incoming stimuli while ignoring others. Individuals have the ability to selectively choose to what they will respond. Individuals also have the ability to prioritize stimuli and their responses to these stimuli. Selectivity is important for organizing and filtering stimuli, especially at times when the amount of incoming stimuli becomes so great that an individual could not possibly respond to all of it. Selectivity is both a conscious and an unconscious phenomenon.

Self: According to **Carl Rogers (1902–1987)**, the conscious **perception** of oneself. *See* **Self-concept/Self-perception**

Self-actualization: In **humanistic psychology**, an individual's fundamental tendency toward maximal realization of his or her potentials, or an individual's desire to "be all they can be" as a person. Characteristics of a **self-actualized** person include self-acceptance, spontaneity, concern for others, autonomy, and **creativity**. Self-actualization is a basic concept in humanistic theories of **personality** such as those developed by **Abraham Maslow (1908–1970)** and **Carl Rogers (1902–1987)**. Self-actualization is the ultimate psychological need in Maslow's hierarchy of needs. *See* Need Hierarchy, Maslow

Self-concept/Self-perception: The ideas, feelings, and attitudes an individual has about himself or herself, or how individuals perceive themselves in general. Self-concept or self-perception answers the question "Who am I?" *See* Self-esteem; Self-image; Self-consciousness

Self-consciousness: In psychology, times when an individual is especially concerned about the reactions of others to him or her. Self-consciousness is a form of heightened self-awareness. In education, students often learn to be self-conscious at an early age, if and when other students and/or teachers laugh at or make fun of them for particular behaviors. The level of self-consciousness tends to rise during **adolescence** due to the physiological and psychological changes that accompany adolescent development. *See* Adolescence; Self-esteem

Self-deception: In psychology, a **defense mechanism** in which individuals deny or disguise the true **motives** of behavior. Self-deception may be unconscious or may result from an individual's inadequate perceptions of a situation or an event. *See* Defense Mechanisms

Self-efficacy/Self-efficacy Expectations: An individual's sense of his or her own capabilities and aspirations. According to **Albert Bandura's (b. 1925)** social learning theory, self-efficacy expectations determine whether or not individuals will attempt certain behaviors, the amount of effort individuals will devote to behaviors, and how long individuals will work on behaviors during difficult periods. Individuals with low self-efficacy expectations limit their participation and give up quickly when things do not go well. Individuals with high self-efficacy expectations do the opposite. Bandura believes that self-efficacy expectations limit overall levels of achievement and career development. He identified four ways self-efficacy and self-efficacy expectations are learned or acquired: 1) performance accomplishments, 2) vicarious learning, 3) verbal persuasion, and 4) physical/affective status. *See* **Social Learning Theory, Bandura**

Self-efficacy Perceptions: In education, the idea that the amount of effort an individual is willing to expend to learn a skill or complete a task is directly related to the individual's perceived ability to do so. Research has shown that individuals who perceive themselves as naturally talented, or "good" at a particular skill or task will expend more effort to achieve successful outcomes than individuals who perceive themselves as having little natural ability.

Self-esteem: In general, how individuals feel about themselves or view themselves, both positively or negatively, or the value or sense of worth individuals place on their own characteristics, abilities, and behaviors. In education, much has been written about the need for building positive student self-esteem, which has been linked to success in academic and non-academic areas of life. In music, studies indicate that self-esteem affects student attitudes toward music and that participation in music may lead to more positive self-esteem. Further, some evidence exists to suggest that positive self-esteem facilitates **academic achievement** in music and non-music classes. *See* **Self-concept; Self-image**

Self-fulfilling Prophecy: In psychology, something being fulfilled or realized simply because it was predicted or expected, or the tendency for individuals to behave in ways that cause their expectations to become reality. In education, studies indicate that **self-fulfilling prophecies** are influenced by other's beliefs and expectations; that is, students often act in accordance with teacher expectations. Furthermore, teachers may actually treat students differently depending on expectations, which further enhances the likelihood of students believing and realizing self-fulfilling prophecies. For example, a teacher who expects certain students to be disruptive and treats these students as if they will be disruptive often find that, in fact, these students are disruptive. *See* **Rosenthal Effect**

Self-image: The image individuals have of themselves based on **perceptions** of how others see them. That is, self-image includes how individuals think others see them, how individuals feel about these perceptions, and how individuals see themselves. *See* **Self-concept; Self-esteem**

Self-improvement: In general, the process an individual undertakes to improve certain areas of his or her life. For example, individuals can improve their physical condition by working out and getting in better shape; they can improve their mental condition by focusing on developing better attitudes about life in general; and they can improve their academic success by studying hard and making better grades. In music education, teachers can use several methods and techniques to improve their own teaching effectiveness, including: 1) videotaping themselves while teaching, then reviewing and critiquing the tape; 2) recording an ensemble or class, then reviewing and critiquing the tape; 3) keeping a journal and reviewing it periodically to detect certain behavioral patterns; and 4) writing out, implementing, and then evaluating the effectiveness of lesson plans.

Self-instruction: The process of talking to oneself in an instructional manner to control behavior. Self-instruction is an aspect of some types of self-control training.

Self-management: A teaching technique in which students set up their own **schedules of reinforcement**, devising their own **reward** systems, and determining the process by which stated **outcomes** are monitored. Self-management enables students to help structure their learning in cooperation with the teacher and offers several advantages over traditional instruction. These advantages include: 1) students may be more committed to achieving educational **goals** because of their involvement in structuring the curriculum; 2) self-management emphasizes the process as well as the product; and 3) self-management provides ample opportunities for **positive reinforcement** strategies. For example, instead of punishing a student for missing an assignment, self-management can be used to monitor study time, to track time spent on assignments, and to set up positive reinforcers to help achieve short-term and long-term goals.

Self-observation/Self-monitoring: The process of systematically observing one's own behavior and monitoring the progress toward changing behavior according to a planned program. Self-observation is an important component in some behavioral therapy programs.

Self-perception: *See* Self-concept

Self-perception Theory: The theory that attitudes and beliefs can be influenced by making observations of one's own behavior. In self-perception theory, individuals judge the way they feel by observing the way they act; in turn, these observations affect how an individual behaves. Self-perception theory is an alternative to cognitive dissonance theory. *See* Cognitive Dissonance Theory; Self-persuasion

Self-persuasion: In psychology, the process by which an individual changes his or her opinion so that it is consistent with behavior.

Self-realization: In psychology, the reconciliation of complementary opposites in an individual's **personality**, such as conscious and unconscious. According to **Carl Jung (1875–1961)**, self-realization is a basic goal of every individual. *See* Self-Actualization

Self-regulation Theory: In psychology, a cognitive theory of **intrinsic motivation** developed by Corno and Rohrkemper (1985) based on the idea that students should learn and use a systematic process for learning new material. Self-regulation theory involves using a systematic process for understanding new material, manipulating ideas about it, relating these ideas to what is already known, and monitoring learning progress. Strategies for helping students self-regulate learning include: 1) having teacher-student and student-student discussions about the new material, 2) learning material in-depth so that networks of knowledge and a deep understanding of the material can be formed, 3) providing positive and constructive feedback and encouragement to promote independent thinking and positive **self-esteem,** and 4) allowing students to control their learning to a greater degree during the learning process.

Self-regulatory Systems/Plans: In psychology, a **person variable** that includes an individual's personal rules, plans, and self-reactions for organizing complex behavior sequences and performing certain behaviors. Self-regulatory systems often include setting goals and rewarding oneself for reaching these goals. According to this system, individuals are motivated by the desire to set and maintain their own internal standards.

Self-serving Bias: In psychology, the tendency for individuals to attribute their successes to talent, effort, practice, or hard work and their failures to task difficulty, luck, or to the influence of other people. Self-serving bias is the tendency for individuals to take credit for the things they do well and to excuse or rationalize their mistakes. In **attribution theory**, self-serving bias is the tendency for individuals to attribute the causes of their own behavior to whatever makes them look the best. For example, individuals often take personal credit for their good actions while they attribute their bad actions to the situation.

Semantic Differential: In psychology, a technique for studying the meanings of concepts or words. Semantic differential involves having subjects rate each word or concept on bipolar scales containing opposite words such as hot/cold with five points in between.

Semantic Memory: Part of the **memory** process that deals with general knowledge, including the meaning of words and language, facts, concepts, and rules. Semantic memory is necessary for the use of language. Semantic memories include the thoughts or understandings that lead to knowledge or action. Semantic memory enables individuals to associate words and their meanings with an understanding of things and concepts. Example: Individuals can identify music as being from the Baroque period because they remember the stylistic features associated with Baroque music.

Sensations: Information received from the environment through the senses, which is relayed to the brain for interpretation (i.e., perception). Sensations are received through the five primary senses: vision, hearing, taste, smell, and touch. Sensations are also facilitated by other physical mechanisms, including **kinesthesis**, **equilibrium**, and other **proprioceptive cues**. *See* **Perception**

Sensing: In Carl Jung's (1875–1961) theory, the process of knowing through the senses. Sensing is one of four ways of contacting or experiencing the world. The other ways of experiencing the world include feeling, **intuition**, and thinking. *See* **Sensations**

Sensorimotor: *See* Piaget's Stages of Cognitive Growth

Sensorimotor Play: A type of **play** that focuses on deriving pleasure from using the senses of touch, taste, hearing, smell, and sight as well as the sense of motion and balance, or **equilibrium**. Playing with food, running around, spinning, twirling, and falling down intentionally just for fun are all examples of sensorimotor play.

Sensory Adaptation: The reduction in sensitivity that occurs with prolonged stimulation. The general idea behind sensory adaptation is that after being around something for an extended period of time, an individual gets used to it and either learns to accept it willingly or becomes relatively unaware of its existence. Example: In music, a student can learn to accept or become indifferent to relatively poor tone quality if they are exposed to poor tone quality on a regular basis. *See* **Desensitization**

Sensory Information Storage: In memory, a brief storage system for information received by the senses from moment to moment. *See* **Sensory Storage; Sensory Register**

Sensory Memory: *See* Sensory Information Storage; Sensory Register

Sensory Register: In the information processing model of memory, where information is held when first received. Information entering the sensory register lasts only a brief moment unless attention is given to it. If attention is not given to information entering the sensory register, it disappears or does not get stored in memory. The sensory register is referred to as sensory memory in the Atkinson-Shiffrin model and includes iconic memory for visual stimuli, **echoic memory** for auditory stimuli, and **haptic** memory for tactile stimuli. All play important roles in the sensory register. Although all of the senses affect memory, sight and sound are the most direct routes for sensory input. *See* **Information Processing Model; Atkinson-Shiffrin Model**

Sensory Storage/Memory: In the Atkinson-Shiffrin model of memory, the idea that each of the senses has a unique storage system for relevant stimuli. For example, **iconic memory** is associated with visual memories, **echoic memory** is associated with aural memories, and **haptic** or tactile memory is associated with remembering information transmitted through feel, body movement, and/or body position. In addition, the ability to remember information as a kind of mental picture or photograph is well documented. This type of photographic memory is called **eidetic imagery**. *See* **Atkinson-Shiffrin Model**

Separate But Equal: *See* **Plessy v. Ferguson; Brown v. Board of Education of Topeka, Kansas**

Sequencing: In education, the order in which information is presented to students. Teaching and learning efficiency is directly dependent upon a teacher's ability to sequence information in a logical manner. In music classes, the sequence of activities and the order in which new or difficult concepts are introduced can be the difference between understanding and confusion. As a general rule, proceeding in a simple to complex manner with specific considerations for experience and/or age level will help facilitate proper sequencing of material. *See* **Pacing**

Sequential Design: In research, a combination of the **cross-sectional** and **longitudinal** designs often used to study developmental research questions. Generally, this design involves starting with a cross-sectional study and includes an initial assessment of individuals of different ages. After some time, usually months or years, these same individuals are assessed again; this is the longitudinal aspect of the design. At this time, a new group of **subjects** is assessed at each age level resulting in a sequential approach to research investigation. Sequential design studies are complex, expensive, and time consuming; however, they can provide information that is impossible to obtain from cross-sectional or longitudinal designs alone.

Serial Memorization: A form of **rote memorization** in which a list of items or a passage of prose or poetry is learned in sequence from beginning to end so that each item or word is a cue to the one that follows. *See* **Paired-associate Learning**

Serial Position Effect: In general, difficulty in memorizing and recalling certain information due to the position of items in a list. Specifically, the serial position effect is the tendency for individuals to recall the first (primacy effect) and the last (recency effect) items in a list better than items in the middle. *See* **Primacy Effect; Recency Effect**

Seriation: The conceptual ability to arrange items in a logical order based on certain criteria or characteristics. For example, seriation may involve arranging toy blocks or crayons according to length, color, or size. According to **Jean Piaget (1896–1980)**, seriation occurs at the preoperational stage of **cognitive** development (two to seven) but is mastered during the **concrete operational period** (approximately seven to eleven). *See* **Piaget's Stages of Cognitive Growth**

Service Learning: In education, learning that results from engaging in volunteer work outside of regular school hours. Joseph Kahne and Joel Westheimer (1996) describe two general categories of service learning programs: those that encourage the goal of change and those that foster the goal of charity. Change programs help students develop a moral sense of caring, including understanding the value of making societal contributions and understanding the importance service learning plays in developing an individual's thought processes. Charity programs help students develop a moral sense of giving through the processes of performing a civic duty and by gaining new, valuable insights and experiences that add to a person's intellectual understanding of life in general.

Set: In general performance, preparatory adjustments or **readiness** for a particular kind of action or experience. Set can be physical and/or mental and is usually a result of instructions and based on experiences. For example, a runner preparing to start a race on command must prepare physically and mentally in order to get off to a good start. In musical performance, the actions musicians take to prepare mentally and physically for a performance usually involves a highly complex set. In psychology, set can also refer to a habitual tendency to respond to a situation in a particular manner. For example, taking a bow to acknowledge the audience's applause is a set behavior. Set is also the second stage of the *Taxonomy of Educational Objectives in the Psychomotor Domain*. In this domain, set specifically refers to being ready to perform mentally (mental set), being ready to perform physically (physical set), and having a favorable attitude about what is being learned (emotional set). *See* **Psychomotor Domain; Response Sets**

Seven Liberal Arts, The: In ancient times, studies through which individuals achieved spiritual and intellectual maturity. The word "liberal" literally means free; thus, the seven liberal arts referred to the seven "free" arts. The notion of free arts can been linked to two factors. First, in the hierarchical society of the Roman Empire, it was believed that the seven liberal arts were only for free men, not for others. Second, study in the seven liberal arts helped free the mind to explore higher levels of thinking and understanding. The division of the seven liberal arts into two subject categories, the **trivium** and the **quadrivium**, has its basis in disciplines of ancient Greece. The trivium was the lower level and included grammar, logic, and rhetoric. These subjects were deemed practical or useful. The quadrivium was the higher level and included arithmetic, geometry, astronomy, and music. These subjects were the most important because they enabled the mind to discover, know, and understand universal truths.

Sex-linked Trait: A **trait** determined by a **gene** transmitted with the same **chromosomes** that determine sex. For example, red-green color blindness typically affects males and is transmitted with the male sex gene.

Sex-role Standards: Behavior that a society considers appropriate based on an individual's gender. Boys and girls are encouraged to adopt varying standards of behavior solely on the basis of gender in American society. For example, boys are often encouraged to be aggressive and masculine, while girls are encouraged to be subdued and ladylike. Whether purposeful or inadvertent, teachers sometimes behave in ways that help promote **sex-role standards**. For example, encouraging boys to play certain games and girls to play others and treating boys with a little less sensitivity than girls are common behaviors that encourage sex-role standards. Some behaviors that promote sex-role standards are detrimental to the learning process. For example, teachers who have preconceived, gender-related notions or expectations of behavior may contribute to **self-fulfilling prophecies**. That is, teachers who believe that boys are more disruptive than girls will probably have disruptive boys in their classrooms. In music education, studies have been conducted regarding masculine and feminine **stereotypes** associated with playing certain instruments. Typically, more girls choose to play flute and clarinet, while more boys choose to play trombone, tuba, or percussion. Certain instruments, such as the saxophone, tend to be more gender neutral. *See* **Stereotypes**

Sex-typing: In general, the process in which boys and girls learn the behaviors, **attitudes**, and expectations associated with being male or female in their culture. *See* **Role**

Shape Constancy: The tendency to perceive the shape of a familiar object as remaining unchanged, regardless of the viewing angle. In other words, an individual's **perception** of an object's shape does not change even though the image projected on the retina does. This ability indicates that object shape is perceived independently of the image it casts on the retina. Shape constancy is easy to understand because it occurs in daily life. For example, individuals are able to recognize the shape of a door as it opens and closes or a car as it makes a turn regardless of their position in relation to these objects. In music, musicians are able to recognize and read musical notation when looking at the notation from various angles. This recognition enables musicians to share music stands, to sit or stand during performances, and to enjoy a large degree of freedom in the music reading process. For the perception of shape constancy to occur, objects must be familiar and/or they must be seen in a familiar context. Lack of familiarity inhibits shape constancy. *See* **Perceptual Constancies**

Shaped Notes: A popular system of notation for **tunebooks** introduced in America by William Little and William Smith in a book entitled *The Easy Instructor* published in 1798. An individual character for each note identifies the syllable. The system may appear on a staff and looks the same as conventional notation except for the shaped note heads, or it may appear on a modified staff. These shapes are designed to indicate the correct pitch syllable to be performed. A different shape was used for each "tone of the scale."

Shaping: In **behavioral psychology**, the process of modifying **behavior** by reinforcing only desired behaviors or by reinforcing related behaviors that ultimately lead to desired behaviors. Shaping involves a technique called **successive approximations**, in which rewards are given for behaviors that are at least close to or in the right direction of the desired behavior. As the shaping process continues and the rewarded behavior becomes more comfortable, rewards are given for behaviors that are even closer to the desired goal. As a result, shaping involves both **differential reinforcement** and a shifting criterion for reinforcement. Most animal acts are built on shaping principles. In education, teachers shape students' behaviors by rewarding them for exhibiting appropriate behavior. For example, teachers may begin to initially shape behavior by rewarding students for exhibiting any behavior related to studying, such as organizing materials or outlining a chapter. Later, rewards may be withheld until students spend at least ten minutes focusing and reviewing these materials. As the length of time is gradually increased before behavior is rewarded, students learn new behaviors. In this example, shaping helps students develop better study habits. Although shaping usually involves rewarding desired behaviors, it can also involve punishment, which can be used in place of **reward** to shape behavior. *See* **Punishment; Shifting Criterion for Reinforcement**

Shifting Criterion for Reinforcement: *See* Shaping

Short-term Memory (STM): In memory, where information that receives attention in the **sensory register** is first stored. Information in STM will be lost unless it is used. If rehearsed sufficiently, information will be transferred into long-term memory (LTM), where it becomes more or less permanent. In 1956, George Miller wrote a famous article entitled "The Magical Number Seven, Plus or Minus Two: Some Limits on our Capacity for Processing Information." In that article, he proposed that an individual can hold approximately seven items (plus or minus two) in short-term memory at any one time. This phenomenon has been proven repeatedly and is accepted almost universally. STM is also referred to as working memory. In the **information-processing model** of memory, **working memory** is the part of memory that deals with current, conscious mental activity. Working memory is constantly receiving new information, so thoughts and memories are either discarded or transferred to the more permanent knowledge base. *See* **Long-term Memory (LTM)**

Sibilants: In singing, hissing sounds in the vocal tone usually caused by a raised tongue position and/or the air stream being directed toward the back of the upper teeth. English sibilants include: *s, z, sh, zh, ch,* and *j.*

Sight Reading: The ability to accurately perform or interpret music notation that has not been seen before. Components of good sight reading include technical mastery of the instrument or voice, the ability to read rhythms and pitches accurately and quickly, and the ability to interpret and perform other musical indications regarding style, dynamics, articulations, and tempi.

Studies on sight reading indicate the following: 1) the ability to sight read and the ability to memorize music are related; that is, students who are able to memorize musical patterns and phrases quickly are usually better sight readers; 2) musical training and experience improve sight reading skills; 3) abilities to sight read are affected by the harmonic context of the melody; 4) music readers tend to fill in missing information and to correct "wrong" information based on previous experience and expectation, a phenomenon similar to what language readers refer to as "proof-readers error"; 5) while sight reading, the eyes move in rapid jerks during which time there is no clear vision. The eyes scan the material very quickly, then pause briefly. It is during these pauses that the material is comprehended; 6) music reading is affected by the type of notation and by the complexity of the notation; 7) the average visual grasp is only three to five notes; 8) the rate of music reading is dependent upon improvement in the ability to grasp rhythmic figures; and 9) skilled music readers observe more dynamic and expression markings than non-skilled readers. Sight reading is closely linked with music reading, and studies on music reading are relevant to the sight reading process. *See* **Music Reading**

Sight Singing Systems: Systems designed to help individuals learn to sight sing, also referred to as pitch reading or melodic reading systems. There are essentially five **sight singing systems** in use today: 1) the letter system; 2) the **syllable system** with fixed "do"; 3) the syllable system with movable "do"; 4) the number system; and 5) the interval system. These five systems fall into three broad categories: 1) fixed systems, which include the letter system and the fixed-do syllable system; 2) relative systems, which include the number system and the movable-do syllable system; and 3) the interval system, in which there is no particular designation for the tones.

Although all of these systems can be effective, some have distinct advantages over others. For example, musicians typically hear pitches in relative terms. Musicians establish the tonality of a piece, and then relate pitches to the key or tonic pitch. Because fixed systems are not relative in this way, some educators believe that fixed systems are inherently flawed. These problems can be avoided by using one of the relative systems since these systems enable musicians to relate one tone to another within any given tonality. In other words, it seems that relative systems such as the movable-do system and the number system are more musically appropriate than fixed systems.

The interval system does not utilize any particular note designations; students generally sight sing using a neutral syllable such as "la" for all notes. The interval system requires students to recognize the distance between notes very quickly as a particular interval. Mastery of this system requires a considerable amount of time and practice. It also tends to put reading into an "intervallic" context and can isolate performers from the concept of tonality since intervals are smaller, more specific units.

The number system is easy to understand and does not require students to learn a system of syllables. It is also easy to transfer across keys and does not present problems with tonality. However, one disadvantage is that the number system cannot satisfactorily deal with accidentals.

The movable-do system seems to be the most popular sight-singing system. It allows the tonic to remain constant, which in turn allows all of the intervallic relationships within the key to remain constant. The movable-do system allows for key changes, accounts for all notes, and is fairly easy to learn, understand, and apply.

Another method for teaching pitch involves the use of hand signs developed by John Curwen. The use of hand signs is popular among some teachers and is typically associated with the teaching method advocated by **Zoltan Kodály (1882–1967)**. Curwen hand signs are most often used at the elementary level. The general idea is that hand signs enable students to derive greater understanding of melody through **kinesthetic** involvement and provide students with visual reference points for placing pitches; however, some research indicates that this may not be the case.

Researchers have shown that the use of sight singing systems and/or syllables can improve musicians' sight reading abilities. However, the application of any system is largely dependent upon individual teaching philosophy, method of application, and personal experiences.

Significance: In general, the importance or meaningfulness attached to or attributed to something or someone. Significance is generally viewed from four broad perspectives: 1) educational, where significance is determined by the practical impact something has on teaching and learning; 2) empirical, where significance is determined through statistical analyses in experimental research; 3) impact on a field of study, where significance is determined by how events, works, discoveries, or performances help define or change a particular discipline; and 4) contribution to a field, where significance is determined based on the way something or someone contributes to a particular field in a global manner.

In research, significance is determined by using various statistical analyses to ascertain whether the differences found are due to manipulation of the **independent variable(s)** rather than to chance alone. Significance of this nature, in and of itself, is not necessarily reflective of how important or meaningful something is in a practical sense. On the other hand, while statistically significant differences may or may not be important or meaningful in a practical sense, important or meaningful differences must be significant. *See* **Statistical Significance**

Significance Level: In research, the probability of rejecting the **null hypothesis** when the null hypothesis is true. Choosing a level of significance or **alpha level** is somewhat arbitrary, and the use of the information gained from an investigation plays a part in making this determination. In studies involving life and death, a high level of significance, such as .01 or .001 is appropriate. In studies not involving life and death, such as determining the effectiveness of a teaching method, a lower level of significance, such as .05 or .10 is sometimes chosen. Interpreting alpha levels is a simple process. If something is significant at the .01 level, it means that the chances are less than 1 out of 100 that the results occurred by chance alone. An alpha level of .001 indicates that the chances are less than 1 out of 1,000 that the results occurred by chance alone and so on. As the alpha level gets larger, the likelihood that researchers will make accurate decisions regarding the null hypotheses decreases. In music research, alpha levels of .05 or .01 are often chosen as significant levels, although levels of .001 are occasionally used. *See* Significance; Statistical Power

Significant Result: In research, a result that leads to a decision to reject the **null hypothesis**, indicating that a statistical difference exists. In other words, a significant result is an outcome of a study that has a low probability of occurrence if the null hypothesis is true. Significant results are generally based on statistical analyses of the data. *See* Significance Level; Statistical Power

Silver Burdett Music Competency Tests: A battery of **criterion-referenced** competency tests developed by Richard Colwell (1979) in collaboration with the Silver Burdett publishing company based on the major objectives of the Silver Burdett music series books for grades one through six. The primary emphases of these tests are placed on aural **perception** of melody, rhythm, form, **tone color**, texture, tonality, and dynamics. Secondary emphases are placed on musical styles, notation, instrument identification, and related arts. The test battery contains three tests divided into six levels for a total of eighteen individual tests. Each level or test corresponds to the respective graded textbook in the Silver Burdett series, and approximately one-third of the material of each book in the series is used. Each test includes all of the necessary instructions, musical examples, and questions and can be administered independently. The **test-retest reliability** coefficients range from .69 to .94 with a median of .88, and inter-item coefficients range from .78 to .97. In addition, norms for percentile ranks and standard scores are provided for each of the eighteen tests.

Similarity, Principle/Law of: A gestalt principle of **perception** that states that when the elements of a figure are equally spaced, similar elements will be seen as a group. That is, **similarity** enables individuals to perceive similar objects as belonging together. Similarity can be based on characteristics such as shape, size, **timbre**, temperature, and color. *See* Continuity, Principle/Law of; Closure Principle/Law of; Proximity, Principle/Law of

Simons Measurement of Music Listening Skills (SMMLS): A **criterion-referenced measuring instrument** devised by Gene Simons in 1974 to assess children's listening skills from kindergarten through grade three. The SMMLS was designed specifically to assess the listening skill objectives included in the Georgia state curriculum guide for the primary grades. The SMMLS contains nine subtests, each lasting about five to eight minutes. The total test takes approximately one hour to complete. The test is appropriate and practical for primary grade children.

Simple Effects: In research, the multiple comparisons required to account for differences among the means in **analysis of variance (ANOVA)** research designs. There are two types of simple effects: 1) **a priori comparisons** and 2) **post hoc comparisons.**

Simple Random Sampling: In research, a **sampling** procedure that enables each member of a **population** to have an equal probability or chance of being included in the sample. *See* Random Sampling

Simple Tone: *See* Pure Tone; Complex Tone

Simplification: A common heuristic strategy in which the number of steps or elements involved in solving a problem is reduced and only the key elements are emphasized. *See* Heuristic

Simulations: In education, instructional strategies centered on constructing and using real-life situations in a simulated environment. Simulations are often used to teach technical skills and are most helpful when learning is impractical or impossible in real-life settings, or when the consequences of making mistakes in real-life settings may be harmful. For example, pilots and astronauts use flight simulators regularly to facilitate learning. Simulations can also be used to facilitate non-technical learning and often involve role-playing. For example, setting up a mock government within the classroom helps students develop a better understanding of governmental functions. The purpose is to learn by doing or experiencing in a more active, life-like environment. Simulations are excellent alternatives to traditional teaching methods and are also fun for students. In music, teachers often arrange for a dress rehearsal or other situation in which students perform a program prior to the actual performance. The purpose is to help students understand what is involved in a real performance setting without actually being in one. Although simulated environments are obviously different from real environments, they are generally quite effective in promoting learning.

Sine Tone/Sinusoidal Tone: A **fundamental** tone with no upper **partials** that produces a simple back and forth **amplitude** wave pattern, or a sustained tone comprised of only one fundamental frequency. Sine tones, also called pure tones or simple tones, do not contain harmonics like complex tones do and are normally produced electronically. Almost all traditional, acoustic musical instruments produce complex tones; however, tones produced by the flute in the very low or high registers are nearly sinusoidal. *See* **Complex Tones; Waveforms**

Singing School Movement: A movement to teach people to sing by note and to improve their singing abilities. The singing school movement began with the establishment of the first singing school in 1717 in Boston, Massachusetts, and lasted into the mid-1800s. Teachers or singing masters would hire out their services to cities and towns for a fee. Classes met from one to five times per week and were often held in churches, schools, or homes. Students, both children and adults, were taught how to read music notation and learned other fundamentals of music. The classes would vary in length from a few weeks to several months. Singing schools were funded entirely by citizens from the private sector; anyone who could afford to pay the teacher could attend.

Single-blind Method/Study: A study in which researchers are aware of which **treatment** the subjects receive and the subjects are not, or when the subjects are aware of the treatment and the researchers are not. *See* **Double-blind Method/Study**

Single-subject Method/Study: In research, a design in which a researcher is working with only one subject. Single-subject experiments are appropriate in counseling and special education environments in which each

subject is evaluated individually to determine what problems exist and what solutions can be applied. Because only one subject is used, issues regarding **validity** and generalizability are a concern. To address these concerns, researchers may repeat the experiment with a number of other subjects in a variety of settings. *See* **Replication**

Site-based Management: In education, the process of involving many people at the school level in decisions about teaching and learning, budgeting, and hiring school personnel. Also called school-based management, site-based management became popular in the 1980s and 1990s and is based on the principle of shared decision-making. The general idea is that the people in a given community most affected by educational decisions should be involved in the decision-making processes. Teachers often serve in leadership roles to help shape the educational programs at their schools. Problems with site-based management have centered around issues regarding the lack of a clear vision or mission, the inability to clearly articulate specific goals, and difficulty in arranging meeting times that are convenient for everyone involved.

Situational Attribution: In psychology, the process of attributing peoples' actions or the causes of their behavior to external or environmental influences. For example, individuals may normally be very rational, yet they may behave quite irrationally when they believe their lives are in danger. *See* **Dispositional Attribution**

Size Constancy: The tendency to perceive the size of a familiar object as remaining unchanged, regardless of the viewing angle. That is, an individual's **perception** of an object's size does not change even though the image projected on the retina does, indicating that object size is perceived independently of the image it casts on the retina. As objects move toward the viewer, their retinal images enlarge, and as they move away from the viewer, their retinal images diminish; yet, those objects are not perceived as changing size. Instead, they are merely perceived as moving toward or away from the viewer. **Size constancy** is dependent upon the familiarity of the object in question and an individual's ability to judge distance. It is easier to estimate distance accurately with familiar objects than it is to estimate distance accurately with unfamiliar objects. In addition, familiar background objects provide important cues that individuals can use to make size comparisons, increasing their abilities to maintain size constancy. Size constancy, like other perceptual constancies, helps maintain consistency in an individual's perceptual environment. *See* **Perceptual Constancies**

Skill: In general, the ability to perform physical and mental actions necessary for task proficiency. Skills are normally developed through practice and training, but are influenced by such factors as knowledge, experience, age, and natural ability. In music, development of performance and non-performance musical skills is generally a lifelong process.

Skill Learning Sequence, Gordon: In Edwin E. Gordon's (b. 1927) music learning theory, one of three learning sequences (skill learning sequence, tonal content learning sequence, rhythm content learning sequence). Gordon identifies two types of skill learning: 1) **Discrimination Learning**, which is learning and imitation that provides readiness for the second type of skill learning, and 2) **Inference Learning**, which is **conceptual learning**. Learning occurs sequentially, where each successive level combines and interacts with previous levels. Every level of learning incorporates all lower levels and sublevels of the learning sequence, and inference learning necessarily incorporates discrimination learning.

Gordon divides discrimination learning into five hierarchical levels and sublevels as follows: 1) Aural/Oral, in which students learn to audiate a listening vocabulary and a performance vocabulary; 2) Verbal Association, in which students learn to name tonalities, meters, and pattern functions; 3) Partial Synthesis, in which students learn to compare and name familiar tonalities and meters based on a teacher's performance using a neutral syllable; 4) Symbolic Association, in which students learn to read and write familiar tonal patterns, rhythm patterns, tonal syllables, and rhythm syllables; 5) Composite Synthesis, in which students learn to read and name familiar tonal patterns, rhythm patterns, tonal syllables, and rhythm syllables. Gordon divides inference learning into three hierarchical levels and sublevels as follows: 1) Generalization, in which students differentiate, perform, read, and write music using aural/oral, verbal, symbolic reading, and writing skills; 2) Creative Improvisation, in which students learn to create music using aural/oral, symbolic reading, and writing skills; and 3) Theoretical Understanding, in which students learn technical aspects of music and come to understand why music is performed, constructed, and interpreted the way it is. In his book *Learning Sequences in Music*, Gordon devotes an entire chapter to describing and explaining his skill learning sequence. *See* Rhythm Content Learning Sequence, Gordon; Tonal Content Learning Sequence, Gordon; Music Learning Theory, Gordon

Skinner, Burrhus Frederick (1904-1990): An eminent American psychologist best known for his theories regarding **behaviorism**. Born in Susquehanna, Pennsylvania, Skinner received his Ph.D. from Harvard University, where he taught from 1948 to 1974. Skinner devised a sound-proof, germ-free, air-conditioned "box" in the mid-1940s called the "Air-Crib," which was supposed to be the optimal environment for raising children.

Skinner described a utopia based on behavioristic principles in a well-known book entitled *Walden Two* (1948). Skinner also received the National Medal of Science in 1968. Skinner's works include: *The Behavior of Organisms* (1938); *Science and Human Behavior* (1953); *Verbal Behavior* (1957); and *Beyond Freedom and Dignity* (1971).

Snyder Knuth Achievement Test in Music: A test designed to assess the **musical achievement** levels of college/university students majoring in elementary education who are required to take music courses as part of their curricula. The Snyder Knuth Achievement Test in music measures the understanding of musical notation. The Snyder Knuth Achievement Test in Music can also be used to establish a basis for remedial work at the high school or college level, or it can be used to assess basic **achievement** at any level. There are two forms of the test (A and B) with an **alternate forms reliability** of .993. Each form has 136 items and 4 parts: listening and seeing, listening, musical comprehension, and tonal memory. **Percentile ranks** are provided for elementary education students. The musical examples come from folk songs. The Snyder Knuth Achievement Test in Music was written by Alice Snyder Knuth.

Social Inhibition: A phenomenon which often causes individuals to perform less well in the presence of other people than when they are alone. Social inhibition is most common when an individual believes that the tasks being performed are particularly difficult. In music, this phenomenon may partially explain why students frequently indicate that they play better during practice sessions than they do during their lessons. **Positive reinforcement** and techniques that help individuals overcome performance anxiety may be used to overcome social inhibition. *See* Performance Anxiety

Social Learning Theory, Bandura: In psychology, a theory proposed by Albert Bandura (b. 1925) suggesting that a significant amount of learning occurs through the **imitation** or **modeling** of and/or identification with others. Social learning theory emphasizes the relationship between social learning and cognition and the dynamic interactions between people and their environments. Bandura's major premise is that a great deal of learning actually takes place in social or group contexts in which individuals modify their behavior as a result of how others in the group respond to them. Social learning theory has been applied to a variety of contexts including the analysis and treatment of behavioral and social problems. In education, students are often influenced by the way their peers react to them. Such influences can be negative as well as positive. *See* **Bandura, Albert (b. 1925)**

Social Motives: In psychology, learned **motives** acquired from an individual's social experiences. Social motives include power, competency, **achievement**, and the need for affiliation.

Social Norms: A society's unwritten rules that govern its members' behaviors and attitudes. Social norms are dynamic, in that they evolve over time. Changes in social norms occur as a result of changing political, social, and religious views.

Social Play: Any type of play with others, typically peers, that promotes and facilitates social interaction. Research indicates that social play is important for the development of social skills among peers in both animals and humans. Social play fosters cooperation, sharing, and maintaining harmonious relationships in a manner that is considered by many to be more effective than learning these skills from parents and siblings alone.

Social Promotion: In education, promoting students to the next grade level to keep them with students of the same age, regardless of past performances or levels of **academic achievement**. Social promotion is typically an implicit policy that has gained approval in some school systems. Legislation and public policy in recent years have discouraged social promotion, although the degree to which the practice has actually been deterred is difficult to ascertain.

Social Psychology: In psychology, the study of an individual's behavior in the context of social situations. Social psychology focuses on how people affect and are affected by other people. Major topics in the field include **conformity**, **cohesiveness**, leadership, social perceptions, group structure, **status** and **role**, and **attitudes** and attitude changes.

Social Reconstructionism: A philosophy articulated in the early twentieth century by Theodore Brameld (1904–1987) and George Counts (1889–1974) based on the belief that systematic and often wholesale changes are needed in education to build a good and just society. Social reconstructionists believe that people are responsible for social conditions and that people can improve the quality of human life by changing the social order. In education, social reconstructionists believe that, through social activism, schools can be created to enable students to address the problems that plague society, typically resulting from ignorance, poverty, and lack of educational and employment opportunities.

Social Referencing: In psychology, a child's **capacity** to use trusted adults as references or **models** to derive situationally appropriate emotional cues. Children often act the way they see their parents acting in social situations, especially when the situation is uncomfortable or new.

Socialization: The process through which individuals in a society learn and internalize that society's rules and **norms**. Socialization helps shape individual characteristics and behavior by providing an environment that trains or pressures individuals into conforming to social expectations. *See* Acculturation; Enculturation

Society for General Music (SGM): A society devoted to promoting general music education. The official publication of SGM is *General Music Today* (*GMT*). The SGM is governed by the **Music Educators National Conference (MENC)**.

Society for Research in Music Education (SRME): Established in 1960 to promote research in music education, the SRME is governed by the **Music Educators Research Council (MERC)**. The *Journal of Research in Music Education* (*JRME*) is its official publication. Anyone who subscribes to the journal is a member of SRME.

Socioeconomic Status (SES): In general, social class or **strata**, typically based on such factors as income, occupation, education, values, and lifestyle. Most commonly, SES is divided into upper, middle, and lower classes, with several variations on this theme. SES is often used as a **variable** in educational research. Studies indicate that students with low SES often perform more poorly than students with high SES in academic classes and in **extracurricular activities**. Studies also indicate that SES influences an individual's physical and mental well-being. In music, research has shown that SES affects music preferences and an individual's level of interest in the arts.

Sociology: The behavioral or social science dealing with group life and social organization in literate societies. Sociology is devoted to the social context(s) in which something happens. Sociology in music is concerned with how music relates to and is influenced by **non-musical** activities common in an individual's **culture** or environment. *See* **Social Psychology**

Socratic Method: A **teaching method** in which students are led to discover and clarify knowledge by engaging in inquiry and dialogues with a teacher. Teachers employing the Socratic method typically ask a series of questions in response to the comments made by students regarding a particular topic or issue. These questions encourage students to analyze or critically examine ideas and issues. The Socratic method enables students to learn or discover errors in their thinking, which ultimately leads to the formulation of clearer ideas and a deeper understanding of a particular issue. The Socratic method is named after Socrates (c. 470–399 BC), a well-known Greek philosopher.

Soft Palate: Also called the velum, the muscular membrane continuous with and attached to the bone of the **hard palate** (or the soft, fleshy back part of the roof of the mouth). In vocal music, the soft palate serves an important function in **phonation**. When raised, it prevents the air from entering the nasal passages during the **articulation** of certain **consonants**. *See* **Hard Palate**

Solfege: An approach to **sight singing** in which each note is assigned a syllable. Researchers have shown that the use of solfege systems can improve musicians' sight singing abilities. Although several solfege systems have been developed, there are two primary approaches in use today: **fixed do** and **moveable do**. In the fixed-do system, the syllable "do" designates the note C and only the note C; other syllables are similarly assigned to other notes. In the moveable-do system, most commonly used in the United States, the syllable "do" is used to designate the tonic of the key or scale being used; again, other syllables are assigned to the other scale degrees accordingly. The syllables commonly used in both solfege systems, in ascending order, are "do," "re," "mi," "fa," "sol," "la," and "ti." Flats and sharps may be designated by saying "flat" or "sharp" after the syllable, or by altering the vowel in the syllable. For example, "re" becomes "ri" to designate it as sharp or "ra" to designate it as flat.

Solfege also refers to one part of a three-branch approach to music learning developed by Emile Jaques-Dalcroze (1865–1950) called the Dalcroze Method. The other two parts of this approach are eurhythmics and improvisation. *See* **Jaques-Dalcroze; Eurhythmics; Improvisation**

Solitary Play: A type of play classified by Mildred Parten (1929), in which children play by themselves. During solitary play, children appear to be unaware of other children playing nearby. *See* **Unoccupied Play; Onlooker Play; Parallel Play; Associative Play; Cooperative Play**

SOMPA: *See* System of Multicultural Pluralistic Assessment (SOMPA)

Sone: In acoustics, a measure of **loudness** based on **subjective** data. The sone scale is based on subjects' perceptions of how loud specific sounds were to them. There is a direct relationship between sones and phons; as the number of sones increases, the number of phons increases and vice versa. *See* **Phon**

Sound Intensity Level (SIL): A physical measure of a sound's intensity or strength. SIL is related to sound pressure level (SPL) and is measured in decibel (dB) increments. Both are virtually identical when the sound waves are traveling in the same direction. In reality, musical performances take place in venues in which the sound **waves** reflect, thus causing the waves to be traveling in many directions simultaneously. This reflection causes slight variations between the SPL and the SIL. *See* **Decibel (dB); Intensity; Sound Pressure Level (SPL)**

Sound Pressure Level (SPL): A physical measure of sound pressure, SPL is related to sound intensity level (SIL) and is measured in decibel increments. Both are virtually identical when the sound waves are traveling in the same direction. In reality, musical performances take place in venues in which the sound waves reflect, causing the waves to travel in many directions simultaneously. This reflection causes slight variations between the SPL and the SIL. *See* **Decibel (dB)**; **Sound Intensity Level (SIL)**

Spaced Practice/Learning: *See* Distributed Practice/Learning

Spatial Intelligence, Gardner: In Howard Gardner's (b. 1943) theory of multiple intelligences, the capacity to create, manipulate, and represent spatial configurations at a very high level. Architects, sculptors, artists, and chess players are said to possess **spatial intelligence**. *See* Multiple Intelligences, Gardner

Spearman, Charles E. (1863-1945): English psychometrician and psychologist well known for his work with **intelligence**. Spearman spent several years in the British army and did not receive his Ph.D. until the age of forty-one under the direction of **Wilhelm Wundt (1832–1920)**. He was also influenced by the work of Francis Galton (1822–1911). **Raymond Cattell (1860–1944)** and **David Wechsler (1891–1981)** were among those individuals who studied under Spearman. Spearman proposed that intelligence was not a simple unitary process. Instead, he felt intelligence could be separated into an underlying **general factor (g)** and a series of very specific factors (s). Among these specific factors were such things as verbal ability, math ability, and even **musical ability**.

Special Education Programs: In education, programs designed to ensure that students with **disabilities** and students who are **gifted and talented** receive effective educational services. **Individualization** and intensive instruction are the two main components of special education. Individualization refers to the process of meeting the needs of every student by planning and adjusting **curriculum** and instruction according to strengths and weaknesses. Intensive instruction involves: 1) actively engaging students in their own learning processes, 2) matching instruction to ability level, 3) providing instructional cues and prompts to facilitate learning when appropriate, and 4) providing detailed feedback on completed tasks.

Special Interest Group: In general, any group that shares particular interests and goals and tries to exert political pressure to advance their causes. Most professional organizations function politically as special interest groups to some degree. *See* Special Research Interest Group (SRIG)

Special Research Interest Groups (SRIGs): In music education, groups that help promote and support research in specified areas. Music education SRIGs are governed by the **Music Education Research Council (MERC)**. Originally, SRIGs were formed in 1978 in areas such as early childhood, instructional strategies, and measurement and evaluation. Today, several SRIGs are active in several areas of music education, including Early Childhood, **Perception** and **Cognition**, **Creativity**, and Gender Research in Music Education (GRIME).

Special-needs Student: A student who has some physical or mental condition that cannot be accommodated appropriately in a normal classroom setting using standard curricula. Special-needs students include those who are physically disabled, mentally disabled, learning disabled, emotionally disturbed, or exceptionally gifted. Accommodations for such students vary widely and can include minor alterations in the standard curriculum, employing the help of a **paraeducator**, and the development of an Individualized Education Plan (IEP). Although legislation and public policy today favor **inclusion** in regular classrooms whenever possible, **segregation** from the traditional school setting to a special school setting where specialized training is available is usually necessary in the most severe cases. *See* Individualized Education Plan (IEP); Learning Disability

Specific Learning Disability: Any **disorder** involving basic psychological processes that adversely affect a student's ability to listen, speak, think, read, write, spell, or perform mathematical calculations. The National Advisory Committee on Handicapped Children defined specific learning disabilities in 1968, and the term was incorporated into the **Individuals with Disabilities Education Act of 1990 (IDEA)**. Specific learning disabilities range from mild to severe, and can include perceptual handicaps, **minimal brain dysfunction**, **dyslexia**, and brain injury. The term specific learning disabilities is used narrowly and does not include: visual, hearing, or motor **impairments**, emotional disturbance, **mental retardation**, or **socioeconomic (SES)**, environmental, or cultural disadvantage.

Spiderweb Model, Eisner: A curriculum model proposed by Elliot Eisner in *The Educational Imagination: On the Design and Evaluation of School Programs* (1985). The spiderweb model is based on the idea that learning will be better facilitated if students are invited to engage in activities rather than being "forced" to engage in activities.

Spiral Curriculum: In education, a principle utilized in some **curricular** designs based on **Jerome Bruner's (b. 1915)** idea that any subject can be taught to a child of any age in an intellectually honest form as long as the **concepts** and materials are presented in an age-appropriate manner. In a spiral curriculum, material is presented to learners several times over the course of the entire educational experience in a variety of settings and complexity levels depending upon the age and experience of the learners. Many educators associate the spiral curriculum concept with **cyclical sequencing.** The idea is that material can be introduced at one curricular point and reintroduced several times throughout the education process. Each time the material is revisited, more information and depth is included to match the intellectual development of the students.

Spiral Model of Musical Development: A model of musical development developed by Keith Swanwick and Jane Tillman in 1986. The model has four levels or loops that ascend, creating the spiral. The loops are age-related, creating stages of development similar to those of **Jean Piaget (1896–1980).** Each loop represents dynamic growth in musical development. The four levels are: 1) Mastery (birth to four), characterized by growth from simply responding to sensory data to manipulative behaviors; 2) Imitation (ages four to nine), characterized by growth from personal behaviors or doing what one wants, to vernacular awareness or becoming more aware of musical conventions; 3) Imaginative Play (ages ten to fifteen), characterized by growth from working with musical conventions and experimentation with these conventions (speculative composition) to the development of an individual musical style (idiomatic composition); and 4) Metacognition (age fifteen and over), characterized by growth from symbolic expression to systematic expression. Each loop of the spiral covers the same content areas and the same general concepts; however, the information is more complex as individuals advance to a higher level in the model. The content areas and the general concepts are age-appropriate at each level. *See* **Spiral Curriculum**

Spiraling: *See* Spiral Curriculum

Split Brain Theory: The theory that the human brain is divided into two hemispheres, left and right, and that each hemisphere controls specific, independent functions. Research has determined that the left hemisphere of the brain is predominantly responsible for verbal, sequential, and logical activities while the right hemisphere of the brain is predominantly responsible for nonverbal, holistic, creative activities. Research has also determined that the two hemispheres communicate with each other via the corpus callosum at the rate of four billion impulses per second, and through this process, the left and right hemispheres function as a whole rather than as two separate and independent processors. Nonetheless, educators and others often refer to math, science, and computer technology as "left-brain" subjects, and art, music, and philosophy as "right-brain" activities.

Split-half Reliability: In statistics, a technique used to determine the **reliability** of a test or measure in which students or subjects complete the test only once. The correct number of responses for the odd-numbered items (one-half of the test) is compared with the correct number of responses for the even-numbered items (the other half of the test) to determine reliability. Split-half reliability can also involve comparing the first half of the test with the second half of the test, depending on the format. In both instances, the resulting statistic is called a split-half correlation. *See* Alternate-forms Reliability; Reliability; Test-retest Reliability; Internal Consistency

Spontaneous Recovery: In psychology, the phenomenon in which a conditioned response that has been extinguished tends to recur on its own after a period of time. The **conditioned response** returns after extinction with no additional conditioning trials. Spontaneous recovery responses extinguish more quickly than the original conditioned responses and may occur several times before extinction is absolutely complete. *See* Extinguish; Extinction

Sputnik I: The first artificial satellite launched into space. *Sputnik I* was launched on October 4, 1957, by the Soviet Union. *Sputnik I* prompted one of the most significant events in the history of American education. Prior to the launching of *Sputnik I*, the United States and the Soviet Union were both working to achieve technological superiority. When the Soviet Union won the "race into space," the American people were shocked. The general feeling across the nation was that the United States was no longer technologically superior to the Soviet Union. The general public demanded answers, and the backlash was dramatic. One result of *Sputnik I* was the reevaluation of the educational system. The general sentiment was that the citizens of the United States were not being adequately prepared to compete in a world where advances in technology and science were believed to be a benchmark of power and prestige. The launching of *Sputnik I* was an important catalyst toward a new era in American education. Between 1957 and into the early 1970s, more attention was given to education than at any other time in history.

Square Wave: In acoustics, a type of **wave** produced by a **complex tone** in which the second **partial** is three times the frequency of the **fundamental** and has one-third the amplitude of the fundamental, the third partial is five times the frequency and has one-fifth the amplitude of the fundamental, the fifth partial is seven times the frequency and has one-seventh the amplitude of the fundamental, and so on.

S-R Psychology: *See* Stimulus-Response (S-R) Psychology

SRA Thurstone Primary Mental Abilities Tests: Published in 1962, tests developed by Louis L. Thurstone (1887–1955) designed to provide both multifactored and general measures of **intelligence**. The tests are based on the idea that intelligence can be divided into multiple factors of primary mental abilities, with each factor having equal weight. These factors include: 1) verbal, perceptual speed, 2) **inductive reasoning**, 3) number, **rote memory**, 4) **deductive reasoning**, 5) word fluency, and 6) space. The SRA Thurstone Primary Mental Abilities Tests are designed for **kindergarten** through college-level students and are published by Science Research Associates. *See* **Thurstone, Louis L. (1887-1955)**

SRIG: *See* Special Research Interest Group (SRIG)

SRME: *See* Society for Research in Music Education (SRME)

Stage Fright: *See* Performance Anxiety

Stage Theory: In psychology, a general term for the belief that growth and development occur in predictable, determinable, and often invariant stages or periods that typically follow a progressive sequence. These stages typically represent qualitative changes in either the structure or the function of an individual, and certain developments must occur before others can occur. That is, stages cannot be skipped. Although growth and development do not occur at exactly the same age in all people, stages do occur within a relatively narrow age range. Stage theories are also progressive. Each stage represents more complex actions and thought processes than the previous stage. Classic stage theories have been devised in several areas, including cognitive development (**Piaget**), moral development (**Kohlberg**), and psychosexual development (**Freud**). *See* Piaget's Stages of Cognitive Growth; Moral Development, Kohlberg; Psychoanalytic Theory, Freud

Staircase Model, Eisner: A curriculum model proposed by Elliot Eisner in *The Educational Imagination: On the Design and Evaluation of School Programs* (1985) along with the **spiderweb model**. The staircase model is based on the idea of organizing learning opportunities in a logical, sequential manner such that an individual can take a sequence of independent steps until a platform is reached. From there, the individual moves on to something else. Education is structured to include many instances of the staircase model. For example, students work to complete first grade before moving on to the second grade, and they progress from elementary school to junior high school or junior high to high school.

Standard Deviation (s or sd): In statistics, a common measure of **variability** defined as the square root of the sum of the squared deviations from the **mean** divided by n or N (number). In other words, standard deviation is the square root of the **variance** and the average deviation of scores in a **sample** from the mean. The standard deviation is generally considered to be the most useful and stable measure of variability.

Standard Error of Estimate: In statistics, the standard error of the differences between predicted values and true values of some measure. Standard error of estimate is useful in interpreting a coefficient of correlation. *See* Correlation Coefficient

Standard Error of Mean: In statistics, the **standard deviation** of the sampling distribution of a **mean** and of certain other derived statistics.

Standard Error of Measurement (SEM): In statistics, the range within which a subject's true test score is likely to fall, or the extent to which an individual's **true score** differs from that individual's obtained score. SEM is related to **reliability**; that is, as test reliability increases, SEM decreases.

Standard Score: In statistics, scores based on the properties of the **normal probability curve**, where the absolute differences between scores are maintained. Standard scores are used to calculate averages and **correlations** yielding the same results as the original raw scores. They are typically used for comparison purposes in testing. Examples: **z-Score**, T-score.

Standard-based Education: An approach to education in which all aspects of the teaching and learning process, including instructional methods, teaching techniques, instructional materials, financial resources, and methods of assessment are driven by or based on achieving a set of predetermined standards. In recent years, more emphasis has been placed on standard-based education in the schools. The creation and/or implementation of "world-class" standards, **national standards** for each subject area, **minimum competency standards**, **high stakes tests**, real-world standards, **discipline-based** standards, and other standards has increased dramatically over the past decade alone. **Accountability** is the primary force driving the move toward standard-based education. Lawmakers, policymakers, school administrators, educators, parents, and the general public are concerned with the quality of education and have demanded that changes be made to help students meet the needs of a changing society. While most agree that having high standards is necessary in education, several important and divisive issues surround standard-based education. These issues include: 1) the content of standards, 2) the roles of teachers and students in the teaching and learning process, 3) the ways in which standards should be used, 4) the ways in which standards should be assessed, 5) ideas regarding uniform standards nationwide, 6) fairness of the standards to minorities, and 7) problems associated with teaching the standards. *See* **Accountability; National Standards, Music Education**

Standardized Tests of Music Intelligence, Wing: A test battery designed to measure **musical intelligence** developed by H. D. Wing in 1939 and reprinted in 1961. The test battery consists of seven subtests, the scores of which can be combined into an overall composite score. The composite score is consistent with Wing's belief in a general factor of musical ability, which was in direct contrast to **Carl Seashore's (1866–1949)** belief in specific, discreet measures of musical ability (Theory of Specifics). The debate over these contrasting viewpoints has been ongoing for decades and is still discussed today. *See* Seashore Test of Musical Talents; Omnibus Theory, Mursell; Theory of Specifics, Seashore

Standardization: In research, using identical procedures, materials, scoring, and interpretation methods with all subjects in the testing process to ensure objectivity.

Standardized Tests: Tests that are or can be used to assess student **achievement** and to compare student performance on a large scale. The use of standardized tests has grown since the 1970s in response to the increased popularity of the **accountability** movement in education. The best-known standardized tests include the **Scholastic Achievement Test (SAT)** and the **American College Test (ACT)** for college admissions. Issues surrounding their use focus on the following questions: 1) Do these tests measure what they are intended to measure? 2) Are these tests fair to all students? 3) Do these tests lead to an overemphasis on teaching material covered on the test? and 4) Are the results of these tests used too generally or liberally to serve political and educational agendas?

Standards: In general, having high expectations for someone or something. In education, standards are educational goals or benchmarks against which progress in an area or areas can be judged. There are many types of educational standards, some of which are broad-based and some of which are more specific. These include: 1) national standards, which are suggested standards for every student across the nation in particular subject areas; 2) state standards, which are suggested standards for every student within a given state; 3) district standards, which are suggested standards for every student within a given district; 4) "world-class" standards, which is a name often associated with standards conceived to help students compete in a global economy; 5) real-world standards, which are standards focused on knowledge and skills that will enable students to function effectively in society; 6) **discipline-based** standards, which are suggested standards for a particular subject area; 7) content standards, which are standards regarding what knowledge students should gain in a given area; 8) performance standards, which are standards regarding what students should be able to do or what skills students should gain in a given area; 9) **opportunity-to-learn standards (OTL)**, which are standards that help ensure that students will be given proper instructional resources that will enable them to learn; and 10) **minimum competency standards**, which are standards that help assure minimal levels of learning. *See* **Standard-based Education**

Standing Wave: In acoustics, when the maximum displacement of a sound **wave** in one direction aligns with the maximum displacement in the other direction. Standing waves are so named because when this alignment occurs, the wave is not moving in either direction, in contrast to traveling waves. All musical instruments produce standing waves because the vibrating string or air column naturally vibrates first in one direction and then in the opposite direction. At some point, these waves, traveling in opposite directions will align, producing standing waves. Standing waves can occur in both transverse and longitudinal waves. *See* **Node; Traveling Wave Theory**

Stanford-Binet Test: Intelligence test developed by **Lewis M. Terman (1877–1956)** in 1916 at Stanford University. The Stanford-Binet test was an American revision of the original test written by **Alfred Binet (1857–1911)**, first published in France in 1905. The primary emphasis of the test remains on verbal skills, although the test has been updated and revised several times.

Stanine Score: In testing, scores based on percentages and related to a **normal curve**. Stanine scores represent areas on a scale that are spaced out evenly along a normal curve. Specifically, there are nine intervals or stanines on the scale, with each stanine representing one-half of a **standard deviation**. The fifth stanine is the middle interval of the scale and represents the middle 20 percent of all scores. On the left side (the lower end of the distribution) of the fifth stanine are located the fourth, third, second, and first stanines representing 17, 12, 7, and 4 percent of all cases respectively. On the right side (upper end of the distribution) of the fifth stanine are located the sixth, seventh, eighth, and ninth stanines also representing 17, 12, 7, and 4 percent of all cases, respectively.

Stapes: The innermost of three small bones that transmit vibrations through the **middle ear** cavity to the **inner ear**. The stapes is also called the stirrup because of its shape. The other two small bones in the ossicular chain are the **malleus** (hammer) and the **incus** (anvil). *See* **Ossicles/Ossicular Chain**

State Boards of Education: State controlled agencies that regulate and control standards for educational practice statewide. State boards also advise governors and legislators in educational matters. All states except Wisconsin have state boards of education, and some states have two boards, including one for elementary and secondary education and another for higher education. State boards perform functions such as establishing minimum standards for student performance, establishing and regulating standards or requirements to assure teacher competence, and making decisions regarding textbook adoption.

State Education Department (SED): A governmental department that acts as an education advisor to the executive and legislative branches of state government and carries out the business-related duties of a state's educational system. These duties include regulating or overseeing the **curricula** of elementary and secondary schools, overseeing college and university teacher education programs, reporting financial matters to the legislative branches of state government, monitoring whether schools comply with state regulations, and administering special programs such as schools for the blind.

State Standards Boards: Government-related boards or commissions that regulate professional practices regarding certification, entry, and exit standards for teachers. Some state boards have final authority over these practices while others serve only in an advisory capacity to state policymakers.

State-dependent Memory: In memory, the tendency for individuals to remember information better when they are in the same physiological or emotional state they were in when they originally learned the information.

Statistical Conclusion Validity: *See* Validity

Statistical Inference: *See* Inferential Statistics

Statistical Power: In experimental research, the likelihood of rejecting **null hypotheses**. The rejection of any null hypothesis is generally determined by statistical testing, and researchers often refer to the power of these tests when determining **statistical significance**. Tests that increase the researcher's ability to make accurate decisions regarding the rejection of hypotheses are more powerful than those that do not. In other words, if a null hypothesis states that there will be no difference and a difference actually exists, then researchers would like the chance of rejecting the null hypothesis to be as great as possible. The greater the chance, the more powerful the test. Certain factors affect power. In general, reducing the level of significance increases the power of the test. In addition, for a fixed level of significance, there is a direct relationship between power and sample size. Specifically, power increases as the sample size increases. Consequently, the greater the number of subjects researchers include in their studies, the less likely researchers are to make poor judgments regarding the null hypotheses. *See* **Significance Level**

Statistical Regression: In statistics, the tendency of extreme scores on a measure to become less extreme (regress toward the **mean**) when the **measurement** is made a second time.

Statistical Relativity: In statistics, a method of labeling that defines deviance based on the frequency of a behavior or characteristic. An average frequency is calculated, and a person's status is compared with that average.

Statistical Significance: *See* **Significance Level**

Status: In **social psychology**, an individual's niche in society's prestige hierarchy, or an individual's standing in society. Status carries with it perceived expectations of **behavior**. The behavior expected of individuals because of their status is often referred to as their "role" in society. *See* **Role; Socio-economic Status (SES)**

Steady-state: In acoustics, a tone that contains no transient partials and is perfectly stable across time. Steady-state tones are often used in acoustical research because they can be controlled; however, musical instruments do not produce steady-state tones.

Stereotype: Biased or prejudiced generalizations, beliefs, or **attitudes** usually based on **ethnicity**, cultural heritage, gender, or religion where individuals are assigned **traits**, usually negative, that they may not possess. Stereotypes are generally preconceived ideas that have developed as a result of and are influenced by several factors including background, experiences, social **status**, and level of education. For example, believing that women should cook and clean house for men, that one **ethnic group** is more intelligent than another, or that overweight people are lazy are typical stereotypes. These and other stereotypes can be particularly harmful. On the other hand, some stereotypes are useful and necessary. For example, parents are stereotyping when they teach their children to avoid people who "look suspicious" or people who are dressed like "gang" members. Parents are also stereotyping when they teach their children that police officers and doctors are good, helpful, and smart. In these instances, stereotypes may be used positively.

Sternhold & Hopkins Psalter: *See* Bay Psalm Book

Stevens' Rule: In acoustics, a rule indicating that the perceived pitch will decrease as the **intensity** of a tone is increased. Stevens' rule is based on a study by S. S. Stevens (1935) in which he investigated the effects of **loudness** on **pitch**. Other research supports Stevens' rule, as long as the predominant **harmonics** of the manipulated tone are below approximately 1,000 Hz. When the predominant harmonics are above 1,000 Hz, questions arise regarding its applicability. *See* Equal-loudness Curves

Stimulus/Stimuli (S): In psychology, anything that elicits a **response**. Stimuli are typically objects or events to which an organism or individual responds, but these also include thoughts and desires. Stimuli and responses can be conscious or unconscious. *See* Response; Behavioral Psychology/Behaviorism

Stimulus Control: In psychology, controlling a **stimulus** that is producing an undesirable response. Typically, stimulus control involves controlling the environment in which the stimulus occurs. For example, if an individual listens to slow classical music every night before going to sleep because it is relaxing, then he or she probably should not listen to slow classical music at work because it is likely to induce sleepiness.

Stimulus Discrimination: In operant conditioning, the tendency for an organism to respond differently to two or more similar stimuli that differ in some dimension. That is, stimulus discrimination occurs when an organism learns to respond to a particular stimulus or operant but not to other similar stimuli. In **classical conditioning**, stimulus discrimination occurs when an organism does not respond to a stimulus that is similar to the **conditioned stimulus**.

Stimulus Generalization: In behavioral psychology, a **response** elicited by a new, previously **neutral stimulus** that is similar to or shares common characteristics with the original **stimulus** used in the **conditioning** process. For example, in **classical conditioning, Ivan Pavlov (1849–1936)** discovered that a dog conditioned to respond to a specific tone would also respond to other tones at lower and higher frequencies. Stimulus generalization may be controlled by extinguishing undesired responses. *See* Extinguish; Extinction

Stimulus Variety: In psychology, the impinging of a wide variety of stimuli or sensory input on the sense organs. Many early theorists believed that stimulus variety was crucial for intellectual development. The general idea was that the more children hear, see, and touch, the more they will want to hear, see, and touch, resulting in increased intellectual growth. Although research indicates that babies and young children who are provided with a variety of sensory input develop more successfully than children who are not, it also indicates that there is an optimal level of sensory variety. That is, too much stimulus variety in a short period of time may overwhelm a child, whereas too little may cause a child to become bored.

Stimulus-Response (S-R) Psychology: In psychology, an approach that emphasizes the relationships between stimuli and responses without considering the influences of mental processes. S-R psychology is typically associated with behaviorism. *See* Behavioral Psychology/Behaviorism; Stimulus-Response Theory

Stimulus-Response (S-R) Theory: In psychology, a theory that stresses the importance of the accumulation of stimulus-response (S-R) associations in defining **learning**. Most behaviorists adhere to stimulus-response learning theories and stress the importance of nurture in the nature/nurture debate. E. L. Thorndike (1874–1949), Ivan Pavlov (1849–1936), John B.

Watson (1878–1958), **Edwin R. Guthrie** (1886–1959), Clark Hull (1884–1952), and **B. F. Skinner** (1904–1990) are well known stimulus-response (S-R) theorists. *See* Behavioral Psychology/Behaviorism

Storage: In the information-processing model of memory, a term used for an organism's internal memory and/or the tendency of information to remain in memory over time. Most theorists believe that **short-term memory (STM)** and **long-term memory (LTM)** are the two main **storage** components of memory. *See* Two-stage Memory Theory; Information Processing Model

Stratification: In **social psychology**, the process of identifying individuals or groups according to **criteria**. Normally, stratification is used when referring to **socioeconomic status (SES)**, a classification system in which people are grouped according to their social **status** or "class." Social **strata** or stratification develops as a result of the value society places on certain criteria, particularly regarding income or occupation. In general, individuals at the top of the social strata tend to be those most valued by society. Stratification usually refers to upper, middle, and lower class, with variations on this general theme.

Stratum/Strata: A subdivision of a population based on specified characteristics of its members. Strata may be based on such factors as age, **race**, gender, **socio-economic status (SES)** or education. *See* Stratified Random Sampling

Stratified Random Sampling: A sampling procedure in which the **population** is divided into **strata** followed by random sampling from each stratum. Stratified random sampling is often used when researchers want the sample to be as representative of the **population** being studied as possible. *See* Sampling; Random Sampling

Structuralist Psychology/Structuralism: The belief that **psychology** should focus on the fundamental or elemental processes of conscious experience. That is, immediate, conscious experience is the proper focus for psychological study. Structuralism was based on discovering the elements of conscious experience, how they were combined, and the causes of such combinations. The three main components of structuralism are: 1) sensations, which include sights, sounds, smells, tastes, and feelings; 2) images, which are typically memories; and 3) affections, which include emotional reactions, such as joy, fear, and love. Structuralists believed that these elements were combined by association into normal conscious experience. Well-known structuralists include **Wilhelm Wundt (1832–1920)** and Edward Bradford Titchener (1867–1927). *See* Introspection

Structure: In education, the organization of information based on relationships or principles that help characterize or define it. Structure helps give meaning to the information being learned. The term structure is also used to describe the basic and fundamental ideas of a subject. That is, structure helps determine course content, curricular design, and course objectives. In psychology, structure is part of **Jerome Bruner's (b. 1915)** theory of instruction. Bruner believed that if a subject is properly structured, information can be presented in a form simple enough that learners can understand it in a recognizable form at any age. *See* Theory of Instruction, Bruner

Structure of Intellect Model: *See* Guilford, Jay P. (1897-1988)

Student Teaching: Usually the culminating experience in teacher education programs, where prospective teachers gain teaching experience by being placed in schools under the guidance of a cooperating teacher and a university/college supervisor. Typically, student teachers begin their experiences by observing the cooperating teacher for a brief period and then teaching on a limited basis. Gradually, student teachers are given more teaching responsibilities and may eventually be given full responsibility for particular classes. Each university or college has specific requirements for student teachers, cooperating teachers, and university/college supervisors.

Student Teams-Achievement Divisions (STAD): A system created by Robert Slavin to promote **mainstreaming**, in which special education and other children are integrated into achievement groups or teams of diverse students. A **reward** system is established to encourage both group and individual achievement. The general idea is for students to work together and to help each other in the learning process, thus reducing destructive competition and equalizing the distribution of positive reinforcers. In traditional classrooms, students who achieve at high levels sometimes receive the majority of the positive reinforcers, while those who achieve at lower levels receive fewer positive reinforcers. Using the student teams approach, all students are recognized for their improvements.

Student Teams-Achievement Divisions (STAD) helps promote the social acceptance of mainstreamed students.

Student-centered Instruction: In education, a type of instruction geared toward helping students discover answers or learn material on their own by organizing information in understandable ways. Student-centered instruction usually involves free and open discussions, in which students are encouraged to provide input and actively participate in the learning process rather than passively listening to teachers present information. In this regard, student-centered classes are more active than passive in nature. *See* **Teacher-centered Instruction**

Subjective Scoring: Test scoring requiring subjective, often complex judgments by the scorer, where "rightness" or "goodness" is often relative to experiences and personal beliefs or biases. Subjective scoring is opposed to objective scoring, where answers are clearly right or wrong. Two examples include grading essay examinations and judging a musician at solo and ensemble festival. *See* **Objective Scoring**

Subjective Tones/Combination Tones: An acoustical phenomenon in which tones that are not actually present in the original sound sources are perceived by the listener. That is, the **fundamental frequencies** of subjective tones are different than the fundamental frequencies of the original sound sources. For example, two tones with different fundamental frequencies sounded simultaneously often produce a third tone, called a subjective tone. The fundamental frequency of this subjective tone is the difference between the fundamental frequencies of the two original tones. Subjective tones are sometimes called difference tones or resultant tones. Although subjective tones are often clearly audible to listeners, they cannot be physically measured. The strength or presence of subjective tones is dependent upon such factors as **frequency, loudness, timbre,** and **duration**. For example, a 400 Hz tone and a 300 Hz tone sounded together would produce a difference tone of 100 Hz. *See* **Summation Tones; Difference Tones**

Subjects: Individuals used in research studies.

Sublimation: In general, a **defense mechanism** that enables individuals to express socially unacceptable impulses in socially acceptable ways. For example, individuals who have disturbing aggressive tendencies might channel their energies into sports, work, or hobbies. In **Sigmund Freud's (1856–1939)** psychoanalytic theory, **sublimation** is viewed as a type of **displacement** that serves a higher cultural or social purpose, such as creating great works of art. For example, Freud suggested that Leonardo da Vinci's paintings of the Madonna were an expression of his desire for intimacy with his mother. *See* Psychoanalytic Theory, Freud; Defense Mechanisms

Substitution: A defense mechanism that enables an individual to maintain **self-esteem** by substituting approved goals and activities that can be carried out successfully for those that cannot. An example of substitution is choosing to perform a solo at a music festival that presents a modest challenge as opposed to choosing a piece beyond an individual's abilities. *See* Defense Mechanism

Successive Approximations: In **behavioral psychology**, a **reinforcement** concept used in shaping behavior, in which the **criterion** for reinforcement is initially set at a level that allows behaviors that are close to or are at least in the right direction of the desired **behavior** or **goal**. As the **responses** become learned, the criterion is again shifted a little closer to the desired goal. This process assures steady progress toward the desired goal and is repeated until the goal is reached. That is, behaviors that demonstrate progress toward a defined goal are **rewarded** to encourage more progress. The process of successive approximations is also referred to as **shifting criterion for reinforcement**. *See* Shaping

Summation Tone: *See* Combination Tone; Subjective Tone

Summative Assessment: In education, **assessment** of a teacher's strengths, weaknesses, and overall level of competence, usually at the end of a specified time period. Summative assessments are typically used to make decisions regarding a teacher's retention, contract termination, promotion, and/or **tenure**. *See* Formative Assessment

Summerhill School: A non-traditional boarding school founded by A. S. Neill that emphasized the free expression of ideas while allowing students to participate in virtually all aspects of **curricular** design. The school places minimal restraints on its students and does not require exams, texts, or even class attendance. Instead, students are allowed to study what they want, how they want, and are free to pursue their interests or talents in a very flexible environment. The general idea is that this kind of freedom enables students to develop healthy attitudes toward learning and emotional well-being. The Summerhill School has served as a **model** for other such schools throughout the world and is a viable alternative to traditional education.

Superego: In **Sigmund Freud's (1856–1939)** three-part theory of **personality**, the part that corresponds most closely to the conscience and to moral standards. Freud believed an individual's superego contains the internalized values of his or her parents and that it always strives for perfection. He also believed that the superego is an uncompromising and punishing conscience that controls through moral scruples rather than through social expediency. *See* **Id; Ego**

Suppression: In psychology, a process or act of self-control in which impulses, desires, tendencies to act, or wishes to perform disapproved acts are kept hidden by an individual. Suppression is a deliberate or conscious effort to hide these desires, and other people are often completely unaware of these suppressed feelings. Suppression and **repression** are often used interchangeably; however, suppression is conscious, and repression is unconscious. For example, a student who consciously keeps homosexual tendencies hidden from others is engaging in suppression.

Survey/Survey Method: In research, one of the oldest and most common **descriptive** techniques for gathering information about a wide range of topics including attitudes, behaviors, and **demographics**. Typically, surveys are pre-designed **questionnaires** sent to a large number of individuals; however, surveys can also be conducted using telephones or computers.

Surveys serve several purposes, including: 1) collecting facts and information about something, 2) identifying positive and/or negative characteristics or attributes about something, 3) facilitating comparisons or evaluations or establishing relationships among several variables, 4) finding out what something is all about so the information can be used in decision-making or planning processes, and 5) helping to determine developments, trends, or changes in something over a period of time. Two basic types of surveys are commonly used: **cross-sectional surveys**, in which information is solicited from individuals once, and **longitudinal** surveys, in which information is solicited several times over a period of time.

When researchers use the survey method, they hope that the individuals who respond will be representative of the population being studied and that they will provide information that will help researchers answer the research questions. When used properly, the survey method is an effective research tool; however, certain types of errors commonly occur. When researchers include too much subjectivity in the evaluation process, validity can be negatively affected. That is, researchers sometimes describe what should or will be rather than what actually is, according to the information collected. Poor sampling techniques can also negatively impact results obtained using the survey method. For example, failure to obtain a representative sample weakens the ability to make accurate statements regarding the population.

Sustained Consonants: In singing, consonants that have a longer degree of sustaining power. Sustained consonants include *l*, *m*, and *n*.

Suzuki Method: A music teaching method devised by **Shinichi Suzuki (1898–1998)**. After watching how easily and naturally children learn their native language, Suzuki concluded that young children had the potential to learn far more than they were learning through traditional methods. Suzuki took many of the techniques commonly used for teaching language to young children and implemented these techniques into his method for teaching music skills. These include observation, imitation, repetition, and gradually developing intellectual awareness of what is being or has been learned. Suzuki's method is based on a sound-before-sight approach to music teaching and learning. That is, students learn to play by ear by imitating a model before they are introduced to musical notation. The Suzuki method is sometimes called the mother-tongue method.

Suzuki Society of America, The: A society devoted to promoting the Suzuki method of musical instruction. *See* Suzuki Method

Syllable System: *See* Counting/Rhythm Syllables System; Sight Singing Systems

Symbolic Association Level of Discrimination Learning, Gordon: *See* Skill Learning Sequence, Gordon

Symbolic Function: According to **Jean Piaget (1896–1980)**, a child's ability to use mental representations in a meaningful way. Symbolic function can be manifested in several ways. First, in language symbolic function involves using words to stand for specific things that are being thought about but are not actually present. Second, **symbolic play** is a type of symbolic function in which children pretend that objects are something other than what they are. Third, **deferred imitation** is a type of symbolic function in which children imitate an action they have seen after some time has passed, even though they can no longer see it. Symbolic function is characteristic of Piaget's **preoperational stage** (ages two to seven) of **cognitive** development.

Symbolic Play: When children pretend that objects are something other than what they are during play. Symbolic play is a type of symbolic function and is characteristic of **Jean Piaget's (1896–1980) preoperational stage** (ages two to seven). Example: A child pretends that a stick is a sword or a guitar. *See* **Symbolic Function**

Symbolic Representation: The third stage of **Jerome Bruner's (b. 1915)** theory of **cognitive** development. According to Bruner, symbolic representation is the stage in which a child is able to translate experience into language; it is a mode of presentation or a method of communication. During this stage, words are used for communication and for representing ideas. Understanding is achieved when an object can be explained through the use of words rather than through actions, which is characteristic of enactive representation, or through pictures, which is characteristic of iconic representation. Symbolic representation enables individuals to make logical connections between ideas and to think more compactly. *See* **Enactive Representation; Iconic Representation; Theory of Instruction, Bruner**

Symbolic Thought: In psychology, a child's tendency to use mental representations, words, and images to represent objects and actions. Children acquire the ability to think symbolically at about age two, during **Jean Piaget's (1896–1980)** preoperational stage (age two to seven). Symbolic thought enables children to remember past experiences, to understand present experiences, and to imagine what the future might be like. *See* **Symbolic Function**

Sympathetic Division: A division of the **autonomic nervous system** characterized by a chain of ganglia on either side of the spinal cord, with nerve fibers originating in the thoracic and lumbar portions of the spinal cord. In music, the sympathetic division is actively involved during periods of **stage fright** or **performance anxiety**. The sympathetic division is active during times of emotional excitement. It increases heart rate, constricts the arteries and digestive organs, heightens emotional response, and causes perspiration.

Syndrome: In general, a group of signs and symptoms that characterizes a particular disease. *See* **Carpal Tunnel Syndrome**

Synectics: A teaching model that seeks to increase students' **problem solving** abilities, **creative thinking**, empathetic sensitivity, and insight into a variety of topics, social situations, or relations. Synectics was developed by William J. J. Gordon, a businessman from Cambridge, Massachusetts. The basic idea behind synectics is for students to make the familiar seem strange by having them stretch their imaginations and think in nontraditional ways. Students work as a team to discover new metaphors and analogies to gain new perspectives on a variety of topics.

Synectics involves several steps. First, students begin with a statement of a problem or topic. For example, a teacher may pose a problem to students about the effects of poor tone quality on the ensemble. Second, students engage in brainstorming or "stretching exercises" that enable students to explore the topic in new ways. This process often involves asking questions about a particular topic and letting students find (or attempt to find) the answers. For example, a teacher might ask the students what effects tone quality has on balance, blend, and pitch. Third, teachers work with students to help them create direct, personal, and symbolic analogies related to the topic that students can relate to empathetically. For example, a teacher may ask the students a question such as "What animal does that poor tone quality remind you of, and why does it remind you of that animal?" Fourth, students share their analogies, insights, and ideas about the topic and develop them by juxtaposing them in unusual ways. For example, if one student associates the tone quality with an elephant and another student believes the tone quality sounds "sick," students may discuss the concept of a "sick elephant." The general idea behind synectics is that it enables students to think about solving problems in new and creative ways.

Synopsis: A philosophical technique in which individuals attempt to build a philosophy by constructing a comprehensive **paradigm** of their views or beliefs. Synopsis also involves building on the work of other philosophers and using the viewpoints of others to support their own beliefs. The purpose of synopsis is verification rather than refutation, as opposed to analysis. Basically, synopsis is a type of philosophy that seeks to prove or show the correctness of a particular belief or set of beliefs. *See* Analysis

Syntax: *See* Musical Syntax

System of Multicultural Pluralistic Assessment (SOMPA): A system developed by Mercer and Lewis in 1978 for adjusting **intelligence quotient (IQ)** tests to compensate for cultural bias. The system takes into account additional behavioral information on each child and adjusts scores accordingly. The following four areas are considered for IQ score adjustment: the family, the neighborhood, the school, and the community. The questions are designed to assess behaviors in each of these areas, and they focus on self-direction, internal control, and complexity. IQ scores may be adjusted upward based on the answers to these questions. Credit is given to **minority** children for performing such tasks as taking care of younger siblings and running errands.

Considerable controversy surrounds SOMPA. Proponents of IQ tests point to problems with **reliability** and **validity**. For example, they point out that the subjective nature of the questions creates problems with reliability and the predictive power of the SOMPA adjustments. In addition, because it is questionable whether the skills assessed in SOMPA relate to school performance, problems with the validity of the system are created. Opponents of traditional **standardized tests** have criticized SOMPA as well. They believe that SOMPA is a small adjustment to a fundamentally flawed system of **intelligence measurement** and would rather see IQ testing eliminated altogether. In short, SOMPA has raised more questions than it has answered, and it has not solved the problems related to the cultural bias inherent in IQ testing.

Systematic Desensitization: In **behavioral psychology**, a therapy technique designed to eliminate or mitigate the effects of anxiety-producing situations. Systematic desensitization usually involves imagining anxiety-producing situations in the mind and associating these situations with pleasant thoughts. Individuals often talk through their fears, which helps them put aspects of the situation in perspective. Sometimes, individuals actually confront fearful situations in reality. This confrontation is usually done in a step-by-step hierarchical manner, in which the individual is either exposed to only a portion of the anxiety-producing situation or is exposed to the entire situation for a brief period of time. Gradually, the individual is exposed to more of the anxiety-producing situation or to the entire situation for longer periods of time. This exposure is accompanied by pleasant thoughts and by rational thought perspectives.

In education, students' inabilities to perform a task at a high level often causes **anxiety**. For example, if students do not do well in math, they may develop anxieties toward math class. In such cases, it is often the fear of failure that causes the anxiety. One way to help students overcome this fear is to provide them with relatively simple problems that they can solve with relative ease and then praise them for a job well done. Helping students feel good about math and showing students that they can do well in math will help students overcome their fear of math. Gradually increasing the level of problem difficulty and giving the students step-by-step strategies for solving problems assists in the desensitization.

Systematic Observation: In research, the process of observing one or more specific **variables** being investigated. Systematic observations can be made in defined or controlled settings, or they can be made in natural environments, depending on the kind of research being conducted. Observations are often recorded using some sort of measuring instrument. For example, a researcher may observe the positive and negative comments made in a particular classroom over a certain period of time. *See* Measurement Instrument

Systematic Sampling: In research, a type of nonprobability sampling in which researchers use a consistent system for selecting **subjects**. For example, using every fifth name on a list of potential subjects or using every other person in a line of potential subjects is systematic sampling. *See* Probability Sampling; Non-probability Sampling

Systematic Variance: In research, **variability** in a set of scores that can be attributed to the **independent variable**. Statistically, systematic variance refers to the variability of a particular group's mean from the overall or grand mean of all subjects in an experiment.

Tabula Rasa: In general, a Latin term for "blank slate," and the general idea that individual human beings are born without "built-in" mental content and that identities are largely defined by events after birth. The idea of tabula rasa falls directly on the side of nature in the nature/nurture controversy. The idea was first advocated by English philosopher John Locke (1632–1704), who believed that the human mind is essentially blank at birth and that information and rules for processing it are the results of sensory inputs or experiences after birth. Because identities are defined by life experiences, each individual is free to define the content of his or her own character through the choice of life experiences. The **tabula rasa** concept is also a component of **Sigmund Freud's (1856–1939) psychoanalysis.** In modern psychology, tabula rasa has a significantly different meaning. In the modern view, the power to effect change through experience lies in society rather than in the self. That is, changing the environment changes the sensory experiences of individuals in the society. *See* **Nature/Nurture Controversy**

Tachistoscope/T-scope: An instrument that permits brief exposures of words, symbols, pictures, or other visually-presented material to an individual. Also called a teaching machine, this device can provide self-instruction by means of pre-designed learning programs that progress at a rate determined by the learner. The machine informs the learner about whether each reply is correct or incorrect. The advantages of the tachistoscopes are that students can proceed at their own pace, receive immediate feedback, and may find the machines intrinsically motivating. Today, computers are more commonly used for such instruction. *See* **Programmed Instruction; Computer Assisted Instruction (CAI)**

Tanglewood Declaration: A symposium that met in Tanglewood, Massachusetts, in 1967 that addressed major issues in music education and "Music in American Society." The symposium was organized by Robert Choate and Louis Wersen and sponsored by the **Music Educators National**

Conference (MENC) in cooperation with the Berkshire Music Center, the Theodore Presser Foundation, and the School of Fine and Applied Arts of Boston University. The focus of the symposium was on music education as an integral part of society. Issues were addressed that related to ways that music education could be improved to better meet society's needs. One important outcome of the conference was that it provided direction for making music education more relevant to the times. The *Documentary Report of the Tanglewood Symposium* contains all of the papers presented at the symposium.

Tanglewood Symposium, The: A music education symposium that was held from July 23 to August 2, 1967, in Tanglewood, Massachusetts. The Tanglewood Symposium was a gathering designed to discuss and define the place of music education in the public school **curriculum** at a time when society was undergoing rapid change. One result of the symposium was the **Tanglewood Declaration**, a document that provided a philosophical basis for future developments in music education.

Task: In education, something a teacher gives students to do as part of the educational process that may be done in or out of class. Having students complete an assignment, memorize a piece of music, or read and outline a chapter from the textbook are all educational tasks. Tasks can also be mundane. For example, straightening up the room, cleaning one's desk, or even sharpening a pencil are all tasks. Educators frequently equate having students actively involved in tasks and task completion with productivity and learning. *See* **On-task; Off-task**

Task Automation: The process whereby actions, groups of actions, or **responses** occur with minimal, if any, conscious thought. Task automation is essential to normal functioning, and many tasks are automated as part of everyday life. For example, routines such as when and how people brush their teeth, comb their hair, get dressed, and eat breakfast are often automated tasks. In music, particularly music performance, automation is necessary for success at any level. For example, a trombone player must know without conscious thought where the slide must be placed and how the embouchure must be set for each note to play any musical passage smoothly and musically. That is, the notes on the page or in the player's mind represent a series of automated tasks that the player must perform. Typically, better performers will have more tasks automated. Task automation allows players to focus attention on higher-level thinking tasks, such as phrasing, dynamics, balance, and blend.

Task Directions: In education, the process of telling students how a task can or should be performed. For example, a teacher can give students a strategy by telling them to complete the following tasks in order: 1) learn and memorize the form of the piece; 2) memorize the first phrase; 3) memorize the second phrase; and 4) perform the first and second phrases together from memory. *See* **Task Response; Task Stimulus**

Task Response: An act that leads to the performance of a task, or an instance of an operation to be performed as part of a given task. Task response involves "doing" according to instructions. *See* **Task Directions; Task Stimulus**

Task Stimulus: The thought process that leads to action enabling an individual to perform a task, or a concept instance that controls an operation to be performed for a given task. Examples: 1) mentally "talking through" the actions or tasks to be done; or 2) using mental pictures to visualize the act or acts of task performance. *See* **Task Response; Task Directions**

Taxonomy: In general, a set of classifications ordered and arranged on the basis of a single principle or on the basis of a consistent set of principles. Taxonomy is sometimes used more liberally to describe any structured arrangement of information, usually in a hierarchical manner. *See* **Taxonomy, Bloom's**

Taxonomy, Bloom's: Fully titled *Bloom's Taxonomy of Educational Objectives in the Cognitive Domain,* a taxonomy of educational objectives that emphasizes the development of **cognitive skills**. The formulation of Bloom's Taxonomy began in 1948 when a group of psychologists interested in **achievement** testing met at a convention of the American Psychological Association (APA). The primary goal was to clarify learning **objectives** and what was expected of the students. These psychologists hoped to provide a convenient system for describing and ordering test items, examination techniques, and **evaluation** instruments. Originally, the psychologists were interested in achievement testing, but they found this to be too limiting. As a result, they decided to look for common terminology for describing and referring to the human **behavioral** characteristics they were attempting to appraise. They were not interested in creating classifications of subject matter; rather, they were interested in the types of human reaction or **response** to the content, subject matter, problems, or areas of human experience that seemed most significant in the learning process.

This group was particularly interested in the types of **learning** that results from the way students are taught. They believed that the discovery of some of the **principles** of ordering learning **outcomes** should define the types of findings that a useful **learning theory** must be able to explain. They also believed it was important to define simple types of learning as well as complex types of learning and to be able to recognize the difference. **Benjamin Bloom (1913–1999)** was responsible for developing the *Taxonomy of Educational Objectives for the Cognitive Domain*. Bloom believed that defining appropriate **goals** was one of the major difficulties confronting educators and that teachers were often too abstract when defining their goals. He believed that goal statements such as "I want to help students realize their full potential as individuals" were too vague, and goal statements such as "My job is to teach math" were too simplistic. Bloom's taxonomy was an attempt to define educational objectives clearly. His goal was to align procedures and materials with instructional strategies. Because the largest proportion of educational objectives fall into the **cognitive domain**, the scope of the project was daunting. *Bloom's Taxonomy of Educational Objectives in the Cognitive Domain* has six levels. They are as follows:

Level One—Knowledge: The lowest level of the taxonomy, it deals with remembering and recall. Students are responsible for defining, distinguishing, acquiring, identifying, recalling, or recognizing information, ideas, material, or phenomena. Students are expected to know specific facts, terms, and methods.

Level Two—Comprehension: The stage in which materials are understood at a level beyond pure recall and the underlying principles of the knowledge can be manipulated. Students must show they understand the material, ideas, facts, and theories. That is, students must translate, transform, restate in their own words, illustrate, prepare, read, represent, change, or rephrase various forms of information. Comprehension may be the most commonly employed level in schools and colleges.

Level Three—Application: The level at which individuals can begin to work independently with the knowledge they have. Students take knowledge and arrive at unique solutions to presented problems. Students must be able to generalize, relate, choose, develop, organize, use, transfer, restructure, or classify various forms of information and apply their knowledge to real situations. At level two (comprehension), individuals understand the ideas. At level three, individuals can demonstrate that they can actually apply their ideas correctly.

Level Four—Analysis: Essentially a more advanced aspect of comprehension, analysis requires individuals to classify or break material down into its components, understand the relationship between these components, and recognize the principle that organizes the structure or the system. That is, at this level students must demonstrate the ability to be able to break apart a particular concept or understanding into its essential components, to identify relationships between the components, and to understand the organizational principles of the components underlying the concept. Analysis involves distinguishing, detecting, identifying, classifying, discriminating, recognizing, categorizing, or deducing various forms of information.

Level Five—Synthesis: At this level, the educational objective is to learn to synthesize material. Synthesis involves making something new, bringing ideas together to form a new theory, going beyond what is now known, or providing new insights. Synthesis also involves being able to take understandings and use them to communicate ideas, being able to take understandings and use them in the formulation of a plan or procedure for accomplishing a task, and being able to determine abstract relations on the basis of this understanding. Students should be able to write, tell, relate, produce, modify, or document various forms of information.

Level Six—Evaluation: The highest level in the taxonomy, it requires the application of all previous levels of knowledge and involves having the ability to make informed judgments about the value or purpose of knowledge. That is, evaluation is the learning of value judgments. Individuals are developing the ability to create standards of judgment, to weigh, to examine, to analyze, and, most of all, to avoid making poor judgments. That is, students must learn to judge, argue, validate, assess, and appraise various forms of information. Evaluation is usually a lengthy process that requires careful examination of the facts.

> Bloom's taxonomy was revised in 2001 and is entitled *A Taxonomy for Learning, Teaching, and Assessing: A Revision of Bloom's Taxonomy of Educational Objectives*, edited by Lorin W. Anderson and David Krathwohl. *See* **Bloom, Benjamin S. (1913-1999)**

Taxonomy of Educational Objectives, Cognitive Domain: *See* Taxonomy, Bloom's

Taxonomy of Learning Objectives, Gagne: The "building blocks" of instruction outlined by **Robert Mills Gagne (1916-2002)** in his book *The Conditions of Learning*. The taxonomy contains five learning outcomes, which include: 1) verbal information; 2) intellectual skills (including **discriminations**, concrete concepts, defined concepts, rules, and higher order rules); 3) **cognitive** strategies; 4) **attitudes**; and 5) motor skills. To achieve these learning **objectives**, Gagne developed the following "nine events of instruction": 1) gaining attention; 2) informing the learner of the objective; 3) stimulating recall of prior learning; 4) presenting the **stimulus**; 5) providing learner guidance; 6) eliciting performance; 7) providing **feedback**; 8) assessing performance; and 9) enhancing retention and transfer. Gagne believed these external conditions or events provide optimal support for the internal processes that occur during learning. They are designed to be used as a guideline for instruction rather than as an absolute formula.

Teacher Education in Music: Final Report (1972): A report based on an examination of collegiate-level teacher education programs in music during the four-year period from 1968-1972. A commission was appointed by then president of the **Music Educators National Conference (MENC)**, Wiley L. Housewright. Its purpose was to review the status of music teacher education programs, to make recommendations for improving these programs, and to identify the qualities and competencies necessary for effective music teaching. The commission published *Recommended Standards and Evaluative Criteria* to help colleges and universities evaluate all aspects of their teacher preparation programs. The *Teacher Education in Music: Final Report* focused on three areas: general education, music, and professional teacher education. In addition, the commission identified three categories of qualities and competencies necessary for effective teachers. These included personal qualities, musical competencies, and professional qualities. The overriding theme in this report was that teachers needed to demonstrate a minimum set level of competence in all areas and that **comprehensive musicianship** should be the goal of all programs.

Teacher Expectations: A teacher's **attitudes** toward and expectations of students' potentials for learning and **achievement**. Several factors have been found to influence teacher expectations. These include social class, **personality**, gender, **ethnicity**, and past **academic achievement**. Research has suggested that as many as 50 percent of all teachers possess one or more **stereotypes** and that these stereotypes can affect teacher expectations, impacting the teaching/learning process.

Teacher Portfolio: A representative compilation of works or products that reflect or display a teacher's knowledge and skills. Teacher portfolios are sometimes used in the evaluation process and may include teacher-constructed handouts, teacher-created tests, and teaching samples or demonstrations on videotape. *See* **Portfolio Assessment**

Teacher-centered Instruction: An approach to teaching in which instruction is provided to students with very little student input, involvement, or discussion. In teacher-centered classrooms, students often sit passively while teachers present information. Lectures, drills, and recitation are typical modes of delivery in teacher-centered environments. Although students may be asked to take a few notes based on the teacher's presentation, students typically sit passively and attempt to absorb the information. Teacher-centered instruction is popular at the college level, particularly for freshmen-level classes. Large class sizes, the need to present a great deal of introductory material in a short period of time, and the maturity level of the students make this type of instruction appropriate. Generally, teacher-centered instruction is less appropriate for younger, more immature students. The term teacher-centered instruction is often used interchangeably with teacher-directed instruction, although teacher-directed instruction implies more student involvement in activities or other forms of practice in order to learn material. The **lecture method** is one example of teacher-centered instruction. *See* **Student-centered Instruction; Teacher-directed Instruction; Expository Method**

Teacher-directed Instruction: A teaching method in which teachers direct instruction through a series of preplanned steps or a lesson plan. Teacher-directed instruction is one of the most common teaching methods and may be considered "traditional" teaching. Components of teacher directed instruction typically include: 1) formulating **goals** and **objectives**; 2) formulating **tasks** and breaking them down into small steps; 3) **sequencing** learning in logical steps; and 4) devising ways to measure whether or not students have learned to master the tasks. Teachers typically introduce a new **concept** or **skill** and explain it to the students, who then practice either under the direction of the teacher or independently. Finally, students are tested in some way to make certain they have learned the skill or concept. Teacher-directed instruction is often used interchangeably with teacher-centered instruction, although teacher-centered instruction implies less overall student involvement in the learning process. *See* Student-centered Instruction; Teacher-centered Instruction

Teacher Unions: Organizations like other labor unions that function to protect the rights and promote the welfare of teachers and the teaching profession. Teacher unions typically negotiate salary schedules and other employment conditions in the **collective bargaining** process. Teacher unions are controversial. Critics argue that unions shield their members from scrutiny and promote or help maintain the status quo. Proponents argue that unions improve public education and maintain and promote high standards. The largest, most well known, and most powerful teacher unions are the **National Education Association (NEA)** and the **American Federation of Teachers (AFT)**. Both the NEA and the AFT have helped shape education. They have been instrumental in increasing teachers' salaries, improving working conditions, raising public awareness of educational issues, and promoting the teaching profession as a whole.

Teaching: The act or process of imparting knowledge, information, **concepts**, and **skills** to people who do not possess them. Teaching takes place at all levels of life, in many different contexts, and in both formal and informal settings. In the home, parents are the primary teachers, and much of what parents do determines what kind of individuals their children are or will be. In formal educational settings (schools) teaching occurs through the interaction of teachers and students and usually involves specific, pre-designated **curricular goals** and **objectives**. Teaching also takes place more informally in school settings. For example, students teach each other through normal, day-to-day social interactions.

Teaching Machine: *See* Tachistoscope/T-scope; Programmed Instruction

Teaching Method: *See* Method

Teaching Music (TM): An official publication for members of the **Music Educators National Conference (MENC)**, which contains a variety of practical ideas for teaching at all levels. It also includes a wide variety of practical articles in specific areas and keeps members informed about relevant activities in music education nationally on a state by state basis. *Teaching Music* is issued five times yearly.

Team Teaching: In education, teaching in which two or more teachers work closely together in planning, carrying out, and evaluating the **learning** experiences of a particular group of students. The idea of team teaching is to vitalize the **curriculum**, develop more confident and competent teachers, and individualize instruction. Students may work in small groups, large groups, or independently, and they often benefit from the diverse experiences of the teachers involved. Team teaching can be used to integrate subject matter across content areas when appropriate so that students gain a more broad-based, interdisciplinary experience.

Technique: In music education, a term referring to some aspect of **pedagogy** or to the way something is done to facilitate the learning process. For example, teaching the proper way to hold a violin bow, teaching how to produce vibrato on the flute, or using humor to make a point all involve techniques. Techniques are usually related to task performance and are commonly associated with **method** or **methodology**, which is a systematic approach for disseminating information based on philosophical beliefs. That is, method is an approach to teaching, whereas a technique may be one aspect of a given method. In music, technique is also frequently used to describe an individual's technical abilities and skills on his or her instrument or voice. For example, an individual who possesses great technical skills and facility is said to have great technique.

Technology: *See* Music Technology; Electronic Music

Telegraphic Speech: In language development, a type of speech in which nonessential words are omitted. A child's first combinations of words are examples of telegraphic speech because they convey a complete idea, but do not typically include extra ideas or words necessary for correct grammar. Examples: "Where ball?" or "Daddy home."

Telephone Survey: In research, a descriptive technique in which researchers contact individuals who are representative of the **population** being studied for the purpose of gathering information by telephone. Typically, telephone surveys involve having researchers ask questions from a pre-planned survey guide pertinent to their study. Although less costly and faster than processes involving mailed surveys or personal interviews, telephone surveys are naturally limited because of time constraints and respondent fatigue.

Temperament: In psychology, inherent dispositions or aspects of **personality** that underlie and affect how one responds or behaves to environmental stimuli. Underlying temperament affects mood, emotions, energy level, sociability, and reactions. Temperament is observed as the characteristic ways individuals respond over time. Fundamental characteristics of temperament are believed to be largely innate, although environmental factors also contribute.

Temperament/Tuning Systems: In music, mathematical systems for adjusting the intervals of a natural scale, or the **pitches (frequencies)** that result from adjustments made to a natural scale. Temperaments/tuning systems are designed to facilitate musical performance in some way.

Different tuning systems have been developed over time. The most well known include: **Pythagorean, mean-tone, just-intonation,** and **equal temperament**. The most commonly used tuning system in Western music is equal temperament, in which the octave is divided into twelve equal parts. Equal temperament was originally developed to enable the pianoforte to modulate freely to all twelve major keys and is built on a system of compromises in which the width of all major thirds is 400 cents. The main ideas of these tuning systems are outlined below.

Pythagorean: A system based on the circle of fifths, in which the fifths are tuned to a beatless 702 cents. When mathematically taken to its entirety (11 fifths), the "leftover" fifth is only 679 cents, or about 23 cents short of a just 702. This is known as the Pythagorean comma. In performance, this resulted in a triad that had a third so badly out of tune that it was not usable.

Meantone: A system in which all of the major thirds are pure and all of the tones are made equal to the mean of a major tone and a minor tone. In other words, the thirds are split in half to get the seconds. It is this averaging process that gives this system its name.

Just Intonation: A system built on "just" or "pure" intervals, in which intervals are related mathematically in such a way that beats are not present when notes are played together. Just intonation is based on the harmonic series and does not involve any unnatural compromise. However, just intonation is very limiting because it prohibits modulation and reduces the melodic and harmonic choices that are usable.

Equal Temperament: The most commonly used system in the Western world in which the octave is divided into twelve equal semi-tones of 100 cents. Equal temperament facilitates modulation to all keys without anything sounding "bad." However, the result is that everything is a bit out-of-tune.

In reality, there can be no "perfect" tuning system for all music. That is, it is not possible to achieve perfect tuning based on any known tuning system. At some point, beats will inevitably result from mistuned intervals in all but the simplest tunes. These mistuned intervals are caused by the fact that the frequencies of some pitches within every scale will not align mathematically with other pitches, when they are played together in certain harmonic contexts. As a result of this inherent problem, attempts to devise better tuning systems have all involved some sort of compromise. That is, systems are designed to mitigate the effects of the natural "out-of-tuneness."

Tenure: A teaching contract guaranteeing that a teacher will be retained each year unless just cause for termination can be demonstrated. Tenure is often referred to as a continuing contract and is most common at the college or university level. Tenure provides job security for professional scholars who may be researching and writing in socially or politically sensitive areas.

Terman, Lewis M. (1877-1956): A psychologist well known for his work with **intelligence** and geniuses, responsible for introducing the Binet **intelligence tests** in the United States. Terman joined the faculty at Stanford University in 1910. In the 1920s, Terman conducted a study of more than 1,500 children who had **intelligence quotients (IQs)** of 140 or higher. Each child was tested for intelligence, scholastic achievement, personality, character, and other interests. These children were also examined medically, and their physical characteristics were measured. In addition, Terman interviewed their parents and teachers to gather additional information on the children. Terman's analysis of the data showed that gifted children were superior in all areas, mentally and physically. That is, not only were children with IQs above 140 academically superior to the average child, they also tended to be taller, healthier, more coordinated, better adjusted, and more popular than the average child. This landmark study remains one of the most influential studies in intelligence. *See* **Gifted and Talented/Giftedness**

Terminal Behavior: A term used in **behavior modification** to describe defined educational **goals** for the whole class or for individual students because they are difficult to observe and measure. Terminal behavior focuses on specific actions or **tasks** a student or class will or will not do when the terminal goals are reached. Terminal goals are defined in objective behavioral terms and are specific in nature. Vague or subjective terms such as "understanding" are not included in the definition of terminal goals. When terminal behaviors are reached, new terminal behaviors are set. Long-range terminal behaviors are achieved by setting a series of short-term terminal behaviors that will help students reach their long-term goals. For example, one long-term terminal behavior might be that students will learn all twelve major scales in a two-week period. The short-term terminal behaviors that could be set to help achieve this goal might be as follows: During the first week, students will learn to play two scales a day from memory. Each day students will review the previously learned scales and add two new scales. During the second week, students will perform all twelve major scales daily with no more than five errors by the end of the first two days, no more than two errors by the end of the third or fourth day, and with no errors on the fifth or sixth days. *See* **Objectives, Behavioral**

Tessitura: The average range of a melodic line or a vocal or instrumental part. That is, tessitura is the range in which most of the notes of a given melody, line, or piece lies. Tessitura is often used synonymously with **range**; however, range refers to the entire distance from the lowest to the highest notes of a given melody, line, or piece of music. *See* **Range**

Test: In education, a collection and/or arrangement of questions or **tasks** that require measurable responses that can be scored in some way. Tests are a common component of the **assessment** process. Four common types of tests or test questions include: true/false, multiple choice, fill-in-the-blank, and essay. In music, tests are often **performance-based**. That is, students are graded on some aspect of demonstrated performance. Test criteria for **evaluation** include tone quality, technical accuracy, rhythmic accuracy, and various aspects of **musicality**, including phrasing and dynamics. *See* Standardized Tests; Achievement Tests; Aptitude Tests

Test of Musicality, Gaston (1957): A test designed by E. Thayer Gaston to measure musicality. First published in 1942, the test was revised in 1950, 1956, and 1957. The test is unusual in that it measures perceptual abilities within a musical context rather than measuring sensory abilities. Test components include: 1) in-depth questions about the test taker, 2) questions about the test-taker's family, 3) questions regarding the test-taker's participation in musical activities, 4) questions regarding music in the home, and 5) a series of **discrimination** tasks. The Gaston Test of Musicality is appropriate for most school-age students. The **split-half reliabilities** given in the test manual are .88 for grades four through six, .88 for grades seven through nine, and .90 for grades ten through twelve.

Test-retest Reliability: In research, a type of **reliability** in which the same individuals are measured at two points in time. Test-retest reliability is a **method** of determining test reliability over time by comparing individuals' test scores on one occasion with their test scores on the same test on a later occasion. If the testing instrument is reliable, an individual's results on both the test and the retest should be roughly the same. Test results may be affected by a variety of incidental factors, such as the emotional state of the test taker or disturbances in the test environment. The more reliable the instrument, the less effect incidental factors have on the results. In addition, there is always the chance that test takers will remember information from the first time they took the test. As a result, alternate-forms reliability is often used. *See* Alternate-forms Reliability; Split-half Reliability; Reliability; Internal Consistency

Thelen's Seven Teacher Images: In education, seven common self-images or self-perceptions of teachers described by Herbert Thelen. Thelen's seven teacher images are as follows: 1) Socrates (c. 470–399 BC), in which the teacher sees himself or herself as a Socratic figure who enjoys argument and debate; 2) the town-meeting manager, who would prefer consensus and cooperation in the class; 3) the master/apprentice, who perceives himself or herself as someone to be emulated and who enjoys playing multiple roles, including parent, teacher, boss, and colleague; 4) the general, who demands obedience and sets rules much like an army general; 5) the business executive, who operates the classroom much like a company; 6) the coach, who views students as members of a team and maintains an atmosphere more like a locker room; and 7) the tour guide, who knows all the information and efficiently imparts information and answers questions.

Thematic Apperception Test (TAT): A **projective test** developed in the 1930s that consists of a set of ambiguous pictures the test taker looks at and then makes up an interesting story about. The pictures include scenes of people such as the faces of a male and a female close together, a boy staring at a violin, and a young man with an older woman. Typically, the test taker is asked to make up a story that includes what events could have led to the event depicted, what is going on in the picture, what the people are feeling and thinking about in the picture, and what will happen in the end. Like other projective tests, the TAT is used to assess **personality** by assessing the way individuals reveal or project themselves through their imaginations. Such tests enable individuals to respond as they wish, and there is no correct interpretation of the pictures. The idea is that individuals will project their thoughts and feelings onto the test, which allows the researcher or therapist to understand each test taker better by gaining insight into an individual's unconscious conflicts. *See* **Projective Tests**

Theoretical Understanding Level of Inference Learning, Gordon: *See* **Skill Learning Sequence, Gordon**

Theory: A speculative explanation or prediction of a phenomenon or phenomena based on a logical interpretation of an organized, cohesive set of related statements, principles, axioms, facts, and/or ideas. Theories provide a **framework** for understanding information or **data** that have been gathered through experimentation, investigation, philosophizing, and/or experience. They also extend thinking beyond the scope of mere facts and observation and provide the basis for future research. Theories can range from simple ideas about why something happens to very complex explanations or interpretations of mass amounts of information. The **validity** of any theory is often determined by whether others in the field can find faults or inconsistencies within the theory or by how well it holds up under scrutiny over time. Of relevance to music educators, many learning theories have been developed through the years; however, no theory has been accepted universally, and no theory provides an explanation for all aspects of learning. Examples: 1) **Edwin E. Gordon's (b. 1927) Music Learning Theory**; 2) **Jean Piaget's (1896–1980) Stages of Cognitive Growth**; 3) **Jerome Bruner's (b. 1915) Theory of Instruction**

Theory and Practice: Considered by many to be the twin pillars of educational disciplines. Theory and practice bridge or connect between the scientific or theoretical side of any particular discipline and the educational or practical side of that discipline. Debates over the relative importance of both in determining **outcomes** are ongoing. In reality, they are both important for growth and understanding within all disciplines.

Theory of Instruction, Bruner: A theory of instruction by **Jerome Bruner (b. 1915)** that focuses on the way information should be taught. Bruner called his theory one of instruction, not **learning**, because it emphasizes the teacher's responsibility for helping students learn. In Bruner's view, a theory of instruction was prescriptive because it prescribes the way a subject can be taught most effectively. By contrast, a learning theory is descriptive because it describes learning after the fact. Bruner's theory of instruction has four major principles: motivation, structure, sequence, and reinforcement. The first principle, motivation, can be intrinsic or extrinsic. Bruner identified four sources of **intrinsic motivation**, including a natural or built-in desire to learn, a curiosity about things, a drive to achieve competence, and a need to work cooperatively with others (reciprocity). Bruner believed that intrinsic motivation could be encouraged by allowing students to solve problems through the exploration of alternatives. The second principle, structure, is based on Bruner's premise that any subject can be taught effectively to any child at any stage of development in some intellectually honest form.

Bruner identified three ways information can be communicated, or three modes of presentation. These include: 1) **Enactive representation**, which involves presenting information through actions rather than words (e.g., hitting a baseball) and is used frequently with young children; 2) **Iconic representation**, which involves the ability to understand information that is presented using pictures or diagrams without action (e.g., using a map to locate a state); and 3) **Symbolic representation**, which involves the ability to translate experiences into language (e.g., describing a musical performance). The third principle, sequence, involves providing instruction in a logical progression, usually from simple to complex, or by moving from the enactive, to the iconic, and finally to the symbolic modes of representation. In other words, Bruner believed that teachers should begin teaching by presenting the material using actions instead of words. Teachers should then present the information using graphs, charts, and other pictorial designs. Finally, Bruner thought teachers should present the material through the symbolic use of language. The fourth principle, **reinforcement**, involves providing learners with appropriate feedback on their efforts. Bruner thought that the timing of the **feedback** was crucial to learning success. If teachers provide feedback too soon, learners will not have time to explore the material sufficiently. If teachers provide feedback too late, learners may learn "wrong" information.

Theory of Specifics, Seashore: In music, a theory proposed by **Carl Seashore (1866–1949),** which views **musical talent** or **musicality** as a series of fragmented or separate abilities rather than an all-pervasive ability that can be described as a "whole" as **James Mursell (1893–1963)** suggested in his **Omnibus Theory.**

Thesis: In general, a proposition, postulate, statement, or idea to be proven or defended. In education, a lengthy paper, essay, or other type of written report presented by a candidate completing work toward a master's degree.

Thorndike, Edward L. (1874-1949): One of America's most renowned educational psychologists, Thorndike studied at Harvard under **William James (1842–1910)** and later taught at the Columbia Teacher's College. Early in his career, Thorndike conducted important laboratory studies on learning with animals as subjects. Using the results of these studies, he constructed the first internally consistent **learning theory**. Thorndike created three major laws of learning: the **Law of Readiness**, the **Law of Exercise**, and the **Law of Effect**. Thorndike believed learning occurs by trial-and-error, and he thought of **learning** as the result of the accumulation of connections between stimuli and responses. He was one of the first psychologists to advocate the use the scientific method in psychology.

Threshold: The transitional point at which a **stimulus** becomes either perceptible or imperceptible. That is, threshold occurs when an increasing stimulus or an increasing difference not previously perceived becomes perceptible or the point at which a decreasing stimulus or previously perceived difference becomes imperceptible. Threshold values are often not absolute; these values vary among individuals and are often affected by context. Threshold values are also dependent in part upon the methods used in determining these values.

Thurstone, Louis L. (1887-1955): An eminent psychologist well known for his work in **intelligence** and one of the developers of the factor approach to understanding intelligence. **Thurstone** received a bachelor's degree in electrical engineering in 1912 from Cornell University, a Ph.D. in psychology in 1917 from the University of Chicago, and did postdoctoral work at the Division of Applied Psychology at the Carnegie Institute of Technology. He taught at the Carnegie Institute from 1917 to 1924 and at the University of Chicago from 1924 to 1952. Thurstone gave sixty different tests of special abilities to large groups of children and then separated those test scores that correlated highly with each other. He discovered from all of these tests that there were only seven underlying correlated groupings or primary abilities. These are: 1) verbal comprehension, 2) word fluency, 3) numerical ability, 4) spatial visualizations, 5) associative memory, 6) perceptual speed, and 7) reasoning. *See* **Thurstone Primary Mental Abilities Tests**

Timbre: In music, **timbre** refers to the tone quality of an instrument that allows one to distinguish the sound of one instrument from another. In science, timbre refers to the characteristics of a sound that enable a listener to distinguish it from other sounds of identical **pitch** and **loudness**. The physical properties of the sound source contribute to timbre by emphasizing some partials and de-emphasizing others. In addition, performance factors such as bow scrapes, tongue distortions, and reed noises contribute significantly to the timbre of the tone. *See* **Transients**

Time-out Room: A special room apart from the regular classroom used to separate disruptive students for short periods of time. Although the use of time-out rooms can be effective in reducing or eliminating disruptive behaviors, excessive use of time-out rooms for behavioral problems can become aversive and ineffective. Time-out rooms are most common at the elementary level.

Tinnitus: A disease of the **inner ear** characterized by a high-pitched throbbing or ringing in the ear.

Tip-of-the-tongue (TOT) Phenomenon: In memory, a common phenomenon characterized by the inability to recall a word or name even though the information is known and even though one feels like the information will be recalled at any moment.

Title I: A federally funded education program for at-risk elementary and secondary students, called Chapter 1 prior to 1994. Title 1 was originally part of the **Elementary and Secondary Education Act (ESEA) of 1965** and was the first bill signed by President Johnson to combat poverty. The program was specifically geared toward meeting the educational needs of low-income, low-achieving students and resulted in the formulation of **pull-out programs** in the public schools. Today, ESEA has been amended with the **No Child Left Behind (NCLB) Act of 2001**. Under NCLB, Title I programs should be designed to prepare students to meet challenging state standards and to further enrich gifted programs. In addition, Title I programs should be school-wide and should obtain funding from a variety of sources. The idea behind Title I is to provide educational opportunities for all low-income students, not only for low-achieving students. *See* **Pull-out Programs**

Title IX: A provision of the Education Amendments of 1972 guaranteeing that "no person in the United States shall, on the basis of sex, be excluded from participation in, be denied the benefits of, or be subjected to **discrimination** under any education program or activity receiving Federal financial assistance." Title IX provides legal protection against sexual harassment and discrimination based on marital or parental status, and extends to students and employees. Although Title IX is best known for its impact on athletic programs, it has also impacted admissions, recruitment, educational programs and activities, course offerings, counseling, financial aid, employment assistance, facilities, housing, health insurance benefits, and scholarships.

Token System: A system of **reinforcement** used by proponents of **behavior modification** in which tokens of varying point values are awarded to students for fulfilling specific **behavioral objectives**. Students generally earn tokens (**conditioned reinforcers**) by achieving **goals** or meeting teacher expectations. The tokens can be exchanged for various kinds of prizes or **rewards** based on their total point value. The token system is sometimes called token economy.

Tonal Content Learning Sequence, Gordon: In Edwin E. Gordon's
(b. 1927) music learning theory, one of three learning sequences (tonal
content learning sequence, rhythm content learning sequence, skill
learning sequence). Tonal content learning sequence is facilitated by
development of a sense of tonality and a vocabulary of tonal patterns. The
tonal patterns used in learning sequence activities are organized according
to tonality classification, such as major, minor, and dorian, and tonal
pattern function, such as tonic, dominant, and subdominant. Tonalities and
tonal functions are sequenced primarily according to familiarity. Major
tonality, for example, is introduced first in both learning sequence activities
and classroom activities because it is the most common tonality in Western
culture and, therefore, the most familiar. Likewise, tonic and dominant
functions are introduced first because they are the most basic tonal
functions in major tonality.

Gordon recognizes the following tonality classifications: Major,
Harmonic Minor, Dorian, Phrygian, Lydian, Mixolydian, Aeolian, Locrian,
Multitonal/Multikeyal, Polytonal/Polykeyal, and Monokeyal. In addition,
Gordon recognizes pattern functions for each tonality classification.
According to Gordon, tonal pattern functions include: tonic, dominant,
subdominant, subtonic, cadential, characteristic tone, chromatic, modula-
tory, multiple, and expanded tonal patterns.

Gordon's outline of his tonal content learning sequence includes
the following levels and sublevels arranged hierarchically. These levels and
sublevels include:

1) MAJOR AND HARMONIC MINOR TONALITIES
   A. Tonic and Dominant Functions
2) MAJOR AND HARMONIC MINOR TONALITIES
   A. All Functions
3) DORIAN TONALITY
   A. Tonic, Subtonic, and Subdominant Functions
4) PHRYGIAN TONALITY
   A. Tonic, Supertonic, and Subtonic Functions
5) LYDIAN TONALITY
   A. Tonic and Subtonic Functions
6) MIXOLYDIAN TONALITY
   A. Tonic and Subtonic Functions
7) AEOLIAN TONALITY
   A. Tonic Subtonic Functions

8) LOCRIAN TONALITY
   A. Tonic, Subtonic, and Median Functions
9) MIXOLYDIAN, DORIAN, LYDIAN, PHRYGIAN, AEOLIAN, AND LOCRIAN TONALITIES
   A. All Functions
10) MULTITONAL/MULTIKEYAL
   A. Multitonal/Multikeyal-Same "do," Multitonal/Unikeyal, Unitonal/Multikeyal, and Multitonal/Multikeyal-Different "do"
11) POLYTONAL/POLYKEYAL
   A. Polytonal/Monokeyal Unitonal/Unikeyal
   B. Polykeyal/Monotonal Unitonal/Unikeyal
   C. Polytonal/Polykeyal Unitonal/Unikeyal
   D. Polytonal/Polykeyal Multitonal/Multikeyal
12) MONOKEYAL
   A. Multitonal
   B. Multikeyal
   C. Unitonal
   D. Multikeyal

In his book *Learning Sequences in Music*, Gordon devotes an entire chapter to describing and explaining his tonal content leaning sequence. Like the other two learning sequences, the tonal content learning sequence is hierarchical; that is, mastery of one skill level provides the readiness necessary to allow one to move on to the next skill level, and so on. *See* **Rhythm Content Learning Sequence, Gordon; Skill Learning Sequence, Gordon; Music Learning Theory, Gordon**

Tone Chroma: In music, the perceptual similarity of tones (or pitch class), typically an octave apart. Tone chroma is one dimension of a two-component theory of pitch, the other dimension being tone height. Tone chroma is graphically represented as the circular dimension of a three-dimensional helix. *See* **Tone Height; Chroma Helix**

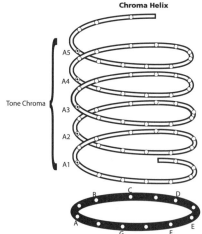

Tone Chroma and Chroma Helix

Tone Color: *See* Timbre

Tone Deaf/Deafness: A term used to describe the general inability to distinguish between two tones in a normal manner or to describe individuals who cannot discriminate between tones. Tone deaf individuals are generally unable to match pitches or sing even the simplest melodic patterns. The cause of tone deafness is not known, but the following factors may be involved: 1) tonal perception, 2) **aural perception**, 3) vocal production, 4) **auditory memory**, and 5) a lack of musical experience and training. The term tone deaf is overused. In fact, although some individuals certainly have limited pitch-matching and pitch **discrimination** abilities, almost everyone can improve these abilities measurably with proper guidance and training.

Tone Height: In music, the perceptual concept of pitch. Tone height is one dimension of a **two-component theory** of pitch, the other dimension being **tone chroma**. Tone height is graphically represented as the vertical dimension of a three-dimensional helix. *See* **Tone Chroma; Chroma Helix**

Tonic Sol-fa: In general, a term used to describe a singing system using traditional **solfege** syllables. Historically, **tonic sol-fa** refers to a specific method of music teaching that began in the primary schools in England. Tonic sol-fa was developed by Eliza (Sarah) Glover (1785–1867) and revised by John Curwen (1816–1880). Tonic sol-fa was based on movable "do" and used a "tone ladder" to teach tonal relationships, followed by the introduction of syllable notation. Time was indicated by the distances between syllables and also incorporated a complex system of commas, dots, and dashes. No staff was used. Teachers in the United States were hesitant to learn a new system of notation, especially one that involved omission of the staff. As a result, tonic sol-fa never caught on in the United States, except as a **mnemonic** device.

Torrance Tests of Creative Thinking: Tests designed by E. Torrance (1966, 1988, 1990) to measure the creative abilities of students in grades K-12. Parallel forms of two tests are available, a verbal content test and a figural content test. Test-takers are given tasks or problem situations and asked to provide written answers or solutions in a specified amount of time. Their written responses are scored according to four theoretical constructs identified by **J. P. Guilford (1897–1988),** including fluency, originality, flexibility, and elaboration.

Toward Civilization: A 1988 report by the **National Endowment for the Arts (NEA)** fully entitled *Toward Civilization: A Report on Arts Education* that described the current state of arts education in the schools, a rationale for including specific arts in the schools, and suggestions on improving arts in the schools. The primary conclusion of the report was that balanced education was essential for all students and for humanity. The report emphasized that the arts were not a universal component of most educational systems and opportunities for art education were not provided to all students. The report included recommendations for strengthening arts education, although support in the form of government funding was and continues to be a barrier to implementing them.

Trace Decay: In memory, a traditional theory of how individuals forget information. Trace decay is based on the idea that learned information actually leaves a physical memory trace that disappears over time if the information is not used. Trace decay is also called trace-dependent forgetting in the **Atkinson-Shiffrin model** of memory. *See* **Decay; Trace-dependent Forgetting**

Trace-dependent Forgetting: In the **Atkinson-Shiffrin** two-process theory of memory, the idea that information stored in **short-term memory (STM)** leaves a physical trace within the brain that **decays** over time. The rate of decay depends on both the amount of time that has elapsed since the information was last used and intervening activities. *See* **Decay; Cue-dependent Forgetting; Two-Process Theory**

Trachea: Commonly called the windpipe, a tube through which air travels from the lungs to the larynx. *See* **Larynx**

Tracking: A process of assigning students who have similar ability levels to specific groups, classes, or programs of study. Proponents of tracking indicate that it enables students to maximize their potentials in the classroom, while opponents argue that the criteria used for grouping students is too narrow and often biased. In addition, opponents feel that tracking results in low **self-esteem**, poor **motivation**, and negative attitudes toward learning for some students.

Trainable Mentally Retarded (TMR): *See* **Mentally Retarded/Mental Retardation**

Trait: A persistent or enduring characteristic or dimension of an individual's **personality** that can be rated or measured. Traits may be viewed as the consistent way an individual responds to stimuli. Although certain traits are commonly found in many individuals, sets of traits or trait combinations are often unique to an individual. *See* Trait Profile; Temperament

Trait Profile: A chart plotting the ratings or measures of an individual's traits on a common scale in parallel rows. **Trait profiles** provide visual representations of individual trait patterns. *See* Trait; Trait Theory

Trait Theory: In psychology, the theory that human **personality** can be characterized by the scores an individual makes on a number of scales designed to represent a **trait** or dimension of personality. In **trait theory**, traits represent continuous dimensions in that they involve various levels or degrees and include qualities such as aggressiveness or sense of humor. Traits differ from types, which represent discontinuous categories such as marital status or education level. Trait theory is often attributed to Gordon Allport (1897–1967).

Transfer: The effects of prior learning on present learning. If prior learning facilitates the learning of a new task, transfer is positive; if prior learning interferes with new learning, transfer is negative. Generally, transfer refers to the process that occurs when individuals use previously acquired knowledge and skills to facilitate the learning of something new. The ability to apply previous learning to new situations and to generalize from one situation to the next is important for positive transfer.

Transference: In **psychoanalysis**, the patient's unconscious tendency to project **attitudes** and attributes possessed by important people in the patient's life, usually a parent or sibling, onto the therapist. When a patient engages in **transference**, both the therapist and patient are often able to gain further insight into the nature of the patient's problems and to whom these problems may be attached.

Transients: Bow scrapes, reed noises, and other non-musical distortions that are common components of the tones produced by traditional, acoustic instruments.

Transition Plan: *See* Individualized Transition Plan (ITP)

Transverse Waves: *See* Waves

Traveling Wave Theory: In acoustics, Georg von Bekesy's modification of **place theory**. Traveling wave theory states that the ear detects sound when a sound impulse sends a **wave** traveling along the **basilar membrane**, and this wave reaches its maximum **amplitude**, displacing the membrane, before falling off sharply. The point at which the wave reaches its maximum amplitude depends upon the **frequency** of the sound. Bekesy confirmed what H. L. F. von Helmholtz (1821–1894) had postulated in place theory; different tones are physically perceived in different areas along the basilar membrane. High-frequency tones are perceived near the base of the **cochlea,** and low-frequency tones are perceived closer to the apex.

Treatment: In research, what is manipulated or done in an experimental study. The term treatment is also used as an adjective to describe the group receiving the manipulation (treatment group or experimental group), in contrast to the control group, which receives no manipulation. In psychology, treatment refers to something done to effect change in an individual or group, usually for the better. *See* **Control Group; Experimental Group**

Trend Analysis: A statistical method used to forecast the future based on past events. Example: Predicting the number of students who will drop out of band this year based on the number who dropped out in previous years, taking into account the expected increase in the number of band students. *See* **Delphi Method; Cross-impact Matrix Method**

Trial-and-error Learning: In education, an expression characterizing a learning process that involves trying different responses until the correct response is found, in contrast to a learning process that involves a pre-planned, systematic approach. Trial-and-error learning is a type of multiple-response learning in which the proper response is ultimately selected out of a variety of possible responses through the influence of **reward** and **punishment**. As a teaching technique, trial-and-error learning can be extremely effective in promoting certain aspects of learning. Trial-and-error learning has been shown to enable students to discover answers or solutions to problems for themselves, which enhances learning permanence and encourages students to think **creatively** and/or **divergently**. In research, trial-and-error sometimes refers to a method of experimentation in which researchers conduct a series of repeated experiments, hoping to achieve desired outcomes.

Triangle Wave: *See* Waveform

Triangulation: In research, the process of cross-checking data by using multiple measures of a concept or attribute to avoid making faulty subjective judgments. The idea behind **triangulation** is that measuring something in several ways or from several different perspectives decreases the likelihood of making erroneous judgments. Example: In a study, if a researcher investigated the effects of praise on the outcome of music instruction based on one criterion, such as improvement in **sight reading** score, and found no significant differences, the results are necessarily limited. That is, all that can be said about the study is that praise does not affect sight-reading scores. Nothing can be said about the effects of praise on improvement in other areas of musical performance, nor can any recommendations be made about whether praise should be used in music instruction. However, if the researcher looked at other criteria as well (triangulation), such as improvement in rhythm or improvement in attitude toward practicing, he or she may find that praise does indeed have a significant effect in at least some aspects of music teaching. In addition, the researcher now has enough information to reach a conclusion and make recommendations that are more accurate and will better benefit the field of study.

Trivia in the Classroom: A teaching technique where teachers ask students questions in a rapid-fire manner. These questions generally call for rote answers. Trivia in the classroom enhances students' abilities to recall information quickly.

Trivium: *See* Seven Liberal Arts

Troubleshooting: In education, a process in which teachers attempt to locate unknown causes of problems. Troubleshooting typically involves a systematic approach to problem solving based on experience and probability. Less often, troubleshooting is done in a haphazard or **trial-and-error** manner in which teachers try different approaches until the problem is, or appears to be, solved.

True Score: An individual's actual score on a **variable** being measured, in contrast to a standard score. True scores are often difficult to attach meaning to, unless the individual interpreting the results is aware of the scoring system for that particular **variable** measure. *See* Standard Score

t-Test: In research, a statistical test used to establish whether or not a significant difference exists between two sample means, or a test that allows comparisons of means between two groups or between the same group of pretest/posttest design. Mathematically, a *t*-test is the ratio of the difference between two **sample means** to an estimate of the **standard deviation** of the **distribution** of differences. A *t*-test is limited because it can account for no more than two levels of an **independent variable**. The most common types of *t*-tests are an independent *t*-test and a related measures *t*-test.

Tufts, John (1689-1750): A minister credited with writing the first music instruction books in the early part of the eighteenth century. Tufts graduated from Harvard in 1708 and served as a minister from 1714 until 1738. His book *Introduction to the Singing of Psalm-Tunes* was first published c. 1714 and was the first music "textbook" published in the Colonies. Tufts is considered by many to be the "grandfather" of American music education, whose goal was to improve church singing by teaching congregations how to read by note in the "regular" or "correct" way instead of the "usual" way, using the lining-out method. Tufts developed a system of notation based on tetrachords, or the division of the octave into two halves, E-F-G-A and B-C-D-E. Tufts' system was later adapted in the development of the "**shape note**" system in which four separate note-head shapes were used to indicate **solfege** syllables.

Tunebook: Books used for music singing and instruction, especially popular in the late 1700s and early 1800s during the **singing school** movement. Tunebooks were typically some combination of choral collection and music textbook. This format had been used as early as the mid-1500s with the *Sternhold and Hopkins Psalter* (1562), which included sections on theoretical instruction. John Tuft's *Introduction to the Singing of Psalm-Tunes* and Thomas Walter's *The Ground Rules of Musick Explained or an Introduction to the Art of Singing by Note,* both published in the early eighteenth century, were among the first tunebooks in the Colonies that also functioned as music textbooks. Tunebooks were used to teach the "correct" or "regular" way of singing by note. Before these and other tunebooks became widely used, the popular method of church singing was lining out, or the "usual" method, in which the congregation repeated each line of psalm by imitation using a melody learned by rote.

The amount of pedagogical material in tunebooks varied greatly, particularly over time. Some included only fundamental information on music reading, while others included more advanced and complex music theory. By the late 1800s, many tunebooks had lesson plans. Although tunebooks contained many types of choral pieces, psalm tunes and hymns were most common. Fuging tunes, lively tunes in two parts, were also common. Tunebooks are still available today, although they were most popular until about the mid-1800s.

Tuning System: *See* Temperament

Tutors: Individuals who provide special instruction, usually on a one-to-one basis. Tutors are often employed on the recommendation of teachers or by parents to help improve **academic achievement** in one or more areas.

Two-process Theory: *See* Two-stage Memory Theory

Two-stage Memory Theory: In the **information-processing model** of memory, the theory that memories are encoded and stored in at least two stages, **short-term memory (STM)** and **long-term memory (LTM)**. In short-term memory, memories last from a brief moment to about one minute. In long-term memory, memories may last a lifetime. *See* **Cue-dependent Forgetting; Trace-dependent Forgetting**

Tympanic Membrane: Also called the **eardrum**, the membrane that separates the **auditory canal** from the **middle ear**. The eardrum is located at the inner end of the auditory canal and vibrates in response to sound **waves**.

Type A Personality: A type of person who is competitive, aggressive, driven to achieve, impatient, angry, or hostile. *See* Type B Personality

Type B Personality: A type of person who is easygoing and relaxed. *See* Type A Personality

Type I Error: One of two main error types in **experimental research**, when the researcher makes an incorrect decision to reject the **null hypothesis** when, in fact, the null hypothesis is actually *true*. Incorrect decisions often relate to poor **research design** and improper **sampling** techniques.

Type II Error: One of two main error types in **experimental research**, when the researcher makes an incorrect decision to accept the **null hypothesis** when, in fact, the null hypothesis is actually *false*. Incorrect decisions often relate to poor **research design** and improper **sampling** techniques.

Type Theory: In psychology, the theory that human beings can be classified into a limited number of classes or types based on common characteristics. That is, individuals can be placed into classes or types because they share common characteristics that set them apart from other classes or types. Type theory includes categorization based on type only, which are discontinuous categories such as gender or marital status. Type theory does not account for traits, which are continuous dimensions of character, such as **intelligence** or aggressiveness. *See* **Trait Theory**

Uu

Ultrasonic: A term used to describe any sound with a **frequency** above the **range** of human hearing. Typically, this range includes sounds above approximately 20,000 Hz. *See* **Infrasonic**

Unconditional Positive Regard, Rogers: A concept used by Carl Rogers (1902–1987) to describe an environment in which individuals are accepted for who they are without condition. Although Rogers used the term in association with person-centered therapy, it is also applicable to educational environments. Rogers thought it was important for teachers to give their students unconditional positive regard. According to Rogers, unconditional positive regard, **empathy**, and **congruence** are the three necessary and sufficient conditions for successful learning. *See* **Rogers, Carl (1902-1987)**

Unconditioned Response/Reflex: In psychology, any **response** that can be elicited automatically by the presentation of a certain **stimulus** without any training or learning (i.e., a reflex). The term is often associated with **classical conditioning.** In Ivan Pavlov's (1849–1936) classic experiment, a dog naturally salivated (unconditioned response) when presented with meat powder (unconditioned response). Pavlov then paired the presentation of the meat powder with the presentation of a tone **(neutral stimulus),** even when it was presented without the meat powder. The unconditioned response was the natural response used as a basis for conditioning.

Unconditioned Stimulus: A term used in **classical conditioning** for any **stimulus** that elicits a particular **response** automatically, without training or learning. For example, the cold air is an unconditioned stimulus that causes the body to shiver (unconditioned response). In **Ivan Pavlov's (1849–1936)** classic experiment, a dog naturally salivated (**unconditioned response)** when presented with meat powder (unconditioned stimulus). Pavlov then paired the presentation of meat powder with the presentation of a tone (**neutral stimulus**). Over time, the dog learned to salivate (**conditioned response**) to the tone (**conditioned stimulus**), even when it was presented without the meat powder. That is, the tone had become a conditioned stimulus.

Unconscious Motives: Unconscious needs or desires that determine an individual's behavior, even though the individual is either completely unaware of them or is aware of them only in some distorted or indirect form. For example, students sometimes have a desire to disrupt class because of an unconscious need for attention. In reality, the separation between conscious and unconscious motives is not always clear, and many motives have both conscious and unconscious aspects.

Unconscious Processes: Psychological processes guided by unconscious motives that affect behavior such as **fear of failure**, or physiological processes that occur unconsciously or automatically, such as circulation and metabolism. *See* Unconscious Motive

Underachievers: Individuals who have the potential and capability to perform specific tasks at a certain level, yet cannot or do not perform at this level for some reason. Research shows that **achievement** and **motivation** are closely linked and that underachievers tend to possess qualities or traits that diminish or eliminate motivation for success. Such traits include the unwillingness or the inability to work hard or to focus on the task at hand. *See* Overachievers

Unique Trait: In trait theory, a trait that exists in only one individual. Gordon Allport (1897-1967) believed, in the strictest sense, that all traits are unique. *See* Common Trait; Trait Theory; Cardinal Traits; Central Traits

Univariate Statistics: In research, statistics appropriate in **experimental designs** where researchers are analyzing only one **dependent variable**. Several **univariate tests** are commonly used in music education research. These include: 1) **Chi-Square (x^2),** which compares observed verses expected outcomes; 2) *t*-tests, which allow comparisons of means between two groups or between the same group in pretest/posttest designs; and 3) Analysis of Variance (ANOVA), which is used when assessing more than two levels of an **independent variable** and can be extended to account for more than one independent variable simultaneously. There are also multivariate forms of ANOVA. *See* Analysis of Variance (ANOVA)

Univariate Tests: *See* Univariate Statistics

Universal Education/Schooling: In general, the process of providing all citizens with a free education to promote the common good of society. The concept of universal education has been around for centuries in various forms; however, in the United States, the first universal tax-supported system of free schools developed in the mid-1800s, and were known as **common schools**. The concept of universal education is also known as the Jeffersonian ideal, because it was Thomas Jefferson (1743–1826) who envisioned an America in which every person had equal access to a free public education. The general belief was that universal education would enable every individual to find a job and to become a productive member of society. The creation of common schools was a step toward universal education, because they were intended to serve all of the children in a given area. Common schools offered instruction in reading, writing, and arithmetic to children of all social classes. **Horace Mann (1796–1859)** served as the secretary to the Massachusetts State Board of Education from 1837 to 1848 and was a well-known proponent of the universal education concept. He believed that tax support for universal education was essential for improving educational opportunities and that the welfare of American society was directly dependent upon how well-educated its citizens were. The ideas of Jefferson and Mann helped pave the way for universal education and public schools as we know them today.

University/College Supervisors: Individuals at the university or college level who arrange and supervise **student teaching** experiences. University/college supervisors are responsible for tracking the progress of student teachers through systematic observations and discussions with student teachers and **cooperating teachers**.

Unobtrusive Measure: In research, a measure of behavior that is made without the subject's awareness.

UPDATE: Applications of Research in Music Education: A publication of the **Music Educators National Conference (MENC)** that focuses on practical applications of research in general music, choral music, and instrumental music. UPDATE also contains information on special topics in music education, and is published twice per year. UPDATE was established in 1982 by Charles Elliott at the University of South Carolina.

Valid: In education, the general idea that a discipline is worthy of formal study or inclusion in **curricula**. Within any particular discipline, content is **valid** if it is deemed to be a legitimate or significant part of that discipline. For example, learning musical notation, **solfege**, or **counting systems** are valid areas of study in music education. In research, a test or measure is considered valid if it measures what it is supposed to measure. *See* Validity

Validity: Generally, the extent to which test instruments measure what they are supposed to measure (content validity). Other types of validity include: 1) criterion-related validity (also referred to as concurrent validity), which refers to whether one test relates to another test that has already produced valid results; 2) construct validity, which is evaluated by investigating what qualities a test measures or by determining the degree to which certain explanatory concepts or constructs account for performance on the test; 3) face validity, which refers to whether something "looks good"; 4) predictive validity, which is the degree to which the predictions made by a test are confirmed by the later behavior of the subjects tested in an experiment; 5) statistical conclusion validity, which addresses the possibility that erroneous conclusions may be the result of a poor statistical procedure or a procedure done with too few subjects; 6) internal validity, which refers to whether the variance is caused by the treatment or due to faulty study design; and 7) external validity, which refers to the approximate validity with which conclusions are drawn about the generalizability of a causal relationship to and across populations of persons, settings, and times.

Value: In general, a theoretical construct used to describe how much or how little personal worth something has. Value can be positive or negative, and it often determines how hard an individual is willing to work for something. Value has also been identified as a person **variable**. In this context, value usually refers to an individual's subjective likes and dislikes. In cognitive motivation theory, value is one of two overriding determinants of behavior, the other being expectancy. This theory supposes that when an individual expects or anticipates something of value, value becomes **positive incentive** motivation. That is, because an individual values something, they will work to obtain it. *See* Cognitive Motivation Theory; Expectancy

Variability: In statistics, the manner in which scores are dispersed around some central value, such as the **mean**. *See* Range; Standard Deviation (s or sd); Variance (s²)

Variable: In psychology, a characteristic that varies from one individual or group to the next according to the situation or context. In **experimental research**, the term **variable** is commonly used to describe the measured and controlled conditions in an experimental study, called the dependent and independent variables, respectively. Typically, the independent variable is actively controlled or manipulated in some way by the experimenter and is the causal half of the cause-and-effect relationship. The dependent variable is a measure of the subject's response and is the effect half of the cause-and-effect relationship. *See* Person Variables; Control Variable; Dependent Variable; Independent Variable

Variable Interval Reinforcement Schedule: A schedule of reinforcement that involves providing **reinforcement** after a certain period of time has lapsed. This period of time varies randomly within a specified range. For example, reinforcement may be given after thirty seconds, ninety seconds, ten seconds, and then seventy-five seconds. In all schedules of reinforcement, the term **variable** refers to "changing" and the term interval refers to "time." Research has shown that the variable interval reinforcement schedule typically produces low rates of responding. *See* Schedules of Reinforcement

Variable Ratio Reinforcement Schedule: A common schedule of reinforcement that involves providing **reinforcement** after a variable number of unreinforced responses. The number of unreinforced responses between reinforcements varies randomly. For example, reinforcement may be given after two responses, eight responses, four responses, and ten responses. In all schedules of reinforcement, the term **variable** refers to "changing" and the term interval refers to "time." For example, playing a slot machine is based on a variable ratio reinforcement schedule in that they "pay off" after a variable number of attempts. *See* Schedules of Reinforcement

Variance (s²): In research, the sum of the squared deviations from the **mean**, divided by N (n) – 1. **Variance** is a way of seeing how scores deviate or vary in a **distribution**. *See* Standard Deviation (s or sd)

Velar: In singing, the consonants formed by arching the back part of the tongue and pressing it against the **velum** or **soft palate**. These consonant sounds include: *k*, *g*, and *ng*.

Verbal Association Level of Discrimination Learning, Gordon: *See* Skill Learning Sequence, Gordon

Verbal/Linguistic Code: In memory, a technique in which concrete objects are recoded or associated with words to facilitate **storage** and **retrieval** of information in **long-term memory (LTM)**. People learn to associate things with the words we attach to them. For example, the word saxophone is associated with a particular musical instrument, while the word pig is associated with an animal. These language associations are learned, and a child just learning to speak could be taught that a "saxophone" is really a "pig" and think nothing of it. In short, verbal codes relate to language and semantics, and they enable people to store an almost infinite amount of information in long-term memory. *See* Memory

Verbal Imagery: Mental images evoked by words. Verbal images are **subjective**; they vary from person to person. Verbal images can be visual or conceptual. Visual images evoked by verbal stimuli are usually associated with a particular event in an individual's past experiences or memories. Conceptual images evoked by verbal stimuli contain an individual's subjective mental representations, thoughts, or ideas based on one's experiences. Musicians utilize verbal imagery regularly. For example, describing a clarinet tone that is bright, pinched, and thin would bring to mind a particular and likely unpleasant clarinet tone quality to most musicians. *See* Imagery

Vestibular Sense: A sense that operates in addition to the five senses: touch, taste, smell, sight, and hearing. Vestibular sense allows individuals to maintain a sense of balance or equilibrium despite changes in body position. Gymnasts and dancers have a highly developed vestibular sense. Strictly speaking, the vestibular sense enables individuals to maintain balance without using the five classical senses.

Vicarious Learning: Learning that occurs by observing the behaviors of others and noting the consequences of those behaviors. Vicarious learning is typically associated with learning that occurs in informal settings as opposed to learning that occurs in structured environments. Vicarious learning is often associated with things that individuals "pick up" during the course of everyday life.

Vision 2020, MENC: *See* Housewright Symposium

Visual Discrimination: The act of distinguishing one visual stimulus from another. Visual discrimination enables an individual to distinguish an oboe from a clarinet or one breed of dog from another. Visual discrimination is a common component in **stage theories** of **child development**. *See* Aural Discrimination

Visual Imagery: A mental picture or conception of something that is not physically present. That is, visual images occur exclusively within the brain. In music, researchers have investigated the visual images that music elicits under a variety of conditions. Typically, these images are expressed as colors (chromesthesia), pictures, or words. *See* Chromesthesia

Vocal Interviewing: In choral music education, the process of evaluating students' voices primarily to determine the part (soprano, alto, tenor, or bass) each student will most easily and naturally sing.

Vocational-Technical Schools: Schools that provide students with the education and training necessary to enter specific trades or careers following graduation. Vocational-technical schools offer a wide-range of programs, including automotive repair, building construction, child care, cosmetology, data processing, drafting, electronics, food production, graphic and commercial arts, horticulture, law enforcement, management, masonry, and a variety of health-related fields. These schools integrate academic course work with technical training and are most commonly available to students after they graduate from high school or pass a high school equivalency test (GED); however, most high schools offer vocational and technical programs.

Voluntary National Tests (VNTs): Proposed voluntary assessment tests intended to inform students, parents, and teachers about students' performances in fourth-grade reading and eighth-grade mathematics relative to the standards of the **National Assessment of Educational Progress (NAEP)** and the Third International Mathematics and Science Study (TIMSS). The VNTs were suggested by President Bill Clinton in his January 1997 State of the Union Address. The Clinton administration and other proponents of VNTs believed that testing students in two critical subjects at critical times in the education process would be beneficial in at least two important ways. First, parents and educators would know if their children were meeting **national standards**, and communities would know if their schools were meeting the standards. Second, this knowledge could be used as a basis for improving instruction and raising standards. Critics have identified several potential problems with VNTs. First, some believe that the tests would lead to increased federal control over educational programs traditionally controlled by state and local entities. Second, many believe that such tests are potentially damaging to disadvantaged and **minority** students if test scores are linked to high-stakes consequences. Third, opponents believe that the tests are unnecessary and would not have a positive effect on student performance. In addition, the fact that the federal government could not regulate how states and local entities would utilize the test results is also problematic. *See* **High Stakes Tests**

Volunteer Bias: In research, the tendency for subjects who volunteer for a study or research project to affect the outcome because of bias or preconceived ideas about the study or project. Volunteer bias is a threat to validity that can be avoided by using a representative sample of randomly selected subjects. *See* **Validity**

Voucher: An allotment of government money provided to parents in the form of scrip or coupons to help pay for their child's education. Vouchers enable parents to send children to the schools of their choice, including **private** and **parochial schools**, as long as these schools meet minimum governmental standards. Although the idea of using vouchers in education has been around since the 1950s, it was not until the 1990s that some states began issuing vouchers. Proponents believe that the voucher system provides parents with freedom of **school choice** and positively impacts the quality of schools. Opponents argue that vouchers encourage many parents to remove their children from public schools. This population shift can result in a public school system comprised mainly of low-income children who, for a variety of reasons, cannot take advantage of the voucher system, creating a wider gap between the quality of instruction offered at various schools.

Vygotsky, Lev Semyonovich (1896-1934): An eminent Soviet psychologist well known for his views concerning the influence of society and culture on development. Vygotsky was educated at the University of Moscow, where he studied philosophy and linguistics. Vygotsky's views were opposed to those of **Jean Piaget (1896–1980)**. Specifically, while Piaget believed that development could be explained in a series of **cognitive** growth stages characterized by a child's abilities to "do" something, Vygotsky believed that social and cultural factors and the interaction between the child and other, more experienced individuals influenced a child's development significantly. Vygotsky also believed that instead of focusing on what a child could do now, it would be better to focus on how to lead a child to learn new things. According to Vygotsky, learning occurs best within a cooperative or collaborative context in which a more experienced person guides learning. Vygotsky worked at Moscow's Institute of Psychology from 1924 until 1934, when he died of tuberculosis. His best known works include *Thought and Language* (1934) and *Mind in Society: The development of higher psychological processes* (1978, revised).

Wait Time: In education, the amount of time that a student is given to answer a question after it has been asked. Studies have shown that many teachers wait about one second before taking further action. This action can include giving the student clues, rephrasing the question, calling on other students to respond, or answering the question themselves. Other studies have shown that when the wait time is extended to between three and five seconds, students are more likely to provide longer and more appropriate answers. In addition, a longer wait time increases the number of student-initiated questions; however, wait time should be adjusted according to the activity. For example, shorter wait times may be appropriate for activities involving drill, short-answer, or review activities (**lower-level questions**), while longer wait times may be more appropriate for activities that involve detailed responses or the demonstration of conceptual understanding (**higher-level questions**).

Waldorf Schools: Alternative schools that emphasize creative play rather than the structured acquisition of specific learning skills. Waldorf Schools were developed based on the research of Rudolf Steiner (1861–1925). These schools encourage young children, typically of elementary school age, to learn through **imitation** and by engaging their senses. Supporters of Waldorf schools believe that engaging in creative play helps develop healthier and more vital children. They also believe that forcing children to focus on intellectual demands robs them of their health and vitality and actually weakens their powers of judgment and practical intelligence later in life. There are more than one hundred Waldorf Schools in North America. *See* **Alternative Schools**

Watkins-Farnum Performance Scale (WFPS): The most widely known test of musical performance achievement. Written by John Watkins and Stephen Farnum in 1954, the WFPS is most often used to assess **sight-reading** skills at the secondary school level. Two forms of the WFPS are available, A and B. The forms have a **reliability** of .953. Each form contains fourteen melodies; each melody is written at a specific level of difficulty. Each new melody is more difficult than the preceding one. Students are asked to sight read each melody until they can no longer proceed without making errors in every measure of any particular exercise. A standardized **measuring instrument** is used to assess students' errors and for computing test scores.

Watson, John B. (1878-1958): The founder of **behaviorism**, Watson attended Furman University at age sixteen and received a Ph.D. in psychology in 1903. At one time, Watson was psychology's most vocal critic of subjectivism, mentalism, and **introspection**. Watson was a strong believer in the importance of environmental factors as opposed to hereditary factors in **shaping** virtually all human behavior. He believed that learning resulted from an accumulation of **stimulus-response** connections, or what he called habits. Watson was a strong advocate of **Ivan Pavlov's (1848–1936) classical conditioning** and utilized this method in his study of the acquisition of fear. *See* **Behavioral Psychology/Behaviorism**

Waveform: Generally used synonymously with **waves**, any of the variety of visual or graphic representations or forms that waves produce on electronic equipment. The most common waveforms are: 1) **sine waves**, which contain only one **partial**; 2) **square waves**, which contain only odd partials of relative **amplitudes** in phase; and 3) **sawtooth waves**, which contain all

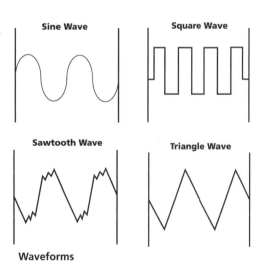

Waveforms

partials, 1, 2, 3, 4, etc., of relative amplitudes in phase; and **triangle waves**, in which the second partial has three times the **frequency** and one-ninth the amplitude of the **fundamental**, the third partial has five times the frequency and one twenty-fifth the amplitude of the fundamental, and so on.

Wavelength: In acoustics, a physical measure of a tone's **period**. Wavelength is the distance between two equivalent points in adjacent cycles of the **wave**. The length of the period corresponds to the wavelength. In other words, a tone that has a short period will have a short wavelength, and a tone that has a long period will have a long wavelength.

Waves: **Periodic vibrations** or disturbances produced by a vibrating body. When the vibration of the waves travels in the direction of the disturbance, the waves are longitudinal. For example, the waves produced by brass instruments are longitudinal, because the vibrations travel through the instrument in the same direction as the vibrating source. When the vibration of the waves travels perpendicular to the direction of the disturbance, the waves are transverse. For example, when string players draw the bow across a string at a ninety-degree angle (perpendicular), transverse waves are created. An understanding of longitudinal waves is more important for musical purposes because most musical instruments produce longitudinal waves. The term waves is also used synonymously with **waveform** to refer to any of the variety of graphic representations or forms that waves produce on electronic equipment.

Wechsler Intelligence Scales: Individual **intelligence tests** developed by **David Wechsler (1896–1981)**. Wechsler developed the Wechsler Adult Intelligence Scale/Revised (WAIS; WAIS-R), the Wechsler Intelligence Scale for Children/Revised (WISC; WISC-R), and the Wechsler Preschool and Primary Scale of Intelligence/Revised (WPPSI; WPPSI-R). These tests are administered by trained examiners to one individual at a time. Each test yields three scores: 1) verbal IQ, 2) performance IQ, and 3) full-scale IQ. Wechsler believed that many intelligence tests placed too much emphasis on verbal items. As a result, he included a performance section in his tests that measures an individual's visual motor abilities.

Wechsler Adult Intelligence Scale/Revised (WAIS; WAIS-R): An **intelligence test** developed for adults by **David Wechsler (1896–1981)** in 1955. The test was revised in 1981 and is now called the WAIS-R (revised). WAIS is administered by trained examiners on an individual basis and takes approximately one hour to complete. Wechsler developed this and other intelligence tests for children in response to **Alfred Binet's (1857–1911)** intelligence tests that relied heavily on verbal items. The Wechsler tests produce three scores: 1) a verbal score, 2) a performance score, and 3) a full-range score. On the WAIS-R, verbal **intelligence quotient (IQ)** is determined by the following six tests: 1) information, 2) comprehension, 3) arithmetic, 4) digit span, 5) similarities, and 6) vocabulary. Performance IQ on the WAIS-R is determined by the following five tests: 1) picture arrangement, 2) picture completion, 3) block design, 4) digit symbol, and 5) object assembly. Wechsler's tests have been used to evaluate personality characteristics as well as IQ. Such personality characteristics include 1) **defense mechanisms**, 2) ability to cope with stress, and 3) the general mode of handling life's situations.

Wechsler Intelligence Scale for Children/Revised (WISC; WISC-R): An intelligence scale developed for children ages six to sixteen by **David Wechsler (1896–1981)** in 1949. A new version was introduced in 1974 for children ages five to fifteen and is now called the WISC-R (revised). The test is administered by a trained examiner on an individual basis and takes approximately one hour to complete. The WISC and WISC-R have a **mean intelligence quotient (IQ)** score of 100 and the **standard deviation** is 15. The IQ range on the WISC-R is from 40 to 160.

Wechsler Preschool and Primary Scale of Intelligence/ Revised (WPPSI; WPPSI-R): An intelligence scale developed for children ages 4 – 6.5 and one half years by **David Wechsler (1896–1981)** in 1963. The test was first published in 1967 and revised in 1989. The age range for the WPPSI-R is 3 – 7.3 years. It is a standardized measure of intellectual abilities in young children. The test is administered by a trained examiner on an individual basis and takes approximately one hour to complete.

Wechsler, David (1896-1981): An eminent psychologist in the area of intelligence testing and test construction. Wechsler studied at City College of New York and Columbia, earning his masters degree in 1917 and his Ph.D. in 1925. Wechsler is most well known for devising a series of individual **intelligence quotient (IQ)** tests. These include the Wechsler Adult Intelligence Scale (WAIS; WAIS-R), the Wechsler Intelligence Scale for Children (WISC; WISC-R), and the Wechsler Preschool and Primary Scale of Intelligence (WPPSI). Wechsler defined **intelligence** as "the global capacity of an individual to think rationally, to act purposefully, and deal effectively with his environment." All of the Wechsler tests report three separate scores including a verbal IQ, a performance IQ, and a full-scale IQ.

Wertheimer, Max (1880-1943): Founder of the gestalt school of psychology in the early 1900s, Wertheimer received a Ph.D. from the University of Würzburg in 1904. Wertheimer criticized the **structuralists** and their insistence that all psychological phenomena should be analyzed into the smallest possible parts. He felt that the whole was more than merely the sum of its parts. To Wertheimer, in order to understand psychological phenomena, one had to study all of the parts together in their particular gestalt. Wertheimer's first studies were in the area of **perception**. Later he became interested in education and the principles of **learning**. He insisted that educators should teach for understanding rather than relying on repetition and **rote learning**. *See* Gestalt Psychology

Whole Learning: An approach to **learning** that involves first presenting an overview of all material and of the general **concepts** to be learned before studying more specific parts in greater detail. Whole learning is based on the idea that looking at the "whole" first enables learners to understand the detail better because they have a conceptual **framework** for reference. The whole learning approach is in contrast to the part learning approach where material is first learned in small chunks and later pieced together into a whole. *See* Whole-part Controversy

Whole-part Controversy: In education, the debate regarding whether instruction should be presented in a holistic manner or in a series of separate steps or parts that lead to the whole. The whole-part controversy is also referred to as general-to-specific or specific-to-general, because these terms are reflective of the teaching approach used. Educators have debated this issue for centuries, and studies can be found to support both views. In reality, most educators use a combination of both approaches.

Wilks' Lambda, Bartlett's: In research, the most common statistical test employed in research designs involving canonical analysis and Multivariate Analysis of Variance (MANOVA). Wilks' Lambda is used to determine if differences exist among the groups on multiple **dependent variables**. *See* Multivariate Analysis of Variance (MANOVA)

Wing Standardized Tests of Musical Intelligence: Also referred to as the Wing Musical Aptitude Test, a battery of seven tests designed to measure music **aptitude** and preference. The test was initially published in 1939 with revisions in 1957, 1960, and 1961. The seven tests include:

1) analysis of chords, 2) **pitch discrimination**, 3) pitch memory, 4) rhythmic accent, 5) harmony, 6) **intensity** (loudness), and 7) phrasing. The first three tests measure music aptitude, while the other four measure music preferences. The tests were designed to identify children who were musically talented and who would be well suited for instrumental performance at the secondary level. The test battery takes approximately sixty minutes to complete.

Woods Hole Conference: A historically important conference held at Woods Hole on Cape Cod in 1959 whose primary purpose was to identify the problems with science education in primary and secondary schools and to recommend solutions to these problems. The original idea behind the Woods Hole Conference came from the Education Committee of the National Academy of Sciences, which had been examining ways to improve science instruction in the schools. The conference was supported by several other entities including the U.S. Office of Education, the Air Force, and the RAND Corporation.

Approximately thirty-five people, including scientists, scholars, physicists, biologists, mathematicians, historians, psychologists, and educators attended the ten-day conference. It was one of the first times that such a widely representative group had met to discuss the future of American education. The topics of discussion included: 1) the learning process and its relevance to education; 2) current conceptions of teaching and learning; 3) curricular content; 4) curricular design; 5) the sequence and timing of instruction and learning; 6) teaching methods; and 7) the structure of subjects.

Jerome Bruner (b. 1915), was the Director of the Woods Hole Conference. Bruner's book entitled *The Process of Education* is his account of what took place during the conference. To this day, it remains one of the most influential books in education. According to Bruner, four themes emerged from the conference: 1) the role of structure in learning and how it may be central in teaching; 2) the **readiness** for learning; 3) the nature of **intuition**, which is the intellectual technique of arriving at plausible but tentative formulations without going through the analytic steps; and 4) the desire to learn and the ways in which learning may be stimulated. These themes are discussed in detail in *The Process of Education*.

The timing of the Woods Hole Conference was ideal because following the Soviet launch in 1957 of *Sputnik I*, the government had recommitted itself to assuring excellence in education. As a result, unprecedented amounts of resources were poured into educational programs over the next decade. Although the main thrust was on improving science and technology, the arts did receive some support during this time. Many educators and scientists at the Woods Hole Conference recognized the need for a balanced **curriculum** that included music and the other arts. This recognition was an important step in affirming the rightful place of music education in public school curricula. Of particular importance, was the fact that music was recognized as being an important part of curricula by such a distinguished group of non-music educators at one of the most influential conferences in history. *See* **Jerome Bruner (b. 1915)**

Word-association Experiment: An experiment designed for studying associative processes in which a **subject** responds to a **stimulus** word by saying the first word that comes to mind as quickly as possible. *See* **Pair-associate Learning**

Working Backwards: A heuristic technique that begins with the desired result or outcome and involves progressing backwards to learn or discover the initial information. For example, a student may know the answer to a mathematical equation without knowing how he or she arrived at the answer. Working backwards may help the student confirm the accuracy of the answer or to develop a deeper understanding of the problem and of the process leading to its solution. *See* **Heuristic/Heuristic Method**

Working Memory: *See* **Short-term Memory (STM)**

Working Through: In psychoanalysis, the process of helping people discover the emotional roots of their problems or conflicts and then re-educating them by letting them face the same conflicts repeatedly in a controlled environment. The general idea of working through is that through repeated exposure to problems or conflicts, individuals can learn to understand the underlying reasons for the problems or conflicts and respond and react in more appropriate ways. Once individuals learn to master these problems or conflicts in a controlled environment, they can **transfer** this mastery to real-life situations. *See* **Psychoanalysis/ Psychoanalytic Method; Freud, Sigmund (1856-1939)**

Wundt, Wilhelm (1832-1920): A German psychologist and founder of the structuralist school of **psychology**, Wundt was educated in Europe and received his M.D. from the University of Heidelberg in 1856. Wundt created the world's first laboratory of psychology at the University of Leipzig in 1879. He believed that psychology should be devoted to the study of the basic elements that make up conscious experience. Wundt is best known for developing a technique called **introspection**, which involves looking within oneself to discover these basic elements. Wundt trained subjects to use introspection, which enabled him to study these elements. These subjects looked within themselves and reported all of their most fleeting and minute thoughts, feelings, and sensations. Wundt's goal was to take psychology out of the field of philosophy and give it a sense of scientific respectability. *See* **Introspection**

Yale Seminar on Music Education (1963): A federally funded arts education seminar held in New Haven, Connecticut, in 1963 to discuss development in the arts, including music education. The thirty-one conference participants included professors, scholars, and only a few music educators. Claude V. Palisca, professor of music at Yale, was the seminar director.

The Yale Seminar was driven by the National Science Foundation (NSF), not by arts organizations. The NSF and science educators felt that the interests of science were not best served by unbalanced **curricula** overloaded with science courses. They also recognized the importance of the arts and music to the students' total educational experience, and they wanted to improve the instruction in these areas.

The participants outlined six major criticisms of the musical material being used in music education programs. The central theme in these criticisms was that the quality of the music used in education was poor. The criticisms and recommendations were outlined by Michael Mark in his book entitled *Contemporary Music Education* (1996) on page 44. The following criticisms were made regarding musical material available for education: 1) It is of appalling quality, representing little of the heritage of significant music; 2) It is constricted in scope. Even the classics of Western music—such as the great works of Bach, Mozart, Beethoven, do not occupy the central place they should in singing, playing, and listening. Non-Western music, early Western music, and certain forms of jazz, popular, and folk music have been almost altogether neglected; 3) It stunts the growth of musical feeling because it is so often not sufficiently interesting to enchant or involve a child to whom it is presumed to be accessible. Children's potentials are constantly underestimated; 4) It is corrupted by arrangements, touched-up editions, erroneous transcriptions, and tasteless parodies to such an extent that authentic work is rare. A whole range of songbook arrangements, weak derivative semi-popular children's pieces, and a variety of "educational" recordings containing music of similar value and type, are to be strongly condemned as "pseudo-music." The more often artificial music is taught to children, the more often they are invited to hate it. There is no reason or need to use artificial or pseudo-music in any of its forms; 5) Songs are chosen and graded more on the basis of the limited technical skills of classroom teachers than the needs of children or the ultimate goals of improved hearing and listening skills. This is one of the causes of the proliferation of feeble piano and autoharp accompaniments and of "singalong" recordings; and 6) A major fault of the repertoire of vocal music stems from the desire to appeal to the lowest common denominator and to offend the least possible number. More attention is often paid to the subject matter of the text than the quality of the music.

In addition to the criticisms regarding the quality of music, the conference participants believed that music teachers spent too much time on performance-related activities and not enough time on development musical understanding. According to Mark, in order to counteract their criticisms of the materials used in music education and of the unbalanced emphasis on performance drill in school ensembles, the following recommendations were made: 1) The basic goal of the K-12 music curriculum should be musicality through performance, movement, musical creativity, ear training, and listening; 2) School music repertoire should be broadened to include the best Western and non-Western music of all periods; 3) More emphasis should be placed on music that is authentic and not artificial in concept; 4) An enlarged repertoire should be made available in useful formats (kits or packages); 5) Sequential listening experiences need to be developed for elementary and junior high school students, and high school students should take music literature courses that require intensive experiences with representative works; 6) Performance activities should include ensembles such as concert bands, orchestras, and choirs for which an authentic and varied repertoire has been developed; 7) Marching and stage bands should be offered to encourage students to participate in other ensembles; 8) Small ensembles are specially important because they require more intense participation and are relevant to future adult musical activities; 9) Keyboard instruction should be available free of charge and accompanied by basic musicianship and theory courses; 10) Advanced theory and literature courses should be available to students who can benefit from them; 11) The increasing disparity between professional and school music should be reduced by bringing musicians, composers, and scholars into the schools; 12) Students should be given insights into how professionals think and work, and professionals should be given opportunities to help develop musicality in young people; 13) School programs should take advantage of professional and highly competent amateur musicians who might serve in various capacities and community-centered ensembles that can lend support and assistance to school programs; 14) Opportunities for advanced music study should be made available to all talented students throughout the country; and 15) Opportunities for advanced music study in metropolitan centers should be made available to all talented students throughout the country.

The Yale Seminar did not lead to wholesale changes in music education for two main reasons. First, for the most part the participants were not music educators, and, second, the seminar had too little representation from the **Music Educators National Conference (MENC)**. One outcome of the Yale Seminar was the Juilliard Repertory Project, a project designed improve the quality of literature used in music education programs. *See* **Juilliard Repertory Project**

Yankee Tunesmiths: A group of New England composers who wrote in a "new" style that was uniquely American. Yankee tunesmiths significantly influenced American music and music education, and many were singing masters in addition to being composers. Most of these composers were not educated musicians and actually taught music as a secondary profession or as an **avocation**. The music of the Yankee tunesmiths was harmonically simple and rhythmically strong. Composers of this school include: **William Billings (1746–1800)**, Andrew Law (1748–1821), Supply Belcher (1751–1836), Daniel Read (1757–1836), and Oliver Holden (1765–1844).

Year-round School: Schools that offer traditional **curricular** instruction in a year-round format instead of the traditional nine-month format. Some year-round schools operate on a single-track scheduling system while others operate on an overlapping multi-track system. In a single-track system, all students get the same scheduled breaks, usually two to three weeks four or fives times a year. In a multi-track system, students in the same school have different break schedules, so that the school building is being used for instruction throughout the entire year. Proponents of year-round schools indicate that they are cost effective, while opponents indicate that keeping schools in session during the summer months actually costs more. The precise effects of year-round schools on **academic achievement** have not been determined.

Young Composer's Project: One of the many new programs that originated during a period of intense educational change in America. When the Soviet Union launched *Sputnik I* in 1957, demonstrating its superiority in space technology, America's reaction was to reevaluate public school education. Conferences, seminars, and symposia were held throughout the nation to find ways to improve education. In addition, the amount of money spent on public education increased dramatically. As a result, numerous educational programs or projects were developed in all areas of education in the decade following the launching of *Sputnik I*. The Young Composer's Project was one of these programs. Funded by the **Ford Foundation** and founded in 1959, the Young Composer's Project was a union between composers and public school music programs. Proposed by Norman Dello Joio (b. 1913), the project placed young composers, under age thirty-five, in public school systems serving as composers-in-residence. These composers were to write music for the schools' performing ensembles, expose students and teachers to new music, and expand the repertoire. It was believed that music teachers and students would embrace contemporary music as they learned to understand it. Thirty-one composers participated in the project from 1959 to 1962. The initial success of the program resulted in additional proposals from the **Music Educators National Conference (MENC)**. In 1962, the Ford Foundation awarded MENC a $1.38 million grant. With that grant, MENC initiated the Contemporary Music Project for Creativity in Music Education (CMP). The Young Composer's Project was continued under the title Composers in Public Schools. *See* **Contemporary Music Project (CMP)**

Zz

z-Score: In statistics, a number that results from the transformation of a raw score into units of **standard deviation (*s* or *sd*)**, equal to the difference between the raw score and **mean** divided by the standard deviation. The z-score is measured in standard deviation units and indicates where a score lies in terms of its distance above or below the mean. *See* **Standard Score**

Zeigarnik Effect: In psychology, the idea that individuals are more apt to remember unfinished **tasks** than completed tasks. Memory is believed to be enhanced by the thought that a job has been left unfinished. The Zeigarnik Effect is named after Bluma Zeigarnik (1900–1988), a Russian psychologist who first described the effect in 1927. She conducted experiments after observing the behaviors of restaurant wait staff. Waiters and waitresses seemed to be able to remember large numbers of food orders, but could not seem to remember to refresh coffee after the meals had been served.

Zero-based Budgeting: A budgeting process in which all expenditures are required to be justified each fiscal year. Schools must justify their money requests for each aspect of the **budget** every year; no assumed carryover is in effect from one year to the next. Zero-based budgeting is in contrast to the more traditional practice of basing the current year's budget on the previous year's budget with slight modifications.

Zero-exclusion Principle: In education, a fundamental premise of the Individuals with Disabilities Education Act (IDEA) of 1990 stating that all students must receive a **"free and appropriate public education" (FAPE)** regardless of the nature or extent of any **disability** the student may have. The general idea is that no student with a disability can be rejected for educational services regardless of the nature, type, or extent of the disability. *See* Individuals with Disabilities Education Act (IDEA)

Zone of Proximal Development: A term used by Lev Semyonovich Vygotsky (1896–1934) to describe the difference between the potential development and the actual development of a child. Potential development is that which would occur without collaboration or assistance, while actual development occurs with the help of an adult or more capable peer.

Textbooks and Reference Books by Subject Area

Music Education

Abeles, H., C. Hoffer, and R. Klotman. (1994). *Foundations of music education* (2d ed.). New York: Schirmer.

Abramson, R., L. Choksy, A. Gillespie, and D. Woods. (1985). *Teaching music in the twentieth century*. Englewood Cliffs, NJ: Prentice-Hall.

Anderson, W. M., Jr., and P. S. Campbell. (1989). *Multicultural perspectives in music education*. Reston, VA: Music Educators National Conference.

Anderson, W. and J. Lawrence. (2001). *Integrating music into the elementary classroom* (5th ed.). Belmont, CA: Wadsworth.

Atterbury, B. (1990). *Mainstreaming exceptional learners in music*. Englewood Cliffs, NJ: Prentice Hall.

Birkenshaw-Fleming, L. (1993). *Music for all: Teaching music to people with special needs*. Toronto, ON: Thompson Music.

Boardman, E. (Ed.). (1989). *Dimensions of musical thinking*. Reston, VA: Music Educators National Conference.

Campbell, P. and C. Scott-Kassner. (1995). *Music in childhood*. New York: Simon and Schuster Macmillan.

Carder, P. (1990). *The eclectic curriculum in American music education*. Reston, VA: Music Educators National Conference.

Choksy, L. (1988). *The Kodaly method* (2d ed.). Englewood Cliffs, NJ: Prentice-Hall.

Choksy, L., R. M. Abramson, A. E. Gillespie, and D. Woods. (1986). *Teaching music in the twentieth century*. Englewood Cliffs, NJ: Prentice Hall.

Colwell, R. J. (1992). *The teaching of instrumental music*. Englewood Cliffs, NJ: Prentice Hall.

Colwell, R. J. (Ed.). (1991). *Basic concepts in music education, II*. Niwot: University Press of Colorado.

Cooksey, J. (1992). *Working with the adolescent voice.* St. Louis, MO: Concordia.

Cooper, G. and L. B. Meyer. (1961). *The rhythmic structure of music.* Chicago: University of Chicago Press.

Creston, P. (1961). *Principles of rhythm.* New York: Franco Colombo.

Davies, J. B. (1978). *The psychology of music.* Stanford: Stanford University Press.

Ernst, K. and C. Gary. (Eds.) (1965). *Music in general education.* Washington, D.C.: Music Educators National Conference.

Floyd, M. (1996). *World musics in education.* Brookfield, VT: Ashgate Publishing.

Gordon, E. (1989). *Learning Sequences in Music: Skills, Content, and Patterns.* Chicago, IL: GIA Publications, Inc.

Graham, R. and A. Beer. (1980). *Teaching music to the exceptional child.* Englewood Cliffs, NJ: Prentice-Hall.

Guidelines for Orff-Schulwerk Training Courses Levels, I, II, III (1980). Cleveland, OH: American Orff-Schulwerk Association.

Hodges, D. A. (Ed.) (1980). *Handbook of music psychology.* Lawrence, Kansas: National Association for Music Therapy.

Hoffer, C. (1993). *Introduction to music education.* Belmont, CA: Wadsworth.

Jaques-Dalcroze, E. (1976). *Rhythm, music, and education.* Trans. H. F. Rubenstein. New York: Arno Press.

Jorgensen, E. R. (1997). *In search of music education.* Urbana: University of Illinois Press.

Kaplan, M. (1990). *The arts: a social perspective.* Rutherford, NJ: Fairleigh Dickinson University Press.

Kohut, D. L. (1985). *Musical performance.* Englewood Cliffs: Prentice-Hall.

Laban, R. (1971). *Mastery of movement.* London: MacDonald and Evans.

Leonhard, C. and R. House. (1972). *Foundations and principles of music education* (2d ed.). New York: McGraw-Hill.

Machlis, J. (1977). *The enjoyment of music: An introduction to perceptive listening.* New York: W. W. Norton.

Madsen, C. (Ed.). (2000). *Vision 2020.* Reston, VA: MENC.

Madsen, C. H. and C. K. Madsen. (1974). *Teaching/Discipline: a positive approach for educational development* (2d ed.). Boston, MA: Allyn & Bacon.

Mark, M. L. (1986). *Contemporary music education.* New York: Schirmer Books.

Merrion, M. (Ed.). (1989). *What works: instructional strategies for music education.* Reston, VA: Music Educators National Conference.

Miles, R. (Ed.). (1997). *Teaching Music through Performance in Band.* Chicago: GIA.

___. (1998). *Teaching Music through Performance in Band* (Vol. 2). Chicago: GIA.

___. (2000). *Teaching Music through Performance in Band* (Vol. 3). Chicago: GIA.

Mursell, J. L. (1927). *Principles of music education.* New York, NY: MacMillan.

Regelski, T. (1981). *Teaching General Music: Action Learning for Middle and Secondary Schools.* New York: Schirmer.

Schaberg, G. (Ed.). (1988). *Tips: Teaching music to special learners.* Reston, VA: MENC.

Schleuter, S. L. (1984). *A sound approach to teaching instrumentalists.* Kent, OH: Kent State University Press.

Spector, I. (1990). *Rhythm and life: The work of Emile Jaques-Dalcroze.* Stuyvesant, NY: Pendragon.

Suzuki, S. (1969). *Nurtured by love: A new approach to education.* Trans. Waltraud Suzuki. New York: Exposition Press.

Swanwick, K. (1988). *Music, mind, and education.* London: Routledge.

Tait, M. J. and P. Haack. (1984). *Principles and processes of music education: New perspectives.* New York: Teachers College Press.

Thompson, K. and G. Kiester. (1997). *Strategies for teaching high school general music.* Reston, VA: MENC.

Tuttle, F., L. Becker, and J. Sousa. (1993). *Characteristics and identification of gifted and talented students.* Washington, DE: National Education Association.

Volk, T. M. (1998). *Music, education, and multiculturalism: Foundations and principles.* New York: Oxford University Press.

Walters, D. L. and C. C. Taggart. (1989). *Readings in music learning theory.* Chicago, IL: GIA.

Warner, B. (1991). *Orff-Schulwerk: Applications for the classroom*. Englewood Cliffs, NJ: Prentice-Hall.

Wiggins, J. (1991). *Synthesizers in the elementary classroom: An integrated approach*. Reston, VA: MENC.

Yarbrough, C. and C. Madsen. (1980). *Competency-based music education*. Englewood Cliffs, NJ: Prentice Hall.

Music Education History

Birge, E. B. (1966). *History of public school music in the United States*. Washington, D.C.: Music Educators National Conference. (Original work published 1928).

Goodman, H. A. (1982). *Music education: Perspectives and perceptions*. Dubuque, IA: Kendall/Hunt.

Keene, J. A. (1982). *A history of music education in the United States*. Hanover, NH: University Press of New England.

Leonhard, C. and R. House. (1972). *Foundations and principles of music education* (2d ed.). New York: McGraw-Hill.

Mark, M. L. (1982). *Source readings in music education history*. New York: Schirmer.

Mark, M. L. and C. L. Gary. (1992). *A history of American music education*. New York: Schirmer.

Rainbow, B. (1989). *Music in educational thought and practice: A survey from 800 BC*. Aberystwyth, Wales: Boethius.

Sunderman, L. (1971). *Historical foundations of music education in the United States*. Metuchen, NJ: Scarecrow.

Music Education Philosophy/Educational Philosophy

Alperson, P. (Ed.). (1986). *What is music? An introduction to the philosophy of music*. New York: Haven.

Bowman, W. D. (1998). *Philosophical perspectives on music*. New York: Oxford University Press.

Broudy, H. S. (1954). *Building a philosophy of Education*. Prentice-Hall: Englewood Cliffs, N.J.

Colwell, R. J. (1970). *An approach to aesthetic education*. Urbana: University of Illinois, ERIC Document Reproduction Service.

Copland, A. (1957). *What to listen for in music*. New York: McGraw-Hill.

Dewey, J. (1916). *Democracy and education: An introduction to the philosophy of education*. New York: Macmillan.

——. (1933). *How we think*. Boston: D. C. Heath.

——. (1979). *Art as experience*. New York: G. P. Putnam's Sons (Original work published 1934).

Elliott, D. (1995). *Music Matters: A new philosophy of music education*. New York: Oxford University Press.

Fowler, C. (1994). *Music! Its role and importance in our lives*. Mission Hills, CA: Glencoe/Macmillan.

Hanslick, E. (1957). *The beautiful in music* (G. Cohen, Trans.). Indianapolis: The Liberal Arts Press.

Hume, D. (1874). *A treatise on human nature*. London: Longmans.

James, W. (1907). *Pragmatism and four essays from The Meaning of Truth*. New York: Longmans, Green and Co.

Jorgensen, E. R. (1997). *In search of music education*. Urbana: University of Illinois Press.

Kant, I. (1929). *Critique of pure reason*. London: Macmillan.

Kohli, W. (1995). *Critical conversations in philosophy of education*. New York: Routledge.

Langer, S. K. (1942). *Philosophy in a new key*. Cambridge, MA: Harvard University Press.

——. (1953). *Feeling and form*. New York: Scribner's.

Lock, J. (1894). *An essay concerning human understanding*. Oxford: Oxford University Press.

Meyer, L. B. (1956). *Emotion and meaning in music*. Chicago, IL: University of Chicago Press.

——. (1967). *Music, the arts, and ideas.* Chicago: University of Chicago Press.

Reimer, B. (1989). *A philosophy of music education* (2d ed.). Englewood Cliffs, NJ: Prentice-Hall.

Schwadron, A. A. (1982). *Aesthetics: Dimensions for music education* (2d ed.). Wakefield, NH: Longwood.

Swanwick, K. (1988). *Music, mind and education.* London, England: Routledge.

Whitehead, A. N. (1929). *The aims of education and other essays.* New York: Macmillan.

Sociology/Social Psychology

Bandura, A. (1986). *Social foundations of thought and action: A social cognitive theory.* Englewood Cliffs, NJ: Prentice-Hall.

——. (1997). *Self-efficacy: The exercise of control.* New York: Freeman.

Bandura, A. and R. H. Walters. (1963). *Social learning and personality development.* New York: Holt, Rinehart & Winston.

Darwin, C. (1872). *The expression of the emotions in man and animals.* London: John Murray.

Farnsworth, P. R. (1969). *The social psychology of music* (2d ed.). Ames: Iowa State Press.

Hargreaves, D. and A. North. (1997). *The social psychology of music.* New York: Oxford University Press.

Honigsheim, P. (1989). *Sociology and music* (2d ed.). (K. P. Etzkorn, Ed.). New Brunswick, NJ: Transaction Press.

Kaplan, M. (1990). *The arts: A social perspective.* Rutherford, NJ: Fairleigh Dickinson Press.

Myers, D. B. (1990). *Social psychology* (3d ed.). New York: McGraw-Hill.

Nieto, S. (1996). *Affirmity diversity: The sociopolitical context of multicultural education* (2d ed.). White Plains, NY: Longman.

Shepherd, J. and P. Wicke. (1997). *Music and cultural theory.* Cambridge, UK: Policy Press.

Tocqueville, A. (1956). *Democracy in America*. New York: New American Library.

Vygotsky, L. (1978). *Mind in Society: The development of high psychological processes*. Cambridge, MA: Harvard University Press.

Educational Psychology

Allport, G. W. (1937). *Personality: A psychological interpretation*. New York: Henry Holt.

Anastasi, A. (1968). *Psychological testing* (3d ed.). New York: Macmillan.

Anderson, M. (1992). *Intelligence and development: A cognitive theory*. Oxford: Blackwell.

Ausubel, D. P. (1963). *The psychology of meaningful verbal learning*. New York: Grune and Stratton.

——. (1968). *Educational psychology: A cognitive view*. New York: Holt, Rinehart & Winston.

Bandura, A. (1969). *Principles of behavior modification*. New York: Holt, Rinehart & Winston.

——. (1986). *Social foundations of thought and action: A social cognitive theory*. Englewood Cliffs, NJ: Prentice-Hall.

——. (1997). *Self-efficacy: The exercise of control*. New York: Freeman.

Berlyne, D. E. (1960). *Conflict, arousal, and curiosity*. New York: McGraw-Hill.

Bloom, B. S. (1956). *Taxonomy of educational objectives: Handbook 1. Cognitive domain*. New York: David McKay.

Boring, E. G. (1950). *A history of experimental psychology* (2d ed.). New York: Appleton-Century-Crofts.

Dweck, C. S. (1999). *Self-theories: Their role in motivation, personality and development*. Philadelphia: Psychology Press.

Eisner, E. (1979). *The educational imagination: On the design and evaluation of school programs*. New York: Macmillan.

Gagne, R. M. (1977). *The conditions of learning*. New York: Holt, Rinehart & Winston.

Galton, F. (1883). *Inquiries into human faculty and its development*. London: Macmillan.

Gardner, H. (1982). *Art, mind and brain: A cognitive approach to creativity*. New York: Basic Books.

———. (1983). *Frames of mind, the theory of multiple intelligences*. New York: Basic Books.

———. (1993). *Multiple intelligences*. New York: Basic Books.

———. (1999). *Intelligence reframed: Multiple intelligences for the twenty-first century*. New York: Basic Books.

Goleman, D. (1995). *Emotional intelligence: Why it can matter more than IQ*. New York: Bantam Books.

Good, T. L. and J. E. Brophy. (1990). *Educational psychology: A realistic approach* (4th ed.). New York: Longman.

Gordon E. (1971). *The psychology of music teaching*. Englewood Cliffs, NJ: Prentice-Hall.

Green, B. and Gallwey, T. W. (1986). *The inner game of music*. Garden City, New York: Anchor Press.

Greer, R. D. (1980). *Design for music learning*. New York: Teachers College Press.

Guilford, J. P. (1956). "The structure of the intellect." *Psychological Bulletin, 53*, 267-93.

Guthrie, E. R. (1935). *The psychology of learning*. New York: Harper & Row.

Hilgard, E. L. and G. H. Bower. (1981). *Theories of learning* (5th ed.). Englewood Cliffs, NJ: Prentice-Hall.

Hull, C. L. (1943). *Principles of behavior*. New York: Appleton-Century-Crofts.

———. (1951). *Essentials of behavior*. New Haven, CT: Yale University Press.

James, W. (1890). *Principles of psychology*. New York: Henry Holt.

Jung, C. G. (1918). *Studies in word association*. London: Heineman.

———. (1933). *Modern man in search of a soul*. New York: Harcourt Brace Jovanovich.

Koffka, K. (1924). *The growth of the mind: An introduction to child psychology*. (Trans. R. M. Ogden). New York: Harcourt Brace Jovanovich.

——. (1935). *Principles of gestalt psychology.* New York: Harcourt, Brace.

Kohler, W. (1929). *Gestalt psychology.* New York: Liveright.

——. (1969). *The task of Gestalt psychology.* Princeton, NJ: Princeton University Press.

Krathwohl, D. R., G. S. Bloom, and B. B. Masia. (1964). *Taxonomy of educational objectives: Handbook 2. Affective domain.* New York: David McKay.

Lefrancois, G. R. (1988). *Psychology for teaching.* Belmont, CA: Wadsworth.

Lundin, R. W. (1967). *An objective psychology of music* (2d ed.). New York: Ronald.

Madsen, C. K. and C. A. Prickett. (1987). *Applications of research in music behavior.* Tuscaloosa: University of Alabama Press.

Madsen, C. K., R. D. Greer, and C. H. Madsen. (1975). *Research in music behavior.* New York: Teachers College Press.

Maslow, A. H. (1987). *Motivation and personality.* New York: Harper & Row (Original work published 1954).

McClelland, D. (1955). *Studies in motivation.* New York: Appleton.

——. (1985). *Human motivation.* Chicago, IL: Scott Foresman.

Mercer, C. D. (1987). *Students with learning disabilities* (3rd ed.). Columbus, OH: Charles E. Merrill.

Miller, G. A. (1956). "The magical number seven, plus or minus two: Some limits on our capacity for processing information." *Psychological Review, 63,* 81-97.

Miller, P. H. (1989). *Theories of developmental psychology* (2d ed.). New York: W. H. Freeman.

Montessori, M. (1913). *The discovery of the child.* New York: Ballantine Books (1980 reissue).

Myers, D. G. (1996). *Exploring psychology* (3d ed.). New York: Worth.

Olson, G. B. (chair), et al. (1987). *Music teacher education: Partnership and process.* Reston, VA: Music Educators National Conference.

Papalia, D. E. and S. W. Olds. (1990). *A child's world.* New York: McGraw-Hill.

Pavlov, I. P. (1902). *The work of digestive glands.* (Trans. W. H. Thompson). London: Charles Griffin.

——. (1927). *Conditioned reflexes* (G. V. Anrep, Trans.). London: Oxford University Press.

Piaget, J. (1928). *Judgment and reasoning in the child* (M. Warden, Trans.). New York: Harcourt, Brace.

——. (1952). *The origins of intelligence in children.* New York: International University Press.

——. (1953). *Logic and psychology.* Manchester: Manchester University Press.

——. (1972). *The principles of genetic epistemology* (W. Mays, Trans.). New York: Basic Books.

Radocy, R. E. and J. D. Boyle. (1988). *Psychological foundations of musical behavior* (2d ed.). Springfield, IL: Charles C. Thomas.

Rogers, C. (1951). *Client-centered therapy.* Boston: Houghton Mifflin.

Schoen, M. (1940). *The psychology of music.* New York: Ronald Press.

Shuter-Dyson, R. and C. Gabriel. (1981). *The psychology of musical ability* (2d ed.). New York: Methuen.

Simpson, E. (1966). *The classification of educational objectives.* (Report No. OE5-85-104). Washington, D.C.: United States Office of Education.

Skinner, B. F. (1938). *The behavior of organisms.* New York: Appleton-Century-Crofts.

——. (1953). *Science and human behavior.* New York: Macmillan.

——. (1971). *Beyond freedom and dignity.* New York: Alfred A. Knopf.

Spearman, C. (1927). *The abilities of man.* New York: Macmillan.

Sprinthall, N. A. and R. C. Sprinthall. (1990). *Educational psychology: A developmental approach* (5th ed.). New York: McGraw-Hill.

Summerhill, A. S. (1960). *A radical approach to child rearing.* London: Hart Publishing.

Terman, L. M. (1916). *The measurement of intelligence.* Boston: Houghton Mifflin.

——. (1925). *Genetic studies of genius: Mental and physical traits of 1000 gifted children.* Stanford, CA: Stanford University Press.

Terman, L. M. and M. A. Merrill. (1937). *Measuring intelligence*. Boston: Houghton Mifflin.

Thorndike, E. L. (1911). *Animal intelligence*. New York: Macmillan.

——. (1927). *The measurement of intelligence*. New York: Bureau of Publications, Teachers College, Columbia University.

——. (1932). *The fundamentals of learning*. Englewood Cliffs, NJ: Merrill/Prentice Hall.

Thurstone, L. L. (1935). *Vectors of mind*. Chicago: University of Chicago Press.

——. (1938). *Primary mental abilities*. Chicago: University of Chicago Press.

Tolman, E. C. (1932). *Purposive behavior in animals and men*. New York: Century.

Torrance, E. P. (1970). *Encouraging creativity in the classroom*. Dubuque, IA: W. C. Brown.

Vygotsky, L. S. (1997a). *The collected works of L. S. Vygotsky: Vol. 3. Problems of the theory and history of psychology* (R. W. Rieber and A. S. Carton, Eds.; R. Van Der Veer, Trans.) New York: Plenum.

——. (1997b). *Educational psychology* (V. V. Davydow and R. Silverman, Trans.) New York: Plenum.

Watson, J. B. (1914). *Behavior: An introduction to comparative psychology*. New York: Holt.

——. (1925). *Behaviorism*. New York: Norton.

——. (1928). *Psychological care of infant and child*. New York: Norton.

Wechsler, D. (1944). *Measurement of adult intelligence* (3d ed.). Baltimore: Williams & Wilkins.

Wertheimer, M. (1959). *Productive thinking* (Michael Wertheimer, Ed., enl. ed.). New York: Harper.

Wilson, F. R. and F. L. Roehmann. (Eds.) (1990). *Music and child development*. St. Louis, Missouri: MMB Music.

Wundt, W. (1874). Principles of physiological psychology (2 vols.). London: Macmillan.

General Education

Abbs, P. (1994). *The educational imperative: A defense of Socratic and aesthetic learning*. London: Falmer Press.

Arends, R. I., N. E. Winitzky, and M. D. Tannenbaum. (2001). *Exploring Teaching: An introduction to education* (2d ed.). New York: McGraw-Hill.

Banks, J. A. (1988). *Multiethnic education: Theory and practice* (2d ed.). Boston: Allyn & Bacon.

——. (1991). *Teaching strategies for ethnic studies* (5th ed.). Boston: Allyn & Bacon.

Banks, J. A. and C. A. Banks. (Ed.). (1995). *Handbook of research on multicultural education*. New York: Macmillan.

Bevevino, M. M. et al. (1999). *An educators guide to block scheduling*. Boston: Allyn & Bacon.

Bloom, A. and Bellow, S. (1988). *The closing of the American mind*. New York: Simon and Schuster.

Bloom, B. S. (1956). *Taxonomy of educational objectives: Handbook 1. Cognitive domain*. New York: David McKay.

Boyer, E. L. (1995). *The basic school: A community for learning*. Princeton, NJ: Carnegie Foundation for the Advancement of Teaching.

Brophy J. E. and C. M. Evertson. (1976). *Learning from teaching: A developmental perspective*. Boston, MA: Allyn & Bacon.

Bruner, J. (1963). *The process of education*. New York: Routledge, Chapman and Hall.

——. (1990). *Acts of meaning*. Cambridge, MA: Harvard University Press.

——. (1996). *The culture of education*. Cambridge, MA: Harvard University Press.

Chomsky, N. (1968). *Language and mind*. New York: Harcourt Brace Jovanovich.

Conant, J. B. (1959). *The American high school today*. New York: McGraw-Hill.

Dewey, J. (1902). *The child and the curriculum*. Chicago: University of Chicago Press.

Eisner, E. W. (1979). *The educational imagination*. New York: Macmillan.

——. (1982). *Cognition and curriculum*. New York: Longman.

——. (1985). *The art of educational evaluation*. Philadelphia, PA: Falmer.

——. (1990). *The role of discipline-based art education in America's schools*. Los Angeles: Getty Center for Education in the Arts.

——. (1998). *The kind of schools we need: Personal essays*. Portsmouth, NH: Heinemann.

Eisner, E. W. (Ed.). (1985). *Learning and teaching – the ways of knowing. Eighty-fourth yearbook of the national society for the study of education*. Chicago: The University of Chicago Press.

Freiberg, H. J. and A. Driscoll. (2000). *Teaching strategies*. Boston: Allyn & Bacon.

Gage, N. L. (1978). *The scientific basis of the art of teaching*. New York: Teachers College Press.

Gardner, H. (1973). *The arts and human development*. New York: John Wiley and Sons.

——. (1983). *Frames of mind, the theory of multiple intelligences*. New York: Basic Books.

——. (1991). *The unschooled mind: How children think and how schools should teach*. New York: Basic Books.

——. (1993). *Multiple intelligences*. New York: Basic Books.

——. (2000). *Intelligence reframed: Multiple intelligences for the twenty-first century*. New York: Basic Books.

Goleman, D. (1995). *Emotional intelligence: Why it can matter more than IQ*. New York: Bantam Books.

Good, T. L. and J. E. Brophy. (1991). Looking in classrooms (5th ed.). New York: Harper Collins.

Goodlad, J. (1983). *A place called school: Prospects for the future*. New York: McGraw-Hill.

——. (1990). *Teachers for our nation's schools*. San Francisco: Jossey-Bass.

Hardman, M. L., C. J. Drew, and M. W. Egan. (1999). *Human exceptionality*. Needham Heights, MA: Allyn & Bacon.

Hargreaves, A. (1994). *Changing teachers, changing times: Teachers' work and culture in the postmodern age*. New York: Teachers College Press.

Hashway, R. M. (1998). *Assessment and evaluation of development learning.* Westport, CT: Praeger.

Heubert, J. P. and R. M. Hauser (Eds.). (1999). *High stakes testing for tracking, promotion, and graduation.* Washington, D.C.: National Academy Press.

Hilgard, E. L. and G. H. Bower. (1981). *Theories of learning* (5th ed.). Englewood Cliffs, NJ: Prentice-Hall.

Hirsch, E. D. (1988). *Cultural literacy.* New York: Vintage Books.

Holt, J. (1995). *How children fail.* Boulder, CO: Perseus Book Group.

Houston, W. R. (Ed.). (1990). *Handbook of research on teacher training.* New York: Macmillan.

Johnson, J. A. et al. (1996). *Introduction to the foundations of American education* (10th ed.) Boston: Allyn and Bacon.

——. (2003). *Essentials of American education.* Boston: Allyn & Bacon.

Joyce, B. and M. Weil. (1996). *Models of teaching* (5th ed.). Boston: Allyn and Bacon.

Kauchak, D. P. and P. D. Eggen. (1993). *Learning and teaching* (2d ed.). Needham Heights, MA: Allyn & Bacon.

Kohl, H. R. (1970). *The open classroom.* New York: Review/Vintage.

McLaughlin, M. W. and R. S. Pfeifer. (1988). *Teacher evaluation.* New York: Teachers College, Columbia University.

McNergney, R. F. and J. M. Herbert. (1998). *Foundations of education.* Needham Heights, MA: Allyn & Bacon.

Mercer, C. D. (1987). *Students with learning disabilities* (3rd ed.). Columbus, OH: Charles E. Merrill.

Montessori, M. (1913). *The discovery of the child.* New York: Ballantine Books (1980 reissue).

National Commission of Teaching & America's Future. (1996). *What matters most: Teaching for America's future.* New York: Teachers College Press.

New American Schools. (1999). *Working toward excellence: Examining the effectiveness of new American school designs.* New York: Teachers College Press.

Nieto, S. (1996). *Affirming diversity: The sociopolitical context of multicultural education* (2d ed.). White Plains, NY: Longman.

Ornstein, A. C. and T. J. Lasley II. (2000). *Strategies for effective teaching* (3d ed.). New York: McGraw Hill.

Queen, J. A. (2003). *The block scheduling handbook.* Thousand Oaks, CA: Corwin Press.

Ravitch, D. (2000). *Left back: A century of failed school reforms.* New York: Simon and Schuster.

Robbins, P., G. Gregory, and L. E. Herndon. (2000). *Thinking inside the block schedule.* Thousand Oaks, CA: Corwin.

Rokeach, M. (1960). *The open and closed mind.* New York: Basic Books.

Schlechty, P. C. (1991). *Schools for the 21st century.* Hoboken, N. J.: John Wiley & Sons.

Silberman, C. A. (1971). *Crisis in the classroom.* New York: Random House.

Sizer, T. A. (1984). *Horace's Compromise: The dilemma of the American high school.* New York: Houghton Mifflin.

Skinner, B. F. (1968). *The technology of teaching.* New York: Appleton-Century-Crofts.

———. (1971). *Beyond freedom and dignity.* New York: Alfred A. Knopf.

Curriculum/Reports

Adler, M. J. (1982). *The paideia proposal.* New York: Macmillan.

America 2000. (1992). Washington, D.C.: U.S. Department Education.

The Arts and Education: Partners in achieving our national educational goals. Washington, D.C.: National Endowment for the Arts and the United States Department of Education.

Arts, Education and Americans Panel (1977). *Coming to our senses: The significance of the arts for American education.* Panel report, David Rockefeller, Jr., Chairman. New York: McGraw-Hill.

Ball, C. (Chair), et al. (1982). *Graduate music teacher education report*. Reston, VA: Music Educators National Conference.

Boyer, E. L. (1983). *High school: A report on secondary education in America*. New York: Harper & Row.

Boyle, D. (Ed.). (1973). *Arts IMPACT: Curriculum for change*. University Park, PA: Pennsylvania State University Press.

Carnegie Task Force on Teaching as a Profession. (1986). *A nation prepared: Teachers for the twenty-first century*. Hyattsville, MD: Carnegie Forum on Education and the Economy.

Choate, R. A. (Ed.). (1968). *Documentary report of the Tanglewood Symposium*. Washington, D.C.: Music Educators National Conference.

College Entrance Examination Board (1983). *Academic preparation for college: What students need to know and be able to do*. New York: The College Board.

Colwell, R. (1970). *The evaluation of music teaching and learning*. Englewood Cliffs, NJ: Prentice-Hall.

Comprehensive Musicianship: The Foundation for College Education in Music (1965). Washington, D.C.: Music Educators National Conference.

Consortium of National Arts Education Associations. (1994). *National Standards for Arts Education: What Every Young American Should Know and Be Able to Do in the Arts. Content and achievement standards for dance, music, theatre, and visual arts; grades K-12*. Reston, VA: Music Educators National Conference.

Contemporary Music Project for Creativity in Music Education. *Comprehensive musicianship: An anthology of evolving thought*. Washington, D.C.: Music Educators National Conference.

Dewey, J. (1956). *The child and the curriculum and the school and society*. Chicago and London: University of Chicago Press.

Dobbs, S. M. (1992). *The DBAE handbook: An overview of discipline-based art education*. Santa Monica, CA: Getty Center for Education in the Arts.

Education Commission of the States. (1999). *Comprehensive school reform: Five lessons from the field*. Denver, CO: Education Commission of the States.

Eisner, E. W. (1994). *Cognition and curriculum reconsidered* (2d ed.). New York: Teachers College Press.

Erbes, R. (1992). *Certification practices and trends in music teacher education* (4th ed.). Reston, VA: Music Educators National Conference.

Holmes Group (1986). *Tomorrow's teachers: A report of the Holmes Group.* East Lansing: Michigan State University.

Klotman, R. H. (chair), et al. (1972). *Teacher education in music: Final report.* Washington, D.C.: Music Educators national Conference.

MENC. (1994). *The school music program, a new vision: The K-12 National standards, PreK Standards, and What they mean to music educators.* Reston, VA: Author.

Multicultural Arts Education: Guidelines, Instructional Units and Resources for Art, Dance, Music and Theatre, Grades K-12 (1993). Orlando: University of Florida.

Music Educators National Conference. (1987). *Music teacher education: Partnership and process.* Reston, VA: Author.

National Advisory Council on Education Professions Development. *Competency based teacher education: Toward a consensus.* Washington, D.C.: National Advisory Council on Education Professions Development.

National Assessment of Educational Progress (1970). *Music objectives.* Ann Arbor, MI: Author.

National Coalition for Music Education (1991). *Building support for school music: A practical guide.* Reston, VA: Music Educators National Conference.

National Commission on Excellence in Education (1984). *A nation at risk: The full account.* Westford, MA: Murray Printing Co.

National Commission on Music Education. (1991). *Growing up complete: The imperative for music education.* Reston, VA: Music Educators National Conference.

National Education Goals Panel. (1994). *The national education goals report 1994.* Washington, D.C.: U.S. Government Printing Office.

National Endowment for the Arts. (1988). *Toward civilization: A report on arts education.* Washington, D.C.: National Endowment for the Arts. Foreword by F. Hodsoll.

Olson, G. B. (chair), et al. (1987). *Music Teacher Education: Partnership and Process.* Reston, VA: Music Educators National Conference.

Opportunity-to-Learn Standards for Music Instruction: Grades PreK-12. Information on what schools should provide in terms of curriculum and scheduling, staffing, materials and equipment, and facilities. Reston, VA: Music Educators National Conference, 1994.

Performance Standards for Music: Strategies and Benchmarks for Assessing Progress Toward the National Standards, Grades PreK-12. Sample assessment strategies and descriptions of student responses at the basic, proficient, and advanced levels for each achievement standard in the National Standards. Reston, VA: Music Educators National Conference, 1966.

Perspectives on Implementation: Arts Education Standards for America's Students. A discussion of the issues related to implementation of the standards and of strategies for key constituencies that need to be involved in the process. Reston, VA: Music Educators National Conference, 1994.

Rockefeller, D., Jr. (Chair). (1977). *Coming to our senses: The significance of the arts for American education.* New York: McGraw-Hill.

Rodosky, R. (1974). *Arts IMPACT final evaluation report.* Columbus, OH: Columbus Public Schools.

The School Music Program: A New Vision. The K-12 National Standards, PreK standards, and what they mean to music educators (1994). Reston, VA: Music Educators National Conference.

Schubert, W. H. (1986). *Curriculum: Perspective, paradigm, and possibility.* New York: Macmillan.

Schwadron, A. A. (1965). *Comprehensive musicianship: The foundation for college education in music.* Reston, VA: Music Educators National Conference.

——. (1982). *Aesthetics: Dimensions for music education* (2d ed.). Wakefield, NH: Longwood.

Summary Statement: Education Reform and the Arts (1994). Reston, VA: Music Educators National Conference.

Task Force on Education for Economic Growth. *Action for excellence: A comprehensive plan to improve our nations' schools.* Denver: Education Commission of the States.

Task Force on Music Teacher Education for the Nineties (1987). *Music teacher education: partnership and process.* Reston, VA: Music Educators National Conference.

Teacher Education Commission (1972). *Teacher Education in music: Final report.* Washington, D.C.: Music Educators National Conference.

The Vision for Arts Education in the 21st Century. The ideas and ideals behind the development of the National Standards for Arts Education (1994). Reston, VA: Music Educators National Conference.

Music Psychology and Perception/Cognition

Backus, J. (1969). *The acoustical foundations of music.* New York: Norton.

Bamberger, J. (1991). *The mind behind the musical ear.* Cambridge: Harvard University Press.

Bekesy, G. Von (1967). *Sensory inhibition.* Princeton, NJ: Princeton University Press.

Brophy, T. S. (2000). *Assessing the Developing Child Musician: A Guide for General Music Teachers.* Chicago: GIA Publications, Inc.

Butler, D. (1992). *The musician's guide to perception and cognition.* New York: Schirmer.

Campbell, M. R. (2001). *On musicality & milestones.* Urbana-Champaign: University of Illinois.

Campbell, P. S. and C. Scott-Kassner. (1995). *Music in childhood: From preschool through the elementary grades.* New York: Schirmer Books.

Davies, J. B. (1978). *The psychology of music.* Stanford: Stanford University Press.

Deliege, I. and J. Sloboda. (1996). *Musical beginnings: Origins and development of musical competence.* Oxford: Oxford University Press.

Deutsch, D. (Ed.). (1982). *The psychology of music.* New York: Academic Press.

Documentary report of the Ann Arbor symposium (1981). Reston, Virginia: Music Educators National Conference.

Documentary report of the Ann Arbor symposium. (1983). Reston, Virginia: Music Educators National Conference.

Dowling, W. J. and D. L. Harwood. (1986). *Music cognition.* Orlando, FL: Academic Press.

Gardner, H. (1983). *Frames of mind, the theory of multiple intelligences*. New York: Basic Books.

——. (1993). *Multiple intelligences*. New York: Basic Books.

Gordon, E. (1971). *The psychology of music teaching*. Englewood Cliffs, NJ: Prentice-Hall.

——. (1989). *Learning Sequences in Music: Skills, Content, and Patterns*. Chicago, IL: GIA Publications, Inc.

Hall, D. E. (1991). *Musical acoustics* (2d ed.). Pacific Grove: Brooks/Cole Publishing.

Hargreaves, D. J. (1994). *The developmental psychology of music*. New York: Cambridge.

Hargreaves, D. and A. North. (1997). *The social psychology of music*. New York: Oxford University Press.

Hodges, D. A. (Ed.) (1980). *Handbook of music psychology*. Lawrence, Kansas: National Association for Music Therapy.

Jourdain, R. (1997). *Music, the brain, and ecstasy*. New York: William Morrow.

Krumhansl, C. L. (1990). *Cognitive foundations of musical pitch*. New York: Oxford University Press.

Madsen, C. H. and C. K. Madsen. (1974). *Teaching/Discipline: A positive approach for educational development* (2d ed.). Boston, MA: Allyn & Bacon.

Miller, G. A. (1956). "The magical number seven, plus or minus two: Some limits on our capacity for processing information." *Psychological Review*, 63, 81-97.

——. (1962). *Psychology: The science of mental life*. New York: Harper & Row.

Mursell, J. (1934). *Psychology of music*. New York: W. W. Norton.

——. (1938). *The psychology of school music teaching*. Morristown, NJ: Silver Burdett.

Radocy, R. E. and J. D. Boyle. (1988). *Psychological foundations of musical behavior* (2d ed.). Springfield, IL: Charles C. Thomas.

Schoen, M. (1940). *The psychology of music*. New York: Ronald Press.

Seashore, C. E. (1938). *Psychology of music*. New York: McGraw-Hill.

Serafine, M. L. (1988). *Music as cognition: The development of thought in sound.* New York: Columbia University Press.

Shuter-Dyson, R. and C. Gabriel. (1981). *The psychology of musical ability* (2d ed.). New York: Methuen.

Sloboda, J. A. (1985). *The musical mind: The cognitive psychology of music.* Oxford, England: Clarendon.

Stevens, S. S. and H. Davis. (1938). *Hearing: Its psychology and physiology.* New York: John Wiley.

Swanwick, K. (1988). *Music, mind, and education.* London: Routledge.

Walters, D. L. and C. C. Taggart. (1989). *Readings in Music Learning Theory.* Chicago: GIA Publications, Inc.

Conducting Books

Demaree, R. W. and D. V. Moses. (1995). *The complete conductor.* Englewood Cliffs, NJ: Prentice-Hall.

Fuchs, P. P. (1969). *The psychology of conducting.* New York: MCA.

Garretson, R. L. (1998). *Conducting choral music.* Englewood Cliffs, NJ: Prentice-Hall.

Green, E. A. H. (1997). *The modern conductor.* Englewood Cliffs, NJ: Prentice-Hall.

Labuta, J. A. (1995). *Basic conducting techniques.* Englewood Cliffs, NJ: Prentice-Hall.

Phillips, K. H. (1997). *Basic techniques of conducting.* New York: Oxford University Press.

Rudolf, M. (1994). *The grammar of conducting.* New York: Schirmer.

Research

Arts Education Research Agenda for the Future (1994). National Endowment for the Arts and United States Department of Education. Washington, D.C.: U.S. Government Printing Office.

Ball, M., W. R. Borg, and J. P. Gall. (1996). *Educational research: An introduction*. White Plains, NY: Longman.

Barnes, S. H. (1982). *A cross-section of research in music education*. Washington, D.C.: University Press of America.

Berz, W. L. and J. Bowman. (1994). *Applications of research in music technology*. Reston, VA: Music Educators National Conference.

Bogdan, R. C. and S. K. Biklin. (1998). *Qualitative research for education* (3d ed.). Boston: Allyn and Bacon.

Burgess, R. G. (Ed.). (1985). *Issues in educational research: Qualitative methods*. London: Falmer Press.

Campbell, D. T. and J. C. Stanley. (1966). *Experimental and quasi-experimental designs for research*. Chicago, IL: Rand McNally.

Colwell, R. (Ed.). (1992). *Handbook of research on music teaching and learning*. Reston, VA: Music Educators National Conference.

Creswell, J. W. (1998). *Qualitative inquiry and research design*. Thousand Oaks, CA: Sage.

Denzin, N. K. and Y. S. Lincoln. (Eds.). (1994). *The handbook of qualitative research*. Thousand Oaks, CA: Sage.

Glesne, C. (1999). *Becoming qualitative researchers* (2d ed.). New York: Longman.

Isasc, S. and W. B. Michael. (1984). *Handbook in research and evaluation*. San Diego, CA: EdITS.

Lehman, P. R. (1968). *Tests and measurements in music*. Englewood Cliffs, NJ: Prentice-Hall.

Madsen, C. K. and C. H. Madsen. (1978). *Experimental research in music*. Raleigh, NC: Contemporary.

Phelps, R. P. (1980). *A guide to research in music education* (2d ed.). Metuchen, NJ: Scarecrow.

Thurstone, L. L. (1947). *Multiple factor analysis*. Chicago: University of Chicago Press.

Weitzman, E. and M. Miles. (1995). *Computer programs for qualitative data analysis*. Thousand Oaks, CA: Sage.

Williams, D. and P. Webster. (1996). *Experiencing music technology: Software, Data, and Hardware*. New York: Schirmer.

Tests and Measurement

ACT Assessment. American College Testing Program.

Advance Placement Examination in Music. Princeton, NJ: Educational Testing Service.

Aliferis, J. (1954). *Aliferis Music Achievement Test: College Entrance Level*. Minneapolis: University of Minnesota Press.

Aliferis, J. and J. E. Stecklein. (1962). *Aliferis-Stecklein Music Achievement Test: College Midpoint Level*. Minneapolis: University of Minnesota Press.

Avar, W. (1954). *Musiquiz*. Los Angeles, California: Period Record Company.

Beach F. A. (with H. E. Schrammel). (1939). *Beach Music Test*. Emporia, Kansas: Bureau of Educational Measurements, Kansas State Teachers College.

Bentley, A. (1966). *Musical ability in children and its measurement*. New York: October House.

Boyle, J. D. and R. E. Radocy. (1987). *Measurement and evaluation of musical experiences*. New York: Schirmer.

Colwell, R. (1969). *Music achievement tests*. Chicago: Follett Educational Corp.

——. (1979). *Music Competency Tests*. Morristown, N.J.: Silver Burdett.

Drake, R. M. (1957). *Manual for the Drake Musical Aptitude Test*. (revised edition). Chicago: Science Research Associates.

Ennis, R. H. and E. Weir. (1985). *Ennis-Weir Critical Thinking Essay Test*. Pacific Grove: Midwest Publications.

Ennis, R. H. and J. Millman. (1985). *Cornell Critical Thinking Test, levels X and Z*. Pacific Grove: Midwest Publications.

Farnum, S. (1969). *The Farnum String Scale*. Milwaukee, WI: Hal Leonard.

——. (1969). *Farnum Music Test*. Riverside, RI: Bond Publishing Company.

Gaston, T. (1957). *A Test of Musicality*. Lawrence, Kansas: Odell's Instrumental Service.

Gordon, E. (1965). *Musical Aptitude Profile*. Chicago: GIA Publications, Inc.

——. (1979). *Primary Measures of Music Audiation*. Chicago: GIA Publications, Inc.

——. (1982). *Intermediate Measures of Music Audiation*. Chicago: GIA Publications, Inc.

——. (1989). *Advanced Measures of Music Audiation*. Chicago: GIA Publications, Inc.

——. (1991). *Iowa Tests of Music Literacy (revised)*. Chicago: GIA Publications, Inc.

Graduate Record Examination (GRE) Advanced Music Test. (1951). Princeton, NJ: Educational Testing Service.

Gronlund, N. E. and R. L. Linn. (1990). *Measurement and evaluation in teaching* (6th ed.). New York: Macmillan.

Guildford, J. P. (1954). *Psychometric methods*. New York: McGraw-Hill.

Hoover, H. D., S. B. Dunbar, and D. A. Frisbie. *Iowa Test of Basic Skills, Form A*. Itasca, IL: Riverside, Publishing.

Hovey, N. *The Selmer Band Manual Quizzes*. Elkhart, IN: H. & A. Selmer.

Jones, A. (1949). *Music Recognition Test*. New York: Carl Fischer.

Knuth, W. E. (1967). *Achievement Test in Music*. Monmouth, Oregon: Creative Arts Research Associates.

Kwalwasser, J. (1927). *Kwalwasser Test of Music Information and Appreciation*. Iowa City: Bureau of Educational Research and Service, University of Iowa.

——. (1953). *Kwalwasser Music Talent Test*. New York: Mills Music, Inc.

Kwalwasser, J. and G. M. Ruch. (revised 1927; last reprint 1952). *Kwalwasser-Ruch Test of Musical Accomplishment for Grades Four Through Twelve*. Iowa City: Bureau of Educational Research and Service, State University of Iowa.

Kwalwsser, J. and P. W. Dykema, P. W. (1930). *K-D Music Tests*. New York: Carl Fischer.

The National Teacher Examinations—Music Education Portion (1957). Princeton, NJ: Educational Testing Service.

Oberlin Test of Music and Art. No author. Princeton, NJ: Educational Testing Service.

The Praxis Series: ARTS (1994). Princeton, NJ: Educational Testing Service.

The Praxis Series: Core Battery Tests and Multiple Subjects Assessment for Teachers (1994). Princeton, NH: Educational Testing Service.

Roid, G. H. (2003). *Stanford-Binet Intelligence Scales (5th ed.)*. Itasca, IL: Riverside Publishing.

Scholastic Achievement Test (SAT). College Entrance Examination Board.

Seashore, C., D. Lewis, and J. Saetveit. (1960 revised). *The Seashore Measures of Musical Talent*. New York: The Psychological Corporation.

Simons, G. (1974). *Manual for Simons Measurement of Music Listening Skills*. Chicago: Stoelting Company.

Snyder Knuth, A. (1968). *Snyder Knuth Music Achievement Test*. Monmouth, Oregon: Creative Arts Research Associates (CARA).

Stevens, S. S. (1951). *Handbook of experimental psychology*. New York: Wiley.

Sullivan, Tiegs, and Willis. (1959, 1963). *California Test of Mental Maturity*. California Test Bureau.

Terman, L. M. and M. A. Merrill. (1960). *Stanford-Binet, Third Edition, Form L-M*. Itasca, IL: Riverside Publishing.

Thurstone, L. L. (1962). *SRA Thurstone Primary Mental Abilities Tests*. Chicago: Science Research Associates.

Tilson, L. M. (1941). *Tilson-Gretsch Musical Aptitude Tests*. Gretsch Mfg. Co.

Torrance, P. E. (1990). *Torrance Tests of Creative Thinking*. Bensenville, IL: Scholastic Testing Service, Inc.

Watkins, J. G. and S. E. Farnum. (1954). *The Watkins-Farnum Performance Scale, Form A: A standardized achievement test for all band instruments*. Milwaukee, WI: Hal Leonard.

Wechsler, D. (1946). *The Wechsler-Bellevue Intelligence Scale, Form II*. New York: The Psychological Corporation.

——. (1949). *Manual for the Wechsler Intelligence Scale for Children*. New York: Psychological Corporation.

——. (1955). *Manual for the Wechsler Adult Intelligence Scale*. New York: Psychological Corporation.

——. (1967). *Manual for the Wechsler Preschool and Primary Scale of Intelligence*. New York: Psychological Corporation.

Weymuth, R. W. (1986). *The development and evaluation of a cognitive choral music achievement test to evaluate Missouri high school students*. Unpublished doctoral dissertation, University of Miami, Coral Gables.

Wing, Herbert D. *Wing Musical Aptitude Test*. (1968). Herbert D. Wing. Cambridge, England: Cambridge University Press.

Additional Resources

Web Sites

American Association of Colleges for Teacher Education (AACTE): www.aacte.org

American Association of School Administrators (AASA): www.aasa.org

American Bandmasters Association (ABA): www.americanbandmasters.org

American Choral Directors Association (ACDA): acdaonline.org

American College Testing Program (ACT): www.act.org

American Educational Research Association (AERA): www.aera.net

American Federation of Musicians (AFM): www.afm.org

American Federation of Teachers (AFT): www.aft.org

American Music Conference (AMC): www.amc-music.com

American Orff-Schulwerk Association (AOSA): www.aosa.org

American Psychological Association (APA): www.apa.org

American School Band Directors Association (ASBDA): www.asbda.com

American Society of Composers, Authors and Publishers (ASCAP): www.ascap.com

American String Teacher Association (ASTA): www.astaweb.com

Association for Supervision and Curriculum Development (ASCD): www.ascd.org

Association for Technology in Music Instruction (ATMI): www.atmi.music.org

Association of Waldorf Schools of North America (ASWNA): www.awsna.org

Carnegie Corporation: www.carnegie.org

College Band Directors National Association (CBDNA): www.cbdna.org

The College Entrance Examination Board: www.collegeboard.com

College Music Society (CMS): www.collegemusicsociety.org (login required)

The Complete Guide to the Alexander Technique: www.alexandertechnique.com

The Conductors Guild: www.conductorsguild.org

Dalcroze Society of America (DSA): www.dalcrozeusa.org

Education Commission of the States (ECS): www.ecs.org

Education International: www.ei-ie.org

Educational Resources Information Center (ERIC): www.eric.ed.gov

Educational Testing Service (ETS): www.ets.org

The Ford Foundation: www.fordfound.org

Getty Center for Education in the Arts: www.getty.edu

The Gordon Institute for Music Learning: www.giml.org

Graduate Record Examinations (GRE): www.gre.org

Interlochen Center for the Arts: www.interlochen.org

International Association for Jazz Education (IAJE): www.iaje.org

International Clarinet Association (ICA): www.clarinet.org

International Double Reed Society (IRDS): www.idrs.org

International Horn Society: www.hornsociety.org

International Society for Music Education (ISME): www.isme.org

International Trombone Association (ITA): http://www.its-web.org

International Trumpet Guild (ITG): www.trumpetguild.org

International Tuba and Euphonium Association (ITEA): www.iteaonline.org

Laban/Bartenieff Institute of Movement Studies (LIMS): www.limsonline.org

Learning Disabilities (LD) online: www.ldonline.org

The Montessori Foundation: www.montessori.org

Music Educators National Conference (MENC): www.menc.org

Music Teachers National Association (MTNA): www.mtna.org

National Assessment Governing Board (NAGB): www.nagb.org

National Assessment of Educational Progress (NAEP): www.ed.gov/nces/naep

National Association for the Education of Young Children (NAEYC): www.naeyc.org

National Association for the Study and Performance of African-American Music (NASPAAM): www.naspaam.org

The National Association of College Wind and Percussion Instructors (NACW-PI): www.nacwpi.org

National Association of Schools of Music (NASM): www.arts-accredit.org

National Association of Teachers of Singing (NATS): www.nats.org

National Band Association (NBA): www.nationalbandassociation.org

National Board for Professional Teaching Standards (NBPTS): www.nbpts.org

National Center for Education Statistics (NCES): www.ed.gov/nces

National Center for the Study of Privatization Education (NCSPE): www.ncspe.org

National Congress of Parents and Teachers (PTA): www.pta.org

National Council for the Accreditation of Teacher Education (NCATE): www.ncate.org

National Endowment for the Arts (NEA): www.nea.gov

National Education Association: www.nea.org

National Flute Association (NFA): www.nfaonline.org

New American Schools Development Corporation (NASDC): www.nasdc.org

No Child Left Behind (NCLB): www.ed.gov/nclb

North American Saxophone Alliance (NASA): www.saxalliance.org

Office of Special Education and Rehabilitation Services (OSERS): www.ed.gov/osers

Organization of America Kodaly Educators (OAKE): www.oake.org

Percussive Arts Society (PAS): www.pas.org

President's Committee on the Arts and the Humanities (PCAH): www.pcah.gov

The Society for American Music (SAM): www.american-music.org

Suzuki Association of the Americas (SAA): www.suzukiassociation.org

United States Department of Education (USDOE): www.ed.gov

Voluntary National Tests (VNTs): www.ed.gov/nationaltests

Professional Music and Music Education Organizations/Associations

American Bandmasters Association (ABA)
1521 Pickard
Norman, OK 73072-6316
405-321-3373 • www.americanbandmasters.org

American Choral Directors Association (ACDA)
545 Couch Drive
Oklahoma City, OK 73102
405-332-8161 • www.acdaonline.org

American School Band Directors Association (ASBDA)
227 North 1st Street
P.O. Box 696
Guttenberg, IA 52052
563-252-2500 • www.asbda.com

American Society of Composers, Authors and Publishers (ASCAP)
One Lincoln Plaza
New York, NY 10023
212-621-6000 • www.ascap.com

American String Teacher Association (ASTA) &
National School Orchestra Association (NSOA)
4153 Chain Bridge Rd.
Fairfax, VA 22030 • www.astaweb.com

Conductors' Guild, Inc.
P.O. Box 18398
Richmond, VA 23226
804-553-1378 • www.conductorsguild.org

Council for Research in Music Education (CRME)
School of Music, University of Illinois
1205 W. California
Urbana, IL 61801

Interlochen Center for the Arts
P.O. Box 199
Interlochen, MI 49643-0199 • www.interlochen.org

International Association of Jazz Educators (IAJE)
P.O. Box 724
Manhattan, KS 66505-0724
785-776-8744 • www.iaje.org

International Clarinet Association (ICA)
P.O. Box 5039
Wheaton, IL 60189-5039 • www.clarinet.org

International Double Reed Society (IDRS)
Norma Hooks
2423 Lawndale Road
Finksburg, MD 21048-1401
410-871-0658 • www.idrs.org

International Horn Society (IHS)
Heidi Vogel, Executive Secretary
P.O. Box 630158
Lanai City, HI 96763-0158 • www.hornsociety.org

International Society for Music Education (ISME)
ISME International Office
P.O. Box 909
Nedlands, WA 6909 Australia
+61-8-9386-2654 • www.isme.org

International Trombone Association (ITS)
1 Broomfield Rd
Coventry CV5 6JW
UK • http://www.its-web.org

International Trumpet Guild (ITG)
David Jones, ITG Treasurer
241 East Main Street #247
Westfield, MA 01086-1633 • www.trumpetguild.org

International Tuba and Euphonium Association (ITEA)
ITEA Treasurer
2253 Downing Street
Denver, CO 80205
303-832-4676 • www.iteaonline.org

Music Educators National Conference (MENC)
The National Association for Music Education
1806 Robert Fulton Drive
Reston, VA 20191
800-336-3768 • www.menc.org

National Association of Schools of Music (NASM)
11250 Roger Bacon Drive, Suite 21
Reston, VA 20190-5248
703-437-0700 • www.arts-accredit.org

National Association of Teachers of Singing (NATS)
4745 Sutton Park Court, Suite #201
Jacksonville, FL 32224
904-992-9101 • www.nats.org

National Band Association (NBA)
118 College Drive #5032
Hattiesburg, MS 39406
601-297-8168 • www.nationalbandassociation.org

National Endowment for the Arts (NEA)
1100 Pennsylvania Ave., NW
Washington, D.C. 20506
202-682-5400 • www.nea.gov

National Flute Association (NFA)
26951 Ruether Avenue, Suite H
Santa Clara, CA 91351
661-250-8920 • www.nfaonline.org

North American Saxophone Alliance (NASA)
Kenneth Tse, Membership Director
School of Music
University of Iowa
Iowa City, IA 52242 • www.saxalliance.org

Organization of American Kodaly Educators (OAKE)
1612-29th Avenue South
Moorehead, MN 56560
218-227-6253 • www.oake.org

Percussive Arts Society (PAS)
701 NW Ferris Avenue
Lawton, OK 73507-5442 • www.pas.org

Society for American Music (SAM)
Stephen Foster Memorial
University of Pittsburgh
Pittsburgh, PA 15260 • www.american-music.org

Suzuki Association of America (SAA)
P.O. Box 17310
Boulder, CO 80308 • www.suzukiassociation.org

Professional Journals/Magazines

Acoustic Guitar
P.O. Box 767
San Anselmo, CA 94979

American Educator
555 New Jersey Ave NW
Washington, D.C. 20001

American Music Teacher (AMT)
Music Teachers National Association (MTNA)
The Carew Tower
441 Vine Street, Suite 505
Cincinnati, OH 45202-2814

American String Teachers (ASTA)
American String Teachers Association (ASTA)
57 Antioch Pike
Nashville, TN 37211

American Suzuki Journal
P.O. Box 17310
Boulder, CO 80308-7310

ASCAP Playback
One Lincoln Plaza
New York, NY 10023

British Journal of Music Education
Cambridge University Press
100 Brook Hill Drive
West Nyack, NY 10994-2133
845-353-7500

Bulletin of Historical Research in Music Education (HRME Bulletin)
311 Bailey Hall
University of Kansas
Lawrence, KS 66045-2344

Bulletin of the Council of Research in Music Education (CRME)
School of Music, University of Illinois
1205 W. California
Urbana, Illinois 61801
217-333-1027

Choral Journal
American Choral Directors Association (ACDA)
P.O. Box 6310
Lawton, OK 73506-0310

The Clarinet
International Clarinet Association (ICA)
1406 Lowden Avenue
Wheaton, IL 60187

Contributions to Music Education
Department of Music
306 Haydn Hall
Case Western Reserve University
Cleveland, OH 44106-7105

Current Musicology
Department of Music
Columbia University
614 Dodge Hall, MC 1812
New York, NY 10027

Down Beat
P.O. Box 906
Elmhurst, IL 60126
800-535-7496

Educational Leadership
Association for Supervision and Curriculum Development (ASCD)
1703 N. Beauregard Street
Alexandria, VA 22311

Flutist Quarterly
National Flute Association (NFA)
204 West Road
Salem, CT 06420-9052

General Music Today (GMT)
Music Educators National Conference (MENC)
1806 Robert Fulton Drive
Reston, VA 20191

The Horn Call
International Horn Society (IHS)
William Scharnberg
College of Music
University of North Texas
Denton, TX 76203

The Instrumentalist Magazine
200 Northfield Road
Northfield, IL 60093
847-446-5000

International Journal of Music Education (IJME)
ISME International Office
P.O. Box 909
Nedlands 6909, WA
Australia
++61-(0)8-9386-2654

International Trumpet Guild Journal
Publications Editor
522 Westview Drive
Manhattan, KS 66502

ITEA Journal
International Tuba and Euphonium Association (ITEA)
Jason Roland Smith
School of Music
Ohio University
440 Music Building
Athens, OH 45701

Jazz Education Journal
International Association for Jazz Education (IAJE)
P.O. Box 52
St. Bonaventure University
St. Bonaventure, NY 14778

Journal of Aesthetic Education, The
College of Education
University of Illinois at Urbana-Champaign
1310 South Sixth Street
Champaign, IL 61820

Journal of Band Research
American Bandmasters Association (ABA)
Troy State University Press
Managing Editor
Troy, AL 36082

The Journal of Historical Research in Music Education (JHRME)
School of Music
Arizona State University
Tempe, AZ 85287-0405

Journal of Music Teacher Education (JMTE)
Music Educators National Conference (MENC)
1806 Robert Fulton Drive
Reston, VA 20191

Journal of Music Theory Pedagogy (JMTP)
C/O Dr. Alice Lanning
Carnegie Building 100
University of Oklahoma
Norman, OK 73019
405-325-3967

Journal of Research in Music Education (JRME)
Music Educators National Conference (MENC)
1806 Robert Fulton Drive
Reston, VA 20191

Journal of Singing
National Association of Teachers of Singing (NATS)
4745 Sutton Park Court, Suite 201
Jacksonville, FL 32224

Journal of the Conductors Guild
5300 Glenside Drive, Suite 2207
Richmond, VA 23228-3983

Kodaly Envoy
National Office of O.A.K.E.
823 Old Westtown Rd.
West Chester PA 19382-5276

Montessori Leadership
International Montessori Council
1001 Bern Creek Loop
Sarasota, FL 34240

Music Education International
ISME International Office
P.O. Box 909
Nedlands 6909, WA
Australia
++61-(0)8-9386-2654

Music Educators Journal (MEJ)
Music Educators National Conference (MENC)
1806 Robert Fulton Drive
Reston, VA 20191

Music Magazine
American Federation of Musicians (AFM)
1501 Broadway, Suite 600
New York, NY 10036

Orff Echo
A.S.O.A.
P.O. Box 391089
Cleveland, OH 44139-8089

Percussive Notes
Percussive Arts Society (PAS)
701 NW Ferris Avenue
Lawton, OK 73507-5442

Philosophy of Music Education Review
Indiana University Press Journals
601 N. Morton St.
Bloomington, IN 47404-9907

Psychology of Music
38 Westfield Road
Hosbury, Wakefield
West Yorkshire, WF4 6EA UK

Psychomusicology
Center for Music Research
Florida State University
Tallahassee, FL 32306-2098

Renewal Magazine
Association of Waldorf Schools of North America (AWSNA)
3911 Bannister Road
Fair Oaks, CA 95628

The Saxophone Symposium
North American Saxophone Alliance (NASA)
Thomas Smialek, Editor
Penn State University, Hazelton
76 University Drive
Hazelton, PA 18202-1291

School Band and Orchestra Magazine
50 Brook Road
Needham, MA 02494
781-453-9310

Strings
P.O. Box 767
San Anselmo, CA 94979
415-485-6946

Teaching Music (TM)
Music Educators National Conference (MENC)
1806 Robert Fulton Drive
Reston, VA 20191

UPDATE: The Applications of Research in Music Education (UPDATE)
Music Educators National Conference (MENC)
1806 Robert Fulton Drive
Reston, VA 20191

Wind Player Magazine
P.O. Box 2750
Malibu, CA 90265
800-946-3305

The Woodwind Quarterly
The Music Trader
23916 SE Kent-Kangley Road
Maple Valley, WA 98038
425-413-4343

Young Children
National Association for the Education of Young Children (NAEYC)
1509 16th Street NW
Washington, D.C. 20036-1426

About the Authors

Mark C. Ely is Professor of Music at the University of Utah, where he is Director of Music Education and Saxophone Performance. Ely holds a Master of Music in Saxophone Performance from Western Michigan University where he studied with Trent Kynaston, and he earned a Ph.D. in Music Education from Ohio State University. He was Director of Bands in the Ross County Public School System in Ohio, where he taught elementary, junior high, and senior high instrumental music. Ely presents regularly at national and state conferences and has several publications to his credit.

Amy E. Rashkin is an attorney with a private practice in Salt Lake City, Utah. She holds a J.D. from the S. J. Quinney Law School in Salt Lake City, Utah, a Masters degree in Music Education from the University of Utah, and an undergraduate degree in Music Performance from the University of Wisconsin-Madison. Prior to practicing law, Ms. Rashkin taught high school and middle school instrumental music in the Salt Lake City area and continues to be involved in music and music education as a performer and adjudicator. She has presented at state music education conferences and has published several articles in music education and law journals.